FLEMISH ART

Translated by
JOHN CAIRNS
BART CLAES
JERI LIZABETH FACKELMAN
TONY LANGHAM and PLYM PETERS
TOM LINDSAY
LINDA VAN THIELEN

Design by
LOUIS VAN DEN EEDE

This 1988 edition published by Arch Cape Press,
a division of dilithium Press, Ltd.,
distributed by Crown Publishers, Inc.
225 Park Avenue South, New York, New York 10003

Printed and bound in Italy

ISBN: 0-517-66530-1

h g f e d c b a

Jacket:

Hans Memling, *Salome*, detail from the left wing of *The mystic Marriage*
of St Catherine, 1479. Bruges, St John's Hospital.

Frontispiece:

Hubert and Jan van Eyck, *The Adoration of the Lamb*, 1432. Ghent, St
Bavo's Cathedral.

FLEMISH ART
FROM THE BEGINNING TILL NOW
CAME ABOUT ON THE INITIATIVE OF
AND IN CO-OPERATION WITH
THE FLEMISH GOVERNMENT

GASTON GEENS

President

KAREL POMA

Vice-President

And the Communal Ministers

PAUL AKKERMANS
JACKY BUCHMANN
ROGER DE WULF
MARC GALLE
JAN LENSSENS
HUGO SCHILTZ
RIKA STEYAERT

FLEMISH ART
From the Beginning till Now

Under the direction of

HERMAN LIEBAERS
VALENTIN VERMEERSCH
LEON VOET
FRANS BAUDOUIN
ROBERT HOOZEE

Assisted by

Piet Baudouin, Wim Blockmans, Helena Bussers, Lieven Daenens, Dirk De Vos,
Hubert De Witte, Erik Duverger, Jean-Pierre Esther, Ria Fabri,
Jeanine Lambrechts-Douillez, Maurits Smeyers, Monique Tahon-Van Roose,
Jean Van Cleven, Stéphane Vandenberghe,
André Van den Kerkhove, Carl Van de Velde, Christine Van Vlierden

Arch Cape Press
New York

CULTURE IS THE EXPRESSION of a pattern of civilization. It finds its expression in any human creation whatsoever. It reflects the identity of a nation, as this has grown and matured throughout the centuries. Art is probably the most subtle exponent of this identity.

Flemish art was mostly at its height during periods of economic boom and general prosperity. This fact confirms the argument that artistic life flourishes at the most when it is based on a firm and stable economic frame. However it is one of the characteristic features of the Flemish nature that even in times of crisis and privation, great works of art were created, out of which an irresistible vital urge and a firm wish to restore and revive appear.

Flemish art is widely recognized and appreciated. The Museo del Prado in Madrid, the Musée du Louvre in Paris, the National Gallery in London, the Kunsthistorisches Museum in Vienna, the Alte Pinakothek in Munich and the Ermitage in Leningrad – to mention a few – have given a place of permanent honour to Flemish art.

We have stimulated the publisher of this book to lay down the artistic expression of the Flemish identity in such a way that also non-Flemings get access to the partrimony. Thus a worth reading synthesis of the exceptional cultural wealth of Flanders, the historic heart of the Netherlands, is presented.

At the beginning of this study the earliest traces of Flemish art are referred to, namely the Middle Ages, the moment on which all the necessary ethnic components were present in order to discover an own national character. The 'present', which forms the coping stone of this book, does not contain the expressions of art from the most recent history, but concludes with Ensor and Expressionism.

This monumental art-history, of which editions in the most important international languages simultaneously appear, has its accent unmistakably on the plastic arts.

It is indeed primarily to painting and miniature, to architecture and sculpture and to the various branches of the applied arts – furniture, textile, wrought ironwork and gold- and silversmithery – that Flanders owes its world-wide reputation. This has not precluded the fact that ample attention has been devoted to the other expressions of culture and in particular to the liberal arts – these are after all the breeding-ground for creative-artistic forces – in each case with due regard to the political, social and economic aspects. The many connotations of the term 'Flemish' are elucidated in a special chapter.

A broad historical outline is, by way of 'introduction', devoted to picturing the background against which the developments of art in Flanders have to be viewed.

Afterwards, four chapters are devoted to plastic arts during the Middle Ages, the 16th century, the 17th and 18th centuries and the 19th and 20th centuries respectively. Each chapter is preceded by a short survey of historical events during the period in question, in particular of the intellectual history and the non-plastic expressions of art. The choice of the very rich and varied illustrative material – the most complete ever compiled in a book about Flemish Art – has not been confined to works of art kept in Flanders only, but reflects the diffusion of Flemish art throughout the world.

The subject, the way in which it is internationally directed, the devotion and reputation of our historians and art-historians and the quality of editing and printing, grant to this oeuvre the dimension of an ambassadorial message from the government which has taken the initiative for this edition.

FLEMISH ART *from the Beginning till Now*, synthesis of a great past and exponent of great promises for the future.

May this book, as carrier of this message, allow the world to get to know Flanders even better!

GASTON GEENS
President of the Flemish Government

THE SPOT OF EARTH that is called Flanders, is part of the northern Delta of Rhine, Maas and the Scheldt. Flanders, the home of the Flemish people, owes its identity to the Scheldt basin, in the same way as the land of the Walloons is born out of the Maas and the Dutchmen, the third people of the delta, have lived and grown on the junction of both rivers.

In the course of time, periods of cultural wealth occurred on each bank of these rivers alternatedly. These shiftings were not alienating for Flanders, but involved enriching alluvia, which have constituted the Flemish identity.

Art is certainly the most splendid expression of this identity. This book makes the link between the past and the future of Flemish plastic creativity. It offers a panoramic view on a fertile plain which has deserved the name of Golden Delta thanks to the wealth of its towns, monuments and museums and through its emanation on the world, and of which Flanders is the cradle. In this connection, 'Flemish' is geographically defined as the Flemish-speaking part of Belgium including the different expansions and contractions this territory has undergone in the course of the centuries: the county of Flanders with the French wing till it is lost under the reign of Louis XIV, the historical duchy of Brabant with Northern-Brabant and present Walloon-Brabant included, the historical duchy of Loon before it was definitively annexed to the prince-bishopric of Liege. The areas which specifically lived under Flemish influence, such as Tournai, Atrecht and Kamerijk are also discussed.

Without falling into narrow national triumph – there are indeed no reasons why one culture would be 'better' than the other – it is not the least merit of this book that it explains how the patrimony of Flemish art has the largest density on the smallest surface of the whole of Europe.

Now that Europe is uniting to be better integrated into the world and one is beginning to recognize the importance of regions in a united Europe, the moment has come to show what one of these regions, Flanders, has contributed to the art of Europe and of the world.

Our historical links to other European cultures – Italian, Spanish, French, German, Anglo-Saxon and Scandinavian – and the specific vitality of our German-Roman duality explain how Flemish art has made a structural contribution to the diversity and coherence of Western civilization of which this book testifies. It will not surprise the foreign reader that the effort which is made to preserve our cultural integrity, is not a mere complication of daily life in this country, but the result of recognizing the role Flemish culture played on the international scene.

May this oeuvre not only offer a view on Flanders, but also stimulate the Flemish people to respect their patrimony of art. It is not enough to look back on the exceptional rich patrimony which Flanders has produced; the presence of this inheritance on own soil should oblige the present generation to preserve it, make it grow and pass it to the future even of greater value.

This is the task, in name of the Flemish people, of those who are charged with cultural management. The confrontation in this publication which such beauty, and the supposition that so many art treasures have not yet been discovered, illustrates clearly how grand but difficult the task is of those who dedicate themselves to the preservation of our movable and immovable patrimony. The publication of this book is therefore a manifesto of our readiness to stimulate all that contributes essentially to the knowledge and appreciation of Flemish art and of our wish to make a further effort for the highest human values.

It is our utmost wish that this engagement is also taken by the next government.

KAREL POMA
Vice-President of the Flemish Government
Communal Minister of Culture.

Flemish

Compagnie douce et courtoises gens
(Aimable company and courteous folk)
(Anonymous, Middle Ages)

'*Vlaams*' (Flemish) sounds better in all languages other than Dutch, whether it comes from the lips of a bucolic Dutchman or a Neo-Flamingant. *Flamand, fiamminghi, flamenco, flämisch*, Flemish... In the ears of a Frenchman, an Italian, a Spaniard, a Briton or an American it strikes a robust, cheerful note, which many of our northern neighbours have lost – owing to their misconception of the adjective which to them smacks only of dialect. Respect for Flemish art and culture is universal, the only exceptions being of a local character: some myopic inhabitants of Brussels who are scarcely worth a mention. The linguistic fanatics among the *Flamingants* have, however, debased a rich concept in the history of our culture, to a niggling strife against a certainly distorted French culture.

Contrast this with the Spanish expression: '*No hay mas Flandes*' – the exclamation of admiration for the wealth of culture, which did not have to await the powerful impulse from the Emperor Charles V to spread southwards. The Flemish 'occupation' of Spain consequent upon the advent of the Emperor was artistic, cultural and intellectual. Philip II – who only went twice to the Netherlands, first for his Triumphal Entry, subsequently for the abdication of his father, Emperor Charles V – could not resist the seduction of the Flemish Primitives. When the town of Louvain wanted to obtain a favour from him, it presented him with a Madonna – from the hand of Jan Gossaert Mabuse – which now hangs proudly in the Prado as the *Virgen de Lovaine*. In choosing this panel the people of Louvain did not set their sights on the ultimate, but they probably knew that the King would be easily satisfied, as long as he knew that it was a Flemish painting.

Anglo-Saxon reserve is not proof against infatuation with everything that is Flemish. In a very scientifically compiled catalogue of the respected Pierpont Morgan Library, New York, a medieval Latin manuscript is identified as 'Flemish, Liege, 12th century'. Our Walloon compatriots would be wrong to give vent to indignation about this, for it is meant as a genuine compliment. The work in question is one of the exquisite Maasland miniatures. In the cultural history of this eastern part of our country, it is impossible not to speak of the Maas region without in the same breath mentioning the Rhineland. Depending on the mood of the experts, a great many manuscripts of the early Middle Ages have moved from one valley to the other. And to conclude from this that our Liege compatriots are the most germanized of all Belgians, is not such a rash hypothesis. If anybody is charmed by the best violin school in Belgium, *i e* in Liege, he or she is inclined to stifle any protest.

Closer to us, in time and space, is the spontaneous compliment addressed by General de Gaulle to Eugène Baie when the latter had just presented him with an illustrated edition of his *Siècle des Gueux*: "*de Flamand à Flamand, mes félicitations*" (My congratulations, from one Fleming to another)... The Baroque French employed by the French head of state, and that of the Fleming writing in French, exhibit just as many similarities as differences – but this is merely incidental to the present dissertation. Eugène Baie was so impressed by the Flemish genius that he – who had been made a Freeman of Antwerp – criticized the Archives and Museum of Flemish Culture for not having sufficient manuscripts by Hadewych, Jacob van Maerlant, Ruusbroec and others of the same category. Just like that, as if they lie there for the taking. Such utterances nevertheless make out a better case than most scientific analyses.

A final comment on the Middle Ages. Flemish, French, English and German were at that time all languages of equal status from a sociological standpoint. In philological terms, all languages are of equal value, but in the course of the centuries Dutch has fallen behind the other world languages in the sociological field. This is of no significance at all to somebody who speaks Dutch at home (I hesitate between 'Flemish' and 'Dutch'). When the Royal Library published a French translation of medieval Flemish poetry and prose under the captivating title of *Le Cercle des choses* – a literal translation of *Die Cirkel der dinghe* – it offered its readers an anthology of great French poetry and prose, apart from some unavoidable errors in translation inherent in any work of this kind. In the preparation of that book all contributors were struck by the fact that French was so close to Dutch in the Middle Ages – which was even more the case with German and English. A Fleming finds it easier to read Chaucer than a Briton. In such a situation western ideas transcended frontiers more freely than they do today.

However, the book which we are concerned with here deals mainly with the plastic arts in Flanders. The promoters felt that a sound text, compiled by eminent experts, together with offset reproductions of paintings, sculptures and engravings, would be sufficient to detract as little as possible from the original works of art. It is always tempting to dwell for a while on the relation between original and reproduction. Disparagement of reproductions is, at least in western culture, a fairly recent phenomenon. When Rubens painted portraits of Albrecht and Isabella, he kept an original in his studio so as to be able to make copies to order. Today art historians are obsessed by these various examples, to the point of endeavouring to discern an aesthetic hierarchy in them. In most cases this exercise gets no further than a subjective assessment. This is of no importance, except to demonstrate that one does not need to do obeisance to the word 'original' and turn up one's nose at the word 'copy'. Just ask a Chinaman what he thinks about it.

The colour plates and black-and-white illustrations in this book do not, however, escape a critical appraisal of the limitations and potentialities of mechanical reproduction techniques. Since Malraux with his *Musée imaginaire* defied many people's imagination, a large number of thorough-going dissertations have been devoted to the enlargement or reduction of works of art, the isolation of detail, *etc*. Take, for example, the matchless *Earthly Paradise*, which contends for the place of honour in every book on Flemish art, and more often than not has been the subject of reproductive manipulation. Such manipulation has not necessarily to be regarded as pejorative. The original, which has been in Spain since the end of the 16th century, is in a poor condition because the Prado still lacks the necessary facilities for temperature or humidity control. These conditions, plus the huge number of visitors, detract not a little from the pleasure of the attentive viewer. Full-scale reproduction, cut up into small folio format, – such as that offered by John Rowlands in 1974 – has its problems, but even so gives rise to moments of considerable emotion. The same is true of the details wrenched from their context, which Peter S. Beagle accompanied with a lyrical commentary in 1982. Both these American authors provide a superficial assessment of the general works of the Master of 's-Hertogenbosch. Europalia has recently added a third series of intriguing reproductions of detail, but in this case the accent is on the colour fidelity of the photographs by A. Dierick.

By the time that Hieronymus Bosch was painting actively, several generations of Flemish artists had already enriched the world of art north of the Alps with outstanding masterpieces of their own. Not long ago Rogier van der Weyden's small *St George and the Dragon* adorned the walls of the National Gallery in Washington, as one of the thirty greatest works of art to be kept in the United States. In truly American style, the art connoisseur Thomas Hoving said that every square inch had a value of $ 84,500. This has no real significance, but to a Fleming it is heart-warming. And at the time of Bosch our compatriots were still awaiting the advent of Bruegel. The phenomenon, the elusive Bruegel, so Flemish that from Brussels to Vienna, via Naples and New York, he has them all guessing. Everyone comes out with 'his' Bruegel, and everyone is both right and wrong. Genius knows no frontiers. When his consummate graphic work was transported from Brussels to Tokyo – on the occasion of the four-hundredth anniversary of the painter's death – one hundred thousand visitors discovered Japanese prints in those of the most Flemish of all artists – hosts of small figures, high horizons, scenes viewed from a height, *etc*. It was as if, so the Japanese believed in good faith, it was not Pieter Coecke van Aelst (1502-1550) who had been his master; but Hokusai in person, or at least (for those who attach some importance to chronology) a remote ancestor of the Master of Fujiyama.

When the Uffizzi in Florence decided to exhibit pictures in chronological order, without regard to national schools, Hugo van der Goes' *Portinari Altar* was set face to face with Botticelli's *Primavera*. Anybody contemplating the two works has to admit that the Fleming had the edge on the Italian. This must have come as quite a shock. Is the comparison not distorted by the fact that for many people the *Portinari Altar* is the greatest masterpiece among the Flemish Primitives?

In this brief introduction there can be no question of pursuing comparisons from generation to generation. Thus the subtle interaction between Rubens and Velasquez is not mentioned, nor are all the possible following mirror images. In the succession of universal artistic trends, Flemish genius has a place of its own, with a number of generally acknowledged peaks, such as van Eyck, Bruegel and Rubens. Among masterpieces of world standing it is naturally difficult to describe what is specifically Flemish. On the other hand, it is just as certain that they have the stamp of everything that is Flemish in the minds of foreigners. Is the palette to be given pride of place among the specific features? Yes, if compared with that of the Italian grandmasters. Or is it rather a matter of a different concept of reality? Does the subject conjure up a patient analysis in the one case, and a synthesis of form and space in the other?

Is the tension between spirituality and sensuality typical of the painters in the Low Countries? This is something which is frequently asserted. In his *Du génie flamande*, Marnix Gijsen invokes in this connection the testimony of Paul Valéry: "This race is distinguished by a specific combination of passion and languor, of tempestuous activity and a contemplative tendency, which is ardent and patient, sometimes sensual to the point of fury and sometimes wholly detached from the world of perception, withdrawn into the mystic castles secretly built by the soul in the darkness of the mind." Caustically, Marnix Gijsen remarks that the adjectives 'sensual' and 'mystic' do not apply solely to the Flemings, but that their individuality lies in the degree and nature of assimilation and rejection.

In this book, which is intended primarily to fulfil an ambassadorial function, the accent has necessarily to be on the visual arts. Apart from a few references in the commentaries, music and literature have no place. There are, of course, links between the Primitives and the polyphonists. For the painters, however, the transition to the Renaissance did not have the same consequences as it had for the musicians, who did not survive the *Stile nuovo*; despite the fact that the Renaissance in music came from the north, as Robert Wangermée so pithily expresses it. This does no alter the fact that the contemporary influence of Guillaume Dufay (1400-1474), Gilles Binchois (1400-1460), Johannes Ockeghem (1425-1496), Josquin Desprez (1440-1521) and Philippe de Monte (1521-1603) was greater than that of Hugo van der Goes and his colleagues. Today a far more considerable impact is exerted by van Eyck, Bruegel and Rubens. What is a likely explanation?

They are particularly well represented in all the major museums of the world, from the Prado in Madrid to the Kunsthistorisches Museum in Vienna, from the Louvre in Paris to the National Gallery in London, from the Metropolitan Museum in New York to the Hermitage in Leningrad. None of the examples quoted above have been kept in our own country. One does not need to be a chauvinist to deplore the fact that there are too few Bruegels in Brussels (and probably too many in Vienna).

Yet very few of these masterpieces were removed from the country *manu militari*, save for the art raids conducted by Napoleon. The outstanding exception to the rule is Hieronymus Bosch' *Earthly Paradise*. J.K. Steppe has unearthed from an obscure set of archives the harrowing tale of the curator, who was quartered for having hidden the tryptich in the Palace of Nassau. The determining factors in the expatriation of the bulk of the works of art were the 'money power' and the acquisitiveness of foreign potentates, who were probably not so foreign as our 19th-century historians would have us believe. Added to this was the fact that, as with the *Ecole de Paris* in our century, our painters benefited for quite a long time from a form of international snobbery. The king made a purchase, the courtiers followed suit. Van Dyck did best of all out of this state of affairs. Is it mischievous to enquire whether the fame of all these artists would have been so great, if all their works had stayed at home?

Anyone who conjoins the names of Bosch and Bruegel with those of Reynard the Fox and Tijl Uilenspiegel, cannot avoid answering the question whether he has really got to the heart of Flemish genius. The temptation to reply in the affirmative is considerable. Is roguishness the dominant feature of the inhabitants of Flanders? Two well-known masters, Bosch and Bruegel, certainly defy rational description, and two anonymous authors, those of Reynard and Uilenspiegel, are certainly not typical of Flanders only. Does the salient characteristic, then, consist in the sum of these four, in the specific tension between the individual and society? Universal contrasts – virtue and sin, death and life, believer and heretic, freedom and tyranny, master and slave – are moulded into a Flemish amalgam for all the world to behold.

With some reflections on our language and literature this introduction takes another turn. Some names – those of Hadewych, Jacob van Maerlant, Ruusbroec, Reynard and Uilenspiegel – have already been quoted, since life itself, also that of the heart and the mind, cannot be confined to an easel or a stereo set. A pleiad which in a manner of speaking has not survived the separation of the Netherlands in 1585. In the struggle for the emancipation of the Flemish people in the last century – in keeping with the upsurge of Romantic nationalism – these celebrated predecessors proved first-rate brothers in arms. And, inevitably, Hendrik Conscience came on the scene at the psychological moment. A gigantic leap, as it were, from the Middle Ages to nineteenth-century Belgium. The start of the movement was marked by what would today be called an 'inter-community antithesis' (*i e* opposition between Flemings and Walloons). To what extent this was an anachronistic standpoint, the reader can judge for himself.

Hendrik Conscience, a half-Frenchman who wrote in (sub-standard) Flemish, entered the fray with his *Leeuw van Vlaanderen* (Lion of Flanders, 1838). He was followed many years later by Charles de Coster of Brussels, who expressed himself in (good) French, with *La Légende d'Uylenspieghel* (1867). The first of these authors was anti-French, the second anti-Spanish. The first scored an immediate success – reprint after reprint, translation after translation. He soon became internationally famous. The second had his work reprinted only after twenty-five years, and translated for the first time after twenty-eight years had elapsed. Regarding the first, who 'taught his people to read', one might crib André Gide, who – when asked who was the best French poet – replied, "Hugo, alas!" By contrast with Hendrik Conscience's Romantic nationalism, Charles de Coster described a legendary fight for freedom, which is Flemish merely by an accident of history. He employed an archaic language, which is nevertheless wholly readable today. Unless adapted or reworked, Conscience's epic writings are not a pleasure to read. They are outmoded, as is so much nationalistic literature.

In the gas-lit century the principal instrument of literature in our region was French. Numerous are the good writers who expressed the facets of Flemish genius in that language. Take for instance *Les Flamandes*, by Emile Verhaeren. Not only did his verses have an authentic ring in far-off Paris; translations served to disseminate them to the four corners of the earth. With the award of the Nobel Prize to Ghent's Maurice Maeterlinck (1911) an unprecedented degree of recognition was attained. The medieval expression *'pays d'entre deux'* (*viz* a bridge between two contending civilizations, the Latin and the German one) has persisted into our own time.

When Suzanne Lilar celebrated her seventy-fifth birthday, four leading authors came to Brussels from France (including her own daughter, Françoise Mallet-Joris, who makes no secret of her affection for Antwerp) to praise her for her Flemish contribution to French literature and the French language in general. Remarkable, is it not? In the same period Flemish literature 'cleaned' its Dutch usage and contemporaries such as Suzanne Lilar and Marnix Gijsen, who were also friends, stood on an equal footing.

From a sociological point the emancipation of the Flemings had to be anti-French, but from a cultural point it was nothing of the sort. The same phenomenon has been observed throughout Europe. The *Matica Slovenska* in Martin has excited the envy of more than one Fleming. There a language and history circle, on the same lines as our 'Southern Netherlands Society of Language, Literature and History', has developed to such a pitch that it has become the National Library of the Slovaks. That would have happened here too, if there had been, as there, two similar languages of the same status. Here, however, we have a world language side by side with a language of limited diffusion. Moreover, the two languages here are dissimilar, the one being of germanic and the other of Latin origin. When the State University of Ghent was due to be converted into a Flemish institution, *i e* with Dutch as the vehicular language, in the inter-war period – the first Flemish rector, August Vermeylen, was not appointed until 1930 – there was still a minority in Flanders and elsewhere in Belgium who contended that Dutch was unsuitable for higher education. They had never heard of Leyden...

Many people confuse language and culture, and this confusion is still rife in Belgium. Language is an essential aspect of culture: this becomes abundantly clear when two cultures served by different languages are compared with each other. It is far less evident when two cultures have the same language. Bernard Shaw said that the British and the Americans were separated by a common language. For my part it is only too easy to apply this sally to Flemings and Dutchmen. The language itself is ineffective as regards separating the Flemish and Dutch cultures; it is, however, extremely dangerous when the Dutch language is used as a paradigm. Willem Frederik Hermans – a Dutchman living in Paris because, as is alleged by some at the University of Groningen, he feels stifled in the Netherlands – blows hot and cold on the Flemings. In one breath he congratulates us on maintaining the Dutch language in the curriculum of secondary education, which has a different designation in each country, and in another he chides us because a Flemish author can be too easily translated into French. In point of fact, W. F. Hermans is saying the same thing twice over. We badly need to make greater efforts to master our own language. As a Dutchman he does not understand that in the northern part of Belgium the concept of mother tongue has a Freudian dimension. For this we have to thank both stiffnecked Dutchmen and blockheads in Brussels. In Flemings aware of the situation this induces subconscious emotions. Where are they taking us, libidinous Flemings who cannot rid themselves of a mother complex?

Against this history sets another, positive, bastardization. The *'pays d'entre deux'* again: the Flemings regarded as the most (linguistically) latinized of the Germanics, the Walloons as the most germanized of the Latins. We learned this in primary school, and anyone who today says that the teachers were wrong deserves a primary school punishment.

The well-nigh inextricable nature of the relationship between Dutch and French in Belgium dates from long before the time of *"la Belgique sera française ou ne sera pas"* (Belgium will either be French or it won't exist), in the words of the eminent prelate. Why in 1566 did Plantin publish in Antwerp a bilingual edition of *Reynard the Fox*? Why in the 19th century had the embryonic Flemish science to rediscover Reynard? The most meaningful answer to these two questions is to be found in an old socialist ideal of elevating the language of the people, the vernacular, to a standard language. In the 16th century – and not in that century alone – both

French and Dutch were the language of Flemings, but evidently not of the same Flemings. The concept of mother tongue gets us nowhere. By contrast, everything becomes pellucid if the concept applied is that of language of the people. With the establishment of standard Dutch as a real language the problem of translation makes itself felt. The vital need for international diffusion is one that a language spoken by only twenty million people cannot meet. The intermingling of language and translation frequently defies cool analysis. Flemish authors writing in French are a moribund breed, but a tough one, and that is as it should be. Among the younger generation is the poet Frans de Haes, son of the poet Jos de Haes who wrote in Dutch. The former describes the tension in the following terms: "Although Dutch-speaking by birth and partly by culture, I write in French. The eldest son of a Flemish poet, I am gradually coming to use another language so that, thoughts against thoughts, with flashes and acrobatics of ideas, I can cope with the implacable logic of the mimetic rivalry concerning an odd subject: poetry. Just as if I could only obliquely, by a devious route, by a ruse, make my name in the other language. The eternal and yet typically strained relations between son and father, between father and son. All this, and only this, save for an entreaty, a compassion, an intoxication and a laugh." After such a profession of faith, would it be irreverent to suggest that his best poems are the translations from his father's?

When in the heat of the Romantic Flemish movement Prudens van Duyse exclaimed that "the language is the whole people", he missed the mark, as do most slogans. It would be more accurate to say that the people is the whole language, although this was questioned by Richard Minne when he wrote: "The Flemings are now speaking a civilized language; it simply remains for them to become civilized themselves." But he also dared to 'correct' old Flemish proverbs, *e g* in 'East West, home best' (the Dutch version of 'Home sweet home') he changed 'home' in 'South'... Minne's self-criticism contains much wisdom, though, useful in our own ranks nowadays.

If a people presents itself to others, it wants to show off. This happens in this book, too. With the aid of the best of our painters, sculptors and engravers, and, indirectly, of our leading writers and musicians, a picture is presented of a glorious past. Every reader who is not entirely insensitive will have understood that we are continuing to uphold this image. It has demanded not a little courage on the part of the authors to resist the temptation simply to stop after dealing with the 'greats' of the 17th century. They were right, for there is not a single people in the world whose development has followed a linear progression.

The Flemings are a people like any other. In this attempt to seek an identity, what has hitherto been missing is a glance northwards, at the Dutch, who are sometimes dubbed 'Hollanders' by the Flemings. The language has no part as a yardstick of the difference that has developed over four centuries between the Dutch-speakers of the north and those of the south. Protests from the north are of no avail. The differences in language are a hotch-potch of dialects, which have nothing to do with the political frontier. The protests themselves, and not the subject of them, afford an indication of the difference. A Dutchman protests far more readily than a Fleming and that is accounted for – no facile pun intended – by his Protestant origin. There are, of course, Catholics too in the Netherlands – quite a lot, in fact – but the great Antwerp statesman Kamiel Huysmans (1871-1963) hit the nail on the head when he said in his characteristic manner that "even the Catholics in the Netherlands are Calvinists." And this shows where the difference between the Dutchman and the Fleming lies: in the religious residue. Religion is now far from being the factor that it was in the turbulence of the 16th-century wars, but when a Dutchman (a Hollander) and a Fleming (a Belgian) look each other in the eyes, they are aware how 1585 brought about their separation.

What, in the final analysis, is Flemish genius? Let us once again glance towards the north – somebody is always a southerner in relation to somebody else – and admit with due humility that it is difficult to distinguish between Geertgen tot Sint Jans and Memlinc (an 'assimilated' German), but quite easy to differentiate Rembrandt from Rubens. After 1585 the Counter-Reformation here found its supreme expression in Rubens; while there the Golden Age was brought about by a new, powerful bourgeoisie, as mirrored in the works of Rembrandt. But this generally acknowledged difference still does not reflect the position of the Flemings. Perhaps Rubens comes near to defining it in the following letter to his friend Peiresc of Aix-en-Provence: "I have resolved to remarry because I am not yet ready for continence and celibacy; moreover, while it is right to give pride of place to mortification, we can also, putting our trust in Heaven, enjoy the permissible pleasures. I have taken a young wife, of honest but bourgeois parents, although people on all sides have tried to persuade me to make my choice in the Court; but I am afraid of coming up against pride, that vice inherent in the nobility, especially among the women. I want a wife who does not blush with shame when she sees me take up my brushes: in a nutshell, I am too fond of my freedom."

In his *Du génie flamand*, Marnix Gijsen makes the following comment on this letter: "what a splendid example of steadfast harmony, of a sense of proportion and prudence, of balance between mind and senses, which have always endowed the mass of the Flemish people with a feeling of confidence, strength and wealth." The circumstances in which Marnix Gijsen penned his comments were so exceptional that they undoubtedly influenced the author's thinking. In New York in 1943 the 'Ecole Libre des Hautes Etudes' organized a series of lectures on *L'Epopée belge*, in which Marnix Gijsen was invited to talk about the Flemish genius. His address was imbued with the sentiment, which he himself later summed up in the words of his friend, the Dutch poet Leo Vroman: "Better homesickness than Holland". The voluntary exile, whose country was in danger of going surrealist.

Listen first to this passage: "For several centuries the Fleming was humiliated and belittled. The resultant bitterness intensified as the nationalistic faith (nationalistic folly would actually be more accurate) became the cornerstone of European politics. He felt himself to be a second-class Burgundian, a second-class Spaniard, Austrian, Hollander and, to make matters worse, a Belgian of inferior status." And: "But we shall return to Belgium. We shall enter Flanders again. We shall see our fine cities again, the noble cities of Flanders, and Brussels, whose inhabitants were described as far back as the 15th century as '*compagnie douce et courtoises gens*'. Tired of the sight of dead straight thoroughfares, our eyes will once again rest a moment or two on the twists and bends of our streets. Once more the language of our compatriots will ring out loud and clear in our ears. Once again we shall tread the soil and breathe the air of the fatherland. Great and profound will be our joy. But our petty squabbles, our reciprocal narrow prejudices, our ancient and deep-rooted dissensions will also be familiar phenomena. May we at that long-awaited moment remember that our two peoples cherish certain constant values, which have made us together great, powerful and rich."

Is Flanders, is Belgium, of which Marnix Gijsen dreamed in New York during the dark years of the war, so different from the one in which we are living today? Yes and no. No longer does distance lend enchantment to the view. And there is no longer the stench of chauvinism, for nothing is more alien to a Belgian living between the Maas and the Scheldt than the most pronounced feature associated with the French. The superficial contradictions have still not been completely eliminated. But one thing stands out clearly. The Flemings are a people among the peoples of the world; the Fleming is a human being among other human beings. What is regrettable is that it took such roundabout route to arrive at a commonplace – a route with many question-marks along it. But how much worse it would have been if they had been exclamation marks! Every form of nationalism sounds the death-knell of a civilization. *Flandern über alles*? No, thanks.

HERMAN LIEBAERS

Historical survey

A succession of peoples, tribes and cultures has lived in what is today called Flanders for the past 120,000 years. In the 7th and 6th centuries before Christ the Celts conquered the region which was known as Gaul, and which covered most of Western Europe, including present-day Belgium. The last wave of Celts, the so-called 'Belgians', crossed the Rhine westwards in the 3rd century B.C., and settled in the region known as *Gallia Belgica,* between the Rhine and the Seine-Marne area.

In 57 B.C. the Roman Julius Caesar appeared on the scene. A single campaign sufficed to subjugate the Belgians, thus extending the borders of the Roman Empire to the Rhine. With the arrival of the Romans, Celtic civilization began to evolve along Roman lines, the Celts became Gallo-Romans, and Latin took the place of the Celtic dialects. The out-of-the-way corner of the Roman Empire formed by what is now Belgium, was of a great strategic importance and this brought with it a substantial economic development: a thriving and diversified 'middle class' owed its prosperity to the Roman legions stationed along the Rhine and urban centres sprouted up outside the army camps. These cities and villages were linked by a network of highways, which were of crucial importance in supplying the border regions with provisions, arms and tools as well as for the swift movement of troops.

Throughout the entire territory *villae* were established; large domains of which the principal activities were agricultural (although such industries as mining and processing of natural stone and metals were also developed), and *vici,* commercial centres along the major roads. The foundations were thus laid for economic growth of which the traces are still apparent in our time. In Central Belgium, roughly present-day Wallonia, it was the metallurgical industry which set the pace: iron, copper and bronze. In Lower Belgium, today's Flanders, the textile industry became dominant: wool from the numerous flocks of sheep providing the raw material for the highly prized fabrics and articles of clothing (hooded cloaks for example), which were exported as far abroad as Asia Minor.

The Franks (whose name means roughly 'bold') filtered into Roman Gaul in the years 256-257. These Germanic tribes were united in a federation, within which appeared two major sub-groups: the Salic Franks in the north, along the Lower Rhine, and the Ripuarian Franks in the east, along the Central Rhine. The Franks infiltrated into the Roman Empire by enlisting as mercenaries in the elite corps of the Roman army. The decimation of the Roman population resulting from successive wars lent the bellicose Germans from along the banks of the Rhine and the Danube easy access to the Roman legions. By the 4th century the Roman army consisted almost entirely of Germans. The 'barbarians' were able to rise high in the military hierarchy; many Frankish warriors acquired the rank of officer, one of them even made promotion to general.

Afterwards the Salic Franks also settled in tribal groups in the virtually depopulated Roman border territories, especially along the Lower Rhine. In the second half of the 3rd century they established themselves in the Betuwe, the delta area of the larger rivers. Only half a century later they had settled Taxandria, present-day North Brabant, and around 450 they had already expanded so far southwards that Tournai and Cambrai had become Frankish cities.

In this period, from the 3rd to the 5th centuries, the linguistic border must have been established. Sharp as a knife but with no natural frontiers, it still cuts the Belgium of today in two. Historians have yet to answer the question as to when and how precisely this happened. In any case the Franks contented themselves with the effective control of Northern Gaul and the colonization of the marshes and moors of Lower Belgium, without penetrating further into fertile Central Belgium. This had the remarkable consequence that a village to the north of the linguistic border became Germanic and is still Flemish, while a neighbouring village just to the south was, and still is, a part of the Romance world.

With the collapse of the Roman Empire in the 5th century, the Germanic tribes had a free hand on the Continent. Virtually everything in the line of material and cultural heritage built up by the Romans was lost. The centralized Roman Empire crumbled to pieces, people deserted the cities and sought out the protection of the local lords. Feudalism developed: people offered their services and usually a portion of their income as well to the local feudal lord in exchange for his protection. The power structure took on a pyramid form of feudal lords and vassals, with at the bottom the serfs, unfree, bound body and soul to the land.

One such warlord succeeded in extending his power beyond his purely local basis in the region around Tournai: Clovis (ca 480-511), of the Merovingian dynasty (named after a legendary forefather, Meroveus). Using true maffia methods Clovis managed to set aside all the other Salic and Ripuarian Frankish chiefs and forced recognition of himself as the only king of the Frankish nation. The territory which he and his successors ruled, *Francia,* the Frankish Kingdom, contained virtually all of Western and Central Europe.

Quarrels and wars among the Merovingians themselves brought about the disintegration of the Merovingian state. Pippin the Short, Mayor of the Palace – a sort of prime minister – shut the last of the Merovingian kings away in a monastery and founded a new dynasty, named after his father Charles Martel: the Carolingians. His son Charlemagne (768-814) was able to further extend his empire northwards to the North Sea and the Elbe and southwards beyond Rome and to the Pyrenees. From its nucleus in the region of modern-day Flanders and North-Brabant, the kingdom of the Franks had grown to one of the superpowers of the era, alongside the Byzantine Empire and the Moslem caliphate of Baghdad.

Although in 315 Christianity was proclaimed official religion of the Roman Empire, Northern Gaul remained largely heathen at the time of the Frankish conquest. The christianization of these regions was completed only in the mid-7th century through the work of missionaries from Southern and Central Gaul, with such pioneers as Saint Amand (in the areas around the Scheldt and near Liege) and Saint Eligius (Inland Flanders and the region around Antwerp). Many others followed after them, among whom numerous Irish and Anglo-Saxon missionaries.

The religious and spiritual climate in the West was principally influenced by the monastic way of life which orginated from the Near East. Monasteries served to continue and intensify missionary work; between 640 and 730 some thirty monasteries were founded in our area, most of which adopted the Rule of Saint Benedict of Norcia. At the same time the secular structure of the Church was refined, with bishoprics corresponding to the former Roman *civitates,* their capitals serving as the bishops' sees.

The clergy and the monks were at that time the only ones who could still read and write; they were consequently able to monopolize the cultural life of the period. Schools existed only in the cathedrals and in the abbeys, only there did the cultural accomplishments of Roman civilization survive.

The Treaty of Verdun (843) divided the great Frankish Kingdom, after a long period of wars and instability, in three: France, Germany and between them the Middle Kingdom. The disintegration of the Middle Kingdom in 855 led to the formation of, among others, Lothringen, named for King Lothair II and including present-day Belgium east of the Scheldt.

Lothringen was however destined to quickly become the stake in a violent contest between France and Germany. In the beginning of the 10th century the latter prevailed and Lothringen became a German dukedom, thus extending the western border of the German Empire from the Central Rhine to the Scheldt. Five centuries later this border still divided what is now Belgium into a smaller French and a larger German territory.

Along its ever-threatened borders the Frankish kingdom was divided into larger duchies, with alongside them smaller *pagi* or counties, governed by counts. In Germany on the other hand the kings were able to keep their officials under control centuries longer.

Soldiers, professional warriors equipped with horses and armour, were necessary to the princes, whose only means of paying them was land. Once in possession of land however the soldiers, fully aware of their indispensability to the prince, promptly set themselves up as miniature princes. They became lords, the feudal nobility of this new period. New castles literally sprouted out of the ground, and around them a complete political, social and economic microcosm arose. In this way each fortress became a power centre which was, considering the ineffectual siege methods, impregnable save by means of treason or stravation. Thus, even when far outnumbered, relatively less powerful lords were nevertheless able to repulse attacks.

Practically out of the blue, in the extreme northwest of France, amidst the anarchy of the 9th century, arose the county of Flanders, which in a few decades grew to be one of the mightiest principalities of the kingdom. It was the incrusions of the Vikings in northwestern France between 879 and 883 which led to the spectacular birth of the county. While the whole of northwestern France lay in ruin, there was a true exodus, a mass flight of the population, including the notables, towards the south. An exception was the 16-year-old Baldwin, son of the recently deceased count, who retreated with a number of warriors to the 'Flanders district', the region around Bruges. Flanders, etymologically, means roughly 'land won from the sea', which refers to the marshlands around the Zwin, a treacherous landscape, half land, half water, where the Vikings did not even venture an attack.

When Baldwin could safely leave his refuge in 883 he found a political vacuum. With a handful of warriors he established, quickly and encountering no appreciable resistance, his authority over a large territory. His domain extended from the North Sea and the Western Branch of the Scheldt on the one hand to the River Aa and the hills of Artois on the other, corresponding to today's provinces of East and West Flanders (West of the Scheldt), the western part of Zeeuws Flanders, the north of the French *département du Nord,* the area from Dunkirk to beyond Lille. The territory was predominantly Dutch-speaking, with a French-speaking strip in the south, the region of Lille, Douai, Orchies, which later became known as *Flandre gallicante*. The original centre 'Flanders district' gave its name to the new principality of Flanders.

Count Baldwin consolidated his power by constructing fortresses at all strategic points, further enriching himself and expanding his authority by large scale confiscations of properties belonging to landowners who had fled the Vikings. This enabled the count and his successors to maintain peace and order in Flanders in a way unique in all of Western Europe, a fact which proved of vital importance to the economic development of the region.

As, in the course of the 11th century, the imperial authority decayed more and more in Lothringen, Baldwin IV (988-1035) and Baldwin V (1035-1067) began expanding their territory eastwards. After half a century of strife the German emperor finally had to recognize the expansion of the county of Flanders to include the land of Alost (East Flanders east of the Scheldt) and the marshland of 'de Vier Ambachten' along the Western

Branch of the Scheldt. From then on Flanders was subject to two realms, Crown Flanders to France and Imperial Flanders to the German Empire.

The Investiture Contest, the conflict between pope and emperor over the investiture of ecclesiastical offices, changed the face of Europe in the late 11th century. Although the emperor was able to retain most of his authority in Germany proper (until the 13th century), Lothringen splintered around 1100 into a mosaic of principalities. In the region which would later make up modern Belgium were thus created Brabant (duchy in 1106, formed by the counties of Louvain and Brussels plus the march of Antwerp), Loon (modern-day Belgian province of Limburg) around the fortress of Borgloon, Hainaut, Namur and Limburg (which is now the land of Herve, the area around Verviers). The Ardennes were cut up into a series of small principalities, which in time came to be united into the county (later the duchy) of Luxemburg.

Equally as a result of the Investiture Contest it was decided that the bishops in Lothringen, Liege included, were to be elected by the local clergy, although they retained the temporal power over the regions previously entrusted to them by the emperor, the prince-bishoprics. The prince-bishopric of Liege was almost exclusively French-speaking until one of the prince-bishops added the Dutch-speaking region of Loon in 1366 by buying off the rights of its last count. Loon remained attached to the prince-bishopric of Liege until the end of the 18th century.

After centuries of turbulent history a Flemish identity began to define itself, reflected in the art which bore witness to its birth. Between the 9th and 11th centuries the principalities and domains established borders which remained virtually unchanged for centuries afterwards. Dynastic vicissitudes, largely the result of marriages contracted with the acquisition and combination of inheritance in mind, were typical of this new era. This tactic was sometimes successful, but just as often ended in internecine feuds leading to further divisions.

A fundamental point is that the balance of power could and did evolve in opposite directions. In the German Empire the emperors lost all authority over their vassals and as a result the princes of Lothringen saw the means of acting entirely on their own initiative; Brabant in particular moved to become the dominant force in Central Lothringen. In France under the Capetian kings precisely the contrary came to pass and in the 13th century the king was entirely successful in subjecting the Flemish counts to his authority.

The economic development of the time was characterized by a vigorous revival, bringing with it the breakthrough of a money economy in the place of an exclusively land-based economy. Nevertheless the power of the princes remained intact: with the 'aids' and other payments which they could exact from their subjects, they assured themselves new and ample means. This allowed them to exert more authority over the hitherto so unruly knights and feudal lords. In order to accomplish this however, the princes were forced to acknowledge the rapidly growing importance of the cities. In the more economically developed regions, with their numerous, rich and powerful cities, the relations with the prince often led to serious friction and from time to time even to revolts.

With few exceptions, all the present urban agglomerations in our area grew up around castles between the 9th and the 11th centuries. Outside the most important castle gate was invariably the marketplace around which the first merchants, craftsmen and tradesmen built their houses, warehouses and taverns. From these tiny centres in a few centuries time grew the great medieval cities.

Cloth manufacture and trade, aided by a long period of peace and order, became the backbone of urban development in Flanders. The rise of the cloth industry was not everywhere apparent to the same degree, but was concentrated in the Dutch-speaking part of the county, particularly in Ghent and Ypres and to a lesser extent in Bruges. Foreign purchasers were to be found principally in Germany, England and France.

With this Flemish revival in the Scheldt basin went a parallel resumption of economic life in the valley of the Meuse, based chiefly on copper and bronze. This recovery was reflected in an equally spectacular development of art and culture in the area. This boom proved short-lived however; although the presence of *kalmei* (zinc, which was used for yellow copper or brass) in the neighbourhood of Morensnet undoubtedly stimulated the manufacture of copper and bronze, just as it had in Roman and Carolingian times, the basic raw material, copper, had to be imported from the German *Harzgebergt*. When in the 11th and 12th centuries the Germans began to process their copper themselves on a large scale, the cities along the Meuse were unable to compete. Already in the 12th century they were reduced to the level of second-rate agglomerations.

The international economy was dominated by Flanders and Northern Italy. These centres also gave the impetus necessary to stimulate trade and industry in other countries. Flanders offered the world its cloth, the North Italian cities, Venice, Genoa and Pisa imported more and more spices and other highly prized luxury goods from the Middle East. This revival of trade brought at the same time money back into circulation, which broke the monopoly of land as the only source of wealth and power.

At this time, just as in the preceding period, trade with England and the Rhineland (Cologne) remained central to the Flemish economic system. Trade with England became, for a very specific reason, of truly vital importance to Flanders. The wool provided by the flocks of sheep grazing on the polders and in Inland Flanders made the original expansion of the Flemish cloth industry possible. But the local production was soon incapable of meeting the rising demand, and from about 1100 on the industry was increasingly dependent on imported English wool, which was moreover of superior quality. Finally only English wool kept the Flemish looms in action. Had the English at that time processed their wool themselves instead of exporting it, the Flemish economic expansion would have been unthinkable.

Count Charles the Good, end of the 12th century. Lille, Archives départementales du Nord, ms. 10 H 323 fol. 109.

The specific organization of trade with England and the Rhineland changed with time. In the beginning of the 12th century caravans of mules laden with cloth left Arras every year for a long journey through Eastern France and over the Alps to Genoa. This traffic did not last long. Both Flemings and Italians were active in Central France, and around the middle of the century they began to negotiate their trade agreements at the yearly fairs in Champagne, a halfway point for each, which thus grew to become the most important economic meetingplace in Christendom.

At the same time Flemish ships sailed southwestwards to load wine in Bordeaux and salt in the Bay of Bourgneuf. This salt in turn served to stimulate the rise of the Flemish herring fishery, and along with it the development of fishing ports along the North Sea coast, Nieuwpoort and Dunkirk among others.

Around the Baltic Sea the situation also changed rapidly, particularly after the threat of Viking aggressions had been removed. The leading role was played by North German merchants, who, after the deterioration of imperial authority had formed the league of cities destined to become the mighty German Hansa. The Flemings came to them, with Hamburg as the most important port of call, to buy products from Scandinavia and Russia: furs, walrus ivory, resin and the like.

Until around 1250 this was an active trade, that is to say that the Flemish merchants brought their own cloth to the foreign markets and brought foreign products from there to sell either in their own country or at other markets. In the middle of the 13th century this situation changed when the English and German Hanseatics (the league by then included the Rhinelanders as well as the North Germans) began to come to Flanders. The fairs of Champagne were disrupted by political troubles, the Italians in turn found their way to Flanders, the Venetians via the Rhine, the Genoans by sea; the first Genoan galleys anchored in the Zwin in 1277. Flemish trade was forced, with the exception of the Biscaye route, into a passive role; from that point on the foreign merchants came to offer their wares for sale in Flanders, and returned home laden with Flemish cloth.

The consequences of this evolution should not be underestimated. The Flemish cities, until then centres of industry and trade, became predominantly industrial, with one exception, which precisely because of the switchover from active to passive trade, flourished as never before: Bruges. Hitherto a city of lesser importance, but the only Flemish port of any consequence; there it was that foreign merchants came to exchange their wares for Flemish cloth. In a few years time Bruges became the principal trading centre in Western Europe, focal point of the German Hansa and terminus of the English and Italian trade routes.

Brabant also profited from the Flemish economic development. Trade had previously been carried on almost exclusively via the waterways. Where these were absent, or necessitated too great a detour, or where the tolls weighed too heavily, land routes presented an alternative. Thus it was that around 1150 the road from Bruges to Ghent was extended as far as Cologne. This in turn started the cloth industry up in those cities of South Brabant in the neighbourhood of this trade axis, with Cologne and the Rhine as their most important export markets. When at the end of the 13th century it came to an open conflict between Flanders and the French monarchy, the Brabanders managed to squeeze their neighbours out of the French market, which paved the road to prosperity. The most important port in Brabant, Antwerp, was nevertheless of no great significance and lived chiefly by supplying the hinterland of Brabant with fish and salt from Zeeland.

This was also a period of rapid urban expansion. A considerable number of towns in Flanders and Brabant counted more than 5,000 inhabitants in the 13th century, which made them, for that time, impressive cities. A century later Ghent counted 56,000 inhabitants and Bruges 35,000; there were scarcely half a dozen such megalopolises then to be found in all of Christian Europe.

In the 12th century the burghers began to build walls around their agglomerations. At the end of the century every urban settlement had its defensive walls. The fortresses within the city walls instantly lost all their military significance. They were therefore quickly dismantled, bringing the additional advantage to the princes and lords of a considerable profit from the sale of the land thus made available. Only Ghent did not follow this pattern. Around 1180 Philip of Alsace tore down the large castle and parcelled out the land, but at the same time he built the solid Castle of the Counts on the site of the tower. This, however, no longer served as a refuge, but as a means of controlling the often ungovernable townspeople of Ghent.

The cloth industry in the cities of Flanders and Brabant made use of the services of specialized craftsmen, each of whom carried out a particular process (weaving, fulling, dying). Though working at home and with their own equipment, they were not self-employed; rather they were wageworkers in the service of merchant-entrepreneurs, who bought up the wool and sold the cloth.

These merchant-entrepreneurs formed a sort of moneyed elite within the cities: the patriciate. They gained control of the entire administrative and judicial apparatus, and used and abused these powers to further their own interests, at the expense of a 'middle class' of tradesmen and craftsmen, and of the proletariat of textileworkers.

Neither of the latter groups had organized themselves. It was at that time however that the first professional organizations were created, the crafts guilds or trades, which were founded by the urban magistrature (in order, among other things, to facilitate the regulation of workers), and were under the strict supervision of the aldermen and thus of the partriciate, who appointed the deacons and 'finders' (overseers).

It would have unquestionably been possible for the French king to have added Flanders to the crown domain, had he gone about it with more address. However the support which the French governor gave to the partisans of the King was much too conspicuous. These partisans were the *leliaarts* (the urban patriciate and a portion of the nobility), who aroused a growing hatred, and a consequent lack of sympathy towards the occupying French troops and administration. The situation reached the boiling point when on May 18,1302 in Bruges Pieter de Coninc and his followers massacred French soldiers and *leliaarts*. The 19th century romantics called this event the *Brugse metten*.

The revolt soon spread over all of Flanders. Philip IV sent an impressive army of knights in haste, which suffered a crushing defeat on the *Groeningekouter*, on the banks of the Leie before the walls of Courtray. This became known as the Battle of the Golden Spurs, after the numerous golden spurs captured from the fallen French knights and hung as trophies in the Church of Our Lady in Courtray.

The Battle of the Golden Spurs broke the dictatorial power of the patriciate. Via the crafts guilds the 'commons' won a voice in the city administration.

In the 14th century the socio-political shocks followed one another rapidly in Flanders. Between 1323 and 1328 there was a bloodily suppressed peasant revolt in the polder areas. The political turmoil was however chiefly the work of the big cities, principally of Ghent, the weavers and fullers acting as the moving forces behind the unrest. In the revolutionary activities of Ghent, Bruges and Ypres, Ghent was always the instigator, under the leadership of 'captain' James van Artevelde, the first commoner in Western Europe to act on an equal footing with kings and princes. He played a role in international politics until his murder in 1345. The weavers led the city in its rebelliousness from 1337 to 1349, later Ghent resisted Count Louis of Male a full five years (1379-1385), until it could finally lay down arms under honourable conditions.

In the course of that century the cloth industry also declined. The reason for this was relatively simple. Around 1340 the English finally began, at the initiative of Edward III and with the help of Flemish immigrant workers, to process their own wool into luxury cloth, and this at a price with which Flanders was unable to compete.

Much of what happened in Flanders during those years seems particularly irrational in this context: the conflicts between weavers and fullers, the aggressive attitude of the city towards the count, viewed as a scapegoat for events over which he had no control, the abuse of power exercised by the big cities with respect to the smaller centres and the countryside, where every attempt at economic competition was met with brutal repression.

After the death of Louis of Male (1346-1384) his possessions went to his son-in-law Philip the Bold, Duke of Burgundy and a younger son of King John II of France. Neither Philip the Bold nor his successors were the rulers of a united kingdom, since the various counties and duchies over which they ruled retained their autonomy and their own institutions. It was thus thanks to the personal prestige and authority of the dukes of Burgundy that the term 'Burgundian State', debatable in a strict sense, came into use. The legacy of Louis of Male included, among others, Flanders and Artois, an ideal bridgehead for a further Burgundian penetration into the Low Countries. This was primarily the work of Philip the Good (1414-1467) who by his political genius, assisted by the circumstances, added nearly all of modern Belgium (minus Liege-Loon) and a large part of the present-day Netherlands (Holland and Zeeland) to his realm. His son and successor Charles the Bold (1467-1477) allowed his father's work to be lost, although the Burgundian realm in the Netherlands managed to survive the crisis which followed his death.

An important development was the formation of the modern state in all of Europe during this Burgundian century. The strengthening of the monarch's authority was central to this process and even in the Netherlands rich and powerful cities were no longer a match for the prince, who could call upon immense resources. These were used, among other things, to support mercenary armies, whose only function was to consolidate the power of the Burgundian dukes. The old, feudal nobility merged in this system with the high officials to form a new court nobility whose rivalries for the ducal favours might or might not be rewarded by such symbols as the Order of the Golden Fleece.

It is also remarkable that the Burgundian state functioned without a permanent capital; the dukes were indefatigable travellers who journeyed, in company of their central administration, from one city to another. The splendour and magnificence of the Burgundian court aroused the admiration and envy of all Europe. Flemish art flourished as never before and Flanders-Brabant became, despite the current economic crisis, together with Northern and Central Italy, the principal artististic centre in the Christendom of the day. In the region of Liege there was a revival around the production of firearms. In Holland and Zeeland more commercially directed maritime activities (a grain trade with East Prussia or Poland) developed out of the fishery. Flanders and Brabant were in this Burgundian period the most economically developed regions not only in the Netherlands but to the north of the Alps. And yet the crisis hit hardest here. The English cloth quickly superseded the domestic production in the international markets and such cities as Ypres, in the 14th century still the third most important city in Flanders, were completely depopulated as a result.

When the urban cloth industry had died out, the fabrication of the 'new drapery' developed in a spectacular manner in the countryside. The raw material for this new branch was the cheap wool imported by the Spaniards. To begin with this industry was centred in South Flanders (Hondschoote, Armentières, Poperinge). The cities managed however to turn this new rural industry to their advantage, since the raw wool and the finished products passed through the hands of urban merchants.

At the same time another industry remained in existence: the manufacture of tapestries used for decorating the walls of castles and palaces. This grew to be an important industrial branch in 14th century Arras (which gave the Italian name for tapestry: arazzo) and Tournai. In the following century they were confronted with serious competition from Brabant (Brussels) and Flanders (Audenarde, Geraardsbergen).

The reorganization of both regions is amply illustrated by the decline of Bruges and the rise of Antwerp. Bruges had become a European trade metropolis, where luxury cloth was exchanged for products imported chiefly by Italians and Hanseatics. Even though this legion of merchants was further strengthened by Spaniards (wool) and Portuguese (African goods) the importance of Bruges waned. This has too often been ascribed to the silting up of the Zwin, although in the 15th century the link with the open sea was never broken. The real reason for the decline of Bruges lay elsewhere: it no longer commanded the Flemish luxury cloth, nor the English cloth which, banned by the embittered Flemings and Brabanders, had nonetheless cornered the international market.

Antwerp had, due to its location, never become a cloth centre. Although it was the only important port in Brabant the pre-eminence of Bruges had always limited the port of Antwerp to a regional role. Burgundian times however brought a change in this situation.

The 'fairs' of Brabant, organized twice a year in Antwerp as well as in neighbouring Bergen-op-Zoom made their appearance in the 14th century. In the beginning of the 15th century the English merchants arrived there whith their cloth, which was avoided like the plague everywhere else. These goods were exchanged for 'new drapery' and moreover attracted the Italians and Hanseatics from Bruges. At the end of the century the Southern German concerns which exploited silver and copper mines in Bohemia and Hungary arrived to exchange their metals for English cloth. The rise of Antwerp was at that moment directly proportional to the decline of Bruges.

Charles the Bold's daughter and heiress, Mary of Burgundy (1476-1482), to secure her a helpmate, was married in haste to the Habsburg prince Maximilian of Austria (became in 1486 archduke of Austria and its dependencies and in 1493 emperor of the German Empire). Maximilan acted as regent first for his wife (1477-1482), then for his son Philip the Fair (1482-1506), who was the first Habsburg ruler of the Netherlands, and finally for his grandson Charles. Archduke Charles (1500-1558) gained control, thanks to the vagaries of fortune and the marriage policy of his grandfather, of an enormous realm: the Burgundian Netherlands (1506), Spain and its dependencies (1516), Austria and the rest of the Habsburg domains (1519), to finally accede to the title of emperor (Charles V, 1519). Because this realm was practically ungovernable Charles V divided it in two when he abdicated in 1555. The Habsburg domains went, together with the emperor's title, to his brother Ferdinand, whereas control of Spain (with dependencies) and the Netherlands was transferred to his son Philip II. The Netherlands thus remained a collection of autonomous principalities which never formed a Spanish colony in the strict sense of the word. Nevertheless they were treated as a Spanish conquest since Philip II and his successors ruled primarily as kings of Spain.

Charles V added several territories to the Burgundian heritage in the Netherlands: Tournai in 1521, which had formed a French enclave in Flemish territory, the whole of the Central and Eastern Netherlands was annexed in 1524 after a fierce struggle with the dukes of Gelders (Friesland); Utrecht and Overijssel in 1528, Groningen en Drente in 1536 and finally Gelders itself in 1543. In that year the 17 provinces of the Netherlands were united, only to separate again in 1585.

Juridically the Habsburg Netherlands still formed a part both of France and of the German empire. Charles V managed to pry the Netherlands loose from both realms through a series of treaties and agreements and to establish them as an independent and indivisable whole.

During the rule of the Habsburgs, who seldom lived in the Netherlands, the governors-general appeared suddenly on the political scene. They were responsible for the administration and protection of royal interests. The first governor-general Margaret of Austria, an aunt of Charles V, (1518-1530) settled in Malines. Her successor, sister of Charles V, Mary of Hungary (1531-1555), lured by the tempting hunting preserves of the Sonienwoud, settled in Brussels. In this way Brussels became the capital of all the Netherlands until 1585 and afterwards of the South.

Antwerp reached the height of its glory around 1500. This city of yearly markets had grown to such a degree as to bring prosperity to its direct hinterland as well (Brabant, Flanders, Holland-Zeeland).

On August 24, 1501 the foundation for this unparalleled rise was laid. On that day the first Portuguese galleon, full to bursting with pepper and cinnamon, put in at Antwerp. The Portuguese king opted for Antwerp as the distribution centre for the new spice trade (Vasco da Gama had discovered a sea route to India via Africa). Only here the metals needed by his traders were to be found in sufficient quantity. This meant copper for Black Africa and silver for India, delivered by the Fuggers from Augsburg and the Welsers from Neurenberg, who had a virtual monopoly on this trade. Although the turnover in this branch was originally quite modest, within a very short time virtually the total Central European production of these metals was draining into Antwerp.

The Portuguese and Southern Germans earned so much from this trade that they began to buy up the 'new drapery' in unheard-of quantities for sale on their local markets. Along with this the demand for linen also rose enormously, as it was a very pleasant fabric to wear in the tropics; thus the linen industry and the 'new drapery' flourished in the countryside of Flanders and Brabant. The demand for English luxury cloth grew correspondingly, and so quickly that the English were unable to properly finish off their product. Antwerp seized the opportunity and applied itself to the delicate work of finishing and dying. With the contribution of the Italians, who arrived at the harbour city with silk cloth, brocade, gold thread and the like, Antwerp at once added up to an important textile centre.

On the shores of the Scheldt sprouted an El Dorado already numbering some 100,000 inhabitants in 1560, and therefore considered, together with Paris, Venice and Naples, among the largest cities of Christian Europe. The new wealth and increasing activity attract-

23

Leo Belgicus (Lion of the Netherlands), engraving, Jan van Doetechum the Younger, edited by the engraver himself at Rotterdam. The prototype of the Leo Belgicus (at which the map of the Netherlands is drawn in the form of a lion) is the title-print, engraved by Frans Hogenberg of the work De Leone Belgico of Michel Aitsinger, Cologne, 1583 and 1585. It was copied a lot as it was here by Jan van Doetechum, who invented a variant by surrounding the lion with the portraits of the political rulers of the Netherlands for the period from 1555 till 1598.

ed in turn new industries, plus a broad spectrum of artistic occupations (book printing, etching...).

At the time there were no true banks outside of Italy. The money trade was essentially the business of those merchants who, having more money than they cared to invest in goods, wished to profit from it in another manner. In Bruges the Italians arranged their financial affairs at an inn called 'the Beurs', named after the family of innkeepers and brokers who ran the establishment: Van der Beurze. In this way *beurs* (Exchange) became a synonym for banking and was in Antwerp applied to the hall the city government made available to merchants for their financial negotiations.

On the Antwerp Exchange money was principally in demand for loans to the crowned heads of Spain, Portugal and England. There were such considerable sums involved and at such high rates of interest, that the situation grew into the nightmare most dreaded by all financiers to this day: the States could no longer meet their obligations. In 1557 Philip II declared himself bankrupt, the Portuguese king followed in 1560. Philip II arbitrarily blocked all repayments and decided moreover to freeze the interest rate at a paltry five percent.

Antwerp's role as the financial capital of Western Europe was thus ended at a single blow. The Southern Germans and Italians especially suffered heavy losses, whereas the local merchants came through, relatively speaking, without a scratch. Thenceforth the balance of their capital was no longer invested in loans to the state, but used to form temporary 'companies': partnerships with shared capital and shared profit or loss, serving to finance the more risky ventures. In this manner trading companies were formed for Marocco, Sweden, Muscovy (Russia) etc.

The Italians introduced a number of refined trading techniques, among them double-entry bookkeeping, sea insurance, the intensive use of letters of change, to Antwerp where they were adopted by the local merchants. In this context Antwerp played a historic role in passing these techniques (plus the art of gambling with capital in risky enterprises) on to neighbours less well-grounded in them. The rise and prosperity of Holland and England were in this fashion certainly hastened.

In 1517 Martin Luther began his preaching and on July 1, 1523 two Augustinian monks from Antwerp were burned at the *Grote Markt* in Brussels. They were the first religious martyrs in the Netherlands; victims not of the Inquisition as is often incorrectly claimed, but of the temporal authority, in the person of Charles V, who wished to keep his Habsburg domains Catholic.

The Lutherans were people respectful of law and order, offering no resistance to the government. They remained quiet and were concentrated in cities like Antwerp which had a large German population. With the great peasant revolts in Germany in the 20's the anabaptist movement also appeared with all its prophets and their far from uniform doctrines. This Anabaptism first found acceptance in the Northern Netherlands and spread from there into Brabant and Flanders, recruiting followers principally from the lower social classes. More than 90 percent of these Anabaptists were executed, as they were feared by Catholics and Protestants alike on account of their 'communistic' ideals.

A third reformation movement, Calvinism, reached the Netherlands around 1540 via the South. Around 1560 this doctrine was already firmly established in the Flemish West Quarter and had spread to the big cities of Brabant, Flanders and Hainaut. The followers of John Calvin belonged to the nobility as well as to the bourgeoisie or middle classes. They were prepared to defend themselves militarily against their opponents and organized themselves in strong local 'consistories' or church communities, most comparable to the Underground cells of the Second World War. They posed on this account the most serious threat to the government at that time.

Political upheaval was also brewing independently of these religious movements. Philip II gave the high nobility, true to tradition, seats in the 'Council of State' which was supposed to advise and assist the new governor, Margaret of Parma (1559-1567). The real power on the other hand fell into the hands of a semi-official *consulta* of confidants and technocrats, against which the aristocracy reacted violently. Philip II backed down and dissolved the *consulta*, returning the aristocracy to power. They accomplished so little in the way of administration that they began to cast about for means of regaining their waning prestige. The obvious issue was the repeal of the edicts against the heretics. The king reflected long on the matter and when at last he bluntly refused the demands of the high nobility, the decision struck the Netherlands like a thunderbolt.

The high aristocracy discovered to their displeasure that they had lost the initiative to the lower nobility. This was predominantly Catholic, but the Calvinists among them formed a 'confederacy', in order to demand repeal of the edicts against the heretics. On April 5, 1566 they marched through Brussels and presented their demands at the governor's palace. That evening echoed the cry 'Vive le geus'. Political and religious movements had flowed into each other and this osmosis was to bring about the fall of the Netherlands.

The Calvinists saw in this petition proof that the aristocracy was behind them and began, under the protection of armed coreligionists, to hold 'hedge sermons' outside the city walls. These sermons spread from the Flemish West Quarter (June 1566) throughout Flanders and Brabant and initiated the 'wonder years' (1566-1567). Both the governor and the local authorities were compelled to accept this since they had no police force or army capable of repressing it.

On August 10, 1566 Calvinist extremists sprang into action and destroyed the interior of the church of Steenvoorde in the Flemish West Quarter. The 'iconoclastic' movement spread like wildfire through the country and came to violent outbursts in Flanders and in Brabant (Ypres August 15, Antwerp August 20, and Ghent August 22), and also, if less violently, in Zeeland, Holland and Friesland, where the movement died down in mid-September. This iconoclasm proved catastrophic for Flemish art, although such important artistic centres as Bruges, Brussels, Louvain and Malines escaped intact.

SCOPVS LEGIS EST, AVT VT EV QVÊ PVNIT EMENDET, AVT POENA
EIVS CAETEROS MELIORES REDDET AVT SVBLATIS MALIS CAETERI SECVRIORES VIVAT.

De Gerechtigheid (Justice), engraving 23.3 × 29.5 cm, anonymous engraver after a drawing by Pieter Bruegel the Elder, 1559. Brussels, Royal Libary. From the series of seven virtues by Hieronymus Cock, 1559-1561; the original drawing of Pieter Bruegel (dated 1559) can be found in the Royal Libary at Brussels. *Justitia* gives us a detailled (and therefore very precious from the historical point of view) image of the jurisdiction (including the *questuur* or torturing of suspects, and the different ways of execution) in the Netherlands during the 16th century.

The iconoclasm aroused the violent indignation of a broad segment of the population, but armed Calvinists were able nevertheless to seize power or to install themselves alongside the legal authorities in some cities (Valenciennes, Tournai, Antwerp, 's Hertogenbosch, Utrecht, Amsterdam). Margaret of Parma finally sent out an army and the last resistance was crushed in March of 1567.

In Madrid an enraged Philip II decided to deal with the heretics and rebels in the Netherlands once and for all. Thus in August 1567 the Duke of Alba appeared in Brussels with a Spanish army to restore order and to replace the governor.

Most of the Calvinists fled abroad and only a few who had remained behind, the counts of Egmont and Hoorn for example, could be executed as a deterrent to others. Within a very short time however the harsh approach of Alba provoked new tensions.

William the Silent, Prince of Orange, had, from his base in Germany, already made several attempts to liberate the Netherlands. In 1572 he began a double offensive: he himself led an attack from Germany and his brother one from France. In addition a diversionary manoeuvre was carried out from England by the so-called *watergeuzen,* who, although coming into action far too soon (April 1, 1572), were nonetheless able to capture the port city of Brielle in South Holland. General anti-government feeling more than the influence of the Calvinists led cities to open their gates to the *watergeuzen* and other exiles, among them numerous preachers who began converting Holland and Zeeland to Protestantism. The campaigns of William of Orange and his brother failed, but did however keep Alba from concentrating his full attention on the powder keg in the North before October 1572. Holland and Zeeland profited from this respite to organize their resistance and William of Orange bound his fate to that of the two rebellious provinces.

Alba could not definitively crush the revolt and was

27

replaced at the end of 1573 by Don Luis de Requesens who only succeeded in confining the resistance movement to those two provinces. Philip II on his part was obliged to pump more and more soldiers and money into the Netherlands. He was so short of cash however that the payroll for the occupying army remained months behind and the soldiers began to mutiny and plunder. This, of course, only served to increase the hatred for the Spaniards even in those territories remaining Catholic and in Spanish hands.

The death of Requesens (March 4, 1576) led to an enormous chaos in the South. The troops, threatened with pogroms, entrenched themselves in small cities (Alost, Lier...) or in the fortresses of the large centres (Ghent, Antwerp...). The States of Brabant, after the establishment of the States General meant to govern the southern provinces, sought contact with Holland-Zeeland. The 'Pacification of Ghent' was signed by both parties on November 8, 1576, just after the Spanish troops had allowed their 'Spanish fury' to rage over Antwerp (November 4-6). North and South had formed a common front to come to terms with Philip II, but once again religion formed the wedge which drove them apart.

The Calvinists resumed their preaching in Flanders and Brabant and grew extremely influential in a number of cities. Ghent proved a bastion of Calvinism out of which attempts were made to introduce Protestantism into Flanders, Artois and Hainaut. This led to violent reactions on the part of Walloon, Catholic 'malcontents', and the anti-Spanish front began to crumble.

On the first of October 1578 Don Juan of Austria, freshly-installed governor of the Netherlands, died. He was succeeded by the commander of his army Alexander Farnese, Duke of Parma and son of Margaret of Parma. He was not only an outstanding general, but an exceedingly skillful diplomat. On October 4, 1579, with the 'Act of Reconciliation', he succeeded in reconciling Artois, Hainaut and Namur with Philip II. From this base he was able in 1583 to begin his 'reconquista'. Farnese fought a strategically well-conceived war without massacres, providing an honourable retreat for even the most fanatical Calvinists; cities were not stormed but besieged and starved. These tactics were first used in Flanders, where Ypres capitulated on April 7, 1584, Bruges on May 20, Ghent on November 17. Then came Brabant's turn: Brussels fell on March 10, 1585. The battle against Antwerp began in May 1584. The bloodiest battles of the entire Eighty Years' War were fought there and the harbour city capitulated on August 17, 1585. The war was to last until 1648, but after the fall of Antwerp the Spanish advance lost momentum. A few kilometers above the Scheldt city a border was formed and it can be said in hindsight that in August 1585 the Netherlands were divided in two: the Spanish, Catholic South and the independent, Calvinistic North, the republic of the United Provinces.

After 1585 the South experienced an economic revival, but around 1650 came a new collapse. The (expected) revival never arrived, which meant a definitive end to the glory years of Flanders and Brabant within the European framework.

In the second stage of the Eighty Years' War the advantage passed to the North, which thanks to the Peace of Munster or Westphalia booked a considerable territorial gain at the expense of the South: States Flanders (Zeeuws Flanders with Sluis, Axel, Hulst), States Brabant (the present-day province of North Brabant), States Limburg (around Maastricht).

The Protestant successes in the 16th century were chiefly due to the abuses within the Catholic Church. When with the Council of Trent (1545-1563) religious life was reorganized and the Counter-Reformation began, the Southern Netherlands grew in a minimum of time into the bulwark of militant Catholicism in Western Europe. In this way also North and South, 'the Flemish' and 'the Dutch', drifted apart.

The first half of the 17th century was relatively calm in the South, but then Louis XIV (1643-1715) attempted to expand his territory at the expense of the Spanish Netherlands. Once again armies roved through the countryside and Louis XIV eventually accomplished his aim. Artois, Cambrai, Walloon Flanders, parts of Southern Flanders (the region around Dunkirk-Cassel, the north of the present-day *département du Nord*), plus parts of Hainaut and Luxemburg became French. The *regio* Flanders got in this way both its northern and southern borders.

Charles II, King of Spain, died childless in 1700 and left his realm to a grandson of Louis XIV, Philip of Anjou. Thereupon the United Provinces and England rallied round the Habsburg pretender to the throne, Archduke Charles of Austria. The result of this discord was the War of the Spanish Succession (1700-1713), fought for the most part in the Southern Netherlands, with all the unfortunate consequences this entailed.

When Archduke Charles unexpectedly became emperor (as Charles VI) and sovereign of the Habsburg domains, the enthusiasm of his allies swiftly dampened since they saw little good in the transformation of a French-Spanish bloc into an Austrian-Spanish one. It came to a sort of Solomon's judgment: Philip of Anjou retained control of Spain and its overseas territories, while Charles VI was allotted Spain's European possessions (including the Southern Netherlands). Thus in 1715 the South became Austrian, the principal result of which was that the Spaniards in the central administration in Brussels were replaced by rather more efficient Austrians.

The unrest which troubled France in the second half of the 18th century aroused little response in the Austrian Netherlands, where the aristocracy was of small account and the bourgeoisie had little reason for complaint. But then the enlightened despot Emperor Joseph II, little endowed with diplomacy, attempted to completely reorganize social and religious life. This led to a revolt in which the 'patriots' expelled the Austrians and proclaimed the republic of the 'United Belgian States' (January, 1790). The situation deteriorated into chaos and in September of that same year the Austrians reoccupied the Southern Netherlands, after which the new emperor Leopold II repealed the reforms of his predecessor.

The peace which followed was of short duration.

Revolutionary France declared war on Austria and expulsed the Austrians from the Southern Netherlands in the course of 1794. This region was promptly annexed, together with the prince-bishopric of Liege and several smaller principalities.

The French occupation soon aroused resentment, chiefly on account of the measures against the Catholic religion and the introduction of compulsory military service or 'conscription'. On November 12, 1798 the Peasant War broke out in Overmere near Dendermonde, spreading from there to other parts of Flanders and the Kempen, but it was quelled within a few months. Peace returned when Napoleon Bonaparte came to power in France (1799).

The French regime introduced a number of positive innovations. The Southern Netherlands were restructured along French lines. The régions were divided into departments (roughly our present provinces) administered by a perfect (now provincial governor), subdivided into cantons (now: arrondissements) with sub-perfects (now: district commissioners) and finally into municipalities with mayors. A single system of weights and currencies was introduced throughout the country, there was a uniform judiciary, the same system of taxation... In short: the administrative and juridical structures of a modern state, which remain for the most part in force to this day.

Under Napoleon's military dictatorship there was no political manoeuvering room for the bourgeoisie, but this was partially compensated by the disappearance of tariff-walls enabling the bourgeoisie throughout the French empire (which included a large part of Europe) to do good business.

Napoleon was forced to abdicate in 1814 and made his final bow with the debacle at Waterloo. In that same year it was decided that the North, which had actively combatted Napoleon, and the South, which had played no active role, should be reunited in the kingdom of the Netherlands with William I of the House of Orange as its prince.

The South seemd at first content with this arrangement, but the contrasts between North and South had grown considerable. Not only were there religious differences (Catholicism versus Calvinism), but a great deal had changed in the language situation as well, since the Southern bourgeoisie had been – certainly under French rule – largely frenchified. This bourgeoisie however made no resistance to the reunification since it allowed them to conduct business throughout the huge Dutch colonial empire. In the parliamentary democracy of the Netherlands William I held the reins firmly in hand; autocratically, he made a number of decisions which were appreciated neither by the Catholics nor by the anti-clerical faction (later the 'liberals') within that same bourgeoisie.

A banal incident in Brussels on the night of November 25 to 26, 1830 led to a full-scale revolt. William I attempted to occupy Brussels with an army, but was forced to retreat following heavy fighting on the barricades and the rebellion spread to Wallonia, Flanders and even to Dutch Limburg.

In November 1830 a National Congress met in Brussels to give the South – from then on called Belgium – a progressive constitution and a new parliamentary regime. The superpowers which had achieved the reunification, compelled to recognize this definitive separation of the Netherlands, opened negotiations under pressure from Great Britain in particular. Thus came into existence the Treaty of the 24 Articles: Belgium was independent, but eternally 'neutral'. The National Congres invited Prince Leopold of Saxe-Coburg to become king of the newly-founded realm of Belgium; he accepted and was crowned on July 21, 1831.

The Industrial Revolution begun in England made use of complicated machinery, discovered steam energy and intensified both production and consumption of iron and steel. Small workshops gave way to huge factories and this modernization soon caught on in our country. With machines smuggled out of England Lieven Bauwens opened in Ghent the first cotton-spinning mill on the Continent. Although this undertaking was not an unqualified success due to a lack of cotton caused by the Continental Blockade, it was nevertheless the herald of a new era.

The bourgeoisie in particular saw in this process of modernization a means of widening their own horizons and provided the necessary impetus. In this fashion Belgium became the second land, in the footsteps of Great Britain, to enter the industrial era, where a new phenomenon put in its appearance: the factory worker.

Other countries followed this example, so that in the course of the 19th and 20th centuries their relative status changed constantly. Belgium was able to maintain its position reasonably well in this murderous competition, boasting an industrial buildup on a double basis: coal mining and metallurgy. These were supplemented by other industries such as glass and textile manufacture (Flanders, parts of Wallonia). Remarkably, in this rapid evolution, the production of linen escaped mechanization and remained a home industry until the end of the 19th century. Cotton on the other hand was more suited to industrial processing and thus Lieven Bauwen's Ghent grew into a Belgian Manchester, complete with a factory proletariat, slums and all the other related side effects.

Ghent was for that matter the only real factory city in Flanders, where smaller companies and home industry long remained the rule. Wallonia on the contrary developed a broad belt of coal mines and factories stretching from Liege to Mons, which made for a pronounced difference with the North.

For nearly a century and a half prosperity of Belgium was founded on this double basis, while the harbour of Antwerp thrived as never before. When in recent years, however, new technologies appeared and other trends developed in world trade, both the heavy industry in Wallonia and the textile industry in Flanders were undermined, and the need for modernization became manifest. This seems to be somewhat more successful in Flanders than in Wallonia, and a parallel can be drawn with what came to pass during the 14th and 15th centuries in Flanders and Brabant.

With the Industrial Revolution the population skyrocketed: from 3,000,000 inhabitants during the Dutch period to 9,500,000 now, with slightly over 5,500,000 Dutch-speaking and slightly under 4,000,000 French-speaking people. The economic expansion also contributed to cultural, scientific and artistic achievements. Whereas in the 18th century the Southern Netherlands constituted a cultural backwater within Europe, Flemish art has since, although never attaining such heights as in the Burgundian, Renaissance or Baroque periods, nevertheless reached a respectable level of accomplishment.

Political parties, a recent phenomenon in Europe, appeared in Belgium only with the establishment of parliamentary democracy in 1830. Even then there were originally no parties in the strictest sense of the word, but the role of the Church and the consequent discussion around education led to the formation of the liberal party in 1846, which received its counterpart in the Catholic party founded in 1868.

Politics long remained – via a system of poll-tax suffrage – the affair of the wealthier bourgeoisie. With Ghent as forerunner the first (clandestine) unions and solidarity funds gradually took form, to emerge into the open in 1866. In 1885 the Belgian Labour Party was born from various socialist-inspired organizations, whereas the Catholic workers – avers to socialist anti-clericalism – began, from 1890 on, to group together. Since then three large parties (Catholic, Liberal and Socialist) have dominated the Belgian political world.

Much remained still to be done about the universal suffrage demanded by the workers. There were mass demonstrations and riots necessary before the bourgeoisie were prepared to replace poll-tax suffrage by a system of multiple votes in which, on grounds of wealth or diplomas, one person could cast several votes. The principal of one man, one vote and universal suffrage broke through only in 1919, and then only for men, women gaining suffrage only after the Second World War.

The bourgeoisie had been frenchified (and French-speaking) since the beginning of the 19th century, and the short-lived reunification with the North did little to combat this trend. This implied that the institutions (administration, judiciary, army, education...) of the new state were also modelled (linguistically as well) on the French. The Dutch language was thus banned from public life, and threatened even as cultural vehicle. With romantic enthusiasm a handful of intellectuals, principally in Ghent and Antwerp, took up the cause of that language.

The Flemish struggle gradually resulted in a number of concessions, through which Dutch could also be used in public life. Only after the Second World War did this conflict take on serious proportions with the formation of Flemish parties which operated alongside or even against the traditional political parties. When in 1934 the University of Ghent became Flemish (-speaking), this event was generally acknowledged as a milestone in the struggle for Flemish autonomy.

In the 60's the conflict between the two communities took on a new dimension when the Flemish wished to combat the spread of what they called the (French-speaking) 'Brussels oil spill'. The tensions to which this gave rise have still not relaxed; on the contrary, they have been further exacerbated by a certain Walloon agitation, which seems to find favourable soil in the economic disappointments of the South of Belgium.

Valentin Vermeersch
Custodian of the Museums of Bruges

THE MIDDLE AGES

LÉON VOET
Introduction

JEAN-PIERRE ESTHER
Architecture

CHRISTINE VAN VLIERDEN
Sculpture

DIRK DE VOS
Painting

VALENTIN VERMEERSCH
The art of stained glass

MAURITS SMEYERS
The art of illumination

LÉON VOET
Graphic art

LIEVEN DAENENS
Furniture

ERIK DUVERGER
Tapestry and textile arts

VALENTIN VERMEERSCH
Metalwork

HUBERT DE WITTE
Pottery production

Pour che que toute
creature de raison a
noble entendement de
sire et appete sauoir.
z oyr choses nouuelles pour la re
creation et esioyssement de son co
raige. z offr que eus ou recoid des
choses aduenues anchiennement
z meismement des haultes et nobles
proesses et emprises des nobles
hommes proaces et enteures des
haultes et nobles procreations et
lignies. tous preudommes ay ans
entendement esseuet en honneur
quant ilz telz fais oent recoider son
esseuent z esmeuuent en plus grant

perfection de baleur z de proesse.
Est il que a ceste instance moy non
digne. poure de sens. et mieure a le
tendement. debille et foible de ceste
haulte matere mettre a effect. se
non que il me fuist comande come
il est de par mon tresredoubte z tres
puissant seigne. monseigr. philippe.
par la grasse de dieu. Duc de bour
toingne. de lothringue. de brabat et
de lembour. conte de flandres. du
tois. de bourtoingne. palatin de hay
nau. de hollande. de zelande et de
namur. marquis du saint empire.
Seigneur de frize. de salins z de ma
lines. me suy determines z disposes

32

Introduction

A large number of objects fashioned by our distant ancestors have been handed down to us from the Paleolithic, Mesolithic, Neolithic, Bronze and Iron periods; but with the best will in the world, these objects can hardly be considered to be works of art. Moreover, the most valuable are articles imported from abroad.

Belgium became part of the Roman Empire at the beginning of the first century AD, and as such it was incorporated into the Graeco-Roman civilization which had developed around the Mediterranean Sea. However, there was no great breakthrough in culture and art. The Romans introduced the use of natural stone and brick in building; but archaeologists have only been able to uncover a few ruins of the constructions built in Belgium by them and their Gallic-Roman imitators. Articles with any artistic merit made in the area were intended for use by soldiers and tradespeople, whose standards were not especially exacting. For temples and tombs, statues and bas-reliefs were made in stone; and even though they are now the pride of Dutch and Belgian museums, any Roman with a feeling for art would have looked down on them with contempt. The few objects of a more than mediocre quality to be found in Belgium were still – as previously – imported from abroad.

In the 3rd century the civil wars lead to economic, cultural and artistic decay throughout the Empire. The arrival of the Franks did not exactly change this situation. In any economic crisis building is always the first activity to be suppressed. In the north of Gaul, which had by now become the Frankish Empire, the recession was so far reaching – even in the areas that remained Romanized – that the use of stone in building was virtually completely abandoned, and builders went back to using wood. Our knowledge of the material life during the Merovingian period is in fact limited to articles which were found in graves. However, this source soon dried up with the spread of Christianity in the 7th century.

This spread brought with a new culture and civilization. The priests and monks, who were the only people who could still read and write – using Latin for this purpose, to the exclusion of the vernacular languages – took over the intellectual life. It is often assumed, either implicitly or explicitly, that the emphasis in art was now completely dependent on religion. This assumption overlooks the fact that powerful secular noblemen also lived in magnificent dwellings or even palaces which they had built for themselves; and collected valuable articles and ornaments, possibly even real art treasures. However, these buildings have disappeared and their contents have been lost as a result of family or other tribulations. Only in monasteries and churches was there any continuity, and at an early stage 'treasure houses' and libraries were established where the most valuable articles could be kept. Even so, only an extremely small percentage of these treasures have survived.

THE CAROLINGIAN RENAISSANCE
(second half of the 8th century – 9th century)

A revival began in the late Merovingian period, but the cultural and artistic breakthrough only took place under the Carolingians; so quickly and overwhelmingly that it is sometimes referred to – rather exaggeratedly – as the Carolingian Renaissance. The use of brick was not reintroduced, but even in the north important buildings – especially churches and abbeys – were once again built of natural stone. Nevertheless, few of these buildings have survived. They were of modest proportions and most were later destroyed to be replaced by the larger Romanesque or Gothic buildings.

In the cathedrals and abbeys, schools were founded for training the higher ranks of the clergy; with courses in music (which was important for the liturgy) and basic science, as mathematics and astronomy, to compute the date on which Easter fell. The *scriptoria* – writing workshops in these establishments – became hives of activity; Bible and liturgical texts as well as old Roman manuscripts were copied and even original contributions were made: religious and moral tracts, annals (chronological historical notes), and above all, *vitae*, biographies of the local saints and the miracles they had performed.

Irish and Anglo-Saxon missionaries were very active in this cultural development. Under their influence the Merovingian script, an almost illegible adulteration of the late Roman, was transformed – as if by magic – into the beautiful Carolingian minuscule lettering, which is at the origin of our own modern script. Their love of the written word also led to the decoration of handwritten works with beautiful initial letters and miniatures, and they succeeded in spreading this love to the mainland. In the Carolingian *scriptoria* many beautiful handwritten manuscripts originated, with initial letters and illustrations derived from Ancient Roman or Byzantine examples, and interwoven with decorative elements of Merovingian (zoomorphic themes) and Irish and Anglo-Saxon (complicated arabesques and floral motifs) origin.

The churches and abbeys, as well as the palaces, were adorned with sculptures and frescoes; crucifixes, relic casings, book bindings for liturgical works were produced in splendid editions, inlaid with gold and silver, encrusted with gems, decorated with enamel or rock crystal or carved ivory (usually from the walrus or narwhal from Scandinavia). However, only a meagre collection of all this has survived from the entire Frankish Empire. Our knowledge of the art of the

Jean Wauquelin presenting a manuscript to Philip the Good, illuminated page from Jacques de Guise, *Chroniques de Hainaut*, Part I (French version Jean Wauquelin), 290 × 200 mm. Bruges (?), *ca* 1450. Brussels, Royal Library, ms 9242, fol 1.
Commissioned in 1446 by the Duke of Burgundy, the book was illuminated in various stages. In the miniature – which may or may not be by Rogier van der Weyden – that was ordered, Chancellor Rolin and the Tournai Bishop Jean Chevrot are seen on the left. Among the figures on the right is Philip's son, the future Charles the Bold.

Carolingian Renaissance is mainly restricted to architecture – more from the remains of buildings than from any that are still standing – and from manuscripts.

The Carolingian Renaissance spread throughout the Empire, but one of the focal points was in the north: in the valley of the middle reaches of the Rhine and the Maas, the border area between the Roman and German world; so that we also begin to find Germanic-speaking scholars, writers and artists, in addition to Romance-speaking ones. The reason for this is obvious: the centre of power of the Carolingian Dynasty lay in this area and Charlemagne made Aix-la-Chapelle the real capital of his empire – a centre of art and culture which attracted intellectuals and artists from the whole Empire, and influenced the churches and abbeys in this region.

In this process the area now known as Flanders did not play a significant role: the lack of natural stone was a serious obstacle to the development of architecture; there were no bishops living in the area; and apart from St Peter's and St Bavo's in Ghent and St Trudo's in St Trond, there were no important abbeys.

On the other hand, the valley of the Maas – with especially the bishop's city Liege, followed by Maastricht – was influenced by the Emperor's court at Aix. To the south of Flanders (in the Romance areas later known as Artois, Hainault, and Walloon Brabant) bishops did reside at Tournai, Arras and Cambray; and the network of monasteries was much more concentrated there with such important centres as the monasteries of St Bertin (at St Omer), St Vaast (at Arras), Lobbes and Marchiennes (Hainault), Nivelles (Walloon Brabant) and above all, St Amand (at Valenciennes). There *eg* the oldest known French and German literary texts, respectively the *Séquence de Ste Eulalie* and the *Ludwigslied*, were written down consecutively in a manuscript dating from the late 9th century.

THE POST-CAROLINGIAN PERIOD
(*ca* 900- *ca* 1050)

The years from 900 to 1050 were a transitional period in art history. Like so many other transitional periods, it has been variously labelled, depending on the particular specialist's viewpoint. During this century and a half Carolingian art evolved into a style which the 19th century termed 'Romanesque' (initially intended to be a pejorative term: Roman art which had been adulterated). Some specialists simply pass over the 10th century, together with the Carolingian period, as 'Pre-Romanesque'; others continue the Carolingian era into the 10th century and view the Romanesque era as beginning in about the year 1000. German art historians finally called the 10th century and the first years of the 11th the 'Ottonian era'. In fact, the period from *ca* 900 to *ca* 1050 can justifiably be termed 'the Post-Carolingian era'. In all areas the lines of force of the Carolingian Renaissance continued to play a part, until new cultural patterns began to emerge in about 1050 with the now fully recognized Romanesque art.

In the 9th-10th century two great states emerged from the Carolingian empire: France and Germany. During the 9th century France suffered severely from invasions by the Normans; and in addition the country was torn apart in the 10th century by an anarchy, which led to the creation of principalities and seigniories. This was certainly not conducive to a flourishing cultural and artistic life. Intellectual and artistic activity were at a low ebb throughout the kingdom, even a considerable backwards step, when compared to the Carolingian era. In the extreme northwest the counts of Flanders (to which what later became Artois also belonged at that time) were able to maintain law and order, and made it possible to rebuild and reorganize the abbeys with the help of Lotharingian church reformers. Again some work was carried out in St Peter's and St Bavo's Abbeys and particularly in the abbeys and churches in the Romanesque south, although this did not yet amount to very much.

On the other hand, the Carolingian Renaissance maintained its momentum in Germany, which had been spared by the Normans and where the kings (emperors after 962) had managed to retain their power; and it even reached a zenith in the 10th century and at the beginning of the 11th. In this area it was termed 'Ottonian' art and culture after the emperors of the House of Saxony: Otto I, 936-973; Otto II, 973-983, and Otto III, 983-1002. Numerous monuments were erected and there was a singularly prolific production of beautifully illustrated manuscripts (in which the Irish-Anglo-Saxon and late Romanesque sources of inspiration made way for Byzantine influences) and other artistic works already characteristic of the Carolingian era (bronze and copper, inlaid with gold, silver, decorative enamelling and gems; carved ivory).

The focal point of Ottonian art was in the Germanic areas of the empire, *inter alia* Cologne, Trèves, Hildesheim and Fulda, but as in the Carolingian era the Maas valley, with Liege in the forefront, was strongly influenced by this cultural and artistic expansion. The 'Imperial Church' established by Otto I was involved in this to a large extent; the emperors appointed the bishops and many of the abbots in their empire – and in doing so they preferred to appoint German clerics who had been trained in the schools of the Emperor's palace. For example, at Liege and Cambray there was a virtually unbroken line of German bishops throughout the 10th and 11th centuries – with an unquestioning allegiance to the dynasty, but at the same time intellectually endowed and permeated with the pomp and glory of the imperial court.

As a result a feverish building programme got underway in the Maas valley which spread throughout Lorraine; and in the abbey *scriptoria* in this area the artistic and intellectual activities exceeded amply those in the basin of the Scheldt. A great deal of the enamel work, jewellery and carved ivory that is so typical of the Ottonian era, was made in the Maas valley.

Jan van Ruusbroec, (about 1293-1381), working in the convent of Groenendaal, miniature, 15th century. Brussels, Royal Libary, ms 19295-97, fol 2 v° The grand-master of Dutch mysticism takes notes on a wax tablet, which are copied by his assistant on parchment.

34

CULTURAL LIFE DURING THE ROMANESQUE AND GOTHIC PERIODS
(ca 1050-1500)

Art historians divide the late Middle Ages neatly into two long eras: the Romanesque period (*ca* 1050, possibly earlier, to *ca* 1200) and the Gothic period (*ca* 1200-1500). With regard to the Netherlands the 15th century is occasionally called 'the Burgundian era'. However, from a cultural historical point of view, trends can be discerned from the middle of the 11th century, which overlapped and led to new waves less easy to categorize.

THE GREAT CULTURAL AND INTELLECTUAL RENAISSANCE (*ca* 1050-1300) The struggle for the Investiture (1076-1122) put an end in Germany to the Imperial Church and meant the decline of the emperor's power. At the beginning of the Romanesque era important artistic and cultural activities continued there, but they were unable to equal the Ottonian achievements. The Romanesque Maas valley also continued to be fairly active intellectually and artistically for quite a long time. However, when the German bishops and abbots disappeared, the ties with the Empire became weaker and looser. In the 12th century the recession in the bronze and copper industries in the Maas cities finished off the job. From the 13th century the valley lost a great deal of its cultural and economic strength, as well as its prosperity. From the 12th century the cultural and artistic centre of the Low Countries moved from the Maas to the Scheldt valley.

By the 11th century France had passed its worst anarchy and the new dynasty of the Capetians expanded its power. There was an intellectual and artistic flowering which surpassed that of Germany, and which was even felt in the extreme northwest area: in the county of Flanders, from where it trickled through to Brabant. From a cultural point both principalities – Flanders from the beginning and very forcefully, Brabant somewhat later and weaker – became provinces of the upcoming France.

During the 11th-13th centuries a great deal took place that had a profound influence on the cultural development of the Occident and of present-day Belgium. The struggle for the Investiture was actually caused by pressure groups which wished to purify the Church and clerical life. Figures such as Gerard of Brogne and Richard of Saint-Vannes had already been responsible for similar movements in Flanders and Lorraine, in the 10th and the first half of the 11th century. With the reformation, which started at the end of the 11th century in Cluny Abbey (Burgundy), these movements gained in strength throughout western Europe. This led, *inter alia*, to the founding of new monasteries in the countryside as well as in the flourishing cities. Baudouin V of Flanders (1035-1067) founded scores of these religious establishments, both in the Germanic and the Romance parts of his principality. In Lorraine princes and knights were no less active.

In addition, new tendencies led in the 12th century to the appearance of new sorts of monasteries: in the countryside those of the Cistercians and the Premonstratensians; and in the 13th century, those of the Dominicans and Franciscans in the towns. Each and every one of these establishments and institutions formed a new centre of cultural and intellectual life. From the middle of the 11th century the area now known as Flanders started to catch up on the centuries in which it had been left behind.

Intellectual life – which still used the language of the Church, Latin, as its official language – continued during the 11th and 12th centuries, to concentrate on religious thought and experience, with subsidiarily historical annals and chronicles. There were few outstanding achievements in this area; one exception is the account of the murder of count Charles the Good (1127) by Galbert of Bruges – one of the most lively journalistic contributions in all medieval literature.

However, in the 12th century there was a sudden acceleration in higher intellectual streams of thought: the texts of the great Greek philosophers (Aristotle and Plato) and scholars permeated the West via Latin translations of... Arabic translations. Colleges were founded where these texts could be studied and evaluated, which led to the foundation of the universities in the 13th century. In these universities the emphasis was still on theology and philosophy – developed in Paris in the 13th century by Albert the Great and Thomas Aquinas into the system known as 'scholasticism', which remains the basis of Catholic theology and philosophy to this day. Nevertheless, for the first time since Roman antiquity a great deal of importance was again attached to the natural sciences (including medicine) and to law. The first of these higher institutions in western Europe were founded in Paris (Sorbonne), Oxford and Cambridge. The Low Countries had to wait until 1425 before a similar centre of learning was founded in Louvain. But long before that time many intellectuals from Belgium had already gone to the Sorbonne to perfect their education. In numerous places in Flanders grants were given to gifted clerics who lacked the necessary financial means to go and study (for example, in the second half of the century by Canon Arnulf of Maldegem for students from the Bruges region). A number of scholars from Flanders and Brabant even built up considerable reputations as professors at the Sorbonne: the Franciscan Wouter of Bruges; and the Dominicans Willem of Moerbeke, Egidius of Lessen, Hendrik of Ghent, Hendrik of Bats and above all, Zeger of Brabant.

Up to 1000-1050 west European society was predominantly agricultural. All the wealth was produced on the land or came from its revenues. Even the rich and powerful lived on their lands in the most literal sense, and had to pay for services rendered with land or with products from it. Obviously this considerably inhibited many activities, including building and art production. However, from about the year 1000 an economy based on money once again became established, at a time when great piety or even religious ecstasy had taken hold of all levels of society. This expressed itself in generous gifts to churches. Already in the second half of the 11th century the monastic chronicle of St Trond could note that the gifts of money from believers regularly exceeded the abbey's revenue from its lands. More than anything else, this emergence of an economy based on money led around 1050 to an acceleration in the development of the budding Romanesque art and encouraged a tremendous amount of building. Churches and monasteries shot up in the cities and in the country, and secular building was similarly affected.

It was during these years that merchants discovered that they also needed to master the 'clerical' art of reading and writing in their trade. They encouraged the establishment of schools, and in doing this they sometimes found themselves in conflict with the Church authorities. In about 1180 there was actually a 'school war' in Ghent because St Veerle's chapter house, which had a monopoly on education in the city, continued to concentrate on religious matters and refused to devote attention to 'practical' matters like arithmetic. The Count's intervention was needed to reach a compromise which gave the burghers of Ghent the opportunity to found 'free' schools. By all means, schools where the children of burghers (and the nobility) could be educated sprang up during the 12th and 13th centuries in all the towns of any importance. With the arrival of these schools the use of the written word spread; and from the 13th century, whenever any sort of agreement was made either in the cities or in the country, a charter would be drawn up.

Noblemen and burghers began to read for pleasure and in the Low Countries literacy developed to such an extent, that in the 14th century a special script was developed by master writers to write more quickly and cheaply. This was the easy-to-write and yet legible *bastarde* (a script in between the formal script used in books, which had developed from the Carolingian minuscule into the decorative but rather laborious Gothic script in the 13th century, and the italic script used mainly in administration, which was very personal and difficult for outsiders to decipher. *Bastarde* can be either a book script that was written more quickly, or an italic script that was written slower and more regular). All the tools needed for writing – parchment, ink, pens – which had previously been made to the best of their ability by monks or priests for their own use, were now put on the market by specialist traders. From the second half of the 13th century paper was also imported from Spain and Italy for less valuable documents such as notes, registers *etc.*

There was another important side effect of the intellectual awakening of the burghers and the nobility: the monopoly of Latin, which had been the only written language in the West for centuries, was now threatened. Latin still remained the language of the Church and of science; but from the beginning of the 13th century it was gradually replaced in administration by the vernacular languages, and these also became a literary medium. The Low Countries were a border area between the *Dietsche* (Dutch speaking) and the *Walsche* (French speaking) worlds. The historic role played by Godfrey of Bouillon in the First Crusade is largely attributable to the fact that, having grown up in the area near Boulogne, he was bilingual (or even trilingual) and could communicate with the French, as well as with the German and Dutch speaking knights.

Nevertheless, during the 12th and 13th centuries French penetrated the county of Flanders – and to a lesser extent Brabant – as the cultural language of the higher clergy, the nobility and the city patricians; without affecting the man in the street or influencing the Dutch language (apart from the intrusion of a few words borrowed from French, particularly relating to military, legal and economic activities). However, during the 14th century with the struggle against France (and the suppression of the patriciate and the French leaning nobility) a nationalist reaction to this developed in Flanders, spreading from there into Brabant. It got rid of much of these French influence.

In the 12th and 13th centuries there was a remarkable growth in French literature and one focal point was in the Romanesque part of the Scheldt basin, which was undergoing an unparalleled economic revival together with the rest of Flanders. At Arras, Douai, Lille, Cambray, Tournai and Valenciennes, '*Puys* (from the Latin word *podium) de rhetorique*' were founded from the 13th century onwards – the precursors of the Chambers of Rhetoric. The poetic works acted out there were partly of bourgeois nature; though they also borrowed a great deal of material from the trouvères and troubadours who, for the benefit of princes and nobles, told tales of courtly love and of the courage of valiant knights going to the rescue of blushing virgins. One of the most famous French minstrels of the 12th century, Chrétien de Troyes, spent a long time at the court of the Count of Flanders, Philip of Alsace.

This French literature was greatly admired by the Flemish in the north. However, in the Dutch speaking part of the country, there were no amateurs who expressed their feelings in the French language. Despite the extensive French influence amongst the nobility and the more important burghers, the literature was produced in Dutch, even if this literature consisted mainly of translations or adaptations of French models.

In the 11th century a writer from West Flanders wrote a few lines in a manuscript in Oxford, which constitutes the first example of Dutch literature: "*Hebban alla vogala nestas bigunnan / Hinase hi(ce)nda thu*" ("All the birds have begun to nest / except for me and you"). However, it was another century before a knight from Loon (Limburg), Hendrik van Veldeke, who died in 1189, gained a wide reputation for his romances, a 'classical' novel (*Eneit*) and a religious tale (*The Legend of St Servaes*). He was particularly admired in the German speaking area where he made a great impression and eventually settled. After Hendrik van Veldeke the literary life in Limburg came to a standstill. The writing of works in the Dutch language in the 13th century became a speciality of literary scholars in Flanders, and occasionally Brabant. Virtually all of these were 'clerks' (clerics or laymen, 'working' with the pen in one administration or other); with only a few exceptions such as Duke John I of Brabant, whose works include a number of romances, and a few woman writers – Beatrijs of Nazareth (*ca* 1200-1268) and Hadewijch (*ca* 1250?), who were amongst the very first women in Europe to be active in the literary field, with some very praiseworthy results.

These clerks worked through the entire repertoire available in French literature and, like the French models, always wrote in verse: tales of chivalry and courtly love, romances, religious epics, mystical lyrics and the bourgeois genre, which consisted mainly of animal tales and fables. Most of these clerks have remained anonymous except: Diederik van Assenede who adapted *Floris ende Blancefloer*; Zeger Diengotgaf, who also wrote tales of courtly love; 'Willem die Madoc maeckte' (*Madoc* is a Celtic tale now lost), who gained lasting fame with his adaptation of *Vanden vos Reinaerde* (Reynard the Fox); and the clerk who was already then considered to be 'the father of all Dutch poetry', Jacob van Maerlant (1225-1300?).

Much of what was produced deserves no more than a footnote in some scholarly handbook; but a few of the works rise above the general level of mediocrity, such as the chivalric tales, *Karel ende Elegast* and *Walewein*, and Diederik van Assenede's *Floris ende Blancefloer*. 'Willem die Madoc maeckte' wrote with *Reynard the Fox* one of the highpoints of medieval animal epic tales. The Mary legend *Beatrijs* is one of the masterpieces in medieval literature; Hadewijch reached outstanding heights in her mystical lyrics, as did Beatrijs van Nazareth, who was one of the very few 13th century writers to use prose, and who achieved an international level with her mystical laments. The prolific Jacob van Maerlant, who wrote in all the genres, was more significant at a national than at an international level; but he can be credited with familiarizing Flemish readers with problems of natural science, theology and world history in works such as *Der naturen bloeme*, the *Rijmbijbel*, the *Spieghel historiael*, which were usually direct adaptations from Latin. Until that time these subjects had been the exclusive province of a limited intellectual elite.

THE 14th CENTURY   After the revolutionary cultural and intellectual upheaval of the 12th and 13th centuries, the 14th century can be viewed as a time of consolidation. Several new tendencies emerged in Dutch literature. France was no longer the main source of inspiration and as a result Dutch literature was more original, if not superior. Tales of chivalry and courtly love became less popular. The emphasis shifted to didactic and moralizing works; the theatre emerged; although poetry reigned supremely, prose did gain some ground both in a qualitative and quantitative sense.

Flanders, which was torn apart by social unrest, was surpassed as a literary centre by the more peaceful Brabant, while to a modest degree contributions were also being made by the Northern Netherlands. The history writers, who still wrote in verse, included Lodewijk van Veltem (who died in *ca* 1326) and Jan van Boendale (*ca* 1280-1365) from Brabant, as well as Melis Stoke in Holland. Jan Yperman, a physician in Ypres, wrote his *Medicine Boeck* and *Cyrurgie* at the beginning of the century, the first original scientific contributions of any value in the Dutch language. For the theatre, plays of love and passion such as *Esmoreit*, *Gloriant* and *Lanseloet van Denemarken*, and light-hearted farces were produced. Whether or not they were staged at the time remains an unanswered question; but there are

indications that already in the 14th century there were companies active (*eg* at Ypres and Courtrai) which became known as Chambers of Rhetoric during the next century, and for whom the theatre was the primary interest.

Once again the highpoint was achieved in mystical works, particularly those in prose. The pious and religious modes of expression, which in the 13th century already appealed to a wide cross section of the population and had a particularly strong effect on women, continued to move and stimulate the masses in the 14th century. Some works transcended the limits of orthodox religion: so Bloemaerdinne (true identity unknown) was burned at the stake as a heretic. On the other hand, the prolific Jan van Ruusbroec (*ca* 1293-1381) was impeccably orthodox. He lived in Brussels from *ca* 1304-1343 and later in Groenendaal in the *Zonienwoud* (Forêt de Soignes). Many of his works were translated into German and others, translated into Latin, were read and studied in Paris and Oxford, as well as in Erfurt and Subiaco.

A religious revival also took place in the Northern Netherlands under the influence of Ruusbroec and led by Geert Grote (1340-1384), the so-called 'Modern Devotion'. Two parallel movements developed from this: on the one hand, 'the Brothers (and Sisters) of the Common Life', a congregation of clerics and laymen who lived from their labour (particularly the copying of books) and also ran schools in a number of cities; and on the other hand, a new canonical order (called after an abbey near Zwolle, the 'Congregation of Windesheim'). These two movements more especially influenced the north, but not without having side-effects in Brabant.

THE BURGUNDIAN ERA (15th century)   In 1384 the Duke of Burgundy, Philip the Bold, also became Count of Flanders and Artois. The Burgundian Dukes rapidly managed to gain control of the Southern Netherlands – with the exception of Liege and Loon, as well as the wealthiest parts of the Northern Netherlands (Holland and Zeeland) – to form a single state. With the arrival of the Burgundian Dukes the Netherlands (with Flanders and Brabant in the forefront) developed into an art province with an international reputation. After Italy it became the most important centre in Christian Europe. On the other hand, there was no breakthrough in a wider cultural sense, except in a few areas.

In the Middle Ages the princes in the Netherlands had each their own court with their own artists and scholars. However, this did not amount to very much. Lodewijk van Male, Philip the Bold's father-in-law, squandered a fortune on his mistresses, horses and jewels, but his artistic aspirations were not especially high. The Dukes of Burgundy, and particularly Philip the Good, had much more feeling for art and culture; and as rulers of a prosperous nation, they had a lot more

Master of St Catherine, *Multiplication of the Loaves and Fishes*, central panel of *Triptych with the Miracles of Christ*, 113 × 83 cm, last quarter of 15th century. Melbourne, National Gallery of Victoria.

money at their disposal to act as patrons. However, an examination of the court accounts and an analysis of the festivities, which were held at the drop of a hat, tend to suggest that they were rather parvenus who wanted to create an impression with a surfeit of pomp and circumstance – and not always of the best quality. Nevertheless, an abundance of splendid and precious grain could be found amongst the chaff.

Although the Dukes of Burgundy were a branch of the French royal family and remained French to the end in their thoughts and feelings, they did not come to the Netherlands with an entourage of French artists and intellectuals. Moreover, they were constantly in conflict with the French royal family and they certainly did not regard France as a shining example. From the beginning they sought out artists and scholars in their own domains, particularly in the Netherlands, and to a lesser extent in their ancestral home, Burgundy.

Through their patronage the Dukes of Burgundy had a decidedly positive effect on the flourishing Flemish arts of miniatures, painting and tapestry work; and directly or indirectly, they stimulated branches of the other arts. They were also to some extent responsible for the international acclaim accorded to the Dutch School of Music. In the Middle Ages trouvères and troubadours were popular guests at the princely courts, and music and song could also be heard amongst the burghers. Even so, it was above all the churches, and particularly the cathedrals, which formed the most important centres of musical life. Up to the 15th century Paris literally and figuratively called the tune in western Europe; but the episcopal towns of Cambray and Liege also enjoyed great fame, and it was in these centres that the Burgundian Dukes found their first *Kappelmeisters*: the Hainault musicians Guillaume Dufay (from Chimay, *ca* 1400-1474) and Gilles Binchois (from Binche, died in 1466) developed the music-chapels of the ducal courts into unique ensembles, and were commissioned to compose masses, motets and songs to surpass those written in France – and succeeded in doing so. The school of polyphony in the Netherlands gained an international reputation and following. The death of Charles the Bold put an end to the Burgundian court chapel and to the first great school of music in the Netherlands, but its influence continued to be felt throughout Europe. So many Dutch musicians were tempted to go to Italy – to the courts of Milan, Ferrara, Florence and Naples, the Papal *curia* and the Signoria in Venice – that one might almost say that the most important music academies of Italy (which in turn had an international influence in the 16th century) were founded by Dutch musicians. Before this, other great masters, such as the Flemish musician Johannes Ockeghem (who died in 1496) and his pupil, the Walloon Josquin des Prez, introduced the Dutch school of polyphony to the French court.

The influence of the Dukes of Burgundy on other branches of culture was far less significant. They maintained a 'stable' of historians and literary figures who wrote in French. There are a few noteworthy figures amongst the historical writers, but the literary achievements were mediocre. The *librye* of Philip the Good (the treasure and pride of the Royal Library Albertina in Brussels) was one of the three great Libraries of the Christian world at that time, next to the *Laurentiana* of Cosimo de'Medici in Florence, and Nicolas V's *Vaticana* in Rome. It contained a wealth of illuminated manuscripts. In addition to richly decorated Books of Hours and religious works, there was also an extensive section of French literature – which, however, contained a lot of cheap chivalric tales and literature of courtly entertainment.

Without being influenced in any way by these French productions of the court, the burghers of Flanders and Brabant continued their literary activities in Dutch, in the 14th-century tradition. There was an enormous increase in output, but unfortunately the quantity was not matched by the quality in any way. The Chambers of Rhetoric, a term which first appeared in Audenarde in 1441, sprang up everywhere. Every important town had at least one of these chambers. The origins of many of them can be traced back to the 14th-century; although they were not recognized until the next century as organizations acknowledged and often subsidized by the authorities. The associations rapidly attracted the literary activity in the towns. Their *factors* produced an endless stream of Miracle Plays and other religious plays, serious theatre and farces; as well as complicated poems and refrains for the edification and entertainment of their fellow-citizens. The Chambers of Rhetoric contributed enormously to making the Dutch language a flexible instrument of expression; but their refrains were more artificial than inspired, and in acting out the plays the main emphasis was so much on edification that they became quite unenjoyable. One brilliant exception must be mentioned: *Den spyeghel der salicheyt van Elckerlijc*, which was adapted among others in English with the title *Everyman*.

The 'Modern Devotion' continued to influence the minds and hearts of many people; but now that it was aimed at more practical pursuits, including education, the movement's literary production was far below the standard of the preceding century. Again there is one exception: Thomas a Kempis wrote *De imitatione Christi* in Latin. This work was acclaimed throughout Europe and was translated in virtually all the European languages. Thomas a Kempis (1379-1471) was born in Kempen, though he spent most of his life in the monastery of St Agnietenberg near Zwolle.

During the 15th century the sciences taught at the European universities were still geared to theology and philosophy, supplemented with some more utilitarian branches such as law and medicine. After a spectacular development in the 12th and 13th centuries, scholasticism reached a low ebb by the 14th and 15th centuries. Scientific activities assumed a very minor role in the Netherlands, although an important local centre was created in 1425 with the foundation of the University of Louvain.

The Image of the Virgin Mary is splendidly received into Brussels, hanging from a series with the *Legend of Our Lady of Zavel*, 341 × 528 cm, Brussels, 1516-1518, after designs ascribed to Barend van Orley. Brussels, Museums of Art and History.

ARTISTIC DEVELOPMENTS
(ca 1050- ca 1500)

ROMANESQUE ART (ca 1050- ca 1200) The art form which was initially pejoratively termed 'Romanesque art' rapidly began to spread from 1050 onwards, after a lengthy period of gestation. One is obliged to approach the art of this period mainly through the architecture and the sculpture connected with it. After centuries of misinterpretation, Romanesque art is now assigned its true value. The immense and powerful proportions of the buildings and the wonderful simplicity of the statues are once again admired. However, much of what is now considered as a sublime art form is based on the lack of skills of the architects and sculptors, who were struggling to combine two elements with which they were not sufficiently familiar: space and form.

In the Netherlands the focal point of this new development in art lay in the Maas valley, which had already participated in the Ottonian art in the preceding century, and which was therefore able to enter the Romanesque period with high standards. This Romanesque style of the Maas valley, which was itself inspired by the Rhineland, spread further west to Loon and Brabant.

The movement got underway at a later date in the Scheldt valley for a very practical reason – the lack of natural stone. Even as late as 1050 Count Baudouin V used the old Roman *castrum* at Oudenburg as a quarry for his residence in Bruges. However, there were real quarries at Tournai; and from the middle of the 11th century traders from Tournai began to supply the whole of Flanders with their stone, either in its natural state or already worked, transporting it down the Scheldt and its tributaries. Tournai played a vital role in the emergence of Romanesque art in Flanders for another reason, too. It was through this city that the artistic influences, having originated in Provence and Languedoc, passed from northern France into the country, to be assimilated as 'Scheldt Romanesque'. The contrast between Scheldt and Maas Romanesque art can also be seen in the decorative relief sculpture on church portals, the capitals on pillars and in the stone fonts, which were produced in great numbers in workshops both in Tournai and the Maas valley. However, regarding bronze, gold and enamel work used in the decoration of precious reliquaries, the position of the Maas valley was unthreatened and internationally recognized.

Virtually nothing remains of the frescoes on the walls of the churches and castles in the Netherlands. Our knowledge of the painting of the period is limited to the miniatures in the manuscripts. The wood carving, which has survived the centuries and must have been produced particularly in the Maas valley, is also minimal. The carved ivory and filigree work encrusted with gems, which was so typical of the Carolingian and Ottonian periods, became unfashionable, at least in the Low Countries.

GOTHIC ART (*ca* 1200- *ca* 1400) The term 'Gothic' – referring to the Goths who destroyed the western Roman Empire – was also originally a pejorative term for barbaric art. In the course of time it acquired a very different meaning. By about 1200, architects and sculptors had mastered the basic techniques of manipulating space and form sufficiently to embark on new experiments: the buildings became taller and lighter, the statues more realistic.

Gothic art originated in the Ile de France and Normandy, and again via Tournai entered Flanders to penetrate into Brabant. The Maas valley, which had suffered from the collapse of the copper and bronze industries, was left behind and would no longer play an important role as an artistic province. The Scheldt basin (Flanders and Brabant) became the artistic centre of the Netherlands for many centuries. At the beginning of the Gothic period the natural stone from Tournai, together with the architects from this town, formed the mainstay of the region of Flanders; but in the 14th century, this was replaced by natural stone from Brabant, together with architects from this area. The late Gothic period in Flanders used materials and techniques borrowed from Brabant.

The coastal area deserves a special mention. Brick, which had disappeared from western Europe with the late Roman Empire, was virtually rediscovered there, and used for the building of monuments for the first time in Europe. There were reasons for this: there was an abundance of clay in the polderland, and the transportation of stone from the Scheldt basin was rather expensive. In other places in Flanders and Brabant, brick was only used in the 15th century to any real extent. Even then it was used more for ordinary houses than for monuments.

Finally, the unusual wealth of secular buildings should be emphasized: town halls, market halls and belfries. This is not surprising in a country of rich and powerful cities; but it was nevertheless unusual in Gothic Europe, where most of the building activities were directed at churches, monasteries and military constructions. As in the preceding period, the Gothic forms of artistic expression are to be approached through architecture, sculpture (now differentiated into: stone relief sculpture incorporated into architecture; statues of stone, wood, copper or bronze; tombs of stone and copper) and the illuminated manuscripts. In addition, a few examples of the frescoes of this period have survived. In the 12th-13th century a new art form emerged in conjunction with painting: stained glass windows. This art form did not yet achieve the same standards as in the Ile de France, though there were both artists working in this medium and clients for the work.

THE LATE GOTHIC [BURGUNDIAN] PERIOD (15th century) The Burgundian or late Gothic period marks a turning point in the history of art in Flanders, at least in certain fields. As regards form, the direction which had already been taken was still followed. In architecture this resulted in a refined interplay between the elements of building, sometimes termed 'flaming Gothic'; and in the visual arts in a more naturalistic representation which often became rather mannered. All the old and new branches of art which had existed in the preceding period continued to be developed.

Special mention should be made of the emergence in Brabant – particularly in Brussels, Malines and Antwerp – of specialized monumental wood carvings, wooden retables depicting hundreds of figures and illustrating the life of Christ. These were so successful that they soon became important articles for export. They were shipped off in large numbers to France, Germany and Scandinavia.

However, the Netherlands of the late Gothic period received an important place in the annals of European art history by the development of the Flemish miniature to an unsurpassed level; and at the same time by a related art form, painted panels; similarly, there was a phenomenal expansion in the art of tapestry making. All this was stimulated to a considerable extent by the patronage of the Dukes of Burgundy.

The art of the miniature has a long historical background. Originally only found in churches, it has been practised since the 13th century by lay specialists. From the late 14th century, worldly princes in France and elsewhere in Europe competed to outdo each other in splendour and magnificence with beautifully decorated Books of Hours, and similar liturgical works that were used in church. Great artists were commissioned to carry out this work, and from the beginning so many Flemish masters were used that specialists have referred to the Franco-Flemish schools of miniaturists. The Burgundian Dukes also wished to surpass everyone in this field and enlisted the best specialists: the Flemish-Burgundian school of the 15th century forms a high point of miniaturist art. It was also the last stage in this centuries-old art form, which disappeared from the Low Countries and the rest of Europe during the first years of the next century, as did the beautiful manuscripts, with the arrival of the printing press.

Miniatures were mainly intended for a royal clientele. Princes often commissioned their court painters to do these miniatures, and conversely commissioned miniaturists for their paintings. Up to that time most paintings had been carried out by using watercolours on walls. In the late 14th century artists began to use oil paints on panels, a 'discovery' which at the time was virtually unanimously ascribed to Flemish artists. Again the stimulus for this development came from the rulers, and again it were the Burgundian Dukes who precipitated the artistic explosion in Flanders and Brabant. The Flemish Primitives – as modern art historians have described them – did not only immediately rise to international heights, but were easily distinguishable from the very beginning from the other great school of art of that era, the Italians of the *Quattrocento*. The Flemish and Italian artists, as well as the French, started working on panels at about the same time. However, the Italians in departing from frescoes continued to use sweeping brush-strokes even in smaller paintings, paying particular attention to composition; while the Flemish artists, whose starting point had been the miniature, neglected composition in favour of the representation of fine detail and brilliant colour.

Although the art of the Flemish Primitives owed its beginnings to the patronage of the Dukes, it did not – unlike the miniature – remain merely an art of the court; churches and burghers rapidly became an important clientele. Thus, for example, the masterpiece of 15th-century Flemish painting, *The Mystic Lamb* by the van Eyck brothers, was commissioned by a wealthy burgher from Ghent, who paid to have it hung in St Bavo's Cathedral in that city.

The same applied to some extent to tapestry work – paintings in textile, as it were. These were usually of immense dimensions, and were intended to decorate the bare walls of castles, palaces and churches. Again they originated during the late 14th century, namely in Arras and Tournai; and from there moved to Flanders, and especially to Brabant, during the middle of the 15th century. Once more the Burgundian Dukes supported this new artistic industry and helped it through the difficult period with their patronage, but it was not long before the ateliers stopped relying on ducal orders to maintain their production. Tapestries were for the extremely wealthy; but in contrast with miniature art and painting, the production of these paintings in wool continued to be an exclusive speciality of Brabant and Flanders until the end of the 17th century. This meant that anyone in Europe who wished to buy a tapestry had to order it from these areas, and from the 15th century tapestries became one of the most important exported articles of the Low Countries. Finally, a new art form arose in Europe during the 15th century, which immediately became very popular in the Low Countries, where it flourished in the 16th and 17th centuries: graphic art.

One thing remains to be said about the centres where Flemish art was produced in the Burgundian Netherlands. The Dukes did not choose any particular town to be a capital of their empire, and perhaps this is the reason that there was no artistic metropolis which dominated the arts. Specialization took place in some towns for a number of branches of art (retables in Brussels, Malines and Antwerp; tapestries in Brussels and Audenarde; bronze in Malines), and the production of art of a very high quality was greater in some towns than in others, *eg* painting and miniature art in Bruges. Artists and works of art were well represented in all the towns of Flanders and Brabant, with the larger cities in the lead, as Bruges and Ghent in Flanders; Brussels, Malines and Louvain in Brabant. There was one notable exception; Antwerp limped along in the rear. This city was developing during the 15th century as the main trading centre and largest urban concentration in the Low Countries; but the population seemed at first to be more interested in money than in art (except for the retables) and culture. However, at the end of the century, the people of Antwerp turned the tables; and in no time transformed their city into the artistic metropolis of the Netherlands and one of the most important in western Europe.

Jason is knighted by Aeson, his father, miniature from *Histoire de la conquête de la Toison d'Or*, 370 × 280 mm, Bruges, Lieven van Iathem, *ca* 1470. Paris, Bibliothèque nationale, ms fr 351, fol 2.
The manuscript is one of the finest from the collection of the highly exacting Bruges bibliophile Lodewijk van Gruuthuse. It subsequently turned up in the library of the French sovereign. Excellent spatial reproduction and sound colour treatment are its outstanding features.

Architecture

PRE-ROMANESQUE AND ROMANESQUE ARCHITECTURE

FROM ROMAN TO CAROLINGIAN We may start the architectural history of Flanders in Tongres, where the town walls from the 1st and 4th centuries still bear witness to the importance of the oldest town from Roman times. During the Pax Romana, the first building activity in hard materials developed, used particularly for the construction of towns, villas and an extensive road network. This imported architecture is known to us almost exclusively through archaeological excavations. Building in the following centuries was influenced to a great degree by late Roman concepts and techniques. Whereas building in Roman times had mainly a military and civil character, from the Christianization of the 7th and 8th century onwards above all religious buildings were constructed; and these were to a certain degree connected to the conservatism of late Roman traditions. The newly-founded cloisters were very active in the architectural sphere. Only from the 12th century onwards the flourishing of the towns, and their new forms of money economy, changed this state of affairs. The agricultural society, with its feudal power structures, and technically at a very low stage of develop-

ment, produced few significant buildings between the 5th and 10th centuries. Flanders belonged to a marginal area from which – in contrast to France and Germany – few new impulses were generated.

During the Merovingian period, in the 7th and 8th century, some abbeys were erected in the area between the North Sea, the Scheldt and the Somme. In the Scheldt region, the Aquitanian monk Amandus († around 676) was responsible for some important foundations. The buildings, which were still simple, represented a first approach to the later and more extensive abbeys which were to play an influential role in the Romanesque period. In the year 630, St Amandus founded at Ghent St Bavo's Abbey at the confluence of the Scheldt and the Leie. Some decades later, he gave the impulse to create St Peter's Abbey on the Blandijnberg. Both were destroyed by fire and pillage during invasions by the Norsemen in 851 and 879-883.

Inspired, among other things, by the efforts of Charlemagne (768-814) to establish the Holy Roman Empire in the west, architecture followed late Roman and Byzantine artistic influences. The Carolingian art gradually shaded over into the Romanesque. Thus it formed the beginning of medieval architecture, which ranged over more than seven centuries. Henceforth a constant flow of continuity would characterize the cultural development of the Middle Ages which, through foreign influences and fruitful impulses from within the frontiers of the country, remained a striking dominant note in Flemish artistic history.

Crocket capital in Tournai limestone.
In both the Romanesque and the Gothic period this form of capital was generally applied in the Scheldt region.

Antwerp, Our Lady's Cathedral, northern west tower, completed in 1521 by Domien de Waghemakere. The decorative openwork spire of the tower is a feat of skill, typical of late Gothic church architecture.

Bruges, St Donate's Church, 10th century.
Scale model of Carolingian (counts') castle, constructed on basis of scientific examination of soil.

The magnificent palace chapel of Charlemagne at Aix-la-Chapelle, consecrated in 805, was built according to the model of the Byzantine San Vitale at Ravenna (547). This form of central building which, according to Christian symbolism, was the representation in stone of the celestial city of Jeruzalem and of the Holy Grail, gained followers in Charlemagne's empire. The chapel of the counts' citadel at Bruges was erected nearly two centuries later *'naar den Aecsen gewerke'*, as Jacob van Maerlant wrote it in the 13th century in his *Spieghel Historiael*. This Church, dedicated to St Donate, also consisted of a central octagonal space – even though on a more modest scale – surrounded by a double-octagonal vaulted gallery and a tribune on the upper floors. On the west side there was a similar high tower with two side towers, in which spiral staircases led to the upper floors. A small rectangular choir was extended on the east side. This fortified church was probably built on the initiative of the Count of Flandres, Arnulf I the Great (918-964), and bears witness to his zeal in reflecting the Carolingian power.

Most churches in this period were built following the basilican layout which, on the basis of the early Christian traditition, was best adapted to the local methods of building. After all, rural buildings in a large part of western Europe in the early Middle Ages were laid out in the form of a hall with three aisles. The early Christian basilica type, mostly with three aisles, the central aisle broader and higher than the side ones, was in any case to prevail in ecclestiatical architecture in the coming centuries.

THE 'SCHELDT ROMANESQUE STYLE' AND TOURNAI CATHEDRAL By the Treaty of Verdun (843), Charlemagne's empire was divided. The region west of the Scheldt was to form the later County of Flanders and to be a dependency of Western Francia. Flanders came gradually under the influence of the northern French and Norman Romanesque school of architecture, while the region east of the Scheldt was to belong to the architectural school of the Maas valley. In the Scheldt region, which comprised Flanders, Zeeland and parts of Brabant and Hainault, we can point out a

46

Tournai, Our Lady's Cathedral, southern transept, 12th-13th century. Both the height (83 m) and the range of forms of these flanking towers foreshadowed the advent of Gothic architecture.

Tournai, Our Lady's Cathedral, nave, completed in 1171. Up to the Gothic period the horizontal section of the side-walls remained characteristic of church architecture in the Scheldt region.

number of buildings, mainly ecclesiastical, in the so-called 'Scheldt Romanesque style'.

The less favourable circumstances for the transport of building materials played a role that was not negligeable. In contrast to the Maas region and Brabant, Flanders had little natural stone. The sand-limestone quarries in East Flanders (such as those in Balegem and Lede) were not opened up till later. In West Flanders, the greenish field stone (Paniselian siliceous sandstone) was used as in the Carolingian era, as well as the brown ironstone (limonite sandstone), and this meant that elaborate or refined forms of building were difficult. There were sporadic imports of the brown-grey porous tuff stone from the Rhineland; in the western corner and the south of West Flanders, limestone was imported from Artois. In the valley of the Scheldt, the possibility of transporting the dark grey Tournai limestone downstream by ship encouraged the spreading of the Tournai school. Because of the fact that there were little or none skilled stonemasons in the Flemish centres, the stone purchased had been worked in the Tournai quarries. In this way, the architectural forms of Tournai spread widely.

While there was still not so much building in Flanders in the 11th century, there was a breakthrough in activity in the course of the 12th; this was a consequence of the economic prosperity generated by the development of cloth weaving and the corresponding growth of population in towns. In this era, Ghent, Ypres and Bruges

flourished and become powerful trading centres, in which both ecclestical and civil architecture was largely inspired by Tournai. Tournai in the 12th century was one of the central points of Romanesque architecture: economic growth was linked with considerable building activity. The strongly industrialized winning of limestone provided intensive exports to Flanders, Hainault, Holland and even to England. Tournai influenced the architecture of the Scheldt region up to the Gothic period. Moreover, the Counties of Flanders and Hainault were temporarily united from 1192 to 1280. This increased still further the importance of this bishopric.

The building of Tournai Cathedral was started around 1110. In 1171, the year of the dedication, the nave was certainly completed. The present Gothic choir, about which we shall have more to say, was developed only later. The Romanesque part was completely inspired by northern French and Normanic examples, and had a strong influence on architecture in the Scheldt region up to the Gothic period. The rhythmics of the walls, in four horizontal articulations, impart an order to the longitudinally directed interior space, with the choir as the optical terminal point. The orientation towards the east, towards the daybreak and the light, symbolizes the triumph of good over evil, of eternity over death. This horizontal orientation contrasts with the verticalism of the later Gothic. The rational, mathematical relations are also striking. For the master builders,

47

Ghent, former St Bavo's Abbey, monastery building, 12th century.
Left: the facade of the refectory, in which lighting was admitted through a row of narrow windows shaped like round arches; centre: lavatorium. This is a unique octagonal building, adjoining the eastern passage. On the upper storey is a sanctuary, dedicated in 1179, which was accessible from the dormitorium.

Ghent, former St Bavo's Abbey, remains of the chapterhouse, first half of 13th century.
The arches with the pointed or rounded mullioned windows are typical of the Tournai transitional style, *i e* from Romanesque to Gothic.

Bruges, St Basil's Chapel, second half of 12th century.
This lower chapel has three naves of equal height, divided by columns which support the main arch and the ribbed vaults.

Ronse, St Hermes' church: crypt, 12th century.
The central columns with cushion capitals support ribbed vaults consisting of rough-hewn blocks of natural stone.

48

Ghent, St Bavo's Cathedral, crypt. 12th century.
The squat monolithic columns in Tournai limestone have an octagonal shaft, a heavy square base with spurs and a quadrilateral capital with voluted leaves. They support stucco groin vaults with 15th and 16th-century paintings.

Dudzele St Peter-in-Fetters Church, tower ruin, second half of 12th century. Of the Romanesque Church only the southern flanking towers on the western side, erected in green fieldstone (rubble), have been preserved. The brick bell-tower dates from 1713.

the keys of knowledge were to be found in the numbers and their combinations. Mathematics was regarded as the highest of the human sciences. This striving, aimed at a harmony based on mathematical relations, may be regarded as an approach to the later Gothic architecture.

The monumental line of towers on the four corners and the transept of Tournai Cathedral forms a separate and admirable whole, in contrast to the accent on the western building in the Maasland churches. This is one of the most valuable contributions of Romanesque architecture in Europe and may be compared with the – largely destroyed – third abbey church of Cluny (1088-1130), which at the time was the most impressive building in the whole of Christianity.

Tournai Cathedral's mighty group of towers was widely imitated in the Scheldt region. The square crossing towers, accompanied on the eastern side by two flanking towers, characterized the silhouette of the vanished church of St Bavo's Abbey in Ghent. With its basilical layout with five aisles, the western building with two heavy square towers and a double outside crypt, this church constituted an impressive monument. This Benedictine church, with a total length of 115 m, was completed after five building campaigns in the second half of the 12th century. Archaeological studies have revealed that this Romanesque church was inspired both by the Maas and Rhineland school of architecture and by the northern French school. This clearly shows how receptive the builders were to the various influences from outside, and how these influences were worked into new creations. Of this abbey, once the abode of the Counts of Flanders, some characteristic Romanesque parts have still been preserved: part of the cloister (*ca* 1170) with the lavatorium (dedicated in 1179), the refectory and the chapter hall. These buildings show the characteristics of the typical Tournai style: the walls in Tournai sandstone are sparsely broken through by round arch windows, sometimes embellished by small central pillars.

Of the Romanesque building of the former St John's Church in Ghent (now St Bavo's Cathedral) there still remains part of the 12th-century crypt. It is the greatest, and archaeologically the most remarkable, remainder from Flanders of this period. The still older crypt of St Hermes' Church in Renaix has roughly mortared arches and unornamented die capitals in abstract geometrical form. The comparison with the crypt of Ghent Cathedral shows how gradual the inroad of refinement and ornamentation was.

The countryside churches bore witness to outspoken simplicity in ground plan, elevation and ornamentation. The crossing towers, which dominated the basilical structure, were widespread in Flanders. Here we would only mention St John-the-Baptist's Church at Ghent-Afsnee. Working with modest technical resources and scarce building materials encouraged simplicity and sobriety, but also inventiveness. In the Romanesque buildings, the simple solid geometry of the building masses is characteristic. Even in simple constructions in villages or towns, or standing alone in flat or hilly countryside, their closeness and the solidity of their walls radiated monumentality and sturdiness. By the combination of ground plans and space layouts, the master builders certainly applied a system of relations in which square and circle played an important role. Surveys prove that there was a conscious search for proportion and harmony between the various building elements.

ROMANESQUE ARCHITECTURE IN THE COASTAL REGION   In the coastal region, apart from the cruciform church with central tower, more and more importance was attached to the dominating volume of the four-sided west towers, under the influence of Norman art. The west towers were to gain importance in this region particularly in the Gothic period. From the second half of the 12th century, some have been preserved: the largely reconstructed western building of St Peter's Church at Ypres, with the central part flanked by two four-sided stairway towers; the ruined towers of St Petersbanden Church in Dudzele, whose Romanesque western building greatly resembled that in Ypres; the unusual octagonal gable towers of the rebuilt St Peter's Church in Torhout.

So far we have reviewed some examples of churches and abbeys from the Early Romanesque, and Romanesque periods, of which only certain fragments in this style have been preserved. Pure examples of Romanesque ecclesiastical buildings are very rare in Flanders. Most constructions were demolished or adapted in the prosperous Gothic period. Later rebuildings, devastations or radical restorations are the cause of the great scarcity of such buildings. St Basil's Chapel in Bruges is the most flawlessly preserved Romanesque church

Oudergem, Hertoginnendal, St Anne's Chapel, 11th century.

building in the former County of Flanders. It is a double chapel with three aisles on the small ground floor. When it was built in the second half of the 12th century, it belonged to the count's castle of Thierry of Alsace († 1169). The unusual construction, with a bottom chapel accessible to the people and a closed chapel situated above, gives its own special character to this building. Being far away from Tournai, only scarce use is made of Tournai limestone; iron sandstone from Flanders is especially used.

THE INFLUENCE OF MAASLAND ART IN THE REGION EAST OF THE SCHELDT   In contrast to the Counties of Flanders and Hainault, which for a time were united in one region and followed the Tournai and northern French styles, part of Brabant and Limburg stood under the influence of Maasland art. The Duchy of Brabant (from 1106 onwards) and the County of Loon (*ca* 1000) were ecclesiastical dependencies of Liege. Culturally, they were mainly under the influence of the Maasland, where the Ottonian style was imitated in the Carolingian tradition.

The most remarkable and imposing example of this style of architecture in the region is St Gertrude's Church at Nivelles, which was erected in two phases: in the first half of the 11th century and in the second half of the 12th century. It is characterized by a symmetrical, balanced layout with double choir and transept, in which the central situation of the nave is stongly stressed. The rhythm of the internal space of the nave is set by the transversal arches holding up the flat ceiling, and by the use of four-sided pillars and flat walls, briefly interrupted by horizontal mouldings.

In Brabant, a region where the Scheldt and Maas styles shade into one another, many country churches were built, and these strike us particularly by their extreme simplicity. They are mainly three-aisle pillar basilicas, without transept, and with a four-sided tower on the western side; or little churches with one aisle and a tower between nave and apse. The most characteristic village churches in Brabant are found in the Voer valley between Brussels and Louvain and date from the 11th century. St Peter's Church in Bertem is the prototype of rural Ottonian architecture. In the same region we note St Veronica's Chapel in Leefdaal, St Lambert's Church in Arenberg Park in Heverlee and the west towers of St Catherine's Church in Dussel. They were constructed in blocks of ochre-yellow sandstone or brown irregular ironstone. One of the prettiest churches from the 11th century is St Anne's Chapel in Auderghem, a little chapel with a four-sided clocktower, oustanding for its great sobriety and the purity of its proportions.

CIVIL ARCHITECTURE IN THE ROMANESQUE PERIOD   Civil and military architecture in the Romanesque period can be limited to a number of examples in Ghent, in which we also note the direct influence of Tournai. The *Gravensteen* occupies an important place in the history of European fortress building. It is a moated castle surrounded by an elliptical ring-wall with a rampart, and was constructed in 1180 by Philip of Alsace, Count of Flanders. The monumen-

Ghent, Gravensteen, 12th-13th century.
The castle was subjected to a thorough-going restoration from 1894 to 1914, but still, as a unique example in the Low Countries, provides a good illustration of the military power of the counts of Flanders.

tal gateway gives access to the inner court where the mighty keep stands. This keep consists of a storage cellar and two halls situated above one another, and is crowned by a row of battlements and four corner towers. The building is constructed completely of Tournai limestone, with herringbone masonry in some places, and this together with the embellishment of the windows strongly suggests the Tournai style.

In the flourishing economic period of the 12th century, when most houses were still built in flammable materials such as clay, wood and straw, the first dwelling houses began to be built from durable materials. These stone houses, with their massive horizontally articulated and tilted front gables still have a predominantly defensive and closed character. The *Kleine Sikkel* on the Nederpolder, dating from the beginning of the 13th century, is a characteristic example of this. As in the Romanesque churches of the Scheldt, Tournai limestone was used. On the *Graslei* we find the *Stapelhuis* or *Spijker* from the end of the 12th century. The three-storey facade is horizontally articulated to a considerable degree by lists between which are the window openings, divided by a central pillar, in the same manner as in the 12th and 13th-century houses in Tournai. This building with gable-end on to the street, covered with a saddle

Ghent, Korenmarkt, Borluutsteen, early 13th century.
The stepped gable in Tournai stone, with mullioned windows and continuous water-drips, can be compared to the Romanesque warehouse on the nearby *Graslei*. This facade is a reconstruction dating from 1933.

In the Pre-Romanesque and Romanesque periods, cultural life sprang mainly from the abbeys. The Benedictines in particular developed a cloister architecture aimed at closeness and seclusion. The layout of the cloister, with the monastery building arranged round it, is a clear expression of this. The change-over from an agrarian to a commercial economy, concentrated in the emerging towns, brought with it a complete revolution in the urban milieu. Hence forward it were no longer the abbeys, but the prosperous towns that were to play the leading role in the architectural world. This revealed itself in churches, belfries, town halls, town walls and bourgeois residences, which stressed in a specific manner the autonomy that had been gained. Up to and including the 14th century, architecture was the most important form of artistic expression in this new urban society.

It is generally accepted that the choir of St Denis near Paris, built around 1135 under the leadership of abbot Suger, represented the starting point of the new style in Europe. New technical achievements made it possible to build the enclosed church space higher. The use of pointed arches, cross-rib vaults and arch buttresses led to a logically executed construction of exposed structural members, in which the static forces that determined the structure of the building as a whole were made clearly visible. Stress was laid especially on the inner spaces, where the verticalism was in contrast with the longitudinal development of the Romanesque nave and choir. The altar was no longer the terminal point of this movement, but the unreal height towards which all the force and movement was directed. In the outside architecture, which was often less easily visible because of the complicated skeleton building, the towers were stressed as the main element.

The series of cathedrals which, in the first half of the 13th century in northern France, made the new style flourish to a remarkable degree (Soissons *ca* 1205, Reims 1210, Amiens 1220, Beauvais 1227, *etc*) directly influenced the emergence and development of the classical Gothic in Flanders. The growing might of France in the County of Flanders, after the defeat at Bouvines (1214), stimulated the spread of new forms of art. St Vincent's Chapel at Tournai, which connects the bishops' palace with the cathedral, proves that local stonemasons already in the last years of the 12th century accepted and applied the Gothic forms of building.

A NEW REGIONAL BUILDING STYLE: SCHELDT GOTHIC   In the first half of the 13th century, the 'Scheldt Romanesque style' developed, under the influence of northern French Gothic, in the direction of the 'Scheldt Gothic style'. This regional style was developed on the building sites of the bishopric of Tournai, and spread rapidly through the Scheldt region.

Some parish churches in Tournai show some common features of this style, particular to the region, in its transition from Romanesque to Gothic: the accent is on the high four or eight-sided central towers at the intersection of nave and transept; there are round stair tur-

roof, is finished off at the front and back facades with a stepped top, each step of which is covered with a projecting stone. This is one of the very first examples of a stepped gable; a type of facade that was to become immensely popular in the Netherlands during the Middle Ages and for long afterwards, and was strongly to dominate the townscape in Flanders.

The stepped gables of the *Borluutsteen* on the *Korenmarkt* and the *Rijhovesteen* on the *Onderstraat* are related to this *Stapelhuis*. The defensive character of the *Gravensteen* was also taken over in the building of individual residences. In this way, the wealthy patricians who dwelt in these houses, wanted to emphasize their power. The *Geerard de Duivelsteen*, a 13th-century fortress-like patrician residence with a keep, which has been preserved although in a markedly restored form, is directly influenced by the *Gravensteen*.

After a laborious start in the Pre-Romanesque and Romanesque periods, it was not until the 12th century that there were important building activities in Flanders. Architecturally speaking, Flanders was not so far advanced compared with neighbouring countries. There are signs of a much slower development. The influences from northern France and the Rhineland meant that two schools were developing side by side. In the Scheldt region, in fact, the greatest influence came from the bishopric of Tournai, which in turn radiated to the north the northern French and Normanic style of building.

Ghent, view of *St Nicholas' Church and the Belfry.*
The lantern of St Nicholas' Church is a fine example of Scheldt Gothic.
Before the Belfry was built, this high tower was used as the city tower, where
the bells regulated municipal activity in the flourishing medieval city.

Audenarde, Our Lady-van-Pamele Church, 1234 *et seq.*
This cruciform church, with many-sided crossing towers and round stair
turrets on the corners of the transept facade, is a good example of the
dissemination of the Tournai style in the Scheldt region.

rets at the corners of the west and transept facade; at the
outsides of the transom windows in the upper central
nave, an outside gallery is cut out in the thickness of the
wall; the walls of the nave show three horizontal articulations with the dividing arches on round pillars with
knob capitals, and openwork triforium with alternating
single and double columns, and mainly threefold transom windows. Apart from the flat ceilings, cross-rib
vaulting was more and more used.

The massive lantern towers, which directly illuminated the central space where the nave intersected with
the arms of the transept, are frequently found in country
churches in this Scheldt region. Yet, they did not belong
to the pure Gothic; for a long time, the Romanesque
heritage made itself felt. The most striking examples of
this style are St Nicholas' Church in Ghent (*ca* 1200-
1235) and Our Lady's Church in Pamele, Audenarde
(1234 and following years). Related to these are the
central naves of the Our Lady's Churches in Courtrai
and Bruges.

BRICK BUILDING IN THE COASTAL REGION   The
lack of natural stone in the north of Flanders and the
transport of building materials from distant regions
hindered the development of building in the Romanesque period, but also stimulated the search for other
and cheaper solutions. From around 1200, mud or clay
was baked in regular shapes. This new building material, which was very cheap and easy to handle, very quick-

ly came into general use in the Middle Ages and later
periods. The form and colour of this material particular
to the region was to be one of the factors determining the
look of Flemish architecture in the following centuries.
In the Flemish coastal region, from the beginning of the
13th century, both ecclesiastical and civil buildings were
erected in red brick. For bearing elements and for those
carrying heavy loads (pillars, dividing arches) Tournai
limestone was still used. For the fine decorative work,
chalk or sandstone was sometimes imported.

In the polders, we can find some monumental west
towers of early Gothic churches, built completely in
brick. Because of their plasticity, the vertical volumes of
the heavy buttresses at the corners, and the horizontal
connections with blind ogive arches, the towers of the
Our Lady's Churches in Damme, Lissewege and Bruges
are true highlights of our Flemish brick architecture.

In the systematic drying-out and reclamation of the
polders by the great Cistercian abbeys of Ter Duinen
and Ter Doest, a number of large barns came to be built,
also completely in brick. At the summit of its might, the
Abbey of Ter Duinen near Koksijde possessed more
than 10,000 hectares of land in the Flemish coastal
region and in the Zeeland islands, managed by numerous farm outposts. The monumental barns of *Ten
Bogaerde* near Koksijde and *Ter Doest* near Lissewege
give some idea of the economic wealth of these abbeys.
They also played a considerable role in the 13th century
in the spread of brick architecture.

Damme, Our Lady's Church, west tower, second quarter of 13th century. The 43 *m* high tower was in former times surmounted by a spire.

Lissewege, Our Lady's Church, west tower, second half of the 13th century. The 50 *m* high tower is lent a sturdier aspect by the heavy buttresses at the corners. The strongly accentuated verticality is mitigated by the horizontal blind arched niches which span the buttresses half-way up.

Bruges, Our Lady's Church, tower adjoining northern transept, completed first half of 14th century.
The 122 *m* tower is the highest brick tower in the world. It bears witness to the temerity and daring of Flemish architects in the Middle Ages.

THE INFLUENCE OF FRENCH GOTHIC The building of the Gothic choir of the Romanesque Tournai Cathedral (1243-1255) represented for Flanders the beginning of a new revolution in style, in which the classical Gothic in France served as an example. This happened under the important episcopate of Walter van Marvis, in a period in which Flanders and Hainault were governed jointly by the deeply religious and ecclesiastically-minded Countesses Joan (1205-1244) and Margaret (1244-1278) of Constantinople. In the middle of the 13th century, this type of building replaced the regional 'Scheldt Gothic', and the master builders took their inspiration directly from examples in northern France (Amiens, Arras, Braine, Noyon, Reims, St Omer, Soissons, *etc*). Here we may mention a few examples designed according to the French art of cathedral building: the choirs of St Nicholas' Church in Ghent; Our Lady's Church in Courtrai; St Walburga's Church in Veurne; St Saviour's Cathedral in Bruges and St Martin's Church in Ypres.

In Brabant too, French examples were followed. In building the choir of St Gudula's Church in Brussels, started before 1226 on the initiative of Duke Henry I of Lorraine, a choir was for the first time laid out in imitation of the French cathedrals. Here the broader and higher spaces, the development of the deep choirs with choir galleries and side chapels, the high transom windows and the strongly vertical articulation of the walls of nave and choir are characteristic features.

In the realm of religious architecture, Flanders did not play a pioneer role. For the most part, it followed examples from outside the County. This receptive trait of character contrasts with the more autonomous creative power of the civil architecture in the different Flemish towns which, in this period, were among the most important trading centres in Europe.

'BRABANT GOTHIC' While in the County of Flanders ecclesiastical building stagnated after the 13th century, one of the most important schools of building in the Netherlands developed in the Duchy of Brabant in the 14th and 15th centuries. This regional school of building took an active part in the international Gothic movement and successfully extended its influence far beyond the Duchy. After Brabant was added to the Burgundian lands of Duke Philip the Good in 1430, Brussels became the political and cultural centre of the administration, in pomp and splendour, of the Dukes of Burgundy.

Once again, building material played an important role. The yellow sand-limestone, won on a large scale from the numerous stone quarries in the Brussels region, was easy to work. This soft material permitted a wealth of sculptured shapes and openwork tracery . Especially during the 15th and 16th centuries, stonemasons could give in this natural stone almost unlimited rein to their urge for flamboyant decoration.

The first expressions of this regional school we owe

Bruges, Our Lady's Church, choir, second half of 13th century.
The buttressing system with flying buttresses is a technical sophistication, adopted from French cathedral construction.

Veurne, St Walburga's Church, second half of 13th century.
All that actually came to be built during the Gothic period of what had been planned on a grand scale, was the choir.

to some refugee master builders from northern France, such as Jean d'Oisy, Jacques Picart and Pierre de Savoye. It was through them that the many forms of international Gothic penetrated to Malines, Aarschot, Diest, Tirlemont and Antwerp. On various building sites, the itinerant master builders served as expert advisers and thus stimulated the rapid spread of 'Brabant Gothic' to the County of Flanders, Hainault, north Brabant and Zeeland.

Jean d'Oisy, who was in the service of the Count of Hainault, was called to Malines. With the layout of the new choir, the choir gallery and the seven side chapels of St Rombout's Cathedral (1335-1343) – based on the example of the classical French cathedrals – he gave the starting signal for 'Brabant Gothic'. As later, in the choir of Antwerp Cathedral (1352-1356) and by the southern transept arm and side aisle of St Gudula's in Brussels (second half of the 14th century), the choir of St Rombout's in Malines had its own wall layout created, which was typical for this style. The vault ribs grow out of the intricate bundles of pillars, giving a strong rhythm to the various traves and an uninterrupted upwards flight to the linear verticalism. The bays between the dividing arches and the sills of the transom windows are enlivened with rich tracery, so that the posts fit onto these dividing arches and run over the openwork triforium into the mullions of the windows. This triforium zone develops into an extraordinarily varied architectural decoration, in which ogive arches with trefoils and intertwine quatrefoils in continually repeated and identical traceries, to create a balanced and harmonious set of lines. The triforium is often reduced to an openwork

parapet, in front of the continuous gallery cut out in the thickness of the wall in front of the transom windows. In the 15th century, this zone between the dividing arches and the transom windows was filled in a simpler manner with a rhythmically connected series of blind wall niches.

A whole series of churches was built in the Brabant Gothic style from the 14th right to the end of the 16th century. Often work was carried out on the same building over two centuries, with repeated interruptions. Here we would mention the following examples in passing: Diest, St Sulpice's (1321-1533); Halle, St Martin's (1341-1467); Tirlemont, Our Lady-ten-Poel's (1357-1438) and St German's (15th century); Lier, St Gummarus' (15th-16th century); Antwerp, Our Lady's Cathedral (1352-1518).

The traditionalism continued to be manifested in St Jacob's, St Andrew's and St Paul's Churches in Antwerp, where the Brabant Gothic style was consequently adapted up to the 17th century. This style was also successfully imitated outside the county. This happened especially in the 15th and 16th centuries, for example in the nave of St Walburga's in Audenarde, St Martin's in Alost, St Michael's and part of St Bavo's in Ghent, and St Waltrude's in Mons.

The spread towards the north was considerable in extent. Various churches and towers in the Netherlands show the direct influence of the Brabant master builders, among others churches in Breda, 's-Hertogenbosch, Dordrecht, Rotterdam, Delft, Gouda, Utrecht and even Haarlem and Amsterdam in North Holland. The masters of Brabant were also active at various places in the

more nearby Zeeland, for instance in Hulst, Goes, Middelburg, Veere and Zierikzee. And the 16th-century sepulchral church of Margaret of Austria in the Burgundian Bourg-en-Bresse was one of the most distant examples of this famous school.

The masters of Brabant were famous builders of towers. All their attention was focused on the central gable tower. Sporadically, they built two west towers. At the outset, these massive towers had a closed character. Later they were given an openwork silhouette, so that the powerful buttresses and the slender pointed arch windows gradually passed over into an angular relief with countless sculptured ornaments in white stone. This tower layout found its most monumental application in St Rombout's Cathedral in Malines, of which the unfinished stumps of the west tower reach a height of 97 m. The intention had been to crown these towers with a spire 50 m high. But, as so often happened, the height aimed at was beyond the financial resources available. The boldest design was thought out in Louvain, where Josse Metsys proposed three towers on the west side of St Peter's Church, of which the middle one was to reach a height of 165 m. This was a megalomania which was not to be outdone until the 19th century. The cathedrals in Brussels and Antwerp have two west towers. In Antwerp, the northern tower alone was finished off with a 123 m high spire with fine pinnacles and subtle lacework-like octagons. This and the Brussels Town Hall tower are the only Brabant Gothic towers to be completed.

OUR LADY'S CATHEDRAL IN ANTWERP This church merits our particular attention. It is not only the largest Gothic church in the Netherlands, but it is also regarded as one of the most remarkable expressions of 'Brabant Gothic'. Building was started on the new Gothic choir in 1352. This was completed in 1422, and a start was made on the tower. Work on this ambitiously

Diest, St Sulpice's Church, 14th-15th century.
Work on the choir was started in 1321 under the supervision of Pierre de Savoie. The nave, a noteworthy feature of which is that the columns have no capitals, was completed in the 15th century.

Alost, St Martin's Church, 14-15th century.
Commenced in 1481, work proceeded until the year of the iconoclastic riots, 1566. Thereafter this Brabant Gothic church remained unfinished.

Malines, St Rombout's Cathedral, west tower, 1452-1520.
Just as with the 13th-century brick-built west towers in the Flemish coastal area, the heavy buttresses throw into strong relief the verticality of the tower. In the 15th century, however, this structure was richly embellished with fine stonemasonry.

Halle, St Martin's Church, choir, 1398-1409.
The outer walls are characterized by the openwork balustrades and the numerous baldachins and pinnacles with crockets and finials.

conceived cathedral continued almost without interruption till 1518. Different generations of masters masons and stonemasons made their contribution: Jakob
van Tienen (1396-1403), Peter Appelmans (1419-
1434), Jan Tac (1434-1439), Everaert van Veeweyden
(1439-1473) and the families of Waghemakers (from
1473) and Keldermans (from the beginning of the 16th
century). In a well-nigh irresistible drive for renovation,
the Emperor Charles V in 1521 laid the first stone of a
new and still larger choir. But these plans were thwarted
by the fire of 1533.

Up to 1477, this was the only parish church in Antwerp, providing a home for increasing numbers of altars
of guilds and fraternities among the forest of bundle
pillars and in the numerous side chapels. This partly
explains the broad layout with five aisles. Antwerp grew
into the most important centre of trade and culture in
northwestern Europe. The flourishing economic situation of this port and its continually increasing population – by the end of the 15th century there were about
5,600 houses in the town – created the favourable
climate in which such a gigantic church could be built.

The church-fabric drew its income in this vast building activity from various sources: contributions from the parish, the clergy, the town authorities, and not least the faithful themselves. There were contributions – in cash or kind – from individuals, guilds and fraternities, via offertories, collections, bequests and wills, especially on the occasion of important devotions. These made it possible to finance the most comprehensive ecclesiastical building project in the Netherlands.

Antwerp, Our Lady's Cathedral, lantern, 1536.
The construction of the largest church building in the Netherlands spanned the period from 1352 to 1521. The dome at the crossing had just been completed in 1533, when a fire destroyed the roof of the nave and transept. After the fire the lantern was restored by Domien de Waghemakere in 1536.

Antwerp, Our Lady's Cathedral, 1352-1518.
This is the largest church ever built in the Netherlands in the Middle Ages.

58

SOME IMPORTANT MASTER BUILDERS In the Middle Ages, masons, stonemasons and carpenters were united in guilds: these controlled the quality, enforced strict secrecy on professional knowledge, strived for the protection of the profession in certain families, and emphasized the distinction between master and apprentice. This form of protectionism was a considerable hindrance to technical and artistic progress. From the middle of the 14th century onwards, certain master builders worked more independently. This development can be compared with the status of architects of the Italian Renaissance in the *Quattrocento* who, on the basis of their artistic ability and intellectual knowledge, were recognized as fully-fledged artists.

It is noticeable that master builders became less and less attached to their home towns. This trend favoured the spread of 'Brabant Gothic'. Thus Jakob van Gobertingen, an apprentice of the earlier-mentioned Jean d'Oisy from France, worked at the end of the 14th century on building sites in Tirlemont, Brussels and Antwerp. In Brussels he was master of works both for St Gudula's Church and for the left wing of the Town Hall. Jan van Ruysbroeck also worked in various towns. This highly talented master builder had an extremely active career. From 1433 to 1436 he worked at the palace of the Dukes of Brabant. In 1433 he was active in Audenarde. In 1449 he was appointed as master of works for the Brussels Town Hall tower, and in 1451 for St Lambert's Cathedral in Liege. In 1459, Philip the Good appointed him as master builder to the Duke of Brabant, and in this capacity he was active in various princely residences. Till about 1480 he was in charge of the building of the two gable towers of St Gudula's in Brussels. He preceded the master builder Keldermans as a designer of monumental tower constructions.

The Keldermans family provides an outstanding example of the father-to-son succession in the 'Brabant

Antwerp, Our Lady's Cathedral, 1352-1518.
The heavy outlines of the compound pillars and the constantly recurring tracery adornments of the triforium zone are characteristic of Brabant Gothic. The nave was skilfully restored in 1973-1983.

Gothic' style. No less than six generations of this very remarkable family of artists from Malines played outstanding roles in Brabant and Zeeland from the 14th century up to the 1530's. The Keldermans can be compared with the German Parler family of master builders in the 14th century. Jan I Keldermans (*ca* 1345-1425) supplied in 1377-1385 the sculpted coping stones for the Malines Town Hall. His son, Jan II (*ca* 1375-1445) was from 1424 to 1445 *appelgierder* or master of works for St Gummarus' Church in Lier, and was simultaneously town master builder of Louvain and Malines. His son, Andries I (*ca* 1400-1488), as town master builder of Malines, directed the building of St Rombout's tower, which was started in 1452. From 1454 onwards he worked on St Lieven's tower in Zierikzee, and from 1455 onwards on the Town Hall at Middelburg. Antoon I (*ca* 1440-1512), son of Andries I, was appointed, after the death of his father, as town master builder of Malines, and he led the works on St Rombout's tower, Our Lady-over-de-Dijle's and St John's Church. He took over his father's tasks at Lier, Zierikzee and Alkmaar. The sons of Anton I, Anton II († 1515) and Rombout II (ca 1460-1531) extended 'Brabant Gothic' further at the beginning of the 16th century.

All of them, with dogged presistence, passed their creative architectural power from father to son. Probably not one of them lived to see his own designs completed; nor was this their direct aim, since Gothic was first and foremost a community art.

Thus far, we have fixed our attention almost exclusively on ecclesiastical architecture in the Middle Ages. This does not mean that civil architecture was less important. On the contrary, here Flanders can boast of an exceedingly rich heritage. Above all the Town Halls, halls and belfries stressed the autonomy of the growing towns from the 13th century onwards.

HALLS, BELFRIES AND TOWN HALLS The flourishing cloth industry called for the building of large sales areas and storage places. The Cloth Hall in Ypres, erected in the 13th century in 'Scheldt Gothic' style, was the most extensive town building to be erected in the Netherlands during the whole of the Middle Ages. The sloping front facade, 133 m long, has two rows of pointed arch windows and niches. The high, four-sided belfry tower is centrally placed. On the ground level were the storage places for the raw materials and the workplaces, and on the upper floor the sales rooms for the finished cloths. The Bruges hall and belfry, dating from *ca* 1280-1300, are to a certain degree inspired by the Ypres building. But in contrast to Ypres, where the facades were built completely in Tournai limestone, in Bruges the cheaper bricks were used as the main building material. Both buildings have an open inner court. These complexes adequately demonstrate the importance of the western European towns as centres of the cloth industry and trade.

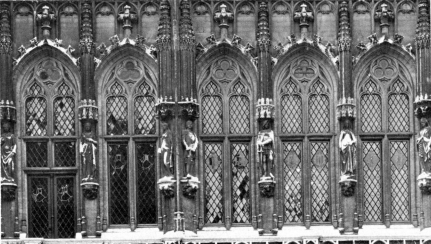

As repository of the town's privileges, assays and the municipal clocks, the belfries in the centre of the fortified towns were the outspoken symbol of the sense of independence and civic pride of the citizens. Most of them date from the 13th and 14th centuries when the Flemish towns of Ghent, Ypres and Bruges were at the summit of their power. Often they were built together with the halls (as was the case in Ypres, Bruges and Malines). Later, particularly in Brabant, the belfry was incorporated in the Town Hall (Alost, Brussels, Audenarde). The Ghent belfry, built in the 14th century, is also remarkable for the fact that the original design for this monument has been preserved.

The Court of Aldermen at Alost, built *ca* 1225, may be regarded as the prototype of Town Hall building in Flanders and Brabant. The rectangular layout, generally with two upper floors, the pointed saddle roof and the corner towers characterized Town Halls in the Netherlands up to the 16th century. Most of them were built

Brussels, Town Hall, 15th century.

Brussels, Town Hall, detail of left wing. Built in 1402-1405 under the supervision of Jacob van Tienen and Jan Bornoy.

Brussels, Town Hall, detail of right wing. Built in 1444-1450 by Jan van Ruysbroeck, who also completed the tower in the period 1449-1454.

Louvain, Town Hall, 1447-1468.
One of the outstanding Brabant Gothic buildings. In the period from 1852 to 1872 the 282 facade and tower niches were filled with sculptures of the Counts of Louvain, the Dukes of Brabant, scholars and artists.

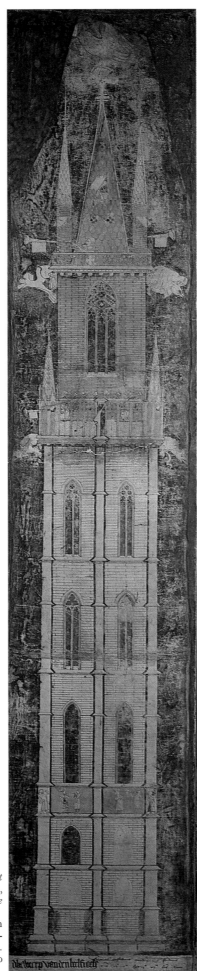

Preliminary design of the Ghent Belfry, parchment, 225 × 40 cm, 14th century. Ghent, *Bijloke Museum.*
An analysis of this original design shows that the actual tower consists of a stack of four squares. The structure of the spire is also based on circle and square.

Ghent, Belfry, 14th century.
The construction did not altogether follow the preliminary design. The coping, originally of wood, was repeatedly broken off and replaced. The present spire dates from 1911-1913.

Bruges, Town Hall, 1376-1420.
This Gothic town hall, the facade of which is entirely in sandlime brick, is conceived as a shrine. From the architectonic standpoint this building provided the basis for a type of town hall, that was to be imitated throughout Flanders in the 16th century.

Bruges, Halles and Belfry, 13-15th century.
This example of brick architecture is of a more sober design than that of the Ypres Cloth Hall. The octagonal white stone coping of the tower was executed between 1483 and 1487; it owed its origin to the influence of Brabant Gothic.

in sand-limestone, which permitted an extraordinary wealth of sculpted ornamentation.

In the Bruges Town Hall (1376-1420), the white stone gable is adorned by high ogive arch windows and lines of sculptures, one above the other, with the portraits of the Counts and Counts and Countesses of Flanders in the niches. For the first time, continuous window niches were applied across both floors. This form of Gothic verticalism, particular to the region, was taken over in house gables up to the 17th century.

Under the influence of Burgundian culture in its luxury and splendour, several rich town hall facades were erected in the 15th century. Because Louvain was losing ground to Brussels politically, these two towns became keen rivals for the building of the most beautiful town hall. Jakob van Tienen, an apprentice of Jean d'Oisy, began work in 1402 on the building of the left wing of Brussels Town Hall. At that time he was undoubtedly the outstanding master builder in Brabant. Under the direction of Jan van Ruysbroeck the work was carried out on the right wing in 1444-1449, and in 1455 the central belfry tower was completed. The building of the Louvain Town Hall began in 1447 under the direction of Matthieu de Layens, based on the original design by Sulpitius van Vorst. With this building, he intended to rival the right wing of the Brussels Town Hall. With the flamboyant ornamentation, the exaggerated use of crowded profiles, crockets and finals, and the strongly sculptural character of the whole, these two monuments represent the high point of 'Brabant Gothic'.

TOWN FORTIFICATIONS, FORTRESSES AND CASTLES Because of the expansions of towns which, particularly in the 19th century, led to major town planning works, there are not so many remains of the medieval town walls and gates, which bore witness to the defendability and peculiarity of the mighty towns in the middle of an agrarian environment. The extent of the walled areas of towns indicates the prosperity of the Flemish and Brabant towns from the 12th century onwards, thanks to the cloth industry. In the 14th century, Ghent was the town with the largest walled area of 644 hectares, and it surpassed or equalled the extent of the most important towns in northwestern Europe. In some Flemish towns there were still town gates, fortified accesses to the enclosed inner towns. These are monumental enclosed buildings, erected in brick or natural stone, with a clearly defensive function, consisting of one or more gates with heavy round towers. We note here the Brussels gate in Malines (*ca* 1300), the Halle gate of the second town walls in Brussels (1357-1383), and the three remaining gates of the original seven at Bruges: the *Ezelpoort* (1369), the *Kruispoort* and the *Gentpoort* (both from 1400-1401). The Broel towers in

Alost, Town Hall and Belfry, early 13th century.
The Belfry Tower dates from 1407-1460. The entire structure was restored at the end of the last century.

Bruges, Cross Gate, built by Jan van Oudenaarde and Maarten van Leuvene, 1403-1406.

Ghent, former Cistercian Abbey of the Bijloke, west pediment of refectory, *ca* 1325.
A masterpiece of brick Gothic architecture in Flanders.

Louvain, Naamse straat, facade of *Van tSestich* House, 15th century.
At the top, which is shaped like a pointed arch, several six-rayed stars were bricked in, together with the LX monogram, as identification of the original occupants, the tSestichs of noble lineage.

Bruges, Genoese Lodge or Saaihalle, 1399 *et seq.*
The use of hard sandlime brick from Brabant and also the shape of the high protective gable – converted in the 18th century into a bell gable – are a manifestation of the desire for a display of power and affirmation of the economic status of foreign merchants in one of the most important trading centres of western Europe.

Courtrai originally formed part of the fortifications of the castle and the town walls. They also formed a fortified bridge over the Leie. These round towers date from the beginning of the 15th century, but were radically restored in 1875.

Originally the castles, surrounded by broad moats, were laid out on an irregular or polygonal plan. The keep stood centrally or formed part of the high defensive walls. The arrival of firearms caused changes in these military buildings. The layout became more compact, with a basic square flanked by corner towers, surrounded by water. Gradually the castles lost their defensive character and were transformed into dwellings.

SOME ASPECTS OF HOUSE BUILDING IN THE MIDDLE AGES   In medieval times, most houses were built in wood, clay and straw. The persistent danger of fire, and the fear of catastrophic town fires, led to strict regulations issued by the municipal authorities. From the 16th century onwards, they banned the building of wooden facades and the placing of thatched roofs. This means that authentic remains of these remarkable wooden buildings are very rare.

The typical form of the wooden upper facade, with the repeated overhangs and the bargeboards with ogive arches or trefoils, influenced the brick facades. The master masons demonstrated their craftsmanship and inventiveness in exuberant verticalizing tracery work with profiled cornices, trefoils, quatrefoils, lozenges and circles. The simple building material – light red brick – was no hindrance to the wealth of forms. Drawings show what extensive use was made by medieval craftsmen of the compasses; a simple instrument with which they created involved tracery.

The fierce competition for building land in the towns was the cause of the narrow and deep building lots. This meant that the houses were built with a narrow top facade or stepped gable on the street side, and this phenomenon determined the streetscape in Flemish towns up to the 18th century. The narrow building sites and the high price of land gave rise to high buildings, too.

The high screen facades evolved from the Romanesque stone houses. They lost their defensive character, but became a symbol of the power and wealth of their inhabitants. In 15th-century Bruges, this type of gable was especially used in the consular houses of foreign merchants.

In the Burgundian era, the aristocracy and the high bourgeoisie modelled their life-style on the luxurious environment of the dukes: the stair towers projecting above the roof in their mansions was an outward sign of their standing in society.

The predominant use of brick in civil architecture is a striking phenomenon. The use of this material particular to the region played a great role in the whole of the Netherlands in the development of their own forms. This typical Flemish building material extended its influence far beyond the frontiers. The resemblance of the architecture in Lübeck, the most important of the Hanseatic towns in north Germany, with which, among others, Bruges had intensive trading relations from the 13th century onwards, is a striking example of this.

65

Sculpture

The astonishing wealth that Flanders was able to amass over the centuries by the excellent artistic creations of its painters and architects, meant that the art of sculpture has so far not been given the necessary attention. Although in the field of sculpture pioneer work was only seldom carried out, Flanders was responsible for a production of high quality that spread, and was valued, far beyond the frontiers.

THE EARLY MIDDLE AGES
(to the end of the 12th century)

The existence of a 'Flemish' art of sculpture in the Middle Ages is difficult to establish. Among the reasons for this are the extreme scarcity of preserved sculptural works of this region, and of the source material available. The ravages suffered by sculpture over the centuries – most catastrophic in the damage caused by the iconoclasts in the County of Flanders and Antwerp in the 16th century – were so radical that it is not possible to form any picture of what sculpture was being produced in the Flemish regions. Because of this, there must necessarily be many gaps in this review, so that much space is given to subjective opinions and judgements. Furthermore, the number of sculptural works known up to this time is not adequate to sketch a stylistic evolution which (at least for the period before 1300) could point to specific Flemish characteristics, let alone to make a choice among the main indigenous works of sculpture.

However, the Romanesque art has an epic character and stands in the sign of the universality of Christianity. It has in the first place an edifying and didactic function which served, via graphic instruction, to stimulate the religious zeal of the early Middle Ages. The same artistic ideal can be found everywhere in western Europe, even though there are slight nuances in the form of expression. Another reason for the absence of sculpture in this early period is the fact that it seldom occurred independently. The design and working of sculpture was closely connected with the art of miniatures and the working of gold and silver, enamel and ivory which flourished to an exceptional degree, especially in the Maas valley. Furthermore, sculpture both

Head of Christ, oak, 28 cm, Maas region or influence thereof (?), ca 1200. Louvain, St Peter's Church.
The Late Romanesque head of Christ belonged to the body on the Brown or Curved Cross which adorned St Peter's Church in Louvain. The sensitive, gentle face depicted here comes very near to the mystic beauty of form achieved by the Carthusians.

in stone and wood can be compared with painting since, originally, it was mostly polychrome and richly ornamented with gilt.

During the early Middle Ages, there were not many centres of sculpture in the Flemish region. Possibly the very remote situation of the Carolingian royal court and the large bishoprics had an inhibiting effect on sculpture which, in spite of being withdrawn from the immediate influence of the great schools of the time, nevertheless learnt from them and was able in its turn to produce highly original masterworks.

The evolution of sculpture proceeded differently in the east and the west of the Flemish region: a clear distinction must be made between the Maas and the Scheldt area. We can speak of artistic production in this period only from towns which were then important centres, such as Tongres and Maastricht for the Maas valley, and Tournai, Ghent and Bruges for the Scheldt area.

The two Limburgs, together with the Campine, Haspengouw and the greater part of Brabant were situated in the immediate sphere of influence of the Maas. Romanesque art in the Maas valley is more important for ivory and metal carving than for stone sculpture. The latter, although closely related to the other artistic activities, lagged far behind in excellence and plastic power. Building sculpture was very vulnerable in this region, since the sculptures principally used a soft sandstone such as the tuff from Maastricht and the valley of the Geer.

In St Trond – one of the early Abbey foundations, a centre of study and culture and, from the point of art history, the equivalent of Stavelot – a tympanum with the representation of the *Majestas Domini* adorned the former burial chapel of the Saints Trudo and Eucherius, which Abbot Wieric had built between 1169 and 1172. This representation of the Christ enthroned in Glory, so familiar to medievals through the ivory book covers and diptyches, which appears in a *mandorla* surrounded by the symbols of the four evangelists, probably resembles the tympanum with the same apocalyptic vision above the entry to the eastern arm of the cloister of St Servate's Church at Maastricht (*ca* 1180). The latter space is less plastically worked out than the altar retable in the same church, dating from the last decade of the 12th century, of which only part is original. The upper arched part, which possibly served previously as a tympanum, represents Christ laying his right hand on the head of the kneeling Peter, and his left hand on that of the patron St Servate.

Apart from the cloister church of Rolduc and that one in Tongres, Maastricht set the lead particularly in the fields of capital sculpture. Apart from basket and chalice capitals, and those with stylized plant motives, fighting animals, misshapen dwarfs and frightful monsters, we also find in the choir and upper gallery of the Our Lady's Church capitals with religious subjects and biblical scenes, such as those with the figure of Balaam.

On another, probably the best-known example, a kneeling figure is offering a chiselled capital to the Virgin. In the explanatory inscription S. MARIA HEIMO, applied under the cover plate, the signature of the

Samson carrying away the gates of Gaza and *Samson taking hold of a pillar of the temple of Dagon,* demi-column in sandstone on which the figure of Samson is carved out in relief, 150 cm, Maas region, first half of 12th century. Nivelles, St Gertrude's Church.
The relationship of the column and the human figure already points in the direction of the new French ornamented portals, which were not imitated until the second quarter of the 13th century, namely in the south portal of St Gervase's Church, Maastricht.

Two frieze fragments and crouching figures, decorative sculpture, Maas region, early 13th century. Tirlemont, St Germanus' Church, western side. A richly worked moulding of twisting vine foliage, emanating from the head of a fool and a monster, rests on a broad profile moulding interspaced with crouching male figures serving as atlantes. The latter have their hands on their knees, while their faces afford clear evidence of a mighty exertion.

Christus triumphans, sculpture, 185 × 181 cm, Maas region, body of Christ, late 11th – early 12th century, painting of later date. Tongres, Our Lady's Basilica.
The peaceful expression of the face on the head slightly inclining away from the light towards the right shoulder, with the high, narrow, straight nose is marred by the gory painting of later date. The figure of Christ with outstretched limbs and broad chest, the anatomy of which is schematically indicated, is entirely symmetrical in design, as is the skirtshaped perizonium, which reaches above the knees.

sculptor is usually seen; but this would be somewhat exceptional in this period. It more probably gives an indication of the donor or patron who presented this and possibly other capitals to the Our Lady's Church.

Dating also from the second half of the 12th century are some thirty historical die capitals on the upper gallery of the west building of St Servate's Church at Maastricht. Amid luxuriant tendrils of plants, laden with fruit, human figures are occupied with manual work, and facing them are demons and monsters gesticulating furiously or fighting with one another. In spite of the roughness in finish, the workshops situated in the Maas valley still managed to produce fine living figures which were symmetrically integrated into their architectural context. Through the flat relief and the ornamental linear folds of the garments, mostly decorative on their own, we can clearly see in building sculpture the transposition of the small sculptures produced by the workshops of the Maas valley ivory-cutters and brassfounders.

The influence of this art also made itself felt in the eastern part of Brabant, in which little sculptural work

has been preserved from this period. On the lintel of the *Samson Porch* (11th century) of St Gertrudis' Church at Nivelles, there is a surprisingly beautiful representation of three scenes from the life of the biblical hero Samson. They make an allusion to the mystery of the passion and the resurrection of Christ. In the middle, Samson holds a lion's muzzle open with his hands; to the right, Delilah cuts off the hair from Samson's head, so that he loses his strength; and to the left the Philistines gouge out his eyes. Two pillar scenes show the same figure, on one side bearing the gates of the temple of Gaza, and on the other shattering a pillar of the temple of Dagon. Similar scenes are also depicted on the portal of Breust (Dutch Limburg). The survival of Carolingian and Ottonian traditions in Brabant during the 11th and 12th centuries is clearly expressed in these examples.

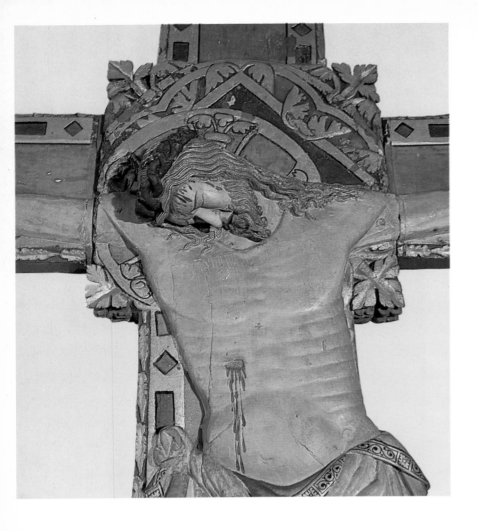

Christus triumphans, oak with remains of original polychromy, 457 × 272 cm, Maas region, 1250-1270. Oplinter St Genevieve's church. The body of the Saviour, which forms a very pronounced curve, is carved in low relief on a wide and richly ornamented cross. Under Christ's feet is an asp, a symbol of the devil overcome by the death on the Cross, and below the asp is the chalice with the Redeemer's blood. At the tip of each of the arms of the cross quatrefoils display the symbols of the Evangelists accompanied by all kinds of monsters and allegorical beings, inclucing Ecclesia and Synagogue. The same motifs were originally reproduced on the reverse side of the Cross.

Sedes Sapientiae, polychrome lime-wood, 160 cm, Nicolaas de Bruyne, Brussels wood-carver, 1442, after a smaller Romanesque Maaslands (?) original, destroyed in 1944 and restored by J. Van Uytvanck, sculptor at Louvain. Louvain, St Peter's Church.

The Romanesque tradition in portal sculpture experienced a lengthy late flowering till far into the 13th century, and this is demonstrated in the round arch portal of the former St Elisabeth's Hospital in Louvain. The same characteristics are also found in the two frieze fragments, which are walled into the early 13th-century west side of St Germanus' Church in Tirlemont and which include figurative sculptural work.

Better preserved are the freestanding Romanesque devotional sculptures, which occur sporadically in the beginning. The iconographic themes which were stressed in the places of worship were the Crucifixion and the Virgin. The former takes shape in great and moving triumphal crosses that bear witness to an exalted religious sense. The absence of any human feeling in the reproduction produces a great spirituality. This is one of the characteristics of the impressive triumphal cross (beginning of the 12th century) of Our Lady's Basilica in Tongres. From the slightly bowed head with the closed eyes emerges a great serenity and an acquiescence in expectation of the Resurrection. It is not the sculpture but the polychrome which, by means of drops of blood, served to visualize the suffering of the Crucifixion. In contrast to this is the more emotional and moving Romanesque *Head of Christ* (last decade of the 12th century) from St Peter's Church at Louvain, probably a fragment from a Crucifixion formerly kept in that place of worship and better known under the name of *Kromkruis* or *Bruinkruis.* This Christ-figure showed the peculiarity that the right arm hung down from the wood of the cross – suggesting that it formed part of a larger sculptural group, depicting the descent from the

cross, further examples of which are found in southeast France, Castile and Italy. On the Romanesque cross of St Leonard's Church at Zoutleeuw, the crucified figure is shown upright with two spikes piercing the feet.

Other products originating in Maas valley workshops are the figure of the crucified Christ from St Denis' Church at Forest near Brussels (*ca* 1160), and the monumental late 13th-century triumphal cross in half embossed sculptural work, coming from the Maagdendal Abbey at Oplinter and now kept in St Genoveva's Church there. Both of these triumphal crosses are more realistic and humane. The body of the Saviour, especially in the late example from Oplinter, is marked by

suffering: the head with the crown of thorns sinks down onto the shoulder, and the two feet placed together are fastened to the cross with one large nail. These elements are characteristic of the after-flowering of Romanesque art in the Flemish regions where the Gothic was gradually to penetrate.

As for most of the crucifixes, the hieratic frontal representations of the Virgin were imported from the workshops of the Maas valley, or were at least strongly influenced by them. The type of the *Sedes Sapientiae* (Seat of Wisdom) evolves from a rigid frontal block view to a more living human representation. In the beginning there was no mutual relation between the stately enthroned Madonna and the blessing infant Jesus, sitting on the lap of his mother. This is the case in the *Sedes Sapientiae* (1160-1180) in the Black Sisters' Cloister at Louvain, of which the head has been replaced by a Romanesque imitation. Another hieratic sculpture of the Seat of Wisdom is the badly damaged Madonna (1150-1160) coming from St Anne's Church at Auderghem, and now preserved in the Museums of Art and History in Brussels.

Flanders, with various important centres such as Bruges and Ghent, forms part of a region through which the middle and lower Scheldt flows. This, from the point of art history, determined a school in the early Middle Ages – as did the Maas region. The southernmost point of Flemish territory in this period was St Bertin's Abbey at St Omer, ravaged by fire and rebuilt around 1093 by the Abbot Jan. On the occasion of this restoration, a whole quantity of sculptural work must have been added, including an ivory *Descent from the Cross*, possibly cut at St Omer in the last quarter of the 11th century. This fairly rare specimen of freestanding sculpture in ivory is an important witness to the English influence which affected northern France in the 11th and 12th centuries – an influence which can also be traced in ivory work cut outside the Maas valley.

In Tournai, the epicentre of the Scheldt region, the art of Romanesque sculpture is more original compared with that of the Maas valley, which retains the Latin tradition in the ancient mould. The importance of the Tournai school and the typically flat aspect of its sculpture can to a great extent be explained by the hard, dark blue-grey stone excavated in the region between the Scarpe and the coast. The winning of this so-called Tournai stone expanded during the 12th century into a veritable industry, in the hands of the Tournai Guild of Stonecutters. It was used for monumental sculpture on places of worship, baptismal fonts and funeral stones. Apart from the numerous decorative capitals of the nave (12th century) of Tournai Cathedral – which represent most imaginatively the world of plants, fantastic animals and historical scenes – particular mention should be made of the badly damaged sculpture of the *Mantilius Porch* (3rd quarter of the 12th century) on the north side of the Romanesque nave. This portal is crowned by two round arches, each surrounded by sculpted bands, which in their turn are inscribed in a three-lobed arch. An extensive iconographic programme is developed in bas-relief, particular to the end of the 12th century. The scenes shown are inspired by the Bible, by history, and

The 'falling' man, historiated capital of the nave, Tournai, second half of 12th century. Tournai, Our Lady's Cathedral.
According to the Borchgrave d'Altena, the historiated capital with the 'falling man' can be understood only if the capital is reversed in the order of thinking. Then it becomes clear that the man sitting on the ground is carrying a column, and it is quite on the cards that the falling man is meant to be the base of the column rather than the capital.

Chastity and Lust, detail of Mantilius door, pilaster figures, *ca* 115 cm, Tournai, late 12th century. Tournai, Our Lady's Cathedral.
Of the representation of the struggle between virtues and vices according to Prudentius on the pilasters of the Mantilius door, only a few groups have been preserved, among which are Chastity and Lust and Humility and Pride. They differ markedly from the customary portrayals. The virtues are not personified by any classical warriors or feudal horsemen, but by young women in the 12th century. Just as in Prudentius's description, Luxuria brandishes the flaming torche while Chastity has a hand raised to hurl a stone at Lust, who has already been wounded in the head.

Mantilius door, portal on the north side of the Romanesque nave, *ca* 1400 × 600 cm, Tournai, 1170-1198 (spiral coupled column added at a later date). Tournai, Our Lady's Cathedral.
In the still legible sculpture of the portal the following themes can be discerned iconographically: the virtues and vices, and the miser and the devil on the pillars; on the archivolts the world of fables and the medieval bestiaries are depicted, and on the keystones above the entrance historical and bible scenes, the theme of which is frequently disputed.

by the fantastic wealth of fables the medieval *bestiaria,* which go back to the *Physiologus.* The figures on the pilasters are more plastically worked out, and they peer shyly from behind the double columns, which were originally not twisted, and which present the *Psycho-machia* or battle of the virtues and vices of Prudentius.

Like the Maas valley, Tournai produced stone baptismal fonts which achieved considerable renown. They were typified by their square or rectangular basins with hollowed-out fonts, standing on a cylindrical foot surrounded by four small corner pillars. The square outer walls of the font are decorated with graphically sculpted friezes, presenting scenes from the Bible or the lives of saints, or limited to architectonic, geometrical and symbolically charged motifs. The archaic, timeless figures, obtained by an exaggerated schematization of forms and the particular attention to the reproduction of details, ignoring proportions, are characteristic of the style of the Tournai workshops. The series production of baptismal fonts exceeded local demand, and Tournai

Baptismal font, Tournai limestone, 99 × 102 cm, Tournai, 12th century. Zedelgem, St Laurence's Church.
The four side-walls of the font basin are adorned with sculptured reliefs. Apart from two heraldically presented animals and soldiers, on the three other sides of the basin are scenes from the legendary life of St Nicholas, such as the legend of the goblet, the story of the three (only two shown here) impoverished sisters and the story of the three murdered children. The same scenes are to be found on the Tournai font at Winchester.

Baptismal font, blue Tournai limestone, 105 × 104.5 cm, Tournai, first half of 12th century, thorough restoration in 19th century. Termonde, Our Lady's Church.
The low reliefs on the lateral faces of the square basins hollowed out in circular form show scenes from the New Testament. Twelve Apostles are sitting together with Christ at the Last Supper. On the other side Saul (Paul) is thrown from his horse after being struck by lightning; Peter, warming his hands by the fire, denied Christ; and on the right Paul and Peter are standing before St Peter's Church in Rome, or the symbolic gate to the Heavenly City of Jerusalem. On each of the other sides are three medallions, with the symbols of Evil and that of Redemption respectively.

baptismal fonts are found not only in the Scheldt region at Zedelgem near Bruges, at Ghent and at Termonde, but also in the English cathedrals of Lincoln and Winchester.

Another important product exported from Tournai is funeral sculpture, which expanded particularly around the middle of the 13th century. Originally the gravestones were in the form of a trapezium and in very flat relief, simply ornamented with palmettes and stylized leafwork – as on the 12th-century example from the Gruuthuse Museum at Bruges and on a gravestone showing the Tree of Jesse in Lincoln Cathedral. Sometimes the figure of the deceased is also represented in idealized form in bas-relief, as on the gravestone of Bishop Roger in Salisbury Cathedral.

But for the period up to the 13th century, there are only scarce evidences of sculpture at Bruges. For stone building sculpture, Tournai limestone was used for the fragments that have come down to us. This shows that Tournai at that time was an important supplier of stone to Bruges. In this connection, we should mention the arched space (12th century) of the Romanesque St Basil's Church that crowns the narrow passage between the southern annex and the right aisle. On the semicircular arch space the baptism of Christ in the Jordan is represented. Here too we find the same abstracting and decorative treatment, as well as the linear and graphic aspect, derived from the Tournai workshops. The hardness of the stone used made any other sort of treatment difficult. Until this time tympani in this material were only exceptionally found outside Tournai, although it would be rash to attribute to its workshops all sculpture carried out in this hard stone.

Not only for Bruges, but also for Ghent, the rare examples of sculpture that have come down to us provide only a fragmentary insight into the existence of any local sculptural activity. The economic power of the town, the presence of prosperous traders, and of abbeys and cloisters with richly furnished houses of worship point – as for Bruges – to a potential patronage, which would

Baptism of Christ, tympanum in Tournai limestone, 100 cm wide, Bruges (?), mid-12th century. Bruges, St Basil's Church.
As regards the Romanesque period, few testimonies in the field of monumental stone sculpture have been preserved in Bruges. An item of importance is the tympanum above the narrow passage between the southern annex and the aisle on the right of St Basil's Church. The Baptism of Christ in the Jordan constitutes a highly stylized adornment of the semi-circular tympanum.

encourage and promote local production. Ghent too lay in the direct sphere of influence of the Romanesque Scheldt school. Religious factors would have contributed to close contacts between Tournai and Ghent in the architectonic and sculptural fields. For stone sculptures, in any case, the Ghent sculptors obtained their materials from the Tournai and Antoing regions.

Related to the Tournai art of sculpture, which links to the French one, is the bas-relief in Ledic sandstone showing the patron saint (?) (*ca* 1160) of St Nicholas' Church in Ghent, where it was found in 1962 in the course of excavations under the choir. But the Tournai style elements are adapted here in a very personal manner, in which a certain contribution from the Maasland art may be surmised. The profiling of the edge on the right side of this sandstone fragment possibly points to the existence of a lintel, such as the historic lintels with representations of the Saints Bavo and Amandus (*ca* 1160). The fragments of these, which were found on the site of the former church of St Bavo's Abbey, must originally have formed part of a larger group, such as *e g* a choir screen. The scene with the Preaching of Amandus and the Adoration of Christ are clearly connected with the badly damaged representation of a fragment on the other side which, shows how relics placed on an altar were venerated. On another fragment an enthroned bishop is blessing. On the basis of the somewhat inflated features of the figures, they have been labelled as Maasland work. However, this line of argument, is not convicting, in view of the more linear effect without the pure characteristics of Tournai sculpture. Possibly the stylistic ambiguity of these lintels bears witness to a local interpretation of the Scheldt and the Maasland art.

Sculptures that escaped the influence of Tournai were also produced in Ghent, which is proved by some capitals in St Bavo's Abbey, including the example in Maastricht tuff stone showing Samson carrying the gates of Gaza. Stylistic comparisons with the capitals of Maastricht, Rolduc and Tongres, as well as the materials used, lead to the assumption that in St Bavo's Abbey stonecarvers were strongly influenced by Maas valley workshops. This hypothesis is strengthened by the absence of the graphic and decorative effects particular to Tournai sculpture, which were adapted in a personal manner by the sculptors of Ghent.

Sepulchral monument of Hugo II, a Ghent castelan († 1232), Tournai limestone, 100 × 245 × 80 cm, Tournai, second quarter of 13th century. Ghent, Bijloke Museum.
The bed with the recumbent figure is supported at each end by four dogs and stones decorated with foliage motifs. Hugo II is depicted as a knight in full array. The head rests on a cushion borne by two angels under a baldaquinesque canopy, which assumes the form of a reinforcement. His feet rest on a dog as symbol of fidelity.

74

THE GOTHIC
(13th-14th centuries)

Sculpture in the Flemish territory does not appear to have developed independently; therefore with the gradual entry of the Gothic into Flanders during the 13th century, the northern French influence was markedly felt. Like the Maas valley, the Scheldt area was to follow in the wake of the northern French Gothic sculptors. Via the cosmopolitan Bruges, works of art from Tournai, Ghent and Bruges itself were spread far beyond the frontiers in return loads, thanks to the presence of many international trading colonies.

At the outset, Tournai held the monopoly in the Scheldt area. The rich Gothic portals of the cathedrals of the Ile-de-France were imitated when, in the middle of the 13th century, the new portal of Tournai Cathedral was erected. Even more than in the Romanesque period, the sculpture presents the doctrine of salvation according to fixed arrangements, and strives for order and measure. Both in the presentation and the detail, a feeling for realism may be noted.

Where funeral sculpture was concerned, the Tournai workshops evidently produced more original work, in view of the many orders they received from abroad. The idealized figure of the deceased could be engraved in a copper plate, of which the deep grooves were often filled with a coloured paste to increase their expressiveness. A grave plate of this kind was ordered by Birgitta of Sweden for her parents, and was placed in Uppsala

Death and Coronation of the Holy Virgin and *Assumption of Mary with Deësis*, sculpture of the pointed arch in the arch area of the porch of the central ward, 179 cm, third quarter of the 13th century. Bruges, St John's Hospital.
The important renovation of this Bruges porch-sculpture is in the gestures of the apostles, who are standing behind the death-bed of Mary.

Crucified Christ with Mary and John, high relief of the Passion tympanum, Avesne stone, the original polychromy covered with a layer of white lime, 100 × 70 cm, Flemish (Ghent?), 1240-1250. Ghent, St Nicholas' Church.
The high-relief fragments discovered in 1968-69 form part of what from an iconographic standpoint is an exceptional Passion tympanum, which is divided into two horizontal registers. The lower register depicts Christ's Entry into Jerusalem, the Scourging, the Descent into Limbo and the Resurrection. In the upper register are seen the Appearance of Christ to Mary Magdalene, the personification of the Church and the Resurrection of the Dead.

75

Cathedral in 1382. The flat tombstone evolves spatially to a stone tomb that is freestanding or set up in a niche. These two types were preferred by royalty, prominent personages and the higher clergy, who had them placed in castle chapels, church buildings, or houses of worship of cloisters and religious orders. The recumbent representation of the idealized, still living deceased would lean on a coping-stone, carried by lions or dogs. An example of this is the tombstone, executed with great technical skill, with the image of Hugo II, landlord of Ghent (*ca* 1230); temporarily stored in the Bijloke Museum at Ghent and coming from the former Cistercian Abbey of Nieuwenbos, near Heusden.

Mostly the *gisant* is laid on a massive substructure or sarcophagus. On the side walls tribute is paid to the lineage, with coats of arms or portraits of members of the family round the socle, *e g* on the tombstone of Henry I of Brabant in St Peter's Church in Louvain (second half of the 13th century): the figures equipped with the tokens of their social status – knights in their armours and priests in their chasubles – lay their heads on cushions and stare in front of them. Their hands are folded in prayer or hold the insignia of their dignity, while their feet rest on a dog or a lion. The image of the deceased is also set in an architectonic frame, accompanied by angels who fulfil all sorts of functions. In medieval funeral plastic art, the deceased is generally provided with an accompanying text, chiselled round the tomb. Usually these grave monuments were originally polychromed and gilded.

As at Tournai, the monumental sculpture of church buildings at Ghent and Bruges in the 13th century was inspired by French Gothic building sculpture. But in contrast to France, this early Gothic monumental sculpture occurs only rarely in Flemish territory.

Behind the 17th-century brickwork of the west portal of St Nicholas' Church in Ghent, an almost completely sculptured tympanum in Avesnes stone (*ca* 1240-1250) was found in 1968/69. The classical iconography of the Passion and the Resurrection was here, exceptionally, used for the sculpture on the arch area of a portal. In the grouping and treatment of the figures, it is hard to ignore the influence of the ivory plates on the Flemish sculptors. There are also striking similarities between, for example, the personifications of Church and Synagogue and those in the gold and silversmiths' art of the Maas valley. The latter, in the 12th and 13th centuries, spread rapidly via the ornamental reliquaries such as that of St Eleutherius (1247) and of Our Lady (1205), signed by the Maas valley gold and silversmith Nikolaas van Verdun, in Tournai Cathedral. The relationship can also be seen with the northern French monumental sculpture of the cathedrals, imported into Flanders par-

Sedes Sapintiae, oak with remnants of the old polychromy, 87 cm, Maas region studio, mid-13th century. Zoutleeuw, St Leonard's Church.
The group comprising the seated Madonna and the child caressing her can hardly, from an iconographic standpoint, be described as a *Sedes Sapientiae.* The Romanesque hieratic Mother of God and the Early Gothic dignity henceforward give way to a more human, tenderer relationship between mother and child.

ticularly via Tournai. The new Gothic style made itself felt in a greater differentiation of the sculptured surface, as the result of a more linear and rhythmical handling of material.

The arch area of the early Gothic portal (ca 1270-1280), added to the east facade of the central ward of St John's Hospital at Bruges, with scenes from the life of the Virgin, goes back to the Virgin and Last Judgment portals of French cathedrals such as those of Chartres, Amiens and Paris. Only the fillings of the two pointed arches above the double entry, representing the Death and the Assumption of the Virgin, are original – although they have been restored. The idealized realism in the treatment of the figures, their high relief, and the more decorative treatment of the folds of the garments, show certain affinities with French sculpture – as interpreted, however, by local workshops. Also in the Maas valley *Bergportaal* of St Servate's Church at Maastricht (ca 1250), where the classical layout of the Mary Portals has been taken over, the French Gothic was imitated.

The strongly weatherbeaten west portal of St Nicholas' Church in Veurne also dates from the middle of the 13th century. Here, on the archivolts, the twenty-four elders of the Apocalypse are shown in relief, which points to a Last Judgment portal. The *Deësis group*, consisting of the seated Christ with the kneeling Mary and John the Baptist, above the arch space, strongly resembles the *Grand-Dieu group* (2nd quarter of the 13th century) coming from Thérouanne Cathedral and now preserved in Our Lady's Church at St Omer.

Under the influence of the new Gothic current, the Maasland type of the frontal enthroned Madonna begins to 'live'. In the 13th century, both the seated and standing Madonnas assume an unrestrained, natural attitude, and the drapes of the garments become more flexible. Now Jesus sits or stands astride on the lap of Mary or is carried on the left arm, while he plays with an apple or a dove. Other examples – the type of which goes back to the well-known example of St John's Church at Liege – show Jesus in an affectionate gesture, stroking the chin of his mother while she stares gently and dreamily ahead. The latter humane motif was introduced in the west in the first half of the 13th century and goes back to the Byzantine type of the *Glykophilousa* ('the Meek'). This type is found in the seated Madonna of St Leonard' Church at Zoutleeuw, trampling a dragon under her feet – a Maasland motif which was still typical.

Examples of the 14th-century, so-called international Gothic are more numerous. In the courtly, graceful, drawn-out figures of the Madonnas – describing a decorative s-shape – and in the dreamy expressions of the countenance, the head being inclined slightly sideways in a maternal gesture, tribute is paid above all to French mannerism, and partly also to the Bohemian-Luxembourg 'gentle style'. This *dolce stile nuove* was expressed particularly in the freestanding images of Mary. The marble sculpture in Our Lady's Cathedral at Antwerp (ca 1350) with the mannered drapes of the garments and the somewhat contrived attitude is an example of this. The same characteristics are found in the image of Our Lady-of-Scheve-Lee at Malines.

This conventional, worldly style was, around the end of the 14th century, abandoned by the sculptors of the Scheldt region and of Brabant. They strove for more realism, as in the monumental stone statue of St Catherine in Our Lady's Church at Courtray (ca 1380), which is ascribed to André Beauneveu of Valenciennes and was carried out as the result of a commission from Lodewijk van Male for the ducal Chapel.

Towards the end of the 14th century, the portal is adorned by a central image. Thus it appears that the image of the Virgin of the Potterie at Bruges originally crowned the old portal of this hospice. Radical restoration has meant that this miraculous and almost life-size image has acquired an exaggerated accentuation of the attitude of the hip; so that in this decorative s-shape all

Standing Madonna with Child, white marble, 132 cm, school of Maas region, *ca* 1330-1340. Antwerp, Our Lady's Cathedral.
The elegant Madonna with the head-shawl descending to the shoulders corresponds iconographically, and also in the pronounced movement of the hips and in the fall of the folds, to the 14th-century French type of Madonna. There is an affinity between this and the Diest white-marble representation of the Madonna (1344), the original of which is kept in the Metropolitan Museum, New York.

too often, possibly without justification, the so-called mannerism of the Franco-Flemish or international style is seen. The image of the Virgin from Our Lady-ten-Poel's Church at Tirlemont in Brabant also adorned the portal, and is related to the image in Notre-Dame in Paris, too. It is somewhat unusual for this period that the author of this idealized image is known through church bills of 1362 and 1363. Wouter Pans seems also to have been the sculptor of the fourteen large vanished images which were originally set up in niches – separate from one another by small columns – decorating the facade next to the entry of this church.

The Watchman, Tournai stone, originally in Ghent Belfry, *ca* 1337. Ghent, St Bavo's Abbey.
At one time the monumental statue of the tower watchman in armour, together with three others, figured prominently up on the corners of the Ghent Belfry. Apparently a competition was organized for the best design for the sculptural embellishment of this civic building. One of the losing entries is, indeed, still kept in the Bijloke Museum.

The Announcement of John's birth to Zacharias and *The Love Potion of Tristan, Isolde and Brangäne,* corbels in Lede limestone, 29 × 54 × 25 cm, Bruges master (?), 1376-1379. Bruges, Gruuthuse Museum.
These structural sculptures from the pre-Sluterian period are among the best in the series of 16 corbels still preserved in the Gruuthuse Museum, and were originally from the facade of Bruges Town Hall. Here the architectonic constraint is almost surpassed. In their dynamic composition, plastic quality and monumentality, they conform in some measure to the contemporary Parisian sculpture.

In the 14th century, the interior of the church was also provided with sculptures, such as those in the choir of St Rombouts' Cathedral at Malines (1350-1375), which are also carved by Wouter Paus. In the Archbishop's Museum of that town, only three sculptures have been preserved, of which the two figures of the Annunciation to the Virgin clearly point to the School of Rheims.

Apart from the clerics, royalty and nobility, the town magistrates and the patrician families became the main clients of the local sculptors. From the late 13th century onwards, however, the centre of political gravity shifted in a democratic direction: the feudal regime gave way to the power of the towns, in which the patricians were represented to a certain degree. Thus the monumental profane sculpture was also used to adorn new buildings – such as the guild halls, belfries, the town hall or sheriff's house – with sculptures, ornamental building consoles and key vaults. In St Bavo's Abbey at Ghent, there is still one of the four monumental stone warriors in armour which, in 1338, were placed at the four corners of the Ghent belfry. From 1377 to 1385, Jan van Mansdale supplied corner stones for the sheriff's house at Malines, and André Beauneveu supplied eight sculptures for it. For the Town Hall at Bruges, Jan van Valenciennes, with collaboration from other sculptors, made some twenty statues of princes and prophets, together with niches, consoles and baldachins (1376-1379). But during the French occupation in 1792, these Gothic statues on the Town Hall were destroyed because of their royalist connotations. The consoles, including that of Tristan and Isolde and of Zacharias with the Angel, which show the most plastic qualities, still belong to the beautiful style of the Franco-Flemish masters.

In the Duchy of Brabant, which during the 13th century grew into a politically and economically important region, only fragments of the sculpture on civil buildings have been presented. At Louvain, all that remains from the early Gothic period is the *Lakenhalle*, in which capitals with grotesque figures were placed in 1317. Particularly in small plastic monumental features such as cornices, venthole fillings, spouts, *etc* there appears, already at a very early stage, a popular art form with a strongly realistic character. This awareness of the importance of reproducing reality – a feature of the building sculpture of all the Gothic schools – was worked out independently at the end of the 14th century, especially in Brabant. It already heralded the approaching golden age of Brabant sculpture.

St Catherine of Alexandria, alabaster, crown, wheel, hilt of sword and fingers restored and renewed, 186 cm, ascribed to André Beauneveu, 1372-1373. Courtray, Our Lady's Church, Chapel of the Counts of Flanders.
Not only from the point of view of the precious material, but also from that of the actual execution is this Catherine one of the most important sculptures of the 14th century in Flanders. From a stylistic angle it presents a synthesis of sculptural output in the 14th century. While the sculptor employed the traditional formulas, such as the still marked perpendicularity, he achieves a higher degree of plasticity. The design embodies a certain monumentality by making the garment envelope a human body, and not an abstract volume.

THE BURGUNDIAN ERA
(1384 – end of 15th century)

A broader horizon for expansion opened up to Flemish artists when, by the marriage of Philip the Bold with Margaret of Flanders, Burgundy was added to their lands in 1376. The patronage of the Burgundian Dukes was also of considerable importance to sculpture: probably the greatest of these patrons was Philip the Bold. In his ducal atelier at Dijon he took Flemish artists into his service for the sculptural ornamentation of his castles and for the Chartreuse of Champmol. At Dijon the art of sculpture took a new turn. A strong reaction against the formulae of the affected international style gave rise to sculpture of a wholly original realism. In the work of the brilliant figure of the Brabantized 'Claus de Sluter van Herlam' this *ars nova* found its most monumental expression. After the death of Hennequin de Marville in 1389, Sluter was entrusted with the management of the Dijon atelier. Sluter replaced his predecessor's collaborators, recruited from the region of birthplace in Flanders (such as the Ypres sculptors Thomas le Fèvre, and Gillis and Staes Tailleleu) by Brussels sculptors, including Jan van Prindale and Willem Smout.

The portal sculptures of the Chartreuse at Champmol were finished around 1397. The image of the Virgin – with its strongly dramatic balance – is adored by the figures of the founders, kneeling at her side, Philip the Bold and Margaret van Male, commended by their patrons saints, John the Baptist and Catherine. Sluter had found how to give a monumental expression to the traditional *ex voto* type, known from contemporary Flemish and French illuminated manuscripts. This is already a speaking illustration of the *ars nova*: Sluter reproduced the physical traits of the Duke with almost painful accuracy, and tellingly expressed the authoritarian character of the princess, as described by the chronicler Froissart. The sculptures by Sluter dominate the space. They have an existence of their own, no longer subordinated to an architectonic background. He also broke with the archaic arabesque folds that led a life of their own. Under the broad cloaks, he sought for a natural reproduction of the living body.

In 1404, the Well of Life in the garden of the Chartreuse of Champmol was completed. Of this Calvary, erected on a draw-well, only the bust of Christ and the pedestal with the famous figure of Moses have been preserved. The *ars nova* is found in its purest form in the mausoleum of Philip the Bold, the design of which is attributed to Sluter. It was his nephew Claus de Werve, who in 1411 – just five years after Sluter's death

– put the finishing touch to the mausoleum. In contrast to the traditional 'flat mummy type' of Beauneveu, Sluter hit upon the idea of a recumbent figure, plastic in the round, to represent the deceased. The side walls of the socle were worked open into a gallery with arcades, in which a funeral procession of forty figures appears, acting as mourners. Above all in this masterly series of weeping figures Sluter's style triumphs. Here we are struck by the extraordinary expressiveness of the countenances and the natural attitude of the figures with the realistic handling of their garments.

In France – especially in Burgundy – but also in Spain, Sluter's sculpture was imitated until the middle of the 15th century. The monumental tomb of John the Fearless, commissioned from Claus de Werve in 1443, and after his death from Juan de la Huerta of Aragon, is a replica of the tomb of Philip the Bold. Striking likenesses are also shown in the mausoleum, now disappeared, of Cardinal de Brogny (1414) at Geneva, executed by Jan van Prindale; the monumental tomb at Bourges, of Philip the Bold's brother, Duke John of Berry, for which Pauwel Mosselman carried out the mourners; and the tomb of Charles the Noble and his spouse at Pamplona Cathedral, commissioned in 1416 from Jean Lomme of Tournai.

But still this new realistic style did not have spread generally in Flanders and Brabant. However, we must take into account that monumental sculpture has been only fragmentarily preserved. When Sluter was staying in Brussels, a specific realistic style must evidently have existed. This is witnessed by the volume working of the consoles on Bruges Town Hall (now Gruuthuse Museum) supplied in 1379 by the town sculptor Jan van Valenciennes, and that of the sheriff's house at Malines (1383-1385), which was executed by Jan van Mansdale of Brussels.

The fact that the monarchs regularly stayed in the palace on the Coudenberg with their extensive court household, certainly has something to do with the remarkable flowering of sculpture in the second half of the 14th century at Brussels and in Brabant. As at Louvain, the sculptors were grouped together with the bricklayers, stonemasons and stonecutters in the guild of the *steenbickeleren* (stone carvers) called the *Vier Gekroonden* ('the Four Crowned') which received its first statutes in 1368. The only Brussels sculptor known by name, to whom work can be attributed with certainty, is the above-mentioned Jan van Mansdale, alias Keldermans, who became a member of this guild *ca* 1370.

The traditional archaic currents persist in the work of the Master of the Group of Three Kings on the southwest portal of St Martin's Church at Halle, and in the well-known Virgin (1390-1400). Towards the end of the 14th century, the Brussels sculptors also followed a new direction, the impulse for which is often connected with the figure of Sluter. Whether the *ars nova* was started by him or by Brussels and Brabant sculptors, is a matter that still has not been cleared up.

Before Sluter worked in the Duke's atelier with de Marville, he stayed till 1385 at Brussels, where he was apparently entered in the membership list of the guild of the *steenbickeleren*. In spite of Sluter's stay in Brus-

Daniel and Isaiah in dispute, statues of prophets on the socle of the Calvary, 198 cm, sculpture: Claus Sluter, polychromy and gilding: Jan Maalwael, 1402/03. Dijon, Carthusian Monastery of Champmol.
The exuberant draping of Sluter's work is of structural conception. The sculptures are completely independent of the architectonic environment in which they have been erected. By virtue of a certain flexibility the prophets, who are characterized by their strongly individualized facial features, come into contact with each other.

sels, and the fact that he chose Brussels stone carvers as his principal collaborators at Dijon, it is surprising how little the new Dijon style made itself felt in Brabant and Flanders. The author of the rich portal sculpture on Brussels Town Hall remains anonymous. Only five sculpted consoles and eight seated prophets have been spared. Because of the voluminous draperies, the sparkling vitality and above all the strongly individualized faces, characteristic of the new spirit of Sluter's *ars nova*, it is often attributed to this great master – perhaps mistakenly. There is a striking likeness to the design of the consoles of Champmol. But the Brussels prophets are still determined by the architectonic framework, and they are therefore less worked out plastically.

Sluter's sculptural principles are also witnessed to in the *Twelve Apostles* with their speaking, individualized likenesses as characters (*ca* 1410), which stand in the flat niches of the triforium of the choir in St Martin's Church at Halle. The sober character of the garments still show archaic traces.

Although knowledge of painting in the 15th century is far further advanced, for sculpture it is in more of an experimental stage. The new, more realistic design assumed by sculpture in the 15th century is especially characterized by more solid figures, a more plastic play of folds, and more expressive faces. Architecture and painting determined to a great degree design, iconography and style in late Gothic sculpture. When we consider the heights attained by painting in the era of the Flemish Primitives, it is not surprising that the sculptors sought their inspiration in painting. In this connection, there was much emulation in the reproduction of all kinds of pictorial details. *Ca* 1425-1435, Eyckian realism in sculpture was to make way for the more pathetic artistic concept of Rogier van der Weyden. The latter's art of painting in scenes such as the Visitation, the Birth and especially the Passion of Christ, was adapted three-dimensionally in the numerous sculpted groups on the retables and in the bronze sculptures. The *Holy Tomb* in St Vincent's Church at Soignies is a striking example of this magic naturalism with its dramatic strain.

Matthew and Simon, apostolic sculptures on the triforium in the choir, *ca* 175 cm, Brabant master, first decade of 15th century (overpainting of later date). Halle, St Martin's Church.
The draping of the mantle is archaistically Gothic and is the result of study rather than of experience. As compared with the capricious arabesque influence characteristic of the pre-Sluterian tradition, the folds become heavier and angular, as a consequence of which a greater materiality is achieved in the reproduction of the garments. This contrasts with the expressive, energetic aspects of the features which make the apostolic figures living character types.

Seated figure of a prophet, porch-sculpture of the Bruges town hall, ca 60 cm, Brussels, Atelier of the master of the retable of Hakendover (?), beginning of the 15th century. Brussels, Municipal Museum.
One of the eight figures of prophets that once adorned the archivolts of the main porch of the Brussels town hall. There is a striking resemblance to the figure of God the Father in the retable of Hakendover (1400-1404).

Sepulchral monument of Philip the Bold (1342-1404), alabaster, gilt and polychromed, black marble from Dinant, 360 × 254 × 243 cm, Claus Sluter and Claus de Werve, 1385-1410 (numerous restorations and reconstructions of the funeral procession). Dijon, Musée des Beaux-Arts.
The recumbent figure of Philip the Bold has been restored in such a way that it is impossible to recognize Sluter's hand in it. The general conception of the tomb of state is mainly Sluter's.

Collaboration between sculptors and painters was a fact in the 15th century. Furthermore, it was not unusual for painters to supply patterns for works of sculpture. Thus for Louvain Town Hall, the designs for the corbels on the outer facades (1447/48) were supplied by Jacob Schelewaerts, doctor of theology, and Jan van den Phalisen, pastor of St Peter's Church. These were put into plan by the *meester-werckman van de metselerien* (master workman of the constructions) Mathijs de Layens, and the patterns for the sculptors were drawn by Hubrecht Steurbout, the *schildere* (painter).

The monumental sculpture, the funeral monuments, the carved altarpieces, the freestanding sculptures as well as the groups were usually polychromed. There was even particular importance attached to finishing off works of sculpture in this way, and often artists of the first rank were commissioned to paint sculptures. In 1435, no less a personage than Jan van Eyck painted six sculptures on Bruges Town Hall!

Because of the expensive materials (such as gold leaf) with which the painter worked, he generally received a larger fee than the sculptor or stonecutter. To Melchior Broederlam of Ypres, for painting the panels and polychroming the sculpture of the retables made by Jacob de Baerze for the Chartreuse of Champmol (*ca* 1399), the amount of 800 *fr* was paid – twice what de Baerze received for his wood sculpting.

In its function, monumental sculpture remained connected with architecture. Town buildings such as the Bruges, Brussels and Louvain town halls were richly decorated with sculpture and generally admired. Because of the numerous devastations and restorations that followed, up to our own days, we must however take account of the pseudo-character of these town hall facades. The iconography of the facade sculpture of Louvain Town Hall is mainly religious in tendency, and recounts history from Adam and Eve until the life of

Christ. Documents relating to the sculptural ornamentation show a considerable presence of the Brussels *steenbickeleren* at Louvain.

Church buildings were also provided with sculptural decorations in areas of their facades, cornerstones, niches *etc.* A witness to this is St Sulpitius' Church at Diest, for which a rich sculptural ornamentation was provided on the restoration of the choir by Sulpitius van Diest in 1417, inspired by that of St John's Church at 's-Hertogenbosch.

Funeral monuments were erected in many Flemish churches. The 15th century represented the last period in which Tournai sepulchral art flourished, having occupied a prominent place in Flemish sculpture from the 12th century onwards. The gigantic grave monuments went out of fashion, and the gravestones bequeathed to us by the Tournai slab carvers are mostly intended to be mortared into a wall. Judging from their subject, these modest votive tablets can be divided into two categories. On the stones on which the deceased were shown, accompanied by their patron saints, they are shown kneeling at the feet of the Trinity or the Virgin. The votive tablets show scenes from the life of Christ or burial scenes. The importance and extent of

Recumbent statue of Mary of Burgundy († March 27, 1482) free-standing tomb (detail), recumbent figure with cushion: 195 cm, Jan Borreman and Renier van Thienen, ca 1490-1502. Bruges, Our-Lady's Church.
The wood-carver Jan Borreman, who is mentioned in relation with the adaptation of the arms of the original model for this recumbent statue, has possibly delivered to van Thienen the wooden model for this recumbent statue.

these was dependent on who commissioned the stone. With a few exceptions, they were mostly ordered and executed during the lifetime of the deceased, or of the last survivor. In any case, the reliefs appear to be the work of capably trained and experienced craftsmen. The influence of Rogier van der Weyden is also felt in the works of the sculptors of his birth town, the damaged grave relief of Jean Lamelin (†1470), court chaplain of Philip the Good and canon of Tournai cathedral.

The production of the 14th-century mourner type of tomb shifted to Ghent in the first quarter of the 15th century, and there the free mausoleum developed further. In Ghent, various ateliers were located that specialized in funeral sculpture. Among these dynasties of tomb carvers, probably the de Meyere family is the best known. From John III the mausoleum of Margareta van Gistel († 1431) was commissioned, and it was set up in the crypt of St Bavo's Cathedral. The recumbent figure of Margareta is known only from a drawing, which makes it clear that the deceased was reproduced '*al ront naer dleven*' ('lifelike and in the round') according to the Sluter formula. The usual Tournai hard stone seemed unsuited to a three-dimensional plastic design, and thus the preference was given to the softer white Avesnes stone. In the richer grave monuments, mourning figures or religious scenes were depicted on the side walls of the tomb. On the broad sides of the sarcophagus of Margareta van Gistel, we find on each side eight mourning figures, now very mutilated, with coats of arms in bas-relief, carried out in Tournai stone. The expressive attitudes and the speaking countenances point to examples from Dijon. The Crowning of Mary, together with the kneeling Margareta and her husband, both presented by their patron saint, and the Last Judgment adorn the narrow sides. The Dedelinc atelier also enjoyed considerable fame.

For carrying out the grave monument of Michele de France († 1422) in St Bavo's Abbey at Ghent, destroyed during the Iconoclasm, Philip the Good gave the preference to the Bruges artists Gillis de Blackere and Tideman Maes. They were experienced in the working of alabaster. From this material the recumbent figures, the two angels at the head end, and the twenty separate figures of mourners under the baladachins are manufactures. The sarcophagus itself was made from Dinant black marble.

Also located in Bruges were ateliers which were experienced in the making of epitaphs for Bruges families, such as de Baemst and van de Velde (*ca* 1490) in Our Lady's Church. As the Tournai gravestones, their iconography is borrowed from the art of painting.

The brass and bronze funeral sculpture, which is dealt with under metalwork, also belongs to the lapidary ornamentation of the church interior. In so far as sculptors and woodcarvers were involved in making them, we should mention the brass grave monument of Mary of Burgundy (1502) in Our Lady's Church at Bruges. The well-known Brussels sculptor, Jan Borreman, carved a wooden model for this – possibly after a design by a court painter. Especially in the countenance of the lifelike *gisant* the new ideal of beauty, that arose via the realism of late Gothic art, is expressed.

In the 15th century, church furnishings gained in importance. They acquired a serving function in the

Sacramental Tower, Avesne stone, 1250 cm, designed by Mathijs de Layens, 1450. Louvain, St Peter's Church.
A masterpiece in the field of miniature architecture is the hexagonal Sacramental Tower, which was commissioned by the Confraternity of the Holy Sacrament to the plans of Mathijs de Layens. In the six niches above the tabernacle are groups of sculptures the iconography of which is related to the Eucharist. Successively presented are the Crucifixion, the Scourging of Christ, Christ Crowned with Thorns, God's Distress, the Agony of Death and Judas' Betrayal.

church offices. In course of time, these furnishings ornamented with decorative wood carving and sculpture grew into real masterworks of architecture in miniature, such as the pulpita and the sacramental towers. The most beautiful pulpita are found in the Southern Netherlands. They occurred not only in capital and cloister churches, but from the 15th century onwards also in parochial houses of worship. In the late Gothic period the pulpitum reached its highest point in Flanders and Brabant. Sculptures and sculptured groups are set in an architectonic framework and represent the apostles, the passion cycle or the history of local patron saints. The pulpitum of St Peter's Church in Louvain (before 1490) contained at that time sculptures of the Evangelists and the Church Fathers in the tabernacles above the columns. Numerous figures of saints stood in the small niches of the tribune.

Among the church furnishings decorated with sculpture are also the wall tabernacles and the Sacramental towers. In the wall tabernacle of St Martin's Church at Halle (1409), on which there are probably the names of the three donors, the niches are filled with representations of the Washing of Feet, the Last Supper, the Entry of Jesus into Jerusalem and the Agony in the Garden. The oldest preserved sacramental tower is that of St Peter's Church in Louvain, executed ca 1450 on a commission from the Brotherhood of the Holy Sacrament after the plans of Mathijs de Layens.

The sculptural dimension of the choir stalls, which are generally listed under arts and crafts, should also not be ignored. They are found in the choir of houses of worship in which the office was sung or prayed. Particularly worthy of attention is the figurative sculptural work with which this modest furnishing is adorned. The sculptural repertoire provides a 'world of piety and satire'. Religious subjects are reserved for the most visible parts, such as the extremities of the stalls, the crowning of the low cheeks and the backs of the row of high benches. They are also found as knobs on the quarter circular armrests of the partitions and on the little fold-up seats. It was on these *misericordia* – the least noticeable parts of the seating – that popular scenes with a satirical and moralizing trend and proverbs were depicted. The choir stalls of St Saviour's Cathedral at Bruges, which go back to the second decade of the 15th century and were altered many times, are the earliest example to be found in Flanders. The subjects on the fold-up seats, in which there are a number of Eyckian reminiscences, were above all drawn from daily life, paying special attention to the child. All sorts of droll figures, monsters and fabulous beasts sometimes also serve as grips on the partitions, as in the more sober choir stalls of St Peter's Church at Louvain. In this example, the little seats show a remarkable realism. These choir seats were supplied in 1439 by the Brussels artists Nicolaas de Bruyn and Geert Gorys, the former being responsible for the sculptural part, and Gorys for the joinery. The elegant choir seats of St Sulpitius' Church at Diest (1490) were made after the example of the Louvain model, and the small seats of the latter are not without interest, either artistically or as regards the iconography. Noteworthy in this case are the numerous

proverbs that are depicted. The sculpture of the choir stalls of Our Lady's Church at Aarschot (beginning of the 16th century) represents a period of more advanced style, which introduces the final phase of Brabant Gothic.

The rich ornamentation of the choir stalls is stylistically related with the wooden retables. From *ca* 1450 till the disappearance of the Gothic *ca* 1530, sculptors in Flanders, but especially in Brabant, were enormously industrious in the production of the crowded and richly painted altarpieces. Not only were they placed on the high altar of houses of worship, they also richly adorned the altars of the crafts and guilds in transepts, side chapels and even against the pillars. A retable consists of a box, whose internal space was divided vertically (since the 14th century also horizontally) into shelves. In these compartments were placed groups in relief, with shallow profiles, composed of various parts. To give the figures an appearance as realistic as possible, those sculpted groups were worked over with the brush by the painters. Wings closed the whole retable, and these were painted on the outside. These panels were opened on high days, and on the name-days of the patron saint of the church, the craft or the guild on whose altar the retable stood. The glitter of the gold and the polychrome gave a rich appearance to the retable. In the oldest altarpieces, the college of the apostles is shown round the calvary group or the crowning of Mary. A later example of this is the Apostle Retable from the former Beguine Church at Tongres (Limburg, *ca* 1470-1490), now in the Museums of Art and History, Brussels.

The crowded peepshows with their strongly narrative and didactic character exhibit an undeniable imaginative power and recount the story of the Passion, supplemented with scenes from the Childhood of Christ. In the

Yawn one's head off, seat of the choir stalls (detail), ca 21 × 18 cm, Brussels atelier, 1490-1493. Diest, St Sulpitius' Church.
The seats of the choir stalls of Diest are characterized by a strong narrative nature, picturing numerous proverbs and expressions.

The monkey with the convex mirror, carving on the circular arms, incorporated in the final wings, (detail), ascribed to be by Jan Borchmans van Eindhoven and his atelier, 1515-1520, rebuilt in 1911. Aarschot, Our-Lady's Church.

The fox is the crane's guest, seat of the low row of benches of the choir stalls at the gospel side (detail), ascribed to Jan Borchmans van Eindhoven and his atelier, 1515-1525, rebuilt in 1911. Aarschot, Our-Lady's Church.

Two spectators from the Scripture story about the Adulterous woman with Jesus, side wing of the choir stalls (detail), oak, 218 × 500 cm, Brabant, third quarter of the 15th century. Hoogstraten, St Catharine's Church. The figures with the Jewish sugar-loaf hat are watching full of anticipating interest to what Jesus is about to reply to the Pharisees in relation with the sixth commandment. The carving is still fully Gothic in the simple framing of the groups and the sober but strong expressivity of the depicted personages. Especially is the scene with the adulterous woman, the laws of perspective seem of no importance.

St George hung upside down with his head just above a sea of flames, St George retabel (detail, central section), pedestal: 163.5 × 284.5 × 30.5 cm, Jan Borreman the Elder (Brussels), 1493. Brussels, Museums of Art and History.
The masterpiece of the retable sculpture in Brabant was, according to a receipt, produced in 1494 by order of the Louvain Guild of Crossbowmen for the Chapel of Our Lady-of-Ginderbuyten, in the Dijle town.

Passion retable of Claudio Villa and Gentine Solaro, polychromed oak, pedestal: 260.5 × 252.5 × 30 cm, Brussels, *ca* 1460-1470. Brussels, Museums of Art and History.
In the central section the patrons, the Piedmont banker Claudio Villa and his wife, Gentine Solaro, are each depicted with their patron saints.

Pieta, passion retable of the high altar of Strängnäs (detail), Brussels, ca 1490. Stängnäs Dom.

The lamentating group, with the dead body of Christ resting on the lap of Mary, is a pieta-type which is based on the work of Rogier van der Weyden. The figures with their delicate faces and their long-drawn bodies are inspired on the creations of Dirk Bouts.

Mary retables, her life and death are shown, as are her joys and sorrows. St Anne, the mother of Mary, was also particularly honoured, as we see from the St Anne retables. A splendid Brussels example, coming from St Anne's Chapel at Auderghem and now preserved in the Brussels Museums of Art and History, shows the Kinship of St Anne (1500-1510).

Other themes chosen to appeal to the imagination, were the legendary life stories of the patron saints of churches, crafts and guilds, including their cruel tortures. The prototype of these Brabant retables is found in the two oldest known Flemish retables (1392-1399). They were carved at Termonde by Jacob de Baerze, at the order of Philip the Bold, for the Chartreuse of Champmol (Dijon, Museum of Fine Arts). Its panels and carvings were painted by Melchior Broederlam.

Apart from retable centres in the county of Flanders such as Ghent, it was especially the Duchy of Brabant – with famous production centres such as Brussels,

Antwerp and Malines – which were internationally renowned for their carved altarpieces in the 15th century and the first half of the 16th.

The Brussels workshops in particular supplied outstanding work, as is seen in the *Passion Retable* of Claudio Villa and Gentine Solaro (*ca* 1460-70), in which the patrons are shown accompanied by their saints. The influence of the Brussels town painter, Rogier van der Weyden, is especially evident in the pathetic group of the Lamentation over the dead Christ. The *Leonard Retable* at Zoutleeuw by Arnold van Diest (*ca* 1479) shows a striking similarity with the work of the Louvain painter Dirk Bouts. With the Borreman family of sculptors, a high point was reached in the art of the retable. The *St George Retable* was supplied in 1493 by the *best beltsnyder* of Brussels, Jan Borreman the Elder, on the commission of the Louvain Crossbow Guild, for their Our Lady-of-Ginderbuyten Chapel. According to the invoice, this was provided with a double pair of wings, recounting the various grisly martyrdoms and the final beheading of St George. Stylistically, Borreman brought an innovation in the spatial grouping of the personages around the main figure, the figures in the foreground being seen from the back.

Although the Brussels altarpieces were superior in quality, the production from Antwerp was more extensive. The great trade metropolis of Antwerp – which was already producing retable sculpture in the 15th century – was particularly active around the turn of the century, especially in the first decades of the 16th, and sold this production both at home and abroad. Also the centre of Malines – which is better known for its small polychromed devotional statuettes (including the charming Virgins, female saints and those of the Infant Christ) and the typical little closed gardens or *Horti Conclusi* – produced various altarpieces. Small retables, such as the picture retable (*ca* 1500) in the Mayer van den Bergh Museum at Antwerp, present a characteristic appearance. The box is divided into three little chapels, each with the representation of a Malines saint statue.. The art of sculpture at Louvain was limited to the locality and its surroundings.

Economic aspects entering into the production of these altarpieces, such as the distribution of work, rules governing the acceptance of offers, quality control and sales, bring us to the working of guilds and crafts in the 15th century. The sculptors were part of the corporative system in the medieval town. At Louvain, as at Brussels, the wood carvers and the sculptors in stone were united in the craft of the *Vier Gekroonden* or the craft of the *steenbickeleren*. In the towns of Antwerp (originally at

Three episodes from the Life of St Leonard, St Leonard retable (detail, left-hand panel), figures in walnut, pedestal in oak: 140 × 229 × 27 cm, Brussels, 1476–78. Zoutleeuw, St Leonard's church.

As regards the commissioning and design of the retable, in which the legendary life of the patron saint of St Leonard's Church is portrayed, it is known from receipts that the Louvain painter Aert de Maelder conducted negotiations in Brussels. There have been frequent references to the affinity of the painting of Dirk Bouts with the tall figures and their impassive expressions on the reliefs. In particular, the tower-like form of the baldachins point to the Brussels retables.

least), Malines, Courtray and Ghent, the sculptors were
united with the painters, gilders, glaziers and other
artists in St Luke's Guild. At Bruges, on the other hand,
they were incorporated in the Joiners' Guild. The
economic aspects we have mentioned were regulated by
these guilds. Members of various craft guilds were
involved in the manufacture of these altarpieces: the
boxmaker or joiner made the cupboard and possibly also
the wings, the *metselriesnydere* did the decorative
carving, the sculptor supplied the sculpted reliefs and
figures, the painter painted the wings, the decorator
and/or the gilder provided the polychrome for the
whole.

To guarantee good quality and to safeguard the
competitive position, the materials used were controlled
by official guild evaluators, who saw to it that the
relevant guild regulations were observed. If these
materials were approved, they were given a hall-mark.
The latter is found on the sculptural work and on the
retables. The carving or burning of marks on wooden
sculptures is a custom applying only to the large Brabant
towns. For Antwerp, this was a branded little hand for

undecorated woodwork and a castle for the polychrome
and the gold. At Brussels, for the wood used in the
carving, a chasing hammer was punched in; a sheep
between the open legs of a pair of compasses for the
joiner's part, and finally the stamp BRVESEL for the
quality of the polychrome and the gold. At Malines, the
punch with the arms of the town (three palisades) was
used for the woodwork. The stamp MECH LEN, with a
coat of arms between the H and the L, sometimes
replaced by the punched initial M, approved of the
quality of the gold used.

Because of their unusual appearance and quality, these altarpieces were not only sold in the Low Countries. Brabant retables are also found in Germany and in Sweden, including the magnificent Brussels *Passion Retable* (*ca* 1490) decorating the high altar of the church at Strägnäs, and the Antwerp retable (*ca* 1500) at Vaksala, showing the parable of the Wise and Foolish Virgins. That the bulk of such altarpieces was no obstacle to their export can be seen from the examples mentioned above. These peepshows are also found in France, Denmark, Poland, East Germany, Spain, Portugal, Madeira, Italy, England and Austria. We may mention other examples in Finland, Russia, the United States and even in Australia. We also frequently find separate groups and fragments from vanished retables.

More numerous still are probably the isolated devotional carvings and sculpted groups. It was thus that shape was given in the late Middle Ages to the bitter suffering of Our Lord. A high point is represented by the monumental *Calvary Group* of St Peter's Church at Louvain, attributed to the Brussels sculptor Jan Borreman the Elder. In the mourning figures of Mary and John, the pathetic influence of van der Weyden is evident. The *Pietà* or *Divine Distress of Our Lady-of-Ginderbuyten* at Louvain (*ca* 1465), now in the Town Museum, shows Mary with the body of her dead Son. Near the Seat of Mercy – the representation of the Trinity – the body of the Saviour rests in the bosom of God the Father. In one of the niches of the Gothic sacramental towers (*ca* 1450) of St Peter's Church at Louvain, designed by Mathijs de Layens, a *Seat of Mercy* of the type of the Master of Flémalle stands. Another touching scene related with the devotion to the holy places is the *Repose of Christ on the Calvary*, better known under the name of *Christ in Distress* – a theme greatly favoured in Brabant at the end of the 15th century.

The Marian iconography was also enriched by themes such as the Virgin in the halo, resting on the sickle moon. St Leonard's Church at Zoutleeuw – a true sanctuary of Brabant late Gothic art, which was spared from the Iconoclasm and French occupation – possesses such a *Marianum* (beginning of the 16th century), which has preserved its original position. Here Mary is also shown as Queen of the Rosary. Another devotional scene that found much favour at the end of the 15th century is the representation of St Anne – but it would lead us too far if we gave here a summary of the whole legion of saints who populated the churches, public places and houses of the Middle Ages.

It was not the turn of the century that brought an end to the production of the late Gothic sculptors. This was achieved by the Italian Renaissance, which for the time being was penetrating only gradually. Its first traces are found on the masonry work, where the 'new' *antycke* – pure Renaissance decorative forms borrowed from Italy – was incorporated. In the beginning, the public had few interest in the new presentation of the human figure. Pictures and reliefs generally remained true to their late Gothic forms.

Triumphal Group, oak and original polychromy partly preserved and exposed; Christ: 205 × 201 cm; Mary: 180 cm; and John: 178 cm, Brussels (ascribed to Jan Borreman the Elder), *ca* 1490. Louvain, St Peter's Church. The monumental Triumphal Group, consisting of Christ crucified and the mourning figures of Mary and John, is set above the rood-loft in St Peter's Church, Louvain, which was erected in 1488. The Holy Virgin in particular brings out the influence of the pathos of Rogier van der Weyden's art.

Painting

FROM THE EARLIEST TRACES TO THE 14th CENTURY

What has survived of Flemish art – if we may employ the term 'Flemish' in such an early stage in history – is very scarce in the time preceding the 15th century, and can be traced back only as far as the late Romanesque period. It had not yet developed a character of its own, nor – with a few exceptions – did it display the special quality, that was to endow art in the same regions with a fame far beyond the frontiers two centuries later. It consists of examples of local craftsmanswork which accord with the international, later Gothic style, influenced by Byzantine art, which was in vogue at the time. A survey of these oldest relics of pictorial art therefore has more significance as an archaeological documentary than as a historical study of style. It appears to us that the upsurge of Flemish art in the 15th century owed its origin to the royal studios in France, where the finest artists from the Netherlands joined forces in the 13th and 14th centuries; rather than to the local centres, where painting was more monumental in character, moralizing from the Church's point, and only subsidiarily designed to generate any aesthetic revival and refinement.

The earliest material evidence of local painting consists in some murals in the refectory of St Bavo's Abbey in Ghent, discovered in 1889 during restoration operations. These are four monumental representations of saints, executed in somewhat crude brushwork and painted in the niches of the windows. The curvilinear treatment of these Roman-like figures is wholly in keeping with the early Christian and Romanesque Italo-Byzantine style.

The oldest panel painting in the Southern Netherlands is the painted back of the *Triumphal Cross of Oplinter*, which is believed to date from the middle of the 13th century and is of Maastricht origin. This partially preserved piece, still in Romanesque style, also shows the retardation of religious painting, although it was not put on the wall. The same may be said of the *Reliquary of St Odilia*, 1292 (Kerniel, Mariënlof Convent), likewise from the Maas region but perhaps originating from a centre more to the south.

The rise of Gothic art in the 13th century spelled the end of large-scale painting on the smaller wall surfaces in churches. This function was now assumed by stained glass. However, spacious scenes were still executed in monasteries, and also in secular buildings, although no example of such works has been preserved.

Some 13th-century wall paintings, only fragments of which are extant, are found in Beguinage Church at St Trond, St Anne's Church at Aldeneik, the Dominican Church in Louvain and St James's Church in Bruges. These are merely fortuitous specimens of what must have been a decorative and schematic – almost mechanical – form of art.

The same fate has befallen the remaining heritage from the 14th century. At that time the painting craft was consolidating and developing into a well organized and entirely secular vocation. We know that a great deal of painting was done on panels and canvas. The tremendous advance and revival of painting in the 15th century was probably the underlying cause of the disappearance of practically all the older mobile paintings from places of worship, which were systematically replaced by new works. To judge from what has been preserved of the murals of that period, however, it is improbable that panel painting in Flanders displayed features which heralded or made way for the art of van Eyck. There is thus no point in comparing the development of this assiduously executed but mediocre œuvre of craftsmen, who had certainly been thoroughly well trained, with that of paintings by artists of outstanding talent. The latter became established in more intellectual circles, frequently as a result of commissions from royal personages, and not so much in the locality of the artist.

The most impressive mural painting from the 14th century is found in Ghent. It is a *Last Supper* which was made to adorn the refectory of the former Bijloke Abbey around 1330. The high quality of this painting, which is still discernible in spite of the damaged state of the work, calls to mind French painting of the same period. Equally extensive but heavily mutilated murals can be seen in the Dominican Monastery and in St John's and St Paul's Hospices, called the *Leugemete*. All this shows the importance and the perpetuation of the Ghent tradition of painting. In Courtray and Bruges too there were at one time vast murals. However, they have likewise disappeared or been mutilated, apart from a few fragments (*St Louis*, Bruges, Our Lady's Church). To com-

Rogier van der Weyden, *Triptych of the Adoration of the Magi*, detail from central panel, ca 1455. Munich, Alte Pinakothek.

Reliquary of St Odille, 34 × 80 × 23.5 cm, Maas region, 1292. Kolen-Kerniel, Mariënlof Monastery.

plete the picture mention should be made of some mural paintings at Maastricht (1337, Dominican Church), Hasselt (St Quintin's Cathedral), St Trond (Beguinage Church), Anderlecht (*ca* 1400, St Peter's Church) and Halle (Our Lady's Church), all of which testify to a high degree of craftsmanship but were designed in accordance with very traditional, calligraphic patterns, in keeping with the prevailing international style.

THE 15th CENTURY

From several points of view the 15th century is one of the most remarkable in the art history of the Southern Netherlands. A felicitous concurrence of several socio-geographical factors, gave a fillip to the rapid development of a new, two-dimensional art. Together with Italian art, it launched the exploratory movement of western pictorial representation, which spanned the ensuing period right up to the end of the 19th century. This era marks the emergence of painting as an autonomous field. Up to the 14th century illustrative painting, in which we can trace the archetypes of modern painting, had a dual function. It dealt with buildings and with books, respectively in murals and miniatures. The rare examples we still have of paintings on separate panels seem (as regards aspect and style) to have been rather on the lines of monumental art. The two types, although both were created with paint and brush, had no connection with each other, either from a craft, or from a structural or functional point. Wall painting was a monumental art integrated with architecture. While it certainly helped to make the Christian doctrine clear in the churches, it was in structural terms of a decorative, hieratic character. The fresco was more a form of depiction than a picture.

The reverse applied regarding book illustration. The miniature painting, with its aristocratic associations, was not essentially decorative but served primarily to illustrate the subject-matter; and as such it can impress us simply by its presentation as a decorative adjunct to the text of the book. To put it plainly, whereas a church building is not erected for the specific purpose of having its walls painted, a book has no reason to exist unless there is something to read or look at in it. So the innovatory process in the pictorial system, which had been applied for centuries, was developed progressively in miniature art. There were also other, form-related factors which may have stimulated the illusionistic, anti-decorative and anti-hieratic evolution of the miniature: *e g* the small size, which through its clarity of arrangement attracts much more attention to the pictorial element; or the 'window' aspect, which a miniature always has because of its clear-cut edging and which emphasizes the illusionary nature of the depiction. The graduation of the painted image to independence ultimately found expression in material terms too. There came into being a mobile piece of 'wall furniture', specially designed to be used for a painted representation. This was the 15th-century painting now so familiar to us: a panel made smooth as glass with priming and inserted in a frame in the same way as glass in a window-pane, a sort of flat-surfaced kaleidoscope which reflects the same pictorial bewitchment on every wall and every surface.

St Brics, mural, *ca* 270 cm high, late 12th century. Ghent, Refectory of St Bavo's Abbey.

Last Supper, mural, *ca* 950 cm wide, *ca* 1330. Ghent, Refectory of Bijloke Abbey.

merchandise of a private character, even though in most cases it still had a religious function. Few paintings were indeed destined specifically for the court.

The impact of the bourgeoisie on civilization and the economic prosperity of the towns, which had developed so rapidly in the Southern Netherlands, generated the impression that the evolution of painting on a high artistic level underwent a change from miniature art in France in the 14th century, to panel painting in Flanders in the 15th. Demand for quality panel painting in the Southern Netherlands municipalities served to consolidate the painting profession, so that talented artists came into their own far more at regional than at court level. The relation between royal patronage and high artistic quality could no longer be taken for granted.

THE 'FRANCO-FLEMISH' STYLE   This relation still existed in the 14th century, when Paris was the centre of the world of art. The most gifted artists at the Court were in many cases originally from the Netherlands. Their greater vitality and their provincial robustness, which derived both from their very nature and the bourgeois orientation of society in their country of origin, imparted fresh vitality to traditional French miniature painting. There is no evidence of prefigurations or contemporary examples of such high-quality art in their home country, and consequently it may be assumed that it was only in this internationally-minded court milieu that the conditions were created which enabled the talent of these immigrants to develop fully. Indeed, only in these so-called 'Franco-Flemish' miniaturist studios works were produced which by their nature and perfection can account for the panel painting, found around the turn of the century in the Court of Dijon and, subsequently, in the cities of the

Limburg Brothers, *December,* miniature of breviary *Les très riches heures du duc de Berry,* 223 × 134 mm, *ca* 1411-1416. Chantilly, Musée Condé, ms 65, fol 12v.°

Jan Maelwael and Henri Bellechose, *Martyrdom of St Denis,* 166 × 211 cm, between 1398 and 1416. Paris, Louvre.

TOWARDS A PICTORIAL NATURALISM   The trend towards realistic painting, which had started in the 14th century and reached its peak in the early decades of the 15th, coincided with a well-known socio-economic change which, as ever in the history of culture, proved to be its vital stimulus. The new social class which took its place between the common people and the nobility or clergy, namely the urban bourgeoisie, gradually increased in importance and soon became the driving force of society, productive and progressive in both the economic and the artistic sphere. Although the newly moneyed bourgeoisie assumed aristocratic airs, its mentality and outlook were nevertheless different. Precisely in that period naturalism in art made such rapid advances: it may assuredly be described as self-projection of this matter-of-fact middle class. Nor was it a coincidence that the painting developed as a movable *objet d'art*; it could be acquired, ordered, bought and sold by individual people, and was a piece of cultural

Southern Netherlands. It was the consummate artistry and experience of these Netherlandish painters which – at the time of the expansion of the guild movement in their own region – probably brought about the immediate enhancement of quality.

The need for physical expression, for space in which objects became almost tangible, for light and colour with which to portray reality without the aid of lines, was the decisive trend set by these Franco-Flemish innovators. But it never eliminated the mannered style and conventional pictorial expression desired by their patrons. This only happened in the 15th century, when the particularism of regional, urban art ousted the internationality of court painting. The stylistic development of the 14th-century miniaturist school in France, attained its peak in the early years of the 15th century with the highly sophisticated illustrations by Pol, Herman and Jan Maelwael, known as the Limburg brothers (*Les très riches heures du Duc de Berry*, Chantilly, Musée Condé). They came from Nijmegen and were in the service of the Duke of Berry. We know that they kept up their connections with Gelderland. With their perfectionist blend of French elegance, Dutch realism (especially in reproductions of nature and in narrative scenes) and Italian compositional inventiveness, the way had already been cleared, at least to present-day observers, for the coming of Jan van Eyck.

To a large extent the same characteristics can be discerned in the master who around 1409 painted the breviary for the Marshal of Boucicaut (Paris, Musée Jacquemart-André). Possibly the Boucicaut Master can be identified with Jacob Coene, a Bruges painter and miniaturist who was working in Paris and, among other things, illustrated a bible for Philip the Bold.

In the larger-sized panel paintings – in which

Melchior Broederlam, *Presentation in the Temple and Flight to Egypt*, painted exterior of right-hand panel of a sculptured retable by Jakob de Baerze, 162 × 130 cm, 1399. Dijon, Musée des Beaux-Arts.

Norfolk Triptych, portable altarpiece of Bishop of Liege, 33.2 × 32.3 cm (central panel), 33.2 × 13.3 cm (side panels). Maas region, *ca* 1419-20. Rotterdam, Boymans-van Beuningen Museum.

Melchior Broederlam, *Annunciation to Mary*, detail from the painted outside of the left panel of a sculptured retable by Jacob de Baerze, 1399. Dijon, Musée des Beaux-Arts.

Melchior Broederlam, *Escape to Egypt,* detail from the painted outside of the right panel of a sculptured retable by Jacob de Baerze, 1399. Dijon, Musée des Beaux-Arts.

hitherto, as with mural painting, the conventional patterns had been adopted – the modern, more realistic concept was being developed around that time (end of the 14th and beginning of the 15th century), in just as refined a manner as in miniature painting. The destination of this work was not Paris but Dijon, the centre of the new Burgundian empire which had been augmented by the former county of Flanders. Many of the painters similarly came from the Netherlands. The best known of them was the uncle of the Limburg brothers, Jan Maelwael from Nijmegen, who was Court Painter to Philip the Bold and appears to have had connections with the Brussels Guild of Painters. The *Martyrdom of St Denis* (Paris, Louvre) was probably almost entirely by him. It formed part of a series of five altarpieces for the Carthusian Abbey of Champmol, where the Duke of Burgundy was buried. After the death of Maelwael in 1415, Henri Bellechose, who succeeded him as the Duke's chamberlain, is believed to have completed the work. Still lagging behind as regards spatiality, the figures nevertheless stand out individ-

ually, with a plasticity which up to then had been unknown in painting.

MELCHIOR BROEDERLAM AND LOCAL PANEL PAINTING BETWEEN 1400 AND 1420 The most important paintings, however, that were made for Philip the Bold (and, in view of the fact that they were completed at Ypres in 1399, also symbolized the end of the perennial emigration of the best artists from the Netherlands) were the panels of a retable sculpted by Jakob de Baerze, likewise for the Carthusian Monastery of Champmol. The painter was Melchior Broederlam, Court Painter to Lodewijk van Male and subsequently also to Philip the Bold. He had his studio in Ypres, although he seldom appears to have received commissions from the citizenry. The perfection of his execution, the narrative realism of his representation and the spatial integration of the figures brought panel painting for the first time up to the level of book illustration. From then on the painted panel was the painter's most important and influential medium.

99

Even so, other examples of local panel painting in this transitional period were still exceptional and in most cases lacked Broederlam's refinement and sense of realism. There was a timid attempt at volume effect in the partially preserved panel *Scenes from the Life of the Virgin Mary* (Brussels, Museums of Fine Arts). This may be a work done in the Maas region, like the small but technically much sounder *Norfolk Triptych* in the Boymans-van Beuningen Museum (Rotterdam), which certainly originated from the Maastricht-Tongres-Liege diocese, and prefigures the miniaturist work of van Eyck. The *Tanners' Retable* in St Saviour's Cathedral (Bruges), a small portable altar with a snap-to top, was created around the turn of the century. It is one of the rare examples of local painting in Flanders which has survived intact from this period, and one which was still wholly under the influence of the Gothic 'international style'. It is often mentioned as a typical example of pre-van Eyck painting in Bruges, although it could just as well be set in Brabant. A further noteworthy specimen of what, apart from Broederlam's work, was painted at local level is the *Last Judgment*, done for Diest Town Hall (now in the Municipal Museum). It remains an enigmatic piece, because it may have been created several decades later than its style suggests.

MASTER OF FLÉMALLE   So far the modern naturalistic tendencies were limited by the pictural forms, which held sway over a full century of painting. Even Broederlam did not escape from their influence. The interplay of curves in the folds of garments, the concession to unnatural, dance-step-like postures and the schematic, ethereal doll's faces of the figures are, all things considered, a long way off the complete and intense naturalism, which brough the 15th-century generations of Flemish painters international fame overnight.

A further link in this chain of development was the Master of Flémalle. The name devised for him is – somewhat unfortunately – based on the presumed origin of three panels, nowadays to be seen in the Städelsches Kunstinstitut, Frankfurt. According to a 19th-century witness, they originated from the Abbey of Flémalle, but the abbey in question never existed in this small village near Liege. Today he is identified with Robert Campin, a painter whose name is found in archivalia and who, when already a master, settled in Tournai at the beginning of the century. He was the first painter of any importance who did not make a career at court, but in an urban environment. As '*peintre ordinaire de la ville*' he seems to have headed a major artists' studio. Clearly endowed with a combative and intractable nature, he became involved in a rising against the patricians in 1423, took an active part in municipal politics in 1428 and thereafter came repeatedly into conflict with the Town Magistrate on account of his 'anti-Tournai' prac-

Last Judgment, detail with the Damned, *ca* 1520?. Diest, Municipal Museum.

Master of Flémalle, *St Veronica*, 144 × 53 cm, *ca* 1430. Frankfurt, Städelsches Kunstinstitut.

tices. In 1427 Jacques Daret and Rogelet de le Pasture were enrolled among his pupils; in 1432 they both became independent masters. Rogelet may be identified with Rogier van der Weyden. Campin was married to Elisabeth van Stockhem, who was probably related to van der Weyden's wife. The stylistic relationship of the œuvre of the so-called Master of Flémalle with that of Rogier van der Weyden (they constitute, as it were, consecutive phases), the strong link with the work of Jacques Daret too, Rogier's Tournai origin, the family relationship between the wives of Campin and Rogier, as well as Rogelet de le Pasture's apprenticeship to Campin – all these are factors which confirm that the Master of Flémalle and Robert Campin were one and the same person.

What survives of this enigmatic artist must be painted between 1415 and 1440. Campin's art is important not only because it underlays the formal style of van der Weyden, but particularly because it heralded in a monumental manner, even before van Eyck, the advent of the actual 'Flemish Primitives' period. The bourgeois realism, which dissociated itself from the artificiality of court painting and the decorative international style of about 1400, had in Campin its first full-fledged protagonist. Viewed from this angle, Campin's significance in the evolution of painting can be likened to that of Sluter in sculpture. His art is largely oriented towards the physical and the material, and witnesses a capacity for close analytical observation. The world he created was charged with substance, cool and metallic in colouring; the surface is, as it were, filled right up with objects which seem to jostle each other. Illusionism, the new vogue in art, seem to be something he wanted to apply irrespective of any other considerations. This form of hyper-realism, coupled with the lack of orderliness of composition or flexibility of design, became less marked in his later work.

Perhaps the earliest work ascribed to him (ca 1414-1420) is the *Triptych with the Entombment* (London, Courtauld Institute). The manifest relief effect of the group of figures forms a striking contrast with the old-fashioned gold-leaf of the flat background. Other typical examples of his archaic style (ca 1420-1425) are *Nativity* (Dijon, Musée des Beaux-Arts) and *Madonna and Child before Firescreen* (London, National Gallery). Somewhat later is the *Mérode Triptych* with the *Annunciation* (New York, Metropolitan Museum). The ascending perspective, still completely the prisoner of the surface of the painting, is in Campin's work invariably in contradiction with the realistic materiality of the objects. This spatial integration was a problem for which he never really managed to find a satisfactory solution. Around 1430 Campin painted his main work,

Master of Flémalle, *Madonna and Child before Firescreen*, 63 × 84 cm, ca 1420-25. London, National Gallery.

a monumental triptych with a *Descent from the Cross*, of which only a fragment of the right-hand panel, the *Evil Murderer*, has been preserved (Frankfurt, Städelsches Kunstinstitut). The same monumentality is found in the panels depicting the *Holy Virgin* and *St Veronica* in the same museum. These sculptural figures have a physical 'presence' which remained unique throughout the 15th century. There is more flexibility and humanity in his later work, as exemplified by the small *Madonna in Glory* (Aix-en-Provence, Musée Granet), in which the elegantly studied gesture, the more balanced arrangement of figures and objects, and the far more rational filling of space point clearly to van der Weyden.

In this milieu frequently archaic processes were used to delimitate space – such as gold background, starry sky or upward sloping floor-despite an already thoroughgoing reproduction of the anatomical and physionomical features of the figures. This is brought out very strongly in a major anonymous work, which was obviously created under Campin's immediate influence, namely *Virgin and Donor Praying before the Crucified Christ* (Bruges, St Saviour's Cathedral).

Master of Flémalle, *Birth*, 87 × 70 cm, ca 1420-1425. Dijon, Musée des Beaux-Arts.

JAN VAN EYCK If Robert Campin was the outstanding pioneer in the 'realistic emancipation' of panel
painting, his slightly younger contemporary Jan van
Eyck was the first artist to design with an unsurpassed
degree of perfection a system of painting, in which the
particularized material representation of objects enabled
them to be viewed as mutually related and embodied in
a cosmos, which apparently functioned in accordance
with genuine natural laws. Van Eyck did not attempt to
emulate the sculptor as Robert Campin had done, as he
discovered the true function of colour as light, the only
element to be observed by anybody who desired to
fathom the actual appearance of objects. While this
attitude seems elementary in our days of emulsions for
colouring effects in photography, it may be called revolutionary in the 15th century.

Van Eyck was able to create his optical universe by
means of a technique, which gave painting the semblance
of reality. He painted in transparent dilute coats of
colour on a radiant white background. The observer
does not see actually paint, but the light reflected and
filtered by these translucent layers of colouring; just as

Hubert van Eyck (?), *Three Maries at the Sepulchre*, 71.5 × 89 cm, *ca* 1425.
Rotterdam, Boymans-van Beuningen Museum.

Hubert and Jan van Eyck, *The Adoration of the Lamb*, detail of the central
panel, 1432. Ghent, St Bavo's Cathedral.

in the real world the objects are not coloured, but reflect
a definite coloured light as conditioned by their composition. The experience we have for the first time unequivo-
cally in the history of art is of not looking at but
seemingly through the painted surface. This involvement of the real world in the painted world, as though
the two were separated only by the frame of the
painting, is typical of the totally novel a-conceptual
mentality of the artist. It also means that the painted
world, even if the ultimate aim is to express a higher
subject-matter or significance, does not lose its realistic
involvement. There is not a single van Eyck that is
visually less accessible through lack of any fore-

Jan van Eyck, *Madonna with Chancellor Rolin*, 66 × 62 cm, *ca* 1435. Paris, Louvre.

Jan van Eyck, *Arnolfini and His Wife*, 84.5 × 62.4 cm, 1434. London, National Gallery.

knowledge of symbolism or iconography. In van Eyck's work plastic design as a symbol, a concept or a conjuration – which to a certain extent characterizes all archaic art – is entirely a thing of the past.

This even applies to the work with the most complex iconographic programme of the late Middle Ages, the *Mystic Lamb*: a monumental polyptych, completed in 1432, which summarizes the whole Christian doctrine in an illustrative logic. Van Eyck made it into a gigantic *tableau vivant* in which God, angels, Adam and Eve, the Lamb from which sparkling blood gushes out, popes, prophets, holy virgins, horsemen, trees, grass, flowers, air, clouds, buildings, *etc* are of the same luminous confection, all clearly discernible and belonging to the same bright, crystalline world. Even the framework of the lateral panels casts its (painted) shadow on the floor of the room in which the Angel appears to Mary!

Van Eyck was solitarily grand. He did not belong to the craftsmen but through his origin, and even more on account of his capabilities, developed into a socially privileged artist. He probably came from a family of painters of high status from the Maas region, Maaseik is his presumed birthplace. His brothers Hubert and

Lambert were also painters, and their sister Margareta is also believed to have practised the profession. No known work can be attributed to any of them, unless the *Mystic Lamb*, which according to an inscription on the frame was begun by Hubert. Because of the relationship with the central panel of the Ghent retable the *Three Maries at the Sepulchre* (Rotterdam, Boymans-van Beuningen Museum) may have come from Hubert's hand, too.

In contrast with Campin, Jan van Eyck was invariably to be encountered in court circles. If Campin was the first full-fledged artist whose background was the guild, van Eyck was the last court painter of any significance. Not only in this respect parallels can be drawn with the Maelwael family; by reason of his training too, probably in the family circle, he was a sort of ultimate exponent of the trend described above. But at the same time, because of his more modern ideas, he imparted maturity to a movement which had been germinating for a number of years.

After initially serving as Chamberlain and Court Painter to Jan van Beieren, Count of Holland at The Hague, he was engaged in 1425 after the latter's death

Jan van Eyck, *Madonna with Canon Joris van der Paele,* 141 × 176.5 cm, 1436. Bruges, Groeninge Museum.

to perform the same duties for Philip the Good and settled in Lille. The Duke had a high regard for him and entrusted him as his confidential agent with secret diplomatic missions abroad. Thus in 1428/29 he was a member of the ducal delegation sent to Portugal, to prepare the way for Philip's marriage to Isabella, the daughter of King Juan. While there he painted the portrait of the future bride. From 1432 he lived in Bruges, the new city of residence of the Duke, which would be the abode of talented artists throughout the century. There he stayed until his death in 1441.

There is no record of his activities as court painter. This work was for the most part of a utilitarian nature and ephemeral; although no court portrait of the Duke, which he certainly must have painted, has survived. He also executed to a limited extent commissions for the higher clergy, the wealthy bourgeoisie and the nobility. It is for this work that van Eyck has gone down in history. It undoubtedly offers a one-sided image of this *pictor doctus,* as he was called, partly because it was all produced in the last ten years of his life. Had his earlier work been of a different, more narrative and miniature-like character, as some people have premised? The small

On the following pages:

Jan van Eyck, *Portrait of Margareta van Eyck,* 41.2 × 43.6 cm, 1439, Bruges, Groeninge Museum.

Rogier van der Weyden, *Portrait of a Young Woman,* 36 × 27 cm, *ca* 1455. Washington, National Gallery, Mellon Collection.

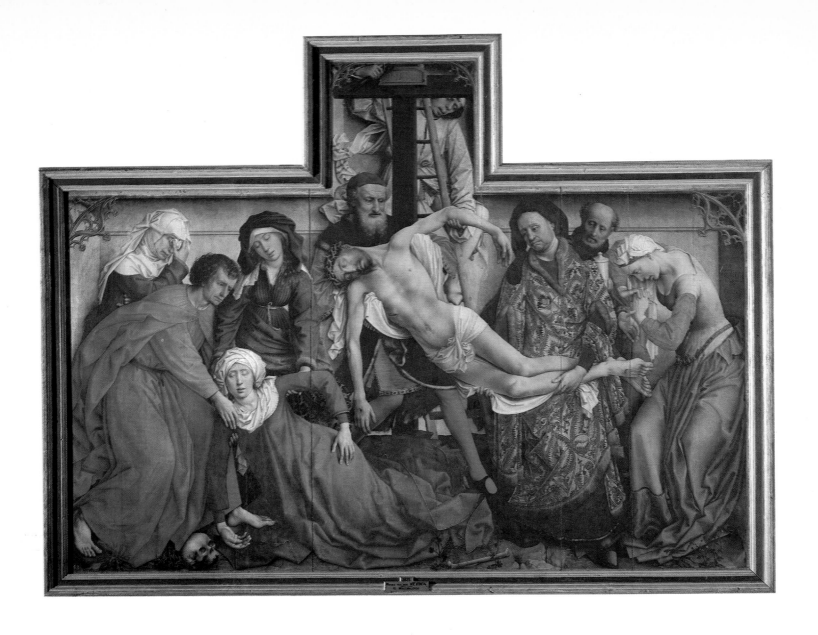

panels depicting the *Crucifixion* and the *Last Judgment* (New York, Metropolitan Museum) could in that case belong to this earlier phase of his style development, just like some miniatures of the so-called *Hours of Turin*.

After 1432, however, his work was confined almost entirely to occasional paintings for private use, and frequently calls to mind rhetoricians' pieces. It includes bust portraits and mementos with the necessary allusions, sometimes in the form of a personal gift, *Portrait of Tymotheus* (1432, London, National Gallery) or *Portrait of Margareta* (1439, Bruges, Groeninge Museum), the painter's wife, probably painted on the occasion of her birthday, as well as *Portrait of Jan de Leeuw* (1436, Vienna, Kunsthistorisches Museum); intimist Madonna representations, in many cases showing the person who had commissioned the work at prayer: the *Madonna with Chancellor Rolin* (Paris, Louvre); a wedding portrait: *Arnolfini and his Wife* (1434, London, National Gallery); a foundation panel in a private chapel: the *Madonna with Canon Joris van der Paele* (1436, Bruges, Groeninge Museum). Most of these paintings are signed in full, bear a motto and – sometimes cryptogrammatically – are dated, as if it was a painted document which also, with the maker's latent self-assurance, was intended to be a 'charter of ingenuity' for posterity. Is not van Eyck here a kind of early

Rogier van der Weyden, *Deposition*, 220 × 262 cm, *ca* 1435. Madrid, Prado.

Rogier van der Weyden, *Jean Bracque Triptych*, 34 × 62 cm (central panel), 34 × 27 cm (side panels), *ca* 1451-52. Paris, Louvre.

Renaissance figure in the north? His interest in antiquity, which finds expression in the use of Greek letters, his knowledge of science and technology, which for instance opened the way for a new application of oil-paint technique (some of the older historians call him the 'inventor' of this technique), his literary erudition and the many extra-artistic activities at the court are evidence of this enlightened humanist attitude.

Because of this exceptional, elitist position van Eyck did not give rise to a real school with imitators of his style, although he had a far-reaching and fundamental influence on all great Flemish painters of the 15th and 16th centuries. Apart from some free imitations which might be attributed to journeymen in the studio, only the œuvre of Petrus Christus owes anything substantial to van Eyck.

ROGIER VAN DER WEYDEN   Of a younger generation and with a completely different artistic background, Rogier van der Weyden, in contrast with van Eyck, virtually imposed his range of forms on painting throughout the second half of the 15th century. Rogier de le Pasture, as he was originally called, was born in Tournai in 1399 or 1400. He was trained by Robert Campin, to whom he became apprenticed in 1427. In 1432 he acquired the status of independent master and shortly afterwards settled in Brussels, where in 1436, already under the Dutch name van der Weyden, he was made City Painter and where he died in 1464.

The œuvre now attributed to Campin bears such a resemblance to the early works of van der Weyden that at one time it was believed to be youthful work of the latter. Although this theory is accepted by hardly anybody now, it has thrown into relief the solid Tournai painters' tradition, which through the personality of van der Weyden radiated a tremendous influence on all art centres in the Southern Netherlands. Those who are familiar with the œuvre of Jan van Eyck will notice the archaic, more Gothic nature of van der Weyden's scenes. Yet his art was far from being behind the times. In a particularly intelligent manner he succeeded in adopting the hieratic, sacral power of the earlier medieval art, and combining it with the new naturalistic achievements of both Campin and van Eyck. Van der Weyden revived and strengthened the formal concept 'style', (as a pattern or formula for a figurative representation), which had been weakened considerably by the growth of realism; as well as the contemplative concept 'icon' (as a symbolic or archetypal projection of a spiritual subject), but did so using true-to-life form.

The *Deposition* (Madrid, Prado) for example, is composed of flesh-and-blood figures, but is conceived as fitting into the two-dimensional surface of the painting. It is abstractly composed – and not only as a consequence of the flat gold background – so that the vitality of the realistically portrayed figures seems completely frozen at the outset. This impression is closely connected with the heavily linear design. Van der Weyden revived the designing of absolute images which could be grasped by the mind – not, as earlier, pictorial syntheses of the unapproachable divinity but of human passion: this was a further aspect of the humanizing tendency in the 15th century. Whether the subject was a weeping, hand-wringing Magdalene, the despair of the damned by the Last Judgment or a mother fondly embracing her child, Rogier van der Weyden turned them into sentimental symbols. These were with unusual rapidity assimilated and applied by his contemporaries, both in and far beyond the Netherlands, as a sort of pictorial vocabulary. Ever since, even the dullest devotional painting or print has invariably owed something to Rogier van der Weyden's imagery.

In his earliest work van Eyck's influence is sometimes apparent. A case in point is the intimate and pictorially conceived *Diptych with the Holy Virgin and St Cathe-*

Rogier van der Weyden, *Lamentation,* 111 × 95 cm, *ca* 1551. Florence, Galleria degli Uffizi.

Petrus Christus, *Lamentation,* 98 × 188 cm, 1460? Brussels, Museums of Fine Arts.

112

rine (Vienna, Kunsthistorisches Museum). The tense, abstract lines of the rigid composition and the spiritual intensity of his later work, as illustrated for the first time in the aforementioned *Deposition* (*ca* 1435), reached their climax around 1445-1450 when he painted the *Last Judgment* (Beaune, Hôtel-Dieu) and the crystal-clear icon-like *Jean Bracque Triptych* (Paris, Louvre). In 1450 he undertook a journey to Italy on the occasion of Holy Year. He stayed in Rome and possibly also in Ferrara. His contacts with Italian art are reflected in a remarkable manner in the *Lamentation* (Florence, Uffizi), a symmetrically composed *expositio* for the tomb on the Tuscan model (Fra Angelico). That period was also the prelude to a number of refined, sharply outlined and soberly composed portraits of Burgundian noblemen, some of them forming a diptych with a *Madonna and Child*. The *Laurent Froimont Diptych*, the *Portrait of Anthony of Burgundy* (both in Brussels, Museums of Fine Arts) and the *Portrait of a Young Woman* (Washington, National Gallery) are among the finest examples. The milder, more elegant tone of these portraits and Madonnas is also specific to some major compositions that he painted in this period, such as the brilliant, mature *Adoration of the Magi* (Munich, Alte Pinakothek).

DEVELOPMENT AND EXPANSION OF THE FLEMISH SCHOOL OF PAINTING   The second half of the 15th century is dominated by the work of five outstanding personalities. Each in his own centre with a highly original skill and psychology differing markedly from one to the other, they determined some part of the image of painting in Brabant and Flanders after the pioneers. Building on their inherited technical and spiritual wealth, they added new dimensions and accents or created new syntheses. They were Dieric Bouts in Louvain, Hugo van der Goes in Ghent and Petrus Christus, Hans Memling and Gerard David (three torch-bearers of succeeding generations) in Bruges.

Four of them were immigrants: Bouts, Christus and David came from North Brabant and Holland, Memling from Germany. This was not an unusual phenomenon at that time. It was due not only to the prosperous economic situation in the Southern Netherlands, but also to the now widespread fame of the Flemish School of Painting. These immigrants integrated completely and their assimilation of the local tradition resulted in an original and refreshing blend of style, which itself in turn was characteristic of the region.

PETRUS CHRISTUS   The oldest of these figures is Petrus Christus. In 1444 he acquired Bruges citizenship and settled in that city as an independent painter. He appears to have come from Baarle (probably the small town to the south-east of Breda). His style and manner of signing and dating – he was actually the only one to adopt this custom – are so similar to that of van Eyck, that one has to assume that some time before his citizenship of Bruges he was already there as the latter's apprentice and assistant. Leaving aside a number of sporadic imitations of van Eyck by anonymous masters, his œuvre is the only one in which the echo of van Eyck

Petrus Christus, *Portrait of a Carthusian*, 29 × 21 cm, 1446. New York, Metropolitan Museum.

Petrus Christus, *Madonna and Child in Interior*, 69.5 × 58 cm, *ca* 1455. Kansas City, Nelson Gallery and Atkins Museum.

Petrus Christus, *St Eligius and the Engaged Couple* (detail), 1449. New York, Metropolitan Museum, Lehman Collection.

– not in a fundamental manner but as to form, although immediately recognizable – continued to reverberate. This œuvre consists today of about 25 paintings, some of which radiate a rather simple but attractive solidity of workmanship. The miniaturized finish and clear expressiveness of it will no doubt have pleased right-minded and positively thinking citizens of that time.

The two earliest dated paintings, the *Portrait of a Carthusian* (New York, Metropolitan Museum) and the *Portrait of Edward Grymston* (London, National Gallery), both of 1446, show how close Petrus still was to his teacher at that period. The sensitive use of light and the hypnotic 'presence' effect are characteristic. Even so, he cannot be called an imitator. Although at a later stage he also borrowed other examples and in particular seized on the successful motivistic inventions of Rogier van der Weyden, such as those in the *Lamen-*

tation (Brussels, Museums of Fine Arts), this eclecticism did not harm the individuality of his disposition. This specific character displays unmistakable Dutch traits, which sometimes makes a comparison with Albert van Ouwater or Dieric Bouts (the Haarlem School!) so surprising. He brought into being a quite specific, self-contained world, in which the light is cold and the atmosphere rarefied, in which space and volume are considerably simplified, but the laws of perspective are clearly observed. Petrus Christus can in fact be regarded as the first painter to the north of the Alps who applied the central perspective almost perfectly and systematically (the earliest example is the *Annunciation* of 1452, Bruges, Groeninge Museum). Did he have more than casual contacts with Italy, as is perhaps rightly argued, and is Antonello da Messina's Eyckian technique in turn possibly to be accounted for by these contacts? The doll-like figures also obey the same stereometric laws: round and heavily shaded, their volume appears to have first been conceived in grey values and then converted into colours (the *St Eligius and the Engaged Couple*, 1449, New York, Metropolitan Museum, Lehman Collection; *Madonna and Child in Interior*, Kansas City, Nelson Gallery and Atkins Museum).

115

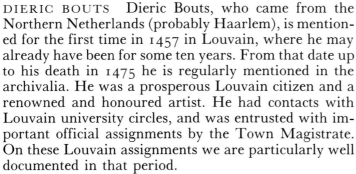

Petrus Christus, *Annunciation*, 88.5 × 54.8 cm, 1452. Bruges, Groeninge Museum.

Dirk Bouts, *Last Supper Triptych,* left-hand panel, above: *Meeting of Abraham and Melchizedek;* below: *Paschal Lamb;* right-hand panel, above: Manna; below: *Elijah fed by the Angel,* 180 × 151 cm (central panel) 88.5 × 71.5 cm (four side panels), 1467. Louvain, St Peter's Church.

DIERIC BOUTS Dieric Bouts, who came from the Northern Netherlands (probably Haarlem), is mentioned for the first time in 1457 in Louvain, where he may already have been for some ten years. From that date up to his death in 1475 he is regularly mentioned in the archivalia. He was a prosperous Louvain citizen and a renowned and honoured artist. He had contacts with Louvain university circles, and was entrusted with important official assignments by the Town Magistrate. On these Louvain assignments we are particularly well documented in that period.

The triptych depicting the *Last Supper* was commissioned in 1464 by the Brotherhood of the Holy Sacrament for St Peter's Church, Louvain, where it can still be seen. It was completed in 1467. Previously, around 1460, he had painted, for a certain Gerard de Smet, presumably a member of the same Brotherhood, the *Erasmus Triptych* (also still in St Peter's Church). We are also well documented concerning the *Scenes of Justice* (Brussels, Museums of Fine Arts). These were

commissioned in 1468 by the Louvain magistrature for the council chamber of the City Hall. The work was originally conceived as a four-panel painting, but Bouts died before he could complete the second panel. From the same source we learn that a second work for the City Hall, a *Last Judgment* triptych, had been completed by the time of his death. The lateral panels are usually identified with the *Road to Heaven* and the *Descent of the Damned* (Lille, Musée des Beaux-Arts).

His early style and consequently also his training are shrouded in mystery. The *Virgin Mary Retable* (Madrid, Prado) is dated around 1445 and displays features which clearly point to the Haarlem School. The compositions, however, are largely inspired by van der Weyden. Although Bouts was obviously not trained by van der Weyden, he has as the latter's spiritual heir in Louvain a significance similar to that acquired by Memling in Bruges. The profound earnestness, the power of dramatic expression and the plastic tautness of van der Weyden's art made an indelible impression on

the young Bouts, when he arrived in Brabant from provincial Holland. Indeed, one of Rogier van der Weyden's main works, the *Deposition* (Madrid, Prado), was on display in Louvain at that time. Nevertheless, Bouts invariably assimilated this influence, as well as that of van Eyck, in a highly individual fashion. It is precisely this blending of Southern Netherlands realism, monumentality and dramatic effect, with the more level-headed mood lyricism of Northern Netherlands art, that accounts for the consecrational and somewhat mysterious character of his paintings.

With Bouts there is always a certain archaism, not only in spatial design but also in the positioning, postures and movements of the figures. Although he delimits space in a rational manner by means of a strictly applied perspectivist line, the third dimension never really seems to be there. This is due to the very high vanishing point, the motley distribution and overlapping of colour surfaces or volumes, and the relief-like silhouettes of the figures. This plane aspect is, however, offset and deepened by the unusually rich and saturated colouring and by the unaffected fidelity to nature, which is perceptible particularly in the evocative reproduction of atmospheric situations. This quality was also conspicuous earlier, and perhaps more than now, so much that the 16th-century Louvain historian Johannes Molanus refers to Bouts as 'an innovator of landscape painting'. On the religious level his subject-matter is always very close to the Bible, which certainly associates him with the purifying tendency of the *Modern Devotion*.

Dirk Bouts, *Birth,* third scene from *Virgin Mary Retable,* 80 × 56 cm, *ca* 1445. Madrid, Prado.

Dirk Bouts, *Ordeal by fire,* detail from second panel of *Justice of Emperor Otto,* 1471-1473. Brussels, Museums of Fine Arts.

Dirk Bouts, *Justice of the Emperor Otto,* two scenes of justice with *Beheading of the Count* and *Countess's Ordeal by Fire,* 324 × 182 cm (each panel), 1471-1475. Brussels, Museums of Fine Arts.

In the iconographic field too we find in Bouts' work some innovations which are directly related to the theological trends in Louvain University. Leading theologians provided him with ideas which he could develop in his painting. In the *Last Supper* for instance, the main theme is not Judas' betrayal or the Apostles' communion, but the establishment of the Sacrament, the actual dedication of the bread. This iconographic conception is wholly in harmony with sacral solemnity, the inherent pathos and the contemplative, investigative character which permeates his entire œuvre. Bouts is the painter of life's mysteries, approached from the point of view of an introvert: human feelings, motives and passions seem to be merely latent for him, suffocated in their intensity and with the way to direct emotional contact barred. In this respect his representations have a natural symbolism. As contemplated by the painter, the world and what happens in it become transcendental.

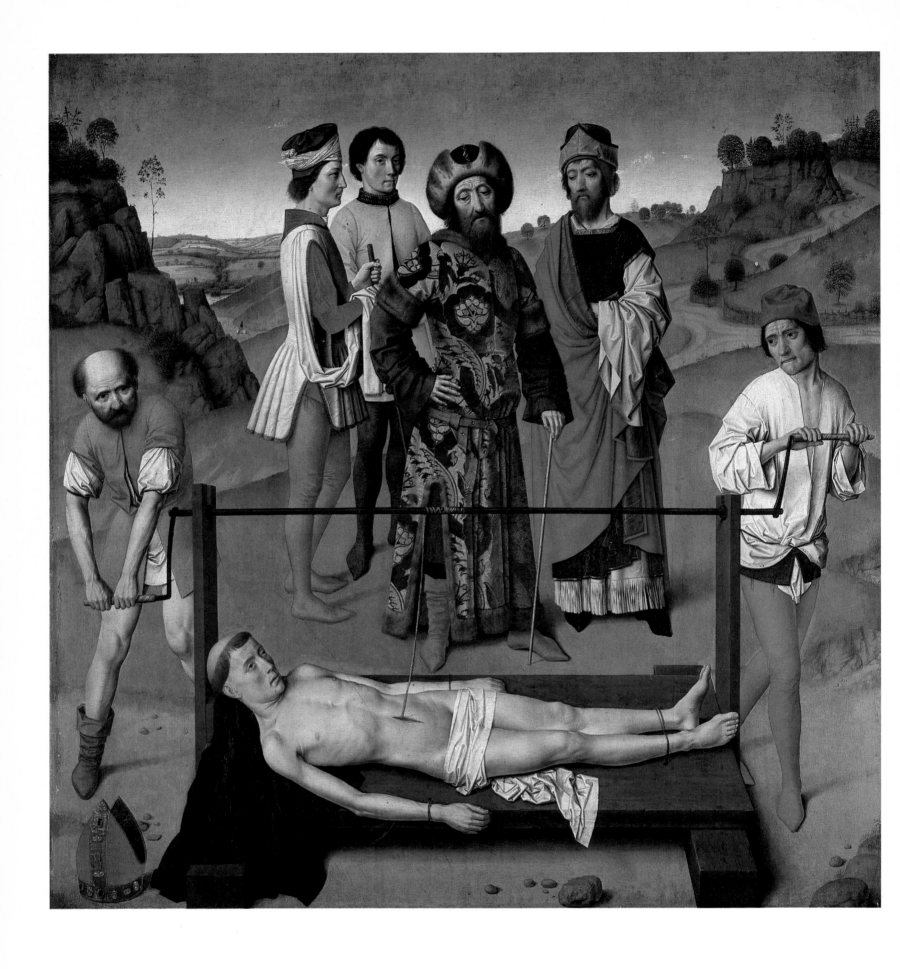

Dirk Bouts, *Triptych with Martyrdom of St Erasmus,* central panel, 82 × 80 cm, *ca* 1460. Louvain, St Peter's Church.

Dirk Bouts, *The Torture of St Hippolyte,* 91 × 91 cm, central panel of a triptych, *ca* 1475. Bruges, St Salvator's cathedral.

Hugo van der Goes, *Adoration of the Magi*, 150 × 247 cm. Berlin-Dahlem, Staatliche Museen.

Hugo van der Goes, *Portinari Triptych,* detail from central panel with *Adoration of the Shepherds, ca* 1475?. Florence, Galleria degli Uffizi.

HUGO VAN DER GOES   The artistic phenomenon of this generation was, however, Hugo van der Goes, who worked in Ghent. Albrecht Dürer later rightly spoke of him in the same breath as van Eyck and van der Weyden. He was probably born around 1430, but as to his origins we are completely in the dark. The likelihood is that he came from a family which had immigrated from the Northern Netherlands. In 1467 he became a freemaster in Ghent and was soon highly regarded as a painter. The striking gap in Ghent's art history between the death of Hubert van Eyck and the advent of Hugo van der Goes (merely through lack of extant material evidence) certainly does not help to place and interpret his style in a Ghent context. However, from the ano-nymous large-scale mural (1448) in the Meat Market it can be seen that there existed in Ghent a mature tradi-tion of pictorial virtuosity and monumentality. This mural presents the *Birth of Christ* and was influenced by both van Eyck and the Master of Flémalle. The Tournai

influence of the latter, which finds expression in both the types of personage and the heavy, space-filling figures, is frequently seen in van der Goes's work; so it must have been directly exerted on Ghent painting to the exclusion of Rogier van der Weyden.

A second important anonymous Ghent work that somewhat bridges up the gap to van der Goes is the large *Calvary Triptych*, kept in St Bavo's Cathedral. This work, which owes a great deal to the *Mystic Lamb*, prefigures the seriousness, the dramatic staging and also the capacity for creating evocative landscapes which are van der Goes' attributes. The painter of this highly refined *Calvary* is frequently identified with Giusto da Guanto or Justus van Gent (presumably Joos van Was-senhove), who worked at the Court of Urbino in 1473. The latter's work seems, however, too crude and clumsy to warrant this presumption in any way. It is true that before he went on his journey to Italy, this Joos van Wassenhove stood surety for Hugo van der Goes in the purchase of his mastership. From that time (1467) until 1478 van der Goes can be shown to have lived in Ghent. In 1468 he contributed to the celebrations held to mark the marriage of Charles the Bold to Margaret of York. In Ghent too he frequently undertook similar decorative assignments.

In 1480/81 he was called upon to go to Louvain to assess the status of Dieric Bouts' unfinished *Scenes of Justice*. Whether this involvement with Bouts' estate explains the fact that he painted the left-hand panel of Bouts' *Hippolytus Triptych* (Bruges, St Saviour's Cathedral) remains an open question. He spent the last four years of his life as a lay brother at the Augustine Red Cloister (Soniënwoud, Brussels). According to the diary of a fellow-brother, Gaspar Ofhuys, he died there insane in 1482 after continual attacks of depression. The tendency to involve this psychological condition in the interpretation and even the dating of his paintings has frequently led to one-sided conclusions. Thus there is still no consensus about the evolution of his work, the style of which showed fairly wide fluctuations for that time. His œuvre was reconstructed on the basis of the monumental *Portinari Triptych* (Florence, Uffizi), commissioned by the representative of the Medici Bank in Bruges, Tommaso Portinari, for the family chapel in Santa Maria Novella Church in Florence. It is still the only surviving work that is connected by sources of olden times with the name of the painter.

Like van Eyck, van der Goes is a phenomenon on his own, an artistic giant. He disclosed a world that, through his psychological rectitude, still leaves a non-conformist impression today. There was no 15th-century painter in whom intent, individual vision, and realization seemed so closely bound up with one another

as in Hugo van der Goes. He was the only one who could, within the nevertheless essentially static and contemplative design of that time, produce movement – not just fixed as a gesture or posture, but filmily evocative. This clearly indicates a very special form of empathy and a highly developed 'pre-imagination' which enabled the artist to maintain the freshness of the initial concept throughout the various stages of painting. This almost corporeal involvement in the subject-matter or motif of the painting, coupled with a clearly emotional self-projection, marks him out as the earliest in the series of more modern artistic personalities such as Rembrandt, Goya and Ensor.

Of his training or apprenticeship nothing is known. Some work reveals a strong van Eyck influence. The rich material, the monumental plasticity and the luminous colouring in the *Adoration of the Magi* (Berlin, Staatliche Museen) call to mind the *Mystic Lamb*. In addition there is such a strong Italian feeling for three-dimensionality and southern elegance, that it seems as though the painting was preceded by a study journey in Italy.

Through the harmonious line flow, the relief-like

Calvary Triptych, detail from central panel, Ghent Master, *ca* 1465. Ghent, St Bavo's Cathedral.

Hugo van der Goes, *Death of Mary,* 147.8 × 122.5 cm. Bruges, Groeninge Museum.

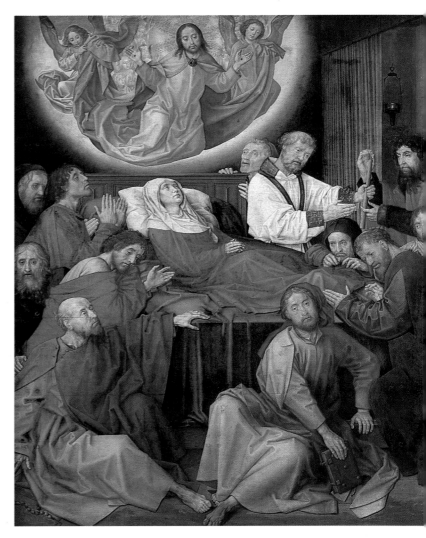

Hans Memling, *Last Judgment Triptych,* 222 × 160 cm (central panel),
222 × 80 cm (side panels), 1467. Gdansk, Muzeum Pomorskie.

aspect of the volumes and the more abstract approach,
other work is clearly under the spell of the formal
expressiveness of the Master of Flémalle and Rogier van
der Weyden. The *Death of Mary* (Bruges, Groeninge
Museum) has – in spite of the visionary restlessness with
which the scene is impregnated – an archaic, Gothic
flatness and graphic tension. The same harmonious line
flow is found in the *Adoration of the Shepherds* (Berlin,
Staatliche Museen).

His propensity for expressive remodelling or for
character painting (especially in later work such as the
Portinari Triptych) anticipates genres that did not come
fully into their own until the 17th century. Van der Goes
had an almost 'proletarian' preference as regards motifs:
rustic types, heavy and raw hands, stubbly chins, 'typical' wrinkled old heads with heavy beards, humid and
autumnal landscapes with bare trees, a bundle of straw,
and so on. His colouring is generally speaking very

sonorous, deep, with rich and vivid tones and above all
creative of atmospheres. In the most expressive work he
sometimes employs acrid contrasts between colour surfaces and chalky skin tones. He likes to highlight the
roundness of the shapes, soft glowing effects, as if the
world was illuminated by one huge candle. This technique comes out strongly in a number of paintings in
mat tempera on thin canvas, a genre that van der Goes,
to judge from the relatively large number of extant
pieces, must have exploited a lot (*Lamentation Diptych,*
New York, Wildenstein Gallery, and Berlin, Staatliche
Museen).

Van der Goes had a tremendous influence on painting
in the last quarter of the 15th century. Painters such as
Geertgen tot Sint Jans, the Master of Moulins (Jean
Hay) Gerard David, Albrecht Bouts and the Ghent-
Bruges miniaturist artists are profoundly marked by
him.

HANS MEMLING   Of the same generation as Hugo van der Goes, but totally different as to training and character, Hans Memling conditioned for thirty years the image of painting in Bruges after Petrus Christus, so that his style has become a symbol of this city and its love of pageantry.

In the Bruges registry of citizenship we read that on 30th January 1465 a certain 'Jan van Memmelinghe', born at Seligenstadt, became a citizen of Bruges. In 1480 he was among the 247 richest inhabitants of Bruges, who had to lend the city money to help finance Maxi-

Hans Memling, *Scenes from the Life of the Virgin Mary*, 80 × 180 cm, 1480. Munich, Alte Pinakothek.

milian of Austria's war against France. In the obituary of the painters' guild we find his name among those of the other deceased painters, saddle-makers, glaziers *etc*, respectfully preceded by the title 'Master' used as an epithet. There are now throughout the world about ninety panel paintings which are with complete certainty ascribed to Memling. Despite his German origin, Memling's painting can certainly not be called German. Nor is it Bruges painting, although viewed in retrospect it brought into being a typical Bruges style.

In Bruges Memling introduced van der Weyden's slender, aristocratic design. Bruges was a receptive centre, where artistic talent frequently came from other areas but where it developed to the fullest extent. Jan van Eyck was a Limburger, Petrus Christus came from North Brabant and Memling too was a foreigner. Would it be too daring to presume that Bruges attracted or invited Memling in one way or another? The most famous artist in the Southern Netherlands at that time was Rogier van der Weyden, who was City Painter in Brussels. Undoubtedly Memling was a pupil of his, and perhaps his best and most gifted: the relationship of style

127

cannot otherwise be understood. Seven months after Rogier van der Weyden's death Memling became a citizen of Bruges and thus left Brussels. Did the fact that Memling was never registered as a member of the Bruges painters' guild, although he was obliged to do so for professional reasons, have anything to do with a 'privileged' entry into the city?

If we may interpret the incomplete date on a tombstone in the *Last Judgment* (Gdansk, Muzeum Pomorskie) as 1467, this grandiose triptych is the earliest painting of Memling's known to us. By comparison with his later work, it manifests his entire personality. It seems as though the painter was only a colourer and modeller of a separately conceived and meticulously drawn pattern, so independent and lacking in interpretation does his manner of painting appear in relation to the subject-matter.

The *Last Judgment* was commissioned by the Florentine Angelo Tani, the official representative of the Medici Bank in Bruges. His successor, Tommaso Portinari, was also among Memling's clientele. A brief survey of his patrons accounts for the character of his paintings and the social context in which they have to be viewed. The Italian bankers were not the only foreigners to order paintings from him. Heinrich Greverade, a mer-

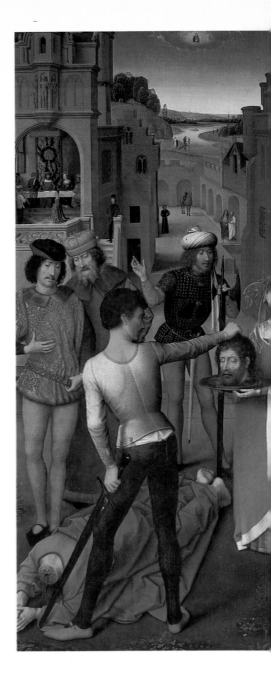

Hans Memling, *St Ursula's Reliquary,* 87 × 91 × 33 cm, 1489. Bruges, St John's Hospital, Memling Museum.

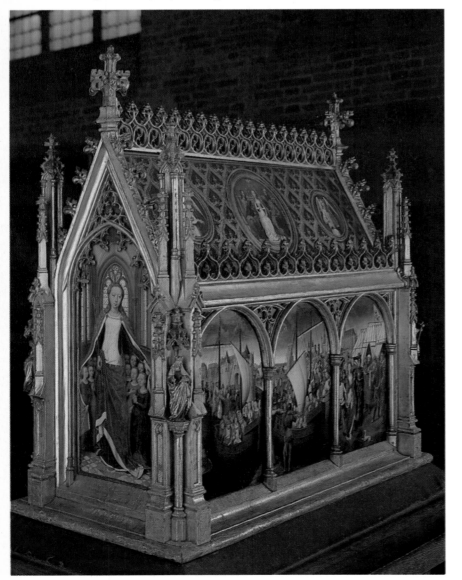

Hans Memling, *Johannes Triptych,* left-hand panel: *Beheading of John Baptist;* central *panel: Madonna and Child surrounded by St John the Baptist, St John the Evangelist, St Catherine and St Barbara;* right-hand panel: *St John the Evangelist on Patmos,*172 × 172 cm (central panel), 172 × 79 cm (side panels), 1479. Bruges, St John's Hospital, Memling Museum.

chant and banker in Lubeck, was supplied by Memling with an imposing *Crucifixion Triptych* (Lubeck, Sankt-Annen-Museum). On another triptych we see John Donne of Kidwelly, who was in the service of Edward IV, together with his wife and daughter (National Gallery, London). In Bruges itself Pieter Bultync, a member of the guild of tanners, presented the guild chapel in Our Lady's Church with a painting depicting *Scenes from the Life of the Virgin Mary* (Munich, Alte Pinakothek). In St James's Church stood the large *Willem Moreel Triptych,* the person in question being a wealthy citizen and important local politician (Bruges, Groeninge Museum). Leading traders such as Jan du Celier and in particular Jakob Floreins have been donors (Louvre, Paris). Maarten van Nieuwenhove, a future burgomas-

ter, had himself depicted in pious prayer before the Virgin (Bruges, St John's Hospital). In addition to bankers and politicians, merchants and guilds, there were some clerics, all associated with St John's Hospital as either brothers or sisters and in most cases from the same families or circles, who always called on Memling for paintings. Jan Floreins, the brother of Jakob, and Adriaan Reins each possessed a small triptych in the Hospital. On the high altar of the Hospital Church stood the large *Johannes Triptych*. In addition, two sisters had a shrine constructed in order to accommodate the reliquaries of St Ursula. For this Memling painted eight small panels depicting the legend of the saint, incorporated as window frames on the four sides of this miniature building. All these works of art are now in the old Hospital.

Memling thus did his painting for just one social class – the bourgeoisie who had become wealthy through a flourishing economy. What he painted and how, therefore accorded completely with an ideal image that this group conceived, and in which he also wanted to reflect his inherent narcissism. What Memling produced seemed an earthly paradise or, conversely, a celestial

extension of what prosperity and stability had already conferred upon the bourgeoisie as a foretaste on earth. Memling created blissful vacuums, transcendant but humanly attainable, in which physically uniform, well-shaped human beings – actually human angels – display their everlasting individual good fortune. Memling's paintings were reassurring in terms of religion. Fear of God, fear of life or passion are eliminated from even the most gruesome subjects by his serene narrative style. By virtue of its predominantly static, spatially delimited and ideal nature, this work is designated as an early form of classicism. Italian influence may have been a factor here, although conversely Memling also inspired Italian masters.

In this atmosphere of bourgeois self-satisfaction, portraiture too recorded an almost democratic expansion for that time. Everyone who could pay wanted his features embodied by Memling's brush. Some thirty such works are known to us. In many cases these bust portraits are combined, as a diptych or triptych, with a Madonna and Child being worshipped by the subject of the portrait. This frequent addition by Memling of a devotional dimension to a portrait must again be seen in

Hans Memling, *Adoration of the Magi,* central panel of *Floreins Triptych,* 57.2 × 64.5 cm, 1479. Bruges, St John's Hospital, Memling Museum.

Hans Memling, *Portrait of a Man,* 30.1 × 22.3 cm. The Hague, Mauritshuis.

the light of that ideal bourgeois aspiration for worldly luxury, compatible with a lifestyle that could be justified on religious grounds. In contrast with Rogier van der Weyden – who took the portrait, sometimes as an autonomous genre, out of the animated context by highlighting the features against an indefinite, dark surface – Memling usually put his figures in a bright open space, which in depth merged idyllically into a luxuriant green wooded landscape under an azure-blue sky.

In 1480 a certain Jan Verhanneman was officially apprenticed to Memling. In 1483 there came a second pupil, Passchier van der Meersch. Their work may perhaps be found among the dozens of extant anonymous paintings in Memling's style, painted with less perfection but with just as serene an atmosphere.

When Memling died in 1494 Bruges already had a new talent – not one of his pupils, but a painter who had earned his spurs ten years previously. So Gerard David of Oudewater had had the opportunity to observe and admire Memling.

GERARD DAVID   Wholly in line with the Flemish tradition outlined above, this emigré from Holland turned up in Bruges in 1484. He was admitted as a freemaster at the time that Memling set the tone in the art of that city. David soon assumed the latter's leading role and remained into the early years of the 16th century the model for the younger Bruges painters, such as Ambrosius Benson, Adriaan Isenbrant and Albert Cornelis, who continued to subsist on his style until the middle of the century. Gerard David may have had his training in the Northern Netherlands. In his work the attention to landscape, the use of a cool, bright illumination and the introverted character of the dramatic aspect are unmistakably attributable to this training (Haarlem tradition?).

In Bruges he created a sort of stylistic recapitulation of the work of his great predecessors van Eyck, van der Weyden and Memling. In particular, the technically perfect finish, the faultlessly smooth depiction of *e g* a relief or a fold in a cloak, the depth and saturation of the

colours and the propensity for isolating objects in space show that David must have learned a lot from Memling during his first few years in Bruges. His earliest style, uninfluenced by Memling, can be observed in the still very 'Dutch' *Triptych of Christ Nailed to the Cross* (London, National Gallery, and Antwerp, Museum of Fine Arts). He is cooler, more objective, more down-to-earth than Memling. While no doubt influenced by van der Goes in the formal treatment of his realism, in his attitude towards his subject he frequently displays an irritating insensitivity, lacking in psychological interpretation. Having a predilection for spatial experiments with diagonals, in which the perspectivist vanishing lines begin to strike one as an artifice, and a decorative interest in Italian motifs (festoons with fruit motif, *putti*, medallions), he is an early example of the growing Renaissance influence on Flemish painting.

All these characteristics are epitomized in the *Judgment of Cambyses*, a scene from justice dated 1498, painted for the Court of Sheriffs in Bruges Town Hall. This gigantic diptych depicts the Persian story of the judge Sisamnes who was punished by flaying – a gruesomely realistic scene designed to instil perennial incorruptibility into the sheriffs. If this work, by its strong volume effect and its intended naturalism, already marks a step in the direction of the 16th century, the *Birth of Christ* triptych – although it had probably never been done earlier – exudes fully the rarefied atmosphere, so characteristic of the century of the 'Flemish Primitives'. It is also one of the most remarkable of landscape and botanical evocations to have been created in the painting of that time.

As a leading and well-to-do citizen, Gerard David presented in 1509 a large painting by his own hand to the Convent Church of the Carmelite Nuns of Sion in Bruges, to be used as a retable for the high altar. On this altarpiece the painter, with the representation of the *Madonna Surrounded by Saints* (Rouen, Musée des Beaux-Arts), immortalized himself together with his wife on the left and on the right between the saintly

Gerard David, *Arrest of Sisamnes,* left-hand panel of diptych of scene from justice with *judgment of Cambyses,* 182.3 × 159.2 cm, 1498. Bruges, Groeninge Museum.

figures. This is the first self-portrait that can conclusively be classed in Flemish painting.

THE MINOR MASTERS The highlights of the painting history in the 15th century are determined by a handful of artists, most of whom were unaffected by strong environmental influences or local corporative methods. In many cases the origin and the perfection of their style are not demonstrable. They appear like comets above industrious members of regional guilds. For the most part they were immigrants who were also high up in the social scale. Historians of the Middle Ages often bring the personal talent and the individual contribution of these artists – something that cannot be explained historically – back to the, sometimes excessively corporative, craftsman level of the profession.

That among the hundreds of names of painters which have been handed down to us via the archives there should lurk great masters whose work has been lost, is certainly an illusion. Of the local average output in the Southern Netherlands some 4,000 (at a rough count) have been preserved, almost all of which have remained anonymous. Among them are fascinating compositions, many of a naive charm, with the accent on the narrative, some affording evidence of a clever miniature-like technique. Although these masters developed individual but very schematic and stereotyped methods, their inventive-

Gerard David, *Birth of Christ Triptych, 130 × 96.5 cm* (central panel), 134 × 43 cm (side panels). Bruges, Groeninge Museum.

ness springs mostly from the famous examples, from which they systematically compiled their paintings. They provide an image of the guilds' average offerings and knowledge of their craft, that was handed down from master to pupil. The majority can be placed in the last quarter of the 15th century, perhaps because the output of paintings in the preceding decades had not yet recorded such an enormous expansion. Of their far more modest output only a few examples have survived the passage of history. A survey of the most important of these still anonymous painters corrects the perfectionist image, that the masterpieces offer us of the production in that period. They are designated by an invented name whereever an œuvre can be attributed to them.

From 1475-1480 two minor masters left an appreciable output behind in Bruges. They did not merely follow in the wake of Memling; although the ingenuous atmosphere and bright colours of their scenes, which are reminiscent of plates in an exquisite picturebook, evoke the same blissful world. The Master of the Legend of St Ursula painted the well-known legend of this saint (Bruges, Groeninge Museum) around 1480, that is to say, a decade before Memling's shrine of St Ursula. It is a naive and fresh miniature world on panel, stereotyped but with plenty of vitality and visual directness. The Master of the Legend of St Lucy exhibited the same simplified but very illustrative style. In his case, in its imitative soundness, this resulted sometimes in a surprisingly meticulous execution. The *Mary Queen of Heaven* (Washington, National Gallery) and the *St John on Patmos* (Rotterdam, Boymans-van Beuningen Museum), which until recently was actually thought to be a Bouts, are highlights in his œuvre. Both these masters made their own compositional devices or stylistic features of van der Weyden, Bouts and van der Goes, which at that stage of development points to a far-reaching blend of the available stylistic patterns from the various centres. As a result, the regional characteristics frequently became obscure. This is the case with the Master of 1499, who in a style strongly influenced by van der Goes scrupulously adopted an Eyckian example as his model in the *Diptych of the Abbot Christiaan de Hondt* (Antwerp, Museum of Fine Arts). He may have worked both in Ghent and Bruges. Other painters such as the Master of the Baroncelli Portraits, carried on their craft in the city of Memling.

To judge from what has survived, the average output in Ghent seems to have been somewhat smaller and generally speaking less painstaking. An exception is the Master of the Khanenko Adoration, active around 1500, clearly an imitator of van der Goes who imparted an archaic note to his fleshy Madonnas by grafting them on the types created by the Master of Flémalle. The small triptych depicting the *Adoration of the Kings* (St Omer, Musée-Hôtel Sandelin) is a real gem in which the sturdy van der Goes figures seem to be somewhat out of breath. Van der Goes' influence makes it probable that this painter worked in Ghent. This is however not certain, just as in the case of the anonymous master who painted a *Triptych of the Martyrdom of St Hippolytus* (Boston, Museum of Fine Arts). It likewise has a basic typology deriving from van der Goes, but on the other hand, a flat,

Master of 1499, *Diptych of the Abbot Christiaan de Hondt,* left-hand panel: *Madonna in Church;* right-hand panel: *Abbot Christiaan de Hondt at Prayer,* 31.5 × 14.6 cm, (each panel), 1499. Antwerp, Museum of Fine Arts.

decorative approach to flora and landscape, which we find chiefly in Brabant circles. The van der Goes influence in Brabant is perhaps related to his stay there in the Red Cloister in the Zoniënwoud at the end of his life.

The painting of the Brussels School from about 1470 to 1500 can be typified by some triptychs resulting from cooperation between several masters. This method, in which each painter was responsible for one panel, was peculiar to Brabant. Three scenes from the *Life of St Géry* (dispersed among the museums in The Hague, Dublin and Paris) probably belong to the same ensemble, the first two panels having been painted by the Master of the Legend of St Barbara and the third by the Master of St Gudula (named after St Gudula's Church in Brussels, which is shown in the background). The Master of St Barbara reveals, in addition to the influence of van der Weyden, the persistent influence of the medieval narrative style, specific to many minor masters of that period. In the case of the Master of St Gudula a reaction is noticeable in an unusual search for expressiveness and dynamism and a tendency to distortion, traits which foreshadowed the mannerism of the following century.

Similar collaboration by several painters brought into being the *Triptych with the Miracles of Christ* (Melbourne, National Gallery of Victoria). The central panel, depicting the *Multiplication of the Loaves and Fishes*, was painted by the Master of the Legend of St Catherine, an assiduous and inflexible imitator of Rogier van der Weyden. The left-hand panel, *Marriage at Cana*, which includes the entire Burgundian-Habsburg dynasty seated at table, is attributed to the

Master of *the Legend of St Lucy, John the Evangelist on Patmos*, 68 × 64 cm, late 15th century. Rotterdam, Boymans-van Beuningen Museum.

Master of St Barbara, *St Géry and Idolatry,* scene from a series including the *Legend of St Géry,* 97 × 69 cm, last quarter of 15th century. The Hague, Mauritshuis.

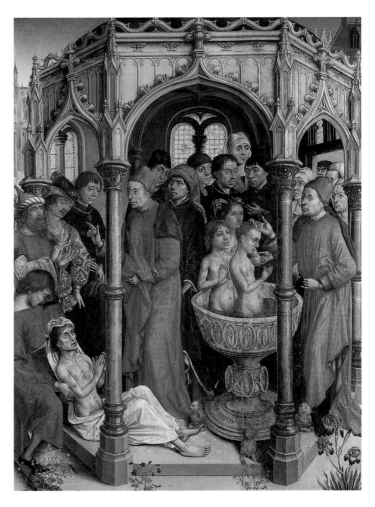

Master of St Barbara, *St Géry cures a Leper and administers Baptism,* scene from a series including the *Legend of St Géry,* 97 × 69 cm, last quarter of 15th century. Dublin, National Gallery of Ireland.

Master of the Portraits of Princes. This painter did much work for the court and some of his prized portraits of courtiers are well known, notably the *Portrait of a Young Man of the Fonseca Family* (Rotterdam, Boymans-van Beuningen Museum). The scene in the right-hand panel is set in the vicinity of the Master with the Embroidered Foliage, although it has greater pictorial qualities. A more typical work by this painter, who derived his name from the carpet-like foliage painted mechanically and flat, as if it was a decor sewn up stitch by stitch, is the *Madonna in a Landscape* (Amsterdam, formerly in the Proehl Collection). Like the Master of the Life of St Joseph (five large *tondos* dispersed among the museums of East Berlin, Munich and New York), he worked in Brussels around the turn of the century. The smooth expressionless figures with arid, rounded forms point to a certain rigidity of style, which was beginning to be exhibited by the offshoots of the century of the Primitives.

FLEMISH PAINTERS ABROAD   A number of artists, after being trained in the Southern Netherlands, were attracted by foreign patrons and developed their careers for the most part in a foreign country. While there, they frequently induced a composite style among the native artists who worked in their entourage. Conversely, their own style and technique were soon imprinted with the taste and habits of their country of adoptions. In contrast with the 14th century, no longer the very best painters landed in this way in foreign courts and cities. The fame of the Flemish School was, however, an obvious recommendation. Many names of such migrants are well known, but unfortunately little work can be associated with them. Lodewijk Allyncbrood belonged to the Bruges guild of painters in 1432/33 and 1436/37. From 1439 up to his death he was found in Valencia. The Eyckian triptych depicting *Scenes from the Life of Christ* (Madrid, Prado) is assumed to be by him.

Barthélemy van Eyck, doubtless descended from the renowned family of Maasland painters, was in the service of King René of Anjou from 1447 to 1472. The evocative illustrations in some allegorical literary works written by 'le bon Roi René' himself, such as *Cuer d'amours épris* or *La Théséide,* are probably from the hand of that artist. The Master of the Aix Annunciation, named after a triptych in Eyckian *trompe l'œil,* the

136

Master of St Gudula, *St Géry preaches before King Lothair,* scene from a series including the *Legend of St Géry,* 95 × 68 cm, last quarter of 15th century. Paris, Louvre.

central panel of which represents the *Annunciation* (Aix-en-Provence, Eglise de la Madeleine), must also have been the work of an emigré Flemish painter. Some people have suggested a connection with Clément van Eyck, who like his brother Barthélemy resided in Provence.

Around 1472/73 the Duke of Urbino, Federigo da Montefeltro, sent for a Ghent painter who in Italy was called Giusto da Guanto. This Justus van Gent is probably Joos van Wassenhove, a friend of Hugo van der Goes. He painted an altarpiece for the Corpus Domini Brotherhood in Urbino, the *Communion of the Apostles* (Urbino, Palazzo Ducale) and a series of *Portraits of Famous Men* (Urbino, Gallerie Nazionale delle Marche, and Paris, Louvre) for the Duke's study. The basic characteristics of his style bear a marked relation to the anonymous *Calvary Triptych* described above in St Bavo's Cathedral, Ghent. The execution is, however, less refined and tarnished by a somewhat clumsy assimilation of Italian monumental principles.

A painter also stamped with the Ghent tradition, albeit only because he must have been apprenticed to van der Goes, is Jean Hay. Although we know him only

by his French name, he was designated in that country 'Teutonicus', which suggests that he originated from the Netherlands. He settled at Moulins, where in 1494 he painted an *Ecce Homo* (Brussels, Museums of Fine Arts) for Jean Cueillette, who was the Duke of Bourbon's receiver-general. His great qualities, which set him in the forefront of painters in van der Goes' sphere of influence, are brought out fully in the celebrated *Triptych of the Glorification of Our Lady* (Moulins, Cathedral).

More inventive than Justus van Gent but of the same stamp, from the point of origin, development of style and his career as court painter in a southern country, is the figure of Juan de Flandes, whom we find in 1496 in the service of Isabella of Castille at Burgos. His surname is unknown. A number of features of his work point to Hugo van der Goes and the miniaturist known as the Master of Mary of Burgundy. He may therefore have had his training in Ghent circles. His earliest Spanish works were intimistic and on a small scale, as in the beautifully clear-cut *Adoration of the Kings* (Cervera de Pisuerga, Church). He evolved in the first decade of the 16th century, after the death of his eminent patroness, towards a freer, coarser but more expressive dramatic style with more direct and evocative brushwork. The panels for the retable of the high altar of Palencia Cathedral depicting the *Life of Christ and the Virgin* (1509) are an example of this trend.

At the time that Juan de Flandes entered the service of Isabella of Castille, a court painter had already been working there for four years, namely Michiel Sittow, also trained in Flanders. A native of Reval, he had his apprenticeship in Bruges from 1484 to 1488 and turned up in Spain in 1492, remaining in the service of Isabella until 1502. From that period date three panels of modest dimensions which formed part of a series of forty-seven, dedicated to the *Life of Christ and the Virgin* and destined for the Queen's oratory (*Ascension*, Earl of Yarborough Collection; *Assumption*, Washington, National Gallery; *Coronation of the Virgin Mary*, Paris, Louvre). All the other panels still in existence and scattered over the world appear to be made by Juan de Flandes. Here Sittow reveals himself as an accomplished miniaturist with a style clearly influenced by Memling. The royal portraits ascribed to him, which he is believed to have done at a later stage when he was successively at the Courts of London, Reval, Copenhagen, Malines and Valladolid, already show a style akin to that of Jan Gossaert, which can hardly be reconciled with the miniature scenes. He died at Reval in 1525.

The art of stained glass

THE MOST RAVAGED FORM OF ARTISTIC ACTIVITY   The art of stained glass is beyond doubt the monumentally applied art for which the quantity surviving from the past is in inverse proportion to its historical vitality, and the quantity of production. As in France, another leading country in this discipline, the rise and flourishing of the art of stained glass in Flanders was closely connected with architecture, and more particularly with the emergence and development of the Gothic style. The Gothic building skeleton, in which the breaking open and dissolving of the walls was one of the main architectural features, evidently lent itself to the art of leaded stained glass.

Thus these colourful windows with their often involved tracery or mullion patterns belonged among the significant elements, both decorative and constructive, of the architecture of the late Middle Ages. Because of their wealth of symbolic capacity, the glass windows – together with the arts of wall painting and sculpture – played an important part in the iconographic programme, which provided the faithful with a plastic and educative environment in the churches and places of worship of the Middle Ages. Apart from its functional and decorative significance – closing off the space and letting in light – the glass window of the Middle Ages had, in consequence, also an important iconographic and devotional role to play.

Not merely because of the very close craft relations between the painters and the glaziers, but also because of the decisive role of the painting itself in influencing style, the art of stained glass evolved towards the end of the Middle Ages to what was undoubtedly the most figurative and pictorially rich decorative form among all the artistic activities of the Middle Ages. However, the brittle and fragile nature of the material, and the many cases of destruction by fire, storm and armed conflict, have seen to it that very few medieval glass windows have been preserved for us today, either *in situ* or elsewhere; although according to written sources the art of stained glass in Flanders appears to go back long before the oldest surviving remains – from the 14th century – right to the Carolingian and Romanesque periods. There are also some authors who see a sort of continuity between the profane art of glazing of the Gallo-Roman and Merovingian periods, and the stained glass – developing from non-figurative to figurative art – of the high and late Middle Ages.

Stained-glass window of Vilain van Immerseel, Rombaut Keldermans van Leuven, 1475-1476. Lier, St Gummarus's Church.

Stained-glass window of the Schoonvorst family (coat of arms), Southern Netherlands, between 1387 and 1398. Zichem, St Eustace's Church. Detail.

Stained-glass window of the Schoonvorst family. Christ on the Cross, Southern Netherlands, between 1387 and 1398. Zichem, St Eustace's Church. Detail.

Stained-glass window with Virgin and Child. Brabant studio, second half of 14th century (?). Louvain, Municipal Museum, previously in Louvain, Beguinage Church.

THE 14th CENTURY   Apart from some small glass windows or fragments of windows from the 13th century (attributed to the Rhenish and French schools) the oldest remains of stained glass, presumably from the Southern Netherlands, belong to the collections of the Museums of Art and History in Brussels. They date from the 14th century and illustrate the view taken by, among others, archival witnesses that they were already in this period very capable glass painters active in Flanders; but that their style was international or cosmopolitan and still strongly under French influence.

The only glass windows from the 14th century preserved *in situ* are at Tournai, Louvain and Zichem. The three windows in question with representations of saints (St Catherine, St John the Baptist and St John the Evangelist) in Tournai Cathedral have been radically restored and renewed, as have so many old examples or groups. The 14th-century Mary Window in the Beguinage Church at Louvain is attributed to the Brabant school, and the most important Flemish glass ensemble to have survived the ravages of time since the end of the 14th century is without doubt the triple *Schoonvorst* window in St Eustace's Church at Zichem. The crucified Christ, the lamenting madonna and St John are each reproduced at the same height in a tabernacle structure of stained glass.

Stained-glass window with Siegbert's victory, Arnold van Nijmegen, Netherlands, *ca* 1500. Tournai, Cathedral.

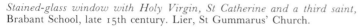

Stained-glass window with Holy Virgin, St Catherine and a third saint,
Brabant School, late 15th century. Lier, St Gummarus' Church.

THE 15th CENTURY The finest hour of Flemish medieval stained glass was in the 15th century. While the early 15th-century examples – such as the glass in Bruges Town Hall and the great ensemble at Halle – still betray the cosmopolitan or international style of the 14th century, in the second half of the Burgundian era and up to the beginning of the 16th century, a growing pictorial and realistic trend can be ascertained. It was brought about – among other things – by the omnipresent influence of the Flemish Primitives who, by the way, often illustrated stained glass windows or stained glass medallions in their compositions painted on panels.

For some important 15th-century ensembles, we also know the names of the glaziers. The small angel windows, in fish-bladder shape, which came from Bruges Town Hall and are now preserved in the Gruuthuse Museum, date from about 1400; they are thought to be the work of the Bruges glaziers Christiaan van de Voorde and/or Jan de Rynghel. The great four-part glass Vilain-van Immerseel window (1475/76) in St Gummarus' Church at Lier with the representations of St Gummarus, St Rombout, the donors and their patron saints, is the work of the Louvain glazier Rombout Keldermans, who apparently worked under the influence of his great fellow-townsman Dirk Bouts.

The most important glazier in the Southern Netherlands at the turn of the 15th/16th centuries was, without a doubt, Arnout van Nijmegen, who also worked at Rouen and afterwards at Antwerp. Together with a few local masters he created, around 1500, the magnificent series of glass windows in Tournai Cathedral with historical scenes connected with the bishopric. Here too there is an undeniable relationship with contemporary painting.

The same applies to a number of anonymous Flemish glass ensembles from the end of the 15th century: four windows of the Brabant school including the monumen-

tal coronation of the Virgin in the already-mentioned St Gummarus' Church at Lier, the equally pretty Mary window in St Peter's Church at Anderlecht, clearly influenced by Hugo van der Goes, the Flemish-Burgundian window of the Antwerp school in the Burgundian chapel at Antwerp, dating from 1497, and the no less pictorially influenced double window from the former painters' chapel at Bruges, now exhibited in the Gruuthuse Museum. In spite of the outspokenly mannered attitude of the two personages – St George and St Michael – the influence of the elegant art of Hans Memling can still be felt in this double window from Bruges; as it can in the glass windows of the Sacred Blood Chapel at Bruges, also from the late 15th century. These princely windows, with the decorative portraits and the angels bearing the arms of Mary of Burgundy and Maximilian of Austria, were unfortunately removed from their places and transferred in the 19th century to the Victoria and Albert Museum in London.

But already, even in the 15th and 16th centuries, Flemish glaziers were appreciated in other countries. Arnout of Nijmegen, for example, worked in France, Bernard Flower in England, Arnao de Flandes in Spain and Hendrik van den Broecke in Italy. One last important Flemish glass window ensemble, this time one that has been preserved *in situ*, is that of St Martin's Church at Halle. But this series of more than twenty windows dates from the beginning of the 15th century – a foundation in the year 1408 by Count William IV of Hainault and Margaret of Burgundy. The graceful idealized style of the personages betrays, in fact, more the cosmopolitanism of the 14th century than the pictorial realism of the late 15th which, at the beginning of the 16th century – even in the art of stained glass – was very gradually to make way, via elements of decoration and composition, for the new style of the Renaissance.

The art of illumination

The illumination of manuscripts is an important witness to the pattern of expectation of medieval man: the decorating of codices responded to a need determined by the broad context in which these books functioned. Indeed, the illumination goes along with the content of the manuscript to which it belongs. In that case, it illustrates a text with the aim of clarifying or synthesizing it, or providing a visual translation which makes it penetrate deeper into the mind and take root there. Thus miniatures can have a teaching content just as well as the text, and can even be 'meditable' i e point out to the reader truths relating to his moral life and his ultimate destination. Moreover, they form an outstanding aid in stressing the exalted value of a text and in making its spiritual dimension visible. Thus the miniatures were signs and symbols, referring to the quality of the written word, the wealth of inspiration or authority of the author; as well as to the importance of the books in education or study, liturgy or devotion. Finally, illumination is a suitable medium to attract the reader's attention and to clarify the internal structure of the text; in this context, enlarged initial letters play an important role.

In view of the fact that illumination, as a bearer of meaning, is used in many kinds of texts to refer to very exalted religious and ethical concepts; and that – in medieval terms – the visible must lead to the invisible, it does not reproduce reality. This explains the particular character of Pre-Romanesque, Romanesque and even to a large extent Gothic art: reality is situated on an unsubstantial level, and the deformation of the human figure, the denial of perspective, and the unnatural use of colour are all means of allegorizing. Not the individual nature of things, but rather their essence and significance, needs to be made perceptible. Not until around 1400 is there a significant change in man's attitude to the world around him. Without the allegorizing dimension of the image completely disappearing, we notice a gradual progress to more realistic presentations – and the culminating point of this progress coincides with the end of the history of book illumination.

Obtaining books for liturgy, devotional reading or study was, from the outset of organized monasticism, a constant concern for every religious community. For this purpose, they set up their own monastic *scriptoria*, which were to remain in existence as exclusive centres of production until *ca* 1200. They produced codices for their own use or for outsiders. The illumination of these manuscripts was very often carried out by the religious themselves, but as the required talent was not always available in a monastery, it was sometimes necessary to hire outsiders for temporary tasks – often ambulant artists. To a great extent these were laymen who were often versed in other disciplines, such as fresco painting, sculpture, enamel or ivory work, and who produced only occasionally book illuminations.

In northern France – a region blessed with early Benedictine monastic culture – the workshops occupied, already since the Carolingian period, a privileged place in the field of book illumination. Here, since the middle

Initial B (Beatus vir) from Second Bible of Charles the Bald, 430 × 395 mm, St Amand-les-Eaux. Paris, Bibliothèque nationale, ms lat 2, fol 234.
The interlacing, the stylized heads of the animals and the line made up of points have been taken from Anglo-Irish miniature art. They endow the letter with an irrational and labyrinthine character, and are designed to emphasize the content and sublimity of the word of the Bible.

Manuscript page with only one letter on it (Adam), from *Bible* (Part 4), 535 × 500 mm, St Amand-les-Eaux, *ca* 1150. Valenciennes, Bibliothèque municipale, ms 4, fol 4v°.
The dovetailing of the vine-foliage motifs into an ensemble filling up a page and the combination with the beginning of the text may be said to be a device specific to the illuminator, Sawalo, monk of St Amand. At the top he signed his work: *Sawalo monacus Sancti Amandi me fecit.*

Scene from the life of St Omer, miniature from *Vita Sancti Amandi*, 315 × 210 mm, St Omer, late 11th century. St Omer, Bibliothèque municipale, ms 698, fol 34.
The intense veneration of the saints and relics in the 11th and 12th centuries gave rise to luxuriously executed *vitae*. The broad framings around the scenes in this example produce an effect of powerful relief and of monumentalism. The fan-shaped drapery heightens the dramatic force.

Christ and the Church, miniature from *Alardus Bible*, 490 × 346 mm. St Amand, pre-1097. Valenciennes, Bibliothèque municipale, ms 10, fol 113. The Song of Songs begins with an allegorical representation of Christ and the Church as Bridegroom and Bride. The unity of the two figures is accentuated by the circular frame, and by the nimbus surrounding the two heads. The sober colouring and the graphic style are eloquent of the poetic character of the text.

of the 9th century, the Franco-Insular or Franco-Saxon style flourished. The name indicates the numerous borrowings in this style from the Anglo-Irish art of the British Isles. The consequence of this was the rejection of the figurative – which was precisely one of the new acquisitions of Carolingian art – in favour of the purely decorative. Initial letters and frameworks are adorned with interlaced ribbon-work ending in stylized heads of animals. The play of lines and the ornamental use of gold and other colours reinforce the irrational qualities of this decor. The character of this insular style, however, is somewhat weakened by a more classical sense for clarifying structures, which tends to give the impression of a cold precision. *Evangeliaria* and *sacramentaria* in this style were created for numerous northern French churches and abbeys.

This style is encountered for the first time in manuscripts from St Amand-on-the-Scheldt's Abbey. The most beautiful example is provided by the Bible of Charles the Bald (Paris, National Library, ms lat 2), created between 871 and 877 for this monarch and subsequently left by him to St Denis' Abbey. The Franco-Saxon style was also used in the *scriptoria* of St Vaast's Abbey at Arras and of St Bertin's Abbey at St Omer.

The Norsemen's invasion led to a break, which was restored only from the end of the 10th century onwards. Now every important abbey had its own *sciptorium*, and some of these, stimulated by the head of the monastery or by the librarian, excelled by an extensive and careful production. But the activity of these workshops was incoherent, and various influences prevailed. This can be illustrated by the example of the St Bertin's manuscripts. While originally Carolingian and even Pre-Carolingian forms persisted, a significant change occurred as the consequence of a special situation. For the restoration of monastic libraries in England after the ravages of the Norsemen, Carolingian manuscripts from northern French abbeys were used as models. Mainly on this basis, around 950 the so-called Winchester style arose, characterized by animated drawings in which the figurative and decorative elements were drawn in inks of one or more colours, sometimes thrown into relief with some light touches of colour.

It was precisely this form of art which returned to northern France to enrich the Franco-Saxon style. Abbot Odbert of St Bertin's (968-1007) not only invited English monks for illumination work, but he himself left behind some twenty manuscripts which bear witness to his great talent, including a Psalter with glosses (Boulogne, Municipal Library ms 20), a collection of the lives of saints (*ibidem*, ms 107) and an Evangelium with collects for the whole of the church year (St Omer,

Municipal Library, ms 342 *bis*). The historized initials and the full-page illustrations show animated personages, swathed in garments with somewhat formalized folds, but these contribute to the animation by their flowing character. Although the influence of the so-called Winchester style is evident here, this art cannot entirely be divorced from the Carolingian and the Franco-Saxon. Even Ottonian elements are found in it. But the various ingredients were worked by Odbert and his collaborators into such a unity, that we may speak of a style proper to this Abbey, which persisted there for a long time.

While in St Bertin's the book illumination bore the stamp of one man, we see a more heterogeneous group of artists at work in St Vaast's Abbey. A Bible from the second quarter of the 11th century (Arras, Municipal library, ms 559) occupies a central place in this production. Six artists collaborated on the numerous illustrations. Although they are carried out with considerable dash, no synthesis of style is attained here, so that both English, Carolingian and some late antique influences can be recognized. As to the iconography, we may speak of a great wealth in which a remarkable unity is obtained on the basis of a powerful imagination. Allegorical representations contribute considerably to the originality of this manuscript.

The extent to which the older concept could continue to penetrate, and a foreign contribution could determine the art of northern France, is shown by an *Evangelarium*, carried out *ca* 1050 in Corbie Abbey (Amiens, Municipal Library, ms 24). The portraits of the evangelists show the nervous, restless design particular to the Carolingian school of Rheims. Then the solid character of the figures recalls the oldest sculptures from Toulouse. An equally distinct style is found in a *Life of St Omer*, carried out in the abbey dedicated to that saint at the end of the 11th century (St Omer, Municipal Library, ms 698). The origin of the fiercely gesticulating personages, with garments that spread open like a fan, is uncertain. Some compare them with the wall paintings of Vic and the illuminations from Moissac. Others see in them a late interpretation of the Ottonian style. In any case, the design of the two latter manuscripts contributed strongly to the formation of Romanesque art in book illumination.

THE TWELFTH CENTURY:
GIVING SHAPE TO THE INVISIBLE

In the field of the luxury book, the 12th century was a time of incomparable activity. Various influences still remained at work. The rich and warm colours, and the drapery whose folds were accentuated by sinuous lines, were an adaptation of the Byzantine manner of articulating the body. Moreover, similar style elements brought about a certain unity in Romanesque art. The Byzantine inspiration also gave wide dissemination to a repertory of decorative formulae. This is seen, for example, in a manuscript with works of St Augustine, created in northern France from Holy Sepulchre's Abbey at Cambray (Cambray, Municipal Library, ms 559). It contains initials with animated monstrous crea-

St Amand in Paradise, miniature from *Vita et miracula Sancti Amandi*, 300 × 210 mm, St Amand-les-Eaux, *ca* 1150. Valenciennes, Bibliothèque municipale, ms 501, fol 31.
Two allegorical figures, Love of God and Love of One's Neighbour, bear Amand, accompanied by a host of companions, up to heaven. Angels hold censer and crown in readiness. The geometrical construction, the studied schematization and the use of colour accentuate the visionary character.

tures. By the action of contrast, they reinforce the purity of the teaching content of the texts they introduce, and promote the awareness of evil and its consequences.

In this century we witness a last flaring-up of the English influence. Around 1150, the so-called Winchester style is, in fact, uncommonly evident in the *Evangeliarium* of Cysoing (Lille, Municipal Library, ms 33). Shortly before this, Liessies Abbey produced a gospelbook of which only two portraits of evangelists remain (Avesnes, Archaeological Society Museum). It is typical for the Romanesque style that the hierarchical importance of these inspired authors is accented by secondary figures in the surrounding frame: a minute Abbot Wedricus in all humility hands the inkpot to St John, a gigantic figure filling the whole page. Noteworthy is the stiff use of drapery, which accentuates the shape of the figures, and the application of a broad continuous line encircling the figures; this gives them a certain metallic hardness. On these pages we can rec-

SŦS GREGORIVS

ognize the same hand as in the Bible of Lambeth Palace in London, produced in England; and we may deduce that this artist also worked on the Continent.

The abbeys in the Scarpe valley, namely St Amand's, Marchiennes and Anchin, reached a high level of achievement during the second quarter of the 12th century. The first-named convent undoubtedly dominated by the quantity and quality of its production. The Alard Bible can be dated already before 1097 (Valenciennes, Municipal Library, ms 9-11); it charms by its delicate linear style, the limited and hesitant range of colours and the allegorical representations adapted. Connected with the extension of the abbey library, around the middle of the century, is Sawalo, the only illuminator of St Amand's known by name. In some forty codices with a striking decorative unity, his hand can be recognized. The showpiece of this series is a Bible in five parts (*ibidem*, ms 1-5) each volume of which opens with an ornamental page signed by the artist, including the beginning of the texts. The background is filled with copiously curling tendrils in which small, lively personages are very imaginatively incorporated. It is not impossible that some influence has come from Islamic ivories.

The evolution of the St Amand's style is best followed in various copies of the life of the abbey's patron. Moreover, the great attention paid to the lives and miracles of the local saints is a general phenomenon. These texts were not only used in the liturgy, but the copies, often richly illuminated, accented the prestige of the saints and the abbeys placed under their protection. The first *Vita Amandi* (*ibidem*, ms 502) dates from the second half of the 11th century. This *vita* is illustrated by forty-two epic scenes, in which Carolingian reminiscences are still at work. The artist has an obvious sense of how to present man and nature in movement, by which he achieves an unusually high degree of drama.

As a masterpiece from St Amand's around the middle of the 12th century we can count another *Life* (*ibidem*, ms 501). The full-page miniatures are based on older manuscripts with the same content; but by escaping from the prevailing layouts, the Romanesque style is here crystallized at a culminating point, which at the same time constitutes the approach to the Gothic. The main quality is probably the harmony between form and content; between the spiritual charge of the themes and the ceremonious character of the personages. Equally striking is the decorative harmony of the smooth and pure colours, which causes the figures to move in a solemn but unreal world.

A last *vita* (*ibidem*, ms 500), started by Sawalo, was completed by an artist who, in the scenes from the *Life of Amand*, introduced a new trend by the striking plasticity, suppleness and movement of the personages in order to give expression to their inner inspiration; such expression was completely lacking in Sawalo. There is no doubt that this phenomenon comes from the lessons of Italo-Byzantine art, of which this illuminator understands not merely the technique but also the spirit. This trend can also be found somewhat later, *e g* in a handsome portrait of St Gregory, intended as frontispiece for a collection of his letters (Paris, National Library, ms lat 2287). The saint, painted in strong colours, is enthroned as a monumental figure. By a distortion of the relations between head, hands and body, the superhuman character of this Doctor of the Church is accentuated.

In the sister abbeys of Marchiennes and Anchin, the same texts were copied and ornamented more or less simultaneously, and this even meant that copyists and illuminators were exchanged. Thus we find the same style, in which there is a strong and understandable influence of St Amand's. Thus during the second quarter

St Gregory, miniature from Gregorius, *Letters*, 465 × 320 mm, St Amand-les-Eaux, second half of 12th century. Paris, Bibliothèque nationale, ms lat 2287, fol 1 v°.
Pope Gregory, the author of the book, is presented as a teacher. Here graphic lyricism has made way for a sense of the monumental; achieved by strong colours, the unusual proportions of the figure and an arrangement of folds with a modelling function.

Scenes from Genesis, illuminated page from the *Bible*, 505 × 350 mm, Marchiennes, second quarter of 12th century, Douai, Bibliothèque municipale, ms 1, before fol 1.
The page-high initial I (*In Principio*) is enchanced by the *Creation of Adam and Eve, the Fall of Man, the Expulsion from Paradise* and *the story of Cain and Abel.* Such an illustrative formula is found to an increasing extent in Bible manuscripts from the Romanesque period onwards.

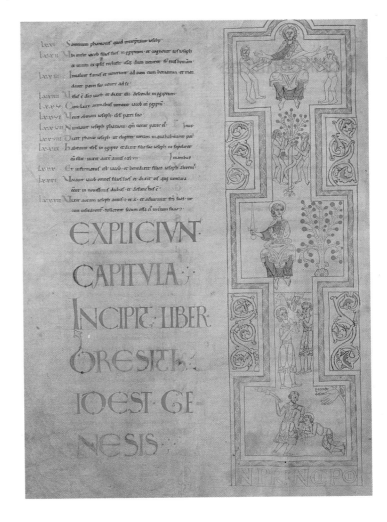

The Evangelist Luke, miniature from *Evangeliarium* of Hénin-Liétard, 325 × 205 mm, St Omer, Abbey of St Bertin, first half of 12th century. Boulogne, Bibliothèque municipale, ms 14, Part 2, fol 5.
The demi-medallions present the Annunciation to Mary and to Zacharias. The heavily stylized drapery, with the garments accentuating the shape of the body, is found outside northern France too, and brought about a certain unity in Romanesque art after 1100.

of the 12th century, a Bible was produced in both abbeys, derived from the already mentioned Alard Bible (Douai, Municipal Library ms 1 and 2). Remarkable in these are the enlarged initial letters with vegetable, animal and human figures. The beginning of Genesis is also ornamented with scenes of the Creation, integrated in the monumental corpus of the initial *I* of *In principio.*

Around 1150, this art attained a high level of quality, as we can see in a commentary on the psalms by St Augustine (*ibidem,* ms 250) from Marchiennes abbey. At the beginning of the book glitters a hieratic portrait of the author, seated on a throne and swathed in brilliant liturgical garments. In the frame, the patron saints of the abbey are depicted in medallions. The portrait of the

author served as model for a similar miniature in a manuscript from St Martin's Abbey at Tournai (Paris, National Library, ms lat 2288).

In St Bertin's Abbey, in the first half of the 12th century, countless manuscripts were illuminated. An *Evangeliarium* intended for Hénin-Liétard Abbey (Boulogne, Municipal Library, ms 14) represents to perfection the particular style of this convent: round, smiling faces of somewhat mannered personages with strongly stylized draperies, betraying the Byzantine influence. On the other hand, the insertion of half medallions in the scenes with portraits of the evangelists refers to the book illumination and enamel art of the Maas and Rhineland.

Borrowings from the Maasland technique and the Byzantine repertory of illustrative and decorative patterns remain characteristic for some late 12th-century manuscripts from St Bertin's. We refer among other things to a Bible and a *Moralia in Job* by Gregory (St Omer, Municipal Library, ms 1 and 12) in which – apart from large initials with interlacings and leafwork, fabulous creatures, representations of humans and animals – there are also some illustrations going back directly to Byzantine models, including female figures with a medallion in front of the chest, in which we can recognize the type of Theotokos Blacherniotissa. Foreign formulae of this kind, which because of their hieratic character lend themselves very well to the invocation of the invisible reality, were not unknown in other northern French illuminating workshops either.

In conclusion it may be said that it is difficult to speak of one single tradition in these northern French workshops. Even in one and the same abbey, we find different currents that are not so much the consequence of a chronological evolution, but rather of the diversity of influences and the inequality of the talents working in these *scriptoria.*

A manuscript important in more than one respect saw the light in St Omer, also from St Bertin's Abbey. This is the *Liber Floridus,* compiled *ca* 1120 by Lambert, a canon, whose autograph has been preserved (Ghent, University Library, ms 92). This compilation shows the revival of encyclopedic literature and of allegorical thinking. The work is illustrated with diagrams and with scenes, often somewhat antiquated, still reminiscent of the art of St Bertin's in the 11th century or of Byzantine models. The fact that this codex was still copied up to the 16th century underlines its fundamental and lasting character.

Benedictine *scriptoria,* higher up on the Scheldt, also began to attract attention in this period: apart from that of the still young St Martin's Abbey in Tournai, the St Peter's and St Bavo's Abbeys in Ghent in particular are

The devil riding Behemoth, illuminated page from Lambert de St Omer, *Liber floridus,* 370 × 204 mm, St Omer, *ca* 1120. Ghent, University Library, ms 92.
In this compilatory work, presented by the author as a 'shrub in bloom', attention is also paid to the events of the end of time: the domination of the Anti-Christ. The Romanesque propensity for stylization lends itself splendidly to bringing out Behemoth and its rider vividly as inescapable reality.

DIABOL SEDENS SVPER BEHEMOT

ORIENTIS BESTIAM
SINGVLAREM ET
SOLAM:
IAN
TIXPM̄,

Behemoth est belua & animal quadrupes dentium imanitate
armatum · & linguam exerit · habens cornua arieti similia
& ei cartilago q̄si lamine ferree habens testiculos pplexos
& pedes animalis cuius ossa sunt sic fistule eris: ht aute̅ cau-
dam draconis atroce̅ & longam quasi cedrus · Cauda quibus
ligat · dentibusq̄ uulnerat · Huic mille motos herbas
quibus pascit fenum sic bos comedens & fluuium absorbens · Sub-
bra enim dormit in secreto calami in locis humidis · Anim̄
origine exortus? ipso transeunte peribit · Significat aut̄ dia-
lu. qui de excelsis ad ima ruit & pmerito suo in aial brutu̅ c-
fecus est · Significat etiam antixp̄m pditiois filiu̅ in fine uenturu̅
Qui in̄tū poterit coopante diabolo pdx gen humanū · & nouissimo se ipsū;

Illuminated page from Augustine, Homilies on Psalms 1-39, 465 × 325 mm, West Flanders, *ca* 1200. Bruges, Seminary, ms 16/196, fol 168 v°.
This manuscript, originating from Ter Doest, illustrates the studied sobriety of the Cistercian Codices: geometrized vine and leaf-foliage motifs, executed with a pen in a small number of colours, constitute the basic data. However, the different combinations in each case made possible an infinite series of variations.

of increasing significance. The activity of the scribes and illuminators in St Peter's Abbey can already be illustrated in the 11th century by a collection of simply ornamented texts referring to St Ghislaine, who founded St Ghislaine's Abbey in Hainault (Mons, University Library, Fonds Ancien, ms 27/221). The art of illumination in St Bavo's is reflected in a *Sacramentarium* from the end of the 12th century (London, British Library, ms 16949). A comparison of the calvary with the canon of the contemporary miniatures from the Maasland, shows that the Ghent illuminator painted less mannered figures which are also flatter in appearance.

After the emergence of the Cistercian order in about 1100, it started production in its own convents. While the followers of Benedict regarded illumination as an enrichment of the text, the White Friars strove in principle after an elemental simplicity as an expression of humility, so that attention should be diverted as little as possible from the spiritual content of the text. Manuscripts from rich libraries such as those of Clairmarais, Ter Duinen and Ter Doest illustrate this. From this last abbey come four parts of St Augustine's homilies on the psalms (Bruges, Great Seminar, 16/19 - 19/193). The decorated initial letters, in varying shapes, are in many colours, either with a layer of paint or drawn with the pen in different inks. These initials are formed or surrounded by decoratively intertwined leaf and tendril work which, in spite of the stylizing, gives it great vivacity. This codex belongs with some thirty others, all intended for Ter Duinen and Ter Doest, in a group produced by the Cistercians between 1190 and 1220.

If we travel east of the Scheldt region in Romanesque times, we have to deal with a very strong current from the Maasland, a region from which a powerful influence radiated at this time. This can be noticed, for instance, in a group of manuscripts produced *ca* 1120-1150 in the Benedictine Abbey of Affligem. This special state of affairs is also found in codices made for Premonstratensian cloisters in Brabant. Thus, in Park Abbey (Heverlee) some decades after the foundation (1129) a manuscript workshop was set up. In the history of Romanesque book illumination, a Bible in three parts (London, British Library, Add ms 14788-90) is of special significance both iconographically and stylistically. The manuscript, according to a colophon *ca* 1148, was produced for Park Abbey; but there is no indication that it was illuminated there. But if this were the case, it is probable that for this work talented artists were recruited from elsewhere. In any case, the ornamentation is closely related to that of bibles from the Maasland, and within this group it even assumes a key position. This last example illustrates once more the fact that, because of the mobility of manuscripts and artists, the exchange of styles, pictorial layouts and ornamentation was a fundamental characteristic of these times.

EARLY AND HIGH GOTHIC: STYLIZED COURTLINESS

The period around 1200 was of great significance for book production. Because of changes in the material culture, the emergence of towns, universities and profane literature, increasingly cast in the vernacular languages, a growing demand for books was felt. Not only in the consumption but also in the production of books, the laity was henceforth involved to an important degree. To be able to meet the increased demand, lay workshops with book illuminators now arose, and these displaced the monastic workshops. This change coincided with a stylistic renewal in which the Romanesque style gradually passed into the Gothic. Connected with political and economic circumstances, a striking shift took place from northern France to the north of the county of Flanders; and the Maas and Sambre region, which had played such an eminent role in the previous period, was now definitely surpassed by the Scheldt country.

The situation sketched above was in fact reflected in the production of illuminated psalters in centres such as Bruges and Ghent. The religious renewal, directed at

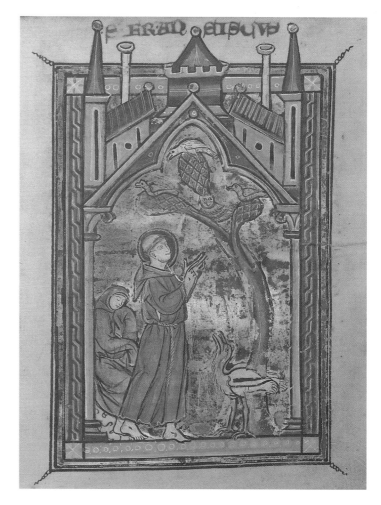

Scenes from Genesis, manuscript page with only one letter on it (*In Principio*), from *Park's Bible,* 430 × 305 mm, North French and Maas region influence, *ca* 1184. London, British Library, Add ms 14788, fol 6 v°.
The ligature IN introduces the story of the Creation. It is linked with all kinds of scenes which illustrate the text. The overall effect is one of decorative unity.
Such a manuscript, a blend of many influences, illustrates the problematic nature of miniature art in Romanesque Brabant.

St Francis preaching to the birds, miniature from *Psalterium,* 145 × 105 mm, Flanders (Bruges ?), 1260-1270. Bruges, *Seminary,* ms 55/171, fol 95.
The illuminators of this psalter were aiming at innovating the iconography by inserting scenes with Franciscan and Dominican saints, which also served to underline the role of the mendicant orders in the spirituality of that time.
The limited use of colour and the architectural copestone produce a strongly decorative effect.

Doubting Thomas – The Choral Song, illuminated page from *Psalter* of Gewijde van Dampierre, 107 × 73 mm. Northern France, *ca* 1277-1275. Brussels, Royal Library, ms 10607, fol 149 v°-150.
The minuscule manuscript, possibly composed for the Count of Flanders, is an example of the wide-scale production of luxuriously conceived psalters in early Gothic style, in which illumination had a functional role. The repertoire of drolleries was drawn upon profusely over several decades.

personal prayer, certainly had something to do with the success of these books, even among the laity. Naturally this was also connected with the purchasing power of the upper classes, so that the production of luxurious psalters even overtook that of such a leading centre as Paris.

The high point of production is without a doubt situated in Bruges between 1240 and 1270. We find in the psalters renewed and refined repertories of illustrations in initials or full-page miniatures. We can distinguish cycles with apostles, with the figure of David as reputed author of these psalms, with scenes from the life of Christ or of saints. The inclusion of Franciscan and Dominican saints is a typical Bruges creation, and it also underlines the role of the religious orders in the spiritual life of that time.

These illuminations are remarkable for their rich blue-red colour contrasts and the glittering gold backgrounds. While originally German and English influences can still be noted in the monumental character of the figures, in the minute detail and the two-

151

dimensional approach – from the middle of the 13th century onwards – the French contribution lead to a greater animation in the courtly, elegant personages and in the attempt to suggest depth. The way in which the colours spread over large surfaces so as to cause strongly decorative effects, as well as the black outlines, point to the influence of stained glass windows. The gold and the radiant colours also form an allegory of the spiritual light, and contribute to a great degree to transposing these scenes into an unworldly reality. Attention was also beginning to be paid to the marginal decoration which, originally very stiff in character, was to become increasingly more supple and extensive. This phenomenon illustrates the striving for decorative effects, particular to the Gothic.

Following the examples from Bruges, psalters were created in Ghent, Brabant and the frontier region between Flanders and Artois. A beautiful example of this last group is the Psalter of Gewijde van Dampierre, Count of Flanders (Brussels, Royal Library, ms 10607). It came into being between 1266 and 1275, and brings together a synthesis of Bruges models and Parisian and local influences. The manuscript also owes its charm to the presence of drolleries in the margins. This sort of marginal decoration with its figures or scenes from everyday life, or drawn completely from the imagination, has absolutely nothing to do with the content of the books; and they are charged with humoristic, satirically

moralizing or even burlesque undertones. The drollery came into being at that time more or less simultaneously in England and in northern France. From there it spread rapidly over other regions, and it did not soon disappear from book illumination.

From the last third of the 13th century till the beginning of the following century, Ghent took over the lead from Bruges. Among the reasons for this jump ahead was a new synthesis of high quality between the French and the Bruges style described above. A missal from the Ghent St Peter's Abbey (Ghent, Bijloke Museum, ms 60-1) gives a good picture of the situation around 1280, a moment at which a considerable degree of maturity had been reached. One full-page miniature depicts at the top a Calvary, and below the three Marys at the empty grave, harmoniously combined within an architectural construction. The warm red and blue, as specific Gothic colours, also form strong contrasts here. Although a French influence cannot be denied, yet the illuminator avoided the inclination to elegance and affectation by a sense for realism, both in the solid figures and in the reproduction of the grief of the main personages. But these attainments in the realm of expression were not absolute, as is proved by the comparison with another Ghent codex, the *Ceremoniale Blandiniense* (Ghent, University Library, ms 233), a manual for the liturgical ceremony, made for St Bavo's Abbey *ca* 1322. As a subject we find here the same full-page illustrations; yet the well-considered and emphatic nature of the subject in the missal has given place to a more subtle and charming design, stressed by a lighter colouration and a greater attention to the decorative. It is difficult to describe this change as a consequence of an evolution within a strict Ghent context. Beyond a doubt, there is direct involvement of the new trend which could be noted in Paris circles around 1320-1330, and more especially in the work of Jean Pucelle.

That inspiration also came from elsewhere is shown by a group of manuscripts, in which the strongly developed and luxuriant architectural elements in the frameworks betray an influence of the English art of illumination. The key manuscript in this series is a *Roman du bon roi Alexandre* (Oxford, Bodleian Library, ms 262), illuminated *ca* 1325-1335 by Jean de Grise, among others. Probably more important than the text illustrations, which are not of great quality, are the drolleries at the foot of the page, in which we see reflected the manners and customs of the time. The place of origin of the manuscripts belonging to this group is uncertain. Some think of Bruges, others opt for Tournai. In the latter town, a series of illuminated codices was produced with the historical and poetic works of the old and blind Abbot of St Martin's there, Gilles li Muisis (1331-1353). They were illuminated around the middle of the century by Pierart dou Tielt. In a realistic and emphatic manner, he presented a very animated picture of dramatic events of that time.

We have already referred to the production of psalters in Brabant. The art of miniature was also practised around the Duke's court. Around 1378, the illuminator Jan van Woluwe was in the service of the Duchess Joan, although manuscripts decorated by him are not known.

The Birth of St John the Baptist, loose miniature from the *Beaupré/Antiphonary,* 303 × 200 mm, Northern France. Brussels, Royal Library, ms II 3634².
The importance of Northern France in the late 13th century is born out by a number of codices, such as the *Antiphonary* of the Cistercian Abbey of Beaupré, Geraardsbergen. It contains two series of three volumes each, parts or loose pages of which are now distributed over various libraries.

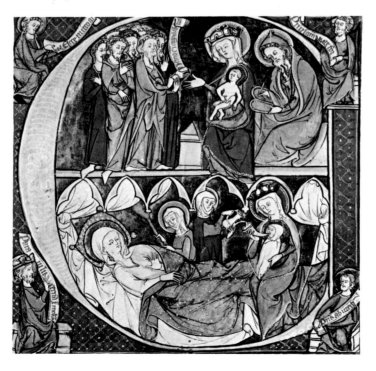

Christ on the Cross – The Three Maries at the Sepulchre, miniature from *Missal,* 150 × 94 mm, Ghent, *ca* 1280. Ghent, Bijloke Museum, ms 60-1. Although the quality of such a miniature is inconceivable without French influence, the illuminator nevertheless chooses expressiveness in preference to the formal grace of his models. The black lines which mark the contours and the angular folds play a major part here.

Christ on the Cross - The Three Maries at the Sepulchre. Miniature from the *Ceremoniale Blandiniense,* 145 × 88 mm, Ghent, *ca* 1322. Ghent, University Library, ms 233, fol 70 v°.
Although thematically the miniature conforms with that from the *Missal* originally in St Peter's Abbey, Ghent, in this case the illuminator's fluent drawing lays more stress on elegance than on dramatic expression. This is attributable to the influence of a new trend in Parisian miniature painting, in the early part of the 14th century.

FROM 1350 TO 1445:
THE BREAKTHROUGH OF REALISM

Under the influence of urban culture, the art of the Netherlands laid more stress on the reproduction of reality from the second half of the 14th century onwards. But this progressive current was 'threatened' by the International Style from Paris. This style grew up in a courtly environment with artificial life-styles, and showed a mannered character. Although the influence was very great, it was also powerfully opposed. On the one hand, artists who had emigrated from the Netherlands weakened the courtly trend in the French environment; on the other, the infiltration of the Parisian style was opposed in the Netherlands.

The phenomenon of employing Flemish illuminators in French court circles during the second half of the 14th century and the beginning of the 15th probably deserves special emphasis. In the Parisian environment they brought about a synthesis between French-courtly, Italianate-intellectual and Flemish-naturalistic elements, with a clear accent on the latter. One eminent representative is Jan Baudolf from Bruges, the leading artist in Paris between 1368 and 1381. As a court painter, he rejuvenated the local style by returning to the sense for realism and plasticity of Jean Pucelle. André Beauneveu from Valenciennes, a sculptor, painter and illuminator, was in the service of the French monarch Charles V, of Lodewijk van Male and of the Duke John of Berry. Jacquemart de Hesdin also came from northern France. In 1384 he entered the service of the Duke of Berry until, in 1409, he was replaced by the Limbourg brothers. But the most brilliant and progressive genius before van Eyck was the Boucicaut Master, who probably also came from the north (Jacob Coene from Bruges?) and who worked in Paris at the beginning of the 15th century.

In the Netherlands themselves, there were also signs of a great creativity. A high point, both iconographically and stylistically, of the art of illumination in western Europe, is an *Apocalypse in Dietse* (Paris, National Library; ms néerl 3). Each chapter of the Revelations of St John was condensed into one scene, in which the episode was combined in a coherent landscape with an extraordinary feeling for the filling of spaces. Although the artist was aiming at a popular narrative style by the inclusion of little genre scenes, yet at the same time he succeeded in reproducing the irreality of the visions. The codex saw the light *ca* 1400 in south-west Flanders.

In the beginning years of the 15th century, we find in some Flemish illuminators and a number of those acting in England like Herman Scheerre a similar style, which was termed the Channel Style. In it we recognize not only traces of the contemporary or somewhat earlier art of panel painting, more especially of the Ypres master Melchior Broederlam, but also of the Rhineland art.

This phenomenon is hardly surprising, in view of the great mobility and the stylistic and iconographic exchange, which was the very feature of the International Style. A series of manuscripts from the Channel Style group, of which a Book of Hours (Rouen, Municipal Library, ms 3024) forms the main work, is striking because of its broad, illusionistic frameworks, its architectural settings and its popular details in the scenes. They come probably from Bruges. The importance of this town as a sales market was also illustrated by the fact that already at the beginning of the 15th century, there was strong opposition to illuminators from Utrecht who came to sell finished books or loose miniatures at Bruges. It is also of great significance that Abbot Lubrecht Hautscilt of St Bartholomew's Abbey at Bruges presented a treatise on astrology, magnificently illuminated in the town, to none less that the greatest bibliophile of the western world at that time, namely John of Berry (New York, Pierpont Morgan Library, ms 785). Although the miniatures give the impression of having been easily and playfully painted, yet their considerable degree of reality betrays a practised hand.

It says much that the Burgundian dukes, who originally took their cue entirely from the Paris workshops, were from a certain moment onwards attracted by the Flemish production centres. A witness to this conversion is a breviary for John the Fearless, begun *ca* 1410 by a French miniaturist, but finished off in Flanders, probably in Bruges (London, British Library, *Harley* 2897, and Add ms 35811). Moreover, already before 1419, the Duke had a Book of Hours illuminated at Ghent (Paris, National Library, ms nouv acq lat 3055). Some other codices can be considered in this connection, including the somewhat earlier Book of Hours of the Ghent patrician Daniel Rym (Baltimore, Walters Art Gallery, ms W 166). The illumination of these manuscripts occupies a place between the earlier Ypres school and the work of the Master of Guillebert of Metz.

Most of these manuscripts show that the perception of reality had changed: more attention was given to the anecdotal or typifying detail, to the mutual relations between people and to their location in the space. This sense of realism was forward-looking. It was to reach perfection in the art of Jan van Eyck, in whom the *ars nova* was to become integral and absolute.

In the second quarter of the 15th century, a number of anonymous illuminators come into the foreground; and their work gives the impression that the expectations roused by the new trends around 1400 had not, for the time being, been realized. No further progress has been made in the representation of depth; on the contrary, the backgrounds were flatly closed off with chessboard patterns, silvery skies or purple fields with golden scrolls.

Procession of Scourgers, illuminated page from Gilles Li Muisis, *Annals,* 273 × 205 mm, Tournai, Pierart dou Tielt, *ca* 1553. Brussels, Royal Library, ms 1307-1377, fol 16 v°.
The author recounts the local history during the closing years of his life. Miniatures showing Jews burned at the stake, the action of the scourgers and the consequences of the plague highlight the horrors of the year 1349.

The son of Man between the Candelabras and the Seven Churches, miniature from *Apocalypse in Dietsche,* 260 × 190 mm, West Flanders, *ca* 1400. Paris, Bibliothèque nationale, ms néerl 3, fol 2.
This manuscript constitutes a peak in Apocalypse illustration. Unreal, with colours heightened with white, a studied arrangement of the pages, the symbolic intensity of decors and motifs, the unexpected combination of data and the sharply etched outline of the clouds enhance the visionary aspect.

The landscape shows little inspiration, and the human figure is stereotyped. Among the causes for this trend is an influence from France which had an inhibiting and even archaizing effect.

First among the principal illuminators is the long underestimated Master of the Gold Scrolls. This name alludes to the backgrounds ornamented with tendrils, although these are not exclusively typical of his work. Moreover, we are dealing here with a group which can be attributed to Bruges, rather than with a single artist. Stylistically, the attainments from Parisian book illumination from the beginning of the 15th century, and especially from the Boucicaut Master, are united with the *Channel Style* prevailing in the Netherlands. This work was also to be the link leading to the art of illumination intended for mass production, from the middle of this century.

Also schooled in the French environment was the Master of Guillebert of Metz, so-called because he illuminated a manuscript that was copied by Guillebert of Metz who lived at Geraardsbergen (Paris, Arsenal Library, ms 5070). The miniatures are careful, some-what hard in character, and not very expressive. The style appears archaic compared with that of French and even Flemish manuscripts from the beginning of the century. A characteristic feature is the marginal ornamentation with large, plastic acanthus leaves following the Lombardy model, but with drolleries worked into it as a Flemish element. A *City of God* by St Augustine (Brussels, Royal Library, ms 9005-06) made for the counsellor and treasurer of Philip the Good, Gui Gilbaut, illustrates the style in question.

This artist too, and the group to which he belonged, had numerous imitators. Around 1453-1460, an anonymous apprentice – known as the Master of the Privileges

Nimrod orders the construction of Babylon, illuminated page from Augustine, *De civitate Dei* (French translation), 480 × 360 mm, Southern Netherlands, Master of Guillebert van Metz, *ca* 1420-1435. Brussels, Royal Library, ms 9006, fol 2.
The large dimensions of this book, produced for a councillor of Philip the Good, and the particular care devoted to the illumination are evidence to the value of Augustine's tract at that time as a standard-setter in the political development of a state.

The Martyrdom of St Sebastian, miniature from *Breviary*, Bruges (?), early 15th century. Rouen, Bibliothèque de la ville, ms 3024 (coll Leber 137), fol 120 v°.
In this codex, the main work from the Channel Style group, various influences converge. Nevertheless, the tendency towards realism reveals a future-oriented vision.

Daniel in the Lions' Den, miniature from *Breviary*, 158 × 147 mm, Ghent, 1420-1425. Baltimore, Walters Art Gallery, ms w 166, fol 168 v°.
Despite the wilde frame, the illustration extends into the margins. On the left, Daniel Rym, who commissioned the work, kneels before his patron saint. Above, an angel lowers Habakkuk into the den by the hair in order to enable him to bring food to the prophet. This anecdotal detail heralds a new vision of reality.

cité de confusion · nembroth ·

Cy comence le prologue du second volume du liure Intitule de la cité dieu

OMBIEN
que au comencement
de ceste translation
et exposition en
nostre prologue
nous auons prins
a mettre declaracions
et exposicions / et
pas et es lieux qui le desirent · Toutesuoiez
nostre entencion ne fu onques de mettre
ces paroles principalment forz en ce qui
seroit histoire ou de poetrie · Et non pas
de touchier ace qui regarde la theologie
car telz choses ne cheent pas en exposition
quant a nous / mais cheent a desputer a
la chaiere / et a determiner a ceulx a qui il
est prins cest assauoir aux docteurs de
sainte eglise · et a ceulx par qui la foy ca

tholique est soustenue · Et suppose que dieu
nous eust appelle a tel degre que nous en
scussione aucune chose monstrer ce que non
ne nous semble Il pas que si haulte matiere
come de la trinite des declaracions dicelle
de la nature des sains angeles et mauuais
de la creacion du monde des choses celestienes
et supercelestienes come des sherarchies
et autres haultes matieres / qui si subtilment
si haultement et si briefment sont traitees
en ce liure et autres · nous nous dions en
tremettre especialment den parler en francois
non pas pour ceulx qui entendent et lun
et lautre · mais pour ceulx qui sont pur
layz / et qui par chose que nous en deissons
en seroient de rienz plus edifiez ne nentent
droient point lun lautaulte plus que lautre
néant plus que du Ve liure de boece de con

of Ghent and Flanders – worked probably in Ghent on commissions for Philip the Good, among others. Although his miniatures make a somewhat archaic impression because they lack a sense of reality, yet it is precisely this fact that gives them a monumental character.

Thus during the first half of the 15th century, a clear continuity was apparent in the art of illumination in Flanders. But from about 1450 onwards, the work of all the Masters we have named declined gradually, and it was taken over by new workshops. At the same time, the intervention of Philip the Good caused a shift towards certain northern French towns or to Brussels. There was also at a very early stage a distinction between those workshops who worked to meet a demand from the market, and thus made use of traditional working methods, and of tried and tested formulae; and those workshops who obtained commissions from important and moneyed patrons. The latter reached a very high level, technically and artistically.

THE GOVERNMENT OF PHILIP THE GOOD: 'FLEMISH MANNERISM'

Once his political and territorial ambitions had been crowned with success, the Burgundian duke exercised an active patronage that was specially expressed in the field of books: about 650 manuscripts were acquired by him. This feeling for the luxurious book also affected people surrounding him: David of Burgundy, Jean Chevrot, Nicolas Rolin, Guillaume Fillastre, Ferry de Clugny, Anton and Charles van Croy, and others. Here we should not lose sight of the fact that these books were more than showpieces; they also influenced political, religious and moral thinking. It is known, for instance, that Philip the Good had made an extensive collection of works connected with the history and idea of the Crusades. This was bound up with his ambition, which was never realized, to set out to fight the Turks in the East.

From the documents of Philip the Good, the names of countless illuminators in various centres in the

The Battle of Gavere, 23rd July 1453, miniature from *Privileges and Statutes of Ghent and Flanders,* 320 × 230 mm, Ghent (?), Master of the Privileges, post-1453. Vienna, Österreichische Nationalbibliothek, ms 2583, fol 340 v°. The codex, with copies of the privileges and statutes of Ghent and Flanders from 1241 to 1454, was commissioned by Philip the Good after his subjugation of Ghent in 1453. The illustration is characterized by archaisms, but suggests the richness of a tapestry.

The horse is dragged into the city of Troy, illuminated page from Jean Mansel, *La fleur des histoires,* 430 × 300 mm, Valenciennes, studio of the Master of Mansel, *ca* 1455. Brussels, Royal Library, ms 9231, fol 116. The codex relates the history of the world from the Creation to the ascension of Charles VI to the throne of France in 1380. The illuminator, employing a continuous narrative style, condenses each of the various chapters into a single scene.

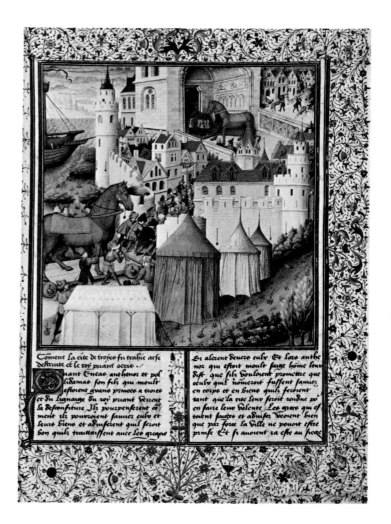

Netherlands have come down to us. In spite of some differences, illumination was nevertheless characterized by common features, such as the realism which was shown especially in the rendering of landscapes. Although the personages are individualized, yet they often show affected attitudes or artificial gestures. But it is probably typical for this to be more of a regressive trend, explained by the fact that the illuminators were striving for a 'courtly' art.

Looked at from the socio-economic angle, we now find the *librariër* ('librarian' should not be taken in its actual meaning) coming to the fore, sometimes as copyist or author, assuming the responsibility for the production of the book, yet handing the work out to various specialists.

A first group of manuscripts can be assigned to the figure of Jean Wauquelin from Picardy, who settled in Mons before 1428 and was active there as librarian, author, translator and copyist. Around 1450 he produced for Philip works including *Les chroniques de Hainaut* (Brussels, Royal Library, ms 9242-44), a

Histoire de Girart de Roussillon (Vienna, Austrian National Library, ms 2533) and a *Histoire d'Alexandre* (Paris, National Library, ms fr 9342). Some fifteen illuminators worked on these and other codices. The realization of the three parts of the *Chroniques de Hainaut* mentioned above illustrates several decades of the history of book illumination in Flanders. The first part opens with a frontispiece in which the codex is offered to the Duke, surrounded by his counsellors and courtiers. This scene, a witness to the almost sacral value of the book in the Burgundian environment, is often attributed to Rogier van der Weyden. In any case, it is of extremely high quality, and was to serve as model for countless later miniatures of the same subject. The rest of this volume is illuminated by different hands, while the two remaining volumes were finished off only after Philip's death, at the request of Charles the Bold.

Also of importance is the *Girart* manuscript we have mentioned above. This history of the first Burgundian duke who "defeated the French monarch twenty times over", is a witness of the political aspirations of Philip

Nobility and clergy arguing with the people about the burial place of Girart de Roussillon, illuminated page from *Histoire de Girart de Roussillon* (prose version by Jean Waquelin), 400 × 300 mm, Brussels (?), Girart master (Dreux Jehan?), post-1448. Vienna, Österreichische Nationalbibliothek, ms 2549, fol 177 v°.
The outstanding qualities of this splendid manuscript from both a stylistic and an iconographic point of view are accounted for by the concordance of its subject-matter with the political ambitions of the patron, Philip the Good, *i e* the upholding of a nationalist policy for Burgundy.

Manuscript page with only one initial on it (letter s), illuminated page from *Miroir de la salvation humaine,* 290 × 190 mm. Flanders, Jean Miélot, 1448-1449. Brussels, Royal Library, ms 9249-50, fol 1 v°.
Design from the hand of the copyist and compiler Jean Miélot, commissioned by Philip the Good. The *Speculum humanae salvationis,* which sets the place of Man in the history of God's deeds, aroused exceptional interest in Burgundian court circles.

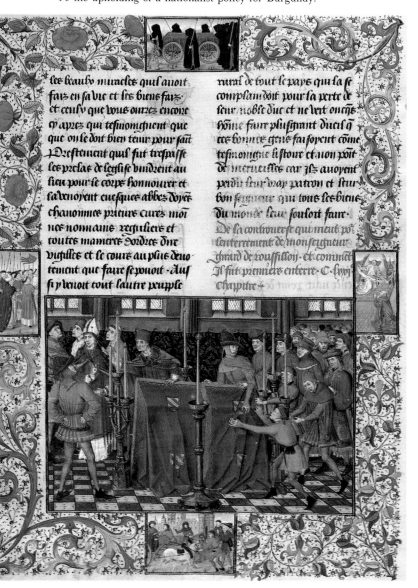

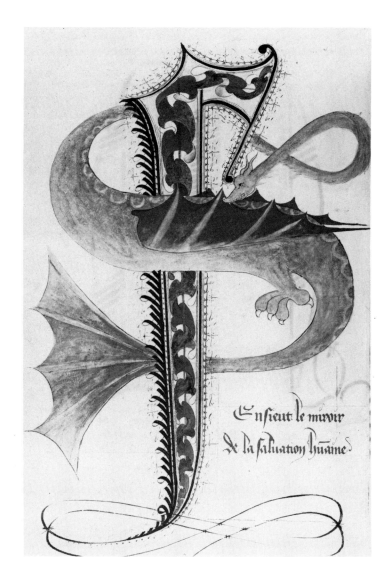

Dieu le souuerai
commencem̃t et
luminere parfaite.
en quoy toutes
choses visibles et
inuisibles passees presentes et ad
uenir manifestement et apertement
ment apparent. Et deuez sauoir
que du mouuement et uerberation
de celly pur air et pure lu
niuer naist la parolle dieu. car
parolle nest aultre chose que uoip
fourmee par uerberation et par

mouuement dair. Et sachies q̃
dieu est sa parolle, et sa parolle est
dieu. Et est ceste parolle complie
et parfaite par iii. souueraines
dictures, sans lesquelles dictures
la parolle dieu, cest a dire sa datte
ne puet estre acomplie ne parfaite
entierment. Et por ce dist pla
tons, que ces iii. dictures sont un
souuerain bien principal, le ql
est commencement de tous aultres
biens, et de qui toutes choses prẽ
dent commencement et perfection

the Good, who took side very fiercely against the French royal house of the time. Part of the illumination was carried out by a progressive artist who is known as the Girart Master. His harmonious colouration has such a great power of light that we are inclined to speak of a modern impressionist technique. This work also shows the influence of van der Weyden, which is expressed in *e g* the solemn portrait character of the personages.

A number of manuscripts were carried out in a related style, which permits the assumption that they come from a large workshop which can be located in the town where Philip resided, Brussels. There are also many factors to support an identification of the Girart Master with Dreux Jehan. This illuminator of French origin was from 1448 to 1464 in the service of the Duke, where he rapidly acquired the title of *valet de chambre*. Dreux Jehan also appears to have been involved in the execution of works by Jean Miélot. Between 1449 and 1454, the latter followed Philip the Good as a secretary on all his travels; and in particular he compiled for the Duke a large number of works, especially connected with spirituality. Apart from luxuriantly illuminated copies, there remain also minutes or drafts, copied by Miélot himself and illuminated with pen drawings and with large initial letters, animated by colouring. An example of this is a version he worked on of the *Miroir de la salvation humaine* (Brussels, Royal Library, ms 9249-50) which saw the light in 1448/49. Minutes of this kind were probably submitted to a client for approval; and they are important because from them we can follow from close at hand the conception of a manuscript and of its iconographical working-out.

At Valciennes, the librarian Jan Mansel compiled *La fleur des histoires* in 1447. Various copies of this have been preserved. The most richly illuminated comes from the *librye* of Philip the Good (Brussels, Royal Library, ms 9231-32). The anonymous artist, known as the Master of Mansel, had certainly had contacts with French illuminators, of which he used models. His scenes, painted in soft colours, are worked out as narratives: different episodes of a story, divided by little paths, rivers and rocks, are combined on one miniature, giving it the richness of a hanging. A second hand brought the realistic style of his predecessor to greater maturity in this manuscript. The narrative system was taken over, but the different components were connected to one another in a more natural way. The elegant personages all express their own individuality; and the landscapes with their delicate tones contribute a wealth of dreamy atmosphere.

This illuminator was earlier identified with Simon Marmion, praised by the humanist Jean Lemaire de Belges in his *Couronne Margaritique* as the 'prince of

illuminators'. This artist from Amiens was active at Valciennes as illuminator and painter from 1458 to 1484. In the latter capacity, the St Bertin's Retable is attributed to him, and was subsequently used as a point of reference for other miniatures. But this identification is disputed. It is true that the work attributed to him does form a coherent whole of exceptional quality. Some are inclined at the present time to regard the Marmion style as a 'concept' at most, and the work belonging to it is ascribed to different hands. This style was to persist for four decades. The last traces of it are found *ca* 1470-1480 in the late Marmion, alias the anonymous Master of Louthe, so-called after a codex intended for a member of this English family (Louvain-la-Neuve, University Library, ms A3).

From more than one point of view, the work of the Master of Wavrin stands outside traditional production. This artist worked in particular between 1455 and 1466 at Lille for Jean, lord of Wavrin and counsellor of Philip the Good. The illuminator was employed in a workshop specializing in romances of chivalry; for which the traditional medium – parchment – was replaced by paper, and the painted scenes replaced by pen drawings with light colour washes. In spite of the sketchy and synthetic character, he showed himself to be a lively and amusing narrator because of the vivacious expressions of the mannered personages. His work is astonishingly modern in appearance, partly because of his somewhat critical and mocking attitude toward the old-fashioned romance of chivalry, although at the time these strongly took the fancy of the royalty, the nobility and even the bourgeois.

Intervention of an angel in the fight between Charlemagne and Doon, miniature from David Aubert, *Chronique et conquêtes de Charlemagne,* 420 × 290 mm, Audenarde, Jan de Tavernier, 1458-1460. Brussels, Royal Library, ms 9066, fol 132 v°.
Jan de Tavernier also illuminated for Philip the Good a breviary and an example of the *Miracles de Notre-Dame* in a translation by Jean Miélot. The extensive miniature cycles were in each case executed by a delicate but consummately controlled grisaille technique.

The Earthly Paradise, illuminated page from *Le livre des sept âges du monde,* 440 × 300 mm, Flanders, Simon Marmion, *ca* 1460. Brussels, Royal Library, ms 9047, fol 1 v°.
The transcription of this commentary on the story of the Creation was entrusted by a member of the Croy family to Jacquemart Philavaine, of Mons. The illumination is by Simon Marmion. The vivid miniature evokes God's resting on the Seventh Day, when the Creation had been completed.

As a witty narrator, Jan de Tavernier is practically second to none. Originally active at Tournai, and subsequently at Ghent, he received commissions from Philip the Good at Audenarde from 1455 onwards. His main work is undoubtedly *Les Chroniques et conquêtes de Charlemagne* (Brussels, Royal Library, ms 9066-68), compiled *ca* 1458 by the copyist and scribe David Aubert. The illustrations in grisaille technique betray a nervous style of drawing. The personages move in a space with a convincing effect of depth. With their bony countenances, marionette-like character and affected attitudes, the author sometimes arrives at the brink of caricature. His predilection for details makes this manuscript an anecdotal picture chronicle. The technique described, which he also used in other manuscripts, was not in any way inferior. Because of the absence of colour, it had the further advantage of preserving the unity between picture and text.

In Bruges, book production profited plentifully from the position of the town as a trading metropolis. This success is manifested not only in the production and large-scale distribution of certain types of books, such as Books of Hours, the ornamentation of which was copied even in other countries; but also in the fact that around 1454 in this town a guild of librarians was constituted under the patronage of St John the Evangelist. This guild united all concerned in book production. In view of the fact that – up to that time – the only other guild of this sort was in Paris, it may be assumed that books occupied an important place in the whole economic activity of Bruges and the Netherlands.

Indissolubly connected with this town are the Turin-Milan Hours (Turin, University Library, burnt in 1904; Turin, Civic Museum), which was actually started for the Duke of Berry. Some of the later executed miniatures are of such quality that they were attributed to Hubert and to the young Jan van Eyck, or at least regarded as an early work by the latter and by an imitator. The accurate and detailed landscapes and interiors, the realism of the personages, the intensive palette of colours and the familiarity with the reproduction of light could apparently not be explained in any other way. Yet it is more than probable that the manuscript was completed only later, between 1440 and 1450, in Bruges, in a workshop that had access to Eyckian and even post-Eyckian models. Other manuscripts were also made in the same workplace, including the Llangattock Book of Hours, made *ca* 1450 for Folpard van Amerongen of Utrecht and Geertrui van Kemseke from Bruges (Malibu, the P. Getty Museum, former Ludwig collection, ms IX.7).

For the illumination of the second part of the *Chroniques de Hainaut*, which we have already mentioned,

Entry of Maldegarius into Hautmont monastery while it is still under construction, miniature from Jacques de Guise, *Chroniques de Hainaut,* Part II (translation by Jean Wauquelin), 290 × 200 mm. Bruges, Willem Vrelant, *ca* 1468. Brussels, Royal Library, ms 9243, fol 106 v°.
The miniatures in this part of the *Chroniques* form the starting-point of the compilation of Willem Vrelant's wide-ranging oeuvre catalogue. A quarter of a century of Bruges miniature painting is dominated by him.

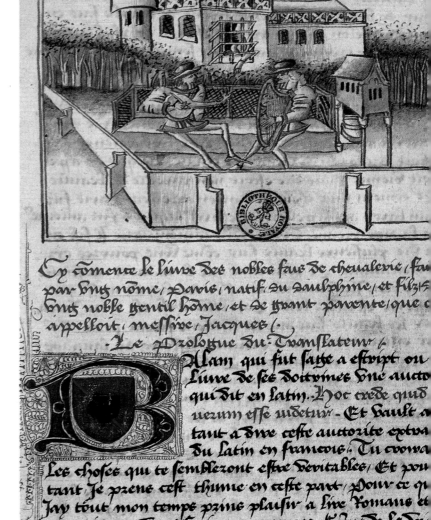

162

Charles the Bold paid in 1468 a certain Guillaume Wielant. This man is identified with Willem Vrelant from Utrecht. It is certain that from 1454 till his death in 1481 he was established in Bruges, where he seems to have monopolized the production of, in particular, religious tracts and Books of Hours. He is characterized by lacking a sense of reality, and this is expressed in his predilection for unconnected and awkward architectural constructions; his personages are stiff, with friendly but expressionless faces. His somewhat limited palette is dominated by blue; the colours are spread in areas without nuances and with some sharp touches. In spite of the routine character of a great deal of his work, it can nevertheless be said in his favour that among the numerous Books of Hours from his workshops – which were also destined for foreign countries, including England and Catalonia – there are many which are striking for their refined design and their radical iconographic renewal.

The third part of these *Chroniques de Hainaut* was provided with decorations by Loyset Liédet. During his stay in Bruges from *ca* 1469 till his death in 1479, he specialized in romances of chivalry and historical works such as the History of Alexander (Paris, National Library, ms fr, 22547), of Charles Martel (Brussels, Royal Library, ms 6-9) and of Renaut of Montauban (Brussels, Royal Library ms 5072-75 and Munich, Bavarian State Library, Cod Gall 7). His work suffered from the numerous commissions he received, and is thus unequal in quality. Because of the slender, wooden and apparently petrified figures, he has been called the 'Dirk Bouts' of the illuminators; although this remark stresses merely an external phenomenon, and not any spiritual relationship. Certain motifs and elements of composition lead us to assume that he was influenced by the works of the so-called Simon Marmion, of whom he may have been an apprentice.

Liédet brings us already right into the period of

The Annunciation, miniature from *Llangattock breviary,* 264 × 184 mm, Bruges, *ca* 1450-1460. Malibu, Paul J. Getty Museum, ms Ludwig IX.7 fol 58 v°.
The figures were copied from the *Annunciation* on van Eyck's *Mystic Lamb* triptych. Other reminiscenses in this codex of Eyckian or post-Eyckian prototypes confirm the close link between painting and miniature work in this Bruges studio *ca* 1450.

The Birth of St John the Baptist – The Baptism of Christ, illuminated page from the *Turin-Milan breviary,* 280 × 200 mm, Bruges, *ca* 1440-1445. Turin, Museo civico, fol 93 v°.
A meticulous detailing of all objects, the realism of the figures, the suggestion of space and the depth of the landscape make up the fascinating qualities of this manuscript. They are to be explained only by the enriching influence exercised by the work of Jan van Eyck on Bruges illuminators' studios.

government by Charles the Bold. Several illuminators worked for him and his spouse, including the Master of Margaret of York who – between 1470 and 1480, first at Brussels then at Bruges – illuminated spiritual works. More important is the Master of Anton of Burgundy, now identified with Philippe de Mazerolles. Of French origin, he settled at Bruges from about 1460 to 1490, where he enjoyed the favour of the Duke. Into this circle, where the book illumination of Vrelant and Liédet tended towards rigidity, he brought new life. He imported from France the method of suggesting interiors and landscapes with a few bold lines. But his creation of depth is incoherent. Yet he was steeped in the Flemish art, including that of Hugo van der Goes, both as regards form and content; like him, he succeeded in reproducing deep emotions. This is shown in a copy of the *Facta et dicta memorabilia* of Valerius Maximus, a successful work of compilation with exempla concerned with moral and philosophical concepts, which was made for Anton of Burgundy (Berlin, State Library, Depot Breslau, 2 Bd 2). The most remarkable book is also a *horarium* on black parchment (Vienna, Austrian National Library, ms 1856) which, after the defeat of Charles in Grandson or Murat in 1476, came into the possession of Galeazzo Maria Sforza. The dark medium mentioned above permitted spectacular enamel-like effects to be obtained, with a strong effect of *chiaroscuro* which heightens the dramatic expression.

The Master of the Dresden Prayer Book continued the Mazerolles style at Bruges from *ca* 1480 to 1500. With a predilection for calendar illustration, he contributed to numerous *horaria*. His work is characterized by the fact that the courtly personages are replaced by heavy figures of rustic appearance, with robust hands and feet. He depicted dramatic events in a touching manner, but this did not prevent him spicing his work playfully with pithy and even humouristic details. His backgrounds testify to a good knowledge of the rendering of perspective. This illuminator maintained relations with other workshops in Bruges and Ghent, and also formed the link with the Bening workshop, which was to play a dominant role in Bruges from 1500 onwards.

In the preparations for the final phase of Flemish miniature art, the town of Ghent unexpectedly played a prominent role. Two artists came to the forefront.

Example with respect to luxuries: the bath-house, illuminated page from Valerius Maximus, *Facta et dicta memorabilia,* Bruges, Philippe de Mazerolles, *ca* 1470. Berlin, Staatsbibliothek Preussischer Kulturbesitz, Depot Breslau, 2 bd, fol 244.
This compilation contains anecdotes from Roman and Greek history which are treated so as to illustrate a moral or philosophical concept. The bath-house, where concern for hygiene was frequently combined with amorous trysts, was an established institution in Bruges in the 15th century.

Coronation of Charles Martel in Rheims, miniature from *Histoire de Charles Martel,* Part I, 410 × 295 mm. Bruges, Loyset Liédet, *ca* 1470. Brussels, Royal Library, ms 6, fol 298 v°.
In 1463 David Aubert copied for Philip the Good in four volumes a prose version of the history of Charles Martel which he had compiled. Loyset Liédet, whose illustrations have a high documentary value, was assigned by Charles the Bold, Philip's successor, the task of illumination, which was started in 1468.

The Bearing of the Cross, miniature from *Breviary,* 250 × 180 mm, Bruges, Philippe de Mazerolles, pre-1467. Vienna, Österreichische Nationalbibliothek, ms 1856, fol 69 v°.
The breviary was presented to Charles the Bold by the town of Bruges in 1467. Use of a parchment dipped in a black dye-bath enabled the illuminator to enhance the epic subject-matter of his scenes with luminous colours.

landum etiam luxuria
malum qm accusare
aliquo facilius est
quam vitari operi nro inserat. Non
quidem ut ullu honorem rapiat
sed ut seipsum recognoscens ad
penitentiam mpxelli possit. iungat
illi libido qm ex hiisdem viciorum
pmapune oritur neq; a reprehende

aut ab emendatione separent. deu
mentis errore conexe. translateur.
En ceste partie valerius commence
son ix.e livre qui est des dits z des
fais dignes de memoire de la cite
de romme z des estrangiers. ouql
apres ce que valerius es viij.e livre
precedent a determine des vertu z
operatione vertueuses. en ce ix.e

Lieven van Lathem spent most of his career since 1454 in this town as a freeman. He died in 1497. He illuminated codices both for Philip the Good and for his successor, and received commissions from bibliophiles such as Lodewijk van Gruuthuse and Anton of Burgundy. Although his personages correspond to somewhat stereotyped formulae, yet they are executed in a masterly and animated manner. Into the flower-strewn margins are worked spicy drolleries, and from these we may assume that van Lathem was in contact with the Northern Netherlands Master of Catherine of Cleves. The presentation miniature, the formal design of which was established in the first volume of *Les Chroniques de Hainaut*, was developed further by this artist: where originally the events were shown in a closed space, there was now an open room. Moreover, van Lathem painted his figures smaller so that interiors, townscapes or landscapes could become relatively larger. It is particularly in respect of the latter feature that this illuminator occupies a place of honour. In his sensibility for the reproduction of the atmospheric, van Lathem was possibly under the influence of the reputed Simon Marmion and of the Girart Master. Combined with dazzling colouration, the work of this Ghent artist attains a high level.

Birth of Christ, miniature from *Breviary of Bona Sforza,* 131 × 93 mm, Ghent, Gerard Horenbout, *ca* 1517-1521. London, British Library, Add ms 43294, fol 82 v°.
The manuscript, started *ca* 1490 for Bona Sforza, widow of the Duke of Milan, was later finished by Gerard Horenbout for Margaret of Austria. This illuminator succeeded in adapting his work, as to both style and format, to that of his Italian predecessor.

Madonna in Church, miniature from so-called *Breviary of Mary of Burgundy,* 225 × 163 mm, Ghent, Master of Mary of Burgundy, *ca* 1470-1480. Vienna, Österreichische Nationalbibliothek, ms 1857, fol 14 v°.
The 'window effect' by which the space in the foreground of the scene intensifies the feeling of depth behind the opening constituting the window, is one of the most important devices by which this anonymous illuminator revived Flemish miniature painting in a final phase.

His fellow-townsman, the anonymous master of Mary of Burgundy, active between 1470 and 1480, has rightly been called the most gifted and original illuminator of the late Middle Ages. He interpreted traditional themes in a wholly new manner. First of all, he understood how to reproduce the atmospheric perspective in northern European art. Then he made use of attainments from the contemporary Ghent panel painting; he clearly took over elements from the work of Hugo van der Goes and from the Master of the Calvary of St Bavo, alias Justus van Gent. The illuminator collaborated with Nicolaas Spierinc, who was established in Ghent since 1476 as a calligrapher in the service of Charles the Bold. This copyist succeeded in attributing decorative qualities to the writing and even to give it a three-dimensional aspect; which was all the more important at a moment when the miniatures, by their striking effect of depth, were beginning to break out of the parchment flagrantly. The most beautiful example is an

Adoration of the Magi – Procession of the Three Kings, illuminated page from *Breviary of Engelbrecht van Nassau,* 148 × 80 mm, Ghent, Master of Mary of Burgundy, *ca* 1477-1490. Oxford, Bodleian Library, ms Douce 219-220, fol 145 v°-146.

The scenes are viewed, as it were, through openings cut out in a wall with niches in which realistic bowls, pitchers and cups in earthenware and glass are exhibited. The proximity of these objects intensifies the effect of depth in a landscape which has been deliberately painted hazily.

horarium which is generally connected with Mary of Burgundy (Vienna, Austrian National Library, ms 1857), to which the artist added four miniatures of exceptional quality. Famous examples are a Madonna in the church and a Nailing to the Cross, framed by an architectural construction – in the first case, the scene is even seen through an open window – which creates a special effect of depth. He illuminated another Book of Hours for Engelbrecht of Nassau (Oxford, Bodleian Library, ms Douce 219-220). In this codex of small format, the Master succeeds in accentuating the mood of an event or the disposition of the figures by a suitable decor. He convincingly represents a nocturnal event such as the betrayal by Judas. The drolleries, which show hunting scenes or a tourney, and run through on successive pages, confirm his considerable ingenuity. The identity of this artist was and remains a riddle. An old hypothesis identifies him with Alexander Bening, but his stylistic and intellectual relationship with van

der Goes makes it equally possible to deduce an identity with the latter. Almost all the illuminators of the next generation were to be influenced by this artist.

In the manuscripts mentioned we find marginal decorations of a completely new type: a fully thought-out decorative formula, which was still to persist for some fifty years, but at the same time was to introduce the swan song of the art of illumination.

THE SO-CALLED GHENT-BRUGES SCHOOL: REALITY SURPASSED

The most typical characteristic of this new marginal decoration, is the replacement of the flowering acanthus painted on the bare parchment, by strongly naturalistic and individualized motifs which cast shadows on a coloured background. But apart from the borders with accurately reproduced flowers and plants, the reader is also surprised by ornamental margins into which are worked letters, pilgrimage badges, shells, precious stones, jewels or household ceramics. The rich colour effects, the illusionistic virtuosity, the surprising *trompe l'œil* and the eye-catching details make these margins into captivating still-lives.

A second characteristic is formed by the realistic

TAVOA PRYMEIRA

landscapes, the endlessness of which is enlarged by the fact that the frameworks we have described above accentuate the depth by a window effect. The three-dimensional reality is so strongly approached, that it even interrupts the unity between the decoration and the flat text. In the painting itself, a detailed narrative realism predominates. Events from within and without are combined in simultaneous pictures. The range of colour is enriched with pastel tints; and this not only softens the whole to a certain degree, but favours an even closer approach to reality. In short, this art manifests a new attitude towards reality.

This so-called Ghent-Bruges style arose *ca* 1470-1480. The Master of Mary of Burgundy and his entourage had a considerable part in the emergence of this new concept which broke through from 1480 onwards; not

only in the whole of the Netherlands but even far beyond, so that the term 'Ghent-Bruges style' is a misleading one. Nonetheless, Ghent and Bruges grew into international centres into which commissions flowed from various regions of Europe. Thanks to the marriage of Mary of Burgundy with Maximilian of Austria, there was also considerable interest from the world of the Habsburgs. Princes, courtiers, clerics, merchants and prosperous citizens ordered Books of Hours and prayer books, or other types of books, in the new style: Isabelle of Castile and her daughter Juana, William Lord Hastings, chamberlain of the English monarch Edward IV, James IV of Scotland, Maximilian of Austria, Cardinal Albrecht of Brandenburg, Dom Fernando of Portugal, and so many other anonymous bibliophiles, whose codices are now numbered among the showpieces of numerous collections. This Ghent-Bruges style exercised so much fascination that foreigners, including those in the Iberian Peninsula, went into the business of dealing in Flemish Books of Hours, and that miniaturists from abroad avidly adopted the new manner of ornamentation.

It is typical that these workshops – in order to be able to speed up production – repeated motifs and pictorial

Genealogical Table of the Kings of Aragon, illuminated page from *Genealogy of the Infante Dom Fernando of Portugal,* 559 × 394 mm, Bruges, Simon Bening, 1530-1534. London, British Library, Add ms 12531. fol 4.
Part of this genealogy was carried out by Simon Bening for Dom Fernando, brother of the Portuguese sovereign, through the intermediary of Damião de Goes, a humanist and diplomat in the Netherlands. In the strong presence of the figures and the tactile value of the whole work, the illuminator competes with the panel painters of his time.

St Gertrude in her living room – The Saint distributing alms, illuminated page from *Hortulus animae,* 214 × 155 mm, Bruges, Simon Bening, 1510-1520. Vienna, Österreichische Nationalbibliothek, ms 2706, fol 290 v°.
This devotional book was copied from a Strasbourg print of 1510. The entirely original illumination is comparable as regards richness and quality with numerous other codices which at that time consolidated the primacy of the manuscript over the printed book.

Scenes from the Life of Jesus, illuminated page of a quadriptych (detail), 680 × 520 mm, Bruges, Simon Bening, *ca* 1525. Baltimore, Walters Art Gallery, ms W 442.
In this quadriptych Bening produced a complex but supremely coherent and penetrating cycle of the life of Jesus. In the effort at innovation creative use was made of graphic and printed models.

layouts, and exploited existing sources such as panel paintings or engravings by using them as models. But this phenomenon should not be regarded as a negative point. It is inherent in late Gothic book illumination and in no way excludes a high level of quality.

Here three illuminators stand out above the rest: Alexander Bening, his apprentice Gerard Horenbout and his son Simon Bening. The former was in 1469 proposed as a member of the Ghent guild of painters (which included also the illuminators) by Hugo van der Goes and Joos van Wassenhove. Although in 1486 his name was entered in the Bruges guild of librarians, yet he continued to live in the Leie town until his death in 1519. No manuscripts can with certainty be attributed to this artist. As we have already mentioned, some authors identify him with the Master of Mary of Burgundy. Recently he has been identified with the Master of the Older Prayer Book of Maximilian I, so-called after a manuscript that was illuminated for this monarch (Vienna, Austrian National Library, ms 1907). The

hand of this anonymous artist can be recognized in some twenty manuscripts from around 1480 to 1510. His roots are clearly in Ghent: he worked with great skill in the spirit of the Master of Mary of Burgundy. His work also relates to that of Hugo van der Goes; we recognize in it the same combination of great spatial depth with static figures which are placed, strongly detailed, in the foreground. Finally, he also borrowed motifs from Gerard David.

Gerard Horenbout, also known as painter, carto-grapher and hanging designer, is found in 1487 in the membership lists of the Ghent guild. But he also worked in Bruges and Antwerp where, in 1520, he received a visit from Albrecht Dürer. In 1514 he became court painter of Margaret of Austria; but six years later he emigrated with his family to England where, until his death around 1540, he was in the service of Henry VIII. He gave his daughter Suzanna, also a miniaturist, in marriage to the monarch's treasurer. *Ca* 1495, Horen-bout – among other things – collaborated on a brevier

August or September, loose miniature, 152 × 102 mm, Bruges, Simon Bening, *ca* 1540. London, Victoria and Albert Museum, Salting ms 2600.

September or October, loose miniature, 152 × 102 mm, Bruges, Simons Bening, *ca* 1540. London, Victoria and Albert Museum, Salting ms 2600 v°. The universality of Simon Bening as an artist is also evidenced by his calendar prints, of which these examples mark the culmination. Reality as seen is transformed by poetic vision, in which the deep landscape eclipses the human aspect.

The Month of March, illuminated page from the *Mayer-van den Bergh Breviary,* 224 × 160 mm, Flanders, *ca* 1510. Antwerp, Mayer-van den Bergh Museum, ms 946, fol 2 v°. The luxurious breviary, perhaps produced for export to Portugal, orginated through cooperation between the leading masters of the late Ghent-Bruges School. Scenes depicting saints and work in the garden illustrate the month of March in the calendar.

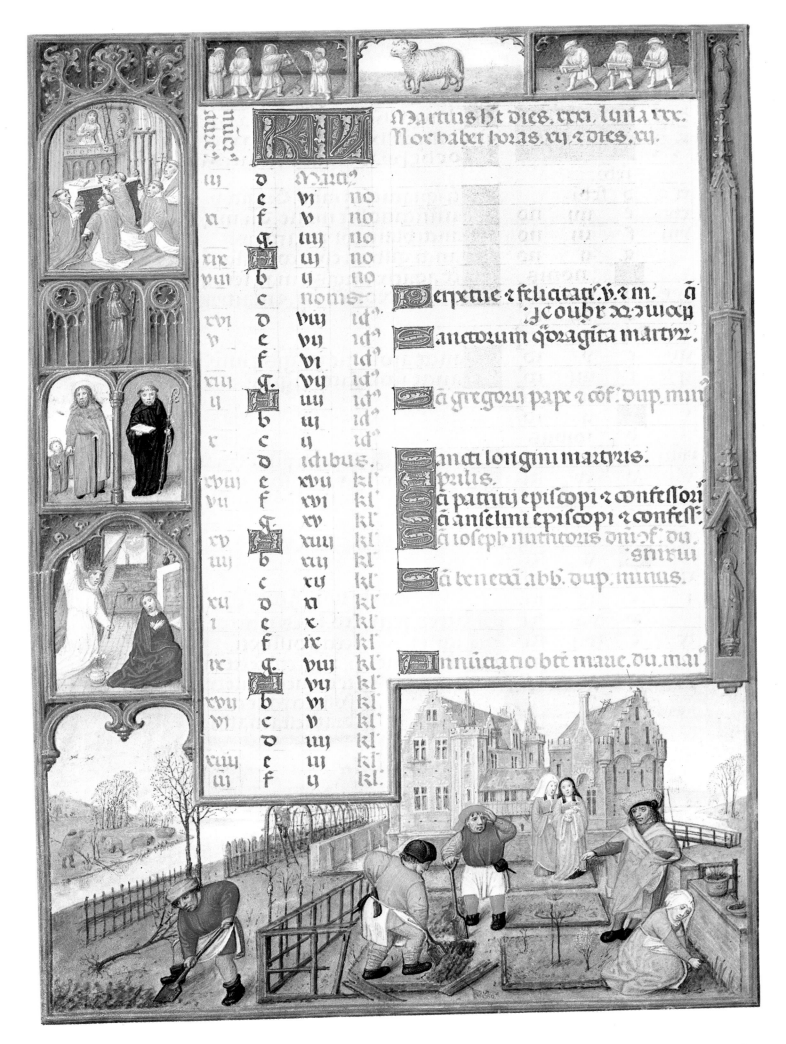

The Lover awakes and walks about in the garden, illuminated page from *Roman de la Rose,* 394 × 292 mm, Bruges (?), Master of he Breviaries of *ca* 1500, *ca* 1490-1500. London, British Library, Harley ms 4425, fol 7.
This version of a popular allegory, one of the three examples illuminated in Flanders, astonishes by the vastness of its format and the richness of its iconography. The romantic atmosphere is evoked by enchanting decors, courtly figures and exotic costumes.

ordered by Francisco de Rojas, Spanish Ambassador to the Netherlands, and offered by him to his Queen (London, British Library, Add ms 18851). His hand can also be recognized in the Sforza Book of Hours (ibidem, Add ms 34294). This is in fact a Lombardic manuscript to which he added miniatures for Margaret of Austria. He also had a part in the Book of Hours for James IV of Scotland (Vienna, Austrian National Library, ms 1897). With rich palette and great mastery of detail, this illuminator strove for charm of narration. The individualization of his personages, with their effect of animation from their strikingly expressive physiognomy, greatly contributes to this.

In 1508, Simon Bening became a freeman in Bruges. As the last in the line of the great Flemish illuminators, he synthesized the acquisitions of Flemish Primitives such as Hugo van der Goes and Gerard David. Bening also used the new inventions of miniaturists as the Master of Mary of Burgundy, and borrowed models from the Master of the Older Prayer Book of Maximilian I. He illustrated numerous Books of Hours, the greatest example of which is undoubtedly that

belonging to Cardinal Albrecht of Brandenburg (Malibu, the P. Getty Museum, former Ludwig collection, ms IX. 19). This prelate possessed several Flemish manuscripts, and it is very significant that Nikolas Glockendon, at that time the leading illuminator in Nuremberg, decorated codices for Cardinal Albrecht, taking the work of Simon Bening as example. The qualities of Bening as a figure painter are expressed to the full in the Stein Quadryptich (Baltimore, Walters Art Gallery, ms W 442): four parchment pages each with sixteen scenes from the Life of Mary and the Passion. Both through the narrative coherence and through the use of half figures, this series radiates a penetrating power. Such monumental figures, strongly in the foreground, and with a great impact on the observer as *Andachtsbild*, were already starting to appear in Books of Hours around 1480.

For Dom Fernando of Portugal, the brother of King John II, Bening completed *ca* 1530-1534 a genealogy (London, British Library, Add ms 12531). This codex, of exceptional dimensions, was begun in Lisbon by Antonio de Hollanda. On the pages given him to finish off, Bening painted a family tree with sculptural qualities: the figures are flesh and blood humans, situated in a tangible space. Bening showed himself to be one of the most gifted landscape painters. With a growing feeling for depth and obvious poetic sensibility, he was able, particularly in his calendar prints, to reproduce the changing character of the seasons. These paintings surpass the art of a contemporary such as Joachim Patinier, and point the way ahead to the art of Breughel.

It is assumed that the three artists mentioned above collaborated around 1510 on the *Breviarium Mayer van den Bergh* (Antwerp, Mayer van den Bergh Museum, ms 946) and some time later on the *Breviarium Grimani* (Venice, Marciana Library). This giant among Flemish manuscripts contains more than a hundred full-page miniatures. The paintings ascribed to Alexander Bening are more archaic in effect than those by his collaborators. The calendar scenes were probably executed by Horenbout who took as a basis the illustrations by the Limbourg brothers in the *Très Riches Heures* of the Duke of Berry, then in the possession of Margaret of Austria at Malines. But because of the more naturalistic quality of persons and landscapes, these paintings appear somewhat more prosaic than those of his illustrious predecessors. Simon Bening's contribution in this breviary can be recognized by the qualities we have already described.

It appears from what has been said that the illumination of codices was not confined within town boundaries: Ghent and Bruges artists combined their talents. In this final phase, the phenomenon of mutual collaboration cannot be sufficiently emphasized. Apart from the three artists mentioned, a large number of other illuminators of varying degrees were working, some of whom were painting very conventional miniatures in an academic manner. Most of these have not been identified. Some illuminators of good quality are the somewhat Memlingesque Bruges Master of the Prayer Books (*ca* 1500), whose most original work is not a religious one, but a richly illuminated and iconographically very inventive *Roman de la Rose* (London, British Library, Harley ms 4425) made before 1500 for Engelbrecht of Nassau, and the Master of Edward IV of England, who was in the service of Lodewijk van Gruuthuse, but also accepted commissions from the English court. Often many illuminators are hiding behind these anonymities, and it is not always possible to make strict distinctions between the hands involved in manuscripts. This is because of the organisation of work by the craft-guild.

Although it has been less studied, we must not lose sight of the fact that also in a Brabant centre such as the economically emerging Antwerp, illuminated manuscripts were being made. This also applies to Malines, certainly after Margaret of Austria had installed herself there as governor of the land. Beautiful music albums were produced in her entourage. The Master of Charles V was active between 1510 and 1530 in Brussels or Malines, probably in connection with the Habsburg court.

Although a Master such as Simon Bening – who only died in 1561 – was for a long time able to maintain himself in an unrivalled position, a turn of the tide can be observed from the twenties of this century onwards.

The miniatures more and more assumed the shapes of little independent paintings, and thus the relation between writing and decoration was lost. The emergent Renaissance attempted to renew the decorative language, particularly in the field of frameworks and marginal decoration, but without much enthusiasm or success. Different was the emergence of the art of printing. Since the time of Philip the Good, the demand for books had become so large that there was a search for more economical working methods, *i e* cheaper and faster production. The imitation of engravings, and even the practice of sticking prints into manuscripts, were the consequences of this. The publication since around 1460 of successful types of illustrated books such as *Biblia pauperum, Ars Moriendi, Apocalypse* and *Speculum humanae salvationis* in the form of block books, springs directly from this situation. Thus we see that this invention was less spectacular than it might appear. In any case, it was thoroughly prepared for in book illumination, and those who made the block books doubtless came from among the illuminators. The 'democratization of bibliophily' in this period was to lead to the emergence of the real art of book printing. Clearly this caused a crisis in the world of the manuscript, which was doomed to disappearance.

Seed-time (October) – Wedding Procession (April) – Meal at a Baronial Court (January), miniatures from *Brevarium Grimani*, 280-215 mm, Gerard Horenbout, 1510-1520. Venice, Biblioteca Marciana, ms lat XI 67. Through Antonio Siciliano, an envoy in Flanders in 1514, the codex came into the possession of Domenico Grimani, patriarch of Aquileia. The calendar prints demonstrate how models a hundred years old and executed in courtly style are converted into realistic and more tangible forms.

173

174

Graphic art

Graphics is essentially the technique of using a medium specially prepared for the purpose to make a number of impressions on another medium (paper, exceptionally parchment). These impressions could be distributed as loose prints, but they also formed (until photomechanical reproduction came into being in the 19th century) the only possibility of being able to visualize the contents of a book. Loose print and book illustration were carried out and printed in the same way; but illustrations were meant to clarify the contents of a book, while loose prints existed on their own. From the art historian's point, graphic art has through the centuries faithfully followed the art of painting. Not only has it steadily adopted its currents and trends, it also exchanged practitioners.

Graphics can be divided over three forms of expression, each with its own set of laws: relief, intaglio and surface printing. The latter (with lithogravure as the principal representative) was only discovered at the end of the 18th century by Sennefelder. But relief and intaglio printing date from the beginning of the history of graphics, probably with a slight seniority for the first-named.

In relief printing, a medium is prepared so that only the parts in relief take up ink and transfer it to the paper. This medium is, in particular, a block of soft wood on which the parts not to be printed are cut away with a knife. The result is the woodcut which is limited to black and white contrasts (not to be confused with wood-engraving in hard blocks, which allows many more nuances, but which did not emerge until the 18th century).

THE WOODCUT: ORIGINATED IN THE NETHER-LANDS? Graphic art represented by the woodcut must have arisen in the 14th century; and in the 15th century it rapidly conquered a place among the important artistic pursuits. Four centres may be singled out right at the start: the Netherlands, Germany, France and Italy. Concerning the extent and quality of production among these four, the Netherlands make a more than honourable impression; and there the new artistic technique appeared so early and with such intensity, that the cradle of the woodcut may have been there.

In the 13th and 14th centuries, it was usual to print fabrics with cut blocks as a decoration. The oldest preserved example of a woodcut block, the so-called *Bois Protat* (France, *ca* 1370) was very probably used for this purpose. But at the end of the 14th century, people came on the idea of printing with such blocks on paper to make illustrations. The oldest woodcut in Europe dates from 1418 and is located in the Netherlands (*Madonna with Saints*, Brussels, Royal Library). From about the same period and stylistically related, we may note a *Missal of St Gregory* (with 15 lines of Dutch text), a *Last Judgment* and a *Madonna*. In the sources of that time, from the beginning of the 15th century onwards, we find for various towns in the Netherlands (both Flanders, Brabant and the North) many references to makers and sellers of prints, even giving the impression that there must have been a very flourishing trade in such prints (already in 1403, for example, painters complained to the Magistrate at Bruges against the competition coming in from outside the town – *e g* Utrecht is mentioned – from prints dealt in by calligraphers and professional scribes). Unfortunately in the Netherlands in the 15th century (as in the rest of Europe) there are preciously few woodcut prints that have survived time and human carelessness.

Page out of a block-book, wood-cut (coloured by hand), with at the bottom a hand-written explanatory text in a Flemish-Brabant dialect: one of the ten illustrations from the first edition of the *Exercitium super Pater noster,* beginning of the 15th century. Paris, Bibliothèque Nationale (Cabinet des Estampes).

St Anne-the-Threes, wood-cut (printed from a block with replaceable parts); coloured by hand, anonymous Flemish-Brabant wood-carver, middle of the 15th century. Paris, Bibliothèque National (Cabinet des Estampes).

Most of the earliest prints were fairly clumsy (with heavy outlines and little or no shading, to help suggest the picture); but over the years, the woodcutters gained technical competence and their works increased in aesthetic quality. If we take a look over the frontiers into neighbouring countries, it may be said that on the average the Netherlands woodcut print was somewhat at a higher level. The older woodcuts may also be distinguished by other than stylistic criteria from later products: they were pressed onto the inked blocks, as it were, with *frottons*. This printed through deeply to the rear side of the print, and it called for the use of a very watery ink (grey, brown or light pink). Only with the spread of the art of bookprinting could presses be used, reducing the printing through, and permitting the use of a more oily black printing ink.

Not one of the early Netherlands representatives of woodcut printing is known by name. Here and there, an accompanying text, or other indication – criticism of the style, in particular – indicates where the work came from (*Calvary* of ca 1480: *Actum Gandavi* = done at Ghent; the superb *Madonna* with a halo, ca 1460: Dutch text referring to Brabant; pictures of three saints *Hieronymus, Anne, Helen* from about the same period: Bruges) but that is about all.

All the woodcut prints preserved from the 15th century are religious and more especially devotional; their production must be seen in the context of the Modern Devotion, which so deeply affected the people in the Netherlands in the Burgundian era and of the emergence of the Poor Friars and their educational institutions. The 15th-century woodcut print was essentially directed to the masses and aimed at religious experience.

Most woodcut prints are also coloured (by hand or with stencils; often very clumsily with broad strokes), the clear aim being to achieve some resemblance to paintings or miniatures. The pictures themselves reflect the schools of painting and miniatures of the time. It is clear that woodcut printing of the 15th century is to be

regarded as a sideline of contemporary miniature and picture painting. And this raises a very important problem, which we cannot answer adequately, due to lack of information.

In the 16th century we see how, when the woodcut came into being, nearly always two specialists were involved: a designer who supplied the models (drawings made directly onto the block, or on paper that was stuck to the block); and the woodcutter proper, who had to complete the technical job to cut the drawing in relief. It may be assumed that in the 15th century already, and certainly for the better quality prints, something similar happened: painters and miniaturists supplied the form and shape for the woodcuts, and it was only exceptional that the woodcutter was also responsible for the 'idea'.

THE BLOCK BOOKS: AN IMPORTANT SPECIALITY OF THE NETHERLANDS Apart from the loose woodcut prints, there also appeared in the 15th century the so-called 'block books': woodcuts which, in the manner of today's comic strips, represented a certain theme and were bound together in a book (generally with an accompanying text which – in the oldest editions – was added by hand, but afterwards also cut in wood).

Block books were a particularly speciality of the Netherlands, and to a lesser extent of Germany (but under the influence of the Low Countries). Like the woodcut prints, these woodcut books are almost exclusively religious in their orientation. It may be assumed that they also came into existence under the influence of the Modern Devotion, and were in particular the brainchild of the Poor Friars (in the foreword of the *Speculum Humanae Salvationis*, ca 1460-1470, it is expressly stated that the work was intended particularly for the *pauperes predicatores* – the poor preachers). Although obviously for other works other motives may have played a role (thus, for example, the *Legend of St Servatius*, ca 1460, must be connected with the display of this saint's relics at Maastricht in 1461).

Qn ſulbi voirt hoꝛen van rap
mōbyn eñ meluſine die als
doen waren te merment. eñ
loe ghinct vaſtelick ten ſaterdaghe
waert.eñ doen oberch haer meluſi
ne dien ſaterbach. eñ tot die daghe
en habde rapmōbyn nopt gheppint
om haer te ſiene ghelpc hi haer ghe
loeft habde alſt voerſept is.ende en
peyſbe nopt arch noch quaet noch
en habde oec ghet quaet ūmoeden
Qu ſo gheburbet dz een luttel rijts
voer be etène hē quamē nieuwarē
Ciij

bat ſyn bꝛoeder die graue vā foꝛetz
hem quā beſuecke des hi ſeer blide
was.hoe wel batter hem naber hāt
leet was.alſo dat rapmōbyn hier
omme groote ghereetſcap maecte
om ſynen bꝛoebere tontfanghene.
Mette couſtē hi ghinc hē tegēs. eñ
ontfinchē blijbeluckē.eñ doen ghun
gē ſy miſſe hooꝛē.eñ bē bienſt gobs
gebaē ſynbe quamē ſp ter zalen eñ
ghingē eten. daer ſy rÿckelikē ghe
bient warbē Pelas baer begōſt eē
grote bꝛoefhyeit.wāt rapmōbyn en

Page out of a block-book, wood-cut (coloured by hand), with at the bottom a hand-written French explanatory text, one of the twenty-four illustrations of the *Legend of St Servate,* around 1460. Brussels, Royal Library.

Page out of a block-book, wood-cut (with Latin texts carved in the wood; coloured by hand), from an edition of the *Biblia Pauperum;* this edition of the 'Bible of the Poor' should be dated 1464/65. Brussels, Royal Library.

Page from an incunable with illustration, wood-cut (coloured by hand), from Ovidius, *Metamorphoses* (also called *Ovide moralisé*), Bruges, Colard Manson, 1484. Brussels, Royal Library.
One of the thirty-four illustrations by the so-called 'first wood-carver of Bruges', after miniatures in a few Ovidius manuscripts of Bruges (one of these was in the possession of the bibliophile Lodewijk van Gruuthuse of Bruges, now in the Bibliothèque Nationale at Paris).

Page from an incunable with illustration, wood-cut (coloured by hand), illustration from Jean d'Arras, *The strange and beautiful tale of Melusijnen and her family,* Antwerp, Gerard Leeu, 1491. Brussels, Royal Library.
The wood-cut has also served for the announcement of the editor, in which G. Leeu makes publicity for his book – the eldest announcement so far known of this sort (also in the Royal Library at Brussels).

Rivers of ink have already flowed on the subject of the block books. Particularly because the works that can be dated with any certainty are relatively young (*ca* 1460) – thus they came into being after the art of bookprinting and were an anomaly, somewhat behind the times. But this overlooks the fact that the invention of Gutenberg gained a foothold in our regions only in 1473; and the fact that the stylistic characteristics, the use of frottons (with the corresponding watery ink, and the sheets printed so deeply through, that they could be printed on one side only, and had to be glued back to back) *etc* clearly enough shows that the older editions emerged before the art of book printing. We may assume that block books knew their finest hour in the Netherlands between about 1420 and about 1480, when they were effectively displaced from the market by the arrival of book printing.

The Netherlands block books belong to the most interesting and artistically most advanced product of European woodcut art in the 15th century. To list the principal ones, in more or less chronological order: *Apocalypsis Johannis* (6 different editions known, the oldest of which must have appeared around 1420; 48 pages with two woodcuts each); *Exercitium super Pater Noster* (one single edition known, *ca* 1420-1430; 10 woodcuts; Dutch texts in Flemish-Brabant dialects, written in by hand); *Biblia Pauperum* (11 somewhat differing editions known; the oldest *ca* 1420-1430; 40 to 50 pages according to the editions; only Latin texts); *Ars Moriendi (Dat Sterfboeck)* (four different printings and at least 17 editions; the oldest *ca* 1440-1445); *Exercitium super Pater Noster* (2nd edition, *ca* 1450; Dutch and Latin texts now cut in the blocks; probably carried out in Brussels); *Legend of St Servatius* (*ca* 1460; 12 pages and 24 woodcuts; in the context of the display of the saint's relics at Maastricht in 1461); *Speculum Humanae Salvationis* (4 prints: 2 with Dutch and 2 with Latin texts; *ca* 1460-1470); *Canticum Canticorum* (9 pages and 32 pictures; *ca* 1460).

Christus Salvator Mundi, wood-cut, illustration by the so-called 'wood-carver of Haarlem' for Ludolphus a Saxionia, *The book of the life of Our Lord Jesus Christ,* Antwerp, Gerard Leeu, 1488. Brussels, Royal Library.
The work contains about one hundred and fifty illustrations, made by the wood-carver of Haarlem, the second wood-carver of Gouda and the first wood-carver of Antwerp; of which many were already used in the first edition of Ludolphus, 1487, and in the *Suffering of our Lord,* Gouda, Gerard Leeu 1482.

die dꝛie gauē der ſielen.eñ vier gauen
des lichaēs:hier in hopen: die waſſen
moet inder toecomēber ſalicheit amē

Vanden blinden van bethlapde:
Dat lxxrix.capitel

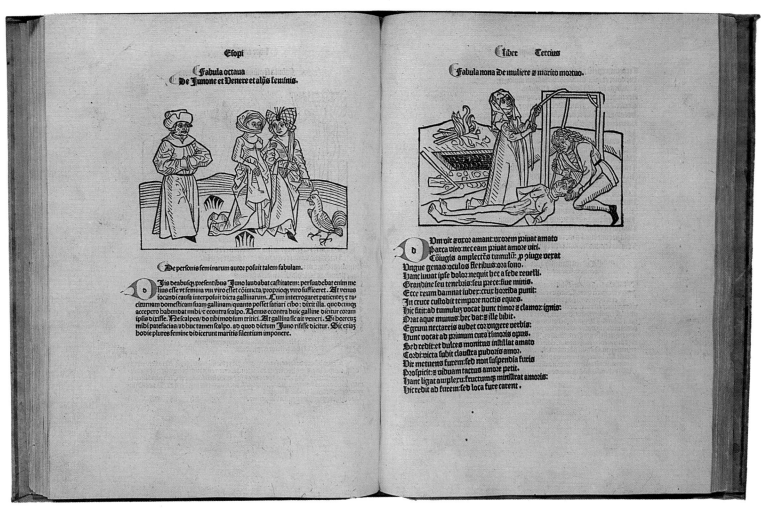

Double page from an incunable with on each an illustration, wood-cut, illustration from *Fabule er vita Esopi, cum fabulis Aviani, Alfonsi, Pagii Florentini et aliorum,* Antwerp, Gerard Leeu, 1486, Flemish-Brabant wood-carver, working after German patterns. Antwerp, Plantin-Moretus Museum.

THE WOODCUT IN THE BOOK ILLUSTRATION Typography came into being in the Netherlands in 1473, and already in 1475 Jacob Veldener published at Louvain the first book illustrated with woodcuts, the *Fasciculus Temporum* by Werner Rolevinck. He found many imitators. There would not be enough space to give the list of Netherlands incunabula in which woodcuts were included: there are several hundreds of them. Suffice it here to indicate that, as the purpose was to visualize the contents of a book, worldly subjects also got their turn, as well as religious ones; and that the focal point of book illustration (and of typography itself) was at the outset situated in the north, and shifted right at the end of the century to Antwerp, where Gerard Leeu, among others, was very active. Leeu may be regarded as the principal publisher of illustrated works in the time of the Netherlands incunabula; he was active from 1477 to 1484 in Gouda where he published some sixty works, and from 1484 to 1492 at Antwerp where he brought the total up to 150 publications – of both the Gouda and the Antwerp production, about half are illustrated, some of them very richly.

Without doubt there was also collaboration between designers (painters or miniaturists) and woodcutting craftsmen in the field of book illustration. But here too, no names are known in either category, so that the specialists have to make do with invented names: First Louvain woodcutter (1475), Utrecht woodcutter (1478-1480); First Gouda woodcutter (1480); Bruges woodcutter (1484); Second Gouda woodcutter (1484); Haarlem woodcutter (1484-1493; a very gifted artist who probably came to Antwerp in 1487-1488 where, until 1492, he provided almost all the illustrations for G. Leeu); First Antwerp woodcutter (1487-1488); Second Antwerp woodcutter, and others.

RELIEF PRINTING IN METAL: A RARELY USED TECHNIQUE Relief printing can also be done with metal (copper or iron). Experiments were made with this process in the 15th century, but it did not become very popular. Technically, it is in fact quite a job to cut away the backgrounds from the metal and leave only the outlines in relief (partly facilitated by leaving the whole very dark – and thus little cut out – and trying to achieve effects of light by only cutting away points: *la manière criblée*). From 1485 onwards, Parisian printers (beginning with Antoine Vérard) began to illustrate their breviaries with metal cuts; but the technique did not take off elsewhere. Loose prints – the so-called scrap pages – are less rare, but they raise a number of questions: all of them are unique pieces, only known in one single copy, and when a text appears on them it is in mirror writing. This gives rise to the assumption that these are not proper prints, but metal plates manufactured by gold and silversmiths with a specific purpose in mind (e g panels for reliquaries, etc) from which a 'rubbing' was taken to serve in the future as a model for similar products.

Whatever that may be, five of the earliest known scrap pages in Europe (around 1445) are strongly related in style, doubtless by the same master, and of very high quality; they may be situated in the Low Countries – one of them has a text in a Dutch dialect of the IJssel region. Some of them have a shield in which there is a heart with a Gothic d in it. But the Master with the Gothic d had hardly any successors in the Netherlands.

INTAGLIO PRINTING: LIMITED TO BURIN ENGRAVINGS AND LOOSE PRINTS   The future of graphics in metal in the Low Countries, as in the rest of Europe, belonged to intaglio printing; in the 15th century it was only represented by burin engraving, i e the engraving of lines on a metal plate (mostly copper) with a burin. These were the lines that retained the ink, while the ink was cleaned off the even surface which remained as a white background. Very fine work can be done with burin engraving, with many nuances (according to the depth of the lines engraved). It is a more refined form of graphics that the woodcut, but it was (and still is) a great deal more expensive, because of the costly medium (a carefully polished copper plate), and the much slower rhythm both in manufacture and reproduction of the prints (needing a special press with a rotary cylinder which, as it were, presses the paper into the engraved and inked lines). Nor is there any possibility here of applying the drawings directly on to the medium. Doubtless in this incunabula age of the burin print, many engravers worked on models from plastic artists; and it was the task of their steady and experienced hands to transfer these models to the metal with more or less precision and art.

Burin engraving, as the scrap pages, must have arisen in the circles of the gold and silversmiths. Around 1430-1450, burin prints begin to appear in Italy, in France (on a very modest scale), in Germany (strongly under Netherlandish influence) and in the Netherlands where – to judge from the style criteria – the oldest known examples can be situated, which bear witness to high quality: the Master of the Death of Mary opens the series ca 1430-1440 (ten prints known), followed by the Master of the Calvary, ca 1445 (nine prints known) and the Master of the Love Gardens, ca 1448 (seventeen prints known). From about 1450 onwards there is an increase not so much in the quality (already very high) as in the quantity, with the very gifted Master w with the Key (so called after the monogram used by him; ca 1450-1470; 83 prints known; probably active in Bruges) and Master FVB (for a time held by the Germans to belong to their country, and christened Franz von Bocholt – now just as arbitrarily rechristened Frans van Brugge; 59 prints known), flanked by figures of less significance (Master of the Banderoles; Master of the Martyr of the 10,000 – with texts in Limburg dialect; Master of St Erasmus; Master of the Dutuit-Mount of Olives, and others).

In the second half of the 15th century, Master IAM was working in Zwolle, and in the same region appeared the first burin engravers known by name in the Netherlands: Israhel van Meckenem the Elder (originating from Limburg or 's-Hertogenbosch; since 1457 at Bocholt) and his son Israhel van Meckenem the Younger (died at Bocholt in 1503; spent some time at Bruges in his youth; less productive than might appear from the 624 prints attributed to him, since he had the habit of getting hold of many plates by other engravers – including Master w with the Key and Master FVB – and putting his own monogram on them).

The burin engravings were intended for a sophisticated and wealthy public which, though it was probably no less devout than the buyers of woodcuts and block books, also had other interests. Apart from the religious subjects, the profane is now very well represented, sometimes with outspokenly frivolous pictures and humorous genre scenes. The copper illustration was very difficult to integrate in the printed book (a problem we shall take up in more detail in the chapter devoted to graphics in the 16th century). Nevertheless, Bruges can claim the credit of having produced the first known work in Europe illustrated with copper engravings: in 1476 Colard Mansion published the *Livre de la Ruyne des Nobles Hommes et Femmes par Jehan Bocace de Certald* with nine burin engravings. But whereas the Italians, from 1477 onwards, published a large number of illustrated works of this type, the Netherlands remained with only this one experiment by Colard Mansion, which moreover was only a half-hearted effort, since the prints were merely pasted up. Only in the 16th century the thread was picked up again, this time better served by technique.

Furniture

Did medieval furniture and interior design in Flanders fulfil a tone-setting function in the evolution of West-European art and culture? This and many other questions concerning Flemish furniture must be answered with circumspection and discrimination; not least because of the fact that in the present state of scientific research (into both archival sources and relics of the period in question) it is scarcely possible to compile a valid assessment of the situation regarding this branch of 'industrial art'. Investigation is further hampered by the numerous copies and forgeries which in the course of time (and especially in the recent past) have swelled our heritage of medieval furniture.

The most comprehensive information we have, is on the medieval corporations which engaged in the manufacture of furniture. In particular, the crafts of the cabinet-makers in the Flemish cities of Ghent and Bruges enable us, throught the archives that have been preserved, to obtain an idea of their work organization and production. The oldest records of the cabinet-makers date back to 1357 in Ghent, and to the second half of the fourteenth century in Bruges. Most of the documents in question relate to lawsuits between the Guild of Cabinet-Makers and other woodworkers. As the carpenters too were entitled to make some types of furniture, the two guilds' operations frequently overlapped, which gave rise to complicated legal proceedings.

To sum up the situation, the cabinet-makers had the exclusive right during the Middle Ages to make various kinds of furniture calling for special assembly techniques (such as square joints, grooves, panelling and gluing). From an agreement signed in 1481 between the Ghent cabinet-makers and carpenters, we learn that the latter had the right to produce "all manner of houses, doors, windows, portals, desks, and further beds, stools, partitions, and wall panelling made on and in walls". The Ghent carpenters were allowed to do this without gluing or sculpting, processes which were the province of the cabinet-makers and the sculptors respectively. From this can be drawn, albeit with a certain qualification, the conclusion that in the Middle Ages furniture for the ordinary people was produced by carpenters; while furniture for the nobility, the bourgeoisie and the clergy was supplied by cabinet-makers.

On the craft training of medieval cabinet-makers in Flanders, very few data are available. The oldest document on the subject comes from the Ghent Guild of Cabinet-Makers, who in 1447 issued provisions concerning the apprenticeship period and the making of a specimen: in order to acquire the status of master, a youngster had to serve a probationary period of four years, and then make a specimen consisting of a square piece of wood "with notches and holes as it behoved".

The Flemish furniture makers' sources of inspiration for techniques and decoration in the Middle Ages are not to be found anywhere in archivalia. Only in the second half of the 16th century, when theoretical books such as Serlio's work on architectonic theory (translated into Dutch and published by Pieter Coeke van Aelst) and Vredeman de Vries' *Différents pourtraicts de menuiserie* (ca 1580) became available, furniture manufacturers were provided with accurate examples. Possibly the medieval cabinet-maker's knowledge of forms and decoration was enshrined in a tradition that derived preponderantly from the architectonic constructions of the master builders.

From a structural point medieval furniture can be subdivided into two types: solid construction, *i e* where the walls are the main supporting element (mostly designated Romanesque in stylistic terms, although still found in the 15th century), and framework construction. Solid construction is characterized by a structure of thick solid wooden planks, joined together and reinforced by iron fittings. Framework construction consists of a skeleton of styles and rules which are assembled by means of a mortise and tenon, the non-structural parts being filled up (by insertion in a groove) with relatively thin panels mostly decorated on the outside.

There is a consensus that the use of relatively thin panels (2-3 *cm*) resulted from the invention of the saw-mill (published around 1250 by Villard de Honnecourt).

Tree-trunk box, 52 × 195 × 50 cm, 14th century. Antwerp, Vleeshuis Museum.
This trunk probably comes from the tower of Hulshout church.

Sideboard, 273 × 120 × 60 cm, Flanders, beginning of the 16th century. Brussels, Museums of Art and History.
The piece of furniture, which comes from the castle of Born near Sittard (Netherlands), is a rare example of a side-board which is arched over with a baldachin. The panels of the storage space, which are open-worked, and the panels of the back were alternately painted in green and red.

Seat, 100 × 110 × 65 cm, 13th century (?). Borgloon, Koolen Cloister.
This seat – which is generally known to be the seat of St Lutgardis – can be compared, as far as the form is concerned, with a late Romanesque or early Gothic seat from choir stalls.

Even so, most 14th-century and early 15th-century furniture displays a Romanesque style of construction. And it is not clear when framework construction was first applied in the designing of furniture. However, panel painting in the early 15th century offers a number of representations of furniture, which show the technical details and construction clearly, and reveal almost without exception framework construction. Must the origin of this type of construction be sought around the turn of the century (*i e* 14th to 15th)?

The panelling of framework construction has, in contrast with the unadorned structural parts, a fascinatingly decorative aspect. A first group – definitely the largest numerically – consists of linen folds. There are various opinions concerning the explanation of the ornamental motif. The usual explanation is that the medieval furniture maker endeavoured to imitate the jagged pattern of torn paper. Viollet-le-Duc felt that the

key lay in the folded-parchment (*Parchemin-plié*) aspect. A technical, but equally contested, version seeks the origin of the linen fold in the triangular form of the cleft wood (which at that time was cheaper than sawn wood).

A second group comprises panels adorned with tracery. This style is an imitation of Gothic window tracings cut from the heart of the panel. Some panels have an openwork (*ajour*) ornamentation, which demonstrates still more clearly the relationship with architecture. Such panels were for the most part affixed to a wooden, sometimes coloured, background. In some cases, too, heraldic coats of arms were inserted in between the tracery. In that connection, attention should be drawn to the not infrequent appearance of the 'Burgundian briquet' in panelling decoration – a clear reference to the Burgundians who at that time were ruling over Flanders.

A third group of panels is ornamented with x-forms (in French, *panneau à cuirs*). These adornments too are

Trunk, 62 × 16 × 63 cm, 14th century. Zoutleeuw, St Leonard's Church.
This trunk in massive building is decorated with nicely drawn down mount. Contrary to the primitive tree-trunk box, this piece of furniture already rests on four legs.

Trunk, 66.5 × 115 × 60.5 cm, Ghent, second half of the 15th century. Ghent, Bijloke Museum.
This is an example of massive building in the art of cabinetmaking of the Middle Ages: big, undecorated planks were joined by cold-weld. The construction is strenghtened by surrounding bail-bands. This trunk probably comes from St Georges' Guild at Ghent.

carved into the heart of the panel, and motifs in the form of foliage or bunches of grapes are set between the x-forms. Particularly noteworthy is the method employed; on most panels it is manifest how first of all a geometrical pattern (mostly lozenge-shaped) was drawn and then the ornament cut out with a gouge (in most cases gouge-marks are still clearly visible.)

Lastly, there is the group of panels in which a decor with representations of figures is carved out of the heart of the wood. For the most part these are iconographic representations of religious scenes. It may be assumed that such panels were found mainly in the 16th century, already heralding the Renaissance in furniture design.

Cradle, supposed to be of Emperor Charles, 83 × 145 × 75 cm, Flanders, end of the 15th century. Brussels, Museums of Art and History.
This is undoubtedly the nicest piece of furniture from the Middle Ages, that has been preserved in Flanders. The sides of the cradle have been painted with the coat of arms of the Duchy of Burgundy. At the bottom of the side the motto of Maximilian of Austria has been painted: 'Keep within bounds with everything'. On the two short sides, two letters M, which are joined by a love-knot, are painted. The double M refers to Maximilian and Mary of Burgundy. The cradle was presumably meant for one of their two children: either for Philip the Fair (born at Bruges in 1478), or for Margaret of Austria (born at Brussels in 1480). It cannot be said for certain whether the cradle has also served for Charles V (grandson of Maximilian of Austria).

Cabinet, 135 × 60 × 45 cm, end of the 15th century. Courtray, Our Lady's Hospital.
This cabinet is probably out of a beguinage.

The material from which the better types of furniture were made in Flanders in the Middle Ages, consisted almost entirely of indigenous oak. Ornamentation was predominantly in the form of low-relief carving and of iron overlay on hinges and handles, frequently wrought in a highly decorative fashion and hollowed out by filing. Although Gothic furniture in Flanders does not as a rule appear to have been coloured, there are a few exceptions, such as the legendary cradle of the Emperor Charles V and the late-Gothic sideboard from Sittard (both in the Museums of Art and History, Brussels).

Of the original medieval bourgeois interiors virtually nothing remains save fragments. By contrast, copious information on the 15th-century interiors is provided by the Flemish Primitives, who with a wealth of detail embodied Flemish interiors with their furniture in their panel paintings. From these we learn that the greatest amount of space in the interior was occupied by the chimney. This was set against the wall and consisted of high-rising cheeks, profiled on the front. At the level of the cowl the cheeks in many cases extended outwards, to form a small socle on which small objects could be placed. Frequently the profile on the front turned out to

be a sculptured diminutive head or figure. On the inclined mantle there was room for a rotary sconce. In the fireplace itself the firewood lay on elegantly wrought fenders. During the summer the fireplace was fenced off by a wooden draught screen secured by copper or iron latches. The wooden ceiling of the interior was supported by main girders and boarding joists. The walls were plastered whitish-grey, and the light entered through one or two openings in which a crossbar window was inserted. In its upper part the crossbar window contained glass in lozenged lead and the lower part was closed off by inward-swinging shutters which rotated on hinges. The floor consisted of small glazed tiles, usually in a chessboard pattern. The furniture was arranged in accordance with the requirements of the activities which took place in the interior.

The earliest reliable relics of Flemish bourgeois furniture date from the 14th century. Pride of place undoubtedly goes to the chest, this being the most convenient type of case furniture, easy to move about, relatively simple to construct and consequently cheaper than any other furniture. The chest served to store documents, clothing and household chattels, and in some cases even provisions. The most primitive chests were

Small cabinet, 100 × 61.5 × 25 cm, end of the 15th century. Antwerp, Vleeshuis Museum.
At the bottom of this cabinet there is a small drawer on which is inscribed: 'Sister Beel van Goer': an indication to the woman owner, probably a nun or a beguine.

Trunk, 74 × 118 × 57.5 cm, end of the 15th century. Bruges, Gruuthuse Museum.
This trunk is an illustration of how much influence medieval architecture had on the art of cabinet-making. Imitations of Gothic tracery were frequently used for decorating the panelling. The constructive parts of the trunk were mostly undecorated.

Seat of honour, 59 × 69 × 45.5 cm, beginning 16th century. Ghent, St Bavo's Cathedral.
The form of the seat of honour dates back to the early Middle Ages. The bended legs end at the top in a gilt apple and at the bottom in a dragon's head. The knots and traceries were originally gilded.

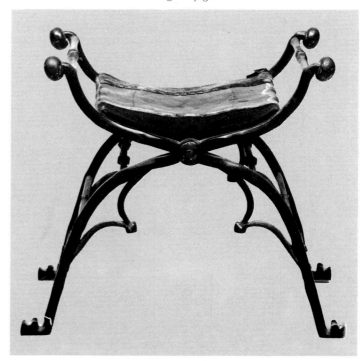

The Annunciation, painting (middle panel from the Mérode Tryptich),
Master of Flémalle, 1427/28. New-York, The Cloisters.
The scene of the Annunciation is enacted in a Flemish interior of the early
15th century. Remarkable in it are the flap-table and the bench, of which the
back can be adjusted.

Small trunk, 15.5 × 37.5 × 25.5 cm, beginning of the 16th century. Brussels,
Museums of Art and History.
This small trunk has on its lid the image of the Maiden of Ghent with the
lion. Around this representation the following inscription has been carved:
'Bear His suffering and sorrow in your heart'. The purpose of this trunk was
probably to keep the files of a guild of confraternity of Ghent.

hollowed out of tree trunks. The lid was fastened to the solid trunk with heavy hinges which, as a reinforcement against cracking, were riveted around the chest. Larger chests were of solid construction, heavy planks being joined together to form a rectangular chest, the structure of which was reinforced by wrought iron strapwork. Closure was usually effected by means of one or more locks. Particularly well-known are the heavy chests in which the municipal authorities kept their charters (Bruges, Ghent); these chests are conspicuous for their superabundance of strapwork and numerous locks.

The chests, which were of framework construction, testify to the decorative inventiveness of the medieval cabinet-makers: linen folds, x-forms and tracery panels impart to the 15th century chests and illustrative character which was already a far cry from the heavy, solid 14th-century article.

Apart from the larger chests, the 15th century was also marked by smaller examples, such as jewel caskets and document boxes. These were of wooden construction and in many cases adorned with leather covering and finely wrought strapwork. The most prestigious piece of furniture in the medieval interior was definitely the dressoir or buffet. Its outstanding feature was its uprightness. In the lower part of the dressoir was an open space, which usually accommodated flagons. The

Cabinet with two doors, 199 × 174 × 73 cm, beginning of the 16th century. Brussels, Museums of Art and History.
This type of cabinet with two wide doors and a door-post occurs at the end of the 15th century. It was constructed especially in the first half of the 16th century, and the panels were often decorated with Renaissance medallion heads. This cabinet comes from Lier.

upper part, which was partitioned off by small doors, served to store valuable tableware. Above the flat top there was room for a water basin and jug required for washing the hands after partaking of the fare.

There was a wide variety of dressoirs. The Bruges crafts' ordinance for 1462, when the Bruges Town Magistrate promulgated a set of rules governing the wages of cabinet-makers' journeymen, lists no less than ten different types of *driesore*. A unique example of the dearest variant, *i e* the one with a baldachin, is kept in the Museums of Art and History in Brussels. Less voluminous were the shallow wall closets, the principal use of which was for storing small objects of value such as documents and prayer books. In the late-Gothic period there emerged the armoire with two or more doors - a type that was to remain in use until well into the 16th century. These chests are characterized by exquisite ornamental panelling (predominantly linen folds) and handles wrought with exceptional skill.

Certain it is that at the beginning of the 15th century the bench with an adjustable backrest acquired a prominent place in the interior. The bench, frequently depicted in the works of the Flemish Primitives, had an open or closed underframe and was set before the open fire in the room. Users of this piece of seating furniture could sit either with the back to, or facing the open fire, as desired, by adjusting the backrest. Chill from the floor was avoided by using a footboard. A bench with a closed high backrest and armrests was placed against one of the walls. In very many cases these benches had a linen-fold ornamentation. Undoubtedly the most prominent types of seating furniture of that time were the three-legged stool and the *driestal* (a more sophisticated version with a high back style and a curved backrest). The slab-end stool was used either as a seat, an occasional table or a kneeling stool; its features being two slabs joined together below by a cross-rail and above by two rails in which religious motifs (such as the monogram of Christ or the Virgin Mary) were carved. If we are to rely on the representations bequeathed to us by 15th-century Flemish artists, the bed also had a leading place in interior decoration. Since no original examples have been preserved, our knowledge of the medieval bed is confined to such plastic representations. The Gothic bed was supported by a pedestal and was composed of a high bedstead and a canopy with overhanging curtains. The canopy was secured to the ceiling with ropes. When not in use, the front and side curtains were drawn back to the corners of the bed and tied together in a ham-shaped bag. Also known from that time are beds with a canopy resting on columns, and beds with a tester adorned by linen folds. There can be no doubt that such beds were possessed only by the better-off classes, who in this way affirmed their status. Most people in the Middle Ages, however, slept in immovable casements or alcoves, which in 15th-century Bruges were constructed not by cabinet-makers but by carpenters.

New-born babes slept in a cradle, usually a wicker basket or a small bed on two runners enabling it to be rocked. By way of exception, a 'state cradle' has been preserved in Flanders – the already mentioned legendary cradle of the Emperor Charles V. From a comparison

Choir stalls, second quarter of the 15th century. Bruges, St Saviour's Cathedral.
In this scenery a few ceremonies of the 13th Chapter of the order of the Golden Fleece took place in 1478.

with the late-Gothic crèches still extant, the construction of the unfinished Charles V cradle can be visualized: the cradle was suspended on an underframe ornamented with architectonic motifs. Its corners too were decorated with architectural imitations.

The medieval table was characterized by a considerable degree of mobility, consisting for the most part of loose planks which were laid on trestles so that they could be put away again after use. Known exceptions are more solid pieces such as the table in the Master of Flémalle's *Mérode Triptych*, which consists of a polygonal top resting on an underframe with slab-ends and runners. In some cases the flap is collapsible and the table can be pushed against the wall with the flap upright.

The lack of comfort during the Middle Ages was more than offset by the use of flexible, thick cushions. Valuable Italian silk fabrics were employed for this purpose. The use of Eastern rugs as floor coverings enhanced the impression of cosiness and luxury in the interiors of the later Middle Ages.

Not so well known, but unrivalled in splendour is the late-Gothic church furniture that adorned Flemish places of worship. This was mainly in the form of choir stalls for sung psalms and offices, which in a unique manner illustrate the cooperation between cabinet-makers and sculptors. These stalls, frequently in two rows, were set up in the choir with two long symmetrical wings against the sidewalls, and a short wing against the back of the organ loft. Each stall consisted of a collapsible seat and a tilting back topped by a circular rail. Between the stalls are intermediate supports. What distinguishes them more, however, is the exceptional artistic value of the sculpture with which they are ornamented: in addition to the architectonic adornments, there are in particular the homely, frequently mocking, diminutive figures and scenes which throw a totally different light on the medieval mentality and environment.

Tapestry and textile arts

TAPESTRY

TECHNIQUES AND USAGE Handwoven tapestries, known in the Middle Ages as *legwerk* and later as *tapisserie* were made on vertical (*haute-lisse*) or horizontal (*basse-lisse*) looms. The difference between these two sorts of weaving cannot usually be detected. In both cases the warp is completely covered by the woof, which determines the play of colours and the pattern of the ribbed weave. The tapestry weaver used cartoons made to the same scale as the woven fabric. The characteristic feature work was that the threads were only incorporated into the pattern, insofar as the design required it.

The cost of tapestry making was extremely high: the progress of weaving was very slow, and the raw materials, especially wool, but also silk, gold thread and silver thread were expensive. Nevertheless, many tapestries were produced and trade prospered in these articles. From the 15th to the 17th century, it was one of the most important industries of the Southern Netherlands. It was found in numerous towns, including Arras, Tournai, Audenarde, Brussels, Ghent, Lille, Edingen, Louvain, St Trond, Herentals, Antwerp, Bruges, as well as in the surrounding countryside.

In the 16th century tapestry weaving was introduced in a number of towns in the Northern Netherlands, often by emigrés from the Southern Netherlands, for example in Middelburg, Delft, Gouda, Schoonhoven. It was also brought by immigrants or by princes (who did not wish to be dependent on imports from the Netherlands) in a number of German principalities, in France

Deer-stalking, hanging (detail) from the series *Huntings from Devonshire*, 409 × 808 cm, Atrecht, about 1440. London, Victoria and Albert Museum.

St John is going to give a description of the visions, shown to him by the angel, to the seven churches of Asia, hanging from the series of the Apocalypse of Angers, about 150 × 230 cm, Paris about 1378, from designs of Jan Boudolf from Bruges. Angers, Castle.

An angel shows to St John the Great Whore of Babylon, symbol of the idolatry, hanging from the series of the Apocalypse of Angers, about 150 × 230 cm, Paris about 1378, after designs of Jan Boudolf from Bruges. Angers, Castle.

Message of the Angel, hanging, 345 × 290 cm, Atrecht, beginning of the 15th century, maybe after a design of Melchior Broederlam. New York, Metropolitan Museum of Art.

(Beauvais and the ateliers of the Gobelins in Paris), in Italy (Florence), Spain (Madrid) and in England (Mortlake).

Even before the 15th century the use of tapestries expanded considerably. They replaced embroidered hangings and silk brocade as wall coverings. A number of episodes from a particular theme would be depicted on four, eight or sometimes even twelve pieces, which together would decorate a chamber. At the court of the Dukes of Burgundy, the *tapissiers* were court attendants responsible for preparing the prince's *camere*, either at the royal residence or when he was travelling. This *camere* referred to a set of tapestries, wall hangings or wall coverings to furnish a room. The tapestries were also used for covering chairs and seats, as well as bedspreads, tablecloths and antependia or fireguards.

Geometric motifs, plants and indigenous or strange animals were depicted on the tapestries. Work containing hundreds of small flowers was known as *millefleurs* tapestry. Later, many tapestries showed landscaped gardens or woodland scenes. There were also many armorid tapestries; and from the beginning there were panels depicting tableaux from the life of Christ and the saints, scenes from the Old Testament, mythology and ancient history. There were genre tableaux, scenes from chivalric tales, and symbolic or allegorical representations. On the other hand, subjects taken from contemporary history were rare.

Visit of Fromons to Girart, hanging (detail) from the series *Gestures from Jourdain de Blaye,* 328 × 380 cm, Atrecht, about 1390-1400. Padua, Museo Civico.

THE ORIGINS The techniques used in tapestry-weaving date back to ancient times, and can be traced as far as Peru and Asia Minor. Coptic examples from the first centuries AD were found in fairly large numbers in Antinoe in Egypt. After the conquest of the Nile valley the Arabs learnt the technique and introduced it in Spain. The *St Gereon* panel from Cologne dates back to the 11th century and is the oldest piece of tapestry in Europe; fragments of it are now kept in Berlin, Nuremburg, London and Lyons. It was probably woven in a monastery in the Rhineland from a Byzantine model. Some characteristic western features include the connecting medallions, as well as the primitively drawn marks and the illustrations of vines. On the other hand, the repeated representation of the fight between a bull and a griffin is a distinctively oriental touch. The dark red and dark green primitive colours are predominant.

Fragments of tapestry dating back to the end of the

191

The Knight gives away his heart, hanging 247 × 209 cm, Atrecht, about 1400-1410. Paris, Musée de Cluny.

12th century were also found in Halberstadt, in lower Saxony. These fragments indicate that church buildings were already being decorated at that time with enormous and festive hangings. Three tapestries are now kept in Halberstadt Cathedral, *viz* the *Abraham* tapestry, the tapestry of the *Apostles* and the *Charlemagne* tapestry. The *Abraham* tapestry is probably the oldest, dating from *ca* 1175-1180, and incorporates the following biblical stories: the Angels visiting Abraham and his wife Sarah, the sacrifice of Isaac, the Archangel Michael fighting the dragon, and finally Jacob's dream. The latter piece has been lost, and is only known through an 18th-century painting. This Romanesque tapestry, more than one metre high and nine or ten metres long, used to hang as a dorsalia above the stalls of the choir of Halberstadt Cathedral. It is made of wool, but linen was used for the white parts of the composition, thus producing vivid contrasts. The work was finely and carefully woven, and the representation is very linear, with virtually no attempt at realistic poses and very little relief work. The antipathy to realistic representation, which is clearly expressed in the *Abraham* tapestry, is further emphasized by the fact that the weaver was not at all concerned with realism in his (or her) use of colour. For example, Abraham's beard is partly blue and partly white, and the donkey is completely red – apart from one yellow hind foot. The dark garments are edged with white and the white parts of the clothing contrast eerily with the tapestry's green background. The vivid outlines of the figures and their wooden movements are characteristic. The rigid, sometimes oval faces and the darkly outlined almond-shaped eyes are also noteworthy.

The fragment representing the *Months of April and May* from Baldishoel in Norway dates from about 1200. The composition is much more primitive than in the above-mentioned fragments. It is an example of local art.

THE GROWTH AND SPREAD   Most probably tapestries were being made in the castles and monasteries of Flanders as early as the 11th century. They were intended to fulfil a decorative as well as a practical function. Some of the inventories of Church institutions from that time mention hangings, but it is not always clear whether or not they refer to tapestries. Making these wall hangings was considered a fitting activity for a particular class of people. It was particularly the wives and daughters of the upper classes, and nuns, who occupied themselves with tapestry work.

By the 13th and 14th centuries the prosperity of the population had greatly increased and there were more rich and well-to-do-burghers. At the same time there

Discussion between Hector and Achilles in front of the tent of the latter, sixth hanging (detail) from a series with the *War of Troy*, 467 × 690 cm, Tournai, about 1472-1483. Zamora, Cathedral.

Julius Caesar as emperor in the senate shortly before the murder, fourth hanging (detail) from a series with the *History of Julius Caesar*, 432 × 750 cm. Tournai, about 1470. Bern, Historiches Museum.

The clipping of the sheep, hanging, 165 × 224 cm, Tournai, about 1460-1475. Brussels, Museums of Art and History.

Susanna and the Elders, hanging, 402 × 336 cm, Tournai, about 1500. London, Victoria and Albert Museum.

was a growing desire for more comfort and luxury. Women were still working at the loom; but by now men were also weaving because women were often unable to meet the demand for their work quickly enough. Unlike the women, whose weaving was often a way of passing the time, men worked day after day to earn a living. They usually came from the cloth weaving industry and therefore initially associated with the linen and wool weavers, though they only worked on tapestries. Later they formed a separate guild of craftsmen. This development had a great effect on production because all tapestry workers were henceforth obliged to be apprenticed for some time, and had to prove that they were skilled. Consequently the quality of tapestry work improved. This progress in the technical field can clearly be seen when one compares the tapestries from Swiss ateliers or from the Alsace region with the well-kown *Apocalypse of Angers,* the pieces of which were woven more than twenty years earlier.

Ferreting, hanging, 300 × 360 cm, Tournai, third quarter of the 15th century.
San Francisco, M. H. De Young Memorial Museum.

The representations used in the work also evolved. There was an increasing number of armorial and pictorial tapestries with a considerably greater number of figures. The cartoons for tapestries were still often produced by the weavers themselves; in certain cases artists were used. For example, the following artists were commissioned to make cartoons: Jean de Beaumez, Jan Maelwel, Melchior Broederlam and Jan Boudolf.

The well-known series which includes the *Apocalypse of Angers* was commissioned in about 1378 by Duke Louis of Angers from Nicolas Bataille in Paris. The cartoons were by the artist Jan Boudolf, from Bruges. Altogether there were seven tapestries depicting ninety representations, all concerning prophetic visions at the end of the world. Some of these gigantic tapestries are still kept at Angers. They bear witness to the technical and artistic skill of the tapestry weavers during the last quarter of the 14th century.

Nicholas Bataille was probably more a merchant than a weaver. The striking differences in the tapestries dating from the same time and delivered by the same merchant, might well be explained by the fact that the cartoons were sent to different workshops to be executed. It is obvious that every workshop would execute the cartoon according to its own insights and interpretation. It is therefore by no means certain that the whole series of the *Apocalypse of Angers* was woven in Paris. In view of the close relationship between Arras and the French capital, it is quite possible that if the Parisian workshops were temporarily overworked, a number of commissions would be passed on to workshops in Arras, and vice-versa. The tapestry merchants in Arras had their own warehouses and agents in Paris as well as in Bruges, and the French nobility preferred to buy tapestries from Arras in Paris, rather than directly from Arras.

Burgundian Coat of arms hanging, about 204 × 820 cm, Brussels, about 1470. Bern, Historisches Museum.

Emperor Trajanus on horseback with at his feet a mother begging for justice, hanging (detail) from the *History of Trajanus and Herkenbald,* 461 × 1053 cm, Brussels, about 1450-1460. Bern, Historisches Museum.

The art of Flemish tapestry-weaving spread across much of Europe. In a number of centres great efforts were made to start up a tapestry industry. The purchasers of these hangings did not usually know the weavers, though they did meet the merchants. This had an important effect on production. In many case the merchant became the weaver's source of income or employer. He exercised a careful and unrelenting technical control over the work produced, and checked to ensure he was making enough profit. He also instructed the weavers as to what theme or subjects should be used in the work. In addition, there was a great deal of competition amongst the merchants themselves, and this also increased the technical and artistic quality of the tapestry. In some towns, halls were even built where the work could be exhibited and sold. The tapestries were also sent to the annual markets, which were attended by merchants from different centres or by their representatives.

Up to then the weavers had worked quite independently, but now their freedom of action was considerably reduced as a result of the guild's regulations and municipal provisions; as well as by the high standards imposed by the merchants. Even the artists started to play a more important role, though the weavers tried to oppose this as far as possible. There was a wide range of subjects, the tapestries were now much larger than before and were usually made from costly materials. The ordinary weaver did not have the means to buy these expensive materials such as gold and silver thread, wool and silk. A skilled weaver would barely do more than a few square inches of his tapestry per day, as the weaving technique was an extremely lengthy process, and it would take a very long time to produce a complete set. The weaver was therefore usually an employee, or he tried to retain his independence and would have to limit his output to making cushion covers, horse blankets *etc.* The tapestry weavers' guilds of Bruges and Ghent were the oldest in the country. Mention was made of the Bruges guild as early as 1302. The guild in Ghent had a charter by 1350, while the weavers in Brussels did not form an independent guild until about 1445.

St Luke paints the Holy Virgin, hanging, 295 × 261 cm, Brussels, first quarter of the 16th century. Paris, Louvre.

Baptism of Christ in the Jordan, hanging from a series with *Scenes from the Life of Christ*, 200 × 175 cm, Brussels, beginning of the 16th century. Vienna, Kunsthistoriches Museum.

THE MAIN TAPESTRY CENTRES UP TO ABOUT 1515 ARRAS   The tapestry weaving centres of Flanders were concentrated particularly along the River Scheldt. The work was carried out in nearly all the old towns north of the present language border. Panels were also woven in Ath, Binche, Lessines and above all in Tournai, but Arras is usually considered to be the oldest and most important centre. The hangings made there were better known abroad than those from any other city, so much so that all tapestry in Italy was referred to as *arrazzo*, and in Spain as *drap de raz*. In English too, the word *arras* became synonymous with tapestry.

Arras had been an important centre for a long time. The wool industry had developed there over the centuries, and architecture, painting and literature flourished there at a very early date. Many prominent merchants trading in cloth lived in the city. It is possible that on their travels abroad they also took tapestries with them. In the neighbourhood of Arras also various plants were grown for dyes, so that a good supply of different colours was always available locally.

The period of great prosperity in Arras continued to some extent until about 1450, but then the city went into decline. The commission of Philip the Good in 1448-1449 for a series with the *History of Gideon* from a workshop in Tournai was, rightly or wrongly, considered to mark the beginning of the decline of the tapestry industry in Arras. In 1456 the municipals of Arras made an appeal to the Duke of Burgundy, complaining that many traders were moving to other towns in Hainault and Flanders. In 1477 the city was destroyed by the army of Louis XI, and this heralded the end of an art form that had flourished in the area. However, tapestries were still made in Arras after 1477, and in fact the looms continued to be in use until 1528.

There were many famous cloth merchants in Arras. They came from families of businessmen who held the most important posts in administration, dealing in and trading all sorts of goods including cloth and wine, and above all tapestries. It is incorrect to think of them as weavers. They passed the orders onto a number of small workshops which were working for them, and they had the necessary capital available, which was very important in this trade. There was always a large choice of woven panels to be found in their homes and warehouses. The most important merchant-tapestry-makers include Huart Walois (born before 1372) and above all Jean Walois, who is believed to have supplied about 1440 the *Devonshire Hunting Tapestry*, (London, Victoria and Albert Museum). There were also André de

Monchy and Michel Bernart. The latter sold a series of tapestries entitled the *Battle of Rozebeke* to the Duke of Burgundy in 1387.

Little is known about the artists who worked for the merchants and weavers of Arras, other than a chance remark in the bills of the Dukes of Burgundy. For example, Jean de Beaumez († 1396) made the cartoons for a tapestry called *The Twelve Apostles and Twelve Prophets*. Melchior Broederlam (born *ca* 1350) delivered a design for tapestries in the castle of Germolles depicting *Shepherds and Shepherdesses*. The design for an *Annunciation* (New York, Metropolitan Museum) could also have been his, as it is very similar to one of his panels in Dijon. Another important cartoon painter was Baudouin de Bailleul († 1464), who was highly praised by Jean Lemaire de Belges. In 1448/49 he produced the design for the above-mentioned *Gideon tapestry*.

Usually all the panels woven between the end of the 14th century and the middle of the 15th are attributed to Arras, but this is incorrect. However, we do know for certain that the *Battle of Rozebeke* was executed by Michel Bernart in Arras in 1387. This gigantic wall hanging was 56 ells (one ell = 27 inches) long and $7\frac{1}{4}$ ells high, it was repeatedly restored and finally lost over the course of the centuries. The last mention of it was in 1576 in an inventory of the Emperor Charles V in which it is described as '*fort vieille et fort usée*' (very old and very worn). Nevertheless, the Dukes of Burgundy were proud of the Battle of Rosebeke, where the rebellious Flemish were defeated by the French king Charles V and Louis van Male. They liked to see this triumph depicted often.

The archives reveal that the looms of Arras also produced tapestries with allegorical representations from works of poetry and chivalric romances, as well as hunting scenes and religious and biblical themes. All of these examples have been lost or have not yet been identified. For example, the *History of Alexander* disappeared. It was believed to have been offered to the Sultan as a ransom for John the Fearless. One set of tapestries consisting of two backcloths that have survived can be identified as work from Arras (Tournai Cathedral). It is a lively representation of episodes in the lives of St Piatus, who brought christianity to Tournai, and St Eleutherius, the first bishop of that city. A 17th-century transcription of a text on one of the fragments from this set, which has now disappeared, proves that these pieces were woven in 1402 in the workshop of Pierrot Feré in Arras for Toussaint Prier († 1437), a canon of Tournai and former almoner of Philip the Bold. The whole history with its dull colours and different scenes is shown on a single tapestry. The figures are short and stocky with almost caricatured faces, and are by no means elegant. The features of the individuals are barely distiguishable except in some of the lesser figures. They are depicted in rows, one above the other, leaving hardly any empty spaces. Neither the artist who made the cartoon, nor the weaver, made any attempt at a pictural composition. The abundance of figures and texts, the lack of any perspective and the extremely high horizontal line are not only characteristic

of work from Arras, but are typical of all the tapestries from the Southern Netherlands until about 1480. On the other hand, the rich architecture and the crowded background are not found in all hangings from other places. Other striking features include the many plain and blue lines in the sky running parallel to the warm to break up the monotony of the sky, and the fern-shaped and heart-shaped leaves and trees with gnarled trunks. There are also often shrubs and flowers in the foreground, water that seems to rise in flames, and paper-like boulders bordering the scenes along the edges.

In the tapestry with the *Saga of Jourdain de Blaye*, which is also believed to originate from Arras, there is much more detail in the landscape with trees and rocks. Some of the tapestries in the Musée des Arts Décoratifs in Paris, with hunting tableaux or with scenes from courtly life, are also believed to have come from Arras, as are the *Knight surrenders his heart* and the *Resurrection of Christ*; the latter two are in the Musée Cluny in Paris. All these tapestries incorporate the general stylistic characteristics not only of work from Arras, but of all work from that period.

TOURNAI   In the middle of the 15th century Arras was superceded by Tournai in the art of tapestry. This old medieval episcopal city played an important role, in ecclesiastical, political and cultural life. Its economy was greatly influenced by the stone quarries in the neighbourhood, which effected the great growth of architecture and even the building throughout the Scheldt basin. Tournai was a very important artistic centre, with a great development of sculpture and painting during the 14th and 15th century. Tapestry-weaving in Tournai can justifiably be dealt with under the heading of Flemish tapestry

There is little information available about the origins of tapestry-weaving in Tournai. Documents dating back to the end of the 13th century already mention tapestry-makers. At the beginning of the next century weavers were producing cushion covers decorated with birds, lions and savages. However, these could hardly be considered as works of art. The question remains whether good quality tapestries were produced in Tournai before the 15th century. The fact that the *History of Piatus and Eleutherius* was commissioned by a canon of Tournai from a workshop in Arras in 1402, suggests that the workshops in Tournai itself did not amount to much at that time.

From about 1433 onwards the tapestry industry expanded enormously. Beautiful and costly tapestries were woven, but towards the end of the 15th century there was a period of decline, which resulted from competition with Brussels. The epidemic of plague which hit Tournai in about 1513 contributed to the demise of the tapestry industry. The weavers and merchants in Tournai undoubtedly did their best to retain their customers and even made gifts to prominent figures, including Margaret of Austria, in the hope of enticing tapestry lovers back to their city. They were unsuccessful, and during the period of religious unrest many weavers even moved away to other areas. Nevertheless, mention was made of the weavers and tapestry work in

The Passion, hanging, 424 × 911 cm, Brussels, about 1460-1480. Brussels, Museums of Art and History.

St John takes leave of his parents, hanging (detail) from a series with the *History of John the Baptist,* 348 × 400 cm. Brussels, beginning of the 16th century. Madrid, Crown Collection.

Tournai during the latter half of the 16th century and even in the 17th century. By attracting workers from other cities they tried to give a new lease of life to this age old industry, but the attempts fell on stony ground.

The outstanding master weavers of Tournai produced some first class work. For example, Robert Dary († after 1458) collaborated with Jehan de l'Ortie from 1449 to 1453 on the *History of Gideon,* a series woven through with gold thread, and based on designs of Baudouin de Bailleul. It took four years to make the eight large tapestries. This set was made to decorate the assembly hall of the Golden Fleece, and was kept in Brussels until the 18th century. In 1794 it was transported to Vienna to protect it from the victorious French troops who were about to enter the country. Since then the pieces have vanished.

One of the most important merchant-tapestry-makers was Pasquier Grenier († 1493). He started working in about 1447 but the period of his greatest activity was between 1460-1477. After 1479 his contacts were mainly with France. At that time he was a wine merchant and it is possible that he was trading hangings for wine. Pasquier Grenier traded in Bruges, Antwerp, Lyons and the Auvergne, and had a factory in Paris. He was not a weaver and is always referred to in documents as a '*marchand de tapisserie*'. Through his intervention a number of famous series of tapestries were procured by the House of Burgundy. In 1459 he sold Philip the

199

Message of the Angel with painted the coat of arms of Hans Tucher from Nuremberg, hanging, Brussels, 1486. Nuremberg, Germanisches National-museum.

Good a *History of Alexander*, in 1461 a tapestry representing *The Passion of Our Lord*, and also a piece depicting *Woodcutters*. A year later he supplied the Duke with a *History of Esther and Assuerus* and a *Knight with the Swan*. When Charles the Bold succeeded his father in 1467 he received a series of tapestries from the magistrate of the *Brugse Vrije* depicting the *History of Troy*. This set was also supplied by Pasquier Grenier.

The best tapestry work from Tournai is justifiably connected with this merchant, as in the case of the above-mentioned *History of Alexander*. Two pieces of this tapestry are still kept today in the *Palazzo Doria* in Rome. These monumental hangings made of wool and silk are richly decorated with gold and silver thread. The first of these depicts the heroic acts in the youth of Alexander, while the second shows the campaigns and fabulous deeds of this conqueror.

The *Caesar tapestries* in Berne, which were once praised as being the most beautiful wall coverings of that period, as well as the *History of St Peter* in Beauvais, were also woven in Tournai. There is no essential difference from the Arras work in these tapestries, crowded with many figures and often showing a number of scenes which merge together with high rows of trees, mountain tops or buildings reaching almost to the upper edge of the tapestry. However, there were developments: there were more round leaves than before and the plants were more systematically incorporated into the composition.

At the beginning of the 16th century a very narrow border was sometimes used round the central picture. Styles of tapestry had evolved considerably and the similarity between work from Tournai and Brussels was much greater. Some of the more striking features included the sculptured pleating of garments, and hats crowned with large ostrich feathers. There were still some important workshops in Tournai. In 1504 Jehan Grenier († 1520), the major successor of Pasquier Grenier, produced a series of tapestries entitled *à la manière de Portugal et de l'Indye*. It was inspired by the voyages of discovery of the day and was very popular with the aristocracy. Clemens Sarrasin was another founder figure of a dynasty of weavers working in about 1504. His hangings included armorial tapestries and a *History of Hercules*. There are references to Arnold Poissonier, also known as de Visscher, from Audenarde, working in Tournai in 1491. In 1510 he sold Emperor Maximilian of Austria a set of tapestries for a room which depicted the *Triumph of Julius Caesar*. When he died he left about 3,000 square ells of tapestry, including a series of *Judith* and a *History of Carrabara*.

AUDENARDE   Meanwhile tapestry work had blossomed in many other towns in Flanders. During the 15th century even Audenarde became an important centre, although most of the workshops were second rate. The tapestry-makers tried to eliminate painters as far as they could, and to use the expensive cartoons they had already acquired as long as possible. Many weavers were working there, and they had already formed a separate craft guild in 1441. The number of apprentices per workshop was restricted to three, which is an undeniable indication of the industry's growth. The weavers were not only working in Audenarde, Pamele and Bevere, but also in about ten neighbouring villages. Even farmers and their families would work at the loom in their spare time and make wall coverings for merchant-tapestry-makers at a very reasonable rate; this led to an enormous production. The farmer would go into town on Sundays and holidays to deliver the work and take home fresh commissions. These country weavers were typical of the Audenarde region.

Mass of St Gregory with the coat of arms of Franz Holzschuher from Nuremberg, hanging, 280 × 235 cm, Brussels, 1495. Nuremberg, Germanisches Nationalmuseum.

BRUSSELS During the first half of the 15th century many panels were woven in the workshops of Brussels, although no work from this period has survived. The *Trajanus and Herkenbald* tapestry came off the loom between 1450 and 1460. This work was based on the *Tableaux of Justice* by Rogier van der Weyden, which adorned the Town Hall of Brussels at the time. The composition of *The Adoration of the Magi* in Berne is also reminiscent of this Brussels artist. The great *Passion tapestry* (Brussels, Museums of Art and History) is probably from the workshop of Gilles van de Putte in the capital. The archaic representation of trees, plants and rocks dates it around 1460-1480. In addition, there are some similarities with regard to the way in which flowers are arranged in the foreground. Documents have shown that the armorial tapestry of Charles the Bold (Berne) was woven by Jan de Haze. He was in charge of a fairly large workshop in Brussels and was also a well-known merchant like Pasquier Grenier in Tournai. His armorial panel dating from *ca* 1470 is a striking illustration of the type of work produced in Brussels during that period. It shows how some motifs and stylistic characteristics were not limited to particular workshops in a particular town, but were common to all Flemish tapestry.

After 1480 Brussels expanded to become the most important centre for tapestry-weaving in the Southern Netherlands. It continued to be so until the end of the 18th century; this was especially because of its favourable position, the large number of trained weavers and the extraordinary development of painting and of various other branches of the arts, which had a beneficial effect on the art of tapestry making.

The work produced in the years 1480-1490 was stylistically very similar to the carved retables dating from that period. The weaving and the finished tapestries were very precise and regular. The technical progress that had been made can be seen in the attempt to incorporate more detail and to depict the figures in a more naturalistic style. Typical examples include the *Allegory of the Holy Virgin as a source of living water* and the *Annunciation*, (Paris, Louvre). The cartoons for these tapestries have been attributed respectively to the Master of the Embroidered Foliage and the Master of the Redemption of the Prado. The composition of the figures within the frame of a retable seems rather illogical. Flowers are anew used in the foreground to complete the composition.

Towards the end of the 15th century there was a reaction against these pictorial tendencies and a monumental style of tapestry weaving developed which continued to be fairly popular until the Italian influence took Brussels by storm. In the first group we find all

History of Herkenbald, hanging (without borders) 387 × 430 cm, Brussels, 1513 from the atelier of Leon de Smet after a design of the painter Philips. Brussels, Museums of Art and History.

kinds of textile ornaments in the tapestries. In a *Mass of St Gregory*, dating from 1495 and containing the coat-of-arms of Franz Holzschuher from Nuremburg, these ornaments are repeated on the floor, on the altar and in the clothing of the figures. The tapestry is also surrounded by a narrow border decorated with gems. A panel showing a scene from the *Life of John the Baptist* (Madrid, Crown Collection) belongs to a second group. These were the so-called 'golden tapestries' which incorporate a lot of gold and silver thread. Finally, there was a third group of a series of tapestries from the entourage of Jan van Roome. He was a painter from Brussels who lived at the end of the 15th century and the first decade of the 16th. The panel depicting the *History of Herkenbald* is based on a design of this artist. It was commissioned in 1513 by the brotherhood of the Holy Sacrament in Louvain, and was woven in the workshop of Leon de Smet in Brussels. The border is decorated with flowers and clusters of grapes and with the symbols of the Holy Sacrament. There is little depth in the composition, which is more decorative and more logical than earlier work. The figures are exceptionally majestic in their long, flowing robes with their deeply sculpted folds. The various scenes are separated from each other by pillars. Another hanging (Brussels, Museums of Art and History) also belongs to this group of tapestries. It depicts the *Discovery of the Cross*. The name KNOEST, shown on the threshold of the building, is the name of the Brussels artist Leonard Knoest, who designed the cartoon for the panel. All of the tapestries still have an individual style. They are not paintings of wool and silk, like for example the fourth tapestry in the series, which depicts the *Legend of Our Lady-of-Zavel* (Brussels, Museums of Art and History). The composition of this work is in the form of a tryptich, and borrows a lot from the art of panel painting. The design is attributed to Barend van Orley and is believed to date from 1517. There seems to be some justification for referring in the 16th century to woven paintings or *tapitsen*.

CARPETS

In the east it was an age-old custom to spread out tapestries on the floor for important occasions. It is quite possible that crusaders, well-to-do diplomats and pilgrims brought back some of these floor coverings to the west. Here they were also used as a mark of honour, sovereignty and wealth; and at the same time they were also valued for their practical and decorative qualities.

Oriental carpets were already imported into Europe from the beginning of the 14th century. Towards the end of the century Turkish and Armenian merchants were granted a licence to trade in carpets on the square in front of St Donate's Church in Bruges. From that point on, interest in these works of art increased and as a result, a thriving trade in imports by Italian merchants developed. Anybody who possessed valuable oriental carpets would be considered to be well-to-do. These carpets were frequently presented to the aristocracy as gifts. In about 1543 Pieter Coecke visited Constantinople, maybe commissioned by the Brussels tapestry-maker Willem der Moyen. It is possible that he hoped

to learn more about the knotting techniques for Turkish carpets, which were already being copied in the Netherlands and sold in the Antwerp merchants' hall.

In the late Middle Ages carpets were being made in a number of towns in Flanders. Initially the decoration was plain and the motifs were very simple. However, during the 15th century they became richer and more complex, though the flat character was retained. Even so, it cannot be denied that oriental carpets had an influence on some of this work, and that they were even faithfully copied. In other carpets the local decoration was used. Paintings by Jan van Eyck, Petrus Christus and Hans Memling, all masters of the Bruges school, often depict carpets which can be identified as oriental carpets, although some experts consider them to be local.

Madonna with Child, painting (middle panel); 27 × 21.5 cm, Jan van Eyck, 1437. Dresden, Gemäldegalerie.
The carpet in front of the throne of the Madonna is decorated with lozenges, which are mutually connected by circles. According to K. Erdmann, van Eyck has depicted this carpet in several of his works, and therefore one can assume that perhaps it was a private possession of the artist. Up till now, one has not been able to find a similar work. Some suppose that it is a Caucasian carpet, but this have never been proved. Perhaps it is a Flemish carpet?.

  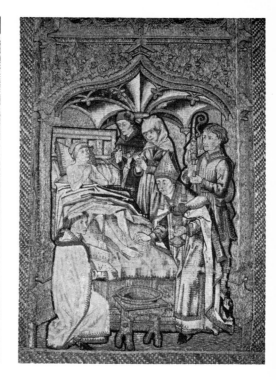

At the left: *The Baptism* and at the right *The Holy Unction,* embroidery (detail) of a cope representing the Seven Sacraments, Flemish, middle of the 15th century. Bern, Historisches Museum.
The representation resembles closely to the painting of the same name by Rogier van der Weyden (Antwerp, Museum of Fine Arts).

St Levinus seated on the throne with in front of him Abbot Hughenois, seated on a praying-stool, embroidered shield of a cope, 57 × 55 cm, Ghent, between 1517/18 and 1534. Ghent, St Bavo's Cathedral.

EMBROIDERY

In the past embroidery has been more successful than any other branch of art industry, with the possible exception of jewellery making. At the peak of the Middle Ages embroidery was done in castles and in patricians' houses, and above all in monasteries, both for domestic use and for local trade. However, from the 13th century onwards skilled craftsmen, both men and women, were working as embroiderers. In some towns these 'painters with the needle' soon formed guilds, which noticeably increased the quality of the work. In Antwerp and in Ghent they formed part of the St Luke's Guild. In Bruges and in Brussels there were enough embroiderers to form their own guild.

Ecclesiastical vestments were often decorated with embroidery, as were the cloths of the aristocracy and the nobility, heralds and guards; banners and sashes were often enhanced with costly embroidery. Even the rooms were decorated with embroidered tapestries or paintings. In some cases the painters made the designs for all these decorations, which meant that their style was reflected in the work. In others the embroiderers were inspired by the work of the Flemish Primitives. The cope with the *Seven Sacraments* (Berne, Museum) from the middle of the 15th century resembles closely the Rogier van der Weyden painting of the same name. Often high sums were spent to embroidery. In 1425 Philip the Good challenged the Duke of Gloucester. As a preparation to the duel, he spent 15,000 pounds. More than three quarters of the sum were used for embroidery. Not only did he count on a victory in the actual battle, he also wanted to outdo his rival with pomp and circumstance.

Little is known about embroidery in Flanders during the Burgundian period. It may have been decorated with animals and with garlands of leaves and flowers. During the 14th century it was common to find figures on canopies. The oldest surviving work is a pluviale dating from about 1300 on which the shield is decorated with a *Calvary* and the sashes with the *Martyrdom of the Apostles.* It is known as English embroidery, which was famous throughout western and southern Europe during the 13th and 14th centuries. Up to 1889 it adorned the Church in Harelbeke, and it is now kept in the Museums of Art and History in Brussels.

During the 15th century embroidery was generally of a higher quality than the so-called *opus anglicanum.* The most noteworthy embroidery dating from this or any other period were the so-called *vestments of the Order of the Golden Fleece,* done in a lazur technique and richly encrusted with pearls and gems. They were probably made in a workshop in Brussels, and were first mentioned in the inventory drawn up after the death of Charles the Bold in 1477. At this time the vestments were kept in two trunks at the house of the treasures of the Golden Fleece in Ghent. They were later transferred to Brussels where they remained until the end of the 18th century. They were then moved to Vienna to protect them from the conquering French army, where they can still be found in the *Schatzkammer.* The vestments are a complete set that was used during church services and consisted of eight pieces: two antependia, of which one was used in front of the altar and behind the candlesticks, three copes or pluvials, one chasuble, one dalmatic and one tunicle. The antependia are executed in the tradition of medieval altar triptychs with a large central composition flanked by two smaller side panels. Different painters such as Jan van Eyck, Robert Campin and Rogier van der Weyden are mentioned in connection with these vestments, although there is no clear indication who actually made the cartoons.

205

Metalwork

ANTECEDENTS AND GENERAL DATA The antecedents of medieval metalwork in the Southern Netherlands are on the one hand the known prehistoric metal cultures from the bronze and the iron age; and on the other hand the Gallo-Roman occupation, in which the working of metal – and especially of bronze – played an important role, and of which quite a number of traces have also been found in Flanders. The study of these oldest metal objects, and of those in the following Merovingian period – almost exclusively burial gifts, such as weapons and jewellery – is still classified as belonging to the field of archaeology. But we find that from the Carolingian period onwards, the custom of burying the deceased with his possessions ended; and that the artistic results of metalwork were no longer to be found in the form of burial gifts, but as liturgical work in bronze and precious metals in the abbeys of that time. It is logical, and also possible to assume from the written sources, that the great Carolingian abbeys already possessed a wealth of liturgical objects; and that there were also gold, silver and coppersmiths among the monks. Yet no important metal objects from this period (9th and 10th centuries) have come down to us. The first material witnesses to the monumental art of metalwork in the Southern Netherlands date from the Romanesque period, when the gold and silversmiths' work could not be distinguished from that of coppersmiths, neither artistically, creatively nor corporatively; at a time when it was not so much Flemish, but rather Maasland art, with some great masters in metalwork, who set the standard for Europe. So let us split up the following discussion of Flemish medieval metalwork, *i e* Romanesque and Gothic metal work, into some product groups according to the four most important sorts of metals: copper, iron, pewter and silver.

Statue in silver of an Our Lady-shrine with the Salvator Mundi, Master Gufkens, beginning of the 15th century. Tongres, Our Lady's Church.

Baptismal of St Germanus' Church at Tirlemont, Maasland 1149. Brussels, Museums of Art and History.

COPPER AND BRONZE

The most important copper artworks from Romanesque Flanders are, without a doubt, the so-called 'Hansa' dishes or merchants' dishes (11th-12th century), which were found at Duffel and Ghent; and the baptismal font of 1149, still decorated with primitive and stylized figures, from St German's Church at Tirlemont, now preserved in the Museums of Art and History, Brussels. These are all anonymous products of an artistic activity still in the development stage, while more especially the Tirlemont baptismal font may be regarded as the work of an indigenous bronzefounder or bellfounder.

From the Gothic period onwards, when the new style, taking its cue from France, also began to manifest itself in metalwork – both in the figurative and decorative aspects – gradually more and more traces are found in Flanders and Brabant of an independent production; although for certain commissions recourse was still had to the Maasland masters and workshops. For Flanders, where Gothic burial art was to become an important field for the application of both cast and engraved copperwork, the most important metalworking centres were the Scheldt towns of Tournai and Ghent, as well as Bruges which acted as a world market for *dinanderie*. The most important Brabant centres of Gothic copperworking were Brussels, Malines and Louvain. Particularly in the last phase of the Gothic, all three of them grew into very productive and artistic metalworking towns.

Eagle, 178 cm, Tournai, atelier of Parent of Poulette, 1411. Tournai, St James' Church.

Choir lectern, end of the 15th century. Tirlemont, St Germanus' Church.

Apostle-figures, about 23 cm, detail of the baptismal font by Guillaume Lefèvre, 1446. Halle, St Martin's Church.

That the Gothic copper or brassfounding tradition got going very early at Tournai – in the 13th century already – is found from the archival testimonies of cast monuments, engraved brasses or tombstones with copper inlay work. For Ghent and Bruges also, particularly from the 14th century onwards, we find written records of the presence – and presumably also the manufacture – of brasses; which also – under the label of Flemish or Bruges school – were exported to distant towns and lands, mostly in Hanseatic Europe. Thus we can still find Flemish or Bruges Gothic brasses in West and East Germany, Poland, Finland and England, as well as in France, Italy, Portugal and Spain. The oldest remaining examples in Flanders itself date from the 14th century. For Ghent these are the monumental brasses in the Bijloke Museum of Willem Wenemaer and Margaretha Sbrunnen, who died respectively in 1325 and 1352; for Bruges the fragments of the brass of Gillis van Namain, from around 1350, in St Jacob's Church. Of the high Gothic sepulchral copper exported from Flanders, one of the most remarkable examples is the brass, adorned with a recumbent metal image of the deceased, of Bishop Hendrik van Bocholt in Lübeck Cathedral, dated 1341.

An equally successful product of the Flemish copperfounders' art, which also found an important sales market abroad (together with many other items of metal church furnishings – baptismal fonts, candlesticks, chandeliers, choir screens and the like) was the medieval lectern, mostly executed in the form of an 'eagle lectern' with a realistic eagle on foot with its wings outspread. Already at the end of the 14th century, the copperfounders' workshops of Tournai produced a large number of copper lecterns; an example of which, dated 1383, may be found in the Musée de Cluny in Paris. Other places abroad where Flemish Gothic lecterns may be found are Norwich in England, Cordoba in Spain and Vizeu in Portugal.

Already from the 15th century onwards, more and more names of master copperfounders and copperworkers, as well as their documented or signed products, have come down to us. Leading metal artists in Tournai at that time were Jehan Parent and Guillaume Lefèvre

to whom, respectively, we owe an eagle lectern of 1411 in St Jacob's Church at Tournai itself, and a magnificent baptismal font of 1442 in St Martin's Church at Halle.

Important names of 15th-century copperworkers for Ghent and Bruges respectively – although none of their works have been preserved – are Jan van Abeele and Thomas Huppyn. An eagle lectern of 1484, probably from Bruges, adorns St Martin's Church at Chièvres.

For the great Brabant copperwork centres of Malines and Brussels too, several names of artists are known to us; evidently together with a number of anonymous pieces, such as the Brabant late 15th-century pelican lectern from St German's Church at Tirlemont. Jan Fierens from Malines, at the end of the 15th and the beginning of the 16th century, supplied two late Gothic masterworks for St Bavo's Church at Haarlem: a monumental pelican lectern, and a choir screen decorated with elegant copperwork. Even in the second quarter of the 16th century, namely in 1527, the Malines metal artist Gillis van den Eynde made a baptismal font in late Gothic style for the church at Zutphen in Holland. The Malines art of copperfounding and bellfounding – which gained steadily in fame – was maintained at a high level, both as regards quantity and quality, by other members of the artists' families van den Eynde,

Cauthals and De Clerck. The late medieval production of Brussels as metalworking centre has left us two great names in particular: Jacques de Gérines and Renier van Thienen, both of whom, according to both archival and monumental testimonies, were particularly meritorious in the casting of fully plastic copper images – mostly after models supplied by carvers.

A considerable amount of copper sepulchral sculpture by these Brussels metal masters has disappeared in the course of time – mostly back into the crucible. But there are three funerary groups (or parts thereof) which still bear witness to the high level of late Gothic style, and the artistic perfection which distinguished the Brussels brassfounders' school: the ten grave statuettes of princes and princesses from the Rijksmuseum in Amsterdam, that have been connected with the work of de Gérines; the mausoleum of Mary of Burgundy in Our Lady's Church at Bruges, designed, cast and gilded respectively by the three Brussels artists Jan Borman, Renier van Thienen and Pieter de Beckere; and the statue of Isabella of Bourbon, mother of Mary of Burgundy, in Our Lady's Cathedral at Antwerp, which cannot be ascribed either to Gérines or to van Thienen, but is attributed to the Brabant school. Another masterwork in copper by Renier van Thienen is the monumental

PEWTER AND WROUGHT IRON WORK

As compared with the copper industry, much less is known about the industry of lead and tin in medieval Flanders. It should be pointed out that in the alloying of a copper work of art, there is usually a quantity of tin – and in the case of brass also a quantity of zinc – present; and that in the metal alloying of a tin object, according to the quality and suppleness of the tin, there is a greater or lesser quantity of lead. One of the oldest remaining examples in Flanders of this tin and lead art is the Romanesque lead candlestick with equestrian figures from *ca* 1200, which was excavated at Bruges and is now preserved in the Gruuthuse Museum. But another similar example was found in a neighbouring country, so here it is only with reserves that we can assume a Flemish manufacturer.

Apart from these examples of medieval light fittings, it can be stated that tin was used particularly as a raw material for eating and drinking implements. In any case, tin kitchen and tableware was a more expensive and less fragile alternative to earthenware in the household. Even liturgical objects such as chalices, patens, ampullae and chrismatoria were often executed in tin as a cheaper alternative to the silver plates and dishes used in worship.

From the Middle Ages themselves there are in Flanders – apart from the written source materials, such as the assays of the tinsmiths who were generally grouped

Sepulchar statues, so-called mourners, coming from the mausoleum of Isabella of Bourbon, South Brabant, 1476. Amsterdam, Rijksmuseum.
From left to right: Albrecht of Bavaria, 1336-1404 (Pseudo Willem VI of Holland); Pseudo Margareta, queen of Sicily († 1479); Pseudo Philips of Nevers († 1415); Female figure with linen cap; Pseudo Jan IV of Brabant, 1403-1427; Female figure with head-dress in V-shape.

Romanesque candlestick, Flanders or the north of France, ca 1200 (?)/ Found by re-paving at Bruges in 1877. Bruges, Gruuthuse Museum.

Easter candlestick, decorated with plastic and dramatically charged statuettes, of 1482-1483 in St Leonard's Church at Zoutleeuw. In the latter church, we can also find some equally beautiful examples of functional late Gothic church metal. Finally, in seeking for the authors of the many copper works from the late Middle Ages that have remained anonymous, both liturgical objects as well as profane or domestic – kettles, combs, dishes, basins, candlesticks, *etc* – we must take account of the fact that a large number of Walloon coppersmiths or *dinandiers* settled in Flanders in the 14th and 15th centuries. Examples are Jean Josès from Dinant, who went to work at Tongres around 1370; Symoen Noël and Jan de Brouwers from Bouvignes who went to live at Antwerp in 1471; and the whole colony of Dinant coppersmiths who, after the devastation of Dinant in 1466, went at the invitation of Pieter Bladelin to settle at Middelburg in Flanders.

in the guilds of smiths, and other corporative texts – very few tin objects that have come down to us. Here and there, as in art collections from Ghent, Antwerp and Bruges, there are still some rare examples of the rectangular or round tin cutting-boards – the so-called *teljoren* – to be found. But most of the examples that have been conserved already date from after the Middle Ages. A few rare examples of tin flagons or beakers from the late Middle Ages are still to be found in the museums of Ghent and Audenarde; while in the Gruuthuse Museum at Bruges we can still find a presumably Flemish tin water-bottle from the end of the 15th century with a lion hallmark. But it is only from the style period after the Middle Ages that more and more tinware has been preserved with marks that allow it to be located.

The metal industry which was least rapidly affected by the developments of time and style, is without doubt the art of wrought iron. Works of art in iron are very difficult to date and to locate, partly because of their very functional character and the less rapid development of their design – except in the case of iron fittings on furniture and woodwork, the dating of which poses less problems. The most beautiful examples of door fittings in Flanders are found on the churches at Tongres and Halle and the town halls of Brussels and Louvain. On the other hand, doors completely in wrought iron are found in the former treasury of the Bruges belfry. This Bruges ironwork, still in the early Gothic style, dates from the end of the 13th century and, according to the town accounts, was made by a smith with the name of Erembald.

Other examples of constructional ironwork were anchoring parts and crowning elements such as crosses, weathervanes, window bars and parapets, locks, handles and doorknockers. Not very many of the pieces that have been preserved of these iron elements, most of which are strictly architectural, can with certainty be attributed to the Middle Ages. On the other hand, the wrought iron crowning of the so-called Metsijs draw-well in Antwerp with its exceptionally decorative shapes, although it represents the late Gothic, probably dates already from the beginning of the 16th century.

Concerning lighting fittings in wrought iron, and the very varied kitchen and hearth ironwork – apart from the more ordinary examples – we can point to some masterworks in Flanders; for example, the late Gothic

Ornament of an andiron with a bronze lion's head carrying a scutcheon. Anonymous brass-founder, beginning of the 15th century. Bruges, Town Hall.

Present-pitcher of Ghent, non-identified tinsmith of Ghent, end of the 15th century. Ghent, Bijloke Museum.

devotional chandelier from around 1500 in the Bishops' Chapel of St Bavo's Cathedral in Ghent, and the Burgundian waffle irons of the 15th century in the Gruuthuse Museum at Bruges. Both in Ghent and Bruges we still find a few characteristic examples, not very decorative but efficient, of iron canons or late medieval 'bombards'. Also in the iron instruments of constraint or torture, the practical and functional prevails over the decorative. The Flemish manufacture of armour and weapons, with Bruges as its principal centre, is one of the many fields of the all-embracing iron industry that has been very inadequately studied so far. Here too, written sources and documents exceed the preserved examples.

Finally we refer to the possibility of finding metal works of art from the late Middle Ages that combine wrought iron with copper or bronze. In this connection we can note two magnificent examples of the artistic heritage of Flanders: the monumental iron dragon finished off with copper plates, anno 1378, serving as a weathervane on the belfry at Ghent; and the 15th-century fire andirons, crowned with copper lions, from the town hall of Bruges.

Chrismatorium in silver in the form of a late Gothic chapel, Cornelis de Bondt, 1486. Paris, Louvre.

Tin case-bottle, Bruges (?), around 1500, Brought up by dredging the Reie at Bruges. Bruges, Gruuthuse Museum.

GOLD AND SILVERSMITHS' WORK

It must be admitted for the goldsmiths' and silversmiths' art in the Southern Netherlands in medieval times, that the centre of gravity of production – both for quantity and quality – was not in Flanders but in the Walloon Maas region. The most important of the examples preserved in Belgium of Romanesque art in precious metals – silver reliquaries and shrines especially – must in fact be attributed to Maasland masters or workshops. It is only from the 14th and 15th centuries onwards that Flemish silversmiths or Flemish works of art in precious metals come to light in the heritage preserved and in historical records. However, a large number of pieces lack hallmarks and have thus so far remained anonymous. But where Bruges is concerned, we can point to the very meritorious 15th-century silverwork preserved in the Gruuthuse Museum and in Jerusalem Church: the *niello* plaquette of Lodewijk van Gruuthuse, the silver fist and bust of Justice, and the Resurrection reliquary, also ornamented with little plastic figures. We find though that the oldest silverwork preserved at Bruges has in fact survived the passage of time with the name of its author. These are the silver sealing stamps of the Bruges town administration, made in 1304 and 1318 by the seal engraver Jan Inghelbrecht.

On the other hand, the silver seal mould – also from the 14th century – of the town of Ghent, preserved in the Bijloke Museum, has remained anonymous. As for

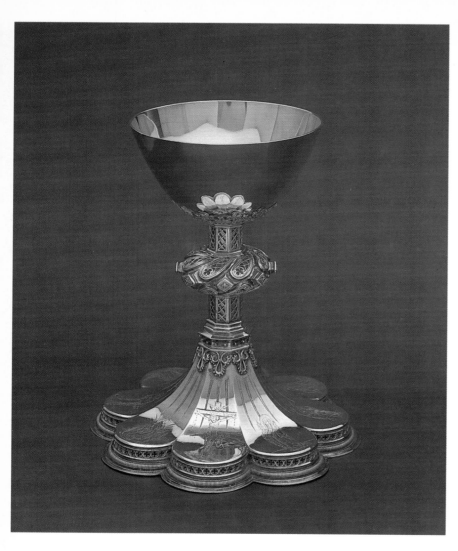

Silver chalice, gift from Gertrudis Beckers, Convent of the *Rijke Claren* at 's-Hertogenbosch, 22 cm, 's-Hertogenbosch, 1493. Malines, Archbishopric.

Bruges, this anonymity applies to some magnificent examples of preserved works of art in precious metals, probably by Ghent artists: the neck-chain of the Ghent gold and silversmiths, ornamented with figurative links (private collection), the pyxis of the *Mariakerke*, decorated with smaltwork, and the similarly decorated small dish from the Courtrai Beguinage; a beaker with lid and a chalice of 1498, now both preserved in London; the Gothic cross reliquary of St Peter's Abbey, probably from Ghent, which in the 17th century was mounted on a Bruges Baroque pedestal.

But one important name of a Ghent silversmith from the late Middle Ages can be retained for the 15th century: Cornelis de Bont, whose name is connected with some masterpieces of 1482 and 1486 respectively: the four luxurious attachments of the Ghent town heralds or shawms (Ghent, Bijloke Museum) in gilded and *niello* silver and enamel; and the small silver chrismatorium, shaped as a small late Gothic chapel (Paris, Louvre).

Apart from the Flemish towns, those of Brabant were very productive at the end of the Middle Ages both for ecclesiastical and lay silver. Names such as those of Gufkens at Tongres, Siger van Steynemolen at Malines and Joos Pauwels at Louvain can all be connected with it in the 15th century. In the figurative parts the lifelike presentation of the personages, and in the non-figurative parts, the architectural forms of the late Gothic, are

Relic of the Holy Katherine. Brussels, 15th century. Louvain, St Peter's Church.

214

One of the four coats of arms, or tokens of the municipal messengers and reed-pipers. Gilt and niello silver, Cornelis de Bont, 1482. Ghent, Bijloke Museum.

Goblet of Philip the Good, rock-crystal, gold, smalt-work, precious stones and enamel. Vienna, Kunsthistorisches Museum.

carried out with great mastery in the precious metal. This is seen from some brilliant but anonymous examples of silver, also of Brabant origin, of the 15th century: a Brussels relic image of St Catherine, preserved in St Peter's Church at Louvain, which can be compared for plastic design and finish with the statuette of St Saviour by Master Gufkens at Tongres; an exceptionally decorative tower monstrance in St Leonard's Church at Zoutleeuw; a silver chalice (1493), no less beautiful, in the Archbishop's Residence at Malines; and a chalice of Brussels manufacture which was presented by Maximilian of Austria to a chapel near Trento in Italy. Finally we note that quite a few luxurious examples of Flemish-Burgundian gold and silverwork – such as jewels, collars of orders, drinking beakers and other items of table silver from the entourage of the Dukes of Burgundy or of the Order of the Golden Fleece – have landed up either at Vienna or via the booty from Charles the Bold at Berne in Switzerland. One of these – mostly anonymous – showpieces is the beaker of Philip the Good, preserved in the Museum of Art History at Vienna, constructed of rock-crystal, gold, smaltwork and precious stones, and adorned with the enamelled emblems of the Golden Fleece.

Pottery production

Although objects in pottery were only seldom made in the Middle Ages as artistic objects, it is nevertheless proper in this review of Flemish art to incorporate a short contribution on them. There are several reasons for this. Already from the stone age (neolithic) onwards, pottery was manufactured and decorated by potters. For archaeologists, it remains until far on into the Middle Ages the most important aid in dating the traces of inhabitation and other archaeological remains found. For this purpose, the technical, functional and morphological characteristics of the pottery are studied, as is the manner of decoration.

On the other hand, in the production of pottery for use, the aesthetic feeling of the potter clearly plays a role. Especially from the moment that a greater diversity of forms of pottery arises – *i e* that for each function (cooking, pouring, drinking, *etc*) a separate shape is made (particularly from the 13th century onwards) – most beautifully decorated pottery is manufactured in Flanders, so that it was exported. Through these exports, potters abroad, *e g* in the Netherlands and Denmark, were in their turn influenced. This decorated pottery consisted especially of utensils for pouring.

In the end, although the greatest part of ceramic production in Flanders consisted of cooking, drinking and pouring utensils, other forms began to emerge in the 13th and 14th centuries. They had a decorative function, in particular a group of roof or ridge ornaments which, as will appear later, can take unsuspected forms.

This condensed review is limited to the main features. Further limitations are implied by the fact that Flanders, during the Merovingian period, but still more during the Carolingian, and even up to the beginning of the 13th, was largely dependent on production centres situated outside the region.

Yet another limit is imposed by the status of investigation (archaeological in particular). Thus for Flanders there is still almost nothing known about pottery production from the Merovingian and Carolingian periods up to the 12th century. Therefore most of the attention in this contribution will be paid to ceramic production in Flanders in the late Middle Ages (13th to 15th centuries), about which we have fortunately learnt more in recent years through excavations and research work.

From a global point of view, however, the study of medieval pottery in Flanders is still in its infancy, but in ten years this situation may have changed. Furthermore, we shall not subdivide the Merovingian and Carolingian periods, but only give the broad lines that apply to them.

THE MEROVINGIAN PERIOD
(5th century – *ca* 750)

Until very recently, the study of Merovingian ceramics in Flanders was exclusively based on very numerous grave findings, *viz* pots that had been buried with the deceased in his grave. This could hardly be otherwise, as up to recent years not a single settlement from the Merovingian time had been located in Flanders, unlike neighbouring countries (*e g* Speyer and Warendorf in Germany, Brebières in France, West Stow in England). But a few years ago, at Avelgem-Kerkhove (West Flanders) work was begun on the investigation of a Merovingian settlement, where excavations so far have revealed a large house with two naves and accompanying barn and granaries, and some buildings with deepened floor level.

These pottery findings at Kerkhove and the Merovingian ones at Semmerzake (East Flanders) prove that not all forms of pottery were put into the graves. In the graves, the pots found were nearly all bicones turned on the potter's wheel, some of them decorated with a roller stamp, rosette ornaments, zigzag motifs *etc*, while handmade pots also occur now and then. In the settlement ceramics, quite a number of the forms found are different from the funerary pottery, *e g* large storage pots, although biconic pots and bowls are also found in the settlement.

Local pottery production must have existed in Flanders; but up to now not a single production place has been found, although they have in the Maas valley (at Huy among other places). Imports are found in Flanders from the Maas valley, north France and the Eiffel region. The handmade ceramics found in Flanders are probably most of local or regional origin. But the Mero-

Statue of riders, oxydized pottery, *Potterierei,* Bruges, second half of the 13th century. Bruges, Museums.

Pitchers, pots and money-box, reduced (grey) pottery, *Potterierei,* Bruges, 2nd half of the 13th century. Bruges, Museums.

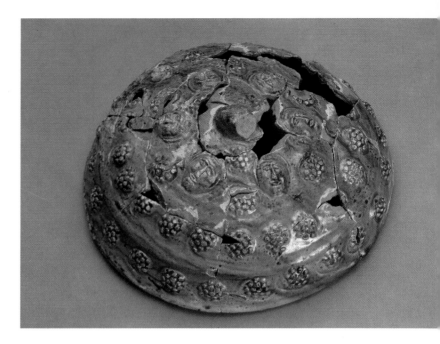

Snuffer, pitcher and spouted pot with lobate decoration, reduced (grey) pottery, Aardenburg, 14th century. Aardenburg, Municipal Museum.

Fire-clock, pitcher and spouted pot with lobe decorations, reducingly (grey) fired pottery, Aardenburg, 14th century. Aardenburg, Municipal Museum.

Casseroles with hollow handle, oxydized (red) pottery, Aardenburg, end of 13th and 14th century. Aardenburg, Municipal Museum.

vingian everyday ceramics are almost unknown, particularly the local production manufactured in earlier (local Romanesque) or later persisting (local early medieval) traditions. Up to now, these have been dated either too early or too late, bringing about an artificial hiatus. This state of affairs can only be remedied by excavating Merovingian settlements which can be properly dated, such as that at Avelgem-Kerkhove.

THE CAROLINGIAN PERIOD
(*ca* 750 - *ca* 900)

AND THE 10th, 11th AND 12th CENTURIES

Neither between the late Roman and the early Merovingian periods, nor between the late Merovingian and the Carolingian ones, is it possible to draw a clear dividing line in respect of local ceramic production.

Changes in a political regime are not necessarily reflected directly in the production of everyday consumer articles. Economic revival, as in the Carolingian period, expresses itself somewhat more directly, particularly in the field of trading relations. As a consequence pottery products, especially those of high quality, were still more than in the Merovingian period imported from production centres outside Flanders. Here we give a review of the most important centres and products.

In the Rhine and the Maas region, centres such as Badorf, Brühl-Eckdorf and Walderberg exported pots and jugs with spouts, frequently ornamented with a roller stamp (with relief-band amphorae as a special form) and sometimes painted red, already from the beginning of the 8th century onwards. From *ca* 900 onwards, red-painted pottery was also imported from Pingsdorf and surrounding production centres, and somewhat later from the south Limburg pottery centres of Brunssum, Schinveld and Nieuwenhagen. Even red-painted pottery (appearing until the end of the 12th century) from Beauvais (France) reached certain parts of Flanders.

From the end of the 11th century up to the 14th, ceramics of high quality were produced at Andenne (Maas valley) and in its direct neighbourhood, and this was distributed over a great part of northwestern Europe. In Flanders, this sort of pottery is found in reasonably large quantities up to the beginning of the 13th century; after which imports of it fell off sharply, possibly under the influence of important local ceramic production. Blue-grey pottery, from production centres such as Elmpt and Brüggen (near Roermond), and *Paffrath* pottery (belonging to the main group of blue-grey pottery), is found in Flanders from the 12th century onwards, but with regional differences in distribution (e g Elmpt pottery is not found in the coastal region).

Pitcher with sliplines, St James' shells and bramble-piles and pitcher with wheel-stamp motif. Highly decorated pottery, Bruges, 2nd half of the 13th century. Bruges, Museums.

Pitcher with vertical sliplines and pitcher with wheel-stamp motif (vine tendrils), highly decorated pottery, *potterierei* – Bruges 2nd half of the 13th century. Bruges, Private collection.

The ordinary, locally produced pottery from the Carolingian period and the following centuries has as its chief characteristic the reducing firing, which gives a grey to greyish-brown colour to the casks. These are mainly cooking pots, shaped by hand and sometimes turned afterwards on the potter's wheel. From the 11th century onwards, we find pottery that has been produced completely on the wheel.

A separate group is the *schelpenceramiek*, so called because fragments of shells were added to the clay as a tempering. Pottery of this sort is found mainly in the Flemish coastal region, but also in Ghent. The *schelpenceramiek*, probably a local product from the coastal region, may be dated in the 12th century.

As for Merovingian everyday pottery, very little is known about local ceramic production in the Carolingian period and further on into the 12th century; in the absence of sufficient excavations of settlements from this period, and of thoroughgoing studies of the small amount of material already excavated. Up to now, the places of production have not been located at all!

THE 13th, 14th AND 15th CENTURIES

In these three centuries a fairly radical change occurs, both in the pottery imported into Flanders, and in that produced locally. From the end of the 12th century to the beginning of the 13th, the red-painted pottery disappears completely; while relief-band amphorae, for instance, are no longer found from the 11th century onwards.

At the beginning of the 13th century, in the Rhine region and the pottery centres of the present Dutch Limburg, the forcing up of the firing temperature brings about the transition to stoneware. In the production of stoneware, the baking temperature attains the sintering

Pot-bellied pitcher, red pottery with white slip-casting and green lead-glaze, *Potterierei* – Bruges, 2nd half of the 13th century. Bruges, Private collection.

point of the clay, *i e* around 1150° to 1250° C, making the fabric very hard and practically impermeable. For this purpose, the sintering point and the melting point of the clay must be sufficiently far apart to avoid accidents in firing, such as the collapse of the pots. Suitable sorts of clay for this purpose are especially found in the Rhineland. During the late Middle Ages, particularly the centres of Siegburg and Langerwehe exported to Flanders. From the end of the 15th century onwards, products from Raeven, Aix-la-Chapelle, Cologne and Frechen also became available.

The stoneware products imported are almost exclusively tableware such as jugs, drinking mugs and cups *etc*; which had an influence on local production: especially the highly decorated pottery consisted predominantly of tableware.

From the middle of the 14th century onwards, majolica is imported from Malaga (southern Spain), mostly ornamented with gold painting (lustre), and still strongly under Arabic influence. In the course of the 15th century, this ware was increasingly imported into Flanders from Manises (Valencia, Spain) and Italy; and less luxurious pottery from Spain and Portugal. The influence of these imports and the immigration of Italian potters to Antwerp at the beginning of the 16th century marks the beginning of Antwerp's own majolica production.

Locally, the usual reducingly fired pottery continued to be produced up to the 15th century. But from the 13th century onwards, the red pottery with oxidizing firing was manufactured; gradually displacing the grey pottery from the market because of its better technical qualities.

These two pottery groups use the same sort of clay but differ in their technique of firing. In reducing firing, the supply of air into the kiln is cut off as much as possible, so that the iron in the iron-containing compounds of the clay is reduced and becomes black. In this process, carbon particles from the combustion gases are deposited on the ceramic and lodge in the pores of the fabric, accentuating still further the grey to grey-black colour on the outside. In oxidizing firing on the other hand, air is freely admitted to the kiln; so that the iron present in the clay is oxidized, producing a red to reddish-brown colour in the fabric. This technique of firing permits the glazing of the pottery, which greatly reduces its porosity. The glaze used is a lead glaze, applied by immersion in a glazing pulp of lead oxide and silicium dioxide, or by sprinkling with lead filings.

THE GREY POTTERY   The grey pottery in the late Middle Ages is fairly hard baked, and mostly has a tempering of fine sand. The main forms occurring are cooking pots, large broad-shouldered jugs, tankards and broad bowls. We can also find firecovers, chamber pots, money-boxes and the like. A certain evolution can be observed in the forms, *e g* the cooking pots in the 13th century are almost spherical with a simple lens bottom. Later pots of this kind have handles and little supporting feet.

In the 15th century, the variety of shapes in grey pottery was considerably reduced, and in general we find only large storage basins and pots. As a simple

Helmeted knight (fragment of a statue of riders), oxydized pottery, Ghent (?), 2nd half of the 13th – beginning of the 14th century. Ghent, Bijloke Museum.

decoration, sometimes a zone of alternating ribs and grooves is applied on the shoulder of broad jugs and cooking pots. Another form is the lobe decoration with thumb and fingers applied on the edge; or on jugs and fireguards, for instance, on the outside of the handle.

We shall return later to the production centres of grey pottery.

THE RED POTTERY   Almost all the shapes occurring in grey pottery were also produced in red, where the variety of shapes is somewhat greater. Thus the important objects we find include frying-pans, dripping pans, small drinking cups, lids *etc*.

An evolution can also be noted in the shape of the red pottery. Thus the almost spherical cooking pots change to the so-called *grapen*, provided with little supporting feet and one or two handles. We also find scalloped or pressed-out feet, sometimes so close to one another that a sort of ring stand is produced. An evolution may also be observed, for instance, in the frying-pans; in the beginning, we only find hollow handles, later they are provided with solid ones. This evolution in shapes is broadly the same for the whole of Flanders, although regional differences may be observed. For instance, the transition from the hollow to the solid handle does not occur everywhere at the same time.

The grey and red pottery was made in the same production centres and even fired in the same kilns, as has been revealed by excavations along the *Potterierei* at

Fragments of ornithomorph roof-decorations, oxydized pottery, *Potterierei –* Bruges, 2nd half of the 13th century. Bruges, Museums.

Bruges. The local pottery for everyday use, *i e* the grey and red pottery including the highly decorated pots (see below), was probably produced in every settlement of any importance (and especially in the towns). Clear traces of pottery industry have so far been excavated only at Aardenburg and St Kwintens-Lennik (14th century), Courtrai and Bruges (2nd half of 13th and beginning of 14th century), Tongres (end of 13th and beginning of 14th century) and Tirlemont (13th-15th centuries).

The most important excavations at a production centre for late medieval pottery were carried out along the *Potterierei* at Bruges. In the second half of the 13th century, this was in fact a quarter devoted to the production of pottery. Three excavations revealed traces of kilns, plus several thousand kilograms of pottery rejects. The production period ran from *ca* 1250 till shortly after 1300. In 1297, the citizens of Bruges began building the second line of town fortifications. These works brought the potters' quarter within the town walls. But as this was an industry presenting fire dangers, it was probably moved to a site outside the town walls.

More than 90 % of the findings at Bruges consist of grey and red everyday pottery, the majority of the ware being red. The remainder consists of the so-called highly decorated pottery, which in fact belongs to the red, oxidizingly fired pottery. It was developed from *ca* 1200, and it is dealt with separately because of its special decoration.

HIGHLY DECORATED POTTERY   The most important characteristics of this group are the decoration and the high quality lead glazing. The lead glazing – and especially the green lead glazing with copper which was developed in the first half of the 13th century – covered the neck, shoulder and most of the body of the objects, and gave them a very luxurious appearance. The combi-

nation of this glazing with a white layer of slib, applied before the glazing, made it possible to obtain special colour effects. The principal decorative patterns are little bands applied in white slib, vertical straight or wavy lines, lozenges or other shapes, scales or flowers applied in white slib, projecting bunches of blackberries or grapes, St James's shells and faces, as well as decoration with a roller stamp (rectangular, fishbone motifs, diamond patterns *etc*, sometimes in combinations). Anthropomorphical decorations, especially the masks on the necks of jugs, are less numerous.

Very seldom complete figures are shown on jugs: especially fiddlers, but also female figures and others, mostly placed between columns supporting a Gothic arch. The only place known so far as producing these so-called 'fiddler's jugs' in Flanders is Bruges. Other examples are known from Welsrijp and Haarlem (Holland) and from Norway, but practically all the modes of decoration found in the highly decorated pottery can also be found in the Bruges production centres. The great majority of the objects decorated in this way are jugs, and thus belong among the tableware. We can distinguish some main groups such as jugs with a high, drawn-out body and an opening in cloverleaf form; jugs with a pear-shaped body; jugs with an almost spherical body and a straight-sided, funnel-like and almost cylindrical neck with turning ribs on the outside; and others with an s-shaped profile.

Also among the highly decorated tableware belong some bell-shaped covers, such as an example from Lampernisse with green lead glazing on a white slib layer; and two examples from Bruges (*Potterierei*), the first with green lead glazing on a white slib layer and decorated with 52 bunches of blackberries and 6 male heads, all protruding in shape; and the second decorated with a star shape with a number of little flowers in, in applied slib. We may also mention dripping pans decorated with applied bands in white slib, little flowers and/or modelled faces on the spout.

A special group of pottery objects, in fact belonging to the highly decorated pottery, the production of which was also revealed along the *Potterierei* at Bruges, are roof ventilators and roof finials. The latter were made especially as decorative objects. They are very striking and can assume various and surprising shapes. Thus at Bruges various pinnacle-shaped finials have been found, as well as large globes on a conical foot (with a height of up to more than 80 *cm*) and finials representing animals, like doves, birds of prey, swans, dragons *etc*. Even horses are shown in roof ornaments. The most unusual form of them are the equestrian statuettes, showing knights, mostly in full suits of armour, seated on horses. Examples of these are found in many parts of Flanders (Aardenburg, Ypres, St Margriete, Malines) but especially in Ghent. A magnificent example was found among the pottery rejects along the *Potterierei* of Bruges.

All these forms can be situated between 1250 and 1350, the high point being the last quarter of the 13th century. The decline probably begins shortly after 1300. From 1350 onwards, decorations in white slib are applied only on plates; and these are found rarely, if at all, in the 13th century. Clear proof of the production of such plates, decorated with ornaments such as birds, was found in Aardenburg. Techniques of decoration continue to deteriorate until they are limited to the application of some lines of slib on ordinary kitchenware such as jugs and cooking pots. Products of this kind were also made at Aardenburg.

The gradual disappearance of the highly decorated tableware shortly after 1300 is probably connected with the emergence of similar products in completely developed stoneware from the Rhineland, which are of superior quality. And probably not by chance the technique of decoration survives only on plates, a form of pottery that was completely lacking among the stoneware.

In Flanders so far only two production centres for the highly decorated pottery have been located, namely Bruges (by far the most important) and Courtrai. The Flemish findings show, however, that similar ware must also have been produced in other towns. Yet the findings decline markedly towards the east of Flanders.

The Flemish production of highly decorated pottery, when it emerged, was very probably influenced to a considerable degree by northwest France (Normandy, Paris *etc*). Dutch production, mainly at Haarlem, as well as the Danish production of highly decorated pottery, can have been influenced by the Flemish. It is also possible that they go back to a common source.

Finally, traces of exports of pottery products from Flanders in the late Middle Ages – both of ordinary everyday pottery and of highly decorated pottery – have already been found along the east coast of England, and thanks to recent excavations, as far north as Scotland.

Basin with white slipdecorations (birds), oxydized pottery, Aardenburg, 2nd half of the 14th century. Aardenburg, Municipal Museum.

Léon Voet
Emeritus custodian of the Plantin-Moretus Museum at Antwerp

THE 16th CENTURY

LÉON VOET
Introduction

JEAN-PIERRE ESTHER
Architecture

CHRISTINE VAN VLIERDEN
Sculpture

CARL VAN DE VELDE
Painting

VALENTIN VERMEERSCH
The art of stained glass

LÉON VOET
Graphic art

RIA FABRI
Furniture

ERIK DUVERGER
Tapestry and textile arts

ANDRÉ VAN DEN KERKHOVE
Metalwork

STÉPHANE VANDENBERGHE
Ceramics

JEANINE LAMBRECHTS-DOUILLEZ
Musical instruments

SEX CVM CHARA HABITAT
MENSES PROSERPINA MATRE

VER

AESTAS

SEX CVM CHARA HABITAT
MENSES PROSERPINA MATRE

SEX CVM DILECTO
CONIVGE DITE MANET

Introduction

In the history of mankind some centuries have had a decisive impact on the continued development of culture. For Europe the 12th-13th century was such a period; the 16th was another, and then the Netherlands – particularly Flanders and Brabant – were foremost among the countries which provided the important stimuli.

THE BACKGROUND   The 16th century was the century of the Renaissance, which had originated during the 14th century and matured during the 15th in Italy. From there it crossed the Alps to gain control of the whole of Europe during the last years of that century. The speed and impact with which this happened were increased by a new medium – printing. After writing, this was the greatest cultural invention of all time, made possible by Johannes Gutenberg of Mainz in about 1440. Together with the printing of books, the graphic art made more visual kinds of expression possible.

The Renaissance is an extremely complex movement fed by numerous sources, which divided into many different streams. At the risk of overlooking a few fine nuances, the powerful secularization of the Italian intellectual elite in the 14th and 15th centuries formed the basis of the Renaissance. In this process widely divergent levels of society became interested in man and his environment, the natural world.

Wherever man looks in new directions, he invariably seeks models which can make his progress easier. In the case of Italy the pioneers of the new movement were completely surrounded by them: the ruins of Greek and Roman antiquity. The germinating movement turned into a 'rebirth of antiquity'. The works of art of antiquity, which concentrated on man and the human body, became a source of inspiration for the new artistic movement. The classical authors were very influential in the intellectual Renaissance, which was termed 'Humanism', because it sought to make man 'more human' (*humanior*) by bringing him into contact with the cultural heritage of the classical world.

In the beginning the humanists tried to purify the degenerated Latin of the Middle Ages, to use again the language which approached that of Cicero, Virgil, Horace and the other great authors of classical Roman literature. At a later stage they started to look for the texts of these authors to republish them, together with commentaries, using the methods of literary criticism which they had developed. In this way the world of antiquity gained widespread familiarity, while lessons for contemporary life were drawn from the classical works.

Humanism was above all a philological and archaeological subject, in which Latin and Graeco-Roman antiquity were central and formed the basis for a new system of education, designed to create the perfect 'man (and woman) of the world' – equivalent to the later English 'gentleman'.

However, a large number of scientific treatises also belonged to this classical heritage, and in view of the increased interest in man and nature, these were studied with particular care and attention. The humanists interested in science were soon surprised to discover, that the highly acclaimed Greek and Roman scientists had made quite a few serious errors. They started to improve and supplement the ancient authorities – initially very carefully and often attacked or criticized by 'scholars' who insisted on the Greek and Roman 'truths'. Together with the emergence of Humanism there was a spectacular development in the natural sciences, which was to raise western civilization in barely four centuries from the level achieved by the Greek and Romans two thousand years ago, to moonwalks and heart transplants.

The new movement found a fertile environment in the Netherlands; and this northern Renaissance spread powerfully to large areas of Europe through the exportation of works of art, the artists themselves, and ideas. It affected Germany, England, Scandinavia and Spain, to a slightly lesser extent France, and even Italy, the country where the Renaissance had originated.

The Renaissance in the Netherlands still focused on the two most prosperous provinces, Flanders and Brabant; and was largely concentrated in the city of Antwerp, which in the 16th century became the largest trading centre in western Europe. Obviously this metropolis could not monopolize all art within its walls. Bruges, Ghent, Brussels, Malines, Louvain *etc* remained active in many fields. However, everything intended for export, produced in these centres, was transported abroad via Antwerp. The city on the Scheldt was extremely important, both in the national and international Renaissance of the 16th century.

Unfortunately, this flourishing period came to a premature halt; religious and political tensions led to an uprising against Philip II and the division of the Netherlands in 1585. The north developed into an independent Calvinist republic, the south remained Catholic and Spanish. The economic centre shifted to the north. This did not entail an immediate intellectual and artistic collapse in the south, nor even a break in artistic activity; but from that time on the Renaissance would follow in the north a new course as a result of the changed political, and especially the religious, climate.

Pluto and Prosperina, dorsal tapestry of a canopy (detail), 419 × 261 cm, style of Michiel Coxcie (1499-1592), Brussels, 1566. Vienna, Kunsthistorisches Museum.

THE ARTISTIC RENAISSANCE IN THE NETHER-LANDS The Italian artistic Renaissance had already gained a foothold in the Netherlands in the late 15th century, and quickly sought to establish itself – though without being able to take over at one fell swoop. The infiltration of the Renaissance took place in small formations and spread order. The Gothic spirit was still deeply rooted in the hearts and minds of the public.

Very few Italian artists of any significance attempted to make a career for themselves in the Netherlands, either during the early stages or later on. Two exceptions were: Jacopo de Barbari at the court of Margaret of Austria at Malines, and Leone Leoni at the court of Mary of Hungary. Their influence on local masters was limited.

Some artists did travel from the Netherlands to Italy. Jan Gossaert of Mabuse was one of the pioneers (1508-1509), and he returned with new forms of expression. Even so, travelling to Italy only became fashionable in the 1530's and 1540's; and the first tourists seem to have been less impressed by their Italian colleagues' achievements than by other things. For Hieronymus Cock these were the ruins of Rome; for Pieter Bruegel the Elder the impressive Alpine scenery.

The first real breakthrough of the Renaissance came via graphic art (Italian engravings and German ones influenced by the Italians), which familiarized local painters, sculptors and engravers with the new ideas from Italy, and influenced in their turn the other arts and crafts.

For quite a few decades the only effect of the early Renaissance was the adoption of decorative elements. Pillars, arches and other architectural elements were based on classical models, and combined with more modern decorative elements such as medallions. They began to swamp the paintings and statues which still retained a Gothic form and spirit; and influenced the decoration of architecture, tapestry work, jewellery, furniture making, ceramics etc. These first contacts resulted in confusion and chaos. Much of what was created in those years may have its personal charm; but it is still no more than kitsch, even though produced with more gusto and expertise than similar articles nowadays.

Only in about 1540 the artists in the Netherlands really started to be infused by the spirit of the Italian Renaissance, partly as a result of the journeys they began to make to Italy. However, even more important were those artists who began to familiarize their stay-at-home colleagues (and the art loving public in general) with 'true' Renaissance art and decoration in their (collections of) prints. This began with Pieter Coecke van Aelst (1502-1550), who from 1539 onwards published a number of richly illustrated treatises in Dutch and in French on architecture and all that was related to it; based on the texts of the old Roman architect Vitruvius, as adapted by the Italian scholar Sebastian Serlio. These treatises were intended – as the introduction explains – for painters, wood-carvers, sculptors and all others who 'delight in classical works'. This didactic task was continued by the highly productive Hans Vredeman de Vries (1527-1606?), who published scores of illustrated albums outlining his Renaissance ideas on a variety of subjects: architecture, sculpture, furniture making, gardens etc. His influence was felt far beyond the boundaries of the Netherlands – especially in Germany, England and Scandinavia.

During the 1540's a singularly Flemish-Italian style of ornamentation emerged in Antwerp, termed the 'grotesque' or 'Floris' style. In 1493 the rooms of Nero's Golden House were excavated in Rome. They were thought to be a grotto (cave), which explains the term 'grotesque'. This strange ornamental style made a tremendous impression, and already in the same year it was used in the Borgias' apartment in the Vatican. People, animals and objects seemed to float in space, connected only by fine threads. The surrealist decor appealed strongly to the imagination of the countrymen of Hieronymus Bosch. They adopted the style, though not without modifying and stylizing it in accordance with Flemish norms. The question of who invented this grotesque Flemish style remains unanswered. For a long time it was thought to have been the sculptor Cornelis Floris, hence the term 'Floris style'; though nowadays it is generally thought to have originated from the engraver Cornelis Bos, who returned to Antwerp from Italy in 1540. At any rate the style was enormously successful and from 1540 began to overrun architecture, furniture making, sculpture, ceramics and anything else that could possibly be decorated. The Grotesque style constituted the most original contribution of the Netherlands, and particularly of Antwerp, to the Renaissance in the north; and although it did not survive the end of the century in a pure form, it did continue to have an effect till well into the 17th century.

The patronage of the Dukes of Burgundy contributed largely to making the Netherlands one of the most important artistic provinces in Europe in the 15th century. However, their Habsburg successors did not spend much time in the Lowlands; and even though some of the governor-generals – above all Margaret of Austria in Malines – were great art lovers, they lacked the financial means to even approach the pomp and glory of the courts of bygone days. Royal patronage in the Netherlands was a thing of the past.

Another part of potential clientele disappeared by the rise of Protestantism. With its vicious attacks on 'idolatry', it led to a temporary reduction in commissions for and from monasteries and churches, even in those countries which had remained Catholic. As a result, and also because of changing fashions, the previous extensive and profitable retable industry completely vanished during the 1540's. In the Netherlands the burghers and the nobility became the most important customers. Henceforth their preferences and desires had to be taken into account, which yielded more worldly art forms.

Charles V on horseback with black coat, wood-cut, coloured by hand, 40.8 × 28.6 cm, carved and edited by Hans Liefrinck (active at Antwerp, 1538-1573). Antwerp, Stedelijk Prentenkabinet.
A similar print by Hans Liefrinck shows Charles V on horseback in armour.

Carolus Par la grace de Dieu/Duc Daultrice/et de Bourgoigne/nasquit à Gand le xxiiij de Feburier, M.D. Et fut coronné Roy des Espaignes le vij de Feburier, M.D. et xvij. Il fut esleu le xxviij de Juing / et puis coronné / Roy des Romains le pj Doctobre, M.D. Et Empereur de Rome le xxiiij de Feburier, M.D. et xxx. Respousa madame Isabel Royne de Portugal le xi Dapuril, M.D. et xxvj laquelle enfanté le Roy Philippe xxi de Maÿ, M.D. xxvij Auquel Dieu tout puissant vueille octroyer tout honneur et victoire. A M E N.

PLV S OVLTR

Imprimé en Anuers sur la rue de Lombars au lieurier blansch par moy Iehan Liefrinck Tailleur de Figures.

This increased interest – another aspect of the new spirit of the Renaissance – compensated, together with growing exports, for the disappearance of royal patronage and the decrease in commissions from the Church. However, it did not extend to all branches of the arts, and there was for example a great decline in sculpture.

These exports took place via Antwerp and many commissions were made through this city, so that it was obvious that many artists were encouraged to settle there. Karel van Mander expressed the spirit of the times strikingly in his *Schilder-boeck* (1604): "The wonderful and celebrated city of Antwerp, prospering as a result of trade, has summoned our most excellent arts unto it and many have come to her, because art likes to be close to wealth". If Antwerp had been rather insignificant in the arts in the 15th century, parallel with its rise as the metropolis of the west, it suddenly became the artistic capital of the Netherlands and one of the utmost cultural centres of western Europe.

The disciplines which were practised in the Renaissance had almost all existed and been carried out in previous periods: obviously architecture, painting on panels (the most popular art form, largely concentrated in Antwerp), stained glass windows, the new graphic art (flourishing spectacularly and also virtually monopolized by Antwerp), sculpture (a relative decline after 1540), work in bronze, copper and iron (to some extent a branch of sculpture), jewellery, tapestry work (still a speciality of Brussels), furniture making and other smaller crafts, including bookbinding. Some of the new artistic crafts which became important in the Netherlands were ceramic and glass work, introduced by Italian specialists in Antwerp; the making of medallions, also filtered through from Italy and produced mainly in Antwerp; the manufacture of musical instruments, particularly harpsichords and organs, again mostly made in Antwerp. A completely new art form thought to have originated in Flanders and Brabant was lace making. On the other hand, the art of the miniature – one of the highlights of Flemish art in the preceding century – rapidly and completely disappeared.

HUMANISM AND SCIENCE   Humanism – the human sciences in a Latin guise – held a central position in 16th-century European culture. The Netherlands played a considerable role in it; the largest concentration of humanists outside Italy relative to the population was found there. At the end of the 15th century, European humanists began passionately to rid Latin of its medieval impurities; at the same time attempting to clear up the abuses in society – and particularly the Church – with the same fury.

The great figurehead of this pioneering stage was Desiderius Erasmus (Rotterdam 1466 – Basle 1536; living in Brabant from 1501-1521). He wrote with much brilliance and irony, using an international readership as a sound-board for his ideas. However, his attacks on the Church were not appreciated, especially when the preaching of Martin Luther (1517) led to the birth of Protestantism. Erasmus was able to leave the Netherlands without being troubled; but Cornelius Grapheus or Scribonius (= the writer, 1482-1558), one of the most prominent members of the humanist circle in Antwerp, who – following Erasmus' example – had criticized the abuses in the Church, was forced to recant in public and dismissed from his post as town clerk in 1522.

The humanists in the countries ruled by Charles V, as well as those in the rest of Europe, became a great deal more circumspect. They left the disputes on Church and society well alone, and transferred their attention to less volatile philological and archaeological subjects. They republished the classical authors, wrote critical essays on them and studied the classical world. In this second stage of European Humanism the Netherlands again produced a figure of international stature: Justus Lipsius (Overijssel 1547 – Louvain 1606).

In the introduction and development of Humanism in the Netherlands and its spread throughout Europe, the University of Louvain played an important role. The new movement rapidly gained ground and became strongly established in it. As early as 1517 the *Collegium Trilingue* was founded at the instigation of Erasmus for the study of the three biblical languages – Latin, Greek and Hebrew. Numerous famous professors taught the *bonae literae* to generation after generation in the various faculties of law, medicine *etc*. However, the greatest interest remained in the faculty of theology and its professors. It deservedly gained international fame through its publications of biblical texts, the Church Fathers, exegeses, *etc*.

The biographies of Erasmus and Lipsius are best read using an atlas – which also applies to many other humanists and scientists from the Netherlands. Obviously some of them preferred to stay at home, but the tremendous mobility of this group of people was quite remarkable. When the troubles started, many Catholics moved to calmer places (Italy, Spain, France, Germany); while the Protestants fled to safety (Germany, England). But even before the iconoclasm in 1566 there was a great deal of movement along the roads of Europe.

Amongst the humanists there were many *amateurs*, and those who stayed at home mainly belonged to this category. The term *amateur* is used here without any pejorative overtone; a large number of them did more and better work than some of the professionals. Theodoor Poelman (1512 - *ca* 1581) from Antwerp for example, a modest fuller and later a customs and excise official, produced in his spare time an impressive series of valuable editions of the classical authors. In some cases they made a more bizarre contribution, like the physician Joannes Goropius Becanus (1519-1572) who, in his work *Origines Antwerpianae*, convincingly proved that Adam and Eve spoke an Antwerp dialect in the Earthly Paradise. With these bold remarks he nevertheless brought a breakthrough in the field of modern comparative linguistics. Becanus was a physician, other amateurs included civil servants, wealthy burghers, artists, printers *etc*, forming a circle of friends, the success of which depended on the dynamism of the people comprising it. A typical example was the first humanist nucleus in Antwerp. Erasmus – who regularly visited Antwerp when he was living in Brabant – became friendly with some of the town officials, whom he

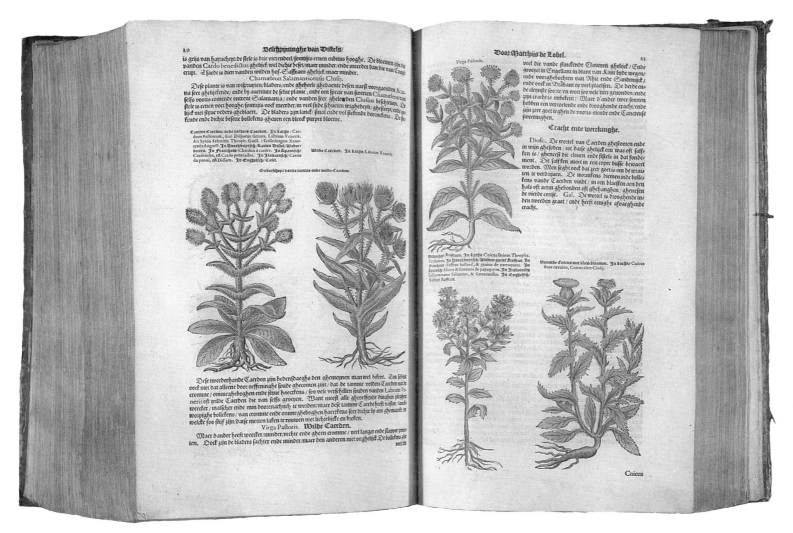

Double page from a botanical essay: Mathias Lobelius (De l'Obel, De Lobel), *Kruydtboeck* ('herbarium'). Antwerp, Christoffel Plantin, 1581, in-folio, wood-cuts coloured by hand. Antwerp, Plantin-Moretus Museum.
The editing of scientific botanical essays, mostly by specialists from the Netherlands, was in the 16th century a speciality of Antwerp publishers, in particular Plantin. The *Kruydtboeck* contains no less than 2187 pictures of plants.

inspired with an active interest in Humanism, and to whom he also introduced Thomas More. The latter wrote his *Utopia* in one of their houses, and published it in Louvain in 1516. Through Erasmus and Thomas More these Antwerp officials warrant a footnote in the history of international Humanism during the movement's pioneering stages: Frans Colibrant, (town clerk from 1513 to 1520), and above all, Pieter Gillis (or Aegidius, town recorder from 1509 to 1532), and Cornelius Grapheus (town clerk from 1520 to 1522). However, Erasmus' departure, and above all the troubles that beset Grapheus in 1521 and 1522, dampened their enthusiasm. In the second half of the century another and even larger circle of humanists, maintaining contacts with scholars throughout Europe, developed round the printer Christoffel Plantin (1520-1598) and the cartographer Abraham Ortelius (1527-1598).

In contrast with these amateurs there were professionals who made their living through humanism and looked for appointments at universities, Latin schools or other institutions; or sought patrons amongst the royal houses of Europe, and the Church. This professional group contained the wanderers, continually seeking better or more interesting jobs, or discovering new horizons in their quest for knowledge. Such a scholar was Nicolas Clenardus (Diest 1493/94 - Granada 1542), one of the foremost experts of this period in Greek and Hebrew, as well as one of the first in Europe to embark upon a scientific study of Arabic; for this purpose he even dared to travel to Morocco (1540-42), at that time quite inimical to Christians.

Many humanists concentrated particularly on the study of the *bonae literae*. The natural sciences also started to become explored; but the total number of investigators in Europe remained rather small. This minority of scientists, which gave Europe an advantage over the other civilizations and laid the foundations of our modern technological society, included a surprisingly large number in the Netherlands. Never before – nor since – had the Netherlands, mainly Flanders and Brabant, formed such an important stimulus for scientific thought. Some of the major figures included Andreas

Vesalius (Brussels 1514 – Zanthe 1564), the father of modern anatomy; Gemma Frisius (Dokkum 1508 – Louvain 1555) who, though a physician, contributed particularly in the fields of mathematics and cartography (in 1533, when he was only twenty-five years old, he developed the triangulation method for mapmaking which still forms the basis of modern geodesy; and he was also the first to show how the problem of computing lines of longitude – something which had obsessed sailors and geographers for centuries – could be easily solved with the use of a chronometer); Gerard Mercator (Rupelmonde 1512 – Duisburg 1594), the most important figure in the history of cartography since Ptolemy; Abraham Ortelius (Antwerp 1527-1598), who published the first modern atlas in 1570 and was a pioneer in the field of the cartography of antiquity; Simon Stevin (Bruges 1548 – The Hague 1620), one of the foremost mathematicians and physicists of his time; and the three great botanists of the second half of the century: Rembert Dodoens (or Dodonaeus; Leeuwarden 1518 – Leyden 1585; educated in Malines); Carolus Clusius (or del 'E(s)cluse; Arras 1526 – Leyden 1609), and Mathias Lobelius (de Lobel or de L'Obel; Lille 1538 – Highgate, London 1616).

Numerous less important figures could be added to this list. To name just two: Michiel Coignet (Antwerp 1549-1623), who wrote a treatise on navigation and another on sines, who manufactured astrolabes, sundials and astronomical timepieces, for which Philip II was an important customer, and who was from 1579 to 1585 the engineer responsible for the fortification of Antwerp; and the Antwerp apothecary Pieter Coudenberg (1520-1584), whose garden, containing over six hundred varieties of plants, was one of the sights of Antwerp, and who totally rewrote and published a treatise on pharmaceutics by the German specialist Valerius Cordus (published in 1568).

Thus scientists and humanists from the Netherlands were very active, with numerous offshoots throughout Europe; though there were no important centres in the Netherlands apart from the University of Louvain. Nevertheless, if not an important intellectual centre, all the threads of the national humanist schools came together in Antwerp to become part of the international cultural movements. This paradox had a very simple explanation: printing.

Printing entered the Netherlands in 1473 simultaneously in the south in Alost (Dirk Martens, with the aid of the German technician Jan van Westphalia) and in the north in Utrecht (Nicolaas Ketelaer). From these two centres it spread through the Low Countries, though during the period of the incunabula (up to 1500) more forcefully in the economically less developed north (eleven centres) than in the more prosperous south (eight centres: Alost and Louvain in 1474, Antwerp in 1481/82, Audenarde, Ghent, Bruges, Brussels, 's-Hertogenbosch; though Alost, Audenarde, Brussels and 's-Hertogenbosch were of minor importance). The majority of the approximately 2,000 titles published in the Netherlands at that time came from the presses in the north. This was actually a fairly modest number compared with the entire production of incunabula, esti-

mated at 30,000 titles; of which 11,000 came from Italy, 9,000 from German speaking countries and 5,000 from France. The institutions of education of the 'Brothers of the Common Life' stimulated both the production and the sales in the north. Compared with the 600 works produced in a small town like Zwolle, Louvain only managed to produce 270, Antwerp 400, and all the other towns in the Southern Netherlands together a paltry 130. In the south Antwerp had the largest output; but the works which were published were mainly aimed at a local readership without high intellectual aspirations, and the contents remained far below the standards of Louvain, Zwolle and Deventer.

However, printing is not only concerned with the reading public. It is a capitalist industry, requiring certain financial means and the possibility of a wide market in order to develop. In its rise to become the metropolis of the west, Antwerp attracted much of the printing industry of the Netherlands to it, from the beginning of the 16th century onwards. Some fairly accurate figures are available for the period 1500-1540: of the 133 printers in the Netherlands, 66 were working in Antwerp; of approximately 4,000 works, 2,250 were printed in Antwerp; after 1540 the hegemony of Antwerp increased further, and between 1500 and 1600 there were no fewer than 271 printers and book dealers in the city.

Together with Venice, Paris, Lyons and Cologne, Antwerp became a prominent book market in Europe at that time. There was an increase in the quality as well as the quantity of the work. In the last half of the 16th century Christoffel Plantin (1520-1589, began printing in 1555) built up the largest printing concern of the time, a capitalist business unparalleled anywhere in Europe. Plantin became a symbol of the international influence of Antwerp in the field of the printed word; but before and together with him, many other printers in Antwerp contributed to transmitting the views of scholars in the Netherlands throughout the Christian world.

CULTURAL AND LITERARY LIFE   The great musicians of the day, like the humanists and scientists, often pursued their careers abroad: Orlandus Lassus (Mons 1532–Munich 1594), the creator of the secular madrigal, who switched to ecclesiastical music at the end of his life when he became the *Kapellmeister* of the electors of Bavaria; Philippus de Monte (? 1521–Vienna 1603), who became the chief *Kapellmeister* of the Habsburgs in Vienna in 1568; Georges de la Hèle (Antwerp 1547–Madrid 1589), choirmaster in Tournai, who became leader of the royal chapel in Madrid in 1581 at the request of Philip II. However, enough important musicians remained in the Netherlands to ensure that the standard of music remained at an international level.

The literary world was less important, although the quantity and diversity of works written in Dutch increased enormously. The printing presses turned out large numbers of moralistic tales in verse, novels in prose, anthologies of poetry and books of songs. However, with a few notable exceptions – such as the moral tale *Mariken van Nieumeghen*, published in Antwerp in

1516 – the quality by no means matched the quantity.

The Chambers of Rhetoric and their *factors* were still very active, concentrating mainly on refrains and plays. They were able to participate in numerous inter-city or regional competitions. However, their refrains remained artificial despite the incorporation of Roman gods, goddesses and other classical elements, and their plays were too moralistic to be enjoyable. Another element also entered the plays, though without improving their quality: Protestant ideas, which cast suspicion on the Chambers of Rhetoric and led to censorship.

Only very few figures rose above the level of mediocrity and introduced new or refreshing ideas. Filips Marnix van Sint-Aldegonde (Brussels 1538–Leyden 1598), the staunch supporter of William the Silent and the author of the biting satire on the Catholic Church *De Biëncorf der Hl. Roomsche kercke* (1569), who is also credited with writing the battle song of the rebels (now the Dutch national anthem) *Wilhelmus van Nassouwe*, may be considered to be the master of Dutch prose in the 16th century. The Antwerp schoolmistress Anna Bijns (1494-1575) wrote in praise of love and religion in the style of the Rhetoricians, though with more passion and fire, and criticized in biting verses Luther and the Lutherans. The Antwerp aristocrat Jan van der Noot (1539-1595), inspired by Ronsard and the *Pléiade*, introduced Renaissance poetry into Dutch literature. However, Marnix van Sint-Aldegonde and van der Noot, as well as others such as the Antwerp schoolmaster and writer Pieter Heyns (1537-1598), also expressed themselves superbly in French.

The Antwerp printers provided the Dutch language with its infrastructure by publishing numerous grammars and dictionaries. The first ones were just lists of words based on foreign, and particularly German examples. The Frenchman Christoffel Plantin produced the first dictionaries in Dutch, worthy of the name. In his attempts to master the language he felt the lack of such a work. He started by collecting fiches, but soon realized that it would be impossible to tackle the job alone, and divided the task amongst a number of Antwerp specialists. The result was the *Thesaurus Teutonicae linguae* (1573). One of the contributors, Plantin's proof-reader, Cornelis Kiliaan (1528/29-1607) became so enthusiastic that he continued the work on his own initiative. In 1574 he published his *Dictionarium Teutonico-Latinum*, which was re-edited in 1588 in a considerably enlarged edition; and which was published again in 1599, thoroughly revised and expanded under the title *Etymologicum Teutonicae linguae*, the basic work for all later Dutch dictionaries.

Architecture

The Renaissance, which culturally connected the end of the Middle Ages and the beginning of the new era, signified for Flanders in the sphere of architecture an amphibious transitional period. The forms of the Italian high Renaissance which, at the end of the 15th century – especially in Florence – ushered in a new high point of western architecture, were applied only slowly and belatedly in the north. In the first half of the 16th century, the progressive elements of the new style were hesitatingly introduced into the late Gothic traditionalism. This led to a hybrid style, in which the Gothic spirit still lingered for a long time. We find the same phenomenon in the *Plateresco* style in Spain and the *Manuel* style in Portugal. This overloaded and ostentatious ornamentation points directly to the Baroque.

Through the patronage of the country's governor Margaret of Austria, who settled in Malines from 1507 onwards, her court developed into a centre for radiating the new humanist culture and Renaissance art. Various scholars and artists were attracted to the court. The new style spread particularly among the nobility and the intellectuals. This meant that Renaissance art presented an outspokenly bourgeois and often elitist character. It was a means of inflating personal prestige.

In architecture, the elements of the new style first appeared around 1515. This was shown, for instance, in the town decorations on the occasion of the Triumphal Entry of the young Prince Charles into Bruges in 1515. As one of the first examples of Renaissance buildings in Flanders, the Recorder's House on the *Burg* in Bruges is often mentioned. This building was erected in 1534-1537 after a design by Jean Wallot. But even before this time, we can point to examples of buildings in the early Renaissance style, such as the palace of Margaret of Austria in Malines (*ca* 1517) and the palace of Henry of Nassau in Breda (*ca* 1510).

In the first half of the 16th century, this art was limited to the use of Italianate ornamentation in a structure that was still predominantly Gothic. Only in the second half pure, classical Renaissance buildings were constructed. Apart from this new artistic stream, which however was not generally adopted, architecture continued using late Gothic forms.

Bruges, Civil Office of the clerck, 1534-1537.
This facade with well-designed vertical and horizontal elements is one of the earliest examples of Renaissance in Flemish architecture. Nevertheless, the tops of the volutes are still decorated with bosses, as they were in late Gothic.

LATE FLOWERING OF THE BRABANT GOTHIC The 'Brabant Gothic' had an exuberant character at the beginning of the 16th century. It was feverishly continued in the ambitiously conceived churches, which were sometimes completed only late in the 16th or in the 17th century. But it was clear that its zenith had been passed. The masons and stonemasons attached more importance to complicated forms and exaggerated ornamentation, than to clarity of arrangement. The de Waghemakere and Keldermans families, continuing the tradition of their predecessors, still played a predominant role in Flanders and Zeeland. The north tower of the Antwerp Cathedral was finished off in 1521-1530 by Domien de Waghemakere and Rombout II Keldermans. Both cooperated on the New Bourse in Antwerp (1527-1531), and on the Town Hall in Ghent, for which they signed the contract together in 1518. In 1517

Audenarde, Town Hall, Hendrik van Pede, 1526-1536.
The detailing of the openwork parapet and the lacework effect of the ridge ornamentation are characteristic of the late (flamboyant) Gothic, while the winged *putti* on the pinacles of the dormer windows betray the influence of the new Renaissance style.

233

Rombout II Keldermans supplied the design for the spire – which was never completed – of St Rombout's tower in Malines. In his work, Flemish Gothic expressed its most extreme forms, and the Renaissance elements were only gradually and timidly applied.

From 1519 to 1539, Domien de Waghemakere and Rombout II Keldermans built the new Court of Aldermen in Ghent. The designs for this monumental project have been preserved. In the flamboyant late Gothic facades, carried out in yellow sand-limestone alternating with blue granite, the abundant sculptural ornamentation is driven to excess. As in so many places, unfavourable political and religious circumstances hindered the completion of these plans. In the extension to the Town Hall, in 1580-1618, there was a resolute choice of the new style.

Antwerp, St Jacob's Church, nave and choir, begun shortly after 1477, only finished in 1656.
This narrow and high church space was built in Brabant Gothic by Herman de Waghemakere the Elder, his sons Domien and Herman and Rombout Keldermans. In spite of the fact that the building took so long, this church shows a pure unity of style.

France, Bourg-en-Bresse, Church of Brou, 1513-1532.
This church was commissioned by Margaret of Austria. In the choir are the sepulchral monuments of Margaret of Austria (left), Philibert de Savoye (centre) and Marguerite de Bourbon (right), which together with the rood screen are of particularly flamboyant Gothic design.

Ghent, *St Bavo's Cathedral, nave and transept*, 1533-1559.
The highly risen cross is vaulted by a star-arch with in the middle a bell-opening. The arch-ribs and the clustered columns are made of sand-lime brick, the arch-panels of brick.

Ghent, *St Bavo's Cathedral*. View in the northern side-aisle from the choir gallery.

Together with the above-named architects, Laureys Keldermans, Hendrik van Pede and Lodewijk van Bodeghem played important roles up to the 1530's. Their works constituted the last expressions of a school that had never lost its vitality. Hendrik van Pede did further work on St Gummarus' Church in Lier and on St Gudula's Church in Brussels. But he is principally known as the designer of the Town Hall at Audenarde (1526-1536), the last in the series of famous Flemish town halls in the late Gothic style.

Lodewijk van Bodeghem deserves to be mentioned as master of works for the sepulchral church of the country governor Margaret of Austria in Brou (Bourg-en-Bresse in Burgundy). This is the southermost monument testifying to the important spread of 'Brabant Gothic'. This mausoleum, built in honour of Margaret's husband Philibert of Savoy, who died young, and his mother Marguerite de Bourbon – her own tomb being placed near to this – was completed with surprising speed (1513-1532). Here too, Renaissance ornamentation was cautiously mixed with the flamboyant play of lines.

Some Antwerp parish churches, such as St Jacob's and St Andrew's, are late examples of the 'Brabant Gothic style'. If the outside architecture mostly remains sober, the inner space is always impressive. Its characteristics are the pointed dividing arches on round pillars with 'cabbage-leaf capitals', the triforium zone reduced to a parapet with late Gothic tracery, and the involved rib vaults with pendant keystones.

St Bavo's Cathedral in Ghent is also an outstanding example of the tenacious Gothic tradition, which would persist for a long time yet. The high Gothic choir with the radiating chapels arose in the course of the 14th and 15th centuries, while the Romanesque nave continued in use. In 1452 the first stone of the west tower was laid, probably built according to the design of Jan Stassins. The spire was not completed till 1534. Only then the Romanesque lower church was demolished; and in 1553-1559, with the inevitable delay, the nave and the transept arms were built.

'Brabant Gothic' was characterized by the predominant use of white natural stone, a thankful material for fine stonemasons' work. In the 16th century, there was increasing use of brick, alternating with this rich material. Above all in the Campines, both building materials were used in alternating layers. A good example of this is the tower of St Catherine's Church in Hoogstraten (1525-1546), after a design by Rombout II Keldermans.

235

Ghent, Graslei, guild-hall of the free shippers, 1530/31.
Modest houses were built in brick, using sand-lime brick only for the elements necessary in the construction. The powerful guilds often had a facade built in natural stone under the influence of the luxuriant Brabant Gothic.

THE GUILD-HALLS AS EXAMPLES OF THE AMBIGUOUS STYLE

More than one guild-hall, symbol of the economic and political power of the guilds at this time, admirably illustrates the transition from the late Gothic to the early Renaissance. Here we shall give only a few examples.

The monumental Meat Hall in Antwerp, built in 1501-1504 for the butchers' guild after the design of Herman de Waghemakere, is still constructed entirely in the traditional late Gothic. The decorative use of the alternating layers of materials and the pointed arch windows with tracery is based on the 'Brabant Gothic' of the region. The many-sided stair towers, with jutting look-out, were also an Antwerp speciality in the houses of the wealthy bourgeoisie. In Bruges too, the style of the shoemakers' guild-hall (1527) derives from local late Gothic architecture. The stepped gable, completely in brick, with the vertical window niches set in separate or combined arched niches, richly ornamented with tracery, is typical of the 16th-century Bruges.

The facades of the guild-halls of the masons (1527) and of the free boatmen (1530) on the *Graslei* in Ghent, both after a design by Christoffel van de Berghe, were built completely in sand-limestone, emphasizing still further the wealth and power of the guilds. Here too the influence of 'Brabant Gothic' is noticeable; although the stiffer skeleton structure, the horizontal mouldings and the shape of the gable tops already point to a slight influence from the emerging Renaissance.

We can see the influence of the Renaissance more clearly in the high granite facade of the house *In den Grooten Zalm* in Malines, the headquarter of the fishmongers, built around 1535 after a design by Willem van Werchtere. Here, the principle of Vitruvius is applied by the superposition of the three orders of columns (Doric, Ionian and Corinthian). But behind the Renaissance ornamentation of the surface, there still lurks a Gothic structure.

The house *De Balans* on the *Grote Markt* at Antwerp, built in 1541 for the cloth-shearers, shows a more classical model. But the awkward piling up of the old architectonic elements (different types of columns, friezes with metopes and triglyphs, obelisks, frontons) gains the upper hand over the clear construction. The design and the proportions are still derived from the Gothic type of facade: a representative characteristic of early Renaissance in Flanders.

Antwerp, *Vleeshuis* (House of the Butchers' Guild) 1501-1504.
This Gothic building was ran up in brick with as decoration the regular use of steatite-layers and continuing window drips in sand-lime brick. This method was used in Antwerp till the end of the 17th century. The multilateral stairtowers with inclining look-out are also a typical Antwerp peculiarity.

THE SPREAD OF THE RENAISSANCE THROUGH THEORETICAL WORKS In contrast to painters and sculptors, many of whom sought direct contact with the new influence by a shorter or longer study trip to Italy, the spread of Renaissance architectural forms in Flanders came in particular from printed books. Only few architects undertook the journey to Italy. Some Italian artists – such as Thomas Vincidor, Alexander Pasqualini and Donato de'Boni Pellizuolo – exercised their influence directly in the Netherlands. But the empirical knowledge, which in the Middle Ages was communicated almost exclusively within the closed building sites and the masons' guilds, could now be widened thanks to the revolutionary progress of book printing. This created an artist of a new type: the intellectually trained and many-sided artist, whose knowledge was wider and whose creative power more personal than that of the medieval master builder.

The works of the Roman architect Vitruvius were published in 1486 in Rome and in 1511 in Venice. Since that time, various translations appeared. From 1539 onwards, Pieter Coecke van Aelst (1502-1550) of Antwerp, published these works in Dutch and French. In that year there appeared *Invention of Columns*, an adaptation of Vitruvius, and *General Rules of the Five Building Manners*, a translation of the fourth volume of the great encyclopaedia published by Sebastiano Serlio. In 1546 he published the third volume of Serlio's series *The most famous Antique Buildings*. After his death, his widow Mayke Verhulst – later the mother-in-law of Pieter Breughel the elder – took over the publishing of the first, second and fifth volumes. These translations met with a wide response and contributed to disseminating the principles of antique architecture over the whole of northern Europe, even as far as England. Their influence is especially marked in Hans Vredeman de Vries (1527-1606 ?) who, in his turn, published model books from 1555 onwards; and in the Antwerp sculptor and architect Cornelis de Vriendt, known as Floris (1514-1575). Both developed their own style which was named after them.

THE TOWN HALL OF ANTWERP The plans for a new late Gothic town hall which were drawn up in 1541 by Domien de Waghemakere, were never carried out. Fresh initiatives were made in 1560 for the building of a new town hall. A working group was set up, consisting of ten artists, mainly sculptors and decorators, and within a short period this group had drawn the plans and had a model made. The advice and collaboration of some foreign artists such as the Florentine Nicolo Scarini and Loys de Foys, the king's architect, may have played a decisive role in this. Cornelis Floris was entrusted with the direction of the works which lasted from 1561 to 1564. Thus the Town Hall of Antwerp is the teamwork of Flemish and foreign artists. It is one of the most important building works in the Southern Netherlands in an indigenous Renaissance style. Taking as a basis the still surviving Gothic tradition, a synthesis was made of the building form of the earlier guild-halls and town halls, and the full-grown Italian Renaissance style. New in this was the horizontal articulation of the main facade, interrupted in the middle by the verticalizing top gable. Equally original was the pictorial use of materials, alternating pink marble with white and blue natural stone. The use of bossage work in the plinth, the superposition of the three orders of columns and the openwork gallery on the top floor are all elements taken over from the Italian *Palazzo*. The polychrome coats of arms and the sculpture contribute to an exuberant impression of luxuriance; a Flemish trait we find both in the Gothic and the Baroque. This achievement was widely imitated in the Northern Netherlands and in Germany.

Antwerp, town hall, maquette, 1560/61. Antwerp, Archaeologic Museums Vleeshuis.
The design for the Antwerp town hall is the result of a committee of internal and foreign artists, who were gathering in this respect from December 1560 till March 1561. These artists were Cornelis Floris de Vriendt, Willem Paludanus, Wouter van Elsmeer, Jean Massys, Lambert van Noort, Jacques du Broeucq from Mons, Jean du Gardin from Lille, Lambert Suavis from Liege, Louis de Foys from Paris and Niccola Scarani from Florence.

Antwerp, town hall, 1561-1564.
This monumental Renaissance facade, with a central part that is typically Flemish and that stands out higher as did medieval belfry towers, was imitated a lot in the North.

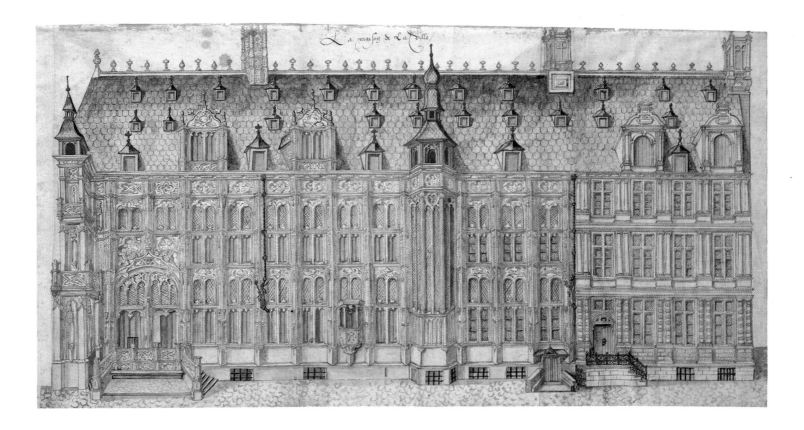

THE SPREAD OF FLEMISH RENAISSANCE IN NORTHERN EUROPE

The 16th century signified, for Antwerp in particular, a high point economically, socially and culturally. But the time of glory was short-lived. The troubles, beginning in 1566 with the iconoclasm and ending for the Southern Netherlands with the capitulation of Antwerp in 1585, put an end to the great fervour for building and drove many Brabant master builders abroad. There, in the last quarter of the 16th century, they spread the 'Floris' and 'Vredeman de Vries style'.

Here the Antwerp family van Steenwinckel played an outstanding role. Laurens van Steenwinckel built the Emden Town Hall in 1574-1576; it was modelled on that of Antwerp. The same high central projection marked the horizontally articulated main facade. Emden, the German port on the North Sea, just beyond the frontier of the Netherlands, was actually an important place of refuge for non-catholic refugees fleeing from the Netherlands. Hans, son of Laurens van Steenwinckel, took refuge in Denmark where he entered the service of King Frederick II, and built various castles and fortresses for him. Among the plans he supplied were those for the Frederiksborg Castle at Hilleröd. From 1582 to 1700 the van Steenwinckels held the office of 'master builder and inspector of the royal buildings' to the Danish royal family.

The Malines master builder Antoon van Opbergen (1543-1611) also fled to Denmark where, from 1577 onwards, he worked on Kronborg Castle near Helsingör. In 1601-1605 he built the arsenal in the flourishing commercial town of Danzig, the most important work of Flemish character in the German Baltic region.

Lieven de Key (1560-1621) of Ghent left his birthplace in 1580 because of his religious convictions and

Ghent, town hall, facades along the Hoogpoort, aquarelle, 69.5 × 104 cm, 1585. Ghent, Bijloke Museum.
This drawing by Lieven van der Schelden represents the facades of the town hall in late Gothic style, from 1519-1539, with next to them the Renaissance facade of the so-called Bollaertskamer, dating from 1580-1582.

Veurne, *Town Hall,* former country-house and belfry, 1596-1628.
At the left we notice the two brick gables of the Town Hall, dated from 1596 and 1612. The in and out-swerving gables are a regional interpretation of the Vredeman de Vries style. At the right we see the belfry tower (1628) and the former House of the Chancellery (1613-1621), testifying of a more classical tendency in Renaissance architecture.

Audenarde, *Episcopal House*, around 1623-1626.
By using blue natural brick to set the front, and because of the strict symmetrical composition of the fronts with superposition of Doric and Ionic columns, this architecture is more associated with the Italian high Renaissance, as propagated by Cornelis Floris de Vriendt.

settled in London; later, in 1591, he went to Haarlem where he was appointed town carpenter and stonemason. There he created various civil buildings such as part of the Town Hall, the Weighing House and the Meat Hall. By their colourful effects and their plasticity with strongly protruding mouldings, they represented a Flemish contribution to the north, and a harbinger of the coming Baroque style.

THE REGIONAL INTERPRETATION OF THE ITALIAN RENAISSANCE AT THE END OF THE 16TH CENTURY

At the end of the 16th century and the beginning of the 17th, preference was often given to a stricter Italianate classicism, attaching more importance to pure architectonic requirements than to ornamentation, and stressing clarity of form. This found expression in Ghent, for example, when the Town Hall was extended by the addition of the so-called *Bollaertskamer* (1580-1582), and in the building of the new wing next to the late Gothic Court of Aldermen (1595-1618). Both facades are strongly accentuated horizontally and show the usual superposition of the three different orders applied to heavy three-quarter columns.

Also the house of the *Kasselrij* in Veurne (1613-1621) and the *Bisschoppenhof* in Audenarde (*ca* 1623-1626) testify to this classical trend under the influence of the 'Floris style', by the use of blue granite and the arrangement of the pilasters or columns. But for the most part, builders stayed with a late interpretation of the Renaissance ornaments on traditional wall structures, long remaining true to the style forms of the region.

The Town Hall at Veurne (1595-1612) is a representative example of this regional interpretation of the Renaissance style, where the aedicula windows and the ribbonwork and scrollwork of the gable tops betray the influence of the 'Vredeman de Vries style'. The use of brick is also particular to the region. The masons' guildhall in Bruges (1621), with its richly painted and gilded pilaster facade and the top gable curving strongly in and outwards, also points to this specific style influence; although in the arch spaces of the top windows there is a stubborn persistence of late Gothic tracery.

CASTLES   To conclude this Renaissance period, we refer to some castles, mostly medieval fortified strongholds converted to residences in the 16th century. They are always very simple in design; they certainly do not vie with the luxury of the famous French chateaux on the Loire. We shall give only three examples from among the wealth of castles in Flanders.

Cleyham Water Castle in Aartselaar still has a 14th-century keep where around 1518-1520 a new residence was erected by Pieter van der Straeten, a friend of Emperor Charles. Its dining hall is adorned by a timbered ceiling in the 'Floris style' (1556).

Rumbeke Castle came into being over various building periods at the beginning and in the middle of the 16th century. With the numerous towers and the facades completely in red brick, it is a characteristic example of a Flemish country castle.

The alternating layers of brick and white natural stone of the Horst Water Castle in St Pieters-Rode are connected with the late Gothic architecture of the region. The irregularly polygonal layout is a relic of the medieval fortress, whose foundations go back to the 13th century. The residential wings date from the 16th and 17th centuries.

Rumbeke, Castle, 16th century.
Built in a regional architectural style, this castle was originally surrounded by moats. These were partly filled in during the 18th century.

Sculpture

During the 16th century Flemish sculpture underwent a complete transformation. Almost a century behind Italy, the Renaissance reluctantly set in in the countries north of the Alps, where the Gothic style was firmly established. The new ideas and the latinization of philosophy and literature were quickly assimilated in Europe through Humanism. In contrast to this, the concepts on form and design of the Italian Renaissance took time to be adopted both in architecture and the visual arts. During the first decades of the 16th century the traditional Gothic style and the progressive movement co-existed in Flemish sculpture.

Only when Cornelis II Floris de Vriendt returned from Italy in about 1539, the Italianate principles were assimilated and a Flemish Renaissance developed, which was particularly successful in northern and central Europe. The Renaissance only flourished in Flanders for a short time. The unfavourable political and religious climate, of which the waves of iconoclasm of 1566 and 1578 were the most striking crisis points, made it difficult for the Renaissance to develop. It rather became a transitional style, which anticipated the more mature forms of the Baroque style.

FLAMBOYANT AND LATE GOTHIC EARLY RENAISSANCE STYLE
(first half of the 16th century)

During the first half of the 16th century the work of Flemish sculptors and wood-carvers was remarkably restricted by tradition. The continuing success of the late Gothic style was largely due to the nature of the works of art that were commissioned. Like those of the 15th century, they had a decorative rather than a monumental function. This tendency was particularly expressed in the interior decoration of places of worship, for which numerous altarpieces, choir stalls, sacramental towers and rood screens were ordered. Biblical stories and lives of the saints were merely an excuse for the execution of opulent works of art, which exhibited great wealth and splendour.

The late Gothic mass-production of altarpieces in Antwerp continued during the first half of the 16th century. The religious themes in the increasingly tall and wide retables were less conducive to devotion, as can be seen in the overpopulated Virgin retable (Antwerp *ca* 1510-1520) in St Laurence's Church in Bocholt.

Mary-retable, oak, renewed polychromy, tray 276 × 246 × 36 cm, Antwerp, 1510-1520. Bocholt, St Leonard's Church.
The retable depicts the life of Mary around the tree of Jesse. Although the verticalism and the architectonic dressing are still strongly late Gothic, the figures already show the beginning of Renaissance.

Partly as a result of Humanism and the Renaissance a new style developed in Antwerp, which was influenced in the 1520's by the contemporary mannerist school of painting. The sculptors aimed at a high degree of realism in their representation of numerous naive figures and lively tableaux, at the expense of mystical and devotional aspects; thus reaching a strong element of caricature, the formulae of which were endlessly repeated. The slender mannered figures seem to writhe with violent gestures. These restless compositions of fashionably dressed figures with imaginative head-gear, seemingly taking part in a dance, can be found in the *Passion* retable of Oplinter (Antwerp *ca* 1530), now in the Museums of Art and History in Brussels. The decorative elements of the early Renaissance were first used hesitantly and later with abandon, though not always in the right way.

Late Gothic mannerism was also expressed in the Brussels altarpieces, which continued to be well-known for their excellent quality. This new trend is evident in the retable depicting the martyrs St Crispinus and St Crispianus (1515-1525), the patron saints of the tanners and cobblers, which was possibly commissioned for the guild altar in St Waltrudis' Church in Herentals. Passier Borreman borrowed the figures from the well-known altarpiece of St George for this exceptionally signed example. The torturers are represented in a more trivial manner and the figures no longer have the calm and sober nature which we find in the work of Jan I Borreman. The event is depicted in a place surrounded by buildings which incorporate elements derived from secular Renaissance architecture. This is still clearer in

The decapitation of the Saints Crispinus and Crispinianus, detail from the retable representing the *Torture of the Saints Crispinus and Crispianus*, non-polychromed oak, 215 × 207 × 40.5 cm, signed by Passier Borreman, Brussels, about 1520. Herentals, St Waltrudis' Church.
The rare iconography leads to the assumption that this retable was made to order. If we compare it with the refined figures from the Retable of St Georges (which had been carved by his father, Jan Borreman the Elder), the personages of Passier Borreman, although they are technically of high quality, show a late Gothic mannerism, in which all inspiration is missing.

General view on the choir benches from the epistel side. Mathys de Wayere, Brussels, 1536-1544, drastically transformed by the Goyers brothers; destroyed in 1944 by bombing and reconstructed by Jozef van Uytvanck (1945-1954). Louvain, St Gertrudis' Church.

Ecce Homo, back of the choir stalls (detail).
The central theme of the choir benches of the St Gertrudis' Church is the Redemption. On the reliefs on the back, which are considered the best part of the performance, scenes from the life of Christ are represented.

the imaginative Italianate background to the tableaux of the Virgin retable in Our Lady-at-Lombeek's Church in Roosdal (Brussels *ca* 1520).

The flourishing mass-production of altarpieces came to an end in the middle of the 16th century. The taste and fashion of the time had radically altered under the influence of the Renaissance; and with the emergence of the Reformation, which denounced images of this sort, the demand for retables decreased considerably.

The relatively small, charming and elegant devotional statuettes, made in Malines, were widely distributed. In addition to artificial flowers and plants, relics and decorative inscriptions, they were popular in the so-called 'Closed Gardens', bearing witness to a naive devotion in hostels and beguinages. For example, the Closed Garden of the Museum of the Commission for Public Relief in Malines (early 16th century) contains the charmingly depicted statuettes of the Saints Ursula and Cathlene, as well as the elderly Elisabeth of Hungary.

From a structural point, the choir stalls of the church of the former St Gertrude's Abbey in Louvain (Brussels 1540-1544) still belonged to the late Gothic tradition. This work, a summit of the flamboyant Gothic style in Flanders, was commissioned in 1540 by the abbot Pieter Was from the Brussels joiner Matthijs de Wayere. The transalpine designs are subtly present in numerous decorative details of the masonry work, the well-balanced structure of the compositions, the extremely flat surface of the carved relief and the figurative sculpture, showing almost classicistic drapery of the garments with ornamental borders.

Rood screens too were overgrown with late Gothic masonry work, following the example of Our Lady's Church in Aarschot (first quarter of the 16th century), characterized by an optimum transparency. Groups of figures depicting the passion of Christ, similar to the sculpture in contemporary retables, appear in the small dark niches of the parapet. Nowhere does the decoration achieve a greater degree of vitality than in the rood screen of St Nicolas' Church in Veurne (now in Dixmude), commissioned from the master sculptor Jan Bertet (1535-1541).

One striking example of the late Gothic requirements of the patrons at a time when the Renaissance was gradually becoming established was the sacramental tower of St James's Church in Louvain (1537-1539). According to the contract with the parish priest Franco de Campo (22nd December 1537), the sculptor Gabriël van den Bruyne was to use the late Gothic sacramental tower of St Peter's Church in Louvain (*ca* 1450) as a model for the new work.

Pulpitum, Brabant, first quarter of the 16th century. Aarschot, Our-Lady's Church.
This is one of the most performed examples of small architecture in Brabant during the late Gothic period, for which the extreme skeletonbuilding and the open-work are characteristic. Testifying of the same pictural spirit are the sculptured groups which adorn the small niches in the parapet and which are clearly related to the retable sculpture of the period from 1500-1525.

Thus the Italian formal repertory infiltrated the deeply rooted late Gothic tradition as a new fashion in art. The transitional style in which the new ornamental designs were assimilated into a Gothic structure can hardly be described as Renaissance art; as the sculptors merely adopted the external features and the formulae of the new language of design in their works, being unable to translate the spirit of the classical *rinascita* in the Italian manner. As a result, the ornamental artists played the leading role. They specialized in making *antycke*, and were therefore known as antique-carvers.

THE SCULPTORS AT THE COURT OF MARGARET OF AUSTRIA IN MALINES (1506-1530)

The true Renaissance could only thrive in an aristocratic intellectual environment rooted in the humanist tradition, able to assess the value of the new art forms inspired by Graeco-Roman antiquity. In the Southern Netherlands the first Renaissance centre was the city of Malines, where Margaret of Austria had her court as the regent, while her nephew Charles V had not reached the age of majority (between 1506 and 1515), and where she was later appointed as the governess. Her extensive court acted as a patron of Renaissance art, and the temporary success of sculpture can largely be attributed to its influence. Therefore, during the first half of the 16th century, Malines was a great centre of attraction for leading artists from other countries, who followed the Italian models in applying the art forms and aesthetic principles of classical art.

As the governess' court sculptor, Conrad Meit from Worms (who worked from 1496-1550/51) settled in Malines in about 1512. Previously he had been introduced to Renaissance art in Wittenberg through his contact with Lucas Cranach, the court painter to the Elector Frederick the Wise of Saxony; and possibly also with Jacopo de' Barbari, a master from Venice, who had lived in Germany for many years as a pioneer of Italian art. Whether Meit also met Dürer is not certain, but he undoubtedly came across Dürer's graphic work.

Meit's statuettes, such as the alabaster figure of Judith (now in the Bavarian National Museum in Munich), date from this period in Saxony. In these figures the Gothic tradition was abandoned and a completely new style emerged. This sculpture is completely free-standing, and the interest in pseudo-antique nude figures of Italian masters such as Barbari is evident in the sparsely clad or nude figures, as with all neophytes of Italianism.

Meit distinguished himself in portraiture in the service of Philip of Burgundy. This new genre had enjoyed great success in Italy since the 15th century, because it expressed the growing consciousness of the human personality. It was thanks to his realistic representation of the human form that Margaret of Austria commissioned him to make a number of statues for three mausoleums (1526-1531) in the church of Brou near Bourg-en-Bresse, which had also been commissioned by her from the Brussels architect Lodewijk van Bodeghem. This large work of sculpture comprised the mausoleums erected for her husband Philibert of Savoy (free-standing tomb in two tiers), who died at a young age, for his mother Margaret of Bourbon (wall-niche tomb), and for herself (hall-tomb). For this prestigious commission Meit was to work from designs by the Brussels painter Jan van Roome. The most important parts, described in the contract as '*les visages, les mains et les vifs*', were to be executed by Conrad Meit himself. He stood clearly on the threshold of the Renaissance with these recumbent alabaster figures, which reveal a remarkable technical skill and are permeated with powerful realism tempered by a quiet dignity.

Apart from his popular cabinet pieces, Meit also showed his skill in portraiture in Malines, his works including the busts identified as Margaret of Austria's and Philibert of Savoy's (London, British Museum). There is some similarity to the melancholy Margaret of Brou in the half figure of Mary (1525) in St Michael's Cathedral in Brussels. Meit spent the last years of his life in Antwerp, where he was enrolled in St Luke's Guild in 1536. However, Meit was not able to assimilate the new Italian style in his portraits or in his nudes.

The saints Ursula, Catharine and Elisabeth of Hungary, enclosed garden, beginning of the 16th century. Malines, Museum van de Commissie voor Openbare Onderstand.
The so-called 'besloten Hofjes' contain, except artificial flowers and plants, banderoles, relics and painted panels, also the so popular typical Malines statuettes which show a slight hip-twist.

His contemporary Jan Mone(t) (*ca* 1485-1550), who came from Lorraine, developed further in the new direction. Before Charles V appointed him as '*artiste de l'empereur*' in 1521, he lived in Aix-en-Provence and in Barcelona, where he worked with the well-known Renaissance sculptor, Bartolomè Ordoñez. There is no documentary evidence whether Mone met the art forms of the *quattrocento* in Italy itself. After a brief interlude in Antwerp in 1520, he settled in Malines permanently in 1524; he secured important commissions from the aristocratic circles of the court, such as alabaster altarpieces and mausoleums which bore witness to a pure Renaissance spirit.

The alabaster retable of St Martin in Our Lady's Church in Halle is Mone's only dated (1553) and signed work. Apart from the emphasis on its vertical structure,

Madonna, marble, 65 cm, ascribed to Conrad Meyt, ca 1525. Brussels, St Michael's Cathedral.
The statue of the divine mother who already anticipates the suffering of her son, is ascribed to Conrad Meyt by J. de Borchgrave d'Altena, based on the fact that she resembles closely to the recumbent statue of Margaret of Austria on her sepulchral monument at Brou.

Sepulchral monument of Margaret of Austria, designed by Jan van Roome (1513-1541) and performed by Conrad Meyt and assistants, 1524-1532. Bourg-en-Bresse, Church of Brou.
This sepulchral monument is, just like that of her husband Philibert of Savoye, a free-standing tomb which consists of two floors on top of which the recumbent statue of the deceased is presented 'au vif' in all his dignity, and at the bottom as 'mort' in a simple mourningdress.

this type of retable is comparable to the most beautiful works of art from the Renaissance in Florence. The horizontal sections are decorated with *tondi*, depicting the seven sacraments. The *horror vacui* decor consists of a collection of Italianate ornamentation: the friezes and pilasters are filled with twining vines in which all the variations of the arabesque motifs are used, together with winged heads of angels and *putti* in high relief.

The mausoleum of Cardinal Guillaume de Croy in St Peter's Church in Edingen (*ca* 1528/29) has been attributed to Mone on the basis of its stylistic similarity. This walltomb is reminiscent of the well-known 15th-century tombs of the humanists Rosselino and De Settignano in Santa Croce's in Florence. Other mausoleums which have been attributed to Mone include those of Anthony de Lalaing and Elisabeth de Culembourg in Hoogstraten and the free-standing mausoleum of Maximiliaan van Hoorn in Kasteelbrakel near Halle.

The Italian ornamentation repertory of the *quattrocento* made a permanent breakthrough in the Southern

245

St Martin's Retable, alabaster, Jan Mone (Jehan Monet), 1533. Halle, Our Lady's Basilica.
Beneath the new Renaissance forms, the Gothic tradition still lingers in the pyramidal construction of the retable. Exceptionally, the liturgical acts of the seven sacraments, in which the Eucharist is central, has been represented.

Recumbent statue of Elisabeth of Culembourg and Antoine Lalaing († 1540), tomb (detail), black marble and alabaster, originally polychromed, 189 × 220 × 350 cm, ascribed to Jan Mone, 1525-1529. Hoogstraten, St Catharine's Church.
The free-standing double tomb, which shows the recumbent statues of the founders of St Catharine's Church at Hoogstraten in full state, must have been closely resemblant to the not preserved tomb of Willem van Croy in the Celestine's Church at Heverlee.

Netherlands with the work of Mone. The well-known small alabaster reliefs with their elegant Renaissance frames and hints of colour and gold, which were produced in Malines on an industrial scale until the 17th century, were very popular. However, these must have originated near the ateliers of Mone and de Beaugrant. The reliefwork on the house retable with the *Adoration of the Magi* (ca 1535-1540, Brussels, Museums of Art and History) is actually closely related to that of Mone.

Mone's fellow-countryman Guyot de Beaugrant (ca 1500-1551) also worked in Malines. In 1526 he was commissioned by Margaret of Austria to build the mausoleum for her brother Franz who had died young. This work was intended for Coudenberg Church at Brussels, but unfortunately has not survived.

De Beaugrant's familiarity with the art forms of the Italian Renaissance is particularly evident in the monumental chimneypiece of the *Brugse Vrije*. This magnificent whole, made of wood, marble and alabaster, was erected between 1528 and 1531 in the council hall of the *Brugse Vrije*; and was based on the design of Lanceloot Blondeel, in honour of Charles V. In addition to five life-size oak statues of the Emperor and members of the Habsburg dynasty, designed by Blondeel, de Beaugrant sculpted the four alabaster winged *putti* in the Italian style of Verrochio; and also carved the alabaster frieze, which depicted four scenes from the tale of law and morality, Susanna and the Elders. The use of *rilievo schiacciato* was entirely new in the Southern Netherlands and was successfully used in Malines until the 17th century. However, this rather classical ensemble contrasts with Blondeel's contribution, which emanates a typical Flemish exuberance.

The figures of the apostles of the former monumental retable of the high altar in St James's Church in Bilbao, are reminiscent of the figures on the alabaster relief. De Beaugrant was commissioned to execute this work in 1537. Although de Beaugrant was very close stylistically to the Italian Renaissance of the *quattrocento* in his own works, he lacked the elegance of an artist such as Mone.

The new forms of art were not only disseminated in the Southern Netherlands by foreign artists who were working in the area and who undoubtedly represented great competition for the local workshops. It was no longer a *conditio sine qua non* for Flemish sculptors to undertake a pilgrimage to Italy, the source of the new style, to come into contact with the Italian Renaissance. Through drawings and engravings they also became acquainted with the pure Renaissance of Florence, Rome, Bologna and Milan.

In this context it is significant that on his diplomatic mission to Rome (ca 1508) Philip of Burgundy chose to be accompanied by the painter Jan Gossaert, who was commissioned to make drawings of the classical monuments. The influence of this journey is clear from Gossaert's design for the much discussed mausoleum of Isabella of Austria (1501-1526), spouse of Christian II of Denmark, which made good use of the Italian art forms. The epitaph of this mausoleum – which has not survived, but once stood in the choir of St Peter's Minster in Ghent – was made by Jan de Heere, who came from Malines and had worked since 1526 in the workshop of the stonecarver-sculptor Jan de Smijtere, who completed the tomb before his death.

The Renaissance designs and motifs were introduced in the Southern Netherlands on a grand scale in the decorations, intended to create a pseudo-classical look in cities on the occasions of the Trumphal Entries, such as those of Charles V in Bruges in 1515 and 1520.

The Italianate art forms were first expressed in the decoration of works in which the late Gothic tradition continued to be used. Some of these hybrid ensembles include the above-mentioned altarpieces from the first half of the 16th century, which helped to establish Renaissance art.

The same tendency is also expressed in the rood screen which was commissioned in 1517 from a workshop in Malines (Kelderman?) by Joris and Nicasius Hackenay, stewards of Emperor Maximilian I, for their parish church of *Sankt Maria im Kapitol* in Cologne. The black marble pillars, the ornamentation of the capitals, the canopies and the friezes, the tondi and the balusters, reveal a master who was consciously striving to follow the new direction in his ornamental decorum. However, despite their Italianate execution, the statues of the saints and prophets, as well as the reliefs, remained faithful to the Gothic spirit of retable sculpture.

Emperor Charles, central figure of the chimney-piece (detail). Bruges, Room of Aldermen of the Vrije.
This life-sized statue was sculptured by Guyot de Beaugrant, after a design by Lanceloot Blondeel.

Chaste Suzanne with the Elderlings, chimney-piece (detail frieze in alabaster), Guyot de Beaugrand, 1529-1531. Bruges, Room of Aldermen of the Vrije.
These four reliefs, representing the moralizing history of Chaste Suzanne, are important to learn about Beaugrant's style. They contrast sharply with the contribution Lanceloot Blondeel made. He misses all sense of clarity in his exuberance in accumulating ornamental motifs.

The source material of the town archivist of Bruges, Parmentier (1949), reveals that apart from the talented Lanceloot Blondeel, another progressive sculptor, Michiel Scherrier, who specialized in both wood and stone, was also at work in the 16th-century Bruges. According to the archivist's documents, this artist was responsible for the execution of the episcopal mausoleum of Jan Carondelet, chancellor of Flanders and archbishop of Palermo, in St Donate's Church (1540-1550). Of the original ensemble, only the alabaster recumbent figure of Carondelet on the black marble tombstone and the copper epitaph plate have survived (now in St Saviour's Cathedral). The magnificently executed alabaster figure of Carondelet, which shows the prelate meditating in a semi-recumbent position, recalls the humanist tombs of Santa Croce's in Florence.

House-Retable, alabastar, wood painted in a dark green and gilt filling-up, 100.5 × 55 cm, Malines, about 1535-1540. Brussels, Museums of Art and History.
The central relief depicts the *Adoration of the Magi* in a luxuriant Renaissance scenery and is, as far as the style is concerned, related to the work of Jan Mone. On the trilateral frame, which is around this relief, ornaments in Floris' style have been glued.

Sepulchral monument of Jan Carondelet († 1544), marble and alabaster, traces of polychromy, recumbent statue: 170 cm; sarcophagus and pedestal: 89 × 190 cm, Michel Scherrier, ca 1545 (severely damaged at the end of the 18th century). Bruges, St Salvator's Church.
Originally the recumbent statue of Carondelet was lying on a sarcophagus in a rounded arch nich, sided by two half columns and crowned by an arch area representing the Last Judgment on top of which is a Deësis group.

HIGH RENAISSANCE SCULPTURE IN ANTWERP
(ca 1550-1585)

When Margaret of Austria, a great patroness of the arts, died in 1530, the seat of government and administration moved to Brussels; so that a large number of artists who had worked in Malines, including Conrad Meit, Rombout de Drijvere, Joos van Santvoort and Willem van den Broecke (alias Paludanus), moved to Antwerp. This city had been flourishing enormously since the beginning of the 16th century in the economic and demographic spheres; and by the middle of the century it had become a prosperous trading metropolis where large numbers of wealthy merchants and traders, both from the Southern Netherlands and abroad, as well as humanists and reformists, came into contact with each other. The latter were responsible for the development of an ideal artistic climate in Antwerp, which attracted artists from every branch of the arts.

Following the Italian Renaissance artists, who sought to provide a scientific and theoretical foundation for their 'craft', a turn of the tide also took place in the conception of artistry in the Southern Netherlands. Leading sculptors gradually began to concentrate on producing designs for many different types of work, and restricted themselves to merely supervising the actual execution of the work. The distinction between the task of the designer or *inventor* and that of the sculptor or carver, became increasingly apparent. The work of Jan van Roome and Lanceloot Blondeel should be considered in this light, when they produced the designs which were elaborated respectively by Conrad Meit in Brou and by Guyot de Beaugrant in Brussels. Jan Gossaert was another *inventor* of funeral sculpture.

The versatile artist Pieter Coecke van Aelst (1502-1550) worked during the first half of the 16th century in Antwerp as an architect, painter and designer of tapestries and stained glass windows; but he was particularly famous as a theorist. His translations of Vitruvius (1539-1541) and Serlio (1539-1553), as well as the publication of his prints and engravings, undoubtedly contributed to the popularization of the grotesque style in the sculpture of the Netherlands. The first manifestation of this new powerful and solid system of decoration – in which iron scroll work was combined with grotesques or the scroll work actually became a grotesque – was in the festive decoration that was erected in 1549 under the supervision of Pieter Coecke and partly based on his designs, on the occasion of the Triumphal Entry of Philip II in Antwerp. The chimney from the *de Moelenere* House (1549), now in the mayor's room in the Town Hall of Antwerp, has been attributed to him, though there is little evidence to support this.

The Renaissance reached full maturity in the Netherlands with the work of Cornelis II Floris de Vriendt (1514-1575). It is significant that the second Renaissance in the Netherlands is known as the 'Floris style'; anticipating the Baroque style in Flanders, which continued to be successful up to the middle of the 17th century. Cornelis Floris managed to impose a specifically Flemish character on the Florentine arabesque style; with which he had become acquainted during his studies in Italy. Departing from the grotesques in the work of Pieter Coecke, and probably also under the influence of the book of moresques by the Antwerp carver of figures Cornelis Bos (1506-1556), he developed a personal style of ornamentation which shows his unbridled imagination and remarkable vitality.

Floris' special creative talents are evident even in the signed, illustrated initials (from 1547) of the *Liggeren* or members' list of the St Luke's Guild in Antwerp (Antwerp, Academy archives of the old St Luke's Guild), and from the engravings with vases (1548) and other series of ornamental prints, which were published in Antwerp between 1554 and 1557. He skilfully assimilated figurative elements such as *putti*, herms, satyrs, wood nymphs and masques in cartouches and scrolls festooned with garlands. After his return from Italy, Floris organized from 1539 a workshop of sculptors on a commercial basis, so as to meet commissions from a large circle of customers very quickly; and as a result Floris became famous particularly in northern and central Europe.

Tomb of Christian III of Denmark, marble and alabaster, Cornelis II Floris de Vriendt, 1568-1575. Roskilde, Dom, Driekoningenkapel. The free-standing tomb of Christian III at Roskilde, the last and most impressive monument that was designed by Floris, is in the form of a hall tomb with a double representation of the deceased: on the heavy pedestal is the recumbent figure and on top of the cover of the six-pillar hall is the kneeling figure in front of a cross.

As a sculptor and designer of mausoleums and ecclesiastical furnishings, Floris strove to produce work of a sober character, and his pieces create a classical impression. He was able to distinguish clearly between structure and ornamentation, and he never allowed the grotesques to overwhelm the architectural form; on the contrary, in Floris' work they emphasize it. In the mausoleums of King Frederick I of Denmark in Schleswig Cathedral (1548) and of Jan III van Merode in St Dymphna's Church in Geel (1554), the plate of the sarcophagus is supported by strong caryatids, a motif based on the Burgundian lamenting figures. In Schleswig they represent the Virtues, and in Geel the bearers are brave warriors, reminiscent of the four kneeling knights of the mausoleum of Engelbrecht van Nassau in Breda.

Floris was also inspired by masterpieces of the Italian high Renaissance. For example, Floris' wall-tomb of Duke Albrecht I of Prussia (1570-1573) in Köningsberg Cathedral could have been influenced by Andrea Sansovino's Sforzamonument in *Santa Maria del Popolo* in Rome. Floris' ornamental free-standing mausoleum of King Christian III of Denmark in Roskilde Cathedral (1568-1575) recalls the tomb of Louis XII in St Denis, which has been attributed to the brothers Antonio and Giovanni Giusti. This typical two-tiered mausoleum displays two images of the dead king: on the upper tier kneeling in full state regalia, and below lying dead.

Although the nine-tiered sacramental tower of St Leonard's Church in Zoutleeuw was still in the Gothic tradition as regards its vertical composition and the sculpted groups, the structure of the work with its broad horizontal sections is clearly evident. This work was commissioned by Maarten van Wilre, Lord of Oplinter, and was erected in 1550-1552. Floris came closer to the Renaissance ideal in the more modest wall tabernacle of Zuurbemde (1555-1557).

Chimney-piece from the house de Moelnere, Antwerp Renaissance, 1544-1549. Antwerp, town hall, Room of the Mayor.
The decorative spectre with caryatids, banderoles, grotesques, lowreliefs picturing religious scenes which are treated in the romanizing style of the middle of the 16th century, shows characteristics which are typical for the Antwerp Renaissance.

The Last Supper, Marc and John, Sacramental tower (detail), 16.60 m, Cornelis II Floris de Vriendt, 1550-1552. Zoutleeuw, St Leonard's Church. Cornelis Floris had agreed on August 13, 1550 to the order of Maarten van Wilre to execute the sacramental tower in the church of Zoutleeuw, which was finished before Whitsuntide. The strong verticality of the nine floors with numerous pillars, corner statues and sculptured relief groups is still of Gothic tradition.

His talent as an architect is unmistakably revealed in the two-tone marble rood screen in Tournai Cathedral, which was erected after the wave of iconoclasm in 1572/73, and which is justifiably considered to be a classical masterpiece of the Renaissance in the Netherlands. The strict architectural use of the classical orders was probably based on the famous *Loggetta* by Jacopo da Sansovino in Venice. On the other hand, the statues and the figurative sculpture are conceived in a more decorative style, and are not really comparable with the expressive sculptures of Jacques du Broeucq of Hainault, which once stood in the rood screen of St Waltrudis' Church in Mons (*ca* 1545).

Because Floris' workshop executed a large number of commissions, and because he trained innumerable pupils who left the country for political and religious reasons, his ornamental style gained widespread recognition in central and northern Europe.

Floris' most independent pupil was undoubtedly Hans Vredeman de Vries (1527-1604), who came from Leeuwarden and worked in Malines and Antwerp in about 1548. This artist distinguished himself particularly as a theorist and creator of decorative designs. The grotesques of Coecke and Floris, as well as the ornamental prints of Ducerceau, were elaborated by Vredeman de Vries into a new decorative system, characterized by a higher degree of abstraction and a less solid appearance. With the publication and popularization of his numerous prints, drawings and pattern-books, as well as reprints and copies of these, he made his mark on the decorative arts of northern Europe up to the 17th century.

Jacob Jonghelinck (1530-1606), who worked predominantly as a bronze caster and medallist, produced more original work. The influence of Floris' ornamental style can only be detected in the heraldic wall decoration of the tomb of Charles the Bold, which Jonghelinck was commissioned to execute by Philip II. It was based on the example of the Gothic monument of Charles' daughter, Margaret of Burgundy, in Our Lady's Church at Bruges (1558-1562).

As a court sculptor, Jonghelinck made a number of statues for the open air, including the sculptures which adorned the court park in Brussels (which have not survived); and the life-size bronze statue of the Duke Alva, intended for the citadel in Antwerp, but destroyed as early as 1574. The Frick Collection in New York possesses a bust of this much hated duke (1577), revealing Jonghelinck's skilful use of this medium.

Pulpitum at aisle-side, black touchstone, rance-marble, alabaster and stucco-work, Cornelis II Floris de Vriendt, 1572-1574. Tournai, Our-Lady's Cathedral.
Being an experienced Renaissance artist, Floris shows how he was able to unite monumentality and ornamentation by a sparing use of statues and decorative motifs.

The Battle of Regensburg (1504) *and the Siege of Kufstein*, mausoleum of Maximilian I (detail from the 24 marble reliefs), Alexander Colyn (sculptor from Malines), after the design of Florian Abel (court painter at Prague), 1562-1566. Innsbruck, Hofkirche.
It is the sculptor from Cologne Arnold Abel who employs Alexander Colyn at Malines. The 24 reliefs in white Carrara marble, which are to represent to the glorification of Maximilian I the high-lights from his life, are meant for the sepulchral monument of this emperor which is placed in a court church is specially designed for this purpose.

A somewhat peculiar sculptor of low reliefs and statuettes for private collectors, was Willem van den Broecke, also known as Paludanus (1530-1580) from Malines, who went to Italy to complete his studies and was registered as a master in St Luke's Guild in Antwerp in 1557. In addition to his extensive oeuvres, which included retables and choir screens, Paludanus made small figurines for the *constcamers* or art cabinets of Antwerp. These comprised mythological scenes and anatomical studies, including the so-called *écorchés*, such as that of St Bartholemew dating from 1569

(Vienna, Kunstgewerbesammlung). Above all in this genre Paludanus paved the way for the Baroque.

Apart from the fact that Flemish sculpture was often exported abroad, a process in which the port of Antwerp played an important role, artists themselves also emigrated; and as a result the Flemish Renaissance – particularly the grotesque style of Floris – spread far and wide. Especially after 1567, when Alva instigated his Blood Tribunal in the Southern Netherlands and the political situation reached a crisis point, a wave of emigration swept through the Flemish artists. Whether most of them left the country because of religious persecution or for political reasons, is not always very clear. The certainty of acquiring commissions, wealth and fame were undoubtedly important motives during this period, when the Reformation had significantly reduced the number of patrons giving commissions; and as a result of the political unrest, there was an economic recession. Nor did the economy improve when the prosperity of the trading metropolis of Antwerp came to an abrupt end with the blockade of the Scheldt in 1585. Bruges artists mostly went to England, while many from Antwerp fled to northern and central Europe.

The success of Floris' work, particularly in Scandinavia and the protestant areas of Germany, *inter alia* through the presence of numerous mausoleums and epitaphs (Roskilde, Herlufsholm, Köningsberg, Schleswig) was undoubtedly due to the fact that many Flemish sculptors using the Floris style were working for German patrons. A few examples will serve to illustrate this.

Alexander Colijn (*ca* 1527-1612) worked sensitively and skilfully in alabaster, following the tradition of reliefs in Malines, the town of his birth. Examples of this can be seen in the twenty-one well-known reliefs depicting the life of Emperor Maximilian I, which decorated the tomb (1562-1566) of the emperor in the Innsbruck *Hofkirche*. Colijn had already worked on the sculptural decoration of Heidelberg Castle, commissioned by Ottheinrich, the elector of the Palatinate. The tomb of the elector Maurice of Saxony for Freiberg Cathedral, was made in the Antwerp workshop of Antoon Zerroen (second half of the 16th century); and the tomb of Edo Wiemken for the parish church at Jever (lower Saxony) was erected by Hendrik Hagart in 1561-1564.

With regard to the emigration of Flemish artists during the second half of the 16th century, the role of noble German mercenary leaders has recently been stressed; these served in the armies of both the Prince of Orange and of Spain. They took Renaissance artists from the Southern Netherlands in service to build and furnish their castles and palaces. In this way the Flemish grotesque style also spread to Germany, for example, through the members of the family of artists Robijn-Osten from Ypres; particularly the brothers Joris (*ca* 1522-1592) and Jan II (*ca* 1525 – after 1600) Robijn, and their cousin Peter Osten (*ca* 1545 – *ca* 1600) gave the style a personal character.

Up to now little attention has been devoted in the history of Flemish art to this emigration of artists from the Low Countries, despite its importance in the spread of the Flemish Renaissance.

Painting

The 16th century was a complex period during which western Europe experienced a number of far-reaching crises in different fields. The art of painting in the Low Countries was profoundly influenced by this. In contrast with the relatively homogeneous style of the Flemish Primitives of the previous century, the first impression one has of the 16th century is rather confusing. The art historians have often explained this as the result of the discrepancy between the surviving tradition of local schools of painting, and the rejuvenating influence of the Italian Renaissance. In this respect, the whole 16th century is seen as a period of imbalance, which only resolved itself at the beginning of the 17th century with Rubens.

However, this theory should be put into perspective. Undeniably the 16th century was determined by the transference of Renaissance ideas and forms, which had evolved in Italy a century earlier. However, this should not be considered as the only significant factor. The commonly held view of 16th-century art in the Netherlands places undue emphasis on the polarization between the so-called autochthonous tradition and a new, wholly imported style. In the past – especially during the 19th century – the influence of Italian art on artists in the Netherlands was often judged to be a negative factor. Driven by nationalistic feelings, many authors saw the imitation of the Renaissance style as a sort of betrayal by the Southern Netherlands artists of 'characteristically' Flemish qualities: precise realism, powerful colouration and a pious Catholicism. In contrast, the works of artists referred to as 'Romanists' or 'Italianists' were described as artificial, anaemic and lacking in content. These painters were often singled out as being responsible for what was felt to be a period of decline in Flemish art. Some even pitied the artists who, 'misled' by the Italian example, had made too little use of their pictorial qualities, which were supposed to be innate to the Flemish!

These views have continued to have their effect up to the present, albeit in a milder form, and less consciously.

In numerous books and articles Flemish 16th-century painting is still divided into 'Italianist' and 'autochthonous' movements. For the latter movement the names that spring to mind are Bosch and Bruegel, and to a lesser extent, painters of landscapes and genre scenes. Artists specifically representing the Italianist trend included, in successive generations, Jan Gossaert, Barend van Orley, Pieter Coecke, Frans Floris, Maarten de Vos and Otto Venius. It should be mentioned in passing that 'Italian Renaissance' here had become a floating concept. Many painters from the Netherlands travelled to Italy to discover a sequence of new styles: the Lombardy school of Leonardo da Vinci, the late representatives of the *quattrocento* in Rome, Raphael and his school, Michelangelo, Titian, Tintoretto, the Florentine Mannerists, *etc.*

However, this is not the only reason why the separation between autochthonous and Italianist, between indigenous and imported art, is largely a fiction. If such a division can be made, it is based more on differences in iconography than in style. It is therefore often difficult to categorize the artists from that period consistently under one movement or the other. To begin with Quinten Metsijs: his religious works are executed in the spirit

Jan Provoost, *The Decapitation of Catherine of Alexandria*, panel, 94 × 68 cm. Antwerp, Museum of Fine Arts.

Pieter Bruegel the Elder, *Hunters in the Snow*, panel, 117 × 162 cm (detail). Vienna, Kunsthistorisches Museum.
This is a part of a series of six, representing *The Months*, in which not only the changing nature is painted in a peerless way, but also the activities of mankind, connected with nature and yet subjected to its forces.

Lancelot Blondeel, *Mary and Child and the Saints Luke and Giles,* canvas, 138 × 98 cm. Bruges, St Saviour's Cathedral.

of the last Primitives, but are inconceivable without the Italian forms. Painters as Jan van Hemessen, Pieter Aertsen and others, who dealt with subjects of widely differing natures, both religious and moralizing genre pieces, also defy such categorization.

In fact, certain characteristics of painting cannot only be explained on the basis of an assumed origin in the local pictorial tradition, or in the imitation of the Italians. One of these characteristics, and possibly the most striking, is the enormous expansion of painting during the 16th century. In the 15th the number of artists – as well as the number of clients – was more limited. Paintings were strictly dependent on their function: as liturgical objects for altarpieces, as representative images for royal portraits, and as status symbols for the powerful clergy, courtiers and wealthy citizens to decorate their homes. In contrast, there was a veritable explosion in the 16th-century production. Panel paintings condescended to the houses of the less well-to-do, traders and merchants; and to the assembly rooms and chapels of their organizations, the guilds. By the last quarter of

the century virtually all surviving inventories of the estates of Antwerp burghers include at least a few paintings. Obviously this expansion in production was accompanied by a corresponding rise in the number of producers, diversifying both in levels of quality and in specialized skills; so that they were able to keep pace with the ever-changing taste of a whimsical public, which wished to see the changes in mentality taking place in that century adequately reflected in the decoration of their homes.

Thus painting to some extent acquired a new function during the 16th century. This evolution took place mainly in the new economic and cultural centre of the Netherlands: Antwerp. During the 15th century the focus was already shifting from Bruges to Antwerp, and more generally from Flanders to Brabant. Philip the Good moved his court to Brussels, where the reigning monarchs or their representatives continued to reside, with a brief interruption when the court of Margaret of Austria came to Malines from 1507-1530. The importance of the court in this cultural and artistic evolution should not be underestimated; but Antwerp plays the title-role during the 16th century, and some time afterwards. It expanded between the middle of the 15th century and the middle of the 16th to become one of the most densely populated and most active cities in Europe. The arrival of a large number of immigrants in the city particularly created an atmosphere of experimentation, which made the other centres in the Netherlands accept Antwerp's cultural leadership during its Golden Age.

During the first half of the century, Bruges continued to make use of its established wealth. Artists such as Jan Provost, Ambrosius Benson and Adriaan Isenbrant continued to provide the rich citizens with the sometimes rather naive religious altarpieces and charming portraits, which their parents and grandparents had commissioned from Memling and Gerard David. The Renaissance motifs were only used as external decoration, even in the work of Lanceloot Blondeel; and only just before 1550 Pieter Pourbus was to introduce the individual dignity of the Renaissance. Other cities with an individual character during the 15th century – Ghent, Louvain and Tournai – became bogged down in provincialism during the 16th century. It was not until about 1570 that the new style emerged in these cities, having then arrived from Antwerp.

We would not mention 's-Hertogenbosch, a market town on the northeastern border of the duchy of Brabant, if Hieronymus Bosch had not worked there between *ca* 1475 and 1516, the year of his death. Neither before nor after Bosch were there artists in this town of his standard, and in order to place him in a stylistic context relationships have been sought with rather diverse phenomena, such as Geertgen tot Sint-Jans, the drolleries of the late medieval miniatures, or the painting of Gelderland and the Rhine region. Although there are no clear points of similarity with the art of the Southern Netherlands in the 15th century, Bosch' art was extraordinarily successful there during the 16th century. The background landscapes constructed from a high viewpoint, and his combinations of human, animal, vegetable and simply fantastic forms into terrifying monsters had a particularly fruitful effect throughout the century – not only on his most original spiritual heir, Pieter Bruegel, and various interesting painters such as Jan Mandijn, Pieter Huys and Gillis Mostaert; but also at a lower level on a series of epigones, whose work sometimes barely rises above the level of folk art. We will return later to these followers of Bosch.

It is striking and possibly significant for the development of his popularity, that Bosch was appreciated early on in the Habsburg circles and amongst the higher aristocracy. In 1504 the painter was paid in 's-Hertogenbosch by Philip the Fair for a *Triptych of the Last Judgment*. According to the inventory of her collection made in 1516, Margaret of Austria also owned works by Bosch; and one of his major works, the *Triptych of the Garden of Earthly Delights*, was probably commissioned by Henry III of Nassau, and was already to be found in his palace in Brussels in 1517. Through Spanish courtiers, this work and others eventually came into the collection of Philip II in his palace of the Escorial.

Hieronymus Bosch, *The Garden of Lusts,* central panel of a triptych, 195 × 220 cm. Madrid, Prado.

Hieronymus Bosch, *The last Judgment,* central panel of a triptych, 127 × 164 cm. Vienna, Akademie der bildenden Künste.

Hieronymus Bosch, *The Earthly Paradise,* left panel of the Triptych of the Garden of Lusts, panel 97 × 220 cm. (detail). Madrid, Prado.

THE RISE OF THE ANTWERP SCHOOL
UP TO THE DEATH
OF QUINTEN METSIJS (1530)

Without losing sight of some interesting phenomena taking place in other cities, such as the court painters of the Habsburgs in Brussels and Malines, the development of 16th-century painting in the Southern Netherlands can be entirely followed in Antwerp. From about 1470 onwards numerous painters arrived there from other parts of the country, attracted by the rapid growth of the city and relying on the opportunities offered by an eager clientele of rich burghers. Particularly with Brussels were there close links during this period. A decree of 1481 gave the members of the Brussels guild the same rights as the free masters of Antwerp to sell their works during the annual markets. Masters from Brussels were welcome guests in Antwerp. In 1493 Colijn de Coter came to paint the vaulted ceiling of St Luke's Chapel in Our Lady's Cathedral, and on this occasion he also became a master in Antwerp; though he later returned to Brussels. Other painters settled in Antwerp, such as Goossen van der Weyden before 1503, a grandson of the great Rogier van der Weyden. An anonymous artist who came to the city early, probably also from Brussels, was the Master of Frankfurt. This name derives from the fact that two of his triptychs, which are still in museums in Frankfurt and were probably commissioned by patrons from that city, might well have been painted there. One indication of his Brussels provenance is the similarity with the work of Hugo van der Goes in the physiognomic types and expressions. The latter had indeed a workshop in the Red Monastery in the Zoniënwoud during the last years of his life. A reliable theory identifies the Master of Frankfurt with Hendrik van Wueluwe, who became a citizen and a free master in Antwerp in 1483. His name crops up repeatedly in the archives of St Luke's Guild between then and the year of his death, 1533. He enrolled a number of apprentices and was appointed deacon of the guild no fewer than six times, first in 1495/96. Possibly this was the occasion when the artist painted his *Self portrait with his wife* (Antwerp, Museum of Fine Arts), which is dated 1496 and bears the coat of arms and the motto of the guild. At this time the Master of Frankfurt was thirty-six years old, *i e* barely five years older than another immigrant to Antwerp, Quinten Metsijs, who was to leave his mark on painting there to an even greater extent. He was born in 1465 or 1466 in Louvain where he was probably trained as a painter, before being enrolled as a free master in Antwerp in 1491/92.

Master of Frankfort, *The Artist and his Wife*, panel, 36 × 27 cm. Antwerp, Museum of Fine Arts.

Quinten Metsijs, *Mary and Child*, panel, 130 × 86 cm. Brussels, Museums of Fine Arts.

Master of Frankfort, *Calvary-triptych*, central panel 116 × 37 cm. Frankfort, Städelsches Kunstinstitut.
On the side panel of this triptych, Klaus Hubracht, a merchant from Frankfort, and his family have been pictured. The anonymous painter (Hendrik van Wueluwe?) owes his pen-name to two triptyches which he painted for commissioners from Frankfort.

Despite the small difference in their ages, the Master of Frankfurt and Metsijs stylistically belong to two different generations; or rather Metsijs underwent an evolution during his career not discernible in his older colleague. This can be clearly seen if one compares two of their major works, which coincidentally have the same subject, *The Kindred of St Anne*. These two triptychs are housed respectively in the Historical Museum in Frankfurt and in the Museums of Fine Arts in Brussels. The composition of the Master of Frankfurt develops in the plane with a remarkable *horror vacui*, which contrasts sharply with the broad open spaces inhabited by Metsijs' figures. The triptych in Brussels was commissioned by the Brotherhood of St Anne in Louvain for its chapel in St Peter's Church and was completed in 1509. The triptych in Frankfurt comes from the St Anne's altar in the Dominican Church in Frankfurt, which was only built in 1492. This triptych is usually dated at about 1504, which seems rather late.

The rest of the Master of Frankfurt's career is more difficult to describe. If he really was Hendrik van Wueluwe, he did not die until 1533, but apart from a few portraits and altarpieces, his work dates from before or not long after 1500, and the attribution of some of these paintings is questionable.

As regards Quinten Metsijs, the situation is quite the reverse. The above-mentioned triptych of 1507/09 is his earliest dated work, though he was already a master in 1491/92. However, there are paintings by Metsijs in a more archaic style dating from this early period, among them several enthroned *Madonnas* (Brussels, Museums of Fine Arts, National Gallery in London *etc*). Gothic verticalism and the decorative use of the plane are still very evident. In the mature work of Metsijs the Madonnas' poses (*e g* the *Madonna Rattier* of 1529 in the Louvre in Paris) are much more naturalistic and the figures are convincingly integrated in the space, giving a fascinating view of an infinite landscape through an

259

Quinten Metsijs, *The Kindred of St Anne*, central panel of a triptych,
225 × 219 cm. Brussels, Museums of Fine Arts.
This is the earliest dated work by Metsijs, painted at Antwerp for the
Community of St Anne in St Peter's Church in his native town, Louvain.

open window. These works bear witness to a completely different religious feeling from that of thirty years earlier. The beauty of man and nature have totally replaced the lack of physical awareness of the Middle Ages. This work can justifiably be termed Renaissance art. The style is already present in essence in the triptych of 1507-1509 and in a second major religious work by Metsijs, the *Triptych of the Lamentation* of 1511 (Antwerp, Museum of Fine Arts). The contrast between Metsijs' early and mature work is so striking, that it can only be explained by his thorough contact with the Italian Renaissance, particularly Leonardo and his school, at the end of the 15th century. In some cases he has even borrowed directly from Leonardo's work, and it is almost inconceivable that Metsijs could have come into contact with these examples outside Italy. There is neither concrete evidence that Metsijs travelled to Italy, nor that he was continuously resident in Antwerp; so he might have left the city for a considerable length of time between 1491 and 1507. A journey to Italy is therefore by no means improbable. Moreover, his knowledge of Italian art is limited to Leonardo and his school, which suggests that he did not go any further than the north of Italy. During this period Leonardo spent most of his time in Milan, where he had many Lombardian pupils. Metsijs has no points of similarity with the Florentines, Umbrians or Romans of the late *quattrocento* (Botticelli, Perugino, Signorelli), and does not seem to have been very interested in classical sculpture.

In this respect his attitude contrasts strikingly with that of Jan Gossaert, a slightly younger contemporary of Metsijs, who made the journey to Rome in 1508/09 on a Burgundian diplomatic mission. He took the opportunity to draw the Colosseum and a number of classical statues, and he was also affected by the recent developments in painting in Rome. The plasticity of the nudes in his paintings-after returning to the Netherlands – is highly reminiscent of Luca Signorelli, whose paintings on the walls of the Sistine Chapel were undoubtedly seen by Gossaert. More than fifty years later Gossaert was still being praised in Lodovico Guicciardini's *Descrizione di Tutti i Paese Bassi* as the artist who had introduced profane mythological scenes, and the nudes which formed part of these, into the Netherlands. One example is his *Neptunus and Amphitrite* of 1516, now in the Staatliche Museen in East Berlin. This type of work did not have an immediate impact in the Southern Netherlands. Gossaert moved to Middelburg and worked mainly for aristocratic and rather exclusive circles, in places like Souburg Castle of

Quinten Metsijs, *Mary and Child,* panel, 68 × 51 cm, Paris, Louvre.

Jan Gossaert, *Neptunus and Amphitrite,* panel, 188 × 124 cm. Berlin, D.D.R, Staatliche Museen, Bode-Museum.

Jan Gossaert, *The Holy Family with angels*, central panel of a triptych, 43 × 31 cm. Lisbon, Museu National de Arte Antiga.
This is an example of the early period, in which Gossaert was a member of the group of Antwerp mannerists.

Master of the Antwerp Adoration, *The Adoration of the Magi*, central panel of a triptych, 29 × 22 cm. Antwerp, Museum of Fine Arts.
Most of the mannerists from Antwerp have remained anonymous. Their most typical works are small piety-triptychs, meant for civil interiors.

Quinten Metsijs, *Triptych of the Lamentation of Christ*, central panel 260 × 270 cm, side panels 260 × 117 cm. Antwerp, Museum of Fine Arts.

Philip of Burgundy, Mencia de Mendoza's Castle in Breda, and sporadically at the court of Margaret of Austria. His activity in Antwerp was restricted to the years preceding his journey to Rome.

The painter born in Maubeuge in Hainault (hence his Latinized signature *Joannes Malbodius*) was most probably the 'Jennyn van Henegouwe', who became a master in Antwerp in 1503 and took on an apprentice in 1505 and 1507. A few drawings remain as evidence of his presence in Antwerp, with inscriptions such as HEN-NINGOSAR (Copenhagen, Print Room) or IENNINAN-WER (Berlin, Print Room), as well as some paintings attributed to him. These are among the earliest examples of the specifically Antwerp style which reached a highpoint between about 1520 and 1540, and which is known as the style of the Antwerp Mannerists. They usually painted small triptychs with subjects from the New Testament or the lives of the saints, intended as devotional pieces for the burghers' homes. In many cases the painted wings of carved wooden retables dating from this period were also executed in this style; with an elegant use of line, slender figures attired in rich, exotic costumes, placed among strange, unrealistic architectural constructions, with much use of changing colours.

Most of the artists of this genre are not known by name. They are referred to as 'the Master of 1518', 'the Master of the Antwerp worshippers' or another appellation; but precisely in the initial stage – shortly after 1500 – a few can be identified: Gossaert was one of these, another was Jan de Beer, who became a master in Antwerp in 1504. A few of his triptychs are now kept in the Brera in Milan and in the Wallraf-Richartz Museum in Cologne. For Gossaert the style was only a passing phase. The late exponents of Antwerp Mannerism tended to degenerate into formalism and a surfeit of decoration.

Let us return briefly to Quinten Metsijs. His mature style was a revelation in Antwerp. Even before the painting of St Anne was completed in 1509, it served as a source of inspiration for Lucas Cranach's triptych of the same subject for Our Lady's Church in Torgau (now in the Städelsches Kunstinstitut in Frankfurt). Thus Cranach must have seen Metsijs at work in his studio during his visit to Antwerp in 1508/09. Dürer's diary

of his journey to the Netherlands in 1520/21 testifies to his great admiration of Metsijs; and in 1526 the master in Antwerp was also honoured by a visit from Hans Holbein the Younger, on his way to England. Apart from the Leonardo-influenced religious works, other aspects of Metsijs' art contributed to his fame: as a painter of profane scenes and of portraits, Metsijs was also an innovator.

The emergence and spread of non-religious themes is a fascinating subject. It clearly illustrates the fact that it is an over-simplification to describe 16th-century painting in the Netherlands as a struggle between local tradition and Italian innovation. On the one hand, the external influences are much more complex; on the other, there was a dynamic force in the movement itself, no constant harking back to the previous century!

One can distinguish two parallel and sometimes inter-related movements in the 16th-century profane iconography. In the first place there are themes based on classical mythology and history. These were popularized by the rediscovery of Latin literature as a result of the texts published by the humanists. There were the so-called *poeteryen* (the name given to them in Flanders in the 16th and 17th centuries), the tales of the poets – particularly Ovid – as they were first depicted in Gossaert's work and gained a lasting popularity with Frans

Floris, shortly after 1550. However, Humanism stimulated the development of profane iconography in another way, *viz* by its moralizing approach. It sought an ethical guideline in classical culture. Examples which could be depicted as an exhortation to proper and moral conduct, were now based not only on religious subjects but also came from the profane sector: from classical literature itself, and from other sources that were more accessible to the public. We are not well acquainted anymore with these sources (literature in local dialect, proverbs and sayings, legend), but their importance cannot be denied. The various starting points referred to here (the Bible, lives of the saints, classical literature, local tradition) were in fact mingled, so the same painters depicted different themes. At this early stage there were no real genre pieces representing daily life. *The Jeweller and his Wife* by Metsijs, painted in 1514 (Paris, Louvre), contains clear moral implications in the contrast between the transitory nature of the earthly riches and the eternal nature of religious values. *Unequal Love* (Washington, National Gallery) warns against credulity and weakness, not without a hint of mockery. Metsijs came across this theme in German prints of the end of the 15th century. Its moralizing spirit is closely related to the writings of Erasmus, and the people who were interested in these paintings must have belonged to the

Quinten Metsijs, *Portrait of Desiderius Erasmus*, panel 50 × 45 cm. Hampton Court, Collection of Queen Elisabeth of England.
The fact that Metsijs was a friend of the leading humanists, is characteristic for the intellectual level of his clientele.

Quinten Metsijs, *The Jeweller and his wife,* panel, 74 × 68 cm. Paris, Louvre.

Quinten Metsijs, *The ill-matched lovers*, panel, 42 × 62 cm. Washington, National Gallery of Art.
The woman has filched the purse from the old man in love and hands it to a grinning jester: a genre-scene with a very clear moralizing content.

humanist circle. In this context the portraits of Erasmus (Hampton Court, Collection of Elizabeth II) and of his Antwerp friend, the humanist and town clerk Pieter Gillis (Collection of the Earl of Radnor), immediately spring to mind. Metsijs painted these in 1517 to send them to their mutual friend, Sir Thomas More. Metsijs' portraits often depict men who are characterized as intellectuals by their accessories (books, writing implements, spectacles). His clients could be found above all amongst these intellectuals.

The constant stream of artists from other cities to Antwerp continued during the 1510's. They adapted to a greater extent to the prevailing taste, and as a result, more continuity was achieved. Most of these artists in one way or another followed the style of Quinten Metsijs. This is certainly true for Joos van Cleve, a native of the eastern border region of the Netherlands, who was enrolled as a master of Antwerp in 1511/12. It is possible but not certain that he first visited Bruges; because two wings showing *Adam* and *Eve* (dated 1507;

Paris, Louvre), of a triptych of which the centre section is missing, are reminiscent of the work of Memling and David. However, from the moment he arrived in Antwerp he was a faithful follower of Metsijs, adopting the latter's compositional schemes, figures and subjects. There are large triptychs by him in the Wallraf-Richartz Museum in Cologne and in the Alte Pinakothek in Munich. One of his very successful themes, repeated in many variations, was *Jesus and John* (one version in the Brussels Museums of Fine Arts); an imitation of a painting by Metsijs (Chatsworth, Duke of Devonshire), based itself on Leonardo. Joos van Cleve's numerous portraits are also similar to Metsijs' work, although he simplified the background to a plain field. As a portraitist his fame spread beyond Antwerp to a number of royal courts; as is demonstrated by his portraits, which include François I of France and Henry VIII of England. Thus he obviously worked abroad for some time, probably around 1530.

In 1516 two other important painters were admitted

Quinten Metsijs and Joachim Patinier, *The Tribulation of St Anthony*, panel, 175 × 173 cm. Madrid, Prado.

Joachim Patinier, *Landscape with the Flight to Egypt,* panel, 17 × 21 cm. Antwerp, Museum of Fine Arts.

Barend van Orley, *Triptych of the Tribulations of Job*, central panel, 176 × 184 cm, side panels 174 × 80 cm. Brussels, Museums of Fine Arts.

to the St Luke's Guild of Antwerp: *Meester Gherart van Brugghe, scildere*. Gerard David had built up a successful career in Bruges and it is not clear whether he continued to be very active during his last years in Antwerp. *Jochim Patenier scildere* also came to Antwerp as a fully fledged master. Only the last nine years of his life, from 1515/16 to 1524, are documented. He died rather early, leaving a wife and three little children. His relationship with Metsijs, who became a guardian over these children, must have been very close. Patinier also worked together with Metsijs: in the *Temptation of St Anthony* (Madrid, Prado), they painted the landscape and the figures respectively. This was an early example of cooperation between specialists, which became common for the next generations of painters and especially during the 17th century. There has been a great deal of speculation about Patinier's early activity. It is certain that he was born in the Maas valley, probably at Dinant. But where was he trained as a painter? In Bruges under Gerard David, in Liege, or in 's-Hertogenbosch under Hieronymus Bosch? The last possibility is suggested by the fact that the so-called 'world landscape' by Patinier has a precursor in the backgrounds of Bosch, rather than in those of David. Patinier designed fantastic landscapes, seen from a high viewpoint, stretching out into depth and disappearing into infinity. His figures, usually belonging to a religious theme, are actually merely a

pretext for creating this world-view. They are minute, as in his *Rest during the Flight into Egypt* (Antwerp, Museum of Fine Arts), otherwise they were painted in by artists like Metsijs, Joos van Cleve or the Master of Female Half-figures.

At the end of this chapter about the first third of the 15th century a brief reference should be made to the importance of the Habsburg Court. Margaret of Austria employed in her court a genuine Italian, Jacopo de' Barbari; and through him the Brussels artist Barend van Orley became familiar with the style of Raphael. In 1517, cartoons arrived in Brussels for the series of tapestries of the *Acts of the Apostles*, which Pope Leo X had commissioned Raphael to design for the Sistine Chapel. These were ten large paintings from Raphael's workshops, of which seven have survived (London, Victoria and Albert Museum), and they were woven in the workshop of Pieter van Aelst. The cartoons made a profound impression on the tapestry designers – including van Orley – as well as on the Brussels painters, by virtue of their large scale conception and the complete mastery of the human form. In his triptych of the *Sufferings of Job* (Brussels, Museums of Fine Arts) of 1521, van Orley copied a figure directly from Raphael, and this sort of imitation was by no means uncommon. In some cases it led to unnatural results.

267

FROM METSIJS' DEATH TO THE TRIUMPHAL ENTRY OF PHILIP II
(1530-1549)

We have discussed the first part of the 16th century in some detail, because the different directions in which painting developed during the rest of the century originated there. It seems rather arbitrary to pick a particular year as a turning point, but the death of Metsijs in 1530 did put an end to a period on which he had made a lasting impression. Metsijs' fame was not restricted to the Netherlands. Already in the 16th century some of his paintings found their way to Italy, and we have already referred to the high esteem in which he was held by Cranach, Dürer and Holbein. His work was highly praised by the general public (a number of anecdotes about him soon began to circulate) and by connoisseurs right into the 17th century. In the well-known *Picture Gallery of Cornelis van der Geest* of 1629 (Rubens' House, Antwerp), Willem van Haecht portrayed the moment in which the proud collector shows the Arch-

dukes Albrecht and Isabella one of his most valued possessions: a *Virgin and Child* by Quinten Metsijs.

During the years following 1530 history painting was not particularly flourishing in Antwerp. Joos van Cleve returned there before 1535, but died in 1540. Jan Sanders van Hemessen, a master in Antwerp before 1525, elaborated the composition schemes created by Metsijs, though his figures are rather solid than idealized. His most characteristic works show some half-figures in the immediate foreground, and on a smaller scale in the background preceding or following episodes of the main theme; this may be based on a religious subject (*e g* the Prodigal Son) or on the moralizing genre pieces. His most important work is the *Triptych of the Last Judgment* in St James's Church in Antwerp, though the date usually attributed to it (*ca* 1635) is difficult to accept. The heroic force of the nudes suggests that the artist was familiar with Michelangelo's *Last Judgment* in the Sistine Chapel, which was only completed in 1541, or at least with a copy of this work. The hypothesis that the small figures in the sky are painted by Pieter Aertsen

Willem van Haecht, *The Art-room of Cornelis van der Geest*, panel, 104 × 139 cm. Antwerp, Rubens' House.
This painting of 1628 shows how much the works of Quinten Metsijs and other elder masters are honoured at Antwerp during the 17th century.

also implies a later date, for this painter from Amsterdam only became a master in Antwerp in 1535/36. Hemessen emigrated to Haarlem in about 1550 and Aertsen returned to his native town in about 1555. During his Antwerp period he produced mainly religious work, including some imposing triptychs for the church of Zoutleeuw, as well as moralizing subjects. His best known works, the pictures of a *Kitchen Maid* (e g Brussels, Museums of Fine Arts), with extensive still life groupings of vegetables, game and other victuals, date from after his departure from Antwerp. Nevertheless, they were known there through Aertsen's nephew and pupil, Joachim Beuckelaar, but this only happened after 1560.

Some representatives of Antwerp Mannerism continued to work in Antwerp in the years following 1530. This school produced Pieter Coecke van Aelst. During his early years he probably worked together with his father-in-law Jan van Dornicke, the putative 'Master of 1518'. In 1527/28 he became a master himself. The works attributed to him are often of an inconsistent

Cornelis Massys, *The Holy Family arriving at Bethlehem*, panel, 27 × 38 cm. Berlin, Gemäldegalerie Staatliche Museen, Preussischer Kulturbesitz.

Pieter Aertsen, *The Kitchen-maid*, panel, 161 × 79 cm. Brussels, Museums of Fine Arts.

quality, which points to an extensive workshop production. As a pupil of Barend van Orley, Coecke was also familiar with Raphael's principle that the originality of the artist lay in the design or *disegno*, and not in the execution of the work, which could be left to other artists. Thus there were no objections to pupils duplicating their master's compositions in replicas and copies. Coecke, who visited both Constantinople and Rome, was very important as an art theorist. He translated Vitruvius' works on architecture into Dutch (*Die Inventie der Colommen*, Antwerp 1539), as well as the works of the Italian architect and painter, Sebastiano Serlio. These books were read avidly by Flemish artists of different sorts.

Quinten Metsijs had trained two of his sons to become painters. After his death, Jan and Cornelis became masters at the same time in 1531/32. Jan, the elder, painted moralizing scenes, with a dubious relation to religious subjects: for example, it is not clear whether the *Merry Company* in Stockholm is a representation of the parable of the Prodigal Son. These borderline cases were characteristic of the fusion of different subjects during this period. Also the distinction between a portrait and a moralizing scene blurred, as in the *Portrait of a couple playing backgammon* by Jan van Hemessen (Collection of the Earl of Crawford and Balcanes).

Not many paintings or drawings of Cornelis Metsijs (or Massijs, the name was spelled differently by consecutive generations) have survived, but there is a larger number of engraved pieces. He was banned from Antwerp in 1544, together with his brother Jan, as a member of the Anabaptists, and probably never returned. A few of his early landscapes (Berlin, Staatliche Museen, monogrammed and dated 1538) are reminiscent of Patinier, but strive for a more naturalistic style by lowering the viewpoint and reducing the fantastic rock formations. In this way landscape painting developed generally during the 1540's with Matthijs Cock and Lucas Gassel. Herri met de Bles, (*Herry Patenier,* as he was named in the list of the Antwerp guild for 1535/36) came even closer to Joachim Patinier; although the latter had been dead for quite a while and could not have been his teacher – the name does not necessarily imply a family relationship. The fantastic character of the backgrounds is the same as in Patinier's work, and Herri created strangely uneven and unstable landscapes, though the viewpoint was lowered. The painting described by van Mander in 1604 of *Monkeys robbing a merchant* (Dresden, Staatliche Kunstsammlungen) is used to catalogue his work.

To mark the end of this second section, in many respects a transitional period, we have chosen 1549: the year in which Philip II made his Triumphal Entry at his father's side in the most important cities of his domains in the Netherlands. This can be justified by the symbolic significance of the change of monarch, which became official in 1555, when the Netherlands definitely became subordinated to Spanish politics. The celebrations which took place for this inauguration were the first opportunities for two artists of the younger generation to put forward their ideas on content and design: Frans Floris in Antwerp, and Pieter Pourbus in Bruges.

THE HIGHPOINT:
FLORIS, BRUEGEL, POURBUS
(1549-1570)

From about 1550 painting in the Netherlands entered a new phase. The classification into various genres (coupled with the specialization of the painters) which had begun earlier, was now elaborated in a more consistent vein. These different specializations were ordered hierarchically. At the top was the history painter, an artist who designed compositions from his imagination. He was expected to be thoroughly acquainted with the themes, whether they were religious, mythological or allegorical. He had to be conversant with architecture, to place his figures in credible settings. The historical accuracy of clothing, footwear and accessories had to be guaranteed. He was expected to have mastered the laws of perspective and anatomy, and to be able to represent complex idealized and emotive contents. In other words, the artist had to work at the level of a scientist or an inventor; he had to be a *pictor doctus*. The master could then appeal to specialists in the various disciplines for the elaboration of his designs, which he would first have roughed out in drawings: background landscape painters, architectural and animal painters.

A painter who could merely faithfully depict what he saw – though much importance was attached to the

Herri met de Bles, *Landscape with a pedlar who is robbed by monkeys,* panel, 59 × 85 cm. Dresden, Staatliche Gemäldegalerie.
The description of this painting in the *Schilderboek* ('Painter's Book') by van Mander allows to take it as the starting-point to compose the oeuvre of this imitator of Patinier.

Frans Floris, *The Fall of the Revolting Angels,* panel, 308 × 220 cm. Antwerp, Museum of Fine Arts.

Frans Floris, *The Holy Family,* panel, 132 × 165 cm. Douai, Musée de la Chartreuse.

accuracy – had a lesser status than the *inventor* of compositions. For this reason portrait, landscape or still life painters were quoted lower than history painters. This did not change in the 17th century, though it in no way hindered the popular success of these 'inferior' genres. Many art buyers were quite happy with simple, easy to understand subjects. During the period under discussion landscapes and still lives did not yet exist as autonomous works of art. They still required a historical setting, though this was often no more than an excuse.

From the second quarter of the 16th century onwards, there was an increasing interest in classical art. We have already seen that Metsijs possibly travelled to the north of Italy and that Gossaert visited Rome almost by coincidence. Jan van Scorel, the founder of the Renaissance in

the Northern Netherlands, travelled to Italy via Germany and Austria between 1518-1520, visited the Holy Land, and even acted as a curator of the collection of his compatriot, Pope Hadrian VI, in Rome in 1523. Michiel Coxcie from Malines was present in Rome from the beginning of the 1530's. He painted frescoes in a style strongly reminiscent of Raphael, in *Santa Maria dell'Anima*, the church of the German and Dutch community in Rome. A few years later Maarten van Heemskerck from the Northern Netherlands and Lambert Lombard from Liege also visited Rome. Their profound interest in classical sculpture is evident from the numerous drawings they made while in Rome. From then on it was thought necessary for anyone who wanted to become a *pictor doctus* to complete his study by

Frans Floris, *The Feast of the Sea-Gods,* panel, 126 × 226 cm. Stockholm, National Museum.
From the middle of the 16th century there is a tendency to paint *poeteryen,* paintings with a mythological subject; especially by Floris.

travelling to Rome, usually right after finishing training in his home town. Frans Floris did so: born in Antwerp in 1519 or 1520, he was trained as a painter by Lambert Lombard in Liege, enrolled as a free master in St Luke's Guild in Antwerp in 1540/41, and he left for Italy shortly afterwards.

Frans Floris' stay in Rome shows typically what attracted many young artists to this city. Some remaining pages of his Roman sketchbooks contain sketches of the antique sculpture he saw there, as well as copies of contemporary Italian painters. The drawings of classical works concentrate on the accuracy of the copied figures with regard to their clothing, footwear, decorative motifs and so on, rather than on the proportions of the statues or their plasticity. For the aesthetic principles, the Italian art was obviously more important: Floris copied works by Michelangelo, Raphael, Giulio Romano, Polidoro da Caravaggio. He also painted when he was in Italy. One of his signed triptychs for a church near Genoa has unfortunately been lost since the beginning of this century.

After his return to Antwerp shortly before 1547 Floris established a workshop, consistently taking into consideration the principles of the Italian art theory of the high Renaissance. The basis of a work of art was the *inventio* or the *disegno* conceived by the artist himself. The execution was sometimes left to other painters, who usually came to the workshop after having completed their training elsewhere. Floris was given his first big commission in Antwerp in 1549, painting all the large canvases for the *Triumphal Arch of the Genoese Nation.* These honoured the heroic deeds of the Emperor and the high expectations of his son, through comparisons with figures and events from classical mythology, in which Charles V and Philip V repeatedly appear themselves. These paintings were just made for the event and have since disappeared. Some of them are still known through copies. They were the typical work of a *pictor doctus* who has total mastery over mythological and allegorical subject matter.

With this work Floris at once became the great specialist in Antwerp. For twenty years (until his death in 1570) he was given all the important commissions for great sacred and profane pictures, sometimes forming an entire cycle. These include a number of altarpieces, such as the one for the highaltar in Our Lady's Cathedral (damaged in the wave of iconoclasm in 1566, restored by the artist himself and enlarged with side panels, but removed in 1581), and for several guild altars. For the citizens of Antwerp he painted a series of paintings with subjects such as *The Labours of Hercules, The Liberal Arts, The Seasons,* or separate paintings such as *The Feast of the Sea Gods* or *The Judgment of Paris.* On the gable of his own house, a luxurious *palazzo* in Italian style, he painted *Pictura, Sculptura* and various other allegorical figures. His large salon was undoubtedly also decorated with a series of his own canvasses.

After a hesitant start in which he probably too closely imitated his models (the Raphael school and Michelangelo, and in his own country Pieter Coecke and Lambert Lombard) Floris developed an individual monumental style with solid, forceful figures. His works dating from

273

after 1560 display signs of a remarkable, though not completely explained evolution towards a greater irrationalism. The figures become more slender, and have a more sensual or even despondent expression. Possibly during these years Floris had come into contact with the school of Fontainebleau through prints. Van Mander, who included an extensive biography of Floris in his *Schilderboek* of 1604 after collecting information about him from his pupils, wrote that Floris could have been the best portrait painter, when he had wanted to. Van Mander based this on a description of a founder's portrait on the wing of an altarpiece. Floris did not often concern himself with this less highly valued genre – he probably considered it beneath him – but his portraits are certainly vivid and natural. Comparable to the portraits, though not drawn from life, were the studies of heads which he painted life-size on small panels, in preparation for his compositions. As far as is known, Floris introduced this method of preparing the production of his workshop, and no other painter after him made as much use of it; some 17th-century painters, including Rubens, followed his example.

The height of Floris' fame and fortune was between 1560-1565. It was no coincidence that these were the final prosperous years for Antwerp. The population was at its greatest, and numbered around one hundred thousand. The wave of iconoclasm of 1566 was the knell heralding the collapse. Floris had run into financial troubles after building his house and went from one lawsuit to another; took to the bottle, according to van Mander, and died in 1570. All his property and effects were publicly sold off. However, his ruin was not an isolated case. In the same year two other great figures, Christoffel Plantin and Hieronymus Cock, also suffered in the financial crisis. The fame of Floris soon diminished. During the first half of the 17th century he was totally overshadowed by Rubens and the Baroque, which – for all that – pushed 16th-century art into the background.

Frans Floris, *Family Portrait,* panel, 130 × 225 cm. Lier, Wuyts-van Campen-Baron Caroly Museum.
Best known under the name *Family of Berchem,* this painting meant a landmark in the development of the family-portrait in the Netherlands.

Pieter Bruegel the Elder was almost a contemporary of Floris, and it is worthwhile to compare these two artists. Bruegel was born between 1525-1530, probably in or near Breda. His productive years as an artist were divided between Antwerp and Brussels. According to van Mander, he was a pupil of Pieter Coecke; but the relationship of Bruegel to this painter, designer and theorist is not very evident from a stylistic point. There is a recent theory that van Mander was mistaken and that the Antwerp landscape painter Matthijs Cock – and not Pieter Coecke – was Bruegel's teacher. This would explain Bruegel's lifelong interest in landscapes, as well as his close links with Hieronymus Cock, the well-known publisher of prints, and brother of Matthijs.

By all means, the earliest documented activity of Bruegel was neither in Antwerp, nor in Brussels, where Pieter Coecke settled for the last years of his life, but in Malines. In 1550 Bruegel painted the wings of an altarpiece that has since disappeared for the guild of glovemakers; working together with Pieter Baltens, a follower of Hieronymus Bosch. In this way a significant link was formed between Bosch and Bruegel, who gave the most original interpretation of the art of this master from 's-Hertogenbosch. In the guild yearbook 1551/52, *Peeter Bruegels schilder* was enrolled as a master in St Luke's Guild in Antwerp. Shortly afterwards he left for Italy, just as a number of other artists had done before him. Possibly Bruegel was accompanied on his journey by a younger colleague, Maarten de Vos. This has been deduced from the fact that they later had mutual Italian friends.

However, the reactions of Bruegel and de Vos to the southern world were completely different. While de Vos – like Floris – was interested mainly in Italian painting and the remains of classical art, even though he had not been one of Floris' pupils, Bruegel immediately fell under the spell of the overwhelming landscape of the Alps. Several drawings have survived in which Bruegel put down his impressions on paper while on his travels. As has been shown recently, Bruegel often imaginatively elaborated these sketches later in his workshop, adding the foreground and figures. Reality, which he captured both precisely and sensitively, was not an aim in itself; but merely a means for expressing his thoughts and feelings in a work of art. In his *Album Amicorum* Abraham Ortelius wrote the following remarkable words in an epitaph for his friend, Pieter Bruegel: *Multa pinxit hic Brugelius que pingi non possunt* (This Bruegel painted many things that cannot be painted). This means that the observer can find more in Bruegel's work than appears at first. The same is true of his predecessor, Hieronymus Bosch, whose 'visions' also provoked a train of thought which would bring an insight into the true meaning of the painting. It is clear that in both artists this meaning can be found in their

Pieter Bruegel the Elder, *The Cross-bearing,* panel, 124 × 170 cm. (detail). Vienna, Kunsthistorisches Museum.

moralistic approach, although the points of view of Bosch and Bruegel are by no means the same. Generally speaking, one might say that Bosch was more inclined to instill in man a fear of God and a sense of piety, in the manner of the late Middle Ages; while Bruegel held a mirror up to man which reflected his sinful, and even more, his irrational and uncontrolled conduct. In this respect Bruegel was obviously a typical 16th-century artist. After Erasmus, the contrast between the illusion of the strength and independence of man, and the reality of his insignificance and impotence, became an ever-present guideline.

Bruegel expressed these thoughts in different ways using a variety of subjects. They were already apparent in the Alpine landscapes, but were also expressed in traditional subjects such as the *Adoration of the Magi* and his *Calvary*, in which the crowd is indifferent to the occasion, although it will determine their fate. Or take the *Fall of the Angels*, in which the rebellion of Lucifer and his angels is a symbol of the insane conceit of man. Following a tradition which arose in Antwerp after Quinten Metsijs, there are also other themes to be found in Bruegel's work in which moralizing thoughts are

expressed. The *Proverbs* of 1559 (Berlin, Museum) gives many examples of absurd aspects of human behaviour, of man's subjugation to sins such as greed, lust *etc*. The *Dulle Griet* (Antwerp, Museum Mayer-van den Bergh) shows how far man shall go to fulfil his greed.

It is not really surprising that only a limited number of congenial characters, for whom these works were intended, were able to comprehend their full significance. Bruegel's paintings clearly belonged in the houses of a rather small group of intellectuals. If a church, monastery, guild or private individual wished to commission an altarpiece, they would turn to the official painters; and from 1550-1570 in Antwerp the official painter was Frans Floris. Obviously he also did works for citizens' houses, but these were conceived in a completely different spirit, *viz* the optimistic, humanist view. Man is glorified as the lord of creation, idealized in the sublime world of the gods of antiquity, the Old Testament, or in the emotional scenes of the New Testament and the admiration for the martyred saints. Compared with these works, Bruegel is far more pessimistic.

Pieter Bruegel the Elder, *Alpine landscape,* pen on paper, 30 × 45 cm. Cambridge, Mass., Fogg Art Museum.
Recent research has pointed out that Bruegel completed his nature impression later in his atelier into real compositions. In this drawing he added the zone below left, with the church tower and the figures, to the mountains.

Pieter Bruegel the Elder, *The Dulle Griet ('Crazy Maggie')*, panel,
115 × 161 cm. Antwerp, Mayer-van den Bergh Museum.

Pieter Breugel the Elder, *Children's Games,* panel, 118 × 161 cm. (detail).
Vienna, Kunsthistorisches Museum.

Pieter Bruegel the Elder, *The Harvest*, panel, 118 × 161 cm. New-York, Metropolitan Museum.

The significance of Bruegel's work was forgotten fairly rapidly. In his followers – especially Pieter Bruegel the Younger, his son – only the narrative element of the subject remained and the moralizing quality was transformed into indifferent mockery. In 1604 van Mander described Pieter Bruegel the Elder as a mere scoffer, who reproduced peasants in their natural habitat in such a way that the paintings could not be viewed without laughing. This can hardly have been the artist's intention, although we do not know exactly how his contemporaries reacted to his work. There is the case of the rich collector, Nicolaas Jongeling, who commissioned both Frans Floris and Pieter Bruegel to decorate his mansion near Antwerp. Unless this man was not aware of any difference in the vision of these two painters, he must have been more interested in their respective artistic qualities. His foremost consideration

was that he wanted works of art in his house; by the way, he also owned a painting by Dürer. Bruegel painted for him a series of six works depicting the theme of the *Months*; Floris had earlier been commissioned to do *The Labours of Hercules* and *The Seven Liberal Arts*. Five paintings from Bruegel's series have survived, including the famous *Hunters in the Snow* (Vienna, Kunsthistorisches Museum) and *The Harvest* (New York, Metropolitan Museum). It is no coincidence that the museum in Vienna still has the largest collection of Bruegel's paintings. His works were gathered by Archduke Ernest of Austria and by Emperor Rudolf II, just as the works of Bosch had come into the Spanish royal collection under Philip II. Like Bruegel's paintings, the works of Bosch were often more assessed in the way in which his followers interpreted them, than according to Bosch' own views.

278

Pieter Bruegel the Elder, *The Parable of the Blind,* canvas, 86 × 154 cm, Napels, Museo di Capodimonte.
'If the one blind man leads the other...' The first one has already fallen into the water, the expression on the faces of those that follow goes from fear and surprise, to unsuspecting and blind trust. Not one of them has seen the church in the background.

Pieter Bruegel the Elder, *Haymaking,* panel, 114 × 158 cm, *ca* 1565. Prague, Narodny Gallery.

The 16th century saw the development of a lot of subjects in painting, while many painters started to specialize in a particular branch. The historical painters were at the top of the hierarchy, while portrait painters were at the bottom – as they did no more than paint from life, not from their imagination. However, they had many clients, for after the 'intellectual' portraits of Metsijs, the generations which followed saw the emergence of portraits of less well-to-do burghers. Many inventories of estates of the second half of the century include portraits of parents and grandparents, which were primarily intended to preserve the memory of these ancestors. This had been true of noble families a century earlier, and now also became commonplace among the common burghers. Portraits were still required in royal circles and court painters were appointed for this purpose. For example, Antonis Mor from Utrecht worked in Antwerp and Brussels for a few years, before going onto the courts of Portugal and Spain. In his *Self Portrait* (Florence, Uffizi) of 1558, he described himself proudly as the painter of Philip, King of Spain, and elevated himself in an inscription as an equal of Apelles. The painters of the simple burgher portraits in Antwerp, such as Willem Key, did not share these pretensions.

Pieter Pourbus is still best known as the portrait painter of Bruges citizens, although it has recently been shown that his importance extends far beyond this. His *Allegory of Faithful Love* (London, Wallace Collection) is reminiscent of the tradition of the rhetoricians and

279

Pieter Pourbus, *Portrait of Pieter Domincle,* panel, 97 × 70 cm. Private collection.

Pieter Pourbus, *Portrait of Livina van der Beke,* panel, 97 × 70 cm. Private collection.

refers to a rationalist morality that indicates a higher intellectual status than might appear at first sight. Pourbus should be seen more as an innovator who introduced the Renaissance to Bruges, rather than as the last of the Primitives of this town, as he is often described.

This survey of the highpoint of Flemish painting between 1550 and 1570 would not be complete without a mention of the lesser known – but not less interesting – painters. Jan Mandijn and Pieter Huys were the most important of Bosch' followers, who also included Baltens. They painted small works without much originality using subjects such as the *Temptation of St Anthony,* which allowed them to depict fantastic and hybrid figures, though without Bosch' disquieting directness.

Landscapes which were still constructed on entirely conventional lines by Patinier and Herri met de Bles, evolved throughout the 16th century towards a more natural style – though this did not necessarily entail that they were true to nature. Matthijs Cock, Cornelis Metsijs, and Lucas Gassel attempted to represent their

landscapes from a lower viewpoint; and to get away from the obligatory succession of brown, green and blue. The breakthrough in this convention came about with Bruegel, who – as in his drawings of Alpine landscapes – used a realistic representation of nature as a starting point, and then transformed it into a total composition. One particularly attractive landscape painter of the same generation was Cornelis van Dalem, a dilettante who painted small, rocky landscapes and architectural pieces remarkable for the tonal, almost monochrome colouration. He left Antwerp in 1565 for religious reasons, and worked until his death in 1573 in the vicinity of Breda.

The 1560's also saw the appearance of paintings of kitchen interiors, after Pieter Aertsen in the previous decade. His nephew and pupil, Joachim Beuckelaar, was a painter of elaborate still lives of vegetables, fruit, game and fish; painted in an iconographic combination which has not yet been completely explained. He painted in Antwerp – which Aertsen had left in 1554/55 – from 1556.

Pieter Pourbus, *An allegorical love feast,* 134 × 207 cm, about 1547. London, Wallace Collection.

THE LATER DEVELOPMENT
(1570-1600)

Towards the mid-1560's the Netherlands were moving into troubled times; the wave of iconoclasm in 1566 was the writing on the wall. Coincidentally the important painters in Antwerp all died within a few years of each other: Pieter Bruegel in 1569; Frans Floris and Hieronymus Cock, the publisher of prints who had been responsible for spreading their work, in 1570. The generation of history painters who took their place was not distinguished by its originality. The most creative of them was Maarten de Vos, who may have travelled with Bruegel to Italy in about 1552. He only became a master in Antwerp about 1558/59, but after this he had a long and productive career there. According to 17th-century sources he worked in Tintoretto's workshop in Venice, and one can certainly detect the influence of Venetian colouration in his work. The bulk of his work consists of the series of altarpieces he was commissioned to paint for the guilds of Antwerp after the iconoclasts in 1566,

Maarten de Vos, *St Paul at Efeze,* panel, 125 × 198 cm. Brussels, Museums of Fine Arts.

Maarten de Vos, *The Triumph of Christ,* central panel of a triptych,
347 × 280 cm. Antwerp, Museum of Fine Arts.
Central panel of the triptych of the Guild of the Old Feetbow, painted in 1590
in accordance with the re-decoration of the guild-chapels in Antwerp Cathedral after 1585.

and even more after the reopening of Our Lady's Cathedral, when the city was conquered by Alexander Farnese in 1585. Other artists from the same period came directly from Floris' workshop and worked in a style which was closer to his. Frans Pourbus the Elder, who was sent by his father from Bruges to Antwerp to be trained by Floris, took the Floris style to smaller towns in the Netherlands (Tournai, Audenarde, Dunkirk). The Francken brothers, of whom Frans the Elder was the more productive, also worked on altarpieces in Antwerp, as well as in their birthplace, Herentals. One rather enigmatic figure was Jacob de Backer, who probably died at a young age, and who painted among others the epitaph for Christoffel Plantin in 1593 (Antwerp, Our Lady's Cathedral). However, this brings us to the end of the century, when Rubens learned the basic principles in the workshop of Otto Venius, in antici-

pation of his journey to Italy to become the *pictor doctus* in the first half of the 17th century.

During the final decade of the 16th century there was also a stagnation in other genres of painting, partly because a number of talented artists emigrated after the fall of Antwerp. Gillis van Coninxlo settled in Frankenthal and later moved to Amsterdam, the brothers Maarten and Lucas van Valckenborch, who were landscape specialists, went east to Frankfurt and Linz. In 1586 Hans Vredeman also left Antwerp. He was a specialist in 'prospective', architectural pieces constructed according to the mathematical laws of perspective. In addition, he was an engineer, a designer of cartoons for tapestries and a cartographer. His name is connected with the specific decorative style, which was popular in various branches of the applied arts and in sculpture during the last decades of the 16th century and the beginning of the next.

Otto Venius, *The Temptations of Youth,* panel, 142 × 212 cm. Stockholm, National Museum.

The art of stained glass

STAINED GLASS ARTISTS AND GLAZIERS The art of stained glass falls under the category of industrial and architectural art; and the new forms of the Renaissance were expressed and elaborated in this art form at a fairly early stage in Flanders, *i e* during the first two decades of the 16th century. In fact the art of stained glass provided an opportunity for the most adventurous painters of the time to exhibit their decorative skills and ideas about composition, by creating designs or cartoons for stained glass windows in accordance with the new artistic ideas. On the other hand, the realistic and individual representation of the figures only continued the pictorial late Gothic art of stained glass windows in the 16th century. All the important painters of the early Renaissance in the Southern Netherlands, such as Jan Gossaert, Jan van Roome, Lanceloot Blondeel, Michael Coxcie, Pieter Coecke, Lambert Lombard, Frans Floris and above all, Barend van Orley, designed single stained glass windows or sets. A number of names of the glaziers themselves are also known, not only from written sources, but also from the works of art themselves. Above all the members of the Renaissance-minded Habsburg court – whose example was followed by many aristocratic families, including the de la Marcks, the Lalaings, the de Croys *etc* – commissioned a large number of stained glass windows to decorate the old places of worship in the Southern Netherlands. Many medieval churches in Flanders were adorned with 16th-century or Renaissance sets of stained glass windows. The stylistic contrast between the usually pronounced Gothic elements of the architecture and the Renaissance patterns in the stained glass windows, particularly of the architectural details surrounding the figures in the panels, add a distinctive dimension to Flemish heritage. Partly because a relatively large number of these stained glass windows have survived, the 16th century in Flanders can be described as the golden age of stained glass. In addition, the range of colours used in 16th-century stained glass windows was more varied and with more nuances, than the glazier's palette of the high and late Middle Ages.

Window of Charles of Lalaing and Jacqueline of Luxemburg, Claes Matthysen, Antwerp school, about 1533. Hoogstraten, St Catherine's Church.

Window of Arnold Streyters, 35th abbot of Tongerlo, Gommarus Loop van Nijvel, Brabant school, 1534-1535 (detail). Lier, St Gommarus' Church.

BRUSSELS AND ANTWERP The two most important centres of stained glass work in 16th-century Flanders were Brussels and Antwerp, where the most progressive pattern painters lived. Aert Ortkens, identified with the famous Aernout van Nijmegen, can be considered to be the transitional figure between the Gothic period and the Renaissance. In fact, Ortkens' first Renaissance stained glass windows were made for export. Another artist whose life and work was spread over the 15th and 16th centuries was the important Brabant master Nikolaas Rombouts, who even became glazier to the court in Brussels. Although there are occasional Gothic motifs in his composition, Rombouts was one of the first artists in the Southern Netherlands to apply the Italian decorative style in his stained glass work. These characteristics are recognizable in a number of preserved sets of stained glass, which can be attributed to Nikolaas Rombouts' workshop: the stained glass window depicting the *Last Supper* by Engelbert II van Nassau, dating from 1503, in Our Lady's Cathedral in Antwerp; the six royal stained glass windows of Maximilian of Austria and his family, dating from about 1516 and 1559, in St Gummarus' Church in Lier, and the royal stained glass windows of Emperor Charles V and his family, dating from about 1520-1530, in the choir of St Michael's Cathedral in Brussels.

The other important sets of 16th-century stained glass windows in the main church of Brussels were made by Jan Haeck – with the exception of the large anonymous stained glass window of Prince Bishop Erard de la Marck, dating from 1528. Jan Haeck came from Antwerp, but in about 1528 he settled in Brussels. He worked from designs or cartoons by either Barend van Orley or Michael Coxcie. The former designed the monumental stained glass windows of Charles V, dating from 1537, and those of Mary of Hungary dating from 1538 – two perfect masterpieces of the mature Renaissance style in stained glass. The collaboration of Haeck with Coxcie, supervised by Barend van Orley

Window of Jeronimus and Jacob Adornes. Flemish school, 1st and 3rd quarter of the 16th century. Bruges, Jerusalem Church.

and Pieter Coecke, produced four other royal stained glass windows in St Michael's Cathedral in the period dating from 1540-1547; depicting François I, Eleonor of Austria, John III of Portugal, Catherine of Aragon, Ferdinand I, Anne of Bohemia, Louis Jagellon and Mary of Hungary. Again the figures are integrated in a perfect Renaissance triumphal arch, similar to that in the windows depicting Emperor Charles V and Mary of Hungary in the same church.

Three other important artists of this period belonged to the Antwerp school of stained glass. Dirk Vellert – who became a master in Antwerp in 1511, and who also painted in oils – left only one composition in Belgium, *viz* the famous and pictorially conceived glass medallion depicting the *Triumph of Time*, now in the Museums of Art and History in Brussels. However, the finest examples of Vellert's work are in King's College, Cambridge, for which he designed many monumental windows. His pictorial style can also be recognized in the work of his contemporaries in Antwerp, particularly in the work of Claes Mathyssen, well-known for the famous stained glass windows of the de Lalaing family (dating from 1528-1532) in St Catharine's Church in Hoogstraten. This church also contains a number of other remarkable sets of stained glass windows from the Renaissance period: the seven royal *Sacramental windows*, made from 1531-1533 by Antonis Evertsoen van Culenborg; and the windows of the *States of Holland*, attributed to the Antwerp school, dated 1532-1535, and possibly based on a design by Pieter Coecke.

Other 16th-century stained glass windows of the Antwerp school can be found in the city itself, *viz* in Our Lady's Cathedral (the *Henry VII window* and the *Dassa-Rockox window*). The third important artist of this 16th-century Antwerp school, Robbrecht van Ollim, completed a stained glass window in Antwerp Cathedral, set up by Antoon and Jan-Jakob Fugger. It depicts

Four heraldic windows from St Elisabeth's Hospital at Lier, Flemish school, 1528. Brussels, Museums of Art and History.

the *Conversion of St Paul,* but has now been thoroughly restored.

OTHER FLEMISH CENTRES   In addition to the sets described above in Brussels, Antwerp, Hoogstraten and Lier, Renaissance stained glass has survived in a few other Flemish centres, although these works are almost without exception anonymous. Nevertheless, they can be described as belonging either to the Flemish or to the Brabant school. The first group includes a few 16th-century stained glass windows in Bruges, like the rather large *Jan de Baenst window* (Our Lady's Church) and the series of *Adornes windows* (Jerusalem Church). As in all of the windows in other centres which depict figures – and obviously as in devotional panel painting – the figures are always shown at prayer, with their respective patron saints behind them. A few typical examples in the Museums of Art and History in Brussels, including a series of heraldic windows dating from 1528 from Elisabeth's Hospital in Lier, belong to the Flemish school. On the other hand, a number of 16th-century windows in the Gothic St Sulpicius' Church in Diest are considered to belong to the Brabant school of stained glass. This also applies to a number of stained glass windows in St Gummarus' Church in Lier, for which the designs are attributed to Goswijn van der Weyden from Antwerp, and the execution to Gommarus Loop van Nijvel of the Brabant school.

Finally we should mention the small number of 16th-century stained glass medallions in Flanders. In these works the lead is used sparingly or not at all in the painted composition. In addition to the famous example by Dirk Vellert, a few of these stained glass medallions in Renaissance style have survived in other Flemish museums, notably in Antwerp and Bruges. In fact, the medallion or circular shape was quite a popular pattern in the Renaissance.

Window of Charles V and Isabella of Portugal, Jean Hack (?), 1537. Brussels, St Michael's Cathedral.

287

Graphic art

In the 16th century, the Netherlands were one of the most active centres of graphic art in Europe; the production being concentrated in Antwerp which, for this artistic activity too, was the metropolis of the west. Antwerp and the Netherlands had an extraordinary degree of influence abroad, but also in their turn digested considerable foreign influences.

THE BREAKTHROUGH OF THE RENAISSANCE The Italian Renaissance conquered Europe in the 16th century, but the Gothic Netherlands maintained a tough resistance. In most artistic activities, the Renaissance influence did not fully penetrate before 1540-1550, including the graphic arts. Flemish and Brabant graphics in the first half of the 16th century were still inspired by the Gothic, even though tinged by Renaissance elements. They were dominated by a figure regarded by many as the greatest graphic artist of all times, Albrecht Dürer. And together with him, other German contemporaries, such as Urs Graf and Hans Holbein, formed a source of inspiration for the masters of the Netherlands.

The German graphic schools rapidly retreated after Dürer and Holbein. The Renaissance graphics that penetrated into Flanders and Brabant around 1540 were this time markedly determined by Italian and French (Italianate) influences. Nevertheless the Flemish and Brabant masters, as well as the other plastic artists, were certainly no slavish imitators, but developed a Flemish style of their own which is clearly recognizable. Technically, on the average, they were on a (sometimes far) higher level than their Italian and French colleagues.

WOODCUT AND BURIN: A REPRODUCTION TECHNIQUE FOR PROFESSIONALS As already stressed in the chapter dedicated to graphic art in the 15th century, the graphic artist himself was generally a professional with a hand trained to cut wood or metal; but he generally took his subjects directly or indirectly from other artists (painters, draughtsmen): directly when the artist provided him with a drawing or other model (often on a commission from a publisher); indirectly when he copied subjects from books or prints (and this generally happened with Flemish woodcuts and engravings, especially in book illustration in which German, and later Italian and French, influences were preponderant).

Albrecht Dürer himself cut in wood and engraved in copper, but only few great painters (e g his Dutch contemporary Lucas van Leyden) followed his example. A typical case is that of Pieter Bruegel the Elder: his magnificent prints are continually cited and reproduced – but in reality this brilliant artist, with only one exception, did not cut any engravings. He was responsible for the 'idea' and supplied the drawings, but they were cut in copper by professional engravers. On the other hand, very few engravers – and only exceptionally – worked according to their own 'ideas' (curiously enough, even when they had made a name for themselves as painters). Graphic art, from the beginnings of its existence, was essentially a reproductive art, and all too often designers and executors are confused.

AN AMATEUR TECHNIQUE: THE EMERGENCE OF ETCHING The relation between the original idea and its execution, however, became somewhat complicated from the beginning of the 16th century onwards, by the emergence of a new technique. Up to that time, graphic art had two main forms of expression: the woodcut (relief printing) and the burin engraving (intaglio). Now a second form of intaglio printing emerged, the etching. German graphic artists seem to have been the first in Europe to experiment with this new method: Urs Graf in 1513, immediately followed by Daniel Hopfer and Albrecht Dürer in person (although he very soon returned to the burin). Lucas van Leyden followed Dürer's example, and stopped in his turn after producing half a dozen prints.

Christ preaching at the bank of the sea, wood-cut, 23.7 × 36.2 cm, Jan Swart (deceased around 1533). Antwerp, Stedelijk Prentenkabinet.

Portrait of pope Paulus III, wood-cut (coloured by hand), 52.6 × 36.2 cm, Jan Mollijns (probably), edited at Antwerp by Hans Liefrinck. Antwerp, Stedelijk Prentenkabinet.

The technique of etching consists in covering a copper plate with a layer of varnish, drawing the desired lines on it with a pointed instrument, and then immersing the plate in an acid bath. Where the point has removed the varnish, the copper plate is etched away by the acid. Thus essentially the technique of etching consists in drawing on a copper plate and leaving the technical execution to a corrosive acid. Compared to burin engraving, etching has some disadvantages: the lines are rounder and equal in depth, which offers less possibilities of nuance; less prints can be made; and after intensive use it is very difficult to re-etch the plate. On the other hand, whereas burin engraving requires lengthy training and considerable technical skill, any dexterous amateur can venture upon etching. And that in fact happened: creative artists, tempted by graphics, expressed themselves almost exclusively in etching; whereas the professionals and semi-professionals – with a few exceptions – scorned the new 'easy' technique.

A typical case is that of Pieter van der Borcht (Malines *ca* 1540 – Antwerp *ca* 1608): after many years of producing designs for woodcuts and, among other things, having supplied many hundreds of drawings to Plantin, he switched over around 1575 to an even more fruitful career as engraver – but devoting himself exclusively to etching (which he had already practised in his youth, when he was 19 or 20).

The list of painters and draughtsmen who expressed original ideas via etching is not so long for the 16th-century Netherlands. Apart from Lucas van Leyden and Pieter van der Borcht, already mentioned, the best are: Dirk Vellert (painter, glazier, active at Antwerp between 1511 and 1544; also has to his credit burin engravings based on his own ideas); Jan Cornelisz.

Portrait of emperor Nero, two-colours print (etching and wood-cut); anonymous master, 1557. Antwerp, Plantin-Moretus Museum.
Etching (framed) on coloured wood-block, tooled for effects of light: one of the 132 images of Roman emperors after antique coins in Hubert Goltzius, *Vivae Omnium fere imperatorum imagines*, Antwerp, Aegidius Coppens van Diest, 1557.

Vermeyen (Beverwijk near Haarlem *ca* 1500 – Brussels 1559); Frans Floris (Antwerp 1516-1570; one of the most renowned painters of his time, but without remarkable achievements as a graphic artist); Nicolaas Hogenberg (Munich 1500 – Malines 1539) and his son Frans (Malines *ca* 1539 – Cologne *ca* 1590; known especially for his hundreds of historical prints which constitute an important source of knowledge for the political history of the time); Hans Bol (Malines 1534 – Amsterdam 1593); Marcus Gheraerts (Bruges 1521 – England before 1604; in England from 1568 onwards); Joris Hoefnagel (Antwerp 1542 – Vienna 1601; from 1576 onwards continually on the move through Europe, he provided many valuable and artistically outstanding pictures of towns for the *Civitates Orbis Terrarum* of Braun-Hogenberg). Some abandoned the activity very rapidly: Jan Gossaert van Mabuse (mentioned in Antwerp in 1503, died at Breda in 1532) gave up after one single etching (and two small burin engravings), just like Pieter Bruegel the Elder.

SOME TECHNICAL AND HISTORICAL REMARKS So in the 16th century, graphics remained essentially a matter for professionals, generally working after models from others, and expressing themselves in woodcuts or burin engravings. Only a few of these professionals practised both techniques: they were either woodcutters or plate cutters (among the few exceptions was Frans Crabbe van Espleghem, active at Malines in the first half of the century). But there was no specialization in prints or book illustration: the graphic artists provided both.

Atelier of an engraver, engraving, 20.3 × 27.3 cm, artist from the atelier of Filips Galle (Theodoor Galle or Adriaan Collaert) after a drawing by Joannes Stradanus (Van der Straet, Bruges 1523 - Florence 1605) (the original drawing can be found in Windsor Castle), end of the 16th century. Antwerp, Stedelijk Prentenkabinet.
From the album *Nova Reperta* ('New Inventions') having 20 illustrations after Stradanus, edited by Filips Galle. This detailed and faithful image of a graphic atelier is the oldest known of, and it is a unique document.

Sculptor noua arte, bracteata in lamina SCVLPTVRA IN ÆS. *Scalpit figuras, atque prælis imprimit.*

The Deluge, etching and engraving, 28.5 × 13.9 cm (second state), Dirk Vellert, 1544. Antwerp, Stedelijk Prentenkabinet.

Another technical comment: quite a few engravings from the 16th century have reached us in a coloured form; but this colouring was done by hand, often by professionals, the *afsetters* (Abraham Ortelius, the great cartographer, started his career as an *afsetter* of maps). But in Germany, in the early years of the 16th century, experiments were made with multicoloured woodcuts (obtained by printing two or more differently cut and coloured wood blocks on top of one another); and the Antwerp master Joost de Necker (summoned to Augsburg, to produce there a series of illustrated publications to the greater glory of the Emperor Maximilian) in a letter of 1512 to the Emperor claims for himself the credit of having been the very first to work with three blocks. But this cumbersome process never became popular, neither in Germany nor the Netherlands, where only a few examples are known for the whole of the 16th century. However, a still more complicated method was worked out in the Low Countries: a plate with etched outlines was printed on a wood block inked with colour for light effects. 132 colour prints of this type were included in the *Vivae omnium fere imperatorum images* by Hubertus Goltzius, published at Antwerp in 1557. Two series, each of six prints, with scenes from the life of Our Lady and Christ, also carried out with this technique (one print dated 1571 and both series with the monogram of Crispijn van den Broeck – probably the designer and not the executor) are still known; but for the rest, this complicated *Spielerei* did not attract many followers.

Malines became an important graphic centre in the first half of the 16th century, when Margaret of Austria established her court there (1515-1530), and for some years thereafter. Bruges, Ghent, Brussels, Liege and – in the north – Leyden, Amsterdam and Haarlem all housed talented graphic artists. But all the threads of graphic production came together in Antwerp, just as for the typographical industry and for the same reasons (capital market, national and international sales possibilities). Even when the artists stayed only intermittently in the Scheldt city, yet they worked mainly for Antwerp clients and exported their products via Antwerp. Far more than other artists, the graphic artists seem to have been wanderers by nature; and many of them turn up abroad, then at home, then at Antwerp, at the most unexpected moments.

Ice sports on the frozen Scheldt at Antwerp, etching, 34 × 49 cm, Joris
Hoefnagel, 1563. Antwerp, Stedelijk Prentenkabinet.
This magnificent view on the roads of Antwerp is also an interesting icono-
graphic document.

Of the several hundred masters active in the 16th century in the Netherlands we can only give the most important names and the broad lines of the evolution.

THE DECLINE OF THE WOODCUT Woodcutting in the Netherlands up to the 1560's flourished to an extraordinary degree, both in the form of loose prints and that of book illustration. But the work was mainly that of anonymous woodcutters; to only a tiny percentage a name can be attached. To limit ourselves to the south: Jan Swart (Groningen after 1500; probably at Antwerp in 1523); Frans Crabbe van Espleghem (Malines, first half of the 16th century; also a copper engraver); Hubert de Croock (printer at Bruges; active between 1518 and 1546 or 1554); Joost Lambrecht (humanist, printer and typecutter; active in Ghent

The miraculous Draught of Fishes, engraving, 22.5 × 29.5 cm, Cornelis Matsijs, (about 1511 - after 1580). Antwerp, Stedelijk Prentenkabinet. After a cartoon of Raphael, design for a hanging from the series *Acts of the Apostles,* woven at Brussels in 1517/18 (the original cartoons of Raphael are now in the Victoria and Albert Museum, London).

The War-Elephant, engraving and etching (second state); 40.1 × 53.5 cm, Hieronymus Cock (probably) after a (lost) painting by Hieronymus Bosch. Antwerp, Stedelijk Prentenkabinet.

The rabbit-shooting, etching, 22.3 × 29.1 cm, Pieter Bruegel the Elder, 1566 (this is the only graphic realization of the artist known so far, the original drawing is in the Collection Fritz Lugt, Paris). Brussels, Royal Library, Print Room.

1536-1553, and at Wezel 1553-1556); Robert Péril (of Liege; active at Antwerp 1530-1540; also the author of the gigantic woodcut in many blocks showing the *Entry of Charles V and Pope Clement VII into Bologna in 1530)* ; Bernard van de Putte (with intervals at Antwerp, active between 1549 and 1580; at Malines in 1573-1578; specializing in maps); Pauwels van Overbeke (published a plan of Antwerp in 1568). Leading publishers of woodcut prints (either cut by themselves or made in their workshop) at Antwerp were Willem Liefrinck (born at Kester in Brabant; active at Augsburg *ca* 1516-1518, and at Antwerp from 1528 to 1543 or 1546), his son Hans Liefrinck (Antwerp or Augsburg 1518; died at Antwerp in 1573; a copper engraver in particular), his apprentices Jan Mollijns the Elder (master in 1532; active till 1558) and Silvester van Parijs (master in 1538, active till 1571). Plantin's account books reveal the names of the artists who cut the countless wood blocks for the *Officina Plantiniana* (and who also worked for other Antwerp publishers): Arnold Nicolai (master in 1550; died in 1585); Cornelis Muller (working for Plantin from 1564 to 1572); Gerard Janssen van Kampen (living at Breda; working for Plantin from 1564 to 1583); Antoon van Lees (master in 1566; died *ca* 1592).

In the second half of the century, woodcutting suddenly declined. First of all in prints, where the more refined burin engraving gained ground so rapidly that by about 1570 it had almost completely displaced the woodcut. The burin engraving was more expensive – but the devotees seemed prepared to pay the difference in price. The woodcut as book illustration held out for a little longer, but here too there was no stopping the advance of intaglio printing (burin and etching): by about 1590 the woodcut played no more than a secondary role in book production (for initials, tailpieces and the like). The great era of the woodcut in the Netherlands (and in the rest of Europe) was finished for good.

Landscape in the Alps, etching and engraving, 36.8 × 48.6 cm, Hieronymus Cock (supposedly made by him, but in any way edited by him), after a drawing by Pieter Bruegel the Elder. Antwerp, Stedelijk Prentenkabinet.

THE BURIN ENGRAVING IN PRINTS Far more modestly than the woodcut, burin engraving made its entry in the 16th century, almost exclusively for prints. It was the north that started off the movement, already in Renaissance style, with personalities such as the mysterious L. Cz. (claimed for a time by the Germans, but now identified as being Lucas Corneliszoon Kunst or de Cock; about a dozen prints known) and the brilliant Lucas van Leyden (Leyden *ca* 1489-1533; 172 prints known). But production rapidly concentrated in the south and in Antwerp. In this first phase we may mention the names of Meester s (Sander – active at Antwerp where he met Dürer in 1520; 400 engravings by him are known); Frans Crabbe van Espleghem (Malines, first half of 16th century; some fifty engravings known, also a woodcutter); Cornelis Metsijs (second son of Quinten; Antwerp *ca* 1510, master in 1531, travelled widely abroad, last heard of in Italy in 1562; 114 prints known).

But the man who, around the middle of the century, was to make Antwerp the great international market for engravings, was Hieronymus Cock (Antwerp 1507 or 1510 – 1570; active as publisher from *ca* 1547 onwards). He was a talented burin engraver and etcher; but above all a shrewd businessman who, from his house *In the Four Winds*, distributed countless prints and print albums (prints bound together illustrating a particular theme; often with a few pages of text, typographically printed). Thus in the world of the print, he acquired the same international fame as his contemporary Christoffel Plantin in that of the printed book. He had the luck (or the power of persuasion) to get Pieter Bruegel the Elder to work for him as a draughtsman. Bruegel was brilliant, both as a designer of prints and as a painter, and he was exceedingly productive. And in his 'stable' Cock was able to assemble a number of the best engravers of that time in Europe (who frequently also worked and published for their own account or supplied book illus-

295

H. Cock · excude · 1557.   F ME   Brueghel · Invent ·

PATIENTIA EST MALORVM QVÆ AVT INFERVNTVR, AVT ACCIDVNT, CVM ÆQVANIMITATE PERLATIO · Lact. Inst. Lib. 5·

Patientia, engraving, 34 × 43.5 cm, Pieter van der Heyden (a Merica) after a drawing by Pieter Bruegel the Elder, edited by Hieronymus Cock, 1557. Antwerp, Stedelijk Prentenkabinet.

The Resurrection of Christ, engraving (first state), 43.5 × 32.4 cm, Filips Galle, after a drawing by Pieter Bruegel the Elder, edited by Hieronymus Cock. Antwerp, Stedelijk Prentenkabinet.

trations), such as the only important Italian master to settle in the Netherlands, Giorgio Ghisi (Mantua 1520 – Antwerp 1582; working for Cock from 1551 onwards). Also among these engravers were Cornelis Bos ('s-Hertogenbosch 1506 or 1510 – Groningen *ca* 1564; master at Antwerp in 1540, but often in Italy before and after that time), Dirk Volkertszoon Coornhert (leading Dutch humanist, Amsterdam 1522 – Gouda 1590), Cornelis Cort (Hoorn 1533 or 1536 – Rome 1578; worked for Cock but did not reside in Antwerp), Pieter van der Heyden (latinized his name to a Merica; Antwerp *ca* 1522-1576, master in 1557), Frans Huys (also a painter; Antwerp *ca* 1522 – *ca* 1562, master in 1546), and Lambert Soetman calling himself Suavius (Liege *ca* 1510 – Frankfurt-am-Main 1574 or 1576; in 1554 at Antwerp).

From *ca* 1517 to *ca* 1567, Filips Galle (Haarlem 1537 – Antwerp 1612) worked for Hieronymus Cock, but then started up his own firm (*In the White Lily*) around 1564. After the death of Cock in 1570, this firm grew to become an equally important international publisher of engravings. Filips Galle was in course of time assisted by his sons Theodoor (Antwerp *ca* 1570-1633) and Cornelis (Antwerp *ca* 1576-1650) and his sons-in-law Adriaan Collaert (Antwerp *ca* 1560-1618) and Karel de Mallery (*ca* 1576 – after 1631) but, with the exception of Adriaan Collaert, their production must especially be situated in the 17th century. There is less clarity on the question of who helped Filips Galle in his heyday.

These two giants left still place for a series of smaller publishers or freelance artists. To name only the more distinguished: Pieter Huys (brother of Frans and especially active as a painter; Antwerp *ca* 1525 – after 1571, master in 1545), Pieter Baltens (Antwerp 1520-1598, master *ca* 1540), Balthasar van den Bos (or Sylvius, 's-Hertogenbosch 1518 – Antwerp 1580; from 1543 onwards at Antwerp), Abraham de Bruyn (Antwerp *ca*

DEBENT IGNARI RES FERRE ET POST OPERARI
IVS LAPIDIS CARI VILIS SED DENIQ3 RARI
VNICA RES CERTA VILIS SED VBIQ3 REPERTA

QVATVOR INSERTA NATVRIS IN NVBE REFERTA
NVLLA MINERALIS RES EST VBI PRINCIPALIS
SED TALIS QVALIS REFERITVR VBIQ3 LOCALIS.

The Alchemist, engraving, 32.5 × 44 cm, Filips Galle (probably), after a drawing by Pieter Bruegel the Elder, edited by Hieronymus Cock (the original drawing, which can be found in the Berlin Print Room, is dated 1558). Antwerp, Stedelijk Prentenkabinet.

1540 – Cologne 1587), Harmen Muller (Amsterdam? *ca* 1550; active at Antwerp till 1596), the monogramist HSD (active at Antwerp between 1546 and 1580), Melchisedech van Hooren (active at Antwerp between 1550 and 1575) and Gerard de Jode (Nijmegen 1509 or 1517 – Antwerp 1591, master in 1547); the latter two specializing in town views and maps.

A very special mention must be made of the three brothers Wierick, Jan (Antwerp *ca* 1548 – after 1615, master in 1572), Hieronymus (Antwerp *ca* 1553-1620, master in 1571) and Antoon (master in 1590, died in 1604). They were among the greatest virtuosi and the most productive of freelance engravers of their time (their total production comprises more than 3000 works); in spite of the fact that their clients had the greatest difficulty in chasing them from the taverns and keeping them working.

THE BREAKTHROUGH OF ENGRAVING IN ILLUSTRATED BOOK   Originally, burin engraving was only

used for prints. At Bruges in 1503, Heynric de Valle published the *Figurae ad devotionem excitantes a Passione Christi* by Dominicus Lupi with some copper engravings that were more than mediocre, and a *Rosarium Virginis Mariae*. In 1551, somewhere in Holland, there appeared the work by the anabaptist David Joris, *Twonder-boeck*, decorated with copper plates. We already mentioned above the 132 camaieu prints, partly in copper, included in the *Vivae omnium fere imperatorum imagines* by Hubertus Goltzius and published at Antwerp in 1557. In 1559, Plantin brought out *La magnifique et sumptueuse Pompe funébre faite aus obseques et funerailles du.. empereur Charles Cinquieme... en la vile de Bruxelles*, with 32 copperplates by the Dutch brothers Jan and Lucas Doetecum (or Duetecum) after drawings by Hieronymus Cock – in fact no more than a print album preceded and followed by a typographically printed text (with versions in French, Dutch, German, Italian and Spanish). Lambert Suavius cut the title print in 1563, after a drawing by Lambert

Portrait of Henry III, King of France, engraving 34 × 23.4 cm, Hieronymus Wierix. Antwerp, Stedelijk Prentenkabinet.

Lombard, for another work by Hubertus Goltzius, *Caesar sive Historiae Imperatorum numismatibus* (followed by similar title prints for other publications by Goltzius in 1566 and 1576).

Thus burin engraving was very slow in penetrating the art of book printing. There were reasons for this. Printed text and woodcuts were easily harmonized in one and the same edition: the same letterpress on the same presses at the same tempo. Intaglio printing (burin engraving or etching) is not only a much more expensive form of graphics, but must be reproduced on a special press at a much slower tempo; if a typographical text was added to the pages, the printer had to use two different presses. Thus there was a technical and a financial problem (between 1575 and 1589 Plantin published a number of liturgical works in a cheap version with woodcuts, and an expensive one with burin engravings: the *Breviarum Romanum* in 4° of 1575 was sold in the cheap form for 3 *fl* and in the expensive form for 4 *fl*. The change of only 7 illustrations, barely 11

by 7.5 *cm*, cost the considerable difference in price of 1 *fl* – equivalent to 2000 of today's Belgian francs). But, as for the prints, customers appeared ready to pay the higher price, and that left only the technical problem to be overcome.

In Italy around 1550-1560, books with copper illustrations were no longer a rarity, but north of the Alps they were not so advanced. It was Plantin who here, as in so many other fields, dared to take the plunge; and in 1566 he brought out the medical treatise of Valverda-Vesalius *Vivae imagines partium corporis humani* with a title print and 42 illustrations, engraved by Frans and Pieter Huys. The following year, in Bruges, Pieter de Clerck brought out *De waarachtighe fabulen der dieren* ('The true fables of the animals') by Edward de Dene, with 108 etchings by Marcus Gheraerts.

The impulse was given. Neither Plantin nor his colleagues had difficulty in finding among the print engravers specialists who were prepared to provide the illustrations in burin or etching. The burin and the etching, practically unused in typographical production in the Netherlands before 1566, had around 1590 almost completely replaced the woodcut.

FLEMISH AND BRABANT MASTERS ABROAD   In the Netherlands, the year 1585 is an important milestone, also in the history of graphics. Neither was there an abrupt break, nor a sudden shift in artistic concepts. But after 1585, also in this artistic activity, Holland – which up to then had only played a modest second fiddle – became a worthy competitor, who rapidly and aggressively threatened the hegemony of Antwerp. This was largely attributable to Flemish and Brabant masters who had settled there, including Pieter Bast (1550-1605), Hans Bol (Malines 1534 – Amsterdam 1593), Jacob de Gheyn (Antwerp 1565 – The Hague 1629) and Crispijn van de Passe (Arnemuiden 1565 – Utrecht 1637, master at Antwerp in 1585).

The troubles (or simply the urge to travel) sent in the later years of the 16th century a swarm of other Flemish and Brabant engravers, both catholic and protestant, over many European countries, where some of them played a vital role. In England, masters such as Thomas Geminus (active 1524-1570), Marcus Gheraerts, Frans Hogenberg and his brother Remigius (Malines *ca* 1536 – in England in 1572 and last recorded there in 1587) and Judocus Hondius (1563-1612) were the first important representatives of the graphic art. In France at the end of the century Antwerp engravers (the first and most important being Thomas de Leu, 1559-1620; in Paris 1576) helped to form the Paris burin school. In the German empire (and to a lesser degree in Italy) – apart from Frans Hogenberg, Joris Hoefnagel, Lambert Suavius and Dominicus Custos (de Coster, son of Pieter Baltens; Antwerp after 1550 – Augsburg 1620) – the de Sadeler brothers were vigorously active: Jan the Elder (Brussels 1550 – Venice 1601; active in Munich, Cologne and Frankfurt; in 1593 in Venice), Egied (Antwerp *ca* 1560 – Prague 1629) and Raphael (Antwerp 1561 – Venice *ca* 1628; with his brother Jan in Munich and Venice), and after them their descendants (Joost, Filips, Marcus and Raphael the Younger).

Furniture

The 16th century was one of the most diverse, as well as one of the most complex periods in the history of Flemish furniture. The furniture of this period still displayed some late Gothic elements, but these were soon replaced by the principles and characteristics of the Renaissance; the latter had originated abroad but were assimilated in an individual and powerful way by Flemish artists and craftsmen.

Although the Renaissance in the Southern Netherlands has been the subject of a great deal of study, furniture was often considered to be a *bête noire*. However, this attitude is quite unjustified as furniture does provide its own illustrations of Renaissance art. This section only deals with the most important aspects of 16th-century furniture, stressing the penetration of Renaissance elements. First we will consider the influence of design books on furniture. This is followed by a survey of the different types of furniture available for storage and seating; as well as a number of references to the interiors where they might have been found, and the incidence of Flemish furniture abroad – which is difficult to assess in the 16th century in view of the small number of surviving pieces. We will confine ourselves to secular furniture, and will only give casual information about cabinet-makers.

The source material to study Renaissance furniture consists of written documents, as well as iconography. Useful information can be found in the archives in household inventories. Compared to the Middle Ages, many more of them have survived from the 16th century; shedding a great deal of light on the names, materials, use and number of different types of furniture in different rooms. It was unfortunately necessary to leave out the guild regulations, the qualifications and the working methods of cabinet-makers. Treatises on architecture and books of designs can provide information about the elements of construction and decorative patterns used. The paintings and prints of the various Flemish Renaissance artists are extremely informative as iconographic sources. They bring to life the image one has of various types of furniture and their use; certainly for less common furniture or for fragments of them.

State-chimney, Lancelot Blondeel and others, 1528-1531. Bruges, Palace of the Brugse Vrije.
Numerous artists, among them H. Closencamp, W. Damast and Guyot de Beaugrant, worked on the execution of the design of L. Blondeel, which contains life-sized wood statues as well as marble and alabaster reliefs. It can be considered as a true *tour de force*.

301

Obviously the most important information is provided by the surviving furniture itself, which is mainly to be found in various museums in Belgium; or in situ, for example in monasteries. These articles of furniture bear witness to the solid workmanship of Flemish cabinet-makers and clearly illustrate the materials, techniques and decoration that were used. Nevertheless, these old pieces of furniture should be studied with some circumspection, bearing in mind the inevitable repair work which has been carried out over the centuries. Similarly, it is necessary to be on one's guard regarding the clever 19th-century copies and skilfully made fakes, which have often found their way into museum collections and have been considered to be authentic.

THE INFLUENCE OF TREATISES AND BOOKS OF DESIGNS ON 16th-CENTURY FURNITURE The principles of Renaissance building were brought to the Southern Netherlands by means of printed Italian treatises on architecture, including the works of Vitruvius and Palladio. The publication of the work by the Venetian Serlio was particularly important. The Dutch translation by Pieter Coecke van Aelst was published in Antwerp in 1539, together with Vitruvius' work, barely two years after the original Italian version, entitled: *The invention of columns with capitals and measurements. From Vitruvius and various other authors, compiled for painters, wood-carvers, sculptors etc.*

These works promoted the application of the correct Roman orders (Tuscan, Doric, Ionic, Corinthian, Composite) with the accompanying decoration and list of capitals, components and classical elements. This applied not only in building, but also in furniture making, which maintained close links with architecture as regards structure, correct proportions and designs. 16th-century architects were well aware of the relationship between architecture and furniture, as they refer to it in the titles of their treatises. In this way, oak furniture was given capitals, pillars or pillasters in accordance with the correct proportions, as well as projecting consoles. Free-standing sculptures such as caryatids and herms added more relief to the furniture.

The centre for the spread of these publications, and above all the books of designs and prints of Renaissance ornaments, has been Antwerp, where in about 1560 the famous work of Hans Vredeman de Vries was published. It was entitled: *A series of fashionable desgigns based on the five Roman orders, for the use of all sculptors and wood-carvers, furniture makers, and all craftsmen, or anyone who loves classical ornamentation...*

This extensive series of imaginative designs and caryatids was often used as a direct example for supporting figures or statues on the frame of oak cupboards, such as those known from iconographic sources. Italian Renaissance elements including grotesques – Italian *groteschi* or wall paintings in 'grottos', subterranean rooms which were discovered in Rome in 1490, and which contained fantastic hybrid human and animal figures – soon reached Flanders. Inspired by this grotesque style, the Antwerp artist Cornelis Floris de Vriendt developed his own decorative style incorporating not only grotesques, but also bosses, fluting, cartouches, masks, satyrs, winged insects, nymphs, birds, dogs, swags of fruit and drolleries. These very characteristic decorative features are collected in a work entitled: *Many variations of grotesques and styles for the use of anyone who practises or loves art*, published in 1556. It was applicable to the ornamentation of oak panels used in cupboards and chests, and also in the decoration of smaller pieces of furniture for storage. Apart from Cornelis Floris, his contemporary Cornelis Bos published an extremely useful work entitled: *A book on the*

Grotesques, Cornelis Floris, copper-plate, 210 × 156 mm, from C. Floris de Vriendt, *All sorts of changes in grotesques*, Antwerp, around 1556.
Among architectonic elements, root-patterns, cartouches with roller-work and mount, there are also festoons of flowers and fruits, brushes, vases, oil-lamps and baldachins, hybrid creatures, sphinxes, exotic masks, horses, insects, birds and snails, together with lobed textile flaps.

many features of moresques... The date and place of publication of this book are not known, but the styles described are very similar to those of Cornelis Floris.

In 1565 a work was published in Antwerp by the famous artist, Hans Vredeman de Vries, entitled: *Grotesques in various styles, very elegant and useful for painters and glass engravers*... which gave examples of many other variations and types of grotesques. Obviously all these books had an influence on Flemish furniture and their models spread to the Northern Netherlands, Germany and Scandinavia; consequently the northern and middle European Renaissance style developed.

In 1583 the versatile Hans Vredeman de Vries published a book in Antwerp, aimed in particular at furniture makers, entitled: *Differents pourtraicts de menuiserie asçavoir Portaux, Bancs, Escabelles, Tables, buffets, frises ou corniches, licts-de-camp, ornements a pendre l'essuoir a mains, fontaines a laver les mains. Propre aux menuiziers et autres amateurs de telle science*... The furniture he proposed incorporated strong lines and had a clear structure, making use of pillars, pillasters, root motifs, spheres, obelisks, ballusters, and decorative carving incorporating masks, moresques and swags of fruit. The designs for court cabinets are particularly striking: each half provides a variation of the same type of furniture. The feeling for size and proportion, the use of a central perspective with two vanishing points in the illustrations, and the concern to achieve the correct perspective in the decoration of the panels and profiles is very evident in this book of designs.

In addition to the above-mentioned book of designs for furniture makers, Hans Vredeman de Vries produced a series of prints with designs for ovals filled with perspective pictures for use as decorative patterns in inlaid work. According to E. Forssmann, the title of this collection of drawings, of which the title page has not survived, would have been: *Twenty pages of perspective and architectural pictures in ovals for ornamental use. Examples for intarsia*. It was published in about 1560.

Rafter-skid, oak, 46.5 × 27.5 × 7 cm, 1556. Brussels, Museums of Art and History.
This rafter-skid is decorated with an exotic male figure which is enclosed by mount, in the style of Vredeman de Vries and Cornelis Floris. Around it, one can notice garlands of flowers, birds and masks, at the bottom is a cartouche which is marked 1556.

Two designs of side-boards, H. Vredeman de Vries, copper-plate, 259 × 193 mm, from H. Vredeman de Vries, *Differents pourtraicts...*, Antwerp, 1583, Antwerp, fol. 10.
The left side-board shows at the left side columns with festoons, fruits, and lion's heads; at the right side pillars with root-patterns; on the doors cartouches with roller-work or geometric mouldings. The cornice of the right side-board has tendril-work with masks, the middle zone has twoo drawers.

Panel, 63 × 19 cm, late 16th century. Brussels, Museums of Art and History.
Panel of a cabinet or possibly part of a frieze, having a mascaron, fine
tendril-work and two half-figures in a Cornelis Floris style.

Door of a cabinet, 43 × 30 cm, 1550, Liege, Curtius Museum.
The door of this dated sacristy-cabinet, coming from St Trond, shows a niche
in the form of a shell, with baluster-like columns in which there is the image
of a Madonna. Above and under the lock there is always a tondo with an
imaginative man's head.

16th-CENTURY FURNITURE FOR STORAGE AND
SEATING   Very few examples of the many pieces of
furniture known by name or by sight from household
inventories or from prints or paintings have survived.
Any knowledge that has been gained about 16th-century
furniture is largely theoretical.

The rooms in the houses of burghers of this period
were fairly large, often arranged around an inner
courtyard in the Italian fashion. The ends of the oak
beams which constituted the ceiling were carved with a
late Gothic profile, or in a Cornelis Floris style with
satyrs, enclosed with ferronerie (Antwerp, private collection), or with scenes borrowed from prints by M. van
Heemskerk (Brussels, Museums of Art and History).

Oak panelling or tapestries covered the wall partly or
entirely. The central feature of the interior of the house
would be a monumental chimney-piece with a fire
surround and the inevitable andirons and English bel-
lows (although the latter term often appears in documents, the significance cannot be confirmed with
certainty). One of the best examples of a magnificent
mantlepiece covering an entire wall and part of the
ceiling is undoubtedly that in the *Paleis van het Vrije* in
Bruges.

Obviously Renaissance rooms contained a great
variety of oak furniture. At the beginning of the 16th
century there were not many new articles of furniture
or changes in their construction. For example, the traditional oak chests with iron hoops and solid locks
continued to be made. Some of these were covered with
leather and lined with lead, and there were also
Duytsche chests and *sluytbancken,* with or without a
lock. It was a long time before the late Gothic decorative
style with panels or vine work was replaced by the
Renaissance style of ornamentation. The masks, imaginary animals, grotesques and arabesques imitated from
Cornelis Floris, emerged reluctantly (Amsterdam,
Rijksmuseum).

There was very little change in the Gothic style in the
structure of the two and four-door cupboards, made in
the first half of the 16th century and known as *schap-
praye* and *cleerschappraye.* The cornice was still slightly

profiled, there was still a frame and panelling, but the carving now incorpated Renaissance motifs. Arabesques or slender garlands of flowers, vases or ribbons surrounded by symmetrically arranged dragons, imaginary animals and birds, alternated with *tondi, i e* medallions of plaited laurel wreaths surrounding the heads of men or women carved in half-relief (Bruges, Pottery museum). These heads had a classical appearance and were often facing each other, or were adapted to the current fashions as the hairstyles clearly reveal (Brussels, Museums of Art and History). Other surviving pieces of cupboards and door panels have shown that in addition to these heads, the range of decoration also included mythological subjects, *e g* Lucretia (Antwerp, private collection), biblical scenes (Antwerp, Museum Mayer-van den Berg), or a tiled floor with a row or arches in perspective (Antwerp, private collection). Also some door panels with Cornelis Floris motifs have survived (London, Victoria and Albert Museum).

In some two-door cupboards there were fluted pillasters on the vertical supports, and many door-posts re-

Renaissance cabinet with two doors, 210 × 180.5 × 70 cm, first half of the 16th century, Brussels, Museums of Art and History.
Panels with antique men and women and profiles in medallions are alternated with fruit-baskets with animals, horns, masks, vases, grotesques. The middle-post is crowned by an image of a saint. Still Gothic of conception are the epistel-panels at the sides of the cabinet.

Decorative wood-carving, state chimney (detail), after the design of Lanceloot Blondeel, 1528-1531. Bruges, Room of Aldermen of the Vrije. The Bruges persons Herman and Willekin Glosencamp, Rogier de Smet and Willem van Damast were employed for the performance of the wainscotting and the wood-carving of this state chimney.

sembled ballusters. Although the ironwork on the locks and hinges was less prominent than during the Gothic period, it remained clearly visible (Brussels, Museums of Art and History). The number of locks on these chests was always mentioned in household inventories. The *trissoor*, a type of chest raised on legs with a door at the front, a drawer and a sort of canopy was still entirely in the Gothic tradition. According to the inventories, these pieces of furniture were often inlaid with other varieties of wood, were gilded or painted, had carved figures and were covered with a fringed, striped silk cover.

One characteristic piece of furniture during the Renaissance period was the court cupboard or *buffet*. This cupboard consisted of a base, sometimes with two doors; and above this there would be a recessed top with three doors and a protruding cornice supported by two pillars, imaginative pillasters – all in accordance with the correct Roman order – or caryatids (London, Victoria and Albert Museum). The door panels were embellished with cartouches or geometrical designs, and in the middle there were sometimes two drawers. These court cupboards were also often inlaid with different types of wood, e g maple, depending on the current fashion. A painting by Abel Grimmer, depicting an interior, shows this type of court cupboard with a pronouncedly curved central section with inlaid rectangular, oval and lozenge-shaped panels. This piece of furniture was not only used to keep the silver, copper or pewter plate; but also served to hold books, arranged on the open lower section.

During the 16th century tables became a permanent feature of any interior. The medieval system with separate tresles and a tabletop was replaced by a solid piece of furniture. Very often the table could be extended with extra pieces which were fixed beneath the large tabletop. They were supported by additional legs, as is evident in the designs of Hans Vredeman de Vries. These legs were shaped like a pillar or a vase, and were connected by four straight pieces of wood or rungs. In imitation of Italian examples, some of these tables had heavy carved supports or tresles (Amsterdam, Rijksmuseum). A number of 16th-century prints show small round tables supported by naturalistically carved goat's legs, which captured the imagination of craftsmen. Three-legged tables and

Three designs of tables, H. Vredeman de Vries, copper-plate, 182 × 259 mm. From H. Vredeman de Vries, *Differents pourtraicts...*, Antwerp, 1583 fol 7. The top table rests on four legs which grow smaller at the bottom and which have root-patterns; the legs of the table in the middle show typical pillars growing into taps and having drop-patterns; the lowest table has legs in vase-form and is extendible. All the legs of the tables are joined by four straight lines.

small low tables or *scabelle* tables with carved and curved legs could also be found amongst the furniture.

There were a number of different pieces of furniture to provide comfortable seating in a 16th-century household. It was still common to warm up by the fire, sitting on oak settles with an adjustable back-rest, which had been used since Gothic times. In order to make these pieces of furniture more cosy, they would be provided with a cloth or a number of square cushions. The cradle would also be placed close to the fire for the wet nurse. Many hours were spent in a wooden armchair or *caquetoire*, a 'talking chair' with a trapezium-shaped wooden seat, a high narrow back and outwardly-angled arms. The front legs were often shaped like Tuscan pillars and were connected by straight rungs, while Doric pillars were incorporated as supports for the arms, showing that once again the correct use of the Roman orders was followed (Amsterdam, Rijksmuseum). Some designs show obelisks and pediments surmounting the high back. The inventories show that Parisian seats and Dutch chairs (two types of chair whose appearance is unknown), chairs for men with ironwork, chairs for women, high children's chairs *etc*, were all common pieces of furniture. In most rooms foot-rests, as well as three-legged stools, with or without a slightly curved back, supported the tired limbs of the less wealthy from the 15th century onwards. These appear in many paintings and prints.

The new piece of furniture was the Spanish chair, which was only found in the interiors of houses of the extremely wealthy, especially in the best room. As its name suggests, this piece of furniture probably originated in the Iberian peninsula and was brought to Flanders during the Spanish occupation, together with Spanish chests, blankets, tables and other household articles. Soon local craftsmen, the so-called 'Spanish chairmakers', began to make this oak chair on four turned legs with a fixed back and an upholstered seat. The legs were jointed, and each section was shaped like a vase, a balluster, or egg or ball-shaped. Eight rungs, arranged in pairs, connected the legs; the top two of these had grooves, while the bottom two were carved like accolades. The back was almost square, the seat rectangular and wider than deep. In the middle of the century the woodwork sometimes incorporated *moresque* features, which probably meant that ivory was used in the inlaid work of the wooden frame, as described in the household inventories. Originally this piece of furniture was upholstered in black, red or brown Spanish leather with embossed designs, which was nailed onto the wooden frame with round-headed copper nails. From the second half of the 16th century the high Spanish men's chairs and low women's chairs were also upholstered with fabric, including green and black velvet. The Spanish chairmakers also used baize with a fringe of the same colour, or *trype*, a velvety woollen fabric, preferably in red. Yellow or blue *corsey* was also incorporated on the back and seat of the chair.

Apart from the Spanish chairs, there were also armchairs, i e Spanish seats with curved wooden armrests supported by uprights. The large number of 16th-century chairs, often described with an indication of the town or country of their origin, also included chairs with cane seats. These chairs were found predominantly in kitchens and back rooms.

There was a large variety of beds, including bedsteads, *lied-du-camp*, *coetse met een bedde*, etc in which the wooden frame, the frieze and the panels were decorated in the contemporary style of Cornelis Floris (Amsterdam, Rijksmuseum). Again Vredeman de Vries produced designs in which the cornice of the canopy was supported by four pillars or pillasters. The bedhead was still surmounted by cartouches and obelisks, while there was a row of vase-shaped balusters at the foot of the bed. There were curtains of damask or *corsey* with valences decorated with tassels hanging from the canopy, and matching the cushions and coverlets, as a protection against the cold and prying eyes. This piece of furniture was still placed in the reception room and was often on a dais, which made it seem even more imposing. *Toeslaande slaapcoetsen*, beds consisting of a large chest with a straw matress, ensured a peaceful night for the common people. Sometimes these beds were painted black and gilded. Coat racks and mirrors set in ornately carved borders containing seated figures, scrolls and

fittings, completed the 16th-century interior (Antwerp, private collection); together with the wooden screens and the sporadically found writing and money tables. The room would be lit by copper and bronze chandeliers, consisting of a single or a double rung of vertical candle holders around a central sphere with a ring below and a figure above. Simple iron or wooden lamps, sometimes gilded or slightly carved, were used together with wooden candlesticks in smaller rooms.

Before concluding this survey, two very interesting items of furniture with *intarsia*, used for storage, should be mentioned. They can be considered as examples of a special type of furniture, and the *intarsia* is crucial in the question where a particular piece originated. The first one, with *intarsia* of different light-coloured and painted pieces of wood, can be considered as a precursor of the well-known 17th-century cabinet (Brussels, Museums of Art and History). Two doors lock twenty-three drawers, divided amongst six sections, and two pigeon-holes. In the corners of the empty cube shape of the two pigeon-holes there are secret compartments, hidden behind a small sprung panel. All the fronts of the drawers and doors were inlaid with vine work surrounding

Secreta, fragment of cabinet with inlaid-work, 40 × 6 cm, around 1600. Brussels, Museums of Art and History.
'Secreta', consisting of 5 oblong drawers, which are concealed behind a square, elastic panel, in the hind corners of the empty cubical space.

Cabinet with inlaid-work, 165 × 120.5 × 48 cm, around 1600, Brussels, Museums of Art and History.
The delicately coloured and perfectly executed inlaid-work on the doors and the drawers, shows patterns which are inspired on the designs of Cornelis Floris, Marc Gheeraerts and Filips Galle. On the fronts of the central panels are the images of a caged goat and dog in perspective.

Inside of the left outside panel, fragment of cabinet with inlaid-work, 60 × 51 cm, around 1600. Brussels, Museums of Art and History.
The inside of the panel is, between others, covered with a vase of flowers, pinks, a balustrade with a parrot, Indians, fruithorns, monkeys, dogs, capped satyrs and tendril-work. Six different frames surround a flowery border in which there are rabbits, an owl and winged creatures.

winged insect-like creatures with spirallig horns, *cornucopiae* of fruit and grotesques. These figures are very reminiscent of the designs of Cornelis Bos and Cornelis Floris, as are the cartouches with scrolls and the imaginary animals. The indians, female torsos under serrated bows and tobacco flowers seem to be inspired by the prints of Filips Galle and Marc Gheeraerts of allegorical scenes of America in 1580-1600. Similar cupboards with more or less the same patterns, materials and inlay technique, were found in many areas of southern Germany (Munich), where there was a great tradition of *intarsia*, following the Italian example. According to the surviving inventories, cupboards with *intarsia* using different kinds of wood could be found in towns in Flanders and Brabant from the end of the 16th century; and the inlay workers in Antwerp were included in the furniture makers' guild from 1543. However, the lack of documents still makes it difficult to specify in which workshop which pieces of furniture were made.

Another interesting piece of furniture with a folding leaf is a late 16th-century piece, similar to a Spanish *vargueño*. This is skilfully inlaid with scenes based on designs of artists such as H. Vredeman de Vries and J. Stradanus, and the cupboard even had a four-line Flemish religious text. The perfection of the technique used suggests the existence of a specialized workshop for this article; but the available data about such a centre during the 16th century are extremely sketchy. Certainly the iconography indicates that it was made in Flanders.

According to research by F. Thirion, the influence of Filips Galle's book of prints, *De Deis gentium imagines aliquot iconicae*, published in Antwerp in 1581, is clearly evident in the carved panels with gods and goddesses of a few Renaissance cupboards which are now in France (Paris, *Musée des Arts Décoratifs*; Cluny). This again shows the international use of designs of Flemish artists, and also shifts the traditional date of these pieces from the middle to the end of the 16th century. Even the designs for the elegant Italianate nudes of the French Renaissance furniture in the so-called *école de Fontainebleau* style were not based on the compositions of artists of the school itself, but rather on prints of designers from the Netherlands.

This concise survey of 16th-century Flemish furniture shows that during this period there was a significant break with the Gothic style. In the first place, Renaissance furniture was influenced by Italian architectural treatises and prints, on which some leading Flemish artists imposed their own character. In turn, the decorative patterns of Cornelis Floris and the books of designs by H. Vredeman de Vries spread to the Northern Netherlands, Scandinavia and Germany. This explains the stylistic similarity between the 16th-century furniture from these regions; but at the same time creates the problem of identifying a particular piece of furniture from a specific workshop. Apart from the Italian one, there was a clearly discernible Spanish influence; particularly as regards the design of some furniture, and to a lesser extent, a French influence. Finally, the Renaissance principles which emerged in 16th-century Flemish furniture as real innovations, developed in a logical way during the 17th century, to be adapted to Baroque norms.

Tapestry and textile arts

TAPESTRY

The Renaissance heralded a new period for tapestry work, an art form which flourished to an even greater extent than before. There were important workshops in Brussels, Audenarde, Bruges and Antwerp, and for a while in Ghent. However, during the first years of the 16th century there was great abuse in the manufacture of tapestries. The district court of Brussels was the first to deal with this. In 1528 an edict was promulgated, obliging weavers to mark any tapestry over six ells long with the town mark. This consisted of two B's, for Brussels and Brabant, with a red shield in the centre. Later the central government published the imperial edict of 1544 which imposed – inter alia – that all large, expensive tapestries had to be signed with the marks of the weaver and the city. The seal of Antwerp depicted a stylized castle, flanked on either side by a small hand, the symbol of the city; for Audenarde the town mark showed the city's shield with a pair of spectacles above; for Bruges it was a Gothic letter B above a spool. In the 17th century it became increasingly common for weavers to use their initials, and later their whole name, to mark their panels on the horizontal or vertical borders of the tapestry. Despite the ordinances the various centres retained their own traditions, customers and the original quality of their work.

During the 16th, and even more in the 17th century and later, the role of the artists who painted the cartoons became increasingly important. The weavers restricted their work more and more to simply interpreting the designs; and later, to reproducing them as faithfully as possible. However, the painters who often received commissions directly from the weaver, usually took the latter's wishes into consideration.

Even during the latter half of the 15th century, a number of hangings were based on cartoons made by Italian painters. These were not only made by Flemish weavers working in Italy, but also in Flanders itself. Nevertheless, great changes were taking place. The humanists were singing the praises of the ancient art of Greece and Rome, being revived in the Italian workshops. Commissions for tapestries based on designs by Italian Renaissance artists influenced the arrival of a new style in tapestry-weaving. In about 1513-1515 Pope Leo X commissioned Raphael to design a series of cartoons depicting the *Acts of the Apostles*. These works of art, which entailed a complete break with traditional Flemish art, give a good idea of the new trends that were developing. Attempts were made to achieve a feeling of depth by producing a large empty space and magnificent skies. The clothing was no longer decorated; and the borders contained series of allegorical figures or scenes

The Avarice, hanging (detail) from a series of the *Seven Capital Sins,* Brussels, middle of the 16th century, with the monogram of Willem de Pannemaker after designs of Pieter Coecke van Aelst. Vienna, Kunsthistorisches Museum.

The miraculous Draught of Fishes, pattern by Raphael for the first hanging from the series of the *Acts of the Apostles,* about 1513-1515. London, Victoria and Albert Museum.

The miraculous Draught of Fishes, hanging from a series picturing the *Acts of the Apostles,* Brussels, middle of the 16th century, after designs by Raphael and with a non-identified weaver's monogram. Spain, Crown Collection.

Death of Ananias and Saphira, hanging from a series representing the *History of Peter and Paul,* 280 × 560 cm, Brussels, 1556-1567 with a non-identified weaver's monogram and after designs which are attributed to Peter de Kempeneer. The coat of arms of François d'Avroult, 56th abbot of St Pieter's abbey at Ghent, and the mark and motto of the convent are woven in the top border of the tapestry. Ghent, Bijloke Museum.

Death of St Paul, hanging (detail) from a series with scenes from the *Life of St Paul,* 417 × 680 cm, Brussels, 1535-1540, after designs of Pieter Coecke van Aelst and with non-identified weaver's monograms. Vienna, Kunsthistorisches Museum.

related to the life of the patron, replacing the earlier decoration which had used garlands of leaves and flowers. It was impossible for the weaver to slavishly reproduce these cartoons; they were viewed as frescoes and flew in the face of Flemish tradition. Even so, Pieter van Aelst, also known as Pieter van Edingen († after 1532), commissioned by the Pope to weave the actual tapestries, was experienced enough to succeed in overcoming any difficulties. He attempted to enrich the designs by filling the foreground and the background with plants, and decorating Christ's garments with golden suns. This set was extremely successful. Pieter van Aelst was appointed tapestry-maker to the Papal Court, and his hangings are still among the most outstanding works of art in the Vatican. Up until the 18th century the *Acts of the Apostles* were a subject for a number of tapestries woven in various workshops in Flanders. The best version came from the 16th-century manufacture of Jan van Tieghem in Brussels.

FALSILOQVO·QVICVQVE·DEVM·FRVSTRABITVR·ORE·
SE·FACIET·POENE·IVDICIIQVE·REVM·ACTA·5

Deer-hunting in the sign of the Virgin, hanging from the series picturing the *Huntings of Maximilian*, 447 × 682 cm, Brussels, about 1525-1540, after designs supposed to be by Barend van Orley and with the weaver's monogram of Jan Ghieteels. Paris, Louvre.

Jacob is welcomed by Joseph in Egypt, hanging from a series with the History of Jacob, 420 × 670 cm, Brussels, second quarter of the 16th century, atelier of Willem de Kempeneere after designs of Barend van Orley. Brussels, Museums of Art and History.

Young Tobias introduces the archangel Raphael as travelling-companion to his blind father, hanging from a series with the History of Tobias, 353 × 450 cm, Brussels, second quarter of the 16th century, after designs of Barend van Orley and with a non-identified weaver's monogram. Vienna, Kunsthistorisches Museum.

During this period artists from Brussels who painted cartoons also produced some valuable work. Barend van Orley (ca 1488-1541) was the foremost exponent of Netherlands Romanism in tapestry work. As a pattern painter he was a pioneer and exercised great influence on later cartoon painters. His designs reveal surprisingly good taste and enormous ingenuity. As a result of the large scope of his compositions, his sense of scale and his familiarity with Raphael's work, Barend van Orley took tapestry work into a new phase of creativity. He created designs for the Passion of Our Lord in Madrid, the Hunts of Maximilian in the Louvre in Paris, the History of Jacob in the Museums of Art and History in Brussels, and for the History of Tobias in the castle at Gaasbeek.

The beautiful festive borders form part of the technique and function of the tapestry, in a most sensitive manner and with very pleasing results. Barend van Orley trained a number of pupils, and other artists followed in his footsteps, such as Lucas van Nevele, who is credited with the designs for a series known as the *Lucas Months*.

Another important painter of cartoons was Pieter Coecke van Aelst (1502-1550), not to be confused with Pieter van Aelst. He worked in Antwerp for many years but spent the end of his life in Brussels. Only three series are definitely based on his designs, *viz* the *History of Josua* (Vienna), the *Life of St Paul* (Vienna and Munich) and the set depicting the *Seven deadly Sins* (Vienna and Madrid). Pieter Coecke's work surpasses Barend van Orley's in both richness and splendour. There is also a great deal of movement in the composition. There is not simply one figure, but a whole crowd of people who are displayed intermingling; they are usually tall, elegant and small footed. He also paid a great deal of attention to the border decoration, which already contains grotesque motifs and iron fittings.

Michiel Coxcie (1499-1592) was undoubtedly an important cartoon painter. He studied the Renaissance style in Rome, particularly the work of Raphael. On his return to Flanders he came to be known as 'the Flemish Raphael'. Nevertheless, his beautiful landscapes belong in the tradition of the art of the Netherlands. For a number of years Michiel Coxcie was the official painter of cartoons for the city of Brussels. His works include designs for a *History of the First Parents* and for a *Story of Noah* (Wawel Castle, Cracow). He was a talented and knowledgeable master, though he was not very independent. His compositions are well balanced, though rather contrived. The beautiful borders with animals of all kinds were enormously successful, and were still copied at the beginning of the 17th century.

The arrest of king François I (detail), hanging from a series representing *The Battle for Pavia*, Brussels, 1525-1531, after cartoons by Bernard van Orley, Napels, Museo di Capodimonte.

Charles V inspects his troups which embark for Tunis near Barcelone, hanging from a series with the *Campaign of Charles V against Tunis,* 520 × 708 cm, Brussels 1712-1721, signed by Judocus de Vos after designs of Jan Cornelisz. Vermeyen of 1546-1548. Vienna, Kunsthistorisches Museum.

Biblical scene, hanging, 310 × 325 cm, Brussels, third quarter of the 16th century, monograms of Franz Geubels and the initials NDW. Amsterdam, Rijksmuseum.

The designs for the series depicting the *Campaign of Charles V against Tunis* (Madrid) were commissioned from Jan Cornelisz Vermeyen (1500-1561) in Brussels. The artist had gone on this expedition himself and incorporated a self portrait in the first tapestry. The soft tone of these works with their predominantly yellow colouration is striking, and their borders are full of moresques, decorative motifs of Moorish origin. The designs for a series depicting the *Fables of Ovid* (Madrid) and for another showing the *History of Vertumnus and Pomona* (Vienna and Madrid) are attributed to him, because in both cases the borders are also decorated with moresques. The last set with its extremely slim figures and rich decoration is among the finest tapestry work of this period.

God's Wrath, hanging from a series with the *Tower of Babel,* 425 × 430 cm, Brussels, about 1560, with the monogram of Leo van den Hecke. Krakau, Wawel Castle.

Month of February with the figure of Neptune who is holding in his one hand a trident and in his other the sign of a fish, hanging from a series of *Twelve Grotesque Months*, 430 × 470 cm. Brussels, third quarter of the 16th century with non-identified weaver's monograms. Vienna, Kunsthistorisches Museum.

Hercules shooting the stymphalic birds with human heads, hanging from a series picturing the *History of Hercules*, 420 × 395 cm, with the city-arms of Audenarde and the weaver's monogram of Michiel van Orley (?), active from 1547 to 1567. Vienna, Kunsthistorisches Museum.

Cartouche with monogram SA of the Polish king Sigismund-Augustus, supported by two satyrs, hanging from a series of five, Brussels, about 1560, with monogram of Leo van den Hecke and with non-identified marks. Krakau, Wawel Castle.

Coat of arms of the Spanish-Basque family de Nagera, of which several representatives were members of the Spanish warehousing company at Bruges, hanging, 278 × 271 cm, city-arms of Bruges and a non-identified weaver's monogragm AL, about 1550. Bruges, Gruuthuse Museum.

Verdure with squirrel, fragment of a hanging from the Room of Aldermen of the Brugse Vrije, with orginally at the top a laurel-wreath with the arms of Charles V, 85 × 142 cm, Bruges, Antoon Segon, about 1528-1530. Bruges, Gruuthuse Museum.

Finally, mention should be made of Peter de Kempeneer (1503-1580), also known as Pedro Campaña. Initially he lived and worked a long way from the tapestry-makers, though he was related to some. He spent a period in Italy and was influenced by the art of Raphael and his school. From 1537 he lived in Seville and other towns in Spain; but in 1564 the old artist suddenly returned to Flanders, appointed as the official cartoon painter for the city of Brussels. The design for a *History of Peter and Paul* with the coats of arms of St Peter's Abbey in Ghent and of Abbot François d'Avroult are believed to be his.

Little is known about the work of the other pattern painters in the second half of the 16th century, who include Denijs van Alsloot († 1625), Hans Vredeman de Vries (1527-1604?) and Lucas de Heere (1534-1584). However, during the last decade of this century there was a definite reaction against the former stylistic norms. The composition became more confused, flatter and more monotonous, with a great deal of conventional filling and a fairly high horizon. It was as though an attempt was being made to return to the ideas that were current in 1500. There is a deliberate lack of movement and depth in the composition, and little realism in the depiction of the flora. The work does not reach the standard of tapestries woven in the middle of the 16th century, also because of the softness and lack of variety in the colouration, and the extremely wide borders with their indistinct designs. The Brussels tapestries were also copied in other centres, but the colouration was usually less rich and the weaving was often coarser and less costly.

It is obvious that master weavers from Brussels played a significant part in the flourishing art of tapestry. The greatest masters of the first half of the 16th century include Pieter van Aelst, Pieter and Willem de Pannemaker, Gabriel van der Tommen, François Geubels and Hendrik Tsas. Some of the well-known families of the second half of the century were those of Jan van Tieghem, Jacob Tseraerts, Leo van den Hecke, Maarten Reynbouts, Jacob Geubels, and Anton, Jan, Jacob and Nikolaes Leyniers. In some cases they formed 'tapestry dynasties' – and as such had the necessary capital at their disposal, as well as the required raw materials, looms and patterns. Their technical knowledge and artistic talent was passed on from generation to generation. However, their work was not sold at home but at the merchants' hall in Antwerp. The weavers from other Flemish manufactures also brought their verdures or their pictorial tapestries to this city; and the export of hangings abroad was an important factor in the success of the tapestry industry as a whole.

Return from the harvest, hanging (detail) from a series of four, with small figures and rural scenes after the style of David Teniers, 305 × 440 cm, Brussels, middle of the 18th century, maybe from the atelier of Pieter van Hecke. Brussels, Museums of Art and History.

CARPETS

From the middle of the 16th century carpets from Ghent, Wervik, Diest and St Trond were traded at the merchants' hall in Antwerp. There is no information available about their decoration and choice of colours. In 1694 the magistrate at Ghent concluded an agreement with Jean Duquesne from Tournai to produce carpets in Ghent; from this it may be deduced that the industry had disappeared there.

EMBROIDERY

During the 16th century there was no fall in the productivity of Flemish embroiderers. In fact, the desire for opulence and magnificence was as great as it had been before. The lazur technique had now been perfected, so that the artists were able to produce pictorial embroidery gradually incorporating elements of the Renaissance style. In some paraments of the period the influence of contemporary painters is clearly visible. For example, the depiction of the famous vellum of 1509 in Lund Cathedral bears a close resemblance to the work of Quinten Metsijs. Possibly this was why it was ascribed to a workshop in Antwerp; this city had become an important centre for the production and trading of embroidery. The scenes became smaller in size from about 1540 onwards as a result of the increasing Italian influence. They were no longer executed in an architectural decor but appeared in circles separated by leafwork. This can all be seen clearly on a chasuble in the Museums of Art and History in Brussels, with a *Mater Dolorosa* in the central medallion.

Brussels continued to be a very important centre. It is probable that the beautiful *antependium of Nassau* (formerly in the Abbey of Grimbergen, now in the Museums of the Art and History in Brussels) was made in a workshop there. Stylistically it dates from the period of Barend van Orley. Its remarkable composition, delicate technique and wonderful use of gold, make it the equal of the beautiful tapestries from Brussels dating from that period.

Embroidery was also done in Bruges, Ghent, Malines, Louvain and Diest, but this branch of the decorative arts flourished particularly in Lier. There was a select group of embroiderers who lived and worked there and their fame spread to the neighbouring towns and abbeys. Frans Ytegem was the official embroiderer at Averbode Abbey from 1534-1538. There was also Gommaar Mynten, whose fame spread far beyond the border. A third famous artist was Gommaar Vervaren, who later moved to Malines. In an Antwerp document he was cited as the best and most industrious master in the Netherlands. Each of these names can be connected with some of the paraments which have survived. In 1559 seven masters from Malines, including Gommaar Vervaren, decided to execute a commission for Emmanuel Philibert, the Duke of Savoy, together with some colleagues from Brussels. This tends to suggest that the techniques were very similar in the different centres and workshops. It also explains the problem of attributing anonymous pieces to a particular region, let alone to a specific workshop.

LACE

At the beginning of the Renaissance it was usual to reveal part of the collar and cuffs of a white linen shirt, and to embellish these parts with matt or open-work embroidery. However, there was a growing tendency to decorate the shirt as well as all the other linen used in the costume – such as the collars, bonnets and handkerchiefs – in a richer, lighter and more transparent fashion. Initially this effect was achieved by simply

The wedding at Cana, the meal at Simon the Pharisee, the meal at Zacheus the Publican and *the Men of Emmaus*, embroidered antependium (without the central scene picturing the *Last Supper*), 60 × 369 cm.
At the left side is the coat of arms of Christoffel Outers, abbot of Grimbergen from 1613 till 1674, and at the right side the arms of the abbey. Both blazons have been fixed on it later on. First quarter of the 16th century after designs from the surroundings of Pieter Coecke van Aelst. Brussels, Museums of Art and History.

The wedding at Cana, embroidered chasuble-cross (detail), about 1525.
Bruges, St Saviour's Cathedral.

cutting away parts of the material or by retaining a few structural or weft threads. The spaces that remained were then filled up with needlework, while the ends of the warp threads were often plaited together in bundles, to form a serrated edge resembling teeth (*des dentelles*). Gradually a technique developed for decorating the border of a woven piece of cloth with separate pieces, because fine linen material was not suitable for being cut or thinned. All sorts of motifs were made with a needle and thread; the piece was attached to paper or rough material, which was later removed. This was the origin of needlepoint lace. At roughly the same time pillow lace was developed as a technical perfection of braiding. The splendour and beauty of a piece was now determined by refined and more complex patterns, and no longer by the glittering effects of gold, silk and silver thread, which had been replaced by white flaxen thread. Pillow lace is made by braiding and crossing a number of threads which come from bobbins. The twisted and plaited threads are pricked onto a lace pillow with pins according to a previously drawn pattern, hence the term 'pillow or bobbin lace', in Antwerp also known as *breynaet*.

Fire-place draping, netting and cut-work bordered with reeled bobbin. 35 × 230 cm, about 1600. Bruges, Gruuthuse Museum.

Frans Floris, *Family portrait*; known under the name *Family of Berchem*, detail: persons with embroidery and lace. Lier, Wuyts-van Campen – Baron Caroly Museum.

Although both techniques were used in Flanders, pillow lace was particularly magnificent there, while needlepoint lace flourished particularly in Italy.

Innumerable women made lace, and for well-to-do ladies it was a way of passing the time. They learned the bobbin technique at a very young age from needlework mistresses, but in some convents lace making was also taught to girls. Lace makers worked for very low wages and never formed themselves into a guild. They owned a few tools necessary for the work, such as a needle and some old material, or some bobbins and a cushion. They were employed by a merchant and were bound by a close credit system: the merchants sold them the thread and lent them the patterns they needed, which he would often design himself. Later on in the 18th century the merchants sometimes bought the patterns in the up-and-coming fashion houses

In 1563 needlepoint lace and pillow lace were already being exported to England from Antwerp. Towards the end of the 16th century this industry had spread all over Flanders. In 1590 the chief magistrate of Ghent issued a decree limiting the teaching of lacemaking; the wealthy burghers could no longer find servant girls to work for a reasonable wage – and it was therefore forbidden for any girls over twelve years of age to occupy themselves with lace making.

The beautiful foot coverlet of the Archdukes Albrecht and Isabella dates from 1599. This is the oldest surviving example of pillow lace from Flanders. Different hands worked on the cover, which explains the uneven technical and artistic quality. It is decorated with all sorts of allegorical, religious and folklore tableaux, numbering one hundred and twenty in all, which in many cases were based on events that took place in Antwerp and Brussels. The border depicts Roman emperors, sibyls and ruling monarchs.

DAMASK

The draw loom was being used in Flanders in the 15th century, and the weaving of damask linen started at that time. This is a shiny cloth with figures and other motifs woven into it. Table linen of this sort was already being woven in Bruges in 1453, and possibly also in Brussels and Tournai. In about 1485 the tick weaver from Ghent Pieter de Vooght made damask serviettes showing the coat of arms of Philip the Fair. Shortly after this (in 1496) the guild of damask weavers, which did not exist yet in any other city, was founded in Courtrai. A few decades later Malines also became an important centre of production. Jacob van Hoochbosch, who came from Ghent, produced table linen there in 1528 for Charles V. It was decorated with the emperor's coat of arms and of the Order of the Golden Fleece, and with images of St Andrew and St James.

The work produced in the 15th century and at the beginning of the 16th was limited, although it was technically and artistically perfect. The price was fairly high and only princes and upper class people could afford it. The damask from that period was decorated with flowers, coats of arms, hunting scenes, scenes from the Old Testament and of the Passion. Some themes from the New Testament were also very common, particularly the *Annunciation*. These subjects were sometimes based on engravings, including German prints.

A serviette with the *Coat of arms of Henry VII*, King of England (1485-1509), dates from the last years of the 15th century (London, Victoria and Albert Museum). The linen is remarkably tightly and finely woven. It is sometimes attributed to Courtrai, and sometimes to the workshop of Pieter de Vooght in Ghent, where this sort of work was woven for Philip the Fair. In the same museum there is also a serviette dating from about 1580 with an *Annunciation* and a remarkably rich border decoration. This work is also attributed to a workshop in Courtrai and is reminiscent of the large brasses. About ten years later the exceptionally beautiful *Table-cloth of Jean Macault* († 1539), counsellor to Charles V, and of his wife Lievine van de Welle († 1547), was woven. It was originally a large work, about 2.5 *m* long, which was later cut up into serviettes. It is decorated with the armorials and patron saints of the clients, and the background is covered with a variety of animals at play and flowering plants.

From the second half of the 16th century Courtrai was undoubtedly the most important centre for the damask industry. The linen was still decorated with coats of arms, diamond shapes and flowers, as well as with religious themes and hunting scenes, and even with allegorical figures. However, during the religious unrest many weavers left the city to settle in Haarlem and other towns. Within a few years the trade flourished there, and the weavers became formidable competitors of the weavers of Courtrai. The question remains whether the Flemish immigrants continued to use the patterns which they had taken with them from their homeland, and which patterns were still being used by the weavers who remained behind. Therefore the work from the two cities is often confused.

From 1590 onwards the Courtrai linen damask industry entered a new phase of prosperity which continued until the middle of the 18th century. After this the industry slowly went into decline because of increasing competition from France, and later from England.

Medallion with at the left *Meleager in love who offers the head of the Calydonian pig to Atalante*, gold-leather, 71 × 110 cm, second half of the 17th century. Private collection.

CORDWAIN

Cordwain is gold-stamped leather which has been worked by hand. It is difficult to determine the origins of this craft but it is believed to have originated long before the 13th century in Ghadames in North Africa, to be taken to Spain by the Moors; hence the Spanish name *Guadameciles*. From Spain the craft spread, inter alia, to Flanders. Cordwain was made from goatskin or sheepskin, although calf hide was also used in Malines from about the middle of the 17th century. The leather was treated with silver and polychrome, and then gilded with a special type of varnish to produce the golden finish. Apart from being colourful, cordwain was tough, hard wearing and easy to clean. Moreover, it was very resistant to damp and a great deal cheaper than tapestry. It was used for tablecloths and fire screens, mantelpieces and wall coverings, antepedia and seat covers.

The first mention of cordwain in Flanders dates back to 1504, when Philip the Fair paid Robinet Lucas in Brussels for producing a chamber of gold leather. It is not known where this wall covering was made, because Spanish gold leather was imported to Flanders well into the 17th century. In 1511 Valentijn Klee appears as a cordwainer in the city archives of Malines, which is justifiably considered to be the oldest centre of this gold leather industry. Nothing is known about his work. In the Malines city museum there are two sheets of cordwain from St Peter and St Paul's Church. They date from about 1527-1530, were probably made in Malines and are the earliest examples of cordwain in Flanders.

325

Metalwork

GOLD AND SILVERWORK

The contrast between the old medieval traditions and the new trends in the development of art during the 16th century is also found in a striking way in the art of gold and silverwork. On the one hand, the late Gothic style, still described as 'modern' throughout the 16th century, continued to be influential far into the 17th. On the other hand, the new Renaissance style, which had fully developed in Italy for more than one hundred years, also penetrated to the countries north of the Alps during the first decades of the 16th century.

This southern style, completely alien to the late medieval and Gothic forms of art, was initially only accepted in the progressive centres open to new ideas; i e at the courts of princes, the high nobility, in the higher clerical circles, and in cities with an international orientation. So Malines, where the regentess Margaret of Austria had her permanent residence from 1506, became the first centre of the Renaissance in the Southern Netherlands. After her death in 1530 this role was taken over by Brussels, where the court then moved permanently, and particularly by Antwerp. This city on the Scheldt developed during the first half of the 16th century into the major trading metropolis of the western world. By far the majority of Flemish secular gold and silver work of the 16th century in the Renaissance style came from workshops in Antwerp. It is not surprising that the Renaissance style was particularly expressed in secular gold and silverwork. The themes, forms and ornaments based on or inspired by heathen antiquity were less suitable for use in church silver.

On the basis of surviving works of art and written documents, it may be stated that Antwerp set the style in the field of gold and silverwork. There were scores of masters working at this craft during the 16th century, and quite a considerable number of these came from other regions, e g Jan van Vlierden from Nijmegen, the van Steynemolens from Malines, Master Alexander from Bruchsal in Baden and Peter Wolfganck from Cologne. However, the gold and silver merchants from Antwerp itself kept their end up too, as will be discussed

below. A number of gold and silversmiths in Antwerp actually became leading merchants and financiers; others also worked as engravers and/or in the mint. Joris Vezeleer, who became a burgher of Antwerp in 1515/16 and died there in 1570, not only played an important role in the gold and silver trade in Antwerp; but also worked as a master in the Brabant mint, where he became the director in 1545. He also became the head of an international trading company, based on family relations and specialized in luxury products: tapestries, jewels and other gold and silverwork, which were often sold directly to the monarchs themselves, such as François I and Emperor Charles V. From a social point of view, Joris Vezeleer was also representative of the wealthy burghers of 16th-century Antwerp; his own art collection shows that he followed the new Renaissance trend. Like many rich Antwerp merchants he had a country estate built in Deurne called *het Lanteernhof*, although this has not survived.

During the first decades of the 16th century the late Gothic style continued to be used in secular gold and

Pectoral cross (front) of Mattheus van Rethen, abbot of Averbode Abbey, gilded silver, precious stones, pearls and enamel, Hiëronymus Jacobs, Antwerp 1562. Berlin, Kunstgewerbe Museum.

State goblet of glass with mount in silver, Reinier van Jaersvelt, 1546/47. Amsterdam, Rijksmuseum.

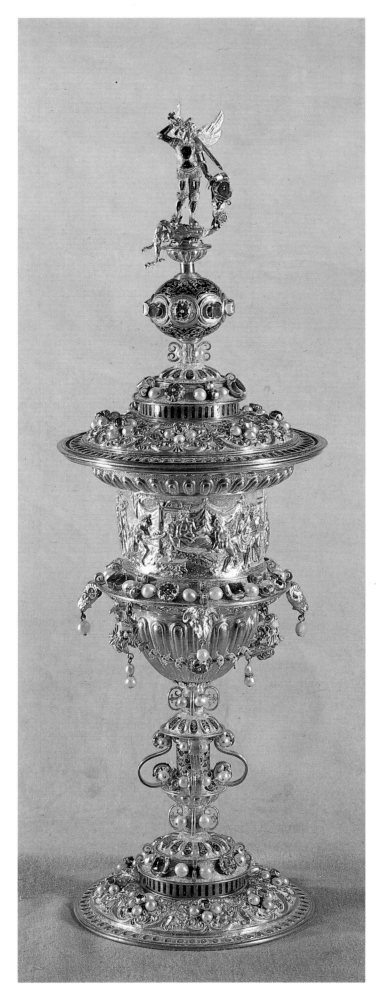

silversmith work in Antwerp. This can be seen in the ornamental standing cup of 1524/25, up to now the oldest known piece of silverwork from Antwerp (Munich, Residenzmuseum). It is similar to the late Gothic type which was found throughout western Europe. Characteristic features include the round foot, the wide calyx-shaped cup, the decoration of late Gothic foliage and the tall, pointed lid. The tableaux embossed on the cup with representations from the lives of the 'Indians', were probably only added later in the 16th century. Renaissance influences, probably coming via Germany, soon left their mark in Antwerp. Both indications in written texts referring to flagons known as *goudronnez à la mode d'Allemagne* (these are embossed ornaments, also known as 'gadroons'), and an ornamental standing cup with a lid from the National Museum in Munich, support this theory. The standing cup made in Antwerp in 1546/47 has a round foot, a baluster-shaped stem and a decoration of bosses and acanthus leaves. It is clearly similar to a type of ornamental goblet that was made in Nuremberg in about 1520, which later became popular in other western European countries.

Far more important was a second type of ornamental standing cup created in about 1530-1540, probably in Antwerp itself, which gained a great and long-lasting popularity, especially in Germany. A round foot with convex curves, a richly decorated stem, a steeply rising cylindrical cup with a curved lip and a rounded lid depicting a miniature replica of the stem, are characteristic of this type of ornamental cup. Decorations with historical or mythological scenes were also typical of the ornamental cups which originated in Antwerp itself. The masterpiece of this group is undoubtedly the *Michael cup* (Vienna, Kunsthistorisches Museum), which owes its name to the fact that a relief figure of the Archangel Michael overpowering Lucifer was added later to decorate the lid. This cup is made of gold and finished in the perfect Renaissance style, richly decorated with pearls, gems and enamel. The cup depicts the pleasures of wine drinking. The *Michael cup* dates from the years 1530-1540 and was traditionally attributed to a French workshop. The great similarity to another ornamental cup dated 1530/31 – made of silver rather than gold – in the Vatican Museum, and which can be attributed to Antwerp with certainty because it bears the hallmark of the city (a hand with a crown), suggests that it is probable that the *Michael cup* was also made by a goldsmith from Antwerp.

From the 1540's the secular work of gold and silversmiths in Antwerp was influenced by Mannerism. This style originated in Rome and Florence in about 1520, and became a European style during the second half of the 16th century through the courts in Parma, Ferrara

State-goblet, known under the name 'Michael's goblet', probably work of Antwerp, 1530-1540, gold decorated with pearls and precious stones, height 51.7 cm. Vienna, Kunsthistorisches Museum.

and Fontainebleau. In the large international cities it was soon adopted on a grand scale, particularly by gold and silversmiths. It was characterized by the unusual and the artificial, bizarre and surprising effects, and its wonderful and exotic subject matter. Prints and pattern books with mannerist designs and ornamentation, often specifically published by and for gold and silversmiths, were largely responsible for the rapid international growth of Mannerism. In this respect Antwerp played an important role. Of particular importance were the designs and models of Erasmus Hornick, a gold and silversmith who worked in Antwerp and later in Nuremberg and Prague; and of other artists from Antwerp or working there, such as Cornelis Bos, Hans Vredeman de Vries and especially Cornelis II Floris de Vriendt (1515-1575). This architect and sculptor was the creator of a typical Flemish mannerist style of ornamentation, which was characterized by remarkably imaginative grotesques (human and animal figures and all sorts of fantastic creatures, combined with and merging into architectural forms, garlands of flowers, scroll work and cartouches). This mannerist ornamentation is found on a number of important pieces of ornamental Antwerp silver from the second half of the 16th century.

The same sort of ornamentation is found on the ornamental goblets with lids from Veere (1548) and of the Archers' Guild of Malmo (1563/64) (which were presented by Maximilian of Burgundy to the Dutch town, and by King Frederick II of Denmark to the guild respectively); and on the beautiful ewers and accompanying basins (1558/59), which were made to commemorate the conquest of Tunis in 1535 by Emperor Charles V (Paris, Louvre). The same Floris style appears in the silver frame of a mirror (ca 1665) from the Rosenborg collection in Copenhagen.

Another beautiful example is the glass inverted conical beaker with a silver foot and lid (Amsterdam, Rijksmuseum). The lid is decorated with the *Triumph of Love* and with the figure of a bear rising from a basket of flowers. This sculpture in silver was made in 1546/47 by the Antwerp silversmith Renier van Jaersvelt.

The mannerist predilection for exotic and wonderful subjects, particularly for the sea, its products and its real or imaginary inhabitants, as well as the intense interest in nature, resulted in the creation of a number of strange and fascinating masterpieces in Antwerp in the middle and during the second half of the 16th century. The most important of these include a ewer, dated 1544/45, probably by Jan or Jeremias van den Heuvele, and a basin, dated 1546/47 by Joris Weyer, both once owned by the d'Aspremont-Lynden family and now in the British Museum in London. The body of the ewer is

Ewer and basin, silver, Jan van den Heuvele (?) and Joris Weyer, 1544/5 and 1546/7. London, British Museum.

Tankard with basin, made in remembrance of the conquest of Tunis by Charles V in 1535. Both are decorated with scenes from this campaign. Made in Antwerp, 1558-1559. Gilt silver, tankard, height 43.5 cm, diameter basin 64 cm. Paris, Louvre.

decorated on one side with Neptune and on the other with Amphitrite. The round basin shows the plague of Egypt and the destruction of Pharaoh's army in the Red Sea in cartouches. In the centre are the coats of arms of the d'Aspremont-Lynden family.

Another remarkable masterpiece in the Antwerp mannerist style is an ornamental cup with a foot and a lid from *ca* 1550 which belonged to the Mildway family (Cambridge, Emmanuel College). The inside of the lid depicts Arion and the dolphin, surrounded by a frieze of sea nymphs and other sea creatures. The rest of the goblet is also richly decorated with real and imaginary sea creatures (sea horses, tritons and sea serpents). The ornamental cup of gilded silver and rock crystal, dated *ca* 1560 (London, private collection) also deserves a mention. It is decorated with the Judgment of Maris, Jupiter and a river god, while the lid bears a representation of the Elements.

Rare natural objects were also often incorporated in the decoration of a variety of ornaments. The ornamental cup described above of *ca* 1560, which was partly made of rock crystal, is an example of this. In addition, coconuts, ostrich eggs and nautilus shells were used. The coconut cup (Deurne/Antwerp, Sterckshof Museum) dating from 1543/44, and the Nautilus cup, (Kassel, Staatliche Kunstsammlungen) dating from 1560-1570, are excellent examples of this. During the second half of the 16th and the first half of the 17th century, a variety of ornamental objects and drinking vessels were made in the shape of birds, particularly owls. A large number of beautiful examples were made in Germany, but also in the Southern Netherlands. These are noteworthy for their naturalistic representations. The so-called *Falcon cup* (Cambridge, Clare College), made in Antwerp in 1561/62, is a beautiful example of this.

Very popular during the second half of the 16th and the 17th century, especially in the Netherlands, Germany and England, were a variety of novelty drinking vessels. They stood on the cup itself so that they had to have a perfect fit *ad fundum*. Examples of this type of work are the well-known *molenbekers* (windmill cups) and *stortebekers* (spilling cups). The windmill cups had cup-shaped bowls and were crowned with a little windmill with a small blow-pipe. The idea was to blow through the pipe to make the windmill go round, and then empty the cup while the sails were still turning. The spilling cups also had a cup-shaped bowl which was attached to a small inner beaker fastened by a catch. When it was used, both of the receptacles would be filled. A lady would offer the large cup to a gentleman, who had to empty it without spilling, and then the gentleman would offer the lady the small cup. The inner cups of some of the spilling cups were made in the shape of a lady with a billowing dress. They were often given as wedding presents. The so-called 'Hansel in the cellar' was a variation on the tazza. It was used to drink the health of an expectant mother. In the middle of the cup there is a small cylinder in which a tiny silver child appears by means of a float when the beaker is filled with wine. This type of playful drinking implement was made especially in the Northern Netherlands, but there are also examples from Antwerp. There is a windmill cup dating from 1603/04 in the Sterckshof Museum, and a spilling cup from the same unidentified master in Bijloke Museum in Ghent.

The gold and silversmiths of Antwerp were internationally renowned. Not only did monarchs, princes, noblemen and clerics place orders there; the work of the gold and silversmiths of Antwerp can also still be found in the Cathedral of Seville, St Peter's Church in Lubeck, and San Lorenzo Church in Genoa. Furthermore, gold and silversmiths from Antwerp worked at the courts of foreign monarchs. For example, Hans van Antwerpen worked at the court of King Henry VIII of England. One

of Hans Holbein's drawings, dated *ca* 1532 (Basle, Öffentliche Kunstsammlungen) gives us some idea of his work. This drawing depicts an ornamental cup with a lid, and is the oldest known design by Holbein for gold and silversmith work. The inscription HANS VON ANT[WERPEN] is engraved on the rim of the cup and the same inscription can be found next to it in mirror image. This can be explained by the fact that in accordance with customary practice, Holbein only completed half of the design, which was then finished off by printing through.

The leading role played by Antwerp should not obscure the fact that important work was undertaken by gold and silversmiths in other cities in the Southern Netherlands, such as Malines, Ghent, Bruges, Brussels, Tournai *etc.* Marc de Glassere, who came from Bruges, worked at the court of Margaret of Austria in Malines. Some written sources suggest that he made a number of silver pieces *à l'anticque* for the regentess. In Ghent, Cornelis Bauwins created the symbol for the Ghent guild of freshwater fishermen in 1519 or shortly afterwards. It depicted their patron saint, St Peter, and the coat of arms of Charles V, together with his motto *Plus Oultre*. Also in Ghent, Jan van Hauweghem made a cup in 1532 in the early Renaissance style. This was probably taken to England by an emigrant and served as a communion chalice in Hethel Church. It is now in the Castle Museum in Norwich. An unidentified silversmith of Audenarde made an owl cup in 1564 (private collection). There is a Brussels coconut cup, dating from 1540, and a nautilus cup from Tournai, both in private collections. The Gruuthuse Museum in Bruges preserves a cross used for swearing oaths, dating from 1562, for the guild of the *cultensteckers* (craftsmen who made cloths and bedding (*culten*) decorated with gold and silver thread).

In addition to ornamental pieces a large amount of simpler household silver was also produced; salt and pepper pots, dishes, bowls, beakers, spoons, candlesticks and so on, but very little of this has survived.

During the 16th century the art of jewellery making also flourished in the Southern Netherlands. Unlike the work of gold and silversmiths, the jewellery was not hallmarked, so it is very difficult to attribute the work to any particular city. Probably much of the jewellery was made at the court of Margaret of Austria in Malines. In any event, a comparison of the two inventories of the regentess' jewel collection drawn up respectively in Granada in 1499 and in Malines in 1531, one year after her death, shows that she added a considerable number of pieces to her collection during her twenty-five years in the Netherlands. However, it is no longer possible to determine what was made by jewellers such as Marc de Glassere and Martin Desabliaux, both attached to the court in Malines, and what was made by local gold and silversmiths from Malines or from other cities in Flanders.

Nautilus-goblet, the shell is set in silver and born by a satyr in silver, made in Antwerp, 1560-1570. Kassel, Staatliche Kunstsammlungen.

For stylistic, iconographic and technical reasons a number of *enseignes* (hat decorations) are attributed to Malines. They are characterized by an unusual degree of realism in the representations, a preference for brightly coloured enamel, and the fact that the figures were made separately and then attached to the gold background with pins, leaving the back unworked. One of these enseignes consists of a circular medallion with a lady standing between a youth and an old gentleman whose advances she seems to be accepting. The inscription is shown between a double cord motif and reads AMOUR FAIT MOVLT [written MONLT] ARGENT FAIT TOUT. The enseigne dates from about 1520 and belongs to the collection of the Metropolitan Museum of Art in New York. There is another one in the Kunsthistorisches Museum in Vienna, which depicts a bust of Charles V and is dated 1520. A third shows Our Lady and the infant Jesus with the inscription MATER DEI MEMENTO MEO. The initials C.I. are engraved at the feet of the Virgin, for Carolus and Isabella. This enseigne was probably presented to Charles V by his aunt, the regentess Margaret of Austria, on the occasion of his marriage to Isabella of Portugal. This piece of jewellery is now part of a pax and is in the treasure chamber of Regensburg Cathedral.

Lock of the cope of abbot Lieven Hughenois, between 1517 and 1535, gilt silver and enamel, diameter 16.2 cm. Paris, Louvre.

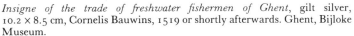

Insigne of the trade of freshwater fishermen of Ghent, gilt silver, 10.2 × 8.5 cm, Cornelis Bauwins, 1519 or shortly afterwards. Ghent, Bijloke Museum.

Jewellery was undoubtedly also made in other towns in Flanders. Mention should be made of the clasp of the choir canopy of Lieven Hughenois, abbot of St Bavo's Abbey in Ghent from 1517-1535. It is made of gilded silver and enamel, has a three-lobed shape and depicts St Bavo, the patron saint of the abbey, seated on a throne and holding a sword and sceptre in his hands. Two angels are crouched holding the coats of arms of St Bavo's Abbey (left) and of the abbot Lieven Hughenois (right) (Paris, Louvre).

A large quantity of jewellery was also produced in Antwerp. However, up to now the archives have only authenticated one single piece as having been definitely produced in Antwerp, *viz* the pendant crucifix commissioned by Mattheus van Rethen, abbot of Averbode Abbey in 1562 (Berlin, Kunstgewerbe Museum). The archives show that the abbot went to the Antwerp gold and silversmith Reinier van Jaersvelt on 15th September 1562. However, he only supplied the pearls and the gems for the crucifix, and passed on the commission to a younger colleague, Hieronymus Jacobs, born in Frankfurt and enrolled in St Luke's Guild in Antwerp in 1560. The design for the cross was drawn by Hans Collaert the Elder. This golden enamelled crucifix consists of two halves, which allowed a reliquary to be placed inside it. The front shows Christ nailed to a small cross, the arms of which are decorated with pearls and gems; two pearls are suspended from the cross arms and three more from the upright. The other side of the crucifix shows the coat of arms of the abbot, with a mitre and crosier above it; as well as his motto NE QVID NIMIS ('Nothing is too much') and underneath, the inscription: AVRO PVRO GEMMISQ[VE] PRECIOSIS D[OMINVS] MATEUS A RETHEN ABB[AS] AVERBODIEN[SIS] ME DE-CORAVIT.

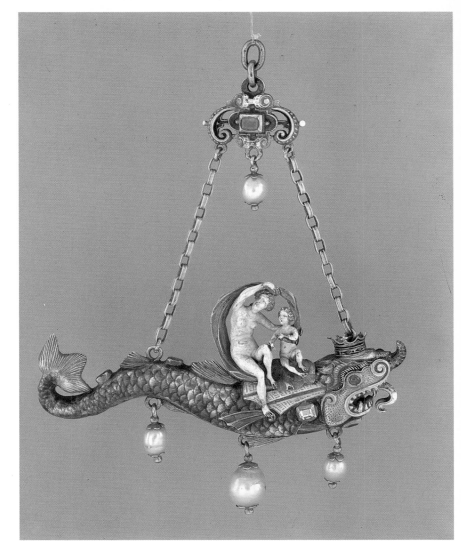

Pectoral cross (back) with the enamelled coat of arms of the abbot van Rethen, his motto and an inscription to make clear that he had the cross manufactured.

Pendentive of Venus and Amor on a sea-monster, gilt and enamelled silver, precious stones and pearls, unknown master, probably Antwerp, around 1580. New York, Metropolitan Museum of Art, Robert Lehman Collection.

Many other pieces of jewellery attributed to Antwerp reveal characteristics of the mannerist style. They depict a variety of sea creatures, dolphins, tritons, mermaids, Neptune and other sea gods. An unusual example of this work, a pendant showing Venus and Cupid sitting on the back of a sea monster, dates from about 1580 (New York, Metropolitan Museum of Art). Hans Collaert the Elder († before 1581), mentioned above, played a leading role as a jewellery designer in Antwerp. Filips Galle had his designs engraved by the jeweller's son, Hans or Jan Collaert (Antwerp 1566-1628), and published these as prints in 1581. In this way Collaert's designs gained international fame and recognition.

This brief outline of the secular work of gold and silversmiths in Flanders, and particularly in Antwerp, shows that the trade flourished during the 16th century. However, only a tiny proportion of the production has survived. Written sources reveal that there was a large number of important commissions, though nothing is known or has remained of them. One of the missing pieces was made by the above-mentioned Antwerp gold and silversmith Joris Vezeleer, who was paid no less than 15,313 Tournai pounds – an enormous sum – in 1532 for '*vaiselle vermeille... cyzelé à anticque... façon de Flandres*', which he made for the French king,

François I. In 1544 Charles V paid him for a gold enamelled crucifix and for a number of '*tables de dyamants*'. In 1582 the city magistrate of Antwerp presented the Duke of Anjou with a golden castle on the occasion of his Triumphal Entry in the city, and gave the members of his retinue two silver basins, two silver ewers, six silver dishes, three silver salt cellars and eighteen silver spoons. Altogether this royal gift cost the city 1,417 pounds and 19 shillings.

The late Gothic style continued to be used throughout the 16th century in church silverware, of which there are numerous examples. These include the monstrance which is believed to have been presented by the king of England, Henry VIII, to St Martin's Church in Halle in about 1513, and was made in a workshop in Brussels; and the monstrance made by Willem van der Mont in 1607/08 in Antwerp for Our Lady's Church in Waasmunster. Both of these works are executed in the late Gothic style and feeling. The fidelity to Gothic forms and ornamentation is not really surprising; because the Renaissance style exalted the individual man and his power as an ideal, while Mannerism dealt with temporal matters and man's pleasure, which was completely in conflict with medieval Christian ideas. In addition, the strong conflicts in religious matters and the

Gilt, silver chalice in Renaissance style, Bruges (?), 1556. Bruges, Potterie Museum.

Sepulchral monument of bishop Jacob van Croy, detail, gilt brass, *ca* 21 cm, about 1518. Cologne, Dom.

religious strife in the second half of the 16th century certainly did not encourage a change in the style of religious silverwork. But some liturgical articles were explicitly commissioned in the Renaissance style. For example, the silverwork on the missal which was made in Antwerp in 1543 by Hieronymus Mamacker, commissioned by Arnold Streijtens, the abbot of Tongerloo Abbey, bears all the characteristics of a classical piece of Florentine Renaissance work. The chrismatory made in 1553 by Jacob Weins, a silversmith in Ghent, for St James's Church in that city, was also made in the Renaissance style. This chrismatory looks like a small box with a semi-circular lid, decorated with foliage, satyrs' heads and a pseudo-classical portrait head. It is one of the oldest examples of this type of object, which became popular during the 17th century, especially in the Northern Netherlands, as a bridal chest. An un-identified silversmith from Bruges made a chalice with clear Renaissance characteristics, which was presented by brother Jan van Verden to St Magdalen's Hospice in 1566 (Bruges, Pottery Museum). The reliquary made in

1571 by Nicolaas Vyzgers, another gold and silversmith from Bruges, was commissioned by the society of the *Damoiseaux* of Tournai Cathedral. Both the shape of the reliquary and the relief figures decorating it are clearly influenced by the Italian Renaissance.

COPPER AND BRONZE, IRONWORK AND PEWTER

During the 16th century the centre of copper and brass work was Brabant. Like gold and silversmithy, it was strongly influenced during the first decade of the 16th century by immigrant masters from Germany. Hieronymus Veldener from Wurzburg settled in Louvain in 1501, where he fulfilled several commissions. In 1518 he probably made the monument for the tomb of Jacques de Croy, bishop of Cambrai, which has not survived; a few years later he made the memorial to this bishop, now in Cologne Cathedral. In 1519 Peter Wolfganck from Cologne, a gold and silversmith mentioned above, who became a free master in St Luke's Guild in Antwerp in 1510, engraved four gilded copper plates with scenes from the life of Our Lady for Our Lady's Cathedral in Antwerp. This work has disappeared, but there is a similar tableau in St Saviour's Cathedral in Bruges. This shows a *Lamentation* with in the background Calvary and the city of Jerusalem. It is signed 'Peter Wolfganck', and judging by the coat of arms shown on the border, it was made for a member of the Spanish De Salamanca family, some of whom lived in Bruges.

As in the Middle Ages, monumental liturgical pieces of brass were made during the 16th century. Some of these adopted the late Gothic style, such as the baptismal font in St Walburgis' Church in Zutphen, cast in 1527 by Gillis van den Eynde from Malines. But other pieces display characteristics of the Renaissance style; such as the baptismal font of the *Grote Kerk* in Breda, which was also cast in about 1530-1540 by a brass smith from Malines. Often the same moulds were used for many decades; for example, the pelican lectern of 1550 in Messina Cathedral is similar to the one in Norwich (1475) and the one in Bornival Abbey (1500). Only the foot of the Messina lectern was adapted to the new Renaissance style.

Sepulchral monument of bishop Jacob van Croy, gilt brass, 112 × 90.5 × 31 cm, about 1518. Cologne, Dom.

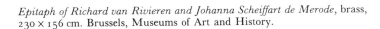

Epitaph of Richard van Rivieren and Johanna Scheiffart de Merode, brass, 230 × 156 cm. Brussels, Museums of Art and History.

One of the most successful Flemish Renaissance creations in brass was the surround of the tabernacle of St James's Church in Louvain. It was cast in 1568 in Louvain by Jan II Veldener, probably based on a design by Cornelis II Floris de Vriendt, and it displays all the characteristics of the imaginative Flemish Renaissance style. This typical style is also expressed in the railing around the tabernacle of Zoutleeuw Church, which was possibly made in 1552/53 by Jan Paus (or Pans) from Louvain; and in the choir lectern cast by Jan Symoens in 1571 in Antwerp (Madrid, Escorial). In 1591, Jan Cauthals from Malines created an architecturally inspired choir lectern with a double book rest, a design which remained popular far into the 18th century.

Apart from monumental copper and bronze work, many household articles, tools *etc* were made: bells, mortar and pestles, candlesticks, candle-snuffers, flat candle holders, holy water bowls, basins, cooking and eating utensils, measuring jugs, weights and so on. Malines was also here the main centre of production in the Southern Netherlands. For generations, families such as the Waghevens, the van den Eyndes, the van den Gheyns, the Cauthals, the Clercks and others, produced work that was famous both at home and abroad.

Also in other Flemish cities copper and bronze pieces were made during the 16th century. For example Marc Le Serre, who cast canons and bells in Bruges, made a Renaissance bell in 1592 for St Basil's Church; it is now in the Gruuthuse Museum. His fellow-townsman and goldsmith Jan Crabbe made a double brass ink-well for the sheriffs of the *Brugse Vrije* in 1556. It is significant that this ink-well was made by a goldsmith. From the 16th century onwards gold and silversmiths increasingly worked with copper as well.

The funereal copper industry, which had flourished during the Middle Ages, especially in Bruges and Ghent, gradually disappeared during the 16th century. With the arrival of the Renaissance and a return to antiquity, marble and other types of stone were preferred for headstones and tombs. Nevertheless, numerous effigies were still made during the 16th century,

Brass door from the now disappeared sacramental tower of St Nicolas' Church at Ghent, late Renaissance style, representing the Calvary, monogrammed L P (Lieven Plumion) and dated 1598. Ghent, Bijloke Museum, height 76 cm, breadth 35 cm.

Two writing-sets in brass, 19.5 × 34 cm. Bruges, Jan Crabbe, 1566.

especially in Brabant. These depict the deceased lying on a cushion in a Renaissance portico, which meant that the old medieval gisant effigy had been adapted to the new Renaissance style. The effigy of Willem van Galen († 1539) in the *Grote Kerk* in Breda is a strange example of this, as is that of Richard van Rivieren and his wife, made in Antwerp in 1554 (Brussels, Museums of Art and History), and in particular, the one of Leonard Bettern († 1607), the abbot of St Trond Abbey (Ghent, Bijloke Museum). According to the inscription, this monumental piece was made by Libert van Eeghem, an engraver and stone mason from Malines. The multi-coloured paste which fills up the drawing is exceptionally well preserved.

Only one copper funeral monument from the 16th century has survived, *viz* that of Charles the Bold in Our Lady's Church in Bruges. It was cast in 1559 by the Antwerp sculptor and medallion maker Jacob Jonghe-linck. It was made in the late Gothic style to harmonize with the monument of Mary of Burgundy, which had been made in 1491-1498 by Renier van Thienen.

The late Gothic style also continued to be used for many years in ironwork. It was only in the second half of the 16th century that the Renaissance influence was expressed in the decoration: s and c-shaped curlicues replaced the late Gothic tracery, and typical Renaissance motifs such as dolphins began to play an important role in secular and religious architecture. The door of the tabernacle of the chapel of the *Gravensteen* in Ghent (London, Victoria and Albert Museum) is a good example of this.

The manufacture of weapons was an important branch of the iron industry. During the 16th century Antwerp also played a major role in this field. A great many weapons and suits of armour were decorated in the city, even though they might not have been made there. The goldsmith, medallion maker and weapon smith Eliseus Liebaerts – who worked in Antwerp from 1557 to 1564, and then in captivity in Denmark until 1569 – made a large number of suits of armour for parades, of a very high quality for both the Habsburgs,

Antoon Claeissens, *Feast*, 1574, panel, 130 × 155 cm. Bruges, Groeninge-museum.

the French and Swedish court, and the Dukes of Saxony. His splendid shield (Paris, Louvre) for the French King Henry II, *ca* 1557-1559, is an excellent example of his craftsmanship. It depicts the siege of the city of Bonifacio in Corsica, surrounded by ornamentation in the typical Floris style. The Sadeler family also manufactured weapons, and halberds and swords are attributed to Emmanuel I Sadeler (Antwerp † 1580). There are also rapier hilts made by Daniel Sadeler in the Victoria and Albert Museum in London.

Pewter work continued to be made for purely functional purposes during the 16th century. In the Netherlands there were no real ornamental pieces in the Renaissance style; like for example the cleverly cast or etched decoration (relief or refined pewter) by François Briot in Montbéliard and by Caspar Enderlein, Nicolaus Horchheimer and Albrecht Preissensin in Nuremburg. However, there are a few decorative dishes dating from the beginning of the 17th century, made by Daniel Do(o)r and Andries de Mangeler I from Antwerp, which have a relief medallion in the centre of the dish, depicting the Archdukes Albrecht and Isabella.

Nevertheless, it is quite possible that ornamental pewterware was made in the Renaissance style. A painting by Antoon Claeissins, dating from 1574 and depicting a banquet of the city magistrate of Bruges suggests that this was the case: one of the figures is holding a larger pewter flagon which is clearly decorated in the characteristic Renaissance style

339

Ornamental basin with monogram of Christ and Moresque decoration, diameter 35 cm, Antwerp majolica, middle of the 16th century. Antwerp, Vleeshuis Museum.

Ceramics

From the late 13th and the early 14th century onwards, Andalusian ceramics were imported to Flanders from Malaga in southern Spain. In the 15th century tinglazed majolica plates, ointment jars and bowls with blue and gold-painting (so-called lustreware) were imported from Manises near Valencia. This valuable Iberian luxury pottery served a mainly ornamental function in monasteries and burghers' houses; and was often decorated with Burgundian coats of arms, inscriptions and ivy motifs. They were brought from the Mediterranean ports to Sluis near Bruges, where they could be traded, free from staple duty. In the first decades of the 16th century tableware with a blue and purple glaze was imported from Calatayud in Aragon; and *cuerda seca* and *cuenca* tiles came from Seville and Talevera de la Reina. Italian polychrome majolica – very important during the Renaissance – was also exported from Faenza, Urbino, Castel Durante, Venice, Gubbio and other centres to Flanders; a few rare examples were discovered during recent excavations.

ANTWERP   At the beginning of the 16th century Antwerp started to play an important economic and cultural role, and this is where the foundation was laid for the manufacture of majolica in the Southern and the Northern Netherlands. The Delft pottery, together with all the other ceramic work classified under that name, later developed from this. Too much has already been written about the so-called Antwerp majolica without any reliable evidence about it. Numerous products from Italy, Spain or France were attributed to Antwerp; but differ from the tableware that has been found there in excavations. Therefore a number of assumptions were in the past considered to be self evident truths, and as a result one error led to another. Majolica which was fired twice and treated with lead and tin glazes was certainly produced in Antwerp at the beginning of the 16th century, and possibly during the second half of the 15th.

Some four Italian ceramic painters settled in Antwerp shortly after 1500. One of these was the well-known Guido di Savini, later known as Guido Andries, recorded in the archives from 1508. In 1531 there is mention of Petrus Frans van Venedigen, and later of Janne Marie de Capua and Joannes Franciscus de Brescia. Guido di Savini died in 1541, after which his widow and some of his seven children took over the business. The floor in *The Vyne* in Hampshire, consisting of four hundred tiles with beautiful busts, is believed to be his. The four-sided and hexagonal tiles made in 1532 for the chapel of Herckenrode Abbey near Hasselt have been attributed to Frans Franchoy, possibly the son of Petrus Frans van Venedigen, on the basis of archives research.

Elements of this remarkable floor are now preserved in museums in Brussels, Amsterdam, Rotterdam and Sevres. Another floor consisting of hexagonal tiles, in Rameyen Castle in Gestel, dates from the same period, *viz* between 1527 and 1538. The work of Jan Bogaert includes the tiled panels depicting the *History of Tobias* in the ducal palace of Villa Vicosa (Portugal) of 1558; and a unique example of its genre is the yellow jug with a lid dated 1562, which also depicts the history of Tobias in three cartouches, finely decorated with grotesque motifs (Brussels, Museums of Art and History).

The well-known polychrome tableau of tiles depicting the *Conversion of St Paul*, dated 1547, with a frame of grotesques and exhibited in the Antwerp *Vleeshuis*, could possibly be attributed to Hans Floris and Jan Bogaert. This famous painting of tiles was acquired before 1890, when it was discovered in the *Kammenstraat* where Guido Andries' workshop had been situated. The composition indirectly refers back to a work by Francesco de Rossi, through imitations by Frans Floris and Eneas Vico. The frame of *putti*, also found on other tiles, is reminiscent of Italian artists from the beginning of the 16th century. On the other hand, the sides have a more specific character, with a decoration

Pitcher with grotesques and episodes out of the life of Tobias (after Cornelis Metsys), Jan van Bogaert, 1562, Antwerp. Majolica, height 37.5 cm. Brussels, Museums of Art and History.

Tile-tableau representing the Conversion of Saulus, Antwerp, work-shop of Andries, 1547. Majolica. Found in the Kammenstraat (Antwerp). Antwerp, Vleeshuis Museum.

of cartouches and *ferronerie* in the Floris style. At first sight this unique tableau gives an Italianate impression. Its representation is extremely emotive, and the composition is built up on a basis of diagonals. From the bottom right and left-hand corners groups of knights are headed for the opening in the background between the woods and the rocky mountains. Damascus can be seen in the distance, with Christ appearing in the clouds.

Not only luxury products were manufactured and exported from the metropolis of Antwerp, but also household articles – such as flat or elongated *albarelli*; syrup jars with floral subjects and slanting cartouches with capital lettering for pharmaceutical use; large and small plates with a chequered pattern and a variety of floral or animal motifs; beakers, bowls, jugs and altar vases, all used for eating, drinking or preserving. One distinguishes white and cobalt blue objects, as well as objects painted in bright colours. Numerous salt dishes represent religious motifs, such as the instruments of Christ's martyrdom or the Madonna with the Infant.

In this context special mention should be made of the famous series of porridge bowls with horizontal three or five lobed open handles, now in the *Maagdenhuis* in the *Lange Gasthuisstraat* in Antwerp. This collection, consisting of sixty-three pieces, was purchased between 1553 and 1587 for the girls' orphanage. The bottoms of these splendid and rare bowls are decorated with a figure of Our Lady, as well as with a variety of busts of men and women. These porridge bowls, possibly made by the potter Michel Nouts, who lived in Antwerp until 1611, used to adorn the wall of the salon in the *Maagdenhuis*, and can be dated at about 1560.

A large number of majolica potters left Antwerp for England, Germany and Holland; especially after the division between the Northern and the Southern Netherlands in 1581, and the fall of Antwerp in 1585. In the Northern Netherlands artistic pottery (later called faience) was manufactured in Amsterdam, Rotterdam, Delft, Haarlem, Leyden, Leiderdorp, Middelburg, Dordrecht, Gouda and Deventer. Initially the ornaments were copied, but during the 17th century the decoration became purely Dutch. Nevertheless, the Chinese influence cannot be ignored, and already from the beginning of the 17th century the well-known Wan-Li style of decoration was used.

GHENT Very little is known for certain about the existence of 16th-century majolica factories in Ghent and Bruges. However, there is some information from rare archives; and some unsigned majolica works have been found, though their provenance is uncertain. The accounts for the city of Ghent of 1534-1538 call one Joos Weyts '*ghaleyer weercman*'. According to some authors this man brought the art of making *gheleyerswerck* to that city. Considering that this is the only known mention of any manufacturer of artistic pottery, this seems rather a premature supposition, not to say a completely unfounded one. Moreover, the pot with a lid and the inscription '*Ghendt A° 1531*' (Liege, Curtius Museum) is made of white clay and has a green and yellow lead glaze; so it can hardly be described as majolica. Thus Weyts' workshop should rather be considered as a temporary pottery, where lead glaze earthenware was manufactured.

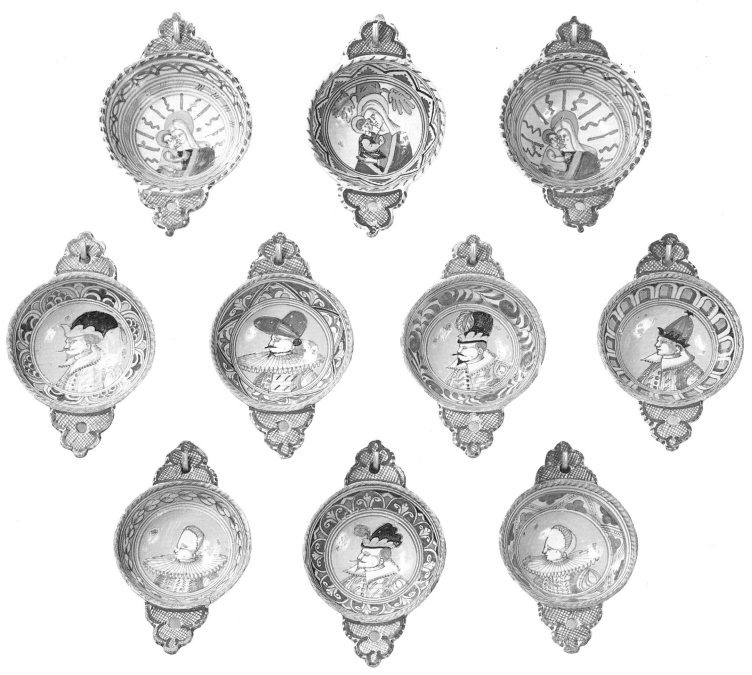

Ten porridge bowls with representations of Our Lady, the Child Jesus and male busts, Antwerp majolica, about 1560 (?). Antwerp, Maagdenhuis Museum.

However, from 1654 to 1674 faience was made in Ghent. Evidence of this can be found not only in the archives, but also from failed pots from this period and even fragments, which were found in 1900 and 1959/60 during excavations in the *Gerard Duivelsteen* and which were attributed to the workshop of Pieter Stockhollem. This faience manufacturer had trained under Pieter Oosterlaen in Delft and had even brought some workers from this city to Ghent. The shards belong to plates with blue paintings, and the decoration consists of sprigs of flowers and concentric circles. In 1667 Stockhollem ran into competition from Gillis van de Vijvere, a burgher in Ghent who had also been in Delft, but no finished products from his workshop have ever been found.

BRUGES According to Henri Nicaise, the above-mentioned Joos Weyts spent eighteen years in Bruges, from 1539 onwards. During the second half of the 16th century there is a record of two *galleyerspottebackers* from Antwerp. In this respect the accounts for the city of Bruges mention Hans Guldens in 1573-1574 and Christiaen van den Abeele in 1576-1578. The latter already left for Amsterdam in 1584 as a result of the religious troubles. If there was ever a manufacturer of majolica in Bruges, which we consider very doubtful, he did not last longer.

As was the case during the late Middle Ages, local potters – especially in urban centres, but also in rural was applied with the graffit technique and included coats of arms, religious motifs and illustrations of proverbs. These were undoubtedly ornamental objects, but they may have had a practical use too. From the end of the 16th century to the beginning of the 18th, not only plates, but also jugs, candle snuffers, beakers, cream jugs, chamber pots, porridge bowls and mugs or three-legged pots were decorated with white slip, which was applied to the unfired clay with a cow's horn by means of the *ringeloor* technique. Initially this method of decoration was believed to be exclusive to the Northern Netherlands. However, recent excavations have shown that these beautiful objects were also produced in Flanders and even in northern France. The ornamentation consisted of geometric figures, coats of arms, figures of animals and humans, and dates. During the last quarter of the 16th century and the first decades of the 17th, beautiful products using a multicoloured slip technique were also made in the Werraland and the Weser area, and it is possible that the contemporary decorative pottery from Flanders is based on that work. This applies particularly to the tableware from Wanfried, Hannoversch-Münden and Witsenhausen, which was also imported to Flanders.

Gallipot or albarello with blue, so-called a fogli-decoration and inscription CO ROSARV. PROVEN. Antwerp (?), second half 16th century; height 17.6 cm; diameter 9 cm. Bruges, Gruuthuse Museum.

Nameplate of a house 'Dit is inde Olifant' ('This is in the elephant'), Antwerp, middle of the 16th century. Majolica 34.5 × 34.5 cm. Found on the front of a house in the *Lange Nieuwstraat* at Antwerp. Antwerp, Vleeshuis Museum.

areas – produced a great variety of oxidized, fired earthenware during the 16th and subsequent centuries; and new types of forms were increasingly being made. Unlike the majolica potters of Antwerp, these ones were not grouped in a guild, but worked quite independently in small businesses. A study of the archives reveals that these potters often passed on their jobs from father to son, or moved to other cities, so that their products are often very similar.

In contrast with the everyday or richly decorated stoneware that was imported in large quantities from the eastern provinces (particularly from Raeren, the Rhineland, and the numerous workshops in the German Westerwald), little or nothing is known about local ceramic work. This type of study is in its infancy, although recent archaeological discoveries in some Flemish cities are very promising. The earthenware that was produced from the 16th century, like the ceramic work of the Middle Ages, was partially or completely covered with lead glaze. In about 1500 plates were commonly decorated and had stands; the ornamentation bears witness to some artistic quality. The decoration

Albarello or gallipot, 7.6 × 15 cm, Antwerp majolica, second half of the 16th century. Private collection.

Other luxury earthenware articles were also imported to Flanders from Friesland, the numerous workshops in the lower Rhine region, Beauvaisis in northern France, or the Saintonge region in the west of France; sometimes to the great annoyance of local potters. However, these were largely exceptions, restricted to the wealthy, who were particularly interested in foreign pottery. Tableware in yellow or white fired clay was made in the Maas valley from Namur up to Liege since the Middle Ages and was imported to Flanders, as mentioned above. During the late Middle Ages, as well as in the 16th and 17th centuries, white fired earthenware, but now with a contrasting decoration of red barbotine was produced there and was glazed with transparent or coloured lead glaze. It is quite impossible to attribute certain pots to a particular centre. From the 16th century German *Hafnerware* (made inter alia in Cologne and in Langerwehe) was brought to Flanders, as was French yellow earthenware. However, it is presumed that local Flemish potters did not only import clay from the Maas region during the post-medieval period for decorative purposes, but that they also manufactured completely new pots from this material. Recent excavations in the city centre of Antwerp particularly bear out this theory; and it is striking that certain local forms were copied exactly in yellow earthenware. Compared with the red ceramic work, there are far fewer examples of this material, which was also oxidized during firing.

Ovens with earthenware tiles, and with warm air introduced inside from a fire in an adjacent chamber, occurred in many important buildings at this time. Late Gothic stoves often borrowed style elements from the architecture of the period, like tracery, pointed arches, and little crenellated towers. During the 16th century these ovens were also found in the burghers' houses, and even in abbeys and monasteries. The influence of etchers and engravers on the decoration of oven tiles soon became evident through ornamental prints and other representations. Both sacred and profane subjects were represented, as well as pillars and columns, proverbs and coats of arms. These tiles, which were made of white or red fired clay, had a white engobe and were then glazed with a green lead that contained copper. Initially it was believed that the tiles used for making the ovens came only from Germany and the Alps. Now, archaeological research has revealed that they were not only transported to Flanders by sea, but were also made to order for the wealthier people in potteries in France and in the Northern and Southern Netherlands. In Belgium these furnace tiles were discovered mainly in the Walloon area, the eastern districts and Luxembourg; but also in Antwerp, Malines, Bruges, Louvain, Ghent, Jette near Brussels, Tongres, Koksijde, Wervik, Mons, Ath and Binche. In the neighbouring province Zeeland, more richly decorated fragments of an oven were found in the ruins of West-Souburg Castle at Walcheren, and also in Middelburg. Of particular interest are the oven tiles made for the lord of Gruuthuse in Bruges, decorated with a combined coat of arms. Found during restoration works at the Gruuthuse Museum, they are clear evidence of the heating stoves constructed from oven tiles based on the German model.

Many historical museums keep some decorated oblong or semi-circular hearthstones which used to adorn the back wall of the fireplace. Although the oldest heat resistant hearthstones probably date from the end of the 15th century, local brickmakers, tile makers and potters started to decorate hearthstones in about 1500, pressing wooden stamps into the soft clay. Heat resistant hearthstones were originally manufactured in the Liege and Tournai areas, and in the region between the Rhine and the Maas. From about 1550 to 1586, these usually unglazed stones were also produced in Antwerp and East Flanders, sometimes marked with the year of their manufacture. In the middle of the 16th century hearthstones were sold in Antwerp, decorated with biblical

Hearth-stone representing Samson who kills the lion, 6.2 × 10.3 × 14.8 cm, Antwerp (?), second or third quarter of the 16th century. Bruges, Gruuthuse Museum.

346

scenes (King David, Samson, a series of the chaste Susanna, the Judgment of Solomon), the lives of the saints, and many different coats of arms. Whether these stones were also made in Ghent and Bruges, to name just two towns, is not known; but the large number of examples found there suggests that they might have been. During the last decade of the 16th and in the 17th century, hearthstones were also made by potters who had moved to the Northern Netherlands, e g in the region of Utrecht. They would be made in Liege and even in Limburg well into the 18th century, when the Rococo style was often used.

Red fired floor tiles were produced in Flanders from the 13th century in the villages near the confluence of the Nete and the Rupel, in the Scheldt valley, Brabant, East and especially West Flanders. They were made in potteries which also produced other building materials, such as flat or round roof tiles. During the Middle Ages the triangular, square, diamond-shaped and occasionally circular floor tiles were usually small, and could be decorated or plain. A deep wedge-shaped groove was cut into the soft clay tile, which was then

filled up with white pipe clay. These so-called 'stamped' tiles had fallen into disuse by the end of the 15th century; being replaced by larger tiles, which were normally not decorated but glazed with a coloured lead glaze. Although these tiles were produced from the post-medieval period until recently and are once again of interest for restoration work, there was a preference during the Renaissance for floors of natural stone and polychrome majolica. Only in West Flanders and in northern France purely decorative inlaid tiles were produced as hearth decoration, reaching a peak in the 18th and 19th centuries.

In any discussion of ceramic work from Flanders, some mention should be made of Torhout. This town in West Flanders produced famous household articles and richly decorated earthenware, but only a few examples have survived. For too long a while all sorts of multi-coloured ornamental ceramic work in the 18th or 19thcentury tradition were attributed to this centre; while they actually originated from Germany, France, England and the Netherlands, or even from Spain, Italy and Hungary. There is some recent *Jugendstil* Torhout earthenware, but objects dating from before 1800 are extremely rare. Moreover, there are only two small fire baskets or jugs with handles showing a signature and the year of manufacture (early 19th century). Although potters were working in Torhout during the early Middle Ages, the information in the archives is complete only from the 17th century. As in other cities the business was usually a family concern.

The most common 'old' Torhout earthenware objects to be found in private collections or in the museums of Antwerp, Brussels, Bruges, Ghent, Torhout, Courtray and St Omer, are small fire baskets, coffee pots, soup tureens, decorative vases, flower vases and richly ornamented water flutes. These fine articles, made with red or yellow clay, were contrastingly decorated with vines, foliage and oak leaves, garlands of flowers and leaves, small animals or human heads.

Fire-cover with face ornament, 28.5 × 41.5 cm, Flanders, second half of the 18th century. Bruges, Gruuthuse Museum.

Fire-pot or hand-basket, 28.5 × 12 cm, Torhout, atelier Willemyns (?), 19th century. Bruges, Gruuthuse Museum.

Fire-pot or hand-basket, 27.5 × 13 cm, Torhout, atelier Willemyns (?), first quarter of the 19th century. Bruges, Gruuthuse Museum.

Basin, red earthenware, white slip decoration with green and transparent lead-glaze. Flanders, 18th century; diameter 23 cm. Bruges, Gruuthuse Museum.

The musical instruments

Musical instruments were not always treated with the appropriate attention. And yet they are an indispensable part of the music making, in other words, of the music-creation. The painter processes his ideas through compositions of colours on the panel or the canvas; the sculptor needs wood, stone or clay to give a tangible form to his expression. The composer moreover requires a medium: the musician who can interpret the written musical notes thanks to an aesthetically developped song-organ or a musical instrument. The quality of the performance bears proportion to the quality of the produced sound.

The problem is indeed very complex: to give testimony of the sound of a particular period, the instrument must not have been altered. A particular sound is the result of proportions and inner construction of the musical instrument. If these are altered because of a different timbre, the original timbre is definitively lost. It happens very rarely that one is able to find musical instruments of the 16th century in their original condition. As far as the Middle Ages are concerned, practically none exists. The only source is the iconography, which can provide information about the exterior form and the circumstances in which it was used, but as far as the inner construction, the materials that were used and the dimensions are concerned, the data are not precise enough and inadequate. The problem of the contribution of musical instruments to the polyphony, has often been mentioned. Most of the time it was accepted that this kind of music was merely vocal.

It is during the 15th century that organ-players are mentioned for the first time, in Italy as well as in the Netherlands. In the court-chapel of the Burgundian-Habsburger sovereigns in the Netherlands, an organ-player regularly appears from 1473 on. The sovereigns themselves gave music their special attention, and much care was bestowed to the music education of princes and princesses. This was the task of the organ-player. The organ was a necessity in the court-chapel. This is clearly proved by the fact that a portable organ was provided. The organ carrier was a fixed element in the court-chapel.

King David among musicians, illuminated page from *Breviarium,* 232 × 159 mm, Master of the Dresden Breviary, *ca* 1495. London, British Library, Add ms 18851, fol 184 v°.
The breviary was commissioned by the Spanish Ambassador Francisco de Rojas and presented by him to Queen Isabella of Castille, who displayed great interest in Flemish art. It contains more than 150 miniatures by various masters.

Country Dance, detail, Pieter Bruegel the Elder, 1568. Vienna, Kunsthistorisches Museum.
Peasants are dancing to the sounds of a bagpipe, as they are often represented on several paintings and hangings from Flemish masters.

WHICH INSTRUMENTS CONTROL THE ART-MUSIC DURING THE 16th CENTURY? Besides the organ, other instruments are mentioned within the neighbourhood of the court. First of all, we shall mention the clavichord, which was played on by the princesses, among them Mary of Burgundy and particularly her daugther Margareth of Austria. The glamour of the court in the Netherlands and the special liking of the sovereigns for music, must have contributed to stimulate the building of musical instruments and more particularly the building of organs, clavichords, virginals, and harpsichords; this around 1500.

We must certainly not forget the other musical instruments besides these of the so-called art-music. As popular instruments the hurdy-gurdy, hommel, jew's harp and especially the bagpipe were widely spread in the Flemish regions. They also have to be mentioned here, because although they are no longer typical for our regions as the tradition has been lost, they can be found very often on Flemish hangings and on this kind of paintings where scenes in an inn or of the country-life are represented. Thanks to the plastic arts and the hangings, we can classify this instrument, which was then widely spread in our regions, into different types.

The Hoefnagel Family, painting (detail), F. Pourbus the Elder, before 1583. Brussels, Museums of Fine Arts.
This is the small instrument which was produced in Antwerp during the third quarter of the 16th century. It used to be placed on a table; the elevations already show the elegant arabesques which are to be found later on too.

As far as the art-music is concerned, a revolution in which the musical instrument plays an important role, occurred at the beginning of the 16th century. Besides the vocal music, room has been given to a number of so-called key-board instruments or, in other words, musical instruments which can be brought to sound by means of keys. On the one side it concerns a composed instrument with pipes, which are blown by a supply of wind (organ), that was mainly meant for religious music. On the other side there are the stringed instruments, in which the string is brought to sound either by a tangent (clavichord), or by a jack (virginals). These later become pre-eminently the musical instruments for the living-room.

Because of a lot of successive alterations, few original organs out of this period were left to us; Flemish clavichords were not preserved. But a sufficient amount of virginals of the 16th century were left to us.

The organ-builders appear to be isolated builders, spread over several towns and often the activity was passed on from father to son. It is also very clear that their production was mainly meant for a community, and more particular for an ecclesiastic community. On the other hand, clavichord and virginals builders are centred around one town: Antwerp and they all are members of one guild: the Saint-Luke's guild. Their production aimed mainly at the prosperous citizens, who were very happy to have themselves portrayed with these musical instruments.

THE CLAVICHORD

Clavichords and virginals bring us to the living-rooms. The sound of these instruments is at its best in small rooms. It is very difficult to distinguish virginal building from clavichord building during the 16th century. At the beginning of the 16th century, only clavichord builders are mentioned within the Saint-Luke's guild; during the second part of the 16th century, there are 'clavicembal-makers'. No instruments from the beginning of the 16th century have been preserved, from the second half there are virginals. This gap can be filled in the iconography by missing examples. We thus come to the conclusion that the mentioned builders of harpsichords, also built virginals. The names of these constructors are noted in the Registers of the Saint-Luke's guild, and although these lists are not complete, they give us an idea of the importance and the number of this branch of art within a guild, which mainly grouped painters: 8 constructors of clavichords are registered. We can clearly see what a Flemish clavichord looked like from a painting of Jan Van Hemessen, 'Maiden at the Clavichord' (1534), which is exposed in the Worcester Art Museum in Worcester (Massachussetts). A clavichord is a stringed instrument with keys within a rectangular resonance-box. By touching a metal tangent, which is fixed at the back of a key, the strings begin to vibrate. This mechanism was depicted very precisely by the painter.

No attention was ever paid to the construction and spreading of this instrument, and it is sad that so few elements can be discovered in this respect. The most important masters are: Jacob Aelbrechts, Hans Van Ceulen, Johan de Hevilez, Joost Kareest, Willem Leest, Pieter de Leyn, Jan Thielen, Pieter Vorenberch.

VIRGINALS

Of great importance though is the fact that out of these work-shops a new instrument arises at about the middle of the 16th century; namely the virginals. What differs is the mechanism through which the vibrating of the strings is induced. As was mentioned before, these masters are referred to as 'clavecimbalmakers' or 'claver-singelmaker'. This term to indicate the trade, occurs for the first time at about the middle of the 16th century in the registers of the Saint-Luke's guild. In 1557, 10 constructors of harpsichords signed a petition, by means of which they were considered as such from now on. To "be received and accepted in the above-mentioned guild", one had to pass a test which consisted out of the "delivering of all materials and tools serving to this purpose, being a square or angular harpsichord, with a length of about five feet, or longer if he wishes it, well and accurately made and respecting the correct measurements, according to the requirements of the work, sweet-sounding and properly pegged and stringed". This proves very clearly that what was mentioned to be a harpsichord, was in fact a virginal. The iconography shows us the musical instrument very clearly in the self-portrait of Catharine van Hemessen, exposed in the Wallraf-Richartz Museum at Cologne. A virginal of Joannes Kareest, dated 1548, is being preserved in the Museum of Musical instruments at Brussels and it has approximately these measurements: 150 cm (5 feet - 143.4 cm).

Joannes Kareest was indeed one of the signers of the petition, together with Martin Blomsteen, Jacob Theeuwes, Aelbrecht van Neer, Hans Dorgelmakere van Keulen, Christoffel Blommesteyn, Ghoosen Carest, Jacob Aelbrechts, Marten van der Biest and Lodewyck Theeuwes, all of them being constructors of harpsichords, living in Antwerp. In this list three names of masters, who are also registered to be builders of organs or clavichords, appear: Hans Dorgelmakere, it is possible that Hans Bos is meant, Jacob Aelberechts and Joost Kareest; the two last ones were noted to be builders of clavichords previously. The fact that a regimentation was drawn up, leads us to the supposition that indeed

Virginals, Joannes Kareest, 1548. Brussels, Museum for instruments. Joannes Kareest, originally from Cologne, was one of the ten persons who signed the request of 1557, to be accepted into St Luke's Guild as harpsichord builders.

an important change had taken place in the construction of musical instruments, a fact of which ten masters became aware. From that moment onwards, the evolution takes place very quickly and in 1575 the name of Hans Ruckers (1533/55-1598) is mentioned for the first time. At that moment he married Adriana Knaeps. He probably came from Germany and he would get famous mainly as the founder of a work-shop, which delivered virginals and harpsichords to the whole of music-making Europe till 1660. This work-shop was established at Antwerp in the Jodestraat, only a few steps away from the place where Rubens would establish himself shortly afterwards. Hans Ruckers was a brilliant craftsman, who totally controlled the laws of acoustics. Already in 1586, it is clear that his instruments are highly estimated. Signed by him, the instruments were worth more than these of any other builder.

As type instrument there is the virginal, which was previously described as 'square', having its key-board at the longest side. The most important kinds are: the 'muselaer' with its key-board more to the right side or the spinet, also called 'scherpen', with its key-board more to the left side and sounding sharper compared to the 'muselaer'.

Further more there is the 'mother-and-child' virginal. This term applies in fact to two instruments of different seize, also varying in so far as the key-board is placed more to the right or to the left. Traditionally, this instrument would be built following the same pattern during the first half of the 17th century.

But let us first take a better look at the decoration of this instrument. It appears that the box was painted with a marble imitation or trompe l'oeil effects. At the

Virginal 'Mother and Child', Hans Ruckers, 1581. New York, Metropolitan Museum of Art.
The 'mother' of this virginal is of the muselaar type. The 'child' can be played separately or together with the 'mother'. Hereto one removes from the last-mentioned the jacks and installs the 'child' in this place, on top of the 'mother'. This is the first time that one can play in two stops.
Above the keys at the right side, one can notice two medaillons, one with the picture of Philip II (right) and one of his wife, Anna of Austria. The instrument was ordered by Philip II and offered to the marquis Oropesa. It was kept in a chapel in Cuzco (Peru).

Virginals, Hans Ruckers, 1591. Bruges, Gruuthuse Museum.
This is the only polygonal virginal of the 'spinet' type with the keyboard more to the left, that has been perserved. It shows typical arabesque decorations with sea-horses around the elevations. On the inside of the top is a motto on glued paper with wood imitations.

inner side, the decoration consists of patches which are fixed on it. The patterns of these can be found in the model-books of those days. Moreover these instruments have been dated. Recently, similar decorations were discovered in houses that were pulled down in the old citycentre of Antwerp. The same patterns were still used for a very long time and if we compare with other applied arts and interior decoration, examples of the same nature can be found. In this way musical instruments can help to give us an idea what the interior in the 16th century was like.

THE ORGAN

Organs can be classified into three kinds; from small to bigger: the portable, the positive and the big church-organ. This church-organ consisted at the beginning out of a principal work, breastwork and later also a back-positive. Big churchorgans already existed in the 15th century. A nice example of these can be found in the breviary of Charles the Bold, which is kept in the Royal Libary at Brussels. From this period, and this also applies to the next century, no more organs exist, except sometimes an empty organ-box. The iconographic documents should therefore be examined very cautiously; the

352

artist does not always represent the details in their correct proportions. But a number of documents exist in Flemish miniatures, through which you can get an idea as far as the general form and the details of key-board and stops are concerned, but the data are not specific enough to allow the definition of the precise pitch.

Pipes can have different forms and produce immediately another timbre. Within one and the same form, they can be built in different successive pitches: this is what is called an organ stop. Different organ-stops provide you with a variety of timbres. Organ stops could be mixed to increase the variety of sounds. In the oldest organs, different organ stops could be made to sound together. The seperate use of the organ stops only occurs from the 16th century.

A positive organ is depicted in the Adoration of the Lamb (before 1432) by the Van Eyck brothers, which is exposed in Saint Bavo's church at Ghent, and also in the wing of the altar-piece with Sir Edward Bonkil, by Hugo Van der Goes (about 1480), exposed in the Holyroad Palace Collection at Edinburgh. These works of art give us some information about these organs, such as the two series of chromatic pipes, the approximate number of keys; but with respect to the pitch, these questions are much more difficult to find an answer to.

During the 15th century, Flanders and Brabant were known to be progressive centres for organ-building. We know of several masters in Bruges, Malines, Ghent, Brussels and Antwerp. They are called upon for organs at Delft in 1429 and at Harlem in 1437. As the most important masters that were active during the period before 1500, we mention Daniel van der Distelen (Antwerp and Malines) and Victor Langhedul (Ypres). The latter became the founder of a family, of which several members chose to become organ-builder and this till the 18th century. In Ghent and Malines, the family Van den Eekhoute was active in 1470 and 1532.

Several masters from abroad were attracted by the cultural prosperity of the Southern Netherlands. In this way Adriaen Pietersz. of Delft became a citizen of Bruges in 1446 and was working successively at Veurne (1448), Antwerp (1449/50) and eventually at Delft (1458).

At the beginning of the 16th century, we have to mention Hans Suys from Nurenberg and Cologne; in 1509 he was ordered to work on the organ of the cathedral of Antwerp. This work meant the installation of 'more rare voices' or organ-stops. Most of the time, he is indentified with master Hans van Keulen, who worked also at Strassburg, Liege, Xanten and Kalkar. He died in Amsterdam in 1543.

As far as the 16th century is concerned, the most important names are those of the families Moors, Brebos and Langhedul. At the recommendation of Bredeniers, organ-player at the court of Philip the Fair, a certain Marc Moors from Lier delivered to the court a manicordium. He was a relative of Jacob Moors, also from Lier, but he had established himself at Antwerp.

His eldest son, Anton (Antwerp about 1420 till before August 1562), already worked for his own account in 1514, and he delivered a positive for the court-chapel of the young Charles V. From 1516 he often worked on the

The Adoration of the Mystic Lamb, panel of the music-making angels, Jan van Eyck, 1432. Ghent, St Bavo's Cathedral.
The angels play on a positive, a harp and a lira da braccio.

organ of the cathedral of Antwerp, from 1524 on he even received a fixed pay. Organs of his hand can also be found at Louvain, Saint Pieter's (1523) and at Dendermonde, Our Lady (1553). He is mentioned to have been repairing at Saint-Omer, Saint-Bertin's church (1527). In 1555 he signed an agreement with the duke Albrecht van Mecklenburg to deliver an organ for the cathedral at Schwerin. This happened probably through his brother Hieronymus Moors (Antwerp 1519 - Schwerin 1598), who became organ-player of Schwerin in 1552. With Joachim II, elector of Brandenburg, he entered into the agreement to deliver an organ for the cathedral of Berlin. Cornelis Moors (Antwerp ?-Antwerp 1556), son of Jacob Moors, was the only one that resided at Antwerp, and there often maintained the organ of the cathedral till 1535-38, and also after the departure of his brother in 1555. At Malines he built the organ of the Saint-Catherine's church (1543) and repaired the organ of Our Lady's church; in 1556 he constructed the organ of the Saint-Walburgis' church at Audenarde.

The Brebos family also originated from Lier and established itself later at Antwerp. This was the case of Gilles († 6.7.1584), in 1556, probably after Anton Moors had left and Cornelis Moors had passed away. He built the small organ on the rood loft of Our Lady's Church (1457/58). This organ was mentioned as an example by the abbot of Averbode in 1562 and by the church-wardens of the Saint-Georges church at Antwerp in 1563. Besides this one, he also built the big organ (1565-1567) and that of the Our-Lady-Brotherhood church (1572-1574). His most important assignment was when he was called to Spain by Philip II in 1579, to build four organs for the Escorial. Moreover he furnished the royal rooms with a home-organ and a portable. His brothers Gaspar and Michiel were also active in Spain, the former being an organ-tuner to the Spanish Court from 1571/72 onwards. Their third brother Hans had already in 1568 left for Copenhagen, where he became organ-builder to the Protestant Court.

The most important assignments of Gilles Brebos are besides the cathedral of Antwerp and Spain: Vere (1551), Herentals 1556-1557), Berchem (1559-1560), Louvain (1560-1561), Averbode (1562-1563), Hoogstraten (1562-1563), Antwerp, Saint-Georges (1563-1564), Malines (1564-1565), Steenbergen, Northern-Brabant (1567-1568).

The last family of organ-builders are the Langhedul's, who were active around 1475-1635 in Flanders, England, Spain and the north of France. Victor Langhedul († Ieper 1513) worked at Courtray, Saint-Omer and Lisle. His grand-son Jan († Ghent around 1592) was active at Lisle (1583) and Paris (1585), where he trained his son Matthijs (Ypres ?-Brussels 1635/36). He would become organ-tuner to the court at Madrid in 1592/99, before establishing himself in Paris. His principal creation was the organ in the Saint-Gervais (1602). In 1605, we find him again at Ypres, Ghent, to the archducal court at Brussels, Antwerp and Tongres. Matthijs Langhedul was one of the founders of the French classical organ, which was built from 1673 to 1700.

The families Moors in Germany, Brebos in Spain and Scandinavia and last but not least Langhedul in France, prove very distinctly what a strong influence the Flemish organ-built had in Europe during this period.

CARILLON

Flanders is also known for its carillons. If we pay a visit to numerous Flemish towns, we are reminded of the fact that the cradle or the carillons lay in Flanders. The belfry was already early supplied with tower-clocks; a bell indicated the hour already during the 14th century. Out of this the warning gradually grew, and by means of four small bells the hour-clock would strike. In the course of time the towers were provided with bells of different size, to be able to announce sad as well as happy tidings. Gradually a melodious warning developped, consisting of a harmonized series of bells. If one connected each bell to a key of the key-board, then the result was the carillon-key-board. This happened during the 16th century and in the following towns the carillons were furnished in this way: Audenarde in 1510, Bruges in 1532, Antwerp before 1541, Ghent in 1533 and Malines in 1556. During the last quarter of the 16th century, pedals were introduced for the heavier bells. Towns and municipalities began to compete to get hold of the heaviest and best chimes.

For the 16th century the most important bell-founders are the Waghevens brothers at Malines and the different members of the Van den Ghein family at Malines, Tienen and Louvain. As far as the Waghevens family is concerned, no less than ten members were active as bell-founders over a period of 100 years. Not only did they supply the whole of the Southern Netherlands with bells, but they also furnished the Northern Netherlands, Germany, England, Denmark and Italy.

The founder Hendrik Waghevens (born around 1425). started a bell-foundry at Malines in 1462. His son, Simon Waghevens (around 1449 - after 1526), succeeded his father in 1483, assisted by both of his half-brothers Peter (around 1470 - 1537) and Georges I (around 1470 - 1537). Georges II (before 1500 - 1539), Cornelis (around 1500 - 1544) and Jacob (around 1500 - 1574) were sons of Peter, Medard (around 1494 - 1557) and Jan (1504 - 1566) were sons of Georges I. Finally there was Michiel, son of Georges II, who like his father, only knew a short career.

The situation is similar with the Van den Ghein family. The founder Willem (Goirle around 1450 - Malines 1533), established himself at Malines in 1506 and started a bell-foundry. His sons Peter I († 1561) and Jan I († around 1543), took over the business and were later succeeded by Anton († 1584), son of Jan I, Jan II (1573) and Peter II († 1598), sons of Peter I. Peter III (1553-1618), son of Peter II took over the work-shop together with his brother Jan III († 1626). Their descendants would still be active as bell-founders till about the middle of our century; from in the 19th century they worked under the name Van Aerschodt. During the 16th century, bells were founded for the Southern Netherlands, but also for the Northern Netherlands, France, Germany, England, Denmark, Sweden, Spain and Portugal.

Frans Baudouin
Emeritus custodian of the Art-Historical Museums of Antwerp

THE 17th AND 18th CENTURIES

LÉON VOET
Introduction

JEAN-PIERRE ESTHER
Architecture

HELENA BUSSERS
Sculpture

FRANS BAUDOUIN
Painting

LÉON VOET
Graphic art

RIA FABRI
Furniture

ERIK DUVERGER
Tapestry and textile arts

PIET BAUDOUIN
Metalwork

STÉPHANE VANDENBERGHE
Ceramics

JEANINE LAMBRECHTS-DOUILLEZ
Musical instruments

Introduction

1585 was a turning point in the history of the Netherlands – and in the artistic and cultural activities of Flanders. After dominating the economy of the Low Countries for centuries, Flanders and Brabant were replaced by Holland and Zeeland. Nevertheless, for another three-quarters of a century the south did relatively well with an artistic and cultural activity corresponding to the prosperous north. However, from 1650-1660 onwards the south rapidly faded away, as a result of new economic and political crises.

LAST EXPLOSION OF ARTISTIC ACTIVITY: THE BAROQUE PERIOD

The political and religious break in 1585 resulted in a shift in the art world and its customers in the Southern Netherlands, and this had far-reaching consequences.

As far as the national consumption of art was concerned, the citizens and the nobility had been the most important purchasers of the country's own works of art during the 16th century. As often happens during a recession when the bourgeoisie is still wealthy but does not wish to invest its capital in commercial ventures, 'investment' in art after 1585 took place on an unknown scale, which in some cases actually became a collecting mania. In the 16th century there had been some private collections, but these had largely been limited to rarities; such as the 'museum' of Abraham Ortelis, famous for its valuable antique coins. These specialist collections became much more common in the 17th century; e g the globes, telescopes and other scientific instruments of Jacob Edelheer (1597-1657), town pensionary of Antwerp, were an international attraction. However, it was characteristic of this new age – and again typical of Antwerp – to find collections of paintings by old and contemporary masters, together with antique works of art, coins, medallions, drawings, engravings etc, which were exhibited in one or more showrooms – the 'art rooms'. Often the owners were so proud of them, that they had them immortalized in paintings, which reproduced their treasures in minute detail – constituting a unique source of information about the history of art in the Netherlands.

The new fashions introduced by the Italians also led to an unprecedented splendour and flamboyance in furniture, wall hangings in gold stamped leather and velvet, and other decorations – which provided a good living for a large number of craftsmen and artists.

Until the end of the 17th century the burghers and nobility continued to be important clients for the national production of works of art, with their own specific desires regarding particular genres and contents. As in the past, a considerable proportion of this 'bourgeois' production could be disposed of to the upper classes abroad. This was increasingly undertaken by specialized art firms – and occasionally by the artists themselves when they went abroad for specific commissions; e g Peter Paul Rubens and Anthony van Dyck, or even the sculptor Artus Quellin, who was invited by the Amsterdam magistracy to decorate their Town Hall (the present Royal Palace).

The burghers and nobility were still important customers, but in the Southern Netherlands they were once more surpassed by the Church. The Counter Reformation recognized again the educational and spiritual value of statues and paintings for church decoration. This had to be produced all the more prolifically, because the Calvinists had not left much behind in many places. Church art flourished once more in the south, with unprecedented brilliance and force. The political and religious schism of 1585 did not entail a radical change in artistic ideas as such. The Renaissance continued in all branches of art until a new movement evolved at the beginning of the 17th century, again originating from Italy. This was the exuberant form of the Renaissance, which came to be termed 'Baroque'.

This art form was expressed in the first place in the construction of new churches and in the decoration of old and new oratories. One particularly gifted painter from the Southern Netherlands, Peter Paul Rubens, became fascinated by the pathos and the strong emotional content of the Baroque art form, which he had discovered at first hand in Italy. From about 1609 Rubens began to adopt this Baroque style in his paintings, and with his great personality and genius he influenced generations of Flemish and Brabant masters. From painting and church decoration the Baroque style also permeated through to tapestry work, engraving and a number of other artistic crafts.

The Baroque art has given Flanders and Brabant a special place in the art history of 17th-century western Europe. They formed a distant outpost of the Italian movement, wedged in between the Northern Netherlands where the Calvinist churches were bare, and Germany and France, where artistic ideas also remained rather sober. The Baroque style was less popular with the burghers for personal use, both in the architecture and decoration of their houses, and in the works of art they purchased. Even Rubens, the great master of Flemish Baroque, could be surprisingly sober in certain genres, such as portrait painting; as were many of his contemporaries, not least his gifted pupil, Anthony van Dyck. The exuberant expression of the Baroque style remained in the Southern Netherlands a religious art form. It did not survive long the death of Rubens; the style soon calmed down and became less excessive. In the course of the 18th century it incorporated the new

Pieter Paul Rubens, *The Reconciliation of the Romans and the Sabines*, detail, oil sketch, 56 × 87 cm. Private collection.

trends, this time originating in France: the Rococo style, and later in that century, classicism.

Much more serious was the fact that after Rubens' death Flemish art soon lost a great deal of its élan and originality. The wars of Louis XIV, the economic recessions, the emergence of important European art centres in Holland, France, Spain and England, which began to dominate the international scene and even acquired customers in the Southern Netherlands, broke its resilience. Already by the end of the 17th century Flemish art had become reduced to a local level. A few branches of the arts resisted more successfully, including sculpture – and especially wood carving – which continued to flourish in church decoration, particularly in an impressive number of pulpits and confessionals. However, by 1700 the great era of Flemish art had irrevocably ended.

THE DECLINE IN INTELLECTUAL, SCIENTIFIC AND LITERARY ACTIVITY

Parallel with the artistic activities of the 17th century, the cultural life of Flanders and Brabant had a final late flowering, though it had fewer pretensions and came sooner to an end. Many humanists and scientists with Protestant sympathies fled from the south before and after 1585, especially to the north, where they played a vital role in the rapid cultural growth. They made an important contribution to the spectacular development of the new Leyden University, founded in 1574, into an international scientific centre. This loss of intellectual potential was only partly compensated for by the return of (re-converted) Catholic scholars to the now peaceful south; such as Justus Lipsius (who left Leyden for Louvain in 1591).

After 1585 Humanism acquired a different character in the south. The Church orders – above all the Jesuits – were instrumental in establishing secondary education; and provided a painstaking teaching of Humanism, but now completely impregnated with a Catholic spirit. This reached and influenced an even wider cross-section than Humanism at the peak of its glory in the 16th century. However, even though the number of authors increased in relative terms (and indeed considerably in cities like Antwerp), their works could at best be considered only adequate, and after 1650 they stopped appearing altogether.

In the south the Counter Reformation once more drew the best elements in religious life and thought. Initially this took place with great gusto at the universities of Louvain and Douai (founded in 1562), but to an even greater extent in the colleges of the Jesuits and other orders; and many bishops and canons were also involved. Once again the threads came together in Antwerp in the printers' workshops. If Christoffel Plantin was the great printer for Humanism, his son-in-law Jan Moretus (active from 1589 to 1610), and his grandson Balthasar I Moretus (from 1610 to 1641) became the great printers of the Counter Reformation in the Southern Netherlands, which they helped to spread throughout Europe. The vast majority of their publi-

cations have now been forgotten; only a few are referred to in footnotes in various reference works on asceticism and piety in the 17th century – or in works of art history. The editions, published by the Moretus family, were indeed often beautifully illustrated – including designs by Rubens – and these engravings became a major source of religious inspiration for generations of artists all over the world, as far afield as Latin America and China.

This religious production came quickly to a halt after 1640-1650. The universities of Louvain and Douai lapsed into silence, as did the colleges of the Jesuits and the other orders. As a result the number of printers in Antwerp diminished sharply; and their production henceforth was aimed only at a local and regional reading public. Only the *Officina Plantiniana* of the Moretus dynasty managed to survive at an international level. In the early years of the 17th century, the Spanish Crown had granted it a monopoly for Spain and its overseas dominions for the production and sale of liturgical works (breviaries, missals and books of hours). After 1640 the *Officina* specialized exclusively in these editions; and until 1764, when the monopoly was withdrawn, hundreds of thousands of these publications were shipped off to the Iberian peninsula – a profitable business which considerably helped the balance of trade in the Southern Netherlands.

Cornelis Jansenius (1583-1638), Bishop of Ypres in 1636, had a tremendous impact with his posthumously published *Augustinus* (1640). It led to the rise of the Jansenist movement named after him, which was particularly influential in France, though it also led to vehement disputes in the Southern Netherlands. Only one religious work of international scope, started in the early 17th century, successfully managed to bypass the difficulties from *ca* 1650 to survive to the present day: the critical edition of the lives of the saints, the *Acta Sanctorum*, which appeared in a seemingly endless series of volumes. This initiative was undertaken by Antwerp Jesuits like Heribertus Rosweydus (1569-1629), Johannes Bollandus (1596-1665), Godfried Henschen (1600-1681) and Daniel Papebrochius (1628-1714). It continued until the dissolution of the Jesuit order in Antwerp by the Austrians (1773), and was then carried on by the Bollandists in Brussels.

Scientific activity did not even manage to get off the ground after 1585. The physician Jan Baptist van Helmont (Brussels 1577-1644) made experiments to show that air is not an indefinable and insubstantial element, but has a concrete structure (including carbonic acid), and also introduced the term and the concept 'gas' in physics. At the beginning of the 17th century the Jesuit college in Antwerp prided itself on its school of 'mathesis', which included a number of famous international names, although most of these soon disappeared abroad: Gregorius van Sint-Vincentius (1584-1667, only lectured in Antwerp from 1617-1621), Carolus della Faille (1597-1654, whose work included a theory on gravitation, but who left for Spain in 1629), Franciscus Aguilonius (1567-1617, the author of the *Opticorum libri VI*, published in 1613 by the *Officina Plantiniana* with illustrations after Rubens, a key work in the field of optics until the time of Newton), Andreas Tacquet (died in 1660), the teacher of Ferdinand Verbiest (1623-1688), the learned Jesuit missionary, who was highly thought of by the Manchu Court in China for his knowledge of mathematics and astronomy. In 1675, the Antwerp beguinage pastor, Frans van Sterbeeck, published a highly acclaimed standard work on mushrooms, *Theatrum fungorum ofte het toneel der campernoelien*. In the 18th century the physician Jan Palfijn (Courtrai 1650 – Ghent 1730) invented the obstetric forceps. However, this is an exhaustive list of all scientists from the Southern Netherlands, who managed to rise above a local or regional level during these two centuries.

With economy and scientific practice, literary activity also moved north to bring about the golden century of Dutch literature. In the first half of the 17th century only a few names can be noted in the south: Richard Verstegen (1580-1540), with epigrams and character sketches; Justus de Harduijn (1582-1636), with religious poetry; Adriaan Poirters (1605-1674), with moralistic tales, including *The World Unmasked*. Again, this was about all. The production of plays managed to survive for a while longer, still performed by the Chambers of Rhetoric, and there were some talented writers like Michiel de Swaen (1654-1707) in Dunkirk, Willem Ogier (1618-1689) in Antwerp, and his daughter Barbara Kerricx-Ogier (1648-1720).

However, by 1700 even this art form had become exhausted. New trends had emerged which led to the decline of the theatrical traditions and spelled out a death sentence for the ancient Chambers of Rhetoric; the public was becoming increasingly interested in seeing the works of the French and Spanish contemporary masters of the European theatre, either in French or in a Dutch translation. Already in the 17th century many foreign theatre groups from France or Italy began to tour through the cities of the Southern Netherlands to introduce music and 'European' theatre. Soon permanent halls were provided for these travelling groups – particularly at the instigation of the city almoners, responsible for public charity and its financing, who were allowed to pocket a percentage of the income of these groups for their works of charity. Thus a musical academy was opened in Antwerp in 1661 (known as the 'Opera' after 1682), followed by a theatre in 1709.

French groups in Flanders and Brabant: this was an aspect of a wider phenomenon which can be largely held responsible for the virtual disappearance of intellectual, scientific and literary activity after about 1650. In the second half of the 17th century Humanism had come to an end. New intellectual movements were emerging in western Europe which were being developed and practised in a new international cultural language: French. In general the bourgeoisie in Flanders and Brabant were reasonably competent in the French language; but unlike Latin, they felt it as a foreign medium which they did not dare to use to express their own ideas. The French influence became increasingly powerful in the 18th century, but still the local elites did not manage to conquer their feelings of diffidence and inferiority. From the second half of the 17th century, they were content to observe what was happening in the intellectual field in Europe, without taking an active part themselves.

Architecture

As in the Renaissance, the new forms evolved within the sphere of influence of the south. The Italian Baroque style, which in Rome had already reached a high point at the end of the 16th century, and experienced an exuberant period of flowering during the whole of the 17th century in most of southern and central Europe, had a strong influence on the Flemish Baroque. While the protestant Northern Netherlands tended to follow the more rational and sober France, Flemish ecclesiastical architecture in the 17th century came completely under the sway of the Italian Baroque, which radiated the renewed power of the catholic church in a whole series of magnificent church buildings. Thus the type of facade of *Gesù* Church in Rome was largely imitated.

ECCLESIASTICAL ARCHITECTURE DURING THE COUNTER REFORMATION

The Flemish feeling for decoration, which often found extravagant expression in the flamboyant late Gothic, continued since the end of the Middle Ages to form one of the principal and lasting characteristics of regional architecture. We have already mentioned how the late Gothic master builders in the 15th and 16th centuries had a predilection for exuberant lacework ornamentations, sometimes to the detriment of clarity of form and architectural purity. In the 16th century, the new Renaissance art was more a style of ornament than a pure architectural expression. In the Baroque period, we find the same tendency towards overloaded ornamentation, as if the local artists were continually concerned with a deep-seated *horror vacui*. This was further reinforced by the specific world-view of the Counter Reformation, which stressed the festively decorative and the rhetorical force of the sensorially perceptible.

While the Renaissance presented an outspokenly bourgeois character, and spread among the nobility and the intellectual artistic class, the Baroque style was more of an ecclesiastical phenomenon. The church authorities, and more particularly the newly founded Jesuit order, used the Baroque to strengthen the purposes of the catholic reform movement as propagated during the Council of Trent (1545-1563). After the fatal religious troubles in the second half of the 16th century, the Southern Netherlands experienced a revival of catholic religious feeling, which expressed its impetuousness in the building of numerous churches. The economic prosperity and political calm under the short but flourishing administration of the catholic governors Albrecht and Isabella (1598-1621) provided the necessary driving force for a renewed artistic upsurge.

Antwerp, *The facade of the St Carolus Borromeus' Church*, engraving, Jan de Labaer. Antwerp, Stedelijk Prentenkabinet.

Antwerp, *St Carolus Borromeus' Church, tower*, 1615-1621.
The tower, which is 58 m high, is built against the choir. The third quadrilateral towerjoint, of the Ionic order, and the cylindrical lantern-tower with Venetian light openings and Corinthian pilasters, is one of the finest examples of Baroque tower-building in Europe.

More so than in the previous period, architects went to Italy to become familiar with the classical language of architecture. In the wake of numerous Flemish painters and sculptors, the architects now went to Rome or to other Italian cities for a study period that often lasted several years. Thus Wenzel Cobergher (ca 1560-1634) spent 25 years in Italy where he was highly regarded as a painter, numismatist and art theorist. In 1604 he returned to the Netherlands to enter the service of the Archdukes Albrecht and Isabella as their principal architect. His brother-in-law Jakob Franckaert (1583-1651), born and bred in Rome, came to the Netherlands in 1608 and also entered the service of the Court. The most important Jesuit architect, Pieter Huyssens (1577-1637), also stayed in Rome, although at a later age and for a shorter period (1626-1627).

Also the brilliant Baroque painter Rubens (1577-1640) stayed in the Italian cities of Mantua, Rome and Genoa from 1600 to 1608, where he showed a great

Antwerp, *St Carolus Borromeus' Church*, drawing, 38 × 26.2 cm, about 1614, supposed to be by Pieter Huyssens. Antwerp, Stedelijk Prenten-kabinet.
The design of the groundplan and the westfront clearly show the strong Italian influence. By the direct assistance of P.P. Rubens, this church got a more explicit Baroque nature. The tower was not built at the west side, but at the choir side.

Antwerp, *St Carolus Borromeus' Church, interior*, 1614-1626.
This interior of one of the earliest Baroque churches in Flanders is very luxurious. It gives a strong space suggestion, mainly because of the galleries above the side-aisles. The high altar is probably made after a design of Rubens.

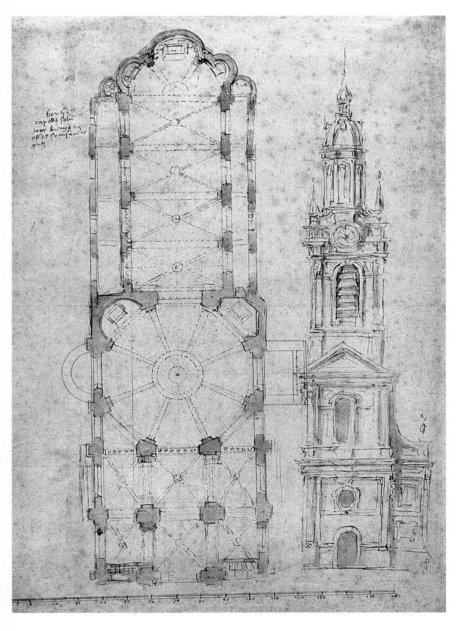

interest in architecture. This resulted in the publication of the pictorial book *I palazzi antichi e moderni di Genova reccolti e disegnati da Pietro Paolo Rubens*, published in two parts at Antwerp in 1622-1623. Before him, Franckaert had published his *Premier livre d'Architecture* in Brussels in 1616. Both works played an undeniable role in spreading Italian classical architecture among local architects and principals. This can be compared with the influence of the model books of Pieter Coecke van Aelst and Hans Vredeman de Vries in the second half of the 16th century. But the pictorial books of Rubens and Franckaert came out at a time when many buildings had already been erected in an early Baroque style. The three architects Cobergher, Franckaert and Huyssens paved the way for the further evolution of Baroque architecture in the Southern Netherlands. In this process, Rubens played a creative and driving role. The Society of Jesus was the great supporting pillar of the catholic church in its fight against the Reformation. In this it was supported by the princes, particularly under the administration of Albrecht and Isabella.

In the first years of the 17th century there was an

Malines, *Beguinage Church*, interior, 1629-1638.
Instead of the traditional columns, Jacob Franckaert used Corinthian pilasters. The rhythmical in and outbending framework between top and bottom part, adds to the light and shadow effects of the vertical and horizontal elements.

Louvain, *St Michael's Church, front*, 1650-1671.
Here the decorative elaboration of the front is even more plastic than that of St Carolus Borromeus' Church at Antwerp. The festive exuberance reaches the pinnacle in the Jesus-monogram surrounded by trumpet-blowing angels under the broken pediment.

explosion of building activity that lasted till around 1640. A renovating force was the direct influence of *Gesù* Church in Rome. The amalgamation of a longitudinal building with a central building (after a design by Giacomo de Vignola, 1568), by which a characteristic effect of space was created, influenced the later Baroque churches in Flanders. In the first Jesuit churches, inspiration was above all drawn from the facade arrangement of this church (a creation of Giacomo della Porta, 1584), where a dynamic effect was provided by the stylish volutes supporting the upper middle part.

However, the layout of the first Jesuit churches still drew to a high degree on medieval traditions; mostly of the basilica type, but without transept, with a polygonal closed choir without choir gallery and side chapels. The vault system was also inspired by century-old traditions: in the beginning of the 17th century, predominant use was made of pointed or rounded arch crossrib vaults, combined with the buttresses that gave the rhythm to the outer facades and side aisles, and where volute-shaped supporting walls took over the function of the Gothic arch buttresses. The verticalism was maintained, both in the spatial effect and in the planes of the facade. The

first signs of this change of style in ecclesiastical architecture may be seen in the works of the Jesuit brother Hoeymaker at Valenciennes and Tournai (*ca* 1600).

In 1615, the building was started of a very important Baroque church in the Netherlands: St Carolus Borromeus' Church in Antwerp, designed by the rector of the *Professenhuis*, the mathematician, philosopher and theologian François d'Aguilon (1567-1617). Special attention was given to the front facade by the exuberant sculpted work which, in comparison with earlier classical church facades, now ushered in the dynamism and theatrical power of the full-blown Baroque. The superposition of the three classical orders, the strongly retreating and advancing parts with vivid light-shade effects, and the alternating use of materials for colour effects give the main facade a festive character, typifying the propagandistic aims of the Counter Reformation. The paintings of Rubens, which were worked into the vault spaces but were lost during a fire in 1718, made this building one of the most beautiful Jesuit churches.

After the death of François d'Aguilon, brother Huyssens took over the direction of the building until it was completed in 1621. On the choir side, a high tower was

Scherpenheuvel, *Our Lady's Basilica*, 1609.
The central construction refers to the Roman influence, under which the designer Wenzel Cobergher came during his long stay in Italy.

Bruges, *St Walburga's Church*, interior, 1619-1641.
The bright colours of the painted walls and arches soften the plastic, Baroque ornamental motifs, and add to the effect of space and the surprisingly high brightness.

erected as symbol of the place where the Holy Sacrament was preserved. The veneration of the Tabernacle played a great role in the Counter Reformation. This four-sided tower, consisting of four sections, shows the superposition of the three orders and is crowned by a round, openwork tambour with a vaulted cupola, over which is a small lantern tower. The form is traditional Renaissance, with elements that refer – among other things – to the works of Serlio and Palladio. The assimilation of these is more powerful, more deeply felt and more plastic. In the creation of this tower, Rubens played a decisive role. The motives and forms he had got to know during his time in Italy were worked by him into a new whole. It is the first tower in the world showing complete Baroque characteristics. Up to the 18th century, its design exercised influence in the Southern Netherlands, and was even imitated abroad.

In the same period, the Jesuits built their cloister church in Bruges, now St Walburga's Church (1619-1641), also after a design by Pieter Huyssens. As in Antwerp, he planned there a monumental tower on the choir side, but this was never completed because of lack of money. The prestigious building works of the Jesuit order led to financial difficulties, and consequently Huyssens was temporarily dismissed as an architect of the order. A recent analysis of St Walburga's Church has shown how a modular system, based on square, circle and cube, was consequently carried out. This systematically built-up space was to create the illusion of a cosmos not bound to matter.

The Baroque style became more sculptural and decorative in the second half of the 17th century, displacing the purely architectural. The front facade of St Michael's Church in Louvain (1650-1671) by the Jesuit Willem Hesius 1601-1690) is a brilliant example of this. All of these churches were designed by members of the order itself. It is typical that they were not trained in the traditional craft system, but had a purely theoretical schooling. The Society of Jesus played a leading role in the evolution of ecclesiastical architecture and the coming into existence of a true Flemish Baroque. This would have been inconceivable without the fructifying role of Wenzel Cobergher who, after his long and successful stay in Italy, introduced the new architectural forms into Flanders. In 1609 he was commissioned by the Archdukes to build Our Lady's Basilica at Scherpen-

Averbode, *Abbey church, front and tower,* 1664-1672 and 1701.
The high front of this Norbertine church shows the effects of the Gothic verticality.

Averbode, *Abbey church, choir,* finished in 1668.
The deep choir, typical for abbey churches, is linked to a circular part, which was meant for the laity. If we compare it to the Baroque church interiors of the first half of the 17th century, the concept of the space is also more vertical.

heuvel. This pilgrimage church has a symbolic heptagonal ground plan with a coordinating central volume, flanked by a series of side chapels. This central building, still tightly arranged, was influenced by the Roman high Renaissance (*e g San Giovanni dei Fiorentini* by Bosio). St Augustine's Church in Antwerp (1615-1618) is also by Cobergher. The west facade is divided horizontally and vertically by broad strips of natural stone, which contrast with the red brick masonry. This play of colours was inspired by indigenous brick and natural stone techniques, and was widely imitated.

Antwerp was the centre *par excellence* for artistic activity, not least in the field of architecture. But other Brabant towns too, such as Brussels, the permanent residence of the Court, and Malines, the centre of ecclesiastical power, experienced considerable building activity. For Brussels, we would mention the Jesuit Church (1616) and the Augustinian Church (1620-1624), both by Jakob Franckaert. In Malines, four important Baroque churches were built in the 17th century. The former Jesuit Church of St Francis Xavier (1670-1677) by Antoon Losson still gives a very traditional effect. The Beguinage Church (1629 – after 1640)

was begun by Jakob Franckaert and completed by Fayd'herbe. The traditional crossrib vault construction was still employed here, but now with Baroque ornamentation.

The sculptor Lucas Fayd'herbe (1617-1687), a pupil of Rubens', played a significant role, particularly after 1660, in the application of the plastic, so-called 'Rubens Baroque'. He is also responsible for the cloister church of Leliëndaal (1662-1672) and the Our Lady-of-Hanswijk's Church (1663-1683). In this building, he experimented with the space combination of a longitudinal building with a central building, in which lighting along the tambour of the cupola vaulting produced the necessary theatrical effects. Because this artist had not benefited from any training as an architect, and tended to prefer decorative working-out to the logic of architectonics, all sorts of technical difficulties arose during the building itself – and alterations and reinforcements had to be carried out to stabilize this hazardous construction.

The victory of catholicism in the Southern Netherlands led to a large number of cloister, parish and country churches being built in the new triumphal style. The Norbertines vied with the Jesuits in the building of

luxurious places of worship. In the abbey church of Averbode (1663-1700), designed by Jan van den Eynde of Antwerp (1620-1702), there was also the search for an amalgamation of longitudinal with central building, aimed at producing spatial effects. This met in an outstanding manner the specific requirements of a cloister church. The smaller circular part was reserved for the people, while the numerous monks took their places in the extended choir. Before this, Pieter Huyssens had realized the same spatial concepts in the Benedictine St Peter's Abbey in Ghent (1629-1722). Here the central cupola is clearly inspired by the *Gesù* and St Peter's Churches in Rome. The abbey church of

Grimbergen, *Abbey church, interior,* 1660-1698.
This abbey church, which was built by the young Norbertine Gilbert van Zinnicq, seems even grander than the one of Averbode. The high pillars with Corinthian heads, the entablature which inclines strongly and the decorated girdle-arches, have all been made in sand-lime brick, while the cupola above the crossing is made out of wood and stucco-work, to avoid the difficulties in building a cupola out of stone, a technique to which one was not familiar in the Southern Netherlands.

Antwerp, *Keizerstraat, Hotel Delbeke,* front of the so-called House of Pleasance on the court-yard, 1659.
The sculpture in the vent-pegs of the round-arches on the ground and in the central roof-chapel on the cornice gives a luxuriant effect to the whole.

Grimbergen (1660-1725), built by the Norbertine Gilbert van Zinnicq (ca 1627-1660) is even more ambitious in design. Here too, a cupola building is combined with a longitudinal layout, resulting in a bright interior.

The following principles applied to all church interiors. By the refined colour nuances, obtained by the use of different materials (white natural stone, stucco, various kinds of marble, painted woodwork and leaf-gold) pictorial effects were obtained that directed the eye immediately to the high altar, the place of liturgy and the presence of the Holy Sacrament. This was underlined still further by the setting up of monumental altar paintings, whereby the strongly coloured and dynamic compositions gave masterly service to the aims of the Counter Reformation.

CIVIL ARCHITECTURE
IN THE 17th CENTURY

Wenzel Cobergher introduced with his designs for the *Bergen van Barmhartigheid* (pawnbrokers) in various Flemish and Walloon towns a new type of facade. These *Bergen* were set up by the Archdukes Albrecht and Isabella as charitable institutions where people could leave their possessions as a guarantee for cheap loans. Cobergher himself was superintendent of these institutions, and as principal master builder he was closely involved in their design. Innovation was provided by several elements inspired by the Italian *palazzi*: the strongly horizontal articulation of the cornices and the rectangular, framed window openings without cross divisions, crowned with frontons and separated by broad walls. They assume an isolated place in the evolution of

Flemish architecture, quite separate from the traditional style of building. Of the twenty *Bergen* that were erected in 1619-1633, we mention here those in Ghent (1622) and in St Winoksbergen in French Flanders (1630).

The great master Rubens, when he built his own house on the *Wapper* at Antwerp, also set the tone for the regional interpretation of Italian Baroque. The inner court was closed off by a monumental portico in natural stone, and this served to connect his own dwelling house with the newly-built studio. The arcade thus formed provided a majestic and theatrical access to the garden, and outlined the perspective view of the ornamental garden pavillion further away. It recalls the Roman triumphal arches, and is worked out in a particularly plastic manner with strongly advancing and retreatig elements, with colour contrasts in the materials used, and with copious use of sculptural elements.

This purely decorative architecture is an excellent example of the personal contribution of Rubens' genius to Flemish architecture. The facades of his studio were also decorated with grisaille paintings of scenes from antique mythology. The subjects testified to Rubens' humanistic interest and gave the illusion of sculpted reliefs. Near his house he had a museum rotunda built, inspired by the Pantheon in Rome, and the model books of Serlio and Scamozzi. This scenic and picturesque Baroque ensemble was created in the period 1611-1627, probably in close collaboration with the sculptor Hans van Mildert. It shows Rubens' creative force and testifies to the exceptional flourishing of culture in 17th-century Antwerp.

The painter Jakob Jordaens, when he built his house and studio in 1640/41, also gave a fully plastic Baroque decor to the natural stone facades on the inner court, even though this was less exuberant than in Rubens' house. The emphasized central doorways of Jordaens' house were admired in Antwerp during the second half of the 17th century. This element often featured in the central projections of some distinguished gentlemen's houses; and united the *porte-cochère*, a balcony window, and a dormer window projecting above the cornice. This is the case, for example, in the Hotel Delbeke in the *Keizerstraat*, where we still see in the main facade the three orders superimposed (1647), and where the facade of the summerhouse on the inner court (1659) is worked out luxuriously by the contrasting use of white sand-limestone and blue granite.

In the Tanners' and Shoemakers' Guildhouse on the *Grote Markt* (1644), we can also observe the classical arrangement. Here the ornamentation of the 'Vredeman de Vries style' is still clearly recognizable. But in contrast to the Renaissance period, the elements were now worked together in a more plastic and dynamic manner. The strict classical elements fitted readily into the Flemish Baroque. However, they were reshaped in an imaginative manner to produce a mobile whole: a quite particular style classified as 'Rubens Baroque'. This style of decoration, in the second half of the 17th century in Antwerp, was quite successful in the so-called 'Spanish porches': these are monumental natural stone doorcases to houses and cloisters, in a fully plastic Baroque style.

Antwerp, *Wapper, Rubens' House,* portico serving as partition between courtyard and garden, 1611-1618.
The different constructional elements have been adopted from the Italian Renaissance. The processing of these materials, which is dynamic and plastic, is typical for the Baroque.

Outside the artistic centre of Antwerp, 'Rubens Baroque' spread mainly in Brabant and East Flanders. As in the late Middle Ages and the 16th century, for the richer facades preference was given to sand-limestone, a thankful material for carrying out sculptural ornamentations. For the omnipresent stepped gables, the traditional brick and natural stone architecture continued to be used. The heterogeneous use of materials gave a colourful and lively accent to even the simplest house facades. In West Flanders – further away from the natural stone quarries – the predominant use of brick tended to tone down the Baroque influence. We find Baroque elements particularly in the decorative parts, mostly carried out in natural stone: semi-relief sculptural work in the arch fields or on the window-bossings, fruit and flower festoons, cartouches which often indicate the date of building, *putti*, oculi and richly worked-out gable tops curving in and out, crowned by frontons and ornamental vases. Another new feature consists of the figurative representations in the sculptural work. They show all sorts of subjects: allegories, mythological scenes, religious motifs, names of houses *etc*.

It is fascinating to record the continued penetration of stone in town architecture. Fear of town fires led the municipal authorities to ban the erection of wooden facades, which had determined the medieval townscape. When the wooden facades were replaced by stone, the overhang on the upper floor was generally taken over, and was decoratively emphasized by an overhanging arch frieze. This element occurred very frequently in 17th-century facades.

As examples of the 'Rubens Baroque' in Flanders, we should also mention the Provost's House on the *Burg* in Bruges (1662-1666) and the monumental entrance of the Fish Market on the *Sint-Veerleplein* in Ghent (1689-1690). But as crowning achievement of this evolution, the series of facades on the *Grote Markt* at Brussels merits our particular attention. It forms the culminating point of Baroque facade architecture in the Southern Netherlands.

During the Nine Years' War against the French king Louis XIV (1689-1697), Brussels came under heavy fire from the French troops in 1695. The guildhouses on the *Grote Markt* were laid in ruins, but completely rebuilt shortly afterwards (1695-1702). The result was an unusual decor, which is especially illustrative in the evolution of style from the full to the classicist Baroque. Certain facades that were not completely destroyed during the shooting, were repaired and renovated. The Italian Renaissance ornamentation was readopted, seen now through the spectacles of Flemish Baroque. This was the case for the houses *Den Cruywagen*, *De Zak* and *De Wolvin*. On the latter facade, built in 1691 from a design by Pieter Herbosch and restored in 1695, the images on the second floor represent Truth, Falsehood, Discord and Peace: a typical 17th-century programme.

The Boatsmen's House *Den Hoorn*, a creation of Antonio Pastorana, dates from 1696. The facade has the form of the stern of a ship, with tritons, sea horses and all sorts of marine symbols; the lines of which, waving in and out, are clearly inspired by Borromini's church facade of *San Carlo alle Quattro Fontane* in Rome. Here we also find early examples of the orders in which the pilasters rise several storeys high; an architectural element from the Italian Renaissance and Baroque, transferred via France and the Northern Netherlands into Flemish architecture, and widely adopted in the beginning of the 18th century and in the later classicism. It can already be seen on the Brussels *Grote Markt* in some facades by Willem de Bruyn: the Tailors' Guildhouse *De Gulden Boot*, *De Engel*, but especially in the monumental facade of the House of the Brabant Dukes, which completely occupies the south side of the market place. The house *De Zwaan*, probably from a design by Cornelis van Nerven, is the facade that shows most French influence.

Antwerp, *Wolstraat 7* and *Oude Beurs 16*, Gate-framings in blue freestone, third quarter of the 17th century. In Antwerp there are a lot of so-called 'Spanish Gates'. They have been conceived in a luxuriant full-plastic Baroque style, typical for the Flemish action urge and fantasy.

Bruges, *Burg, Proosdij*, 1662-1666.
This front, alternately in sand-lime brick and blue freestone and having strongly projecting and recessing mouldings, is one of the rare examples of Rubens' Baroque in West Flanders.

Brussels, *Grote Markt,* north-west side.
From left to right: 'de Vos' ('the Fox', 1699, by architect Corneel van Nerven), 'den Horen' ('the Horn', 1696, by architect Antoon Pastorane), 'de Wolvin' ('the she-wolf', 1691, 1696, by architect Antoon Pastorane), 'den Cruywagen' ('the Wheelbarrow', 1696-1697, by architect Jan Cosyn), and 'den Coninck van Spagniën' ('the King of Spain', 1696-1697, by architect Jan Cosyn).

Brussels, *Grote Markt,* guild houses 'Hertogen van Brabant' ('Dukes of Brabant'), 1695-1698.
The segment-arched pediment and the balustrade have been added in 1772 by architect Laurent Dewez. The sculptures in the arch-field represent Peace, which brings back Trade and Agriculture; this refers to the economic and political prosperity during the Austrian government.

HOUSE FACADES IN THE 18th CENTURY

While Flemish architecture in the 16th and 17th centuries was mainly oriented to Italy, in the 18th it came more and more under the influence of the French Louis styles, but also of the severity of the Northern Netherlands and the playful Rococo of the Austrians. Around 1700, full Baroque changed into a more classical severity with a Louis XIV strain, and this became known as 'classicist Baroque'. From the middle of the century onwards, the Louis XV or Rococo style experienced quite a considerable success, and produced flourishing local variations. And after the end of the century, the Louis XVI style or classicism reached back to the pure classical forms.

The triumphant character of the Counter Reformation made way for the demand for an expression of monumentality and wealth from the bourgeoisie and the moneyed aristocracy, which was manifested in magnificent gentlemen's residences. The revival of the economy and the emergence of new industries, under the Austrian rule, created a climate favourable to the emergence of a new type of housing. In all towns during the whole of the century, numerous gentlemen's houses and stately bourgeois homes were built. Here the 'deep house' – the type of dwelling most frequently encountered since the Middle Ages – was abandoned, and the preference henceforth was for a construction worked out in breadth. The central hall and the place for the staircase determined the symmetrical layout of ground plan and facades. Under the influence of the French life-style, a great deal of interest and money was bestowed on the luxurious appointment of the *salons* with marble chimneypieces, refined panelling and painted wallpaper. Stucco ceilings concealed the cealing beams, and for these, Italian specialists were often called in.

THE CLASSICIST BAROQUE
(*ca* 1690-1740)

As had already happened in the Northern Netherlands – with the works of Hendrick de Keyser and Jakob van Campen – in the last years of the 17th century, stateliness and symmetry gained the upper hand over plasticity and dynamism, and reasonableness over unbridled fantasy. From about 1690 onwards, the Baroque elements were more and more mingled with a classical simplicity. Here the trend of the Northern Netherlands – in particular through the model books of the Amsterdam master builder Philip Vingboons – probably played a greater role than the French school. The corniced facade, sometimes with a higher central projection and punctuated by the Doric, Ionian and Corinthian order, was still frequently used up to the end of the 18th century. In particular the giant order, which in the middle of the 17th century was strongly in demand in the Northern Netherlands, arrived to enrich Flemish architecture from about 1695 (*cf* the *Grote Markt* in Brussels).

Departing from the traditional brick and natural stone architecture, the plastering of facades became fashionable, as a surrogate for natural stone. The painted facades, sometimes plain white or grey, but

Ghent, Korenmarkt, De Wapens van Zeeland (The Arms of Zealand), 1702.
This facade shows on the one hand a typical Flemish character by the play of colours and the plastic effects. On the other, the application of the colossal order testifies of an influence from the classicist Louis XIV-style.

Courtray, Lange Steenstraat, House Ghellinck, 1698.
The house was built for the mayor of Courtray, Jan Baptist Ghellinck on the occasion of his marrigage. Under the influence of the French Louis XIV-style, Flemish Baroque grew to a stricter composition at the end of the 17th century.

often surprisingly colourful, were enlivened by natural stone elements in door and windowcases. In smaller dwellings, the voluted gable with advancing and retreating top developed into a new type: the (bell or bottleneck-shaped) Dutch gable. These remained the fashion up to the end of the 18th century. We give here only a few examples of this trend in style.

The Ghellinck House (1698) in the *Lange Steenstraat* at Courtray still shows the three well-known orders in the central projection, crowned by a segmented arch

fronton. The *Arms of Zeeland* (1702) on the *Korenmarkt* in Ghent is already marked by Corinthian pilasters. The contrast worked out between brick and sand-limestone still relates to the traditional Baroque. But the use of the giant order is a novelty, here presumably under the influence of the regional Louis XIV style in Lille.

The Town Hall of Diest (1726-1731, after a design by Guillaume Kerrickx) is also built in brick with sand-limestone and blue granite worked in. After the French model, it is punctuated by flat colossal pilasters. The windows still have a traditional natural stone cross division, which fell into disuse in Flanders around 1740 to make way for the window with delicate wooden glazing bars, glazed in small panes of glass.

The Unfree Boatmen's Guildhouse (1739, after a design by Bernard de Wilde) on the *Korenlei* at Ghent is a late example of an advancing and receding gable top, still strongly Baroque in design. But the middle projection with chequered corner bands, the ornamental vase in Louis XIV style and the salmon-coloured painting bear witness to local adaptations of the fashion. And the whole looks somewhat antiquated in a time in which the first Rococo motives were emerging.

THE ROCOCO
(*ca* 1740-1765)

The Rococo style marked only a short intermezzo in the evolution of Flemish architecture. Yet there are some interesting examples of it, bearing witness to an original and creative adaptation of French elegance and grace.

The facade construction remained classical, mostly with a horizontalizing effect and a middle projection to which the asymmetrical shell-like motifs were applied only discreetly. The waving lines occurred particularly in the fillings of the frontons – mostly in stucco – and in more or less subordinate elements such as window and doorcases and the capitals of the pilasters. The scrollwork of the cast iron balcony railings above the *porte-cochère*, or the fanlight over the door also contributed to the striving for elegance. The preference was for facades that were plastered or painted in pastel colours. It is noticeable that the Rococo style in Flanders showed an outspokenly regional character.

In Antwerp, Jan Peter Baurscheit the Younger (1699-1768) was the pioneer of the local Rococo style.

Ghent, Kouter, Hotel Faligan, interior, shortly after 1755.
The wall-paintings of this drawing-room, by Emmanuel Pieter van Reysschoot (1713-1772), glorify the matrimonial love of the owners. The frivolous Rococo-style after French taste, testifies however of Flemish character.

Antwerp, *Meir, former Royal Palace,* 1745-1750. Built for the merchant Jan Alexander van Susteren, after a design of the succesful architect Jan Peter Baurscheit the Younger from Antwerp.

After being trained by his father, he was first active in the Northern Netherlands, together with Daniël Marot, a Huguenot refugee and fervent partisan of the new French style. After returning to his birthplace, he introduced a new type of facade, in which the central division is worked out as a slightly marked protrusion with typical rocaille motifs. We mention here four mansions in Antwerp built from designs by J.P. Baurscheit the Younger. The du Bois de Vroylande House (*ca* 1740), 20-24 *Lange Nieuwstraat*, has a central higher door trave. The monumentality of this doorcase – plastically accentuated also by the sculptures flanking the balcony – shows a specific Antwerp characteristic of the Baroque period (also present in Jordaens' House). On the front facade of the Hotel du Bois (1748), 94 *Lange Nieuwstraat*, the second floor is worked out as a *mezzanino*, a recurring characteristic of Baurscheit's later works. Here the luxuriousness of the plastically treated door projection is even more marked.

For Jan Alexander van Susteren he built a splendid mansion on the *Meir* (1745-1750). The main facade, built completely of Bentheimer stone, shows some new features: the axis is crowned by a stylish crest on the Dutch model, and the form of the strongly horizontalizing attic gains a significance all of its own. That the whole of this house bears witness to great luxury and aristocratic distinction is proved by the fact that, in the French period it came into the possession of the Imperial Crown domain, in the Dutch time it was the palace of William I, and with the emergence of the Belgian Kingdom it was made available to the princes.

On the same street, the *Meir*, we find the *Osterriethhuis* (1749) built for the dowager Régine-Thérèse van Susteren-du Bois. It is at the present time the headquarters of the *Bank van Parijs en de Nederlanden*, and of the Mercator Fund. Here too the central, deepened doorcase is crowned with a monumental crest. The cornice is interrupted by fan-shaped garret windows, which finish off the otherwise sober side walls.

Like Antwerp, Ghent also had its own Rococo style. There David 't Kindt (1699-1770) was the most important architect. Influences both from the French school and from the Austrian Rococo here led to an indigenous hybrid style, in which the undulating shell motifs still

Ghent, *Koningstraat, Hotel van Oombergen,* 1746.
This magnificent mansion, designed by David 't Kindt who lived in it himself, is one of the best succeeded examples of the Rococo style of Ghent. Pay attention to a local speciality: the thresholds of the top windows are decorated with lambrequins, which have been cut in stone; a *trompe l'oeil* effect which gives, together with the rocaille-motifs, an elegant liveliness to this symmetric front.

Antwerp, *Osterrieth House,* 1749.
It was built for Lady Régine-Thérèse van Susteren-du Bois after design by Jan Peter Baurscheit the younger.

bore signs of Rococo excess. A heavier and higher extended middle projection, jutting out or turning inwards with curved fronton, characterizes several facades of rich mansions. The facades are mostly plastered, adorned with Corinthian pilasters of the giant order, but sand-limestone facades are also found. Among the extensive series of patrician residences we mention: Hotel van Branteghem (1739) on the *St-Baafsplein*; Hotel van Oombergen (1746) in the *Koningstraat*, now the seat of the Royal Academy of Dutch Language and Literature; Hotel Serlippens (1752) in the *Hoogpoort*; Hotel de Coninck (1755) in the *Jan Breydelstraat*; Hotel Faligan (1755) in the *Kouter*; and the front facade of the Hotel d'Hane-Steenhuyse (1768) in the *Veldstraat*. Of these, the Hotel Faligan is probably the most luxurious example, particularly for its enchanting interiors with wall paintings by the Ghent artist Pieter-Norbert van Reysschoot (1738-1795).

The Rococo style was in fashion in most Flemish towns in the middle of the 18th century, if not always in the same outspokenly exuberant manner as in Antwerp and Ghent. The facade of Our Lady's Hospital (1772) in Audenarde is a late example of this. It came into being at the moment when classicism was being introduced everywhere.

Opheylissem, *Norbertine Abbey, prelature,* about 1780.
The simple side-facade, designed by architect Laurent Dewez, has been erected in brick, while the three accentuating risalites have been cut in sand-lime brick.

CLASSICISM
(*ca* 1770-1795)

Inspired by the French Louis XVI style, the stricter arrangement of the facade came into fashion once more. Here the newly-instituted academies – first in Brussels, Antwerp and Ghent, later in the other important towns – played a stimulating role. This happened under the relatively successful government of Charles of Lorraine (1748-1780), governor-general of the Austrian Netherlands and brother-in-law of Empress Maria Theresa. Through the power of attraction of the Court, Brussels now became the focal point of artistic life in Flanders, where classicism flourished earlier than elsewhere.

Architecture had less of a local character than had been the case in earlier style periods, but was more directed at the international spreading of French classicism. Theoretical works by the Frenchman Jacques François Blondel (*De la distribution des Maisons de Plaisance et de la Décoration des Edifices en Général,* 1737) and of his pupil, the Liegeois Jean-François Neufforge (*Receuil élémentaire d'Architecture,* 1757-1765) played a considerable part in this.

The house facades of the mansions are in general broadly horizontalized and stiffly arranged, often of the giant order, with an accentuated middle part crowned by a triangular fronton. Decorative elements underline the architectural power. For the first time, there is a departure from the deep-seated Flemish tradition of a desire for ornamentation inspired by the Baroque.

Here we shall limit ourselves to some examples in Brussels. On the site of the old *Hof van Nassau*, destroyed in a fire, a new palace was built for Charles of Lorraine (now part of the Royal Museums of Fine Arts). In 1767, the semicircular wing was built after a design by the Court architect Jean Faulte (1726-1766),

still reminiscent of the Rococo, but with a decorative vocabulary such as Ionic pilasters, coats of arms and mythological figures, pointing to the Louis XVI style.

The *Koningswijk*, with the *Koningsplein* and the *Warande*, were designed about 1774-1780 and executed by the French architects N. Barré and Gilles Barnabé Guimard, and the Austrian court gardener Joachim Zinner. The *Koningsplein* reflects French examples (Paris, Nancy, Reims) and is dominated by the temple front of St Jacob-op-de-Koudenberg (by B. Guimard and L.-J. Montoyer). Grandeur and symmetry, as well as perspective views both from the square to the old town lying below, and to the *Warande*, are the basic principles of this homogeneous part of the town. The facades of the Palace of Nations (the present Houses of Parliament) also bear witness to the same spirit. Architecture and town planning are also combined in the Brussels *Martelaarsplein* (1775) by the town architect Claude Fisco (1736-1825). The facades on the square, based on classical models – with the temple fronts, the architrave with triglyphs and metopes, the rams' heads, the attic running through – radiate a cool but harmonious effect.

Finally we turn out attention to the influence of classicism on the country, both for religious architecture and for manor-houses. The Liegeois Laurent Dewez (1731-1812), court architect to Charles of Lorraine, made a study trip to Italy from 1754-1757, where in particular the works of Palladio made a great impression on him and influenced his own creations. His most important works came into being in Wallonia, but also in Flanders he designed several religious buildings, such as St Saviour's Church in Harelbeke (1769-1773) and the Norbertine Abbey of Opheylissem in Brabant, in which the facade of the prelate's house (*ca* 1780) is one of the most classical buildings in Flanders. Here the strongly horizontal character is interrupted by two slightly projecting elements, and above all by the central volume. The cupola which crowns this imposing middle part was rebuilt in the 19th century by Balat, on the model of the Pantheon in Rome.

Leeuwergem Manor-house (*ca* 1745), in the neighbourhood of Audenarde, shows signs of classicism in the construction, the strictness of which is lightened by Rococo ornamentation. In particular the park, laid out in the manner of Le Nôtre, is unique in Flanders.

Wannegem-Lede Manor-house (1784-1786), also in the Audenarde region, was designed by the Court architect Guimard, who came from Lorraine. The architecture of this house is strongly influenced by *Le Petit Trianon* in Versailles (1755) by Jacques-Ange Gabriël (1698-1782) and by the already mentioned theoretical works of J.F. Blondel and J.-F. Neufforge. The main facades are characterized by the theatrical porticos with Corinthian columns. These facades are arranged on the basis of the square and the golden section, which clearly illustrates the rational in this late 18th-century architecture. Together with the ochre-coloured plastering, they strongly recall Palladian villas. This manor-house is one of the purest examples of international rationalism in Flanders.

Brussels, Wetstraat, the Palace of Nations, 1779-1783.
This building, which was designed by architect Barnabé Guimard, is one of the purest classicist examples in the capital.

Wannegem-Lede, *Castle*, 1784-1786.
This classicistic castle was designed by court-architect Gilles Barnabé Guimard for Baron Baut de Rasmon. The central risalite with four Ionic columns and the corniche with four vases, can be described as square. The two side-wings are conceived according to the golden section.

375

Sculpture

When thinking about Flemish art in the 17th century, one's first thoughts are always about the painters. They hold a very privileged position in the artistic hierarchy. In contrast, 17th-century sculpture in the Netherlands has long been passed over in a historical consideration of culture as being of lesser importance. This unjustifiable attitude is gradually changing as a result of the growing interest in the rich heritage of Flemish sculpture and the study of this art form.

At the beginning of the 17th century the prospects for Flemish sculpture were not that brilliant. Obviously the limited economic activity during this period was partly responsible for this. Renaissance elements were incorporated into the products of craftsmen *ad nauseam*; and the first attempts of the important Flemish family of sculptors, the de Noles, to free themselves from this tradition were successful only after Rubens had returned from Italy in 1608. Rubens acted as a powerful catalyst in the development of Flemish sculpture because of his interest in it, his friendship with artists like Frans Duquesnoy and Hans van Mildert, and especially because of his own designs for sculptures. He also succeeded in spreading his Baroque ideas, brought from the south, which were expressed quite well in the works of art on which he worked in close collaboration with the sculptor; *e g* the high altar (before 1621) of St Carolus Borromeus' Church in Antwerp, in which the characteristics of the high Baroque are already discerned.

However, it is normally not possible for a single figure to influence the whole direction of art. The cultural background and the economic context also play an essential role in the development, and make it possible for a genius such as Rubens to realize his talents. The main spiritual impetus driving cultural and intellectual activity during the 17th century was the Counter Reformation. The troubled times of the two waves of iconoclasm (1566 and 1581/82), when most of the churches and monasteries were damaged, were followed by the rehabilitation of Catholicism. Church interiors were renovated in accordance with the liturgic prescriptions of the Council of Trent. This renovation was expressed in the Baroque style, the art form which was most suitable to reinstate the former power and vitality of the Roman Catholic Church, to fan religious fervour, and to bring the lost sheep back to the fold. One could therefore argue that in broad terms the Baroque was the art of the Counter Reformation. This style, with its large gestures, opulence and surfeit of decoration, corresponded to the spirit of the Church triumphant, and could be used as a means of expressing its ideas. It was because of the wealth of statues that churchgoers could identify most intensely with the liturgy, and that the sacraments of the eucharist and confession – which had been threatened by Protestantism – were once more the centre of attention.

An impressive number of richly decorated altars, con-

Antwerp, Interior of the St Carolus Borromeus' Church.
The high-altar in marble was designed by Rubens and sculptured by Hans van Mildert (before 1621). The painting is by Cornelis Schut.

The Fall, ivory high relief, 27.2 × 12.6 cm, Frans van Bossuit, date unknown. Munich, Bayerisches National-Museum.
The ivory-carving of van Bossuit was mainly noted because of the book of Mattijs Pool, which was published in Amsterdam in 1727 and in which seventy engravings represent the works of the sculptor. Characteristic for van Bossuit is – between others – the background which is elaborated with stipple prints.

fessionals, communion-rails and pulpits were commissioned for churches, both in the cities and in the smallest villages. Initially these were conceived in a fairly decorative style, but gradually this church furnishing began to incorporate statues, which were often life-size. These sometimes grandiloquent creations usually fitted in very well in Gothic churches; and obviously also in the interiors and on the facades of the new Baroque buildings. Tombs were also an important part of church furnishing. These compositions, usually in marble, were designed and made by the same artists who made the wooden furnishings. The material used depended on the commission, and no longer signified a distinction between sculptors and wood-carvers. Finally, the almost total disappearance of polychromy should be mentioned. There was one exception to this in the more traditional centre of Malines, *viz* Nicolaas van der Veken, who painted most of his wooden statues.

Secular art was also given a new lease of life. In fact, the Baroque style was the obvious form of expression for exalting the absolute power, bestowed on the ruling monarchs by the grace of God. The Archduke and Archduchess Albrecht and Isabella (1598-1621), resident in Brussels, were known for their love and patronage of art; and many noblemen and wealthy burghers wished to have their portraits made and to possess works of art in their homes. However, in contrast to the large religious output, very little secular sculpture has survived; particularly during the second half of the 17th century the production was poor. This might have been due to the departure in 1656 of Leopold William, the Austrian regent, who was widely known for his love of art. It may have been one of the reasons why many Flemish artists left for Paris. There was certainly plenty of work available on secular commissions at the French court in Versailles.

Flemish artists also emigrated to other countries, a phenomenon that was not restricted to the 17th century. In the first place, this can be explained by their talent, but also by the international character of the art. The lack of commissions at home, and obviously the military troubles which embittered the cultural climate, made many gifted artists try their fortunes elsewhere. Thus many sculptors travelled to Rome to study the art of antiquity, as well as the work of the celebrated Italian masters. Some, like Frans Duquesnoy, actually settled in Rome. After the Renaissance Rome continued to exercise a strong attraction to artists; this city was even an essential link in the process of artistic perfection. The presence of a significant number of Dutch and Flemish artists is shown by their corporation, *de Bent*, which was founded in about 1623 and which included Flemish sculptors as Artus Quellinus the Elder, Michiel van der Voort, Frans van Bossuit *etc.*

The divine Love and the profane Love, plaster low relief, 92 × 50 cm, Frans Duquesnoy, about 1635. Rome, Galleria Spada.
The divine Love beats the profane Love and forces the fallen Amor to be silent. Another Amor is triumphantly holding up a laurel-crown, price of the immortal victory. The Amors resemble those of the antique sarcophagi.

There are three distinct steps in the development of Flemish Baroque: early, high and late Baroque. The term 'early Baroque' refers to the period from 1608 – Rubens' return from Italy – to about 1640. The sculptors of this period freed themselves from the Renaissance with some difficulty. A few of them occasionally succeeded in transposing Rubens' dynamic forms into their sculptures, but only when they worked together with the great painter himself. In other works the compositions remained frontal and symmetrical without inner tension or feeling. In addition, the works were conceived in a decorative style and were usually not very well integrated in a whole.

The single exception to this was Frans Duquesnoy. His style displays such a maturity and such a radical departure from the 1620's that he deserves to be classified among the high Baroque artists, far ahead of his contemporaries.

Hans van Mildert (Königsberg 1588 – Antwerp 1638) settled in Antwerp in 1610. Although a contemporary of Frans Duquesnoy, his creations should be considered as the last examples of the production of the Renaissance workshops; frontal, symmetrical, linear and static. However, when he worked with Rubens, as on the high altar in St Carolus Borromeus' Church in Antwerp – sometimes called 'the marble temple' – he succeeded in expressing the Baroque style in his sculpture. Van Mildert sculpted the vivacious marble angels on either side of the seated Mary, based on Rubens' design for the frame with Corinthian pillars. The rigid style of his youth made way for a more emotional statement.

A large number of sculptors were trained in Antwerp. The brothers Robrecht (Utrecht before 1570 – Antwerp 1636) and Jan de Nole (Utrecht before 1570 – Antwerp 1624) were enrolled in St Luke's Guild of Antwerp, although they worked all over the country. In 1604 Robrecht was appointed "*maistre sculpteur à la cour de leurs Altèzes*" by the Archdukes Albrecht and Isabella. Jan's son Andries de Nole (Antwerp 1598-1638) secured important commissions, *e g* for St Rumoldus' Church in Malines, where he completed with his father and his uncle nine of the twelve sandstone statues of the apostles. The composition was still more or less frontal, and there is little trace of any inner feeling. The gestures are rigid and the garments reveal little or nothing of the anatomy. Nevertheless, the representation is more lively and this is expressed mainly in the ornamentation.

A second family of sculptors from Antwerp was the van den Eyndes. The most important member, Huibrecht van den Eynde (Antwerp 1594-1661) worked predominantly in the churches and abbeys of Termonde, Averbode and Duffel. His most successful composition is the *Faustina group*, probably dating from 1636, in the *Maagdenhuis* in Antwerp. This sculpture heralded the high Baroque period with its lively and natural character. It was exceptional for a work of sculpture dating from before about 1640 to radiate such a charming spontaneity. The standing Infant is stretching his chubby little arms to be taken onto a lap. As the

St Suzanne, statue in marble, at natural size, Frans Duquesnoy, 1633. Rome, Church of St Maria di Loreto al Foro Traiano.
This statue, which has clearly been influenced by antique examples, was ordered to Frank Duquesnoy by the Roman guild of bakers. Originally, St Suzanne was standing at the right side of the altar, and she was pointing with her finger at it.

Maagdenhuis was originally an orphanage for girls, the group can also be interpreted as an allegory of the care of orphans.

At this time the leading Flemish sculptor, Frans Duquesnoy (Brussels 1579 – Livorno 1643) was working in Italy. Frans was trained by his father, Hieronymus Duquesnoy the Elder (? Quesnoy *ca* 1570 – Brussels 1641/42), who had a busy workshop in Brussels.

He received his most important commissions from the Archdukes and from the Church. His monumental sacramental tower (1604) in three sections in St Martin's Church at Alost is one of his few surviving works. This tabernacle still displayed the influence of the style of Cornelis Floris, though some of its statues already incorporated elements of the Baroque. However, Hieronymus owes his fame to the small figure of *Manneken-Pis* (1619), which adorns the fountain on the corner of the *Stoofstraat* in Brussels.

In 1618 his son, Frans, left for Rome with the financial support of the Archdukes Albrecht and Isabella, who awarded him a grant for two years. With his friend Nicolas Poussin, the French painter, he travelled to the Eternal City to study the works of Titian as well as the art of the antiquity, which he followed. He was strongly influenced by the great Italian Baroque sculptor, Bernini (1598-1680), although his work is essentially different. His classical and sensitive work exercised a lasting influence on the sculptors of the Netherlands. His tempered, restful Baroque style was taken up in the Netherlands, for example, by his younger brother Hieronymus, and by Quellinus the Elder, who both trained under him. He was also known as *Frans de Vlaming* or *il Fiammingo*, which shows that he was proud of his Flemish origins. His biographers also called him *fattore di putti*, because no other sculptor manufactured the small cupids more charmingly or spontaneously. This is possibly still the most relevant aspect of Duquesnoy's work. His reliefs with allegorical and mythological tableaux, in which the *putti* play a central role, are certainly among the loveliest and most successful achievements of 17th-century sculpture.

However, his fame was established far beyond Italy in particular by two large scale monumental works, *viz St Susanna* (1633) for Santa Maria di Loreto al Foro Traiano in Rome, and *St Andrew* (1640) for St Peter's in the Vatican. The statue of St Susanna was commissioned by the Roman bakers' guild. Although the classical influence is clearly visible in this beautiful work of art, a number of unusual features testify to Duquesnoy's original and talented creativity: the soft sensitivity of the imposing and idealized expressions, the unclassical hip movement compensated for by the turn of the head, and the dynamic composition. This life-size marble statue immediately became an overwhelming success. Even during Duquesnoy's own lifetime copies and replicas of this work, especially of the head, could be admired in a number of collections. Already before the marble Susanna was placed in the church, Pope Urban VIII commissioned the Flemish artist to produce a design for a statue of St Andrew for St Peter's Basilica. Probably the pope had seen the maquette of *St Susanna*, and had been so enthusiastic that he immediately invited Duquesnoy to work on the decoration of the transept of the basilica. Eventually, four artists – three Italians and *il Fiammingo* – each made a five metre high marble statue for the four niches. *St Andrew* was unveiled in 1640 and was immediately hailed as the very gem of the basilica. The well-balanced composition of this monumental statue, the wonderful way it dominates the space, the classical representation of the superb torso, the deeply felt humanity and the lively folds in the garments, make this one of the masterpieces of sculpture. News of this magnificent creation spread rapidly: a few weeks after it was unveiled, Rubens wrote a passionate letter to Frans Duquesnoy, bewailing the fact that he was too old to travel to Rome; but adding that he hoped to be able to greet him "in his beloved Flemish fatherland"...

Unfortunately Duquesnoy was never to see his country again. From 1639 he was sounded about the post as *sculpteur du roi* by Louis XIII King of France; while Nicolas Poussin, also still in Rome, was proposed for *peintre ordinaire du roi*. Duquesnoy hesitated for a long time before accepting this offer, but Richelieu staked everything on persuading '*Monsieur François le Flamand*'. An apartment was furnished for him in the Louvre, and his fee amounted to 3,000 pounds for a period of three years. In addition, he received 2,000 ducats for his journey. He was asked to train twelve young sculptors, in other words, to found an academy of arts in Paris. Few artists can boast of receiving such a wonderful contract. However, he did not enjoy the fruits of it, as he died in Livorno after a short illness on 19th July 1643; already on his way to France, accompanied by his brother Hieronymus.

One might ask to what extent Frans Duquesnoy should still be considered a Flemish sculptor. In fact, his whole career took place in Italy. However, although he never returned to his fatherland, his indirect influence in Flanders – even on subsequent generations – was very important. The role he played in the training of his brother and the talented artist Artus Quellinus the Elder, was so considerable that he cannot be omitted from any survey of Flemish sculpture.

Many other sculptors could be mentioned for the period of the early Baroque, but these fall outside the scope of this section. However, one event of great artistic importance, in which many artists cooperated, merits discussion, *viz* the Triumphal Entry of the Cardinal-Infant Ferdinand of Austria in Antwerp in 1635. Obviously these historical occasions required temporary decoration.

But after this particular celebration, the *Pompa introitus*, a monumental memorial book was published depicting all the great decorations, the triumphal arches and so-called theatres, with excellent illustrations by the painter Theodoor van Thulden. The designer of the decorative programme was Pieter Paul Rubens. The triumphal arches and theatres which had been erected along the route of the stately procession were truly festive pieces of architecture, constructed partly of durable materials. On no other occasion architecture, sculpture and painting were combined in such a dynamic fashion. The extraordinary project – full of complicated profane allegories complemented with examples from religious iconography – can be considered as the epitome of Flemish Baroque. In addition to well-known painters such as Jacob Jordaens and Hendrik van Balen, numerous sculptors worked on the realization of the project. Huibrecht van den Eynde and Hans van Mildert, who were mentioned above, were involved; as well as Sebastiaan de Neve, Forci Cardon, Erasmus Quellinus and many others.

HIGH BAROQUE

Although the classification of art history into strictly separate periods often does not coincide with reality, the year 1640 is generally considered as an acceptable starting point for the high Baroque period. This does not mean that the year applies to each artist individually. A case in point is the artist, Frans Duquesnoy, whose work displayed all the characteristics of high Baroque in the 1620's. In 1639 Artus Quellinus the Elder returned from Rome and settled in Antwerp; and in 1643 Hieronymus Duquesnoy the Younger (Brussels 1602 – Ghent 1654) came back to Brussels, after having worked in Spain and Italy, which he had left together with his brother Frans. He soon became famous in his native city, and barely two years later (in 1645) he was

Mausoleum of the bishop Antoon Triest, white and black marble, at natural size, Hiëronymus Duquesnoy the Younger, 1651-1654. Ghent, St Bavo's Cathedral.
The bishop, who is represented very realistically, lies half erected on the tomb, beside which two *putti* carrying an hour-glass and a turned-down torche symbolize time and death. The image of the Virgin Mary is related to St Suzanne of Frans Duquesnoy. The text below on the cartouche is the last will of the deceased.

appointed "architect, *statuarius* and sculptor of the court" to replace the sick Jacques Francart. He was not remunerated for this post, although he did enjoy the privileges and exemptions attached to this honorary function.

As the court sculptor, Hieronymus Duquesnoy made in 1650 the marble portrait of the *Archduke Leopold William* (Vienna, Kunsthistorisches Museum,) the son of Emperor Ferdinand II. This Austrian archduke was the regent of the Southern Netherlands from 1647-1656, and he owned an enormous art collection which went to the Viennese court when he died. The bust of the arrogant monarch testifies to Duquesnoy's keen and observant eye and his love of the realistic portrayal of detail; although the work is in no way comparable with the portraits of his contemporary, Artus Quellinus the Elder. The work was signed with the sculptor's full signature and dated, this became increasingly common, especially for portraits. It shows that sculptors were becoming more aware of their individual value and no longer considered themselves as craftsmen, but as free artists.

Hieronymus' style was similar to that of the tempered Baroque of his brother Frans. There was no pathos and there were no grand gestures, but lots of life and movement. His most important achievement was the rather eclectic mausoleum of Bishop Antoon Triest (1651-1654) in St Bavo's Cathedral in Ghent. The prelate had already contacted Frans Duquesnoy – who was still in Italy – at an earlier date with regard to the monument. It is thought that the two *putti* with an hour glass and an inverted torch, symbols of impermanence and death, were based on the terracotta models made by Hieronymus' brother. In the Italian 16th-century style, the bishop is in a semi-recumbent position on his tomb; between a statue of Our Lady, reminiscent of Frans Duquesnoy's *St Susanna*, and one of Christ, inspired by Michelangelo's *Christ* in Santa Maria sopra Minerva, both in Rome. The head of the prelate is portrayed in surprisingly realistic detail. The relation between the three marble figures is explained in the inscriptions. Hieronymus failed to complete the work, because he was arrested by the city magistrate for the crime of sodomy. The court condemned him to be strangled and burnt on the *Korenmarkt* in Ghent.

The most remarkable and original Flemish sculptor of the 17th century, Artus Quellinus the Elder (Antwerp 1609-1668), was a member of a family that produced a number of different artists: five sculptors, two painters and one engraver. His father, the *antycksnyder* Erasmus Quellinus the Elder (bishopric of Liege *ca* 1584 – Antwerp 1640), was particularly well-known for his decorative pulpit (1635) in the chapel of St Elisabeth's Hospital in Antwerp, which still bore strong Renaissance traits. The young Artus was apprenticed to his father in the customary fashion. He went to Rome at a relatively late stage in 1634 to complete his studies at the source. He studied classical antiquity under his compatriot, Frans Duquesnoy. The latter was more familiar with the classical statues than anyone else, because from 1621 (when his grant from the Archdukes terminated) he had to earn his living partly by restoring

Venus, high relief in marble, more than natural size, Rombout Verhulst, about 1652-1658.
Amsterdam, Town Hall, now Royal Palace.
In her left hand, Venus, goddess of love, is holding the apple which she has won by her beauty, while Cupido and Anteros are really locking her in. The pigeon is the bird of Venus and the swan is the animal which pulls her wagon.

Apollo, high relief in marble, more than natural size, Artus Quellinus the Elder, 1650-1653. Amsterdam, Town Hall, now Royal Palace.
The sun-god Apollo, crowned with laurels, patron of the arts, has killed Python, the monstruous dragon, with his lightning arrows. This relief can be found in the southern gallery.

Greek and Roman sculptures. In 1640 Quellinus was accepted as a master in St Luke's Guild in Antwerp. His oldest known work was made there, and already bore the marks of his strong personality, *viz* the coat of arms with the motto *Labore et Constantia* on the gable of Plantin-Moretus Museum, then the residence and workshop of the well-known family of printers and publishers (16th–19th centuries). Two dynamic Rubens' figures, a realistic Hercules and a richly draped lady, represent labour and constance. The same client, Balthasar Moretus, also commissioned a number of portraits of his ancestors, which were placed in the inner courtyard of Plantin's House.

These various works from Quellinus' youth, dating from 1639-1644, reveal the change in Baroque. Rubens' forms had permeated sculpture. Feelings were no longer imposed from outside, but radiate from the statue itself. The compositions bear witness to a harmonious balance between realism and sensitivity – and this applies to both the statues and the decorative motifs. The statue of Mary, known as the *Ara Coeli,* made by Quellinus for St Michael's Cathedral in Brussels, emanates a natural stateliness, as well as sensuousness. The play of light on the surface of the work is infinitely subtle, and it can be considered as a characteristic example of Flemish Baroque.

However, the most illustrious commission he secured came from Amsterdam. He was commissioned to make the sculptures to decorate the inside and outside of the new Town Hall on the Dam, now the Royal Palace, of which Jacob van Campen (1595-1657) had been the architect. This was an opportunity to design a major secular work, and he gave free rein to his almost profane love of nature. He designed large-scale marble reliefs, free standing statues and ornaments, which constitute an extraordinary unity without any trace of mannerism or artificiality. The most remarkable part of this building is the *Vierschaar*, or public court of law. Three reliefs depict tableaux of judgments from the past, by way of example, including the judgment of Solomon; interspaced between four caryatids, half-naked figures of women symbolize punishment and shame. The presence of these four statues, almost trembling with life, could be rather surprising in a room which was used only to pronounce the death sentence.

The Tribunal, public court of justice, Artus Quellinus the Elder, 1650-1652. Amsterdam, Town Hall, now Royal Palace.
The Tribunal was only used for death sentences. The caryatids in marble, which represent punishment and shame, support the architrave of the bench on which the ministers of justice were seated. The town-clerk sat on the chair at the right.

All the decoration in this creation, with its allusions to classical antiquity, is related to Amsterdam. Quellinus was able to design this elaborate and complicated iconographic programme as a well-balanced whole, because of his controlled expression combined with an exceptional technical skill and a classical vision of sculpture. It is not possible to describe the Town Hall fully here, though when it was completed, the building was sometimes called the eighth wonder of the world. The sculptor from Antwerp took more than fourteen years (1650-1664 or 1665) to complete this commission, for which the city council of Amsterdam paid him handsomely. He was one of the few artists to become wealthy. In addition to his own home in Antwerp, he had a *huis van plaisantie* (country seat) in Hoboken. He also enjoyed many privileges in the city of Amsterdam, such as an allowance for housing. Conscious of his elevated cultural task and his eminent artistry, he asked to be exempted in his native city from all the professional, civic and Church obligations laid down by St Luke's Guild and the city council.

383

It goes without saying that his achievements in Amsterdam were not undertaken single-handedly. Quellinus brought a number of sculptors with him from Antwerp, and trained others in Amsterdam. His most important Flemish co-workers in Holland were Rombout Verhulst and Artus Quellinus the Younger, his cousin. Rombout Verhulst (Malines 1624 – The Hague 1698) stayed in the Republic and breathed new life into sculpture in the north. His works include the warm and realistic *Venus*, goddess of love, in the northern gallery of the Town Hall. The signature RVHVLST can be found at her feet. Another work of outstanding quality is the monumental tomb of A. Clant in Stedum Church near Groningen, with a sculpture of the deceased sleeping peacefully on the sarcophagus.

In Antwerp many sculptors worked in Quellinus' workshop. In fact, this was the case in most important workshops, as a well-known sculptor was usually unable to complete large commissions on his own. Quellinus paid so much time and attention to training his apprentices, that it is sometimes difficult to determine whether a work of art from his workshop was made by him, or by one of his colleagues or pupils.

His originality and creativity, as well as his brilliant technical skill, can most easily be assessed from the terracotta models which he designed for the Town Hall. These clay models, which he made personally and which were submitted to the clients for their approval, were considered to be very important. This is quite evident from the fact that a large number of these designs have survived and can now be seen in the Rijksmuseum, Amsterdam. An example is the tympanum of the facade, on which the sea gods paid homage to the virgin of Amsterdam. This model – with a graticulation or a background of squares to facilitate the extension of the sculpture on the stone tympanum – included naiads, Tritons, dolphins and hippocampi, which are modelled in an amazingly lively way and seem full of energy. The

Artus Quellinus the Elder, *Tympane of the front of the town-hall of Amsterdam, now Royal Palace*. Terracotta model, high-relief, 95 × 410 cm, ca 1651. Amsterdam, Rijksmuseum (in loan by the Municipality of Amsterdam).

Portrait-bust of Johan de Witt, marble, 95 cm, Artus Quellinus the Elder, 1665. Dordrecht, Museum.
The portrait of Johan de Witt, Grand Pensionary of Holland, is the last work which Quellinus made at Amsterdam. The psychology of the statesman is depicted with astonishing realism. Quellinus made in the spring of 1665 a one-day trip to The Hague, with the only purpose of modelling the hand to life.

Confessional stall, oak, Pieter Verbruggen the Elder, about 1659. Antwerp, St Paul's Church.
The St Paul's Church contains ten four-figured confessional stalls. Beside the small room for the priest are two angels, who are each holding a paternoster and a crown of roses. At the left of the compartment of the confessant is St Joseph. Biblical scenes are depicted on the continuing wooden panelling.

385

Pan has Amors dancing, terra-cotta high relief, 33 × 69 cm, Lucas Faydherbe, before 1640, Brussels, Museums of Art and History.
Pan is standing in the middle of the dancing Amors, just as Venus was in Rubens' Feast of Venus. The early work of Faydherbe is impressed with Rubens' Baroque, and reflects the same liveliness and delicacy.

first plan for this tympanum was a drawing by Jacob van Campen, but the definitive dynamic arrangement owes everything to the talent and lyrical vision of Quellinus.

In addition to the Town Hall of Amsterdam, Artus Quellinus the Elder also completed other commissions of which the portraits are especially noteworthy. Thus the bust of *Johan de Witt*, now in the museum of Dordrecht, can be considered as one of the most beautiful examples of this genre. It is a masterpiece of realism, and at the same time, of psychological insight. Quellinus did not view this councillor in his official capacity, but as a human being.

Another productive family of artists from Antwerp was the Verbruggens. Pieter Verbruggen the Elder (Antwerp 1615-1686), the founding father of this dynasty, married Artus Quellinus' sister, and also worked together with him; although Verbruggen's ideas about art were more traditional than those of his brother-in-law. The impressive high altar in St Paul's Church in Antwerp was made by him. As prescribed in the Council of Trent, the altar was conceived as the focal point of church liturgy. The monumental construction of black and white marble, approached by broad, majestic steps, dominates the Gothic choir and the whole interior of the church. The statues for this imposing altar were made by his son, Pieter Verbruggen the Younger (Antwerp ca 1640-1691). There is much confusion between father and son, their achievements and their pupils, because they worked together in the same workshop.

Two other Antwerp sculptors deserve a mention as important exponents of Flemish high Baroque: Mattheus van Beveren and Ludovicus Willemssens. Mattheus van Beveren (Antwerp *ca* 1630 – Brussels 1690), a sculptor and a mint cutter, was particularly well-known for the extreme elegance and virtuosity of his ivory carving. Although his work was not signed, it can be attributed to him on the basis of the similarity with his monumental achievements. The prominent family, Thurn und Taxis, commissioned him to make the mausoleum of Lamoraal Claude-François, count of Thurn und Taxis, in Our Lady-of-Zavel's Church in Brussels (1678). This tomb is an allegorical composition in which a gracious female figure, symbol of Virtue, and a grisly greybeard, symbolizing Time, are drawing towards themselves a cartouche with the coat of arms of the deceased. On top of it there is Fame, trumpeting forth the immortal glory of the deceased. This charming white marble group contrasts theatrically with the black background; and the figures are so finely chiselled that it is difficult to believe that they are marble statues.

Like his colleagues, van Beveren was commissioned for a number of large-scale works by the Church authorities of various Flemish cities, including Ghent, Termonde, Brussels, and obviously Antwerp. He was also often commissioned for secular works; for example, the Queen of England now has in her collection a beautiful monument dedicated to the glory of the reign of James II. Hercules and Minerva are crowning the

Memorial monument of James II, King of England, ivory, ebony, silver, tortoise, 180 × 72.3 cm. Mattheus van Beveren, about 1685-1690. Windsor Castle, Collection of Queen Elisabeth II.
Van Beveren was known for his virtuoso ivory-carving, and he was charged with important assignments from abroad. On this showpiece, on which he is supposed to have spent six years, the King of England is represented as Grand-Master of the Order of the Garter, while Hercules and Minerva crown him.

seated monarch, who is represented as the Grand Master of the Order of the Garter. Above him is a statuette of St George and the dragon. Van Beveren used ivory for the human figures, silver for the three lions, and tortoise-shell and ebony for the architectural background. It is not clear under what circumstances this ornament was commissioned. Did James II come into contact with van Beveren during his first period of exile in 1679, or was it commissioned from England during his reign from 1685-1688?

Ludovicus Willemssens (Antwerp 1630-1702), who often worked together with van Beveren in the churches of Antwerp, would also have secured commissions from the English court. According to tradition, Willemssens was the court sculptor of the English king William III, who owned a number of very beautiful statues of his. All this shows that the relations between England and Flanders (and more particularly between London and Antwerp) were extremely fruitful after the 1680's; in fact, a number of Flemish sculptors went to work in England, including Artus III Quellinus and John Nost.

Nicodemus Tessin the Younger, a Swedish architect who visited Holland and Flanders in 1687, called Willemssens "the best, and especially good at sculpting models". Tessin, a great admirer of Italian Baroque and often rather scathing about artists from the Netherlands, obviously had a high opinion of Willemssens' work, and this was by no means unjustified. The latter's terracotta model for *St Martin of Tours*, now in the Museums of Fine Arts in Brussels, is impressive in a monumental way. The way in which the saint holds his gracefully draped cloak is reminiscent of van Dyck's painting for St Martin's Church in Zaventem.

The contrasts used by Willemssens emphasize the emotivity of his figures, which reveal some degree of mannerism and thus anticipate the 18th century. This mannerism is clearly expressed in his works for St James's Church in Antwerp, such as the pulpit and the marble statue of God the Father in the Eucharist Chapel. These two works are dynamic and expressive, but at the same time they have been executed in a surprisingly well-balanced and sophisticated manner.

Apart from Antwerp, where undoubtedly the majority of the sculptors were working, the Malines school also flourished from the second half of the 17th century. The most prominent figure here was Lucas Faydherbe (Malines 1617-1697). From 1636-1640 this gifted sculptor worked in Rubens' workshop. He was the only one of his generation to have such close and lasting contacts with the master from Antwerp, who was full of praise and affection for him. Hence his early work was profoundly influenced by Rubens, whose estate included a number of ivories by Faydherbe. The model – or replica? – in terracotta of one of these works is in the Museums of Art and History in Brussels. The work itself, an ivory relief on which the god Pan makes the cupids dance, is in the Prado, Madrid. The composition is based on Rubens' *Feast of Venus* (Vienna, Kunsthistorisches Museum), though Venus is replaced by Pan in the relief. The sensitive relief of the sprightly cupids is brilliantly executed. Faydherbe also proved himself to be a skilled architect and completed the Beguinage

Church in Malines, begun by Francart, although his contribution consisted mainly of the sculptural decoration. Faydherbe's sophisticated instinct for assimilation enabled him to adapt his work more successfully to the Gothic interiors of churches than some of his fellow sculptors. One striking example of this is the high Baroque portico altar of St Rumoldus' Church in Malines. Notwithstanding the pure Baroque composition crowned by the monumental marble figure of the patron saint (height: 3.75 m), this work is totally integrated in the Gothic choir. It was commissioned by Archbishop Andreas Cruesen, just like his tomb in the same church (1660). This mausoleum, placed in the choir, shows the bishop kneeling and looking at the resurrected Christ. Chronos is behind the prelate, ready to wield the scythe of death; while a winged cherub seems to be attempting to restrain him. The composition, which is characteristic of Flemish Baroque, illustrates the struggle between the terror of death and the Redeemer. The heavy contrast between the realistic and peaceful representation of the archbishop, and the dramatic intensity of the Rubenslike Chronos is also typically Baroque.

Apart from Faydherbe, a number of other sculptors from Malines, all pupils of his, deserve a mention. They include Frans Langhemans (Malines 1661- ca 1720), who worked mainly in Dusseldorf and Cologne; Jan van Delen (Brussels or Malines? – Brussels 1703), Faydherbe's son-in-law and colleague, whose career took place mainly in Brussels; and finally Jan-Frans Boeckstuyns (Malines ca 1650-1734), who worked principally in his native town, unlike the others.

Two figures who fall outside this emotive sphere of Rubens' influence in Malines were Rombout Pauwels, also known as Pauli (Malines 1625 – Ghent 1692), who was greatly influenced by Frans Duquesnoy in Rome, and Nicolaas van der Veken (Malines 1637-1709). The latter, who already belonged to the late Baroque period, carved a number of fine and serene wooden saints' statues, which radiate a tranquil piety. The sober polychromy, which he applied himself, added even more expressiveness, as we remarked earlier.

LATE BAROQUE

In about 1680 there was a change in the forms used in sculpture; they became more expressive, exuberant and theatrical. The solid and muscular bodies of the high Baroque period made way for long and elegant figures, which often seem to defy the laws of gravity. The play of light and dark is full of contrasts and nervous tension, extending the pictorial effect to its furthest limits. The representatives of the late Baroque period were still mainly sculptors from Antwerp. The most important of these was Artus Quellinus the Younger (St Trond 1625 – Antwerp 1700). With his cousin Artus Quellinus the Elder, who influenced him very strongly, he decorated the Town Hall in Amsterdam. In 1654 he returned to Antwerp, where he worked in a number of churches with other colleagues. A brilliant example of this was the high altar (1685) in St James's Church in Antwerp, for which Ludovicus Willemssens and Guillielmus Kerricx chiselled the monumental wreathed columns and Quellinus – who was in charge of the work – made the dramatic statue of the exalted St James. The theatrical effect of depth in the composition is enhanced by the different levels of the marble columns. In 1667 the Jesuits of Bruges commissioned Quellinus to make a pulpit for their church, now St Walburga's parish Church. The iconographic programme was made by the Jesuit Willem Hesius. The graceful caryatid of Faith, which supports the pulpit and stands completely on its own, is quite unique. Some years later, but before 1682, the church council of St Saviour's Cathedral commissioned Quellinus to make the marble statue of God the Father. It crowned the roodloft, which was moved to the west wall in 1935 for liturgical as well as aesthetic reasons. The figure of God the Father is very similar to that of St James in Antwerp and betrays the influence of the classical Laocoon group. The billowing and flapping garments lend an unparalleled dramatic emotion to this statue.

However, not all his creations are so emotionally charged: he also excelled in charming representations, as can be seen *e g* in the frolicking cherubs on the communion-rail of St Rumoldus' Church in Malines; and even more in the graceful statue of *Santa Rosa of Lima* in St Paul's Church in Antwerp. The outlines are so delicately sculpted that they seem to fuse with the surround, creating an almost illusory shape.

Guillielmus Kerricx (Termonde 1652 – Antwerp 1719), like many of the figures discussed above, came from a family of joiners and sculptors. Little is known about his early career. Some authors believe that he spent some time in Paris, but there is no documentary evidence for this. The public registers of St Luke's Guild in Antwerp (the *Liggeren*) reveal that twenty-six apprentices were enrolled under him.

He furnished a number of churches in Antwerp, usually in cooperation, and he also secured an important commission for St Gertrudis' Church in Louvain. His marble mausoleums for the two abbots, A. de Fourneau and A. de Pallant (1714-1715), are decidedly naturalistic. The two prelates are portrayed very realistically, kneeling on a sarcophagus and placed at either side of the high altar (also designed by Kerricx, but unfortunately destroyed during the Second World War).

However, his best work is indisputably the bust of *Maximilian II Emanuel of Bavaria*, governor of the Netherlands (1694), commissioned while Kerricx was the deacon of the guild. The representation of the courtly atmosphere and the interpretation of the subtle haughtiness inherent in this ambitious man, are very close to the French court style, and make this marble bust unique in Flemish art. In this portrait Kerricx anticipates the characteristics of the Rococo style.

Another sculptor whose career ran parallel to that of Kerricx was Pieter Scheemaeckers the Elder (Antwerp 1652 – Arendonk 1714). At the age of ten he was apprenticed to his uncle, Pieter Verbruggen the Elder, and in 1674-1675 he became a free master together with Kerricx. Scheemaeckers was probably the most pictorial and original of the Antwerp sculptors. His work is

Maximilian II Emanuel of Bavaria, marble bust, height 117 cm, Guilliemus Kerricx, 1694. Antwerp, Museum of Fine Arts.
The spiral composition, the contradiction between the stiff armour and the elegant coat, and the casual pose of the hands are features which anticipate the Roccoco.

characterized by attractive small-scale bas-reliefs, which are often found in juxtaposition with his large compositions. The picturesque and even playful character of these reliefs, in which landscape plays an important role, is typical of his style. He secured commissions throughout Flanders, and nineteen apprentices were enrolled under him in Antwerp. His pithy creativeness and fertile imagination were so popular, that he also made designs for other sculptors.

The style of his monumental tombs was characteristic of the late Baroque. Some of his works even anticipate the coming of the Rococo period, for example, the tomb of the Marquis F.M. del Pico de Velasco (1698, now in St James's Church in Antwerp). The spiralling composition of this courtly, rather precious figure would certainly be at home in the 18th-century spirit. These often dramatically laden, allegoric tombs of Scheemaeckers can be considered as precursors of 18th-century English and French funereal sculpture. This is partly explained by the presence of his two sons, both sculptors working abroad: Pieter the Younger in London, and Hendrik in Paris.

The most productive sculptor of this period was Hendrik Frans Verbrugghen (with *h*, Antwerp 1654-1724), the son of Pieter Verbruggen the Elder, and a nephew on his mother's side of Artus Quellinus the Elder. He completed his apprenticeship in the customary fashion in the parental workshop *den Draeck* on the *Steenhouwersvest*. He was enrolled as a free master in St Luke's Guild in Antwerp at the relatively late age of twenty-eight. Like Faydherbe, he worked as an architect, sculptor and ornamentalist; a tradition which was later continued by Guillielmus Ignatius Kerricx, the son of the above-mentioned Guillielmus Kerricx, and by Jan Peter van Baurscheit the Younger. A great deal is known about his activities, because a large number of his drawings and designs have survived. These documents are invaluable for the study of civil architecture and interior decoration, particularly as so many art treasures have disappeared over the years. They are also an inexhaustible source of information for the study of church furnishings; and they witness the unusual indus-

High altar, white and black marble, Artus Quellinus the Younger, Ludovicus Willemssens, Guillielmus Kerricx, 1685. Antwerp, St James' Church.
Several sculptors from Antwerp rendered assistance to this splendid Baroque altar with torsional pillars. The general supervision rested with Artus Quellinus the Younger. He himself chiselled the emotional statue of St James, who is assumed into heaven.

try and originality of this artist, who nevertheless was always running out of money. Some 18th-century authors claimed that he took to drinking. At the end of his life, Verbrugghen's house and belongings were impounded and publicly sold. Whatever the truth of the matter is, he was extremely active from 1678 until his death in 1724. He made innumerable altars, pulpits, confessionals, communion-rails, tombs and church portals.

A typical example of his fertile imagination and skilful technique is the pulpit (1700) in the former Jesuit Church, now St Peter and St Paul's Church in Malines. The figures of the four continents, each with their symbolic animal, carry the pulpit which is adorned with four medallions of Jesuit saints. Two trumpeting Bernini-type angels support the sounding-board. This 'didactic' composition represents the spread of faith throughout the world, and the medallions with portraits remind believers that God's word is being given here from a Jesuit pulpit. What makes this work so attractive is the homogeneous combination of worldly (both ethnographical and zoological) and spiritual elements.

All these figures of the late Baroque period are characterized by an exaggerated emotional expression. The movements become restless, and the serenity of expression is replaced by looks of ecstasy and pathos. The Counter Reformation had entered a new stage: it no longer functioned as a 'war machine' against Protestantism, but gradually lapsed into a sentimental affectedness and a weak piety. In fact, this viewpoint continued to be expressed in sculpture even in the 19th century. It was supported by the traditions of the guilds, which were often passed on from father to son. In addition, the lack of a strong leading personality such as Artus Quellinus the Elder forty years earlier, is very noticeable. As a result religious sculpture, like painting, was increasingly tending towards hollow rhetoric and empty pathos.

Secular art developed differently. It was mostly not so grandiloquent and hollow, but rather responded to a more classical Baroque tendency, which gradually merged into a tempered Rococo style. This controlled approach characterizes the work of, *inter alia*, Gabriel Grupello (Geraardsbergen 1644 – Ehrenstein near Aix-la-Chapelle 1730), who was apprenticed to Artus Quellinus the Younger in Antwerp and later worked for a time in Paris. There he encountered the designs of Charles Le Brun for the chateau and park of Versailles. In 1673 he was enrolled as a master in the Guild of the Four Crowned in Brussels, where he had a prosperous workshop. There are a number of remarkable works dating from this period, such as the *Wall fountain with sea gods* and the two garden statues of *Diana* and *Narcissus*, which are in the Museums of Fine Arts in Brussels. The marble fountain – unfortunately the accompanying grotto has not survived – was commissioned from Grupello in 1675 by the Seafishmongers' Guild in Brussels. The basin, supported by three dolphins, served as a wine cooler for the assembly hall. In the shell there are two sea gods with a double fishtail, and at the top there is a lively *putto*, seated on a fiery seahorse. Rubens' influence is very much in evidence, as is that of Artus

Quellinus the Elder; and even of Bernini, if one thinks of the fountain in the Piazza Barberini in Rome.

The two garden statues of *Diana* and *Narcissus* were commissioned for the palace park of Lamoraal Claude-François, the count of Thurn und Taxis, situated in the vicinity of the actual Zavel, Brussels. The degree of expression of these statues – reminding of some French examples – as well as their majestic characteristics, undoubtedly contributed to the fact that Grupello was appointed first as a court artist of Charles II of Spain in 1688, and subsequently of the elector, John William of the Palatinate in 1695. He moved to Dusseldorf, where he produced a series of life-size statues, portrait busts and medallions for the elector and members of his family. His best known work in Dusseldorf is the statue of John William on horseback. When his patron died, he returned to Brussels, and was appointed court sculptor for Emperor Charles VI.

PRECLASSICISM

Grupello is an artist with a special place in art history. It is difficult to compare his work with that of his contemporaries, such as Michiel van der Voort, Joannes Claudius de Cock and Jan Peter van Baurscheit the Elder. The work of these three figures was predominantly characterized by the dualism between the stormy Baroque style and controlled classical forms. As usual the pendulum of culture saw to the regular alternation of balanced moderation and exalted exaggeration, of thought and feeling. The thoughtful Fleming reacted to the emotionality of the late Baroque by pursuing a controlled and sober style. This could be considered to anticipate neoclassicism, which evolved during the second half of the 18th century. The renewed interest in the art of antiquity and in the temperate, peaceful Baroque style of Frans Duquesnoy, as well as the influence of the ornamental Louis XIV style, played a decisive role in the evolution of preclassicism.

Michiel van der Voort (Antwerp 1667-1737) was enrolled as a master in St Luke's Guild in 1689-1690. Apart from his journey to Italy to complete his studies, van der Voort was very productive in his native city. This all-round artist worked during the fifty years of his career alternately in the late Baroque and in the classicistic style. His series of twelve Baroque apostles for the nave of St Paul's Church in Antwerp is particularly impressive. Each statue is integrated in a carefully elaborated whole. There are clearly visible similarities to Michelangelo's *Matthew* and to Frans Duquesnoy's *Andrew*. The angels of Mount Calvary next to the same church were directly inspired by the angels of Bernini on the Ponte Sant'Angelo in Rome.

The classicistic and rather academic tendency of van der Voort's work is reflected in the majestic and sober tomb with an obelisk for Prosper-Ambrosius, the count de Precipiano (1709), in St Rumoldus' Church in Malines. On the other hand, the pulpit in the same church – although it was designed twelve years later for the Premonstratensian Church of Leliëndaal – was com-

Wall-fountain with sea-gods, white and black marble, height of bottom part 118 cm and of top part 87 cm, Gabriel Grupello, 1675. Brussels, Museums of Fine Arts.
This fountain was ordered in 1675 by the guild of fish-mongers of Brussels. The basin, which is supported by dolphins, was meant to cool the wine. Two sea-gods with double fishtails are sitting in the big shell. The water springs from the nostrils of the impetuous sea-horse and from the right breast of the seagoddess in the basin.

pletely in the late Baroque tradition. It is difficult to recognize the structure of the pulpit through the excess of decorative elements in the composition. A sort of *tableau vivant* depicts the conversion of St Norbert, the Calvary and the temptation of Adam and Eve. The crown of the tree of Good and Evil forms the sounding-board. The whole scenario is depicted with such realism in the opulent decoration that no one could remain unaffected by this work of art. Naturalistic pulpits like this one were made in Flanders until the 19th century.

In addition, M. van der Voort was a skilled portraitist, though only a few of his portraits have survived. The one of *Abraham Genoels* was modelled very realistically and witnesses a deep psychological insight.

Another transitional figure was Joannes Claudius de Cock (Brussels 1667 – Antwerp 1735). This sculptor was apprenticed in the workshop of the Verbruggens,

The Church, terra-cotta design, 80 cm, Jan Peter van Baurscheit the Elder, after 1718. Antwerp, St Carolus Borromeus' Church, Museum for Ecclesiastical Art.

This female figure, symbol of the Church, is the design for the supporting-figure of the pulpit, which was erected in the St Carolus Borromeus' Church at Antwerp after the fire of 1718. The angel with the flashes of lightning and shield strikes down a dragon with seven heads. The pulpit is an example of the transition period from late Baroque to classicism.

and was commissioned by the king-stadtholder William III to decorate the renovated *Prinsenhof* in Breda. In addition to his work as a sculptor, this versatile artist wrote a didactic poem for his pupils. In this treatise he expressed his admiration for classical art and for Frans Duquesnoy. In addition, he pleaded for a more tempered style. This was actually expressed in his own sculptures, fascinating because of the dualism which is always present. On the one hand, he was not able to escape entirely from the late Baroque influence of the Verbruggens; on the other he saw himself as a defender of classicism. This duality is clearly visible in the choir stalls that de Cock made in 1713 for the priory of Korsendonk, part of which is now in the collegiate St Peter's Church in Turnhout. The allegorical figures of women are partly carved in a powerful late Baroque and partly in accordance with the controlled classicistic norms, while the fantastic decorative motifs already anticipate the Rococo style.

Another talented sculptor of this period was Jan Peter van Baurscheit the Elder (Wormersdorf 1669 – Antwerp 1728). He was an important person, honoured with a number of titles, including the sculptor for the king, and later for the emperor – in 1723 he described himself as 'statuarius et architectus Caesaris'. His period of greatest activity was in Antwerp where he was trained, though he also succeeded in securing commissions in Holland and Zeeland. A number of his fine portrait busts have survived, including one of *Philip V*, king of Spain (1700-1701), sculpted at the expense of the city of Antwerp; it can now be found there in the Museum of Fine Arts.

His most important commission in his native city was undoubtedly the restoration of St Carolus Borromeus' Church after the fire of 1718, which destroyed the nave and tribunes. He sculpted wainscottings, confessionals, a communion-rail, the pulpit and the organ case; in which he managed to combine late Baroque and classicistic elements very harmoniously. This dualism is best expressed in the majestic classicistic female figure under the pulpit, versus the late Baroque cherubims hovering around her. In contrast, the ornamentation was clearly influenced by the Louis XIV and the French Regency style. It was probably due to the cooperation of his son, Jan Peter van Baurscheit the Younger (Antwerp 1699-1768) that so many French elements such as shells, rosettes, ribbons and net-work, as well a graceful Corinthian capitals are used in the decoration. The young Jan Peter came early into contact with the buildings designed by the French architect Daniel Marot in Holland. After the death of his father he devoted himself predominantly to architecture.

In this context it is worthwhile to observe a typical phenomenon of the beginning of the 18th century. While a certain decadence could be detected in sculpture, civil architecture was becoming emancipated and was flourishing. Gradually the architects were imposing their will on other artists in areas where formerly the sculptors had dominated the architecture, as in the case of L. Faydherbe and H.F. Verbrugghen.

Another sculptor who generally remained faithful to the late Baroque style, though at the same time strove for a more sober and controlled grasp of form, was Alexander van Papenhoven (Antwerp 1668-1759). He was apprenticed to Artus Quellinus the Younger and became a master in 1698/99. As a *Bildhauer Gesell* he might have worked together with the son of his master, Thomas Quellinus, who had settled in Copenhagen. One of his more successful works was the marble communion-rail, made for St Ignatius' Chapel in St Carolus Borromeus' Church in Antwerp. Another worthwhile work was the most elegant *Venus and Cupid* in Sanssouci Park in Potsdam.

The statue of the blessed *Jordanus*, which he sculpted for the Calvary near St Paul's Church in Antwerp (the former Predicant Church) is nobly executed. This Calvary is an extraordinary 'museum' of statues dating from the first half of the 18th century. Most Antwerp sculptors mentioned above collaborated on this unique work, which was the initiative of two Dominican monks. There are nine bas-reliefs and sixty-three life-size statues in a garden with an artificial rock. The whole work is a gigantic *tableau vivant* in stone, a fascinating insight into popular devotion in Antwerp.

A number of lesser known sculptors are not listed here because of lack of available space. We will therefore limit ourselves to two figures whose work has not received much attention. Guillielmus Ignatius Kerricx (Antwerp 1682-1745), the son of Guillielmus, who was referred to above, collaborated on the Calvary. He was also known as a playwright, painter and architect; although he did not excel in the latter two fields. Pierre Denis Plumier (Antwerp 1688 – London 1721), known as Denis Plumier in England, was apprenticed to Ludovicus Willemssens and continued his studies in Paris. In 1713 he moved to Brussels, where he made the statue of a recumbent river god, *The Scheldt* (1715), for the inner courtyard of the Town Hall; as well as the naturalistic oak pulpit, now in Chapel Church, depicting Eliah in the desert (1721). He was invited to work in London by Lord Cadogan in about 1717. There he designed, *inter alia*, the model for the mausoleum of John Sheffield, Duke of Buckingham (1721), which was preferred to that of James Gibbs. This monument was erected in Westminster Abbey with the help of Peter Scheemakers the Younger and Laurent Delvaux, one of Plumier's former pupils. Despite his early death, Plumier breathed new life into English sculpture. This new style was developed further by the young Scheemakers and Delvaux, who worked for a number of years as partners, and were commissioned to make a considerable number of tombs and busts for English clients.

ROCOCO

In about 1730 a new style emerged from Baroque: the Rococo style. At the end of the 17th century a few Flemish sculptures anticipated this new style, such as the *Portrait of Maximilian II Emanuel of Bavaria* by G. Kerricx. Moreover, a large number of Flemish artists spent part of their apprenticeship in Paris, where they obviously came into contact with the *rocaille* elements of the Louis XIV style. It should be pointed out that in the Southern Netherlands the Rococo style differed from the uncommon elegance and light playfulness of Rococo in Germany and Austria, and was also in no way related to its enchanting variant of the French court. In the Low Countries this art form was middle class and charming: sculptors followed contemporary examples or copied classical works, in most cases treating the pictorial surface in a very skilful manner, without ever achieving the bravery and whimsicality typical of Rococo. This can probably be explained on the one hand by the preclassicistic influence which can be discerned in many works of art at a very early stage, even before the beginning of the 18th century; and on the other hand, by the serious nature and the common sense that characterize the Flemings. Or is the classification used for the international evolution of style inadequate, if applied in this case. Did 17th-century Baroque have such a blinding effect – particularly in Antwerp, the cradle of the movement – that no other current was powerful enough to stand up against it; or was there no new trend in Flanders because there was no leading personality or pioneer to inspire this?

Moreover, the restless and controversial 18th century cannot easily be identified with one or more successive chronological styles. A number of different styles flourished side by side and evolved simultaneously. The individual artist could make a choice from them, depending on the nature and location of his commission.

One typical representative of this kind of art was Walter Pompe (Groot-Lith/North Brabant 1703 – Antwerp 1777), a pupil of Michiel van der Voort. At this time artistic activity in Antwerp was reawakening and attracting some artists from North Brabant and Holland, who could find no other way to become skilled in their profession except by coming to the Southern Netherlands. Pompe settled in Antwerp where he was very productive; his work was quite popular even during his own lifetime. He was especially esteemed for his finely carved figures of Christ in box-wood and ivory, but also for his pithy and sometimes mannered small statues with a more secular character. These works, often made in terracotta, gave Antwerp Rococo its own cachet. However, their charming elegance is typified by a rather middle-class character. On the other hand, Pompe's altars reveal to what extent the Baroque style continued to have an effect on the production of church furniture. The influence of van der Voort is evident, and Pompe's style is almost classical, particularly in his larger statues. Nevertheless, he lacks the dynamic quali-

Mount Calvary, composition of sculptures, at natural size, several co-workers, first half of the 18th century. Antwerp, St Paul's Church.
An artificial rock was built in the garden of St Paul's Church, and one can reach the Holy Grave by the so-called Angels' Lane. The first statue at the entrance pictures St Jordan, sculptured by Alexander van Papenhoven.

393

Justitia, terra-cotta, group of statues, gilt, 107 cm.
In her right hand, Justitia is holding the sword of justice and in the other the balance. On the richly ornamented consoles two *putti* are sitting; the one with a flame, symbol of the purifying force, in his lifted hand; the other with the Roman fasces, which personifies the power over life or death, pressed close to its body. At the bottom a small medallion depicts the self-portait of W. Pompe.

ty of his master and is technically far weaker.

His Antwerp contemporary, Jacob Jozef van der Neer (Antwerp 1718-1794) was a worthy artist. In his work the line between Baroque and Rococo is difficult to draw. His church furnishings are in the Baroque style but the decorative motifs are Rococo. The same applies to Adriaan Nijs (Antwerp 1683 – Temse 1771) and his son Filips Alexander Nijs (Temse 1724-1805), who both worked in Temse Church. It was mainly the son who produced some opulent Rococo works, particularly communion-rails; as in Stekene, Zele and Bazel.

Rococo also flourished in West Flanders. Hendrik Pulinx (Bruges 1698-1781), who became a master at the tender age of seventeen, had a chequered career. He started as a sculptor, but also worked as an architect and opened a manufactory producing fine ceramic ware in the city of his birth, for which he designed quite decorative models. His church sculpture was predominantly in the late Baroque style. His two marble mausoleums for the bishops H.J. van Susteren and J.B. de Castillion, now in St Saviour's Cathedral, were undoubtedly inspired by that of bishop Triest in Ghent. However, Pulinx

quickly started to apply the Rococo style to his brilliantly modelled earthenware.

His fellow-citizen, Pieter Pepers (Bruges 1730-1785), worked mostly in stone. He succeeded in combining the opulence of Baroque and the elegance of Rococo in his own harmonious style. Yet another artist from Bruges, Paul Louis Cyfflé (Bruges 1724 – Brussels 1806), was particularly well-known as a modeller of Rococo figurines in the ceramic manufactory of Lunéville.

NEOCLASSICISM

As mentioned earlier, it is virtually impossible to classify 18th-century Flemish sculpture into well-separated styles. On the one hand, the dynamic spirit of Flemish Baroque continued to be very influential – even in the neoclassicist Godecharle – and on the other, neoclassicism was beginning to emerge strongly. Flemish artists evolved between these two styles. During the second half of the 18th century classicism gradually gained the upper hand. Sculptors rejected dramatic representations and strong emotions, to pursue a certain fixedness and more subtle and aristocratic forms.

Like Rococo, neoclassicism did not develop in the same way in Flanders as in other countries. Nevertheless, it can be discerned at an early stage in the work of H.F. Verbrugghen and some of his contemporaries. Moreover, it can be detected implicitly in the work of most artists throughout the 18th century, and like in Rococo style, often only in the decorative motifs. It was only with the arrival of Godecharle that neoclassicism in the Southern Netherlands had a true representative at an international level. Antwerp was the metropolis of sculpture until about 1750; when it was temporarily replaced by Ghent, Bruges and Nivelles, and particularly by Brussels, which assumed a leading role as the city where the Austrian governors were in residence. It was no longer the Church that awarded the most important commissions; but many came from the court, as well as from the nobility and the rich burghers.

During the 18th century sculptors often secured the largest commissions from abbeys. A single master would often work in two totally different styles in the same church. This was the case with the creations of Theodoor Verhaegen (Malines 1701-1759) for the former Abbey Church in Ninove, a parish church since 1813. These works are clearly characterized by the powerful and exuberant, Rubens-like Baroque, but also by the more controlled expression of classicism. His training by M. van der Voort and J.Cl. de Cock was obviously a contributory factor. One of his *tours de force* is the confessional (1736) in this Abbey Church. This colossal and excessively ornamental construction, in which the various architectural elements can no longer be distinguished, is exuberantly theatrical. The companion piece to this work, made in 1739 by the Brussels sculptor Jacques de Koninck (Brussels 1703 – after 1777), who was a pupil of Jacques Bergé, is just as bombastic. In contrast, Verhaegen's picturesque wooden reliefs for the same church are far more sober and classical. About ten years earlier another sculptor from Brussels, Jan Baptist van der Haeghen (Brussels 1688-1738) had already erected the Baroque, scenographic main altar in the same church, with tribunes, colonnade and two groups of statues.

Jacques Bergé (Brussels 1696-1756) was another sculptor whose work is characterized by the same dualism. He worked mainly in Ninove and Heverlee and is sometimes confused with his Bruges colleague Jacobus Berger, who died in 1701. Bergé studied in Paris in the workshop of Nicolas Coustou, and later in Rome. He sculpted a naturalistic pulpit for the Ninove Abbey Church, now in St Peter's Church in Louvain, which is closely connected with the picturesque pulpits by M. van der Voort. Bergé's extensive commissions (high altar, pulpit, choir stalls, confessions *etc*) for Park Abbey in Heverlee are also executed in a classicistic style. Not many of his secular works have survived, but

Confessional stall, oak, Theodoor Verhaegen, 1736. Ninove, Church of Our Lady-at-Ascension.
The seat of the father confessor is sided by two angels at natural size: the angel with the balance personifies Justice, the one with the chalice personifies Faith. The repentant saints Mary Magdalene and Peter kneel on big volutes while an enormous risen Christ accepts the penance of the sinners.

the best known is the *Minerva Fountain* (1751) on the *Grote Zavel* in Brussels.

During this period the above-mentioned Laurent Delvaux (Ghent 1696 – Nivelles 1778) became a prominent figure. After a period in England he went to Rome, where he studied the art of the antiques and the statues of Bernini. He then settled in Nivelles. From 1733 to his death he was the court sculptor to the Austrian regents. In his rich career he managed to assimilate the stylistic complexity of the 18th century, and to develop a personal mode of expression in which neoclassicism played a major part. It is difficult to classify him as belonging to a particular style, especially as many of his figures – such as those on the pulpit of St Bavo's Cathedral in Ghent – still belong to the dynamic late Baroque style. His best works include the well-balanced and sculptural statues which clearly reveal his admiration of the antiques. A good example is the marble *Hercules* (1770) of the monumental staircase in the former palace of Charles of Lorraine in Brussels.

During the second half of the 18th and even during the 19th century, there were still some meritorious sculptors working in this style. Karel van Poucke (Dixmude 1740 – Ghent 1809) studied at the Academy in Bruges and then travelled to Paris and Italy. With the support of Charles of Lorraine, he secured a number of official commissions there. Eventually he settled in Ghent, where he designed and executed the neoclassicistic mausoleum of bishop G.G. van Eersel (1782-1784) in the Cathedral. The figure representing Faith on this tomb was sculpted by Frans Jozef Janssens (Brussels 1744-1816). This sculptor was appointed as *Inspecteur des travaux publics de l'Administration centrale de Belgique* during the French occupation in 1792. In this capacity he was able to save many statues on the facades of the guildhalls on the *Grote Markt* in Brussels from being destroyed. In Antwerp, Daniel Herreyns, who became a master in 1751, was working for Plantin-Moretus' House, where he sculpted a series of door panels inspired by the elegant ornamentation of the Louis XVI style. Cornelis de Smedt (Termonde 1742 – Antwerp 1815) was particularly well-known for the two monumental confessionals which were commissioned in 1779 by the Premonstratensians for Averbode Abbey Church. Their architectural construction is in the neoclassicistic tradition, though the statues rather reflect Baroque characteristics.

In contrast with the increasingly strong pressure of neoclassicism, a number of sculptors continued the Baroque tradition. Peter Valckx (Malines 1734-1785) and even Jan-Frans van Geel (Malines 1756 – Antwerp 1830) still made church furnishings which can hardly be distinguished from 17th-century works.

The most remarkable figure of neoclassicism was Gilles Lambert Godecharle (Brussels 1750-1835), one of Delvaux' pupils. His work was very similar to French neoclassicism. This is not surprising because in 1772 the young Godecharle was apprenticed to Jan Pieter Antoon Tassaert in Paris, an emigré from Antwerp. That very year he was admitted to the *Ecole académique*, as a result of the patronage of Pigalle. He was able to afford his time spent abroad because of an annual pension paid by Charles of Lorraine.

Godecharle travelled to Berlin, London and Rome, before settling permanently in Brussels. There he designed the facade of the Palace of Nations (1781) and decorated the Royal Castle in Laken (1784). The influence of Clodion and Bouchardon cannot be denied in these creations. Although his work is often extremely decorative, it is not without charm. His astonishingly skilful terracotta models with *putti* reveal his great talent but also his playful character particularly well. The superficiality of the idealized forms and the sometimes rather piquant character of their subjects are both often found in the Romantic salon statues, which were so popular with the 19th-century bourgeoisie.

FLEMISH SCULPTORS ABROAD

It was common to find that artists emigrated fairly early on, *viz* from about the middle of the 17th century, a period of economic and political crises. In Flanders commissions were difficult to find and many sculptors went abroad to seek their fortune. The influence that they had on schools in other countries, and which they experienced in turn in these new surroundings, has up to now only been studied sporadically. However, many Flemish sculptors secured commissions from foreign clients – Frans Duquesnoy is just one case in point – and they often ran influential workshops such as, for example, Artus Quellinus the Elder in Amsterdam.

Martin van den Bogaert (Breda 1637 – Paris 1694), known as Desjardins in France, already worked in Paris before 1661. He was trained in the workshop of Pieter Verbruggen the Elder in Antwerp and he secured most of his commissions, predominantly secular works, from the court of Louis XIV. The same happened to Gérard van Opstal (Brussels 1605 – Paris 1668) who was involved in the foundation of the *Académie Royale des Beaux-Arts* in Paris to replace the deceased Frans Duquesnoy. He was particularly known for his ivory *à-jour* reliefs depicting playful cherubs and bacchanalia. Philippe de Buyster (Antwerp 1595 – Paris 1688) and Sébastien Slodtz (Antwerp 1655 – Paris 1726), who were both trained in Antwerp, also emigrated to France, attracted by the opportunities for employment, and participated in the decoration of a number of palaces that were being built. Both were given the title *sculpteur ordinaire du roi* and enjoyed the accompanying privilege of living in the Louvre. Three of Slodtz' sons also became prominent sculptors in France.

Frans van Bossuit (Brussels 1635 – Amsterdam 1692), a carver of ivory, left for Italy after his training in Brussels and Antwerp. He moved to Amsterdam before 1685 and worked there until his death. His ivory reliefs, inspired by both secular and religious themes, can be found all over the world. Rombout Verhulst, who worked together with Artus Quellinus the Elder on the Town Hall in Amsterdam, also settled permanently in the Dutch Republic. Jan Baptist Xavery (Antwerp 1697 – The Hague 1742), the court sculptor to William IV, lived in The Hague. He also worked for some time in

Kassel, where he was employed by the Count of Hessen.

Josse de Corte (Ypres 1627 – Venice 1679), also known as Giusto Le Corte or Le Court, had a great influence on art in Venice, where he lived from 1657. His work was predominantly religious and represented the style of Bernini in Venice.

The son of Pieter Scheemaeckers the Elder, Pieter Scheemaeckers the Younger (Antwerp 1691-1781) – usually referred to as Peter Scheemakers – emigrated to London. Artus III Quellinus (Antwerp 1653 – London 1686), also known as Arnold Quellin, was another Flemish sculptor to make his career in England. His younger brother, Thomas Quellinus (Antwerp 1661-1709), ran a busy workshop in Copenhagen for twenty years where a number of sculptors, mainly from Antwerp, worked together.

There has been some mention of the cooperation between Denis Plumier, Laurent Delvaux and Peter Scheemakers in London. However, the leading figure in this was undoubtedly Michael Rysbrack (Antwerp 1694 – London 1770). After his schooling by M. van der Voort he went to London in about 1720. The influence of the city of his birth can be detected in all his work. Without him and without Peter Scheemakers – his rival, who regularly tried to poach on his commissions – English 18th-century sculpture would have developed very differently.

Nicholas Millich, who became a master in St Luke's Guild in Antwerp in 1657/58, spent most of his life in Sweden, where his major work was to carve the statues which decorated the staircase and hall of the Royal Palace of Drottningholm. He returned regularly to Antwerp, where he designed in 1680 a new tower for St Paul's Church, which had been badly damaged by fire in 1679.

Guillielmus de Grof(f) (Antwerp 1676 – Munich 1742), also trained in Antwerp, was probably first employed by Louis XIV, but then worked in Munich for Maximilian II Emanuel of Bavaria from 1714. Some of his work displays Louis XIV and Rococo characteristics. One of his masterpieces portrays the elector Maximilian Jozef; a silver votive statue which is now in Altötting Pilgrimage Church.

During the 18th century Paris continued to act as a magnet for Flemish sculptors. Jacob Verberckt (Antwerp 1704 – Paris 1771), a pupil of M. van der Voort, was very active in the decoration of the chateau of Versailles and other royal residences. He too was given the title *sculpteur ordinaire du roi*; and his Rococo ornamentation was extremely successful. Jan Pieter Antoon Tassaert (Antwerp 1727 – Berlin 1788) also went to work there though he did not stay long; because as a result of the mediation of Jean d'Alembert, he was invited by Frederick the Great to settle in Berlin. There he took up the running of the royal workshop for sculpture, in which he taught the important German neoclassicistic sculptor, J.-G. Schadow. Pierre François Lejeune (Brussels 1721-1790) entered the service of the Duke of Württemberg in Stuttgart, after having worked in Rome for many years. Amongst other things he designed models for the famous porcelain manufactory of Ludwigsburg. Pieter Antoon Verschaffelt (Ghent

Sepulchral monument of John Sheffield, Duke of Buckingham, marble (detail), at natural size, Denis Plumier, Laurent Delvaux and Peter Scheemakers, about 1721. London, Westminster Abbey.
The sepulchral monument, designed by Plumier, is made by his former pupil Delvaux and his partner Peter Scheemakers. The composition of the lying duke and his mourning widow at his feet, meant an innovation in the English sepulchral sculpture, which would later often be copied.

1710 – Mannheim 1793) was a very productive artist. One of his works is the bronze Archangel *Michael* at the top of the Castel Sant'Angelo in Rome. In Mannheim he entered the service of the elector Charles Theodore of the Palatinate, who commissioned him to renovate and decorate a number of palaces and to landscape the gardens. In his native city Ghent he realized the mausoleum of bishop Maximilian Antoon van der Noot in St Bavo's Cathedral. Thus he was continuing the 17th-century Flemish tradition by which many sculptors also worked as architects, and concerned themselves with anything remotely or closely to do with the embellishing of a building.

Painting

It is common knowledge that Flemish painting flourished in the 17th century, predominantly in Antwerp, the leading art centre in the Southern Netherlands. This is mainly attributable to one important decision, taken less than a month after the conquest of Antwerp. On 6th September 1585 the municipal council ordered the guilds and crafts to install new altars in place of those which in 1581, during the Calvinist administration, had been either demolished or removed from the churches. In some cases this order was complied with almost at once, but most of the guilds and crafts, on account of the lack of the necessary financial resources, were only able to give effect to it in the course of the 17th century. But the promulgation of this order, which moreover was backed by the church authorities, set in motion a process by which one new guild or craft altar was erected in Our Lady's Cathedral practically every year – as well as in many other churches. Among them was the altar of the Harquebusiers' Guild, for which in 1610-1614 Rubens painted his famous triptych, the central panel of which depicts the *Descent from the Cross*. The chapters and church councils also rose to the occasion, providing new high altars all of which were adorned by impressive altarpieces. And the religious brotherhoods (*confréries*) had likewise altars set up in their chapels.

A considerable stimulus to this was given by the Twelve Years' Truce, enacted on 9th April 1609, which ushered in a period of peace and economic revival. When eventually – after many years of misery and uncertainty – peace was restored, even greater energies than before were devoted to repairing the churches which had been damaged or neglected during the religious disturbances in the previous century; and at the same time to investing them with new works of art. It is also noteworthy that most of the monastic orders, which in 1585 had established themselves afresh – or for the first time – in the cities, erected new churches shortly after the inception of the Twelve Years' Truce, to supersede the small chapels which they had been using up to then. The most outstanding example is the Antwerp St Carolus Borromeus' Church, built between 1615 and 1621, for which Rubens – in addition to two large altarpieces – made together with his assistants no less than 39 ceiling paintings.

Thus as early as 1585, but particularly after 1609, a considerable need arose for altarpieces and religious scenes. In addition, their commissioners wanted them to comply not only with the prescriptions and spirit of the Counter Reformation, but also with the sense of monumentality, demonstrative realistic portrayal and decorative flourish, which characterized the new artistic concepts of their time. Here is to be found the explanation why Baroque (which had sprung up in Italy, with Caravaggio and the Caraccis around 1590-1600) was generally adopted and further developed in the Southern Netherlands, mainly under the impulse of Rubens. This was in contrast to what happened in Holland, where Calvinism banned artistic representations from church buildings, so that painting was geared (as regards both subjects and dimensions) to the requirements of bourgeois interiors. A more intimist, highly original form of art came into being.

P.P. Rubens, *Samson and Delilah* (detail), about 1609-1610, panel, 185 × 205 cm. London, National Gallery.

P.P. Rubens, *The duke of Lerma on horseback*, 1603, canvas, 289 × 205 cm. Madrid, Prado.

Following pages

P.P. Rubens, *Self-portrait at the age of 41 years*, 1623, panel 86 × 26.5 cm. Windsor Castle, Collection of Queen Elisabeth II.

Anthony van Dyck, *Self-portrait as a young man*, about 1621-1622, canvas, 81 × 69 cm. Munich, Alte Pinakothek.

This does not mean, however, that painting in the Southern Netherlands was confined entirely to religious scenes. Here too the wealthy merchants and magistrates liked to adorn their drawing rooms and other places in their houses with paintings which, in addition to dealing with religious subjects, took the form of mythological scenes, portraits, genre pieces, still-lifes, landscapes, *etc*. But these, in contrast with the north, displayed the same stylistic features of the Baroque as the altarpieces in the churches. That, at least, was the case during the first half of the 17th century; for subsequently the differences between the north and the south as regards secular subjects became less marked.

There was another important factor in the tremendous upsurge of Flemish art in the 17th century – the presence of outstanding artists, who were capable of satisfying the huge demand for paintings, and whose talent also enabled them to express themselves in the language of the Baroque style; which, moreover, they endowed with a character that was all its own. Uppermost in the mind here are Rubens, Jordaens and van Dyck; but many others contributed to the prosperity of painting: their works, to be found in dozens of museums and galleries throughout the world, still catch the visitor's eye. Here only the leading artists of this group can be mentioned.

Undoubtedly Rubens determined the unique character of Flemish Baroque. Without wishing to denigrate the artistic contribution and personality specific to Jordaens and van Dyck, nevertheless their art would not have displayed the same aspect that it now possesses, but for the influence which Rubens exerted on them during their formative years. Moreover, his influence was not confined to painting: he also left his mark on sculpture, tapestry, graphic art, gold and silversmithy. As a result of his artistic development the Baroque entered a new phase between about 1610 and 1620. For it was Rubens' work that heralded high Baroque – even before Bernini was to do the same in Italy. Hence Rubens' return at the end of 1608 from Italy to Antwerp, where he immediately embarked on his career, was of profound significance to Flemish art: from that time onwards he changed its course completely.

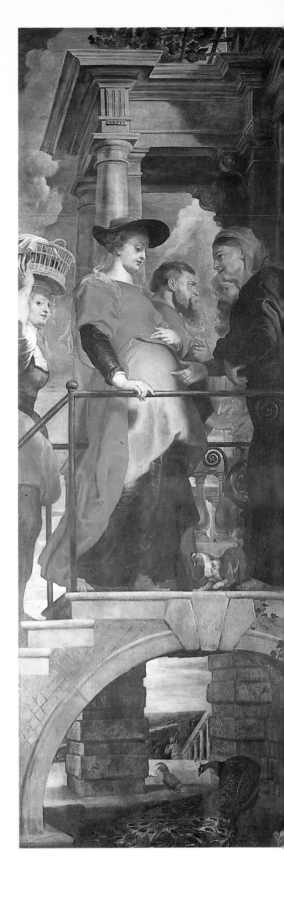

P.P. Rubens, *Triptych representing the descent from the Cross* (central part), *The Visit of Mary to her niece Elisabeth* (at the left), and *The presentation in the Temple* (at the right), 420 × 310 cm (central panel), 420 × 150 cm (side panels). Antwerp, Our Lady's Cathedral.
The central panel was painted in 1611-1612, the side panels in 1612-1614.

P.P. Rubens, *The Gonzaga family in adoration for the Holy Trinity*, 1604-1605, canvas, 381 × 447 cm. Mantua, Palazzo Ducale.

To make this clear we have to examine the artistic trends encountered by Rubens in Flanders on his return, which were still in line with 16th-century traditions. First of all there was the older generation, which included masters such as Ambrosius Francken (1544-1618) and Otto Venius (1556-1625), whose work consisted mainly of altarpieces in a cool classical vein. In their footsteps followed a number of younger contemporaries, such as Hans van Balen (1575-1632), Abraham Janssens (1573/74-1632), Marten Pepyn (1575-

1643) and, somewhat later, Artus Wolffort (1581-1641). Usually the plasticity of the figures in their work is accentuated by contrasts of light and shade, in some cases under the influence of Caravaggio, but gradually a rather more colourful aspect is developed.

In addition there was quite a large number of 'minor masters' at work, most of them imitators in one way or another of Pieter Bruegel the Elder; they included his sons Pieter Breughel the Younger (1564-1638) and Jan Breughel I, known as 'Velvet Breughel' (1568-1635), as

well as Sebastiaan Vranckx (1573-1647), Frans Francken the Elder (1542-1616) and his son, Frans Francken the Younger (1581-1642). The best was undoubtedly 'Velvet Breughel', a specialist in the miniature-like treatment of landscapes, animals and flower-pieces.

It should also be recorded that some of the 'minor masters', primarily Frans Francken the Younger and Willem van Haecht (1593-1637), introduced a new genre into painting, *i e* interiors representing picture galleries. This Antwerp innovation persisted until far into the 18th century and also had many imitators abroad, notably Watteau, Pannini and Zoffany.

Apart from exponents of cool classicism and the minor masters there was a third stylistic movement which had caught on in Antwerp, namely Caravaggism, a fairly 'modern' movement which went back to Caravaggio. Prominent features are the marked contrasts of light and shade, in many cases caused by artificial sources of light (torches, candles, *etc*) and the realism in the portrayal of figures. Rubens and Jordaens themselves experienced the influence of this movement for some time. Caravaggist features are also to be observed in some works by Abraham Janssens, Adam de Coster (1586-1643),

Gerard Seghers (1591-1651) and Theodoor Rombouts (1597-1637). After 1620, however, the two last-named artists changed, under Rubens' influence, to a new design and colouring related with his art.

More lasting success was achieved by Caravaggism outside Antwerp, particularly in Ghent and Bruges. Among the works of the Ghent painter Jan Janssens (1590 – after 1650) are a number of typical *Crowning with Thorns* compositions with very unreal light effect and of a highly dramatic character. The most important representative of this movement in Bruges was Jacob van Oost (1601-1671), who also acquired fame as a portrait painter. Theodoor van Loon (1581/82-1667) worked in Brussels. His *Scenes from the Life of Mary*, in Scherpenheuvel Basilica, are among the most beautiful religious works painted in the 17th century. They were not, however, influenced by Caravaggism but by the school of Bologna.

This group of artists operated entirely outside Rubens' sphere of influence, which was exceptional, as from about 1620 almost all artistic activity underwent the impact of his powerful personality.

Peter Paul Rubens was born in 1577 at Siegen, a small town in Westphalia. His parents had left Antwerp in 1568, some time after the arrival of the Duke of Alva in the Netherlands, when they felt threatened on account of their Protestant sympathies, and found accommodation in Cologne. The period following their settling in Siegen became one of the most dramatic episodes in their protracted exile. After the death of the father, the

P.P. Rubens, *The 'large' last Judgment*, about 1615-1616, canvas, 606 × 452 cm. Munich, Alte Pinakothek.

P.P. Rubens, *The hunt on lions*, about 1621, canvas, 247 × 375 cm. Munich, Alte Pinakothek.

P.P Rubens, *The tribute-money*, about 1612-1614, panel, 141.5 × 189 cm. San Francisco, California, H.M. De Young Memorial Museum.

and *The Transfiguration* (Nancy, Museum). After completing these works in May 1605, Rubens went for a while to Genoa, where in the same year he painted *The Circumcision of Jesus*, still on the high altar of St Ambrosio's. In that same city, where he spent further periods (in 1606 and 1607), he painted portraits of the aristocracy, and collected ground plans and surveys of palaces and churches; which he later had engraved in Antwerp, to illustrate his book *Palazzo di Genova*, published in 1622.

From the end of 1605 however, Rubens spent most of his time in Rome. There he studied sculptures from classical antiquity. At the same time he devoted his best efforts to the execution of an important commission, obtained in 1606, thanks to his influential patrons: namely the painting of an altarpiece for *Santa Maria in Vallicella*, of the Oratorian Fathers, the *Chiesa Nuova*. When the canvas (now at Grenoble, Museum of Fine Arts) was placed on the high altar, it was found to be scarcely visible owing to a troublesome reflection. Rubens then produced a new version, with the changed

mother returned with her children to Antwerp. There the young Peter Paul went for a number of years to the Latin chapter school, popularly known as the *Papenschool*, where he studied the Latin language and literature, and also learned some Greek. Throughout his life he developed his knowledge of classical culture, which certainly affected the way he portrayed his mythological and allegorical scenes. Moreover, his friendship with humanists such as Nicolaas Rockox, Gaspar Gevartius and Peiresc, would arouse in later years his interest in classical antiquity. At the age of fourteen he had to leave school, and soon started to learn the trade of painter. His apprenticeship in Antwerp took him successively into the studios of Tobias Verhaecht, Adam van Noort and Otto Venius. The last-named was undoubtedly the most important of the three. The composition *Adam and Eve in Paradise* (Antwerp, Rubens' House) makes us aware how much affinity his art had at that time with the cool classicism of his teacher.

After having been registered as a master in St Luke's Guild in 1598/99, Rubens left for Italy in May 1600. Almost immediately upon his arrival he was appointed painter to the Court of Vincenzo Gonzaga, Duke of Mantua. But during his stay in southern Europe, which just over eight years, he was not in the duke's court all the time. As early as October 1600 we find him in Florence, and in 1601/02 in Rome for several months. In 1603 he went to Spain on the orders of Vincenzo Gonzaga as the supervisor of a convoy of priceless gifts – including works of art – for Philip II, King of Spain, the Duke of Lerma, his powerful minister, and other influential courtiers. On his return Rubens finally received a major commission from his Duke, who had hitherto given him mainly work of minor importance, *e g* making copies. He painted three gigantic canvases to adorn the choir of the Jesuit Church at Mantua: *The Gonzaga Family's Adoration of the Holy Trinity* (part of which is now at Mantua, Palazzo Ducale), *The Baptism of Christ in the Jordan* (Antwerp, Museum of Fine Arts)

P.P. Rubens, *Portrait of Veronica Spinola Doria*, about 1607, canvas, 225.5 × 138.5 cm. Karlsruhe, Staatliche Kunsthalle.

P.P. Rubens and Jan Breughel I, *Madonna with Child within a garland of flowers and surrounded by angels,* about 1616, panel 185 × 209.9 cm. Munich, Alte Pinakothek.

composition extending over three panels instead of one. This time he painted the scenes on slate, a less reflective materia. They are still to be seen in that very church in Rome. Hardly had they been completed when Rubens learned that his mother was seriously ill. He hurried back from the Eternal City in October 1608. Although he had written to the Duke of Mantua's secretary shortly before his departure that his absence would be of short duration, Rubens never returned to Italy.

When we contemplate the works which Rubens painted during his time in Italy, we perceive during the first two years still the influence of his apprenticeship with Otto Venius. But very soon this is overlaid with r∃w impressions, acquired when he first came to know what the Peninsula had to offer in artistic beauty. In the vast composition *The Gathering of the Gods on Olympus*

(Prague, Hrasdin), probably painted at Mantua in 1602, many features reminiscent of Venius' art can be detected; but also a number of borrowings from antique pictures and sarcophagi, while the colouring is beginning to display Venetian effects. The *Equestrian Portrait of the Duke of Lerma* (Madrid, Prado), painted in 1603 during his first visit to Spain, marks a turning-point in his development: the cool classicism of his apprenticeship gives way to greater freedom in design, and a vibrant but nuanced colouring. The eclecticism with which Rubens tries to simulate the finest achievements of the great Italian masters finds expression in the major compositions which he subsequently produced, in 1604/05, for the Jesuit Church at Mantua. Here we see side by side motifs and stylistic elements which have been borrowed, sometimes from Michelangelo, sometimes from Raphael, Titian or Tintoretto, invariably bathed in a silvery, seductive, Venetian colouring. In the works which he painted in Rome for *Santa Maria in Vallicella* (1606-1608) is added a dimension of heroic monumentality; which he had made his own through his attentive study of antique sculpture.

Dozens of drawings have been preserved on which Rubens copied Greco-Roman sculptures, in some cases several times and from different angles. He also diligently studied the art of Michelangelo, Raphael, Titian, Giulio Romano and many other Italian artists, from whose works he also executed drawings. Year after year – in fact throughout the rest of his career – he resorted to these sketchbooks and portfolios, in which he kept those drawings and copied motifs. It should nevertheless be pointed out that he integrated these borrowings into his compositions in a vivid and original manner, so that we are not always aware that this or that figure derives from an antique or an Italian example.

When Rubens returned to Antwerp at the end of 1608 his mother had already died. Although he probably had the idea of going back to Rome, where he had secured powerful patrons, he decided to settle in Antwerp for good. Most probably the Twelve Years' Truce had something to do with this decision. In September 1609 he became 'Painter to the House of Their Highnesses' Archduke Albert and the Infanta Isabella. But he accepted this office, which afforded him many financial advantages, only on condition that he did not have to live at the Court in Brussels. One month later he married Isabella Brant. On 1st November 1610 he bought a property on the *Wapper* at Antwerp, where his house and spacious workshop were to be built. Probably he did not take up residence here with his family until 1615.

Portrait of Isabella Brant, about 1624, panel, 85 × 62 cm. Florence, Uffizi.

P.P. Rubens, *The defeat of Sennacherib* (detail), about 1612–1614, panel, 97.7 × 122.7 cm. Munich, Alte Pinakothek.

P.P. Rubens, *The sacrifice of Abraham,* 1620, panel, 50 × 65 cm. Paris, Louvre.
Sketch in oils for one of the 39 ceiling-paintings on canvas, meant for St Carolus Borromeus' Church at Antwerp, made in 1620-1621 by Rubens and his assistants, one of them being Anthony van Dyck.

After his return to Antwerp Rubens' art continued to be strongly influenced by Italian examples. Thus the *Raising of the Cross* (Antwerp, Cathedral), painted in 1610, is to be regarded as a powerful embodiment of all he had learned in Italy: the vastness of the composition, which recalls Tintoretto's passion scenes; the sculptural design of Michelangelo in the figures on the central panel; the Venetian colouring, more particularly in the right-hand panel; and Caravaggio's influence, at least in some measure, in the portrayal of the women in the foreground of the left flanking panel. Other new phenomena are a greater impetuosity and an intensified expressivity, hence the years 1609-1612 are usually called Rubens' *Sturm und Drang* (Storm and Stress) period.

The impetuosity did not, however, persist for long. As early as 1611-1614, during which time he painted the *Descent from the Cross* (Antwerp, Cathedral), greater control is perceptible, both in the overall simplification of the composition and in the restful attitudes and gestures of the figures. This was the forerunner of a new style phase, which was called 'classical'. The colouring became stronger; some local colours, clearly brought out

P.P. Rubens, *Apotheosis of Henry IV, King of France and proclamation of the regency,* 1622, panel, 53 × 92 cm. Munich, Alte Pinakothek.
Design for one of the 25 large paintings of the Maria de' Medici-series, painted in 1622-1625, now in the Louvre at Paris.

P.P. Rubens, *Madonna on the throne with the Child and three female saints,* 1633, 260 × 210 cm. Toledo, Ohio, Museum of Art.

within the contours of the garments, are distributed evenly over the entire surface. The design was just as linear and plastic as before; but a bright, uniformly dispersed light softly caresses the sculptural forms, which sometimes stand out as reliefs on a neutral background.

From about 1615 onwards Rubens again turned to the creation of more animated scenes, such as the grandiose *Large Last Judgment* (Munich, Alte Pinakothek), numerous hunting scenes, ecstatic *Assumptions of the Virgin* and imposing scenes from the lives of saints. Although the figures still have a certain plasticity, the contours are no longer so sharply defined. The postures and gestures are more supple, the colouring more variegated. In contrast with his *Sturm und Drang* period, he no longer strove for strong contrasts; nor – as in the classical phase – did he aim at applying local colours within clear-cut outlines; he rather endeavoured to obtain harmonious transitions and colour blendings, sometimes in a dominant bright tint, sometimes in a darker one, but always in a flamboyant and at the same time balanced composition.

Inundated by an ever-increasing number of major commissions, Rubens now called to a greater extent on assistants. From 1617 to 1620 Anthony van Dyck was the foremost of them. Sometimes Rubens entrusted him with the entire execution of works, which he himself had previously designed in oil sketches. For the rest, the extent of the studio's participation varied from work to work. In some cases Rubens left it to specialist assistants

P.P. Rubens, *The Rape of the Sabine Women by the Romans*, sketch in oils on panel, 56 × 87 cm, about 1630-1635. Private collection.

– such as Jan Breughel I ('Velvet Breughel'), Frans Snyders, Paul de Vos and Jan Wildens – to insert certain components, like flowers, animals, still-lifes and landscape backgrounds, in his own work in accordance with his directions. Then again, a particular composition would be executed almost entirely by assistants on the basis of his drafts, sometimes with the exception of some heads or other essential parts, which he painted himself. And another time a composition would be started by assistants, but subsequently so thoroughly worked over by Rubens, that their share in it would be scarcely perceptible. With his organizational talent he will undoubtedly have left much of the material work of minor importance to his studio, which enabled him – even in times of considerable pressure – to produce a number of large-scale paintings entirely on his own.

From about 1620 bright colouring predominated. Rubens no longer employed transitions from light to dark to the same extent as before, but tended to multiply the gradations and nuances within the same colour ranges. Henceforward, both the outline drawings and the colouring were to be more or less 'dissolved' in the rich variegations of this pictorial chromatism.

The ensuing period, which came to an end in 1628, could be called the era of the great series. In quick succession Rubens was assigned commissions for series of paintings, and designs for a range of wall-tapestries. The foremost of them is the afore-mentioned imposing series of no less than thirty-nine ceiling paintings in St Carolus Borromeus' Church in Antwerp, which Rubens turned out in barely a year's time (1621/22), with the aid of some of his assistants, including van Dyck. As the paintings themselves were destroyed by fire in 1718, we now have to rely mainly on the oils sketches from Rubens' own hand, to obtain an idea of the paintings in question. Prophets and saints, in daring foreshortenings and depicted as viewed from below, seem to be floating about in celestial spheres.

For Rubens the new phase also signified a breakthrough at European level. In fact he had already had some orders from abroad, but those he was now receiving were on a far longer scale. First he painted the *Marie de'Medici* Cycle (1622-1625 – Paris, Louvre), consisting of twenty-five vast canvases, in which he transformed in an allegorical fashion the rather banal existence of his principal, the Queen Mother of France,

P.P. Rubens, *The Assumption of Mary*, 1625-1626, panel, 490 × 325 cm. Antwerp, Our Lady's Cathedral.

by means of gods and heroes from classical antiquity. They appear to accompany her on her journey through life into triumphal episodes, the echo of which reverberates as far as Olympus. In 1622 he designed for her son, King Louis XIII, twelve tapestries depicting the *History of the Emperor Constantine*. Another series upon which Rubens embarked in 1625 for Marie de'Medici, having as its subject the life of Henry IV, her deceased husband, was never completed. A number of sketches and some partially finished canvases give an idea of the breadth of vision with which these series were conceived. Political difficulties made it impossible to carry the project through. Even so, these commissions from the French Royal House serve to bring out the virtuosity, with which Rubens applied his talents to the glorification of absolutism.

Meanwhile he produced around 1626/27, this time by order of the Infanta Isabella, the designs for a series of wall-tapestries woven in Brussels, which the Princess donated to the Order of the *Descalszas Reales* in Madrid, the Poor Clares with whom she had spent part of her youth. The impressive ensemble can be considered as a triumphal glorification of the Eucharist and the Roman

Catholic Church, as restored and consolidated by the Counter Reformation.

In addition to the great series, Rubens painted in the years 1620-1628 some altarpieces, which are among the most beautiful that he ever accomplished. The composition is characterized by an even more conspicuous unity than before. It is no longer constructed in accordance with some clearly indicated intersecting diagonals; the figures are now, as it were, subsumed in a *perpetuum mobile* of oscillating movements and countermovements which blend into a festive synthesis. The richness of the extremely variegated colouring contributes to the flamboyant cohesion of the composition. Enormous altarpieces, such as the *Adoration of the Magi* (Antwerp, Museum of Fine Arts), completed in 1624, the *Assumption of the Virgin* (Antwerp, Cathedral) and *The Madonna Adored by Saints* (Antwerp, St Augustine's Church), created in 1628, are peaks of a thoroughly developed high Baroque, which Rubens himself was never to surpass.

In the meantime Isabella Brant, his first wife, had died in 1626; probably as a result of the plague which claimed many victims in Antwerp at that time. More than hitherto, Rubens became involved in negotiations, aimed at securing a new armistice or a peace treaty for the Netherlands. In August 1628 he left on a diplomatic mission for Madrid, where he stayed for some eight months. While there he was assigned a further peace mission, which took him to London, from where he did not return to Antwerp until April 1630.

Although during the long periods he spent abroad Rubens naturally produced far fewer paintings, the diplomatic missions were not without their significance as regards his art. In Madrid he painted portraits of Philip IV and members of the Royal Family. Of more importance, however, was the renewal of his acquaintance with the numerous Titians in the Royal collection, some of which he copied. In London he painted for Charles I of England pieces which included an *Allegory of Peace* (London, National Gallery). Before he left he was commissioned by the King to do large canvases for the ceiling of the vast Banqueting Hall of Whitehall Palace – a mighty work which he did not complete until 1634/35 when back in Antwerp, from where it was sent to London.

P.P. Rubens, *Portrait of Helena Fourment and her son Frans Rubens*, about 1638, panel, 192 × 130 cm. Paris, Louvre.

Following pages:

P.P. Rubens, *The Lamentation for Christ* ('Christ on the straw'), about 1617, panel, 139 × 90 cm. Antwerp, Museum of Fine Arts.
Central panel of the triptych for the epitaph of Jan Michielsen, then in the Cathedral at Antwerp.

P.P. Rubens, *Madonna on the throne with the Child and surrounded by saints* (also called the *Mystic marriage of St Catherine*),1628, canvas, 564 × 401 cm. Antwerp, St Augustine's Church (temporary in the Museum of Fine Arts).

414

A milestone, also from an artistic point, was his marriage on 6th December 1640 to Helène Fourment, who was then barely seventeen years of age. Her enchanting beauty was to inspire him time after time to paint delightful, intimate portraits. We also frequently recognize her in biblical, and especially in mythological, scenes painted during the last ten years of his life, which is usually termed his 'lyrical period'. The number of altarpieces diminished appreciably: the artist seemed to rid himself of all kinds of commissions, in order to depict – now for his own pleasure – subjects that fascinated him. These are mostly mythological scenes, which can be likened to hymns, dedicated to the beauty of women. In 1634 Rubens was requested by the Town Magistrate of Antwerp to design arches for the Triumphal Entry as Governor of the Southern Netherlands of Cardinal Infante Ferdinand, brother of Philip IV, King of Spain – a festive event which took place in April 1635. Thus he had one final opportunity of designing grandiose architectural forms, in an imposing and decorative Baroque style. The actual execution of the canvases adorning the arches, however, was left by Rubens to a whole pleiad of Antwerp painters, who worked from his sketches.

The same procedure was adopted in the case of the sixty-odd large-scale mythological scenes, which Rubens designed in 1636-1638 for the *Torre de la Parada*, the

huntig lodge of Philip IV, in the vicinity of Madrid. Only four paintings (Madrid, Prado) in this cycle – the largest commission he ever received – were done by his own hand. The rest were the work of Jacob Jordaens, Cornelis de Vos, Theodoor van Thulden, Erasmus Quellin and other artists in his entourage. The sketches in oils which he made for this cycle are among his finest. His hand was now so skilled that he had scarcely any trouble, reverting to the wealth of forms which he had composed throughout his life, in embodying his vision on the panel with an astounding dexterity and accuracy.

In 1635 Rubens purchased the country estate *het Steen* at Elewijt, near Malines, where he spent the summer months for the rest of his life. There the softly glowing Brabant countryside inspired him to paint landscapes. Not that he had previously neglected this genre altogether, but at Elewijt the land had a luxuriant variety, and above all a mellowness which awakened a response in his nature.

Peter Paul Rubens died at Antwerp on 30th May 1640. On the altar of the mortuary in St James's Church, where his body was interred, was placed – as he had requested – a painting made during the last years of his life, *Madonna and Saints*. In this splendid work shines the vibrant light that imparted a paradisical aspect to so many of his paintings. Here too he reveals his unrivalled mastery, acquired only after a long apprenticeship both in Antwerp and Italy, which gradually manifested itself with a growing individuality in a continuous evolution of style, persisting even during the last years of his life.

Undoubtedly Rubens was one of the most versatile and productive artists of his time. Practically all genres of painting were exploited by him, and invariably to perfection. He was a great colourist, for whom skilful treatment of colour was an outstanding means of expression; an inspired, imaginative and 'rhapsodic' portrayer of the divine and the human drama, which prompted both Eugène Delacroix and Jacob Burckhardt to compare him to Homer; an artist who achieved a rare equilibrium between a realistic reproduction and an idealizing design, between his unbridled imaginative power and his efforts at harmoniously balanced composition. His influence was not confined to artists of his own time, but is even discernible far into the 19th century, notably in the work of Delacroix and Renoir.

P.P. Rubens, *The Union of England and Scotland (Charles I as Prince of Wales)*, panel, 83 × 71 cm. Minneapolis, Institute of Arts, William Hood Dunwoody Fund.
Sketch in oils, design for one of the large ceiling-paintings of Banqueting House, Whitehall, London, finished in 1634-1635 by Rubens.

Following pages:

P.P. Rubens, *The Garden of love,* about 1632, canvas, 198 × 283 cm. Madrid, Prado.

P.P. Rubens, *Madonna with Child surrounded by saints*, panel,
211 × 195 cm, about 1635-1640. Antwerp, St James' Church.

A few days after Rubens' death Balthasar Gerbier, the English King's *chargé d'affaires* in Brussels, wrote to a correspondent in London that "Jordaens had become the foremost among the painters here". In contrast with Rubens and van Dyck, Jordaens never visited Italy. A contemporary, the German painter Joachim Sandrart, delivered this indictment of the artist: "His works have been criticized in particular on the grounds that he has not seen the antiquities or the works of the leading Italian masters, a fact that he himself acknowledges." This desideratum in his artistic training may, on the other hand, explain why his art remained more closely linked with the life of the people of Antwerp, than the art of Rubens and van Dyck, his more cosmopolitanly-minded colleagues. To put it succinctly, Rubens moved in the humanists' and scholars' world of representations

and ideas; van Dyck was at home in the distinguished and refined circles of the Italian and English nobility and of the Antwerp higher bourgeoisie; while Jordaens' best medium was the life of the well-off middle classes and the Chambers of Rhetoric. With them he has in common his jovial, folksy, sometimes coarse tone, and also his propensity for moralizing.

Jacob Jordaens was born at Antwerp on 19th May 1594. He was thus about seventeen years younger than Rubens, and five years older than van Dyck. His father was a linen trader, a significant factor, for when – after his apprenticeship with Adam van Noort – he was registered as a master in St Luke's Guild in 1615, he was designated a 'water painter'. This meant painting large canvases in water colours; these were used to decorate the walls of rooms, as a sort of *Ersatz* for the much dearer tapestries. His father's trade may have induced him to choose this specialization. Nevertheless, soon he also did oil paintings on canvas or panelling, as some of these date from 1616. In these juvenile works it is usual to find a compact group of figures filling the entire surface of the composition; they seem to be pressed together within the framework of the painting. The plastic forms of the figures are sometimes accentuated by sharp contrasts of light and shade, in most cases evoked by burning candles and torches. Here we can discern the influence of Caravaggio; albeit via Rubens, whose art was his guiding star in other respects, too. In the early works the paint is usually laid on thick and spread out with broad strokes of the brush.

Around 1620 the hitherto conspicuous contrasts of light and shade lose something of their intensity. The compressed grouping of the figures becomes less marked, and in his composition Jordaens achieves more balance. The *Homage to Pomona* (Allegory of Fertility) (Brussels, Museums of Fine Arts), perhaps his most famous painting, illustrates these outstanding features of his style. He did, in fact, paint a number of scenes depicting the Holy Family in something of a genre vein; like his first and most successful genre pieces, such as the *Peasant and Satyr*, a theme to which he was later to revert frequently. These are all paintings of medium size, with which the artist was most at home. They reveal an infectiously optimistic view of life.

The year 1628 marked a turning-point in the development of Jordaens' art. Then he painted his first large altarpiece, *The Martyrdom of St Apollonia* (Antwerp, St Augustine's Church – temporarily in the Museum of Fine Arts), which was soon followed by a number of major commissions from the Church. The height of these canvases forced him here to plan fresh compositional arrangements. The figures were now, as it were, stacked one above the other, to fill the entire surface. Consequently, there are not many effects of perspective or depth to be found. The colouring generally becomes cooler, the folds of the garments more angular, more broken and flatter. Jordaens also ventured upon large

Jakob Jordaens, *The torture of St Apollonia*, canvas, 409 × 213 cm, 1628. Antwerp, St Augustine's Church.

Jakob Jordaens, *Apollo slaying Marsyas*, canvas, 146-117 cm, beginning of the 1620's. Private collection.

mythological scenes and designed some series of tapestries. Most of these works were preceded by bright preparatory sketches in watercolour and gouache; unlike Rubens, who favoured oil sketches on panelling. It seems as though in the years from 1628 to 1640 Jordaens was endeavouring to surpass Rubens in monumentality and Baroque elegance – for the most part in vain, however. His most successful works are medium-sized genres, in which he showed the greatest mastery in surface-filling; such as the excellent versions of subjects which he painted several times, *The King Drinks* (Brussels, Museums of Fine Arts), or *As the Old Sing, so the Young Twitter* (Antwerp). These scenes from the lives of the people and the bourgeoisie, which bear witness to an unconcealed joy of living (and sometimes to a fairly naive bonhomie and a moralizing concern) accord better with his uncomplicated, generous nature and his artistic potential.

After Rubens' death in 1640, Jordaens took his place as the leader of the Antwerp painting school. As a consequence the number of orders increased appreciably: now foreign princes too called upon his talent. Among the commissions was the gigantic canvas *The Triumph of Frederick Henry* (8.50 × 8.20 m), which forms the central motif of the Orange Room in *Ten Bosch* House (near The Hague). This he painted in 1652 at the request of Amalia van Solms, the widow of the stadtholder Frederick Henry, Prince of Orange.

The expansion of orders caused Jordaens to involve more assistants in the work than before. In most cases this did not enhance the quality. Although he occasionally produced striking compositions, his creativity

Jakob Jordaens, *As the old sang, so the young pipe*, canvas, 120 × 192 cm, signed and dated: *J. Jor. fecit 1638*. Antwerp, Museum of Fine Arts.

Jacob Jordaens, *The satyr and the farmer's family,* about 1620, canvas, 174 × 205 cm. Munich, Alte Pinakothek.

Jakob Jordaens, *Tribute to Pomona. Allegory of fertility*, canvas, 180 × 241 cm, signed, about 1623. Brussels, Museums of Fine Arts.

suffered a general decline, even to an increasing extent over the last twenty-five years of his life. The colouring became darker; and a certain rigidity afflicted the design – a trend which became generally perceptible in the painting of the second half of the 17th century, under the influence of classicistic tendencies. The familiar compositional arrangements were employed *ad nauseam*. In 1678 Jordaens died at the age of eighty-four.

In his best years Jordaens also painted excellent portraits, mostly of people in his family circle or his immediate environment. "He aims not only at portraying the features and personal appearance of his models but also, and in particular, at bringing out their human qualities. As though they feel the need to show themselves as they really are, they address themselves directly, and even boldly, to the viewer." (R.-A. d'Hulst).

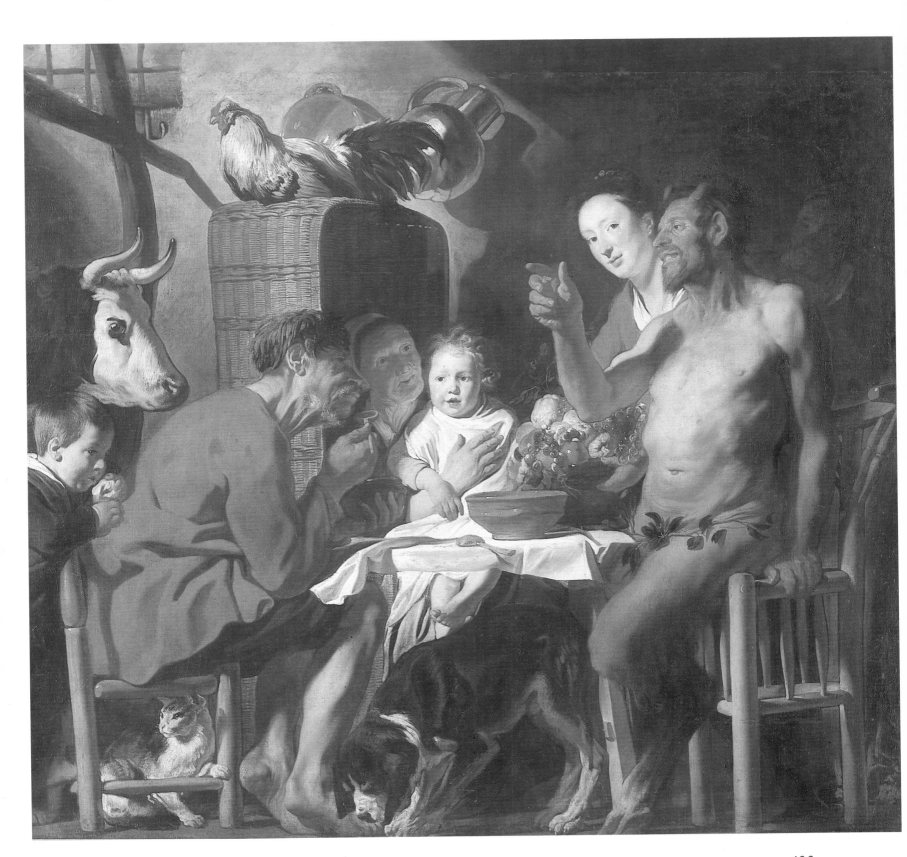

Still more fame as a portraitist was gained by Anthony van Dyck, who indeed specialized mainly in this branch of painting. Born in Antwerp on 22th March 1599, he was apprenticed to Hendrik van Balen as a ten-year-old. He was accorded the status of master in the Antwerp guild of painters in 1618, but before that he had already been active as an autonomous artist, employing several assistants. One of the earliest commissions on which he worked independently was the *Fifteen Mysteries of the Rosary* cycle, in St Paul's Church, Antwerp. The ninth component *Christ Bearing His Cross*, was painted by him, perhaps as early as 1617 (Rubens and Jordaens too each provided a panel for this cycle). From that year onwards van Dyck also worked on several occasions as one of Rubens' assistants. A striking example of this cooperation is the triptych *Le Christ à la Paille* ('Christ on the straw' – Antwerp, Museum of Fine Arts). The central panel, apart from a few heads, was painted by Rubens, while the flanking panels were executed by van Dyck to the former's design. Typical of the young master is the heavy coating of paint, effected with swift, nervous touches; in marked contrast to the even, fluent brushwork of Rubens in the central panel. Rubens' influence is, moreover, very pronounced in the religious and mythological works painted by van Dyck in his first Antwerp period; but they are at the same time characterized by an individual style, a manifest sense of distinction and an aristocratic mastery. Another characteristic is to be found in the whole of his oeuvre: "Rubens had a strong feeling for the plastic forms of his figures wheras van Dyck always thought in terms of line and surface" (Sir Oliver Millar). To bring out this point clearly it is sufficient, for example, to compare van Dyck's *Samson and Delilah* (Dulwich College Picture Gallery) with Rubens' (London, National Gallery). These qualities also find expression in the numerous portraits of members of the Antwerp bourgeoisie.

The natural distinction and the elegant pose which we see in them were to a large extent further developed when the artist, after a few months in London in 1620/21, set out for Italy in October 1621. He remained in that country for about six years. He visited the leading centres (Rome, Florence, Venice) and even Sicily, but his longest stay was in Genoa. There he discovered among the aristocracy a clientele that particularly attracted him by a somewhat reserved dignity and refinement of posture, gesture and attire. As Rubens had done before him in Genoa, he generally painted the nobility full-length, in an interior with imposing columns and luxuriant drapery, suggesting the high rank of the personages concerned. During his stay in Italy the restlessness that drove him from town to town already became manifest.

It was probably in the autumn of 1627 that van Dyck returned to his birthplace. One of the first commissions he was assigned was *The Ecstasy of St Augustine* (Antwerp, St Augustine's Church), an altarpiece which was delivered in 1628. Here the influence of Venetian colouring is unmistakable, which is easy to understand when we consider that the works of Titian had made the greatest impression on him in Italy. Venetian (cobalt) blue predominates, and the figures stand out in turbulent, graceful contours. In his religious works of this period van Dyck broke away completely from Rubens. More than hitherto, there is evidence of a certain frailty and melancholy masked by elegance of design.

The same is seen in some profane paintings. About one of these, *Rinaldo and Armida* (Baltimore, Museum of Art), Sir Oliver Millar wrote: "Van Dyck is constructing a link between the Venetian painters of the previous century and Boucher". The rose-in-bloom flesh tones of Rubens' figures pale in van Dyke's into ivory tints, and the grandiloquent gesture becomes an

Anthony van Dyck, *Portrait of the wife of Theodoor Rombouts (?) and her little daughter,* about 1627-1630, panel, 133 × 91 cm. Munich, Alte Pinakothek.

Anthony van Dyck, *The Assumption of the Virgin, with cherubs who carry the tokens of the suffering of Christ,* canvas, 118 × 102 cm, about 1628-1631. Washington D.C., National Gallery, Widener collection.

Following pages:

Anthony van Dyck, *Marchesa Balbi,* about 1622-1627, canvas, 183 × 122 cm. Washington D.C., National Gallery of Art.

Anthony van Dyck, *Margareta de Vos, wife of Frans Snijders* (detail), about 1620, panel, 130.7 × 99.3 cm. New York, The Frick Collection.

Anthony van Dyck, *Thomas Killigrew and William Lord Crofts* (?), 1638, canvas. Windsor Castle, Collection of Queen Elisabeth II.

elegant, dignified pose. The numerous portraits from this second Antwerp period present the same bourgeois as before, but in nobler postures, and psychologically also more intrusive. They rank among the very finest that were painted in the 17th century.

Despite the success enjoyed by van Dyck in the Southern Netherlands in those years, he was soon on the move again. In March 1632 – following two brief sojourns in Holland – he left for London, where he had honours heaped upon him and was appointed Court Painter by Charles I. While in England he painted countless portraits of members of the royal family and the higher nobility. During these years of feverish activity van Dyck's style evolved to great refinement in the treatment of colour, and to extremely polished elegance of posture. For a brief period (1634/35) he

returned to the Netherlands, but thereafter until his premature death he resided in England again. Prior to this, however, as though driven by a constant feeling of restlessness, he paid a fleeting visit to the Continent, but on 9th December 1641 he died in London, barely forty-two years of age.

Van Dyck had a considerable influence on English portrait painting, not only in the 17th century, but much later as well. A notable instance is provided by the works of Thomas Gainsborough (1727-1788). On the European Continent too the evolution of the portrait in the late Baroque and Rococo periods is inconceivable without van Dyck's example. "But none of his successors attained the supreme distinction, reticence and refinement which made him so aristocratic an artist" (Sir Oliver Millar).

Next in line after Rubens, Jordaens and van Dyck comes Adriaen Brouwer (1605/06-1638). This is because of the high quality of his work and the fact that he introduced – and firmly established – the small-sized genre painting in the Netherlands. He first did small panel paintings in the Bruegel tradition, the most prominent features of which were a fairly large number of figures and quite variegated colouring. Soon his composition displayed more clarity of arrangement, and his colouring a velvety softness, abounding in delicate transitions and fine gradations. At the same time more expression is discernible in the faces of the tipplers, tobacco-smokers and vagabonds on the fringe of society, which were his preferred subjects. Brouwer's prodigious achievement was to depict savage facial expressions and gestures in roisterous scenes, which are at the same time gems of extremely refined colouring.

We have already mentioned that from about 1615 to 1620 only a few artists managed to break away from Rubens' influence. This applied, of course, to van Dyck and Jordaens, who at that time were producing their earliest works. This supremacy not only asserted itself in religious and profane scenes, but also in other areas of painting. A typical example is afforded by Frans Snyders (1579-1657), who initially painted in the late 16th-century tradition; but under Rubens' influence turned to large-scale, dynamic and decorative still-lifes and animal paintings. The hunting scene was exploited with equal zest by his brother-in-law, Paul de Vos

Adriaan Brouwer, *Inn-quarrel around a barrel,* about 1632, panel, 15 × 14 cm. Munich, Alte Pinakothek.

(1596-1678). Roughly the same experience was undergone by Jan Wildens (1586-1653): his early landscapes reflected the transitional style of artists such as Gillis van Coninxloo and Roeland Savery, but in a later stage he executed large vistas, in which the relationship with Rubens' landscapes is indisputable.

Nevertheless, it would be a misconception to set 17th-century Flemish art entirely in the context of Rubens' supremacy. Even before his death artistic development took a course which diverged from his line, and was more attuned to the refinement and distinction of van Dyck's art. For a long time afterwards motifs and compositions were borrowed from Rubens' works, but they were applied in a different spirit. The heroism, fervour and vigour of the great master of the Baroque make way for more refinement and softer colouring. The elegant pose supersedes the broad, rhetorical gesture. The mighty epic is thundered out; idyllic notes are borne in upon us.

Quite remarkably, the new movement manifested itself very early on in the religious and mythological works of Rubens' former assistants: Cornelis Schut (1595-1655), Theodoor van Thulden (1606-1676) and Erasmus Quellin (1607-1678). It can also be observed in one of Rubens' most successful epigons, the highly productive Gaspar de Craeyer (1584-1669), and in other painters of figures, whom Rudolf Oldenbourg called *Enkelschüler* (literally 'descendant pupils') of Rubens. The most prominent of these are Abraham van Diepenbeeck (1596-1675), Jan Boeckhorst (1605-1668), Thomas Willeboirts Bosschaert (1614-1654) and Thedoor Boeyermans (1620-1678).

In portrait painting van Dyck's influence proved to be the strongest: Cornelis de Vos (1585?-1651) was one of the leading specialists in this field. After having painted in Rubens' vein, he was soon drawn towards van Dyck's style. Flemish portrait painters were gaining great renown abroad, e g Justus Sustermans (1597-1681) in Florence, Frans Luycks (1604-1668) in Prague and Jacob Ferdinand Voet (1639-1700?) in Paris and Rome. In the second half of the 17th century a special facet of portraiture emerged in Southern Netherlands art, namely the small family portrait. Its principal initiator was Gonsales Coques (1614-1684), who painted a number of medium-sized and small scenes featuring families dressed up in their Sunday best; the setting being either the garden embellished with sculptures, or the drawing room draped with gilt leather.

Although we assume these figures to be well-to-do citizens, they have something of the 'grandezza' of van Dyck's portraits of aristocrats about them. Coques' innovation met with considerable approval. It was imitated by, among others, Hieronymus Janssens (1624-1693), Gillis van Tilborgh (*ca* 1625-1678) and François Duchastel (1625-1694).

In his genre pieces Joos van Craesbeeck (*ca* 1606-1662) comes closest to Adriaen Brouwer. But other artists generally strive for a certain idyllic distinction, which was a characteristic of the second half of the 17th century. To ascertain this it is sufficient to compare the scenes from everyday life by David Teniers the Younger (1610-1690) or David III Ryckaert (1612-1661) with

Frans Snijders, *Kitchen-scene with young man*, canvas, 138 × 203 cm. Munich, Alte Pinakothek.

Brouwer's panels, with their wild ruffians and habitual drunkards. The bitter grimace and the debauched primitive violence are absent from the formers' paintings, while the colouring is brighter and glossier. Nor are the figures any longer exclusively set in the tavern, the kitchen or the farmhouse; but also in the fashionable houses of eminent citizens. The social life of the upper classes, with its musical interludes, its dancing and banqueting, is now the subject of genre scenes too.

Apart from David Teniers, the already mentioned Hieronymus Janssens, Gillis van Tilborgh and François Duchastel painted works of this kind. In some cases, moreover, these artists tended rather to paint group portraits in genre form. The dividing line between these two branches of art is blurred, and it is not always easy to ascertain in which of the two categories the painters' works have to be placed. The British solve the difficulty by terming them 'conversation pieces'. This designation is, however, of Southern Netherlands origin; it is already found around 1640 in inventories of Antwerp art collections! And was not Rubens' *Garden of Love* styled a *conversation à la mode* in the same inventories? Yet this was also in a certain sense a genre scene with recognizable figures.

A personality apart from the main body of Flemish genre painters was Michiel Sweerts (1624-1664). Born in Brussels, he spent several years in Rome, where he

came under the influence of the cool Neapolitan Caravaggism. In 1656 he was back in Brussels. Thereafter he spent a while in Amsterdam, and then set out with a team of French missionaries for India, where he died at Goa. He left a very poetic oeuvre.

The new vision of man was matched by a fresh concept of landscape. No longer was there the waft of the cosmic breeze which had pervaded Rubens' portrayals of nature, nor were landscapes marked by the grandiose composition and dynamic tension which had lent a Baroque aspect to the perspectives of Kerstiaen de Keuninck (*ca* 1560-1632/35), Joost de Momper (1564-1635) and Jacques d'Arthois (1613-1686). Here too a more restful and idyllic form of painting developed in the second half of the century. This was already heralded in the work of Lucas van Uden (1595-1672), and also in the later work of Jan Wildens, but was given its main expression by David Teniers and Gillis Neyts (1623?-1687?). They painted unpretentious, delicate impressions, sometimes comparable with the soft light and silvery atmosphere of dreamy Dutch landscapes.

The most original landscape painter in the second half of the 17th century certainly was Jan Siberechts (1627 – *ca* 1700). He represented fords where peasant women, carts and cows were making their way across, shepherdesses with their flocks and other scenes from country life. His thoughtful compositions, most of which

David Teniers the Younger, *Wedding-party with dancing and eating farmers* (detail), 1647, canvas, 75 × 112 cm. Madrid, Prado.

give the impression of having been created in the cool of a spring morning, are bathed in an atmosphere of peace and tranquillity. What a contrast with Rubens' animated, cosmic landscapes and with the *furia* of his fluent brushwork! Friedländer was undoubtedly going too far in describing Siberechts as a 'Flemish Vermeer'; yet his comparison works, as to the mood which these paintings awake in us.

The evolution of the still-life parallels that of the other genres. Jan Fyt (1611-1661), the most prominent of the many pupils of Frans Snyders, turned in the 1640's to more contemplative than dynamic paintings of storerooms and spoils of the chase. His animals and fruits, and also his few flowerpieces, testify to his great mastery of brushwork. The various matters – such as rough or downy furs, velvety fruits or worm-eaten wood – are painted with a consummate sureness of touch. The same style was employed by several other artists, notably Pieter Boel (1622-1674).

A major aspect of still-life painting is the flowerpiece. The vases and garlands, of which which Jan Breughel had made free-standing subjects, were further developed by his pupil Daniel Seghers (1590-1661), who became a master in 1601 and shortly afterwards joined the Jesuits. Typical of Seghers are the luxuriant garlands around cartouches, in which usually a religious motif is illustrated, executed by one of the numerous Antwerp

figure painters in his entourage, especially Cornelis Schut and Erasmus Quellin.

So far it can be concluded that Flemish painting up to about the last quarter of the 17th century was tremendously productive. There were, indeed, more than sufficient outlets in Antwerp for the art trade to thrive vigorously. From there vast consignments of paintings and *objects d'art* were sent abroad, as far as Lima and other places in South America. Moreover, Flemish artists themselves sometimes went to foreign markets. Among them were Cornelis de Vos and David Teniers, who put up their works for sale at the St Germain-des-Prés fair in Paris. Gradually the French capital took over Antwerp's role as the leading centre of artistic activity and art trade in Europe. As a result of the acute deterioration of the economic situation during the second half of the century, many painters tried their luck abroad. Notable examples were Peter Boel, who settled in Paris in 1668, and Jan Siberechts, who emigrated to England in 1675. The trend was to continue into the 18th century.

Compared with the 'Century of Rubens' the 18th century was unmistakably a period of decline of painting in the Southern Netherlands. In no way did it set the tone as it had done previously, and in a rather provincial manner it participated in the new artistic

431

Cornelis de Vos, *Self-portrait together with the wife and the two children of the artist*, canvas, 118 × 162 cm, signed and dated 1621. Brussels, Museums of Fine Arts.

the embellishment of staircases and drawing rooms of mansions in his native town. He too is mostly associated with the late Rubensian tradition; though he also borrowed from abroad.

Van Reysschoot also painted scenes in grisaille, a specialization which, in the wake of the Dutch painter Jacob de Wit, found many imitators in the Southern Netherlands. In this field Marten Geeraerts (1707-1791) acquired a great reputation, as a result of which he also provided grisailles for many patrician houses and country dwellings in Holland and Zeeland.

In addition to the history and grisaille painters, mention must be made of a considerable number of artists who might be grouped under the head of 'minor masters'. Most of their work consisted of genres and family portraits in the genre vein, known as 'conversation pieces'. Some of them, such as Jan-Baptist Lambrechts (1680-1732), Peter Snyers (1681-1752) and Peter Angillus (1685-1734) – without question the greatest – occasionally introduced still-life elements, such as vegetables, flowers, fish and game. Others, such as Gerard Thomas (1663-1723) and Balthasar van den Bossche (1681-1715), his pupil, frequently set their genre scenes in sculptors' and painters' studios. Hendrik Goovaerts (1669-1720) did the same, but also painted a *Carnival Festival in a Palace* (1714 – Brussels, Museums of Fine Arts). These artists deserve more attention than has so far been given. In a very specific, somewhat stolidly bourgeois manner, they introduced Rococo into painting at about the same time as Antoine Watteau (1684-1721), but with less refinement and depth.

The same can be said of Jan Jozef Horemans the

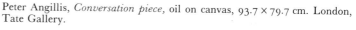

Peter Angillis, *Conversation piece*, oil on canvas, 93.7 × 79.7 cm. London, Tate Gallery.

movements which were developing elsewhere, particularly in France. Although Flemish art still exhibited a character of its own, and was practised by artists of merit, no masters of real genius such as Rubens, Jordaens, van Dyck and Brouwer, or highly talented exponents such as Teniers and Siberechts were there to be found. Even so, the 18th-century Flemish painters have not yet formed the subject of really thorough-going studies.

If, with this reservation in mind, we endeavour to assess the entire output in the Southern Netherlands during the 18th century, we can discern two parallel movements. On the one hand, we find a number of artists who, in the manner of the epigons and *Enkelschüler* of Rubens, to some extent carried on his tradition. Outstanding among them was, indisputably, Pieter Jozef Verhaghen (1728-1811); a highly productive painter who did numerous and sometimes very large canvases for many churches, and also for major Brabant abbeys. However 'post-Rubensian', his altarpieces nevertheless have a character of their own, with an unmistakable 18th-century flavour. Willem Jacob Herreyns (1743-1827) painted along the same lines, continuing to do so into the first decades of the 19th century.

In the same category of history painters must be placed Petrus Norbert van Reysschoot (1738-1795), of Ghent. However, he was better known for large decorative compositions, embodying mythological scenes for

Jan A. Garemijn, *The tea-party*, 1778, canvas, 59 × 93.5 cm. Bruges, Groeninge Museum.

Elder (1682-1759) and his son, Jan Jozef the Younger (1714 – after 1790). They painted scenes from the life of the upper middle class, usually sedate conversation pieces. The most talented representative of this somewhat bourgeois Flemish Rococo was the Bruges artist Jan Antoon Garemijn (1712-1799), who also won distinction with paintings of religious scenes and portraits. In addition, he produced vast landscapes with figures in them, such as *The Construction of the Bruges-Ghent Canal* (1758 – Bruges, Groeninge Museum). The countless small figures depicted are done in a crisp Rococo style. Such large-scale canvases were painted in the second half of the 18th century to adorn walls of drawing rooms, being fitted into the panelling.

Other 'minor masters', but of a different sort, were Theobald Michau (1676-1765), who until far into the 18th century imitated in a charming manner small landscapes with Jan Breughel I figures; and a number of painters of battles and equestrian scenes in which the influence of the Dutch 'horse painter' Philips Wouwerman is sometimes detectable, including Jan Peter Verdussen (1700-1763), Karel van Falens (1683-1733) and Pieter van Bredael (1683-1735).

It should be recorded that several 'minor masters' settled, and were welcomed, in other countries: Peter Tillemans (1680-1754) in England; Alexander Goovaerts (1701-1745) in Mainz; Jan Peter Verdussen

in France. Also worthy of note are the landscapes of the 'Veduta painters' (*vedutisti*) Jan Frans van Bloemen (1662-1720) and Hendrik van Lint (1684-1726), who gained considerable fame in Italy.

From about 1760 a new style, neoclassicism, made its appearance in Flemish painting, exploited by Andries Cornelis Lens (1739-1822) of Antwerp, who while in Rome became acquainted with the aesthetic theories of Winckelmann. His art took its inspiration from the "*edle Einfalt und stille Grösse*" (noble simplicity and calm grandeur), which Winckelmann admired in works of art from antiquity and recommended to artists of his own time. Even so, in the elegance of his figures and the brightness of his colours – perhaps in spite of his own theoretical ideas – Lens remained a child of the Rococo era in which he had grown up. The same is true in some measure of the Bruges artist Joseph Benoit Suvée, who in 1771 won the *Prix de Rome* in Paris. He painted academic portraits and historical and mythological representations in neoclassicistic vein, in which from time to time Pre-Romantic features can already be observed.

We must, however, wait until right at the end of the 18th century before we see a more 'orthodox' and more thorough-going neoclassicism emerge, under the influence of Louis David. This marked the final break with the tradition of Rubens and the Flemish genre.

Christoffel Jegher.

CL

P. P. Rub. delin. & exc

CVM PRIVILEGIIS.

Graphic art

Portrait of a man (Giovanni Cornaro, doge of Venice?), camaieu (= two-colours) wood-cut, 32.2 × 23.4 cm, Christoffel Jegher after P.P. Rubens. This print has been improved by Rubens personally. Brussel, Royal Libary.

Around 1600, the woodcut had practically disappeared. Intaglio printing reigned unchallenged, both in prints and in book illustration. This remained the case in the 17th and 18th centuries. But at Antwerp, the woodcut had one last spectacular flare-up with a master who may be regarded as the greatest European woodcutter of the 17th century: Christoffel Jegher (Antwerp 1596-1652/53; of German origin, his real name being Jegherendorf). In the early years of the 17th century, Pieter Kints of Brussels made a number of woodcuts; and at Antwerp the very meritorious Dutchman Christoffel van Sichem (*ca* 1546-1624) did some work before he returned to the north.

Balthasar I Moretus actually needed a full-time collaborator for his *Officina Plantiniana*, and from 1625 to 1643 he called upon Christoffel Jegher: for illustrations to scientific works that were not too expensive, for cheap versions of liturgical works (but this was limited to one effort: the *Missale Romanum* in folio of 1632), for the 144 portraits of Roman Emperors in two colours, in the fifth part of the collected works of Hubertus Goltzius (reproduced from the 132 portraits published for the first time at Antwerp in 1557, with twelve additional portraits; executed in 1631-1634 although the edition was not put on the market before 1645), for initials, printers' marks, tailpieces and the like. But Jegher attained international fame because he attracted the attention of P.P. Rubens. The great master of Flemish Baroque, as we shall immediately see in detail, ensured European attention for his paintings, by having them reproduced and multiplied as burin engravings. In this connection, he also considered the woodcut, by then hopelessly outdated. Here he was probably influenced by what he had seen in Italy where, for the same objective as Rubens', Titian had surrounded himself with woodcutters. But Rubens only carried out his plan in 1630, when he realized that Jegher could fulfil it and, through the black and white contrasts in the woodcut, could express the dynamism in his works. Jegher did not let Rubens down: his woodcut prints after the master (distributed by Rubens himself)

Hercules kills the hydra, wood-cut (first state), 61 × 35.6 cm, Christoffel Jegher after the painting by Rubens at the Banqueting Hall, Whitehall, London. Antwerp, Stedelijk Prentenkabinet.
A (probably by Rubens) improved print can be found in the Bibliothèque Nationale (Cabinet des Estampes), Paris.

are among the most impressive creations of their kind in the 17th century. The personal interest of Rubens for the works of Jegher is shown clearly enough, by the fact that proofs of woodcuts have been preserved on which Rubens himself had made improvements.

But after Rubens' death, Christoffel Jegher ceased his activity. His son Jan Christoffel Jegher (Antwerp 1618-1666/67) continued in the same style but with less talent (including work for the *Officina Plantiniana*, 1644-1655). Later in the century, Gonzales van Heylen (1661 – *ca* 1730; working for, *inter alia*, the *Officina Plantiniana* in 1694 and 1703-1715) still produced some weak decorative work. And that was practically the end of the art of woodcutting in Flanders and Brabant. The Moretus family had their final woodcuts in the second half of the 18th century executed by, among others, Parisian specialists.

INTAGLIO PRINTING IN THE FIRST HALF OF THE 17th CENTURY Graphics in the 17th-18th centuries, in Flanders and Brabant as in the rest of Europe, was centred around intaglio printing. In these centuries, complicated variants were worked out of the classical forms of expression, burin and etching: the mezzotint or 'black art' (in which the plate was roughened beforehand with a frosting chisel or iron; invented at Amsterdam in 1642 by the German Ludwig von Siegen), and around

435

the middle of the 18th century the *vernis-mou*, the crayon manner and the aquatint. There were virtuoso practitioners of each of these new techniques in Europe, but they did not become very popular in Flanders and Brabant. For the mezzotint we may note the names of Jan van der Bruggen (Brussels 1649 – ?, master at Antwerp in 1678, later in Paris) and Jan Thomas (Ypres?-Vienna?, master at Antwerp in 1640, at Mainz in 1654, in Vienna *ca* 1656). But that was all.

Flemish and Brabant graphic art in the 17th-18th centuries remained attached to burin and etching. As in the previous period, the burin was handled exclusively by professionals working after models from other artists; while the amateurs expressed themselves in etchings, working on their own ideas. Now, however, we also find many etchers (and sometimes burinist-etchers) specializing in the reproduction of works by other artists. As in the 16th century, these professional engravers produced both prints and book illustrations, according to how things turned out.

Many of the masters from the previous chapter continued to produce after 1600. Right up to the end of the 17th century the firm of Galle remained the principal publisher of prints in the Southern Netherlands, and one of the most important in Europe. Filips Galle (1537-1612) was vigorously supported from the end of the 16th century onwards by his sons Theodoor (*ca* 1570-1633, master in 1596) and Cornelis (*ca* 1576-1650, master in 1610), and his sons-in-law Adriaan

Collaert (*ca* 1560-1618, master in 1580) and Karel de Mallery (*ca* 1576 – after 1631, master in 1597).

After the death of Filips Galle, Theodoor took over the management of the firm (1612-1633) to be succeeded by his son Jan (1600-1676, head of the business from 1633 to 1676) and his grandson Norbert (1648-1694, head of the business from 1676 to 1694). But it is symptomatic of the general evolution of graphic art in the Southern Netherlands that from Jan Galle onwards the firm did no more than publish its stocks of old plates (on which the names of Filips and Theodoor were systematically replaced by that of Jan).

Apart from the Galles, there were other publishers of prints active at Antwerp, most of them also engravers: Jan Baptist Vrints (died in 1612, specializing in maps), Martin van den Enden (active *ca* 1630 – *ca* 1645), Gillis Hendricx (active in the same period), Nikolaas Lauwers (*ca* 1600-1652), the family Huybrechts (Huberti), father Jan (1612-1670) and son Cornelis Meyssens (born in 1640, died at Vienna); Frans van den Wijngaerde (1614-1679). But most of these firms, if they reached 1650 at all, declined rapidly after that date.

RUBENS AND THE BURIN ENGRAVING   But that point had not been reached in the first half of the 17th century. At that time, the attraction of Antwerp was still so strong that many foreign masters – particularly Dutch – came to settle in the Scheldt town. In this half century, the Antwerp school of engravers flourished

St Catherine, etching touched-up with burin (third state), 29.3 × 20 cm, P.P. Rubens (with the assistance of a burin-engraver: Lucas Vorsterman?). Antwerp, Stedelijk Prentenkabinet.
This is the only print which can be ascribed to Rubens for certain. A proof which has been improved with a pen (probably by Rubens) can be found in the Metropolitan Museum at New York. The original painting of Rubens was hanging in St Carolus-Borromeus' Church at Antwerp, but it disappeared in the fire of 1718.

Suzanne and the elderlings, fragment (textpart at the bottom has not been reproduced), engraving (second state), 39.2 × 27.9 cm, Lucas Vorsterman after P.P. Rubens, 1620. Antwerp, Stedelijk Prentenkabinet.
The preparatory drawing of Vorsterman is in the British Museum at London.

Rest on the Flight to Egypt, camaieu (= two-colours) wood-cut (second state), 45.6 × 59.6 cm, Christoffel Jegher after P.P. Rubens. Antwerp, Stedelijk Prentenkabinet.
Improved (probably by Rubens) proofs in the Bibliothèque Nationale in Paris, the Rijksprentenkabinet in Amsterdam and the Museum of Fine Arts at Antwerp.

spectacularly, with a production counted among the most beautiful in Europe. The man to be honoured for this is, as for so many other aspects of Flemish Baroque art, P.P. Rubens.

Only one etching (worked over by a specialist with the burin), *St Catherine* (date unknown), can be attributed to the master himself. But he had an uncommon interest in graphics and its possibilities. His aim was threefold. The primary aim was a public relations operation: he intended to make his creations known throughout Europe by means of burin engravings, carried out by carefully chosen masters and under his personal control (various proofs with improvements by Rubens in his own hand have been preserved). He himself directed this distribution, and he ensured that he would obtain the financial profit from it by taking the *privileges* (which we should nowadays call the copyright) for his own account; finally all these prints were accompanied by a text, bestowing the necessary praise on some domestic or foreign personality – which would naturally impress these influential figures, and gain their support for the artist and his works.

Jan-Baptist Barbé (1578-1649), an apprentice of Filips Galle, whom Rubens had got to know in Italy, was probably the first in the series. Others followed: Pieter I de Jode (1570-1634); some apprentices of Hendrik Goltzius from Haarlem such as Willem Swanenburg (in 1611-1612), Egbert van Panderen (1581?-1637?, active at Antwerp *ca* 1606-*ca* 1609), Andries Stock (*ca* 1580 – after 1648), Jacob Matham (1571-1631, stepson of H. Goltzius), Jan Muller (1571-1628), and also the Frenchman Michel Lasne (active at Antwerp in 1617-1620). But this still did not amount to very much.

437

Already very noteworth as a work of art is *Judith and Holofernes*, engraved by Cornelis Galle around 1610. But Cornelis Galle left it at that; probably not because Rubens underestimated his work, but because Cornelis was too occupied with the family business.

The production of Rubens' prints only got into its stride in 1615 with Pieter Soutman (Haarlem *ca* 1580-1657). He worked with Rubens from 1615 to 1624 as a painter but also as a graphic artist, and produced a number of meritorious prints after Rubens, combining the burin with etching. But Rubens was still not satisfied. As he wrote in a letter of 1619: "It seems to me a lesser evil to have the work carried out before my own eyes by a young man who is anxious to do well, than by more talented people who follow their own ideas."

This 'young man who was anxious to do well' was already at work in Rubens' atelier: Lucas Vorsterman (Bommel/Gelderland 1595 – Antwerp 1675) engraved from 1617/18 to 1623 a series of masterworks in which, by his virtuoso technique with the burin, he represented in copper with unequalled skill the essence of Rubens' art – the luminosity of colour. But the relations between painter and engraver soon became strained. Vorsterman suffered from depressions that led to persecution mania, and in 1622 he even made an attempt on Rubens' life. He then emigrated to England and returned to Antwerp in 1630 to work for Anthony van Dyck, among others, but without attaining his earlier heights.

Rubens then called on Nikolaas Ryckemans (before 1600 – ?) who had already engraved his *Palazzi di Genova* (1622) – but his work did not turn out well.

The Adoration of the shepherds, engraving (second state), 28.7 × 44.6 cm, Lucas Vorsterman after a painting by P.P. Rubens for the Dominican Convent at Antwerp, 1620. Antwerp, Stedelijk Prentenkabinet.

Salomon's judgment, fragment (textpart at the bottom has not been reproduced), engraving (second state). 43.3 × 51.4 cm, Boetius a Bolswert after P.P. Rubens. Antwerp, Stedelijk Prentenkabinet.
The original painting by Rubens can be found in the Museum of Copenhagen.

The return from the fields, engraving, 45.5 × 64.2 cm, Schelte a Bolswert after a painting by P.P. Rubens. Antwerp, Stedelijk Prentenkabinet. The original painting can be found in the Palazzo Pitti, Florence.

Nikolaas Lauwers (1600-1652) did somewhat better, but not too much. But finally Vorsterman's place could be occupied by new young talents: Paulus Pontius (Antwerp 1603-1658, working for Rubens from 1624 onwards, master in 1626/27) and the brothers Bolswert (or 'a Bolswert' – their real name being Uyttema): Boetius (Bolsward *ca* 1580 – Antwerp 1633, in 1618 in the Southern Netherlands, master at Antwerp in 1620) and Schelte (Bolsward *ca* 1586 – Antwerp 1659, master at Antwerp in 1625). Together with Lucas Vorsterman they are among the greatest burinists of the 17th century – particularly when they worked after and under the direction of Rubens.

Rubens also played an important role in the book illustration of his time. He provided Antwerp printers, in particular the *Officina Plantiniana* of his friend Balthasar I Moretus, with some dozen of models (drawings and some oil sketches). For the *Officina Plantiniana* (after a first trial in 1608, then only to illustrate a work by his brother Filips Rubens on Roman Antiquity) he already began working in 1613; at the end of his life (1637-1640), when he was plagued by gout, he had the drawings made, after his own ideas, by his apprentice

Erasmus Quellin. Most of them were cut on copper by Theodoor and Cornelis Galle.

In the field of book illustration, Rubens was especially interested in the title print in which, in the allegorical and symbolical manner so beloved by the humanists, he sought to visualize the contents of the books in question, often working out the whole space into a true Baroque painting. Via the *Officina Plantiniana*, these title prints found their way through Europe, providing a source of inspiration.

ETCHING IN THE 17th CENTURY The other masters of the Flemish school of painting showed less interest in book illustration and in the publication of prints under their supervision. Some of them did personally try their hand at graphics but, as might have been expected, they limited themselves almost exclusively to etching.

A special mention must be reserved for Anthony van Dyck. Immediately after his return from Italy in 1626, he began to work on his collection of engraved portraits, the famous *Iconographie* (the full title of which was *Icones principum virorum doctorum pictorum calcho-*

Title-print, fragment (the textpart has not been reproduced), engraving 31.7 × 21.7 cm, Cornelis Galle after a design by Rubens. Antwerp, Plantin-Moretus Museum.
Title-print for Ludovicus Blosius, *Opera*, Antwerp, Officina Plantiniana, (Balthasar I Moretus), 1632.
The original drawing by Rubens (according to some specialists after Rubens), is in the British Museum at London; a proof of the print is in the Bibliothèque Nationale (Cabinet des Estampes) at Paris; the original copper-plate is in the Plantin-Moretus Museum at Antwerp.

Samson opens the mouth of the lion, title-print, engraving, 19.7 × 14.1 cm, Cornelis Galle after a design by Rubens. Antwerp, Plantin-Moretus Museum (where also the copper-plate is kept).
Title-print for Maffeo Barberini (Urbanus VIII), *Poemata*, Antwerp, Officina Plantiniana (Balthasar I Moretus), 1634.

Samson opens the mouth of the lion, drawing (pen in brown on a foundation of black chalk), 17.9 × 13.8 cm. P.P. Rubens (according to some specialists after Rubens), 1634. Antwerp, Plantin-Moretus Museum.
Design for the title-print of M. Barberini, *Poemata*. Antwerp, Officina Plantiniana (Balthasar I Moretus), 1634.

graphorum statuariorium nec non amatorum pictoria artis numero centum ab Antonio van Dijck pictore ad vivum expressae eiusque sumptibus aeri incisae). A first edition with eighty portraits was published between 1636 and 1641 by Martin van den Enden, and increased to a hundred portraits and published in 1645 by Gillis Hendricx. Other editions with supplements and modifications followed. But only about twenty of the hundred portraits were etched by van Dyck himself – and with very few exceptions (such as the masterly portrait of Erasmus) these etchings were worked over with the burin by specialists such as Lucas Vorsterman, Pieter de Jode the Younger, Jacob Neeffs and Schelte Bolswert. Van Dyck also made masterly transformations of some of his own works into etchings, but these too were worked over with the burin. He is truly one of the great masters of his time, both as a painter and as an etcher.

Other prominent painters made but a few etchings before giving up, as Thomas Willeboirts Bosschaert (1614-1654), Gaspar de Craeyer (1584-1669) and Abraham van Diepenbeeck (1596-1675). Theodoor Rombouts (1597-1637), Frans Snyders (1579-1657) and Gerard Zegers (1591-1657) were not much more active. Somewhat more productive were Bonaventura Peeters (with Scheldt views, 1614-1652), Cornelis Schut (1597-1655) and Theodoor van Thulden (1606-1669). Some prints are known by Jacob Jordaens, dated 1652; but they are of such a poor quality, that it may well be doubted whether the master himself was responsible for them. The same holds for some dreary little prints that bear the name of Adriaen Brouwer (1605/06-1638).

Particular distinction as graphic artists was achieved by the landscape painters Lucas van Uden (1595-1672/73), Jan Baptist Bonnecroy (1618-1678) and Gillis Neyts (1623-1687); the animal painters Jan Fyt (1611-1661) and Pieter Boel (1622-1680); and the

440

LVCAS VORSTERMANS
CALCOGRAPHVS ANTVERPIÆ IN GELDRIA NATVS.

Erasmus Rotterdamus.

genre painter David Teniers the Younger (1610-1690, although probably not all the many etchings bearing his name were executed by Teniers himself). Jacob Harrewijn (1660-1740), who was not particularly significant as a painter, was rescued from oblivion by a series of documentary prints on Antwerp. A special place is occupied by the Czech Wenzel Hollar (Prague 1607 – London 1677), who in the course of his ramblings through Europe spent many years in Antwerp (1644-1652). There he produced a number of meritorious prints, often of great documentary interest. This list could be completed with a boring list of artists of the second rank, but they are not responsible for any notable achievements.

DECLINE AND EXODUS IN THE SECOND HALF OF THE 17th CENTURY   Much the same can be said of the professionals (burin engravers and etchers): although up to the end of the 17th century the quantity – the number of masters and the volume of their production – still remained high, the quality began to deteriorate rapidly around 1650. The older generation, active in the first years of the 17th century, and the brilliant burin engravers around Rubens, were already accompanied by weaker masters; and these were followed by figures of still lesser talent. With an uncommon amount of zeal, although with decreasing talent, most of them continued to copy Rubens, van Dyck, Jordaens and other prominent artists. While the first and second generation of engravers still knew their job – such as, apart from Nikolaas Lauwers and Nikolaas Ryckemans (already mentioned in connection with Rubens), Antoon van der Does (1609-1680), Marinus van der Goes (1599-1639), Pieter de Jode the Younger (1606- after 1674), Koenraad Lauwers (1632 – after 1662), Koenraad Waumans (1619-1650), Jan Witdoeck (1615 – after 1642) – the epigones and the epigones of

Portrait of the burin-engraver Lucas Vorsterman (1595–1675), etching touched-up with burin 24.5 × 15.8 cm, Anthony van Dyck (with the assistance of a burin-engraver). Antwerp, Stedelijk Prentenkabinet.

Portrait of Desiderius Erasmus, etching, 24 × 15 cm, Anthony van Dyck, after a drawing by Hans Holbein. Antwerp, Stedelijk Prentenkabinet.

Jupiter and Io, fragment, etching, (first state with at the bottom: *Fac. Iordaens inventor 1652*), 29 × 36.1 cm, Jacob Jordaens (It is not sure that it was Jordaens himself who made this print). Brussels, Royal Libary (Prentenkabinet).

The prodigal son looks after the pigs (also called *The farmyard*), etching, 11.5 × 17 cm, Jan Baptist Bonnecroy (1618-1676). Antwerp, Stedelijk Prentenkabinet.

epigones are only worth mentioning in a detailed book on Flemish graphics.

In parallel with this disappointing evolution, a massive exodus started. While in the first decades of the 17th century, many foreigners had succumbed to the siren songs of Antwerp (and of Rubens), already before the middle of that century a flood of emigration started, dispersing many good and less good Flemish and Brabant masters over Europe.

After 1585, Flanders and Brabant had once more become piously Catholic. Consequently, in contrast to the great emigration in the second half of the 16th century, this time there were relatively few seeking refuge in protestant countries such as Holland – among them Hendrik Bary (*ca* 1625-1707) – and England – including Robert Voerst (1596-1635) and Pieter Lombart (1648-1681). The German Empire too showed no great power of attraction, with only a few exceptions, such as the already mentioned mezzotint specialist Jan Thomas and the painter-etcher Frans de Neve (1606 – after 1688, after a stay in Rome, 1660-1666, active in Salzburg till at least 1688). Strangely enough, also Spain was little in demand (apart from Melchior Christoffels, born in 1615, in Seville). The great flow went to Italy and France, where a few chose Lyons (including Jacob Buys, active after 1660), but most were tempted by Paris. Especially prominent among these was Gerard Edelinck (1640-1707) who, in 1665, was summoned by Colbert to France where he exercised a profound influence on the art of engraving in the late 17th century. But he was preceded by a whole host of fellow-countrymen, who also made their contributions to shaping French graphics in this century: Jaspar Isac

(died in 1654), Melchior Tavernier (1594-1641), Pieter Firens (active *ca* 1650), Pieter van Schuppen (1623-1702), Nikolaas Pitau (1632-1676), Matheus Plattenberg (1606-1660), Abraham Genoels (painter-etcher, 1640-1723, in Paris from 1659 to 1672) and the already mentioned mezzotint specialist Jan van der Bruggen. The attraction of Italy was hardly less, with burin engravers such as Aubert Clouwet (1636-1679), Jacob Blondeau (died in Rome in 1698) and Arnold van Westerhout (1666-1725); and painter-etchers such as Cornelis de Wael (1592-1672), Jan Baptist de Wael (1599 – after 1658), Jan Miel (1599-1663), Valentin Lefebvre (1642-1700) and Jan Frans van Bloemen (1662-1749). The greatest distance was achieved by the Brussels painter-etcher Michiel Sweerts (1624-1664) who ended his days at Goa in India.

In Flanders, towards the end of the century, the graphic arts declined rapidly and abruptly, after the quality also in quantity. But for those who ended their days in the 18th century, there was after 1700 not a single painter-etcher of more than local significance; and even the professionals who still had some idea of how to use the burin or etching needle can, for the whole century, be counted on the fingers of one hand: Richard van Orley, who actually belonged to the past century (1652-1732), Hendrik Diamaer (born in 1685), Frans Pilsen (1700-1784), Lodewijk Fruytiers (1713-1782) and Lambert Claessens (1764-1834).

For three full centuries, the graphic art in Flanders and Brabant had maintained a high level of excellence and had often been a source of inspiration, or at least of admiration for the rest of Europe – but around 1700, it had virtually ceased to exist.

Peasant's kitchen, etching, 15 × 20 cm, David Teniers the Younger. Antwerp, Stedelijk Prentenkabinet.

Dogs, etching, 15.8 × 17 cm, Jan Fijt (from a series of eight prints, representing dogs, edited by Jan Fijt in 1642). Antwerp, Stedelijk Prentenkabinet.

443

Furniture

Like the other applied arts, 17th-century Flemish furniture making flourished because of the thorough craftsmanship and the ingenuity of cabinet-makers, ebony carvers, wood-turners, inlayers and Spanish chairmakers; supported by the expertise, originality and love of experimentation of the theorists. During the Baroque period craftsmen produced a considerable number of original pieces of furniture which can still be admired today, and of which fortunately a large number have survived. The lack of development of 18th-century furniture means that inevitably a different amount of attention must be paid to the two centuries.

This chapter will deal only with the most important aspects of 17th and 18th-century furniture, and consequently a rather simplistic view may arise. First, the influence of books of designs on Baroque furniture will be concisely outlined; followed by a survey of different types of 17th-century furniture for storage and seating, and their places in the interiors of houses. Special attention will be paid to the famous 17th-century art cabinets and their popularity abroad. Finally, the French influence in the 18th century will be discussed, with a description of the changes taking place during this period, as compared with the preceding century.

The source materials for the study of 17th and 18th-century furniture is fairly analogous to that of the 16th century; although a considerable number of pieces of Baroque furniture have survived, including some dated examples, so that a choice had to be made from them.

During the Baroque period Antwerp played a leading role. The city produced influental examples of both ecclesiastical and secular furniture; as did Bruges, where the oak Baroque cupboard developed an individual style.

As in the 16th century, furniture remained sensitive to changes in architecture during the 17th. It was above all the works of Vignola and contemporary publications by J. Francart, *Premier livre d'Architecture...* (published in Brussels in 1617), and the well-known book by Rubens, *Palazzi di Genova* (1622), that inspired the monumental decoration of facades. As the front of a cupboard was conceived as a sort of facade, the charac-

teristics of Baroque architecture such as barley twist pillars, broken pediments *etc* were also used in furniture making. In order to achieve a sense of space – another important 17th-century feature – the corner pillars were often placed at an angle of 45°, so that they would be visible from a number of different viewpoints. This same sense of space accounts for the construction of the perspectives in *cantoren* (art cabinets).

The revised edition of Vredeman de Vries' *Different pourtraicts*, published in Amsterdam by his son Paul in 1630, was particularly useful for cabinet-makers. The (translated) title now read: *Different cabinet designs, including doors, wardrobes, court cabinets, beds, tables, chests, chairs, benches, seats, towel racks, glass cabinets and many other pieces of furniture, all most excellently arranged and drawn.* It now contained four times as many designs as in 1583. In addition to the surviving 16th-century designs and patterns, these pieces of furniture contained new Baroque features, such as bosses, acanthus leaves, oval frames, heads of herms, full figures *etc*, which can be recognized in the surviving furniture. These designs with their wealth of sculpture fired the imagination of the craftsmen, and were a challenge to their skill. Unfortunately no examples identical to the designs have survived, but their influence is very evident. In addition, interesting drawings of furniture – often accompanied by a grand plan, even with indications of the sort of wood to be used – can be found in the work of C. van de Passe Jnr, *Officina arcularia. Cabinet-makers' workshop, including the principle pieces of the art of the cabinet-maker, with the basic designs and decorated with the new inventions, by ...*, which was published in Amsterdam in 1651. The influence of these two books of designs obviously extended to Baroque furniture in both the Northern and the Southern Netherlands.

OAK FURNITURE FOR STORAGE AND SEATING IN THE BAROQUE INTERIOR   The large rooms of the front and the back of the house, linked in an organic way, provided plenty of room for a great diversity of household and ornamental furniture. The 16th-century structure of the high oak cupboard with two doors remained virtually unaltered; but scales, root motifs, lions' heads *etc* were used to decorate the posts (Antwerp, Brouwershuis). The doors were decorated with geometric profiles glued in mitred profiles around a central diamond-shaped motif or a thick wooden 'cushion'. During the first quarter of the 17th century this piece of furniture still rested on straight legs, later on ball feet. The first modest Baroque development was expressed in sculpted cornices, sometimes recessed, and decorated with bosses and ornamental leaves.

The second half of the 17th century saw the development of the famous two-door cupboard with cushions – often a linen cupboard – in which the raised cushions were glued with ebony or walnut, and in which the structure is stressed by pillars. This piece of furniture was especially popular in the Northern Netherlands, but probably it was also made and used in Flanders in the interiors of burghers' houses. In cupboards with four doors the central section, often elaborated as a drawer,

Frans Francken II and David Teniers the Younger, *Art Room,* painting
60 × 90 cm, non-dated. London, Princess Gate Collection.
In the middle of the room a two-door cabinet is displayed. It has an inlaid
vase of flowers on the door panels, ebony root-motifs on the posts and on the
top a damask cloth. In the front at the right, one can see a rectangular table
with a Turkish cloth on it.

was enhanced with rich carving. In this way the division
of the two sections of the cupboard was emphasized.
Sometimes this piece of furniture contained panels
which accentuated the structure in a sober but forceful
manner (Antwerp, Plantin-Moretus Museum).

From 1650 the structure of furniture was overshadowed by complicated floral friezes with a wealth of
cupids and animals. The exuberant Baroque style appears in the semi-relief carved work with sacred and
profane themes, found in the central door cushions or in
the caryatids of the central and side posts. During this
period the *troonkast*, a type of display cupboard, also
developed to the full. A number of examples reveal
imaginative caryatids supporting the cornice of the top
section of the cupboard, which is slightly recessed (Brussels, Museums of Art and History), and which depicts
a particular subject in an allegorical way.

Typical of the second half of the 17th century were
the four-door cupboards from Bruges, usually dated, in
which the top section with two oblong doors is half the
height of the bottom section, with two square doors. The

central or top section was sometimes made into a drawer
(Bruges, Gruuthuse Museum). These pieces of furniture were richly decorated with carvings of figures,
garlands of fruit, geometric designs, as well as historical
scenes and some examples of scenes from daily life
(Bruges, St John's Hospital).

Tall two-door cupboards were also very popular as
practical household furniture for storing services and
silver; these are called court cupboards or *rechbanken*.
Sometimes they had a stepped section at the back for
displaying ornamental china; and the doors would be
inlaid with vases of walnut, cypress or ebony, based on
designs by Paul Vredeman de Vries. Identical
cupboards with the same pattern of flowers can be
recognized in paintings. Consoles and shell motifs were
also used.

Convenient, small hanging cupboards with only one
door – which were mainly used for storing comestibles
such as jam – had a wooden lozenge-shaped lattice above
the small door, simple grooves or pilasters on the posts,
and were often dated (Bruges, St John's Hospital).

Similar to these were the so-called beguines' cupboards, in which the upper door also had lattice work, while the middle section closed with a hinged leaf which could also be used as a dining table, and with another door below this. There were many other pieces of furniture, including serviette presses (Bruges, Gruuthuse Museum) which enhanced the daily comfort of housewives and household staff.

The 17th-century interior was provided with a great variety of pieces of furniture to sit on. The Spanish chair remained the most typical one: this prestigious piece of furniture was found, apart from salons and important living rooms, in assembly halls or reception rooms of official bodies; such as those of town councils (Audenarde, Town Hall), guilds (Antwerp, Brouwershuis), chambers of rhetoric (Antwerp, Vleeshuis), monasteries (Bruges, Bouverie, Potterie Museum; Geel, Old Hospital), abbeys (Tongerlo, Premonstratensian Abbey) or brotherhoods (Beauvoorde, Mergherlynck Castle). Very often these bodies had their gilt or painted coats of arms stamped on the leather back of the chair, sometimes with an inscription. Patron saints, sometimes set in a scene with seals or inscriptions, were preferred in monasteries and hospitals (Bruges, St John's Hospital, St Godelieve's Abbey; St Amandsberg, St Elisabeth's Beguinage). With this decoration the piece of furniture became even more dignified, with a direct indication of its ownership. In guilds and chambers of rhetoric the Spanish chair was considered to be an honourable gift, and was often donated to the entering deacon; like the chair with the inscription by P.P. Rubens, dated 1633 (Antwerp, Rubens' house).

After 1640 the sections of the legs, as well as the eight rungs, were turned in a spiral or 'corkscrew' shape. The legs were connected by only five twisted rungs: the bottom three in an H-shape, while the others were attached in the middle of the front and back (Veurne, Town Hall). The posts at the back of the chair were crowned with the heads of angels or lions. Examples from the Northern Netherlands were very similar to these Flemish pieces of furniture, as were several chairs in the French Louis XIII style, which were upholstered in leather. Important or older people rested in Spanish leather seats, which developed in a similar way as the Spanish chair. The characteristic arm rests of these seats evolved from a straight broad design with baluster shaped supports (Antwerp, Convent of the Grauw Sisters) to a less comfortable curved style. The most

Baroque side-board from Bruges with four doors, 144 × 161 × 63 cm, 1678. Bruges, St John's Hospital.
On the left top door a chemist's interior is depicted, at the right a ward of a clinic with patients who are confined to their beds, the posts represent the Saints Godelieve of Hungaria, Michael and Dorothea. In the middle of the bottom doors John the Baptist and St Augustine are depicted.

Spanish chair in leather, 90 × 44 × 38 cm, middle of the 17th century. Bruges, St Godelieve's Abbey.
The strangulation of St Godelieve has been depicted in a conventional oval medallion. At the bottom is an unknown coat of arms, at the top are two angels carrying attributes for a martyr: a laurel-wreath and a palm-branch. The original stamp has been preserved.

common upholstery was in black, brown or red leather; although velvet or cloth dyed red, green, blue or yellow, were also popular. To match the other soft furnishing, *viz* the curtains or drapes on the beds, the housewife chose to apply damask, *say*, or even tapestry work to the Spanish chairs. Some meticulous households would resort to loose covers, which could be stored away in the court cupboard when not used for a season. In addition to the Spanish ones, there would be Prussian (probably upholstered in blue leather) or Russian (possibly upholstered in a pleasant resin-scented red leather) leather chairs; together with ordinary wooden chairs, which could be decorated with carving.

In most Baroque interiors there would be heavy oak, ball-footed tables. The massive leaves of the tables were supported by four solid ball feet, which were turned on a lathe. These were copied directly from the design book by C. van de Passe. There would be either an animal's claw, or a flattened sphere under the lower cube-shaped section (Antwerp, the former in the Brouwershuis; both in the Convent of the Grauw Sisters). The legs were connected by four straight, fluted rungs or a V-shaped fork. A number of museums, monasteries and abbeys in Flanders possess these tables; some even still use them. Like the legs of the chairs, after 1640, table legs were made with a barley twist. As far as is known, few of the fantastic designs from the design book by Vredeman de Vries have survived. Inlaid work using unusual sorts of wood such as ebony, rosewood, olive and agate wood appeared in smaller ornamental tables; the leaf of the table would be decorated with floral patterns, animals and *putti*; as in the work of Michiel Verbiest, dating from 1689 (Amsterdam, Rijksmuseum).

During the Baroque period beds continued to have a canopy. Similar motifs to those on cupboards were incorporated on the frieze and the other parts of the oak frame (Bruges, Potterie Museum; Brussels, Museums of Art and History). The surrounding sides were still partly enclosed, and the foot of the bed might be adorned with a series of turned balusters. There were also gilt beds or beds made of walnut, sometimes with barley twist posts. All the beds were still enclosed with curtains and richly made up with cushions, a mattress and low hanging bedspreads in heavy materials.

Inlaid state-table, 88.5 × 146 × 88 cm, Michiel Verbiest and Pieter de Looze, 1689. Amsterdam, Rijksmuseum.
The excessively decorated top, showing flowers, animals, *putti*, fruits and the coat of arms of the Neuff-van Eversdijck family, is supported by a magnificently elaborated leg, having curls in a C-form, ram's heads, *putti*, garlands and a cross in X-form.

ANTWERP CABINETS   The fame of Flemish furniture is largely due to the famous Antwerp art cabinets, *viz* the *scribanen* and *cantoren*, which were quite popular throughout the Baroque period. A number of specialized firms – including those of the Boussemart, Forchondt and Musson families – made, sold and exported these luxurious pieces of furniture. These cabinets had rather a limited practical use, but they were the centrepiece of any 17th-century art collection. In fact, the customers for these cabinets – according to the surviving correspondence and the accounts of the above-mentioned family concerns – not only included the Flemish nobility, but also the foremost European aristocrats; such as the Emperor of Germany, the Monarch of Liechtenstein, the Princess of Orange, the Marquis of Lavallière *etc*, as well as the very wealthy burghers. To make these cabinets the Antwerp firms often called upon well-known ebony carvers, gilders, wood turners, coppersmiths, silversmiths and painters. The distribution of these ornamental cabinets was ensured by word-of-mouth advertising by the often moving merchants or noblemen who owned one of them; or by members of the family businesses in branches of the firm abroad.

The first type of cabinet was the *scribaan*, the precursor of which had already appeared in the 16th century. This was a rectangular oak or beech cupboard with ebony pieces stuck on, the front of which was taken up entirely by a series of little drawers distributed over the various sections. The fronts of these drawers were often decorated with tortoise-shell panels with an ivory edge. The cabinets were made both with and without doors (Brussels, Museums of Art and History).

Some of the large scribans were completely covered in ebony, carved with mythological or biblical scenes or decorated with reliefs (Antwerp, Rubens' House, Rockox' House; Brussels, Museums of Art and History). This type is similar to the ebony scribans, attributed to Jean Macé (Paris, Cluny Museum, Louvre). This artist, who worked in Paris, was probably trained in the Southern Netherlands; as his cabinets have roughly the same decorative designs and techniques. In many cases the iconography of his French cabinets was based on 17th-century novels.

Apart from the scribans, the *cantoren*, made in various models, were well-beloved. These rectangular pieces of furniture were usually topped with a gallery of copper balusters. The central small portico shows an architectural frame including a pediment, keystones and pillars. On either side of the central section there would be four or six drawers one above the other, all with an oval cushion surrounded by a copper or silver edge. The fronts of the drawers, the central door and the two doors which could close the cabinet were decorated with ebony and reddened tortoise-shell, characteristic of Flemish furniture. The lower part of the cabinet often consisted of pilasters (Antwerp, Vleeshuis; Bruges, Gruuthuse Museum; Brussels, Museums of Art and History; Amsterdam, Rijksmuseum; London, Victoria and Albert Museum; several German, English and Italian private collections). Behind the central door there was nearly always a *prospectiefke*. This perspective was a

Scriban with ebony glued on it, 186.5 × 168 × 52.6 cm, middle of the 17th century. Brussels, Museums of Art and History.
The engraved representation in the medallions of the four square cushions on the front doors, depict at the left side *Perimele in insulam*, and at the right side *Diana orders an Aesculapius to look after Hippolytus*, after models by A. Tempesta for the *Metamorphoses* by Ovid (G. Derveaux-Van Ussel, 1973).

miniature chamber consisting of three walls, a floor and a ceiling. Mirrors would be glued to the side walls, which were mostly set at an angle of 45° and lined with pillars, creating an optical illusion through the reflections. A number of architectural elements including niches, pilasters, pillars, balusters, architraves and arches were incorporated in this space. This type of construction may be considered as a typical Baroque *Spielerei* (Antwerp, Vleeshuis; Brussels, Museums of Art and History, *etc*).

Compared with the German and Italian cabinets, the Flemish works are distinctive for their definite lines, their sober but delicate decoration and their less massive and dramatic perspectives.

One highly original type of *cantoor*, which was only made in Flanders as far as is known, incorporates small paintings on panels or copper plates (Antwerp, Rubens' House, Rockox' House; Brussels, Museums of Art and History; Amsterdam, Rijksmuseum; London, Victoria and Albert Museum) or even marble (Antwerp, Plantin-Moretus; Amsterdam, Rijksmuseum), which were attached to the fronts of the drawers, the door, the top and the shutters. Numerous miniature painters, including J. Jansens, Ch. van der Lamen, Fr. Fran-

cken II and F. van Neeck industriously painted a wide variety of religious and secular subjects on the *cantoren*, in which a certain division of the work was observed. For example, the landscapes, figures and architectural subjects were painted by different artists (Oslo, National Museum; Brussels, Museums of Art and History; The Hague and London, private collections). In most cases the painted scenes were based on prints from illustrated works, *e g* the famous *Metamorphoses* of Ovid, with copper engravings by A. Tempesta (Brussels, Museums of Art and History; Bonn, Städtiches Museum; London, private collection). Subjects from the Old Testament, including the Creation and the story of Abraham, were often depicted.

Cantor with painted panels, 162 × 97 × 43.9 cm, middle of the 17th century. Brussels, Museums of Art and History.
The paintings on the drawers are borrowed from pictures by A. Tempesta, drawn for the *Methamorphoses* by Ovidius. At the top to the left *Cadmus kills the dragon*, at the right *Race of Atalanta and Hippomenes*. On the inside *Hermes in love with Hersia*, the *parting of Diana to the hunting*, on the flaptop *The judgment of Midas*.

Cantor with drawn ivory panels, 55 × 65 × 35 cm, after 1604. Brussels, Museums of Art and History.
On the doors of the opened *cantor* the *Grammatica*, *Dialectica* and *Musica*, after designs of Maarten de Vos, are to be recognized. In the borders are designs of J. Wierix and H. Collaert. All the fronts of the drawers are decorated with fishing sceneries from the book *Venationis Piscationis et aucupi typii* by H. Bol.

Painted panels based on series of prints with emblemata (Antwerp, Smit-van Gelder Museum; Lisbon, Museu Nacional de Arte) or with allegorical subjects by famous artists such as Otto Venius, were produced in large numbers. According to surviving documents, these cabinets were exported to Cadiz, Lisbon and Seville in large numbers, where they can still be found in local collections in museums. In these painted *cantoren* a second type of perspective can be distinguished, in which the painting is attached transversely in the centre, so that it reflects in both mirrors (Brussels, Museums of Art and History). The bottom sections of these painted *cantoren* frequently consist of large, carved wooden allegorical figures, depicting *e g* the four seasons (London, and Munich, private collection; Antwerp, Plantin-Moretus Museum; Amsterdam, Rijksmuseum).

In another type of *cantoor* the drawers and doors have thin ivory plates attached with scenes depicted in black ink (Brussels, Museums of Art and History; Cologne, Landesmuseum; Baltimore, Walters Art Gallery; Rome, private collection). Again the artists found inspiration in graphic examples, *viz* allegorical prints or hunting and fishing scenes, sometimes found in collected works by well-known designers, particularly M. de Vos and H. Collaert. There has been a tendency abroad to attribute these *cantoren* decorated with ivory and ink drawings to a workshop in Cologne, or to describe them as *stripo lombardo*. However, the identification of the examples, which revealed that both 16th and 17th century prints were used as designs, suggests that these cabinets originated in Flanders. Other examples decorated with embroidery are similar to these *cantoren* with ivory, as regards their structure. On these cheaper pieces of furniture colourful pictures of poultry and dolphins, interspersed with flowers, strawberries and trees, were embroidered with silk, gold and silver thread on a white silk background. Part of it is painted and decorated with copper discs (Antwerp, Vleeshuis, Rockox' House; Brussels, Museums of Art and History).

Only a few plaquettes of engraved silver, which once adorned the cabinets, have survived in Flemish collections (Antwerp, Vleeshuis, treasures of Our Lady's Cathedral; Brussels, Museums of Art and History). Goltzius, Wiericx and Somers cooperated in the design and engraving of these silver plates. Large *cantoren* decorated with them were almost exclusively found in royal households. A few large cabinets, richly decorated with silver plates, have found their way into collections abroad (London, Victoria and Albert Museum; London, private collection); unlike those in Flanders, where the *cantoren* decorated with silver plaquettes are very small (Antwerp, Rockox' House). To complete this list, some were also inlaid with lacquer work and mother-of-pearl, as well as with Florentine work and agate.

As all these cabinees served mainly for storing small valuable works of art, so that they almost functioned like safes, they often had small secret compartments or false bottoms hidden in the structure, which could be built into the cabinet in five different ways. Like the perspectives, the secret compartments were an expression of the extreme principles of the Baroque, consisting of a playful interweaving of complexity and hermetism. This characteristic feature heralded the arrival of the awakening 18th century.

INFLUENCES AND CHANGES IN 18th-CENTURY
FURNITURE Compared with the 17th-century, 18th-
century Flemish furniture enjoys relatively little interest.
More important was the celebrated furniture made in
Liege and Namur, which reached its zenith in the course
of the 18th century. Undoubtedly it spread to Flanders,
and the craftsmen tried to imitate these pieces of furniture locally (St Niklaas, Museum). In Bruges and Ghent
a number of beautiful Rococo and Louis XVI pieces have
survived; they are dated and the maker's name is known.
But there is little knowledge about 18th-century furniture, and therefore any description of its interiors is once
again largely theoretical.

During the first decades of the 18th century, *cantoren*
inlaid with mother-of-pearl and precious stones, as well
as *schrijflayen* (secretaires) with lacquer work, kept
being made. The Spanish leather chair remained an old
favourite; the legs and rungs usually had a barley twist
and the back was a narrow rectangular shape. The seats
were still used by public and ecclesiastical organisations,
which often had the leather backs of the chairs inscribed
(Antwerp, Vleeshuis; Bruges, Gruuthuse Museum).

After the first quarter of the 18th century the artists
were strongly influenced by French styles, once again
popularized through architectural treatises. Even in the
17th century French examples could be found in
Flanders, including designs by Androuet du Cerceau
and Abraham Bosse, who were well-known in these
regions. The book by J.F. Blondel, *De la Distribution
des Maisons de Plaisance et de la Décoration des Edifices
en Général*, published in Paris in 1737, served as a
particularly important guide to 18th-century views on
interior decoration and the accompanying furniture. In
addition to some general information about the architectural aspects of houses and rooms, stucco, murals, colour
schemes *etc*, there are designs for fittings and chandeliers. Pieces of furniture such as consoles, sofas and
court cupboards were assigned a fixed place in the room;
for example, between the windows or on either side of
the fireplace. By means of prints based on designs by
J.-L. Bérain and J.A. Meissonnier, Flemish artists were
familiarized with the new, playful and airy decorative
style of Rococo period which was used, for example, in
wood-carving and marquetry in furniture.

In 18th-century salons, paintings and furniture could
no longer be ascribed an arbitrary place in the room:
certain norms were imposed, as is indicated by
J.F. Blondel. An architect, such as the well-known
J.P. van Baurscheit II, would provide designs for the
decoration of the walls of newly built mansions; and his
cabinet-makers would create especially designed court
cupboards with curved convex doors and shells or asymmetrical rocaille motifs, to match the decoration of the
mantelpiece or the wood-carving above the doors. Unfortunately, no furniture from his houses has survived,
as far as is known.

Initially the high oak cupboards with four doors
consisted of a very high top section and a lower and
somewhat broader base, which was in accordance with
the Louis XIV norms; the large cornice had a pronounced curve with a small head of a herm attached; the
moulded edges of the door panels were also rounded

*Two-door cabinet in Louis XV style,*201 × 168 × 52 cm, A. Pulincx, 1762.
Bruges, Town Hall.
On the door panels there is a fantastic rocaille-motif in which the coat of arms
of Bruges has been processed; an eagle with spread wings, symbol of the
government of the country, crowns this piece of furniture. A. Pulincx got for
this cabinet 40 pounds 5 shilling.

(Bornem, St Bernard's Abbey). Some identified local cabinet-makers gave the door panels of the cupboards curved mouldings decorated with shells, pilasters and acanthus capitals (Ghent, Town Hall). The heavy Baroque two-door cupboard, in which the 17th-century structure can be clearly recognized, was now decorated in the Louis XIV style. The slightly recessed cornice was supported by three pilasters of the composite order, interspersed with garlands and tassels. On the panels of the doors the coats of arms are shown in a geometrically designed cartouche. Naturalistically sculpted lions replace the ball feet, as a survival of Baroque sculpture.

Sculpture is also found in the two-door cupboards in the Louis XIV style, in which the iconography of the figures often refers to the owner of the furniture (Bruges, Town Hall; Ghent, Museum of Decorative Arts). Apart from the asymmetrical decorative shells – either prominently displayed on the door panels or modestly incorporated on the side pilasters – the ornamentation also included C and S-shaped curlicules, small extrusions and stylized leaves of the Rococo style, which reached a peak between 1740 and 1750.

In about 1770 the Louis XVI style began to influence furniture design. Both the two-door cupboard (Ghent, Museum of Decorative Arts) and corner cabinets – which were becoming increasingly common because they were suitable for furnishing smaller rooms – were decorated with vases, joined musical instruments, garlands, ribbons, overlapping laurel leaves, medallions *etc* (St Niklaas, Museum). Oak and walnut were used as veneers as well as ebony and other exotic varieties, while painted and marbled pieces were also very popular. Some corner cupboards had a copper gallery at the top, which was also sometimes found on the chimney-breast to prevent porcelain pots and figurines from being knocked off.

A large number of new sorts of cupboards for a specific use were introduced, including the *vitrine* cupboard, the *chiffonnière*, the *commode* and the *bibliothèque*. They retained their French names, and were considered to be very convenient in 18th-century households. The *secretaire* was decorated with Eastern motifs in the chinoiserie fashion (Antwerp, Vleeshuis). Because of the lack of studies, it is very difficult to identify Flemish examples of these types of furniture.

In the 18th century seating was made more comfortable with the development of new types of seat including the *bergère* (St Niklaas, Museum), *fauteuil* and *canapé*, the protruding frames of which typified the characteristics of the various Louis styles. The curved legs with

Corner side-board, 95 × 96 × 45 cm, about 1780. St Niklaas, Museum.
Practical corner side-board in Louis XVI style having a serrate frame on the top, and overlapping fourlobs on the side-posts. The top sides of both door panels are decorated with continuing garlands which have been shoved through a ring.

Bergère, 11 × 69 × 67.5 cm, about 1780. St Niklaas, Museum.
The comfort of this chair is increased by a high, nicely fitting and curved back, which is directly linked to the seat as well as by the bended arms. The Louis XVI style can be noticed in the form of the profiled frame and in the grooved legs.

carving in the Louis XIV and XV styles, no longer connected by rungs, were especially striking; as was the large back which was joined tightly to the seat. The seat was lower to the ground and was sometimes trapezium-shaped, with large matching cushions. During the Louis XVI period, the legs were again straight and fluted. For the upholstery there was a wide variety of materials during the 18th century, including flowered velvet, silk, damask tapestry, Tournai fabric or embroidery. In many cases allegorical subjects were depicted in needlework; the embroiderer would only be given two weeks to complete one chair cover. Useful stools, *tambouretten* and fire-screens were decorated with matching tapestry or embroidery. Chairs with cane seats were very popular in the dining room and had an open-work back, adorned with motifs in the prevailing Louis style (St Niklaas, Museum).

Many tables with heavily sculpted feet, often made by well-known wood-carvers such as J.F. Allaert, had a white or veined marble leaf. The legs of oak or walnut tables, or of the consoles which stood against the walls of the dining room (for example, for holding the dessert), displayed the characteristics of the various Louis styles. A great deal of time would be spent seated at small oval or round tea-tables in ebony, walnut or lacquer; and any pauses in the conversation might be punctuated by the steady ticking of the large grandfather clock provided with chimes (Ghent, Museum for Decorative Arts), or by a Parisian or London pendulum.

The success of indoor games during the 18th century had an influence on furniture. The increasing passion for card games, including *le biribi*, *le pharaon etc*, resulted in the creation of special card tables such as the *table de quadrille* in walnut with marquetry. Also billiard tables were created.

Beds and four-poster beds, still usually made from walnut, finally moved into bedrooms. Oak examples often had barley twist sections, still retained a canopy and were screened off with drapes. Only one example of an 18th-century bed in the Louis XVI style has survived (Ghent, Museum for Decorative Arts). Rooms were illuminated by candlelight from crystal chandeliers and richly carved wooden chandeliers; the example dating from 1770 is still used in the original way *in situ* (Ghent, Museum for Decorative Arts, formerly the Hotel de Coninck). The designer, F. Allaert, was clearly inspired by the designs of J.F. Blondel.

This brief survey of 18th-century Flemish furniture does show that this period has been unjustifiably neglected, and that it offers rich possibilities for researchers. Finally, it ought to be mentioned that the individual Flemish character and creative force, which is evident from both the theoretical books of designs and the practical manufacture of furniture, declined sharply during the 18th century. The quality of furniture and the skill of the craftsmen was safeguarded until the end of the corporate system, when the *Ancien Régime* collapsed. The increasing industrialization and mechanization of furniture-making during the 19th century gradually put an end to the thorough craftsmanship of Flemish furniture-makers, and the exportation and spread of furniture abroad ceased entirely.

Candelabrum in Louis XV style, diameter 118 cm, J.F. Allaert, 1770. Ghent, Museum of Decorative Arts.
Around the central post, which has been elaborated in a tree with at the top two birds, are four *putti* which symbolize the continents. The eratically bended branches end in animal's heads with highly risen tufts. At the bottom of this exotically inspired candelabrum, a monkey swings on a ring.

Bed in Louis XVI style, 173 × 137 × 203 cm, end of the 18th century. Ghent, Museum of Decorative Arts.
This bed with a loose tester, which was constructed for bishop Lobkowitz, has luxuriant and polychromed carving with garlands, rosettes, crossed torches, bundles of arrows, vases, a horn of plenty, a *caduceus*, a book, a pen and a quill.

Tapestry and textile arts

The crisis which followed the religious troubles, the revolts and depression the halt in trading, the closure of the port of Antwerp and the departure of many tapestry weavers and cartoon painters, brought the tapestry industry to the edge of an abyss. Only during the last years of the 16th century things gradually began to improve. During the following decades it flourished again, though it never equalled the earlier heights of success. A number of prominent artists produced designs for the tapestry industry, although the late Renaissance cartoons continued to be used until the mid-17th century in more or less revised versions and with new borders.

The designs of Peter Paul Rubens (1577-1640) brought about a complete reversal in the art of tapestry-weaving, comparable to the upheaval caused by Raphael's *Acts of the Apostles*. After 9th November 1617 Rubens was commissioned by the Antwerp humanist and tapestry merchant, François Sweerts the Younger, and possibly also by Jan Raes from Brussels, to design cartoons with scenes from Roman history. He chose the *History of Decius Mus*, a subject which had never been used in tapestry making before. This heroic subject captured the attention of tapestry connoisseurs, and would undoubtedly attract many orders. The first set based on the cartoons was made for Franco Cattaneo from Genoa. A completely independent border was added around the tapestries. It was very difficult for the tapestry-makers to execute this sort of large composition, with its exuberant life force and magnificent colouring in wool and silk. All the minor details were reduced to a minimum as the attention was focused on the extremely large and muscular figures.

In 1621/22 Rubens did some sketches in oils for a *History of Constantine* for the use of the Gobelins in Paris. This was followed by cartoons for a *Triumph of the Eucharist*, commissioned by the Archduchess Isabella in 1627/28. As the artist had made use of less depth but more richly attired figures in these sketches, they were particularly suitable for use in tapestry work. The border has an architectural character which forms part of the central composition. It is executed as a rich portal made up of many segments, and surrounds the tableaux depicted within. The architrave is supported by spiralled pillars, the so-called Solomon pillars, decorated with reliefs of angels playing and clusters of grapes. Everything is elaborated to enhance the effect of

Decius Mus consults the Haruspex or priest who sees or guesses the wish of the god from the intestines of sacrified animals, hanging from a series picturing the *History of Decius Mus*. Brussels, 17th century, atelier of Jan Raes after designs by Pieter-Paul Rubens (?). Madrid, Royal Collection.

457

Victory of the Eucharist on idolatry, hanging from a series picturing the *Triumph of the Eucharist*, 490 × 670, Brussels, 1626-1628 signed by Jan Raes and with the monograms of Jacob Fobert and Hans Vervoert after designs by Pieter-Paul Rubens. Madrid, Convent of the Descalzas Reales.

Death of Achilles, hanging (here with unfinished borders) from a series representing the *History of Achilles*, 340 × 375 cm, Brussels, second half of the 17th century, atelier of Gerard van der Strecken after designs by Pieter-Paul Rubens. Kassel, Staatliche Kunstsammlungen.

the main theme of the hangings. There is even no horizontal border at the bottom of the tapestry and the composition is edged with a narrow strip. In the designs for the *History of Achilles*, usually dated between 1630-1635, the border has totally lost its independent character and is closely related to the subject. Herms are shown to the left and right of the central tableau, and at the bottom they give the impression that they are not on a plinth, but in front of one. At the top they are connected by a main structure with *putti* and garlands of flowers, and in the middle there is a richly elaborated cartouche.

Rubens' style was popularized by his pupils and followers, *e g* Cornelis Schut (1595-1655), Theodoor van Thulden (1606-1676), Justus van Egmont (1601-1674) and Jan Boeckhorst (1605-1688),though some relaxation of the style can be discerned in their work. They were more inclined to take into account the flat character of the tapestry. They designed light, clear compositions with a predominant emphasis on detail. The large figures gradually disappeared, so that a more harmonious result was achieved. The heavy borders, which had been inspired by architecture and sculpture, were replaced by edges filled with flowers and plants. The pathos of Rubens' work is completely absent in Jan van den Hoecke's (1611-1651) cartoons for the *Months*, the *Four Seasons*, the *Four Elements* and the *History of Zenobia*. Because of the loving attention to detail and the brilliant flowers, fruit and *putti*, these designs can be

Soliman, son of Bajazet, marries the niece of emperor Manuel, hanging from a series picturing the *History of Tamerlan and Bajazet*, 370 × 395 cm, Antwerp, last decade of the 17th century. Maybe from the atelier of Maria Anna Wauters. Vienna, Kunsthistorisches Museum.

regarded as being amongst the most successful compositions of the period.

The same evolution is revealed in the tapestries designed by Jacob Jordaens (1593-1678), who trained as a *waterschilder* (painter in tempera and watercolours). He was a very gifted artist with a great feeling for decoration. However, he had so much work during his lifetime that he was not averse to transposing the figures and groups from one series of tapestries to another. When he made cartoons for tapestries he sometimes forgot that the figures in the finished woven work had to be reversed... Jordaens is believed to have started making cartoons in about 1620, and some examples of his best and most famous work include the *Story of Ulysses*; the *History of Alexander the Great*, the *Scenes from Country Life*, the *Proverbs* and the *Riding School*. He is also known for his designs for a series of *Famous Women of Antiquity* and for a *History of Charlemagne*. The composition was usually well-balanced and very suitable for the characteristic style of the tapestries.

The painter David II Teniers (1610-1690) also exercised a great influence on the art of tapestry-weaving.

Thousands of tapestries were woven in Brussels, Audenarde, Lille, Beauvais, Aubusson *etc*, known as *fins Teniers* or *Tenières*, depicting scenes of country fairs or peasants returning from work and the market. It is not certain whether David II Teniers produced the cartoons for these, or whether these tableaux are simply based on his paintings. His work was highly decorative with good clear detail, numerous small figures and a rich background, and was very suitable for use in tapestry work. At any rate he and his son, David III Teniers (1638-1685), produced designs for armorial hangings and for allegorical compositions.

At the end of the 17th century two movements could be discerned in the art of Flemish tapestry. In the first group of tapestries, which often depicted mythological and historical tableaux and sometimes religious scenes, the increasing French influence of the Gobelins is clearly visible. An excellent example of this is the beautiful set dating from 1717 showing the fable of the *Triumphs of the Gods* (Ghent, Museum of Fine Arts). It comes from the Brussels workshop of Urbaan (1674-1747) and Daniel II Leyniers (1669-1728) and Hendrik II Reydams (1650-1719). The cartoons were painted by the gifted Brussels artist, Jan van Orley (1655-1735), who was not only inspired by the work of Charles le Brun, but was also influenced by the designs of Charles and Antoine Coypel. These are paintings converted into tapestries: the elegant and idealized figures and the charming layout of the composition, the rich colouring in the foreground and the delicate pastel tints of the background, as well as the excellent use of light, are all evidence of the French influence. The border is filled with floral designs in the Louis XIV style, and is in fact an imitation of a picture frame. These fashionable and charming figures, the lively colours and the landscapes which are built up like theatre sets, can all be seen in a *History of Psyche* and in a series of *Alexander* from the workshop of Jan-Frans van den Hecke, in a *History of Achilles*, signed by Judocus de Vos, as well as in a set with the *Life of Christ* (Bruges, St Saviour's Cathedral) from the workshop of Jaspar van der Borght. They all date from the end of the 17th or the first half of the 18th

century, and they show how the Gobelins increasingly dominated tapestry making in Brussels.

In the second group of tapestries depicting battle scenes, genre tableaux or simple landscapes, the indigenous style survived. These tapestries were woven mostly by Judocus de Vos and by the van der Borght family, and are superior to the tapestries from the workshops of the Gobelins. They are not only remarkable for their decorative effect, but also for their colourful brown and green hues, and the Flemish landscapes in the background. The borders are filled with a wealth of flowers.

During the 17th and 18th centuries the subjects which were used on the looms of the various workshops were largely determined by the trade in tapestries. Copies were certainly being made of the most famous sets from the previous century, but there was often a preference for mythological tableaux from poetry or subjects from Ovid's *Metamorphoses*. Scenes from

The Glorification of Venus, hanging from a series of five, picturing the *Glorification of the Gods*, 408 × 515 cm, Brussels, 1716-1717, atelier of Urbaan and Daniel Leyniers and Hendrik II Reydams, after designs by Jan van Orley and Augustin Coppens. Ghent, Museum of Fine Arts.

The Resurrection of Christ, hanging from a series picturing the *Life of Christ*, 422 × 730 cm, atelier of Jaspar van der Borcht, after designs supposed to be made by Jan van Orley. Bruges, St Saviour's Cathedral.

Greek and Roman history were very popular, but Biblical or religious subjects or themes from contemporary history were less common. In the workshops of Bruges, Audenarde and Brussels many panels with shepherds were woven. The views of gardens and boscages completely took the place of the millefleur tapestries. Tapestry connoisseurs were demanding more and more verdures with small animals or a castle, hunting scenes, battles and allegorical series. However, by the end of the 17th century the *conversations à la mode* were very popular as a result of the French influence.

Despite the great demand and enormous production during the 17th century, the decline of the tapestry industry had then already begun. Silken and velvet hangings – and later, painted canvasses and wall paper – were increasingly used as wall coverings. Gold-leather was particularly popular. Houses had numerous but smaller rooms which were less suitable for tapestries. In addition, there was growing competition from tapestry workshops abroad, usually state manufacturers encouraged by the high taxes on the importation of Flemish tapestries. It is true that production in Flanders was rationalized to some extent and retained a good reputation everywhere, but this was not enough to overcome all the problems. For this reason an attempt was made to adapt the representations to the tastes prevalent in other countries. In some cases foreign tapestries were even copied. Nevertheless, the state of the tapestry industry in the Southern Netherlands gradually became very grave.

The industry collapsed completely after 1750. Jan-Baptist Brandt closed his workshop in Audenarde in 1772. In Brussels Jacob van der Borght was still working and in 1785 he produced four tapestries, though not of an outstanding quality, depicting the *Legend of the Holy Sacrament of Miracles* for St Michael's Cathedral in Brussels. However, in 1794 van der Borght, the last manufacturer of tapestries in Brussels, died. His workshop was closed, and the contents were put up for sale. This put an immediate end to the once famous tapestry art of Flanders. For more than three centuries Flemish weavers not only produced work of high artistic merit, but also played a leading role in this field in a number of countries in Europe.

CARPETS

By the beginning of the 18th century carpets were being made in the Audenarde workshops of François-Guillaume van Verren. They were made for Ter Kameren Abbey near Brussels, and there was an unmistakable similarity with the boscages depicted in the tapestries of that period. This raises the question

Don Quichotte roped to the window of the inn by the maid Maritornes, hanging from a series picturing the *History of Don Quichotte*, 285 × 690 cm, Brussels, 1712-1734, from the atelier of Urbaan Leyniers after designs by Jan van Orley. Brussels, Royal Museums of Art and History.

whether the coarse tapestry that has survived was used for carpets as well as for wall coverings.

EMBROIDERY

During the religious troubles a large number of vestments were destroyed, and this led to an enormous production at the beginning of the 17th century. Antwerp had become the most important centre, but the formidable competition of lace making had to be taken into account even there. The embroiderers increasingly tried to emulate paintings, which is clear from the elaborate pictorial composition of the *Antependium of the former Abbey of Eekhout* in Bruges. This depicts Our Lady with the infant Jesus and the four Latin Church Fathers in five octagonal panels. This rectangular work was made in 1642 by a skilled hand using gold thread and many coloured silks, for the Abbot Nicolas van Troostenberghe.

However, the production of these finely embroidered panels was not normally so prolific. They were often replaced by ribbons, flowers, vines with flowers and fruit, or by symbolic ornaments such as the Mystic Lamb, the monograms of Christ and the Virgin Mary, ears of corn, and grapes. All of these motifs were represented in a very naturalistic style in close embroidery. This also indicates that the embroiderers were influenced by sculpture, and tried to introduce a higher relief into their work. The embroidery was also adorned with pearls, sequins and pieces of coloured glass. Pictures were only found on the shields of the copes and the cartouche of the antependium, or on the secular tableaux which decorated some of the cabinets of art. The so-called *Rubens vestment* of 1629 in St Carolus Borromeus' Church in Antwerp is an exception to this. The front side and reverse contain seven circles showing scenes from the life of Christ and Our Lady. Some of the typical features are the cartouches in black relief which stand out clearly against the embroidered pictures.

During the 18th century the copying of painting and relief work was at its peak. The intrinsic character of embroidery itself was completely lost, although a great deal of interesting work was produced. The cope from St Michael's Church in Ghent, showing the *Baptism of Christ* on the shield, and which dates from the first half of the 18th century, is a charming piece of painting in needlework with delicate and fresh colours. The same can be said of the *Italian Mountain Scene with Gypsies* (Ghent, Bijloke Museum) which was made to adorn the wall of a tastefully furnished room. It is signed: "Michel de Rynck fecit Gandavi 1784". The decorations on clothing were also elegant and colourful, but the embroiderers often lacked individual creativity. They tried as much as possible to copy paintings or the drawings in pattern books.

LACE

During the 17th and 18th centuries lace making flourished, although the production during the last hundred years was more prolific in Brabant than in Flanders. Lace served to adorn a variety of vestments and it was also used by the nobility, rich burghers and even the common people to decorate their clothing and the interiors of their houses. However, from about 1780 onwards there was a temporary shift in fashion and lace was only worn during the feast days.

A large number of people were involved in this industry, including both lay people and nuns. When Duke Cosmo de' Medici visited Antwerp in 1688 he remarked that all the women were rather large and very beautiful, and that they nearly all made lace. Fine lace

463

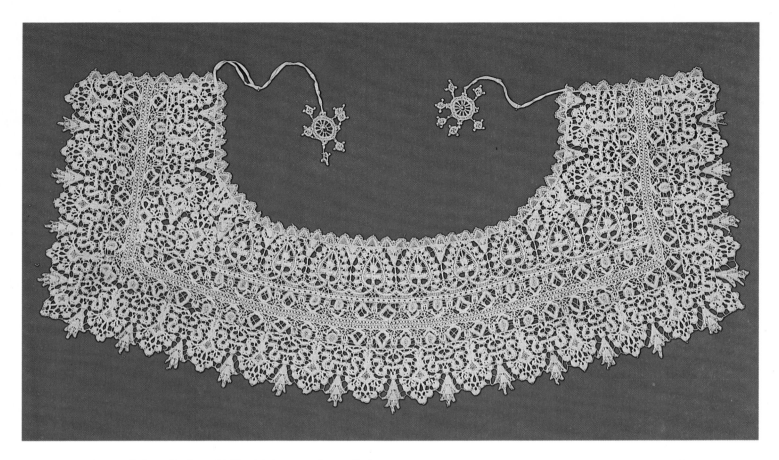

Medicis-collar in so-called van Dyck or old Flemish lace, 40 × 81 cm, first half of the 17th century. Bruges, Gruuthuse Museum.

Our-Lady with St Catharine, Ursula and Barbara, benediction veil in Brussels bobbin lace with ground relief and round darns, 89 × 79 cm, 18th century. Bruges, Gruuthuse Museum.

was made in the cities, while coarser lace was usually made in rural areas. It was exported to France, England and the Northern Netherlands, but Spain was the most important market. From Spain, Flemish lace was even exported to South America.

During the 17th century lace was referred to as 'Flemish lace', though it was made in a number of different centres. It was only at the end of the 17th century and particularly at the beginning of the 18th, that local differences emerged. There are examples of gauze lace from Brussels with a background of hexagonal meshes, which were made at the same time as the motifs. The lace from Malines, also known as 'summer lace' because it was so light, could be identified by its 'frosty' background; while the flowery work from Bruges and Brussels was made without a net background and was also known as duchesse lace.

Nevertheless, there was soon a great deal of confusion, because these regional names no longer referred to the lace from a particular city but rather to a particular type of lace. For example, Valenciennes lace was also made in Ghent, Malines lace was made in Antwerp and Brussels, and Brussels lace was made in Flanders. Holland lace, which is not very transparent, derives its name from the fact that it was transported in large quantities to the Northern Netherlands, and was probably made in Antwerp. English lace also originated in Flanders and Brabant, particularly in Brussels.

TEXTILE PRINTING

Even during the late Middle Ages textiles were being printed in Europe using wooden blocks and printing dyes. It is possible that this was also done in Flanders but there is no information available. Only in the early 17th century Antoon Kint from Antwerp obtained a patent for printing chamois, linen and woollen materials with a variety of decorative motifs. He was also appointed as a satin printer in St Luke's Guild. The printer and publisher of news-sheets, Abraham Verhoeven (1575-1652) from Antwerp, also worked with printed fabrics. In 1618 he taught Cornelis Michielssen from Delft how to print armozeen, a thin and matt taffeta, satin and damask.

In 1650/51 Augustijn de Raucourt became a member of the artists' guild in Antwerp as a fabric printer. He printed various strange figures on ladies' skirts, tablecloths and fire screens, mantelpiece coverings and drapes or curtains for beds and rooms. None of his work has survived but there are some remaining examples of the work of Peter Wouters. In 1675 Wouters was given a patent for printing linen and woollen materials with landscapes and different subjects. He used engraved wooden blocks which were pressed onto the material and were then finished off with chablones. His intention was to produce cheap printed tapestries. These hangings consisted of a number of separately printed linen cloths, which were then stuck together along the seams. In the Museum at Cracow there is a series of seven printed wall hangings signed by Peter Wouters. They depict the *Seven Sacraments* and are very reminiscent of the paintings with the same name by Nicolas Poussin.

After 1689 the cotton printers in Antwerp were obliged to join the painters' guilds. From 1691-1700 there were nine of these, which is an indisputable indication of the flourishing development of this art. In the middle of the following century the Compagnie Beerenbroeck (1753-1813) acquired an exclusive patent in that town with a duration of twenty-five years for printing and painting cotton. A few years later (in 1759) the Prince of Lorraine set up a similar factory in Tervuren. The best known cotton printing workshop in Ghent was that of Abraham Voortman and Frans de Vos. It was founded in 1790 and continued to produce work until about 1890. The work produced was aimed particularly at the requirements of the rural population and the lower bourgeoisie.

CORDWAIN

During the first half of the 17th century there was increasing interest in gold leather among the wealthy burghers. Leather wall hangings and tablecloths were made not only in Malines, but also in Antwerp, Brussels and Ghent. The cordwainers never founded an independent guild; but were always classified with leather workers, tanners, suitcase-makers and goldblathers. The work produced during this period was still rather flat, speckled and partially painted, but this soon changed. In about 1640 embossed gold leather was made in Brussels and later also in Malines. Wooden or copper

Fragment of a wall-clothing with floral motifs, gold-leather pressed in relief, 75 × 59.5 cm, Flanders, last quarter of the 17th- beginning of the 18th century. Bruges, Gruuthuse Museum.

blocks were used, and these were sometimes carved by prominent sculptors. Jan Vermeulen of Malines had blocks depicting a large and a small eagle, vines, and the Five Senses. His fellow-citizen Guilliam de Blaes imitated Holland gold leather, while sheets depicting the *History of Romulus and Remus* were made in the workshop of Martin Sotteau in Brussels. This was the peak of achievement in this decorative art. Partly because of the thriving art trade in Antwerp, cordwain was exported far and wide.

At the beginning of the 18th century allegorical and mythological scenes were still popular. One typical example was the rather clumsily executed work in the Museums of Art and History in Brussels depicting *Neptune in his Chariot*; it was made in about 1710 and was signed by Egidius Jacobs. In most centres the art of cordwain went into a decline. However, in Malines the gold leather workers succeeded in adapting to different successive styles.

During the Rococo period embossed relief gold leather gradually disappeared. Flat decoration became fashionable once again, and the golden shine made way for various painted motifs. In the second half of the century this art form went into a great decline and after the French Revolution the cordwain industry disappeared entirely. The high production costs and the evolution in taste were largely responsible for this.

Metalwork

GOLD AND SILVER

Despite the economic recession in the Southern Netherlands, the demand for gold and silver work remained
very high. The triumphant Counter Reformation invested in brilliant and increasingly large pieces of church
plate. The desire amongst the nobility, patricians and
corporations for opulence was encouraged by the court
of the Archdukes Albrecht († 1621) and Isabella
(† 1633); and after their deaths the demand for ornamental domestic silver continued to be very great.
Following the capitulation of 1585 and the resulting
emigration of many gold and silversmiths to virtually all
parts of Europe, Antwerp ceased to be the international
centre for gold and silver-work. Nevertheless, during the
17th century the Antwerp silver still set the tone in the
Southern Netherlands, both in a quantitative and an
inventive way. Antwerp was the major producer of
church silver for the entire country as well as for the
Catholic missionary parishes in the United Provinces.
Embossed plates and ornaments were made for the
cabinets and looking-glass frames, which were exported
by Antwerp art dealers in large quantities throughout
Europe. Besides famous lineages of gold and silversmiths
such as the Valcks, Rogiers, Lissaus, Lesteens and
Somers, there also came a number of silversmiths in the
city from the Southern Netherlands, including the
prince-bishopric of Liege; such as Guilliam van der
Mont, Guilliam Jacques, Joannes de Fallais, Hendrik
Corbion and Hendrik Dardenne, who returned to Huy
and spread the Antwerp style in the area of Liege.

At the beginning of the century Bruges was an
important centre, with families of gold and silversmiths
such as the Crabbes and the van Nieukerckes. During
the 17th century Ghent gained a larger than local significance with *inter alia* the van Sychens and Lenoirs; as
did Brussels with for instance Joachim de Meyer.

The Church stayed an important client for the gold
and silversmiths of Flanders throughout the 18th
century; though it became common practice to melt
down old articles to make new works of art in more
fashionable styles. Nevertheless, the proportion of
domestic silver increased steadily, notably because ela-

Goblet of state of the St Sebastian's Guild of Diest, (detail), silver, height
45.5 cm, Gaspard Lanoy, Brussels, 1714. Diest, Municipal Museum.

Salt-cellar of state, ivory in gilt silver setting, height 43.8 cm, carving by Jörg
Petel, silver-work by Jan Herck, after a design by P.P. Rubens, Antwerp
1628. Stockholm, Kungl. Husgerådskammaren.

borate and diversified dinner services became the vogue.

From the end of the 17th century the French interpretation of the late Baroque style, and then of Rococo and classicism, became very influential. These imported styles often acquired a touch of their own, especially in Antwerp, though in the 18th century this centre lost its prominent position for ever. At this time the leading cities in Flanders were Brussels, encouraged by the court of the governor-general Charles of Lorraine, and Ghent. High quality silver was also produced in Bruges during the first half of the 18th century, and in Malines towards the middle of it.

FROM LATE RENAISSANCE TO BAROQUE The Renaissance influenced until deep into the 17th century. Some typical examples included the larger reliquaries such as St Dympne's of Geel, with niches flanked by pillars, made in 1630 in Antwerp by Guilliam Jacques; and the reliquary of the Holy Blood in Bruges, in the shape of a hexagonal temple and encrusted with gems, by Jan Crabbe III (1570-1651). The same style can be detected in the cylindrical monstrances, though the Gothic tower is replaced by colonnettes with entablature. However, in spite of the spiral columns and intricate scrolls, the composition was still an accumulation of Renaissance architectural elements; such as in the monstrance of Guilliam van der Mont of 1617 in St Peter's Church in Turnhout, and that of Joos Lesteens of 1631 in St Martin's in Alost.

The Renaissance tradition also continued to have an effect in domestic silver, for example in the cylindrical cups and the octagonal serving trays with engraved and beautifully designed leaf patterns. The fairly flatly chased representation of the *Failed Siege of Bruges in*

Jan Crabbe III, *Relic-shrine of the Holy Blood,* gold and gilt silver, enamel and precious stones, 129 × 61 cm, Bruges 1614-1617. Bruges, Holy Blood Chapel.

Mathias Melijn, *Ambrogio Spinola during the siege of Gulik in 1622,* chased silver, 23 × 54 cm, originates from an art-gallery, Genoa, 1636. Amsterdam, Rijksmuseum.

P.P. Rubens, *Design for the wash-basin of King Charles I of England representing the 'Birth of Venus'*, panel, 61 × 78 cm, 1630. London, National Gallery.

Loys van Nieykercke, *Ornamental basin* representing the *Failure of the siege of Bruges in 1631*, which was contrived by Frederik Hendrik, from the abbey of Tongerlo, chased and gilt silver, diameter 55.5 cm, Bruges, 1631/32. Brussels, Museums of Art and History.

1631 on a large decorative salver by Loys van Nieukercke from Bruges (Brussels, Museums of Art and History) was also faithful to the Renaissance tradition.

Nevertheless, the Baroque style eventually broke through in embossed work. There asymmetric compositions and high relief were used to achieve the desired effect of movement, depth and contrast of light and shade inherent in the new style. This is evident in the scenes depicted on ewers and basins such as *Pilate washing his hands* of 1619, made by Abraham Lissau from Antwerp, of which there is a galvanoplastic replica in Park Abbey at Heverlee; and the *Rape of the Sabine Women* (Toledo Cathedral), embossed in 1627 in Spain by the Antwerp silverchaser Matheus Melijn, who also made the five Genoese Spinola reliefs dating from 1636 (Amsterdam, Rijksmuseum).

The only knowledge we have of the ewer and basin of Charles I of England, chased by Theodoor Roegiers in 1630/31 and later melted down, comes from the engravings of Jacobus Neeffs and from P.P. Rubens' *grisaille* painting for the oval basin depicting the *Birth of Venus from the foam of the sea* (London, National Gallery). The ewer and basin of Rubens himself, dating from 1635/36, are still in the possession of his descendants. The frieze on the ewer depicts *Venus coming onto the land from the sea*, and the oval basin shows *Susanna ogled by the Elders* on the base and the *Four Elements* on the rim (Vorselaar, collection Baron de Borrekens). Another work that has survived from Rubens' collection is a salt cellar with a *Birth of Venus* carved in ivory by Iörg Petel, in a gilt silver setting by Jan Herck with an Antwerp hallmark from 1627/28 (Stockholm, Statens Historiska Museum).

The cylindrical monstrance gained a more Baroque appearance by the addition of two large figures of saints or angels next to the cylinder, flanked by s-shaped scrolls, as in the Antwerp monstrance of 1656 in St Peter's in Turnhout. However, after 1640 the typical Baroque monstrance with a round lunette surrounded by rays became the normal style. The oldest of these have short, pointed, alternately straight and flame-

Jan Moermans, *Halo-ostensorium from the Roman-Catholic Church of St Dominic at Amsterdam,* gilt silver, height 68.5 cm, Antwerp about 1675. Amsterdam, Rijksmuseum.

Jan Moermans, *Halo-ostensorium with figures of Faith, Hope and Love,* gilt silver, height 102 cm, Antwerp, 1687/88, Alkemade, St Peter-in-Fetters Church, Roelof-Arendsveen.

Jan Anthony Le Pies, *Chalice from the R.C. Church of St Dominic at Amsterdam,* gilt silver, height 33.4 cm, Antwerp, 1723. Amsterdam, Rijksmuseum.

Jan Baptist Buijsens I, *Ciborium,* partly gilt silver, heigt 52.5 cm, Antwerp, 1721/22. Amsterdam, Rijksmuseum.

Wierick Somers III, *Relic-shrine of St Gummarus,* chased silver on a wood kernel, height about 100 cm, breadth about 180 cm, depth about 80 cm, Antwerp, 1681/82. At the bottom there are four sitting lions in gilt wood by Lodewijk Willemssens, Antwerp, 1682. On the shrine: silver relic-ostensorium in the form of a tree by Joannes de Fallais, Antwerp, 1666. On the pedestal by J. Lecocqmartin, Antwerp, 1784/85, two sitting angel *putti* in silver by Jan Baptist Verberckt I, Antwerp, 1784/85. Lier, St Gummarus' Church.

shaped rays, with small figures of saints or angels at the bottom; such as in the early example dating from 1641/42 in the village church of Landegem.

Gradually the rays became longer and the figures larger. The Antwerp Moermans' monstrances are easily recognizable and were widely copied. These have two angels kneeling in worship and a large royal crown with a cross above: such as that dating from 1665 in St James's Church in Antwerp, that of 1669 in Westminster Cathedral in London, and that of 1687/88 in San Martin in Noya, in the Spanish province of La Coruña. At the end of the 17th century the dove of the Holy Spirit was shown beneath God the Father, floating above the loosely grouped broad rays of different lengths. The monstrances of the Antwerp silversmith Wierik Somers III have *putti* on the rays and sculptural evangelist symbols at the foot, as in that in Averbode Abbey from 1693/94 and that of St Barnabas' in Niedermörmter/Kreis Kleve (Germany) dating from 1698/99. Somewhat later there was a preference for two large figures placed on the convolutions rising from the stem. A monstrance dating from *ca* 1700-1710 in Our Lady's Church in Maastricht shows two kneeling angels. The one from 1713/14 in St Andrew's Church in Antwerp has the figures of *Faith* and *Hope*, for which the models were made by the sculptor Michiel van der Voort I; within a year Somers made a slightly smaller replica of this monstrance for the village church of Pulle.

The Baroque reliquary shrine was shaped like a tomb, covered with embossed plates depicting scenes and ornamentation, and supported by four diagonal convolutions or animal figures. Sometimes other elements were placed on top of the large tomb, such as an older reliquary horn on the Brussels shrine in the church of the former Ninove Abbey, dating from 1643/44; or the already existing reliquary tree upon St Gummarus' shrine in Lier, made in 1682 by Wierik Somers III of Antwerp. Smaller chests served as a base for a statuette, such as on St Hubertus' shrine, (1646) in Wakkerzeel/Werchter, made by Joachim de Meyer from Brussels; or for a bust, such as on the Antwerp shrine of St Nicholas (1661), by Jan Moermans in Sint-Niklaas.

In the high Baroque chalices the ovoid boss on the baluster stem is replaced by a pear-shaped one. But in many cases the baluster itself is replaced by a group of herms or figures, such as in the Moermans' chalice dating from 1675/76 in the Roman Catholic Church of St Peter in Leyden; or it is replaced by a single figure, as in the chalice with the Holy Church, made in 1698 by Anthoni Le Pies, a silversmith who had left Brussels to settle in Antwerp. He made this for the Jesuits in Leyden, and it is now in St Willibrord's College at Zeist.

FROM LATE BAROQUE TO CLASSICISM After 1700 Flemish gold and silversmiths were greatly influenced by the more classical late Baroque style of Louis XIV of France, through *e g* the illustrated books

Goblet of state of the St Sebastian's Guild of Diest, silver, height 45.5 cm, Gaspard Lanoy, Brussels, 1714. Diest, Municipal Museum.

by Jean Bérain (1640-1711) and the ornamental prints of Daniel Marot (1663-1752), who emigrated to the United Provinces after 1685. The dashing Baroque style had to contend with a more restrained form of expression, stricter lines and well-regulated ornamental patterns in bas-relief or engraving. The impact of this new style was particularly strong on domestic silver. Nevertheless some traditional work was still made at first, though of a more sober nature; such as the Guild Cup of St Sebastian of Diest (1714) by the Brussels silversmith Gaspard Lanoy, who came from Tirlemont.

The style was adopted less rigorously in church silver, and the Flemish late Baroque style continued to be evident in some pieces. It can be detected in the Antwerp chalices with a standing figure by Jan Anthony Le Pies (who always added 'alias Dedalus' after his signature), as in the chalice with *Maria Immaculata* (1707) of the Fraternity of the Rosary at the Black Friars, now in St Paul's Church in Antwerp. The same applies to the reliquary bust of St Amelberga in Temse (1734/35), and to the monstrance of Westerlo (1725) with a representation of the *Last Supper* shown in relief at the bottom in front of the rays, both by the Antwerp silversmith Jan Baptist Buysens I. A particularly impressive piece, decorated with many pearls and rubies, is the 64 *cm* high golden monstrance, donated by the widow of Frans van Beversluys to Our Lady's Church in Bruges

Tankard with three taps, silver, height 40 cm, master from Antwerp, 1772. Deurne/Antwerp, Sterckshof.

in 1725. The upper part of this work is fairly open and airy: vine tendrils are entwined over the slender and separate groups of rays, with a large number of bunches of grapes made of pearls; to the left and right of the stem there are thin wisps of clouds with slender, mannerist enamelled statuettes of the virtues. On the lunula's frame, a similar figure of *Faith* stands between two embossed Baroque *putti* and beneath a crown, glittering with diamonds and rubies. This *Katte van Beversluys,* made by the gold and silversmith Jan Beaucourt (1680-1743), was a prelude to Rococo.

This more elegant style with a preference for slender figures, continuous spiralling movement and asymmetrical rocaille decoration emerged in Flanders from 1740. The French Louis XV style now became decisive for domestic silver, though there are no French models for the jugs with three taps, such as the Antwerp example of 1772 (Deurne, Sterckshof Museum). Typical rocaille work can be found in the Ghent altar set with a cross and six candlesticks, in the former abbey church of St Peter in Ghent, made in 1752 by Matthieu Lenoir; and in the Antwerp ciborium (1763) made by Lambertus Hannosset, which came from the Roman Catholic Church of St Catherine (Amsterdam, Rijksmuseum).

After 1770 the preclassicism of the French Louis XVI style began to become influential, with its predilection for geometric forms – round columns, cubes and circles – and a sober style of ornamentation, consisting of fluted and pearly edges, garlands of laurels, pending from rings or knots of ribbons. The large quantity of work produced, for instance, by Jan-Baptist Verberckt in Antwerp and Pierre Joseph Tiberghien in Ghent, largely accorded with this classicist pattern.

MEDALS

Jan van Montfort († 1649) was the last in a line of famous Renaissance makers of medals in the Netherlands, most of whom worked in Antwerp. He was also employed there in the Mint as a die-sinker and assay-master. As mint-master general, he left Antwerp in 1613 to go to Brussels. The traditional art of medals flourished there and was encouraged by the Archdukes Albrecht and Isabella, and later by the governor-general of the Spanish Netherlands. It was produced mainly by the famous silversmiths and die-sinkers, the Waterloos. Mint-master general Adriaan Waterloos (1599-1681) was the most important Flemish medal artist of the 17th century. As well as striking medals from a cut matrix, they also cast medals from moulds carved in wood or modelled in wax.

The Antwerp silversmith Filips Roettiers I (1596-1669), was the first person in the Southern Netherlands to strike medals systematically with a screw press from dies cut in steel; a procedure which was also gradually being introduced for minting coins. His descendants, some of whom also worked in London and Paris, used the same method up to Jacques Roettiers (1698-1772), the chief die-sinker at the Antwerp Mint.

The most productive medal artist in the second half of the 18th century was Theodoor van Berckel (1739-1808) from 's-Hertogenbosch, who first worked in the

Theodoor van Berckel, *Medal of the Academy of Fine Arts at Antwerp*, front: Effigy of Governor-General Charles of Lorraine, reverse: Allegoric representation of the Fine Arts. Chased bronze, diameter 4.7 cm, Brussels, 1778. Deurne/Antwerp, Sterckshof.

United Provinces and was employed by the Mint in Brussels from 1776.

In general the 17th and 18th-century medals from the Southern Netherlands, whether they were cast or struck, were skilfully made. However, they rarely achieved the high artistic standards of the medals made in the Netherlands during the Renaissance.

COPPER, BRONZE AND BRASS

During the first half of the 17th century Malines maintained its traditional position in this field with the van den Gheyn, de Clerck and Cauthals lineages of bronze and brass workers. The Renaissance manner persisted, as in the baptismal font of Scherpenheuvel (1610) by Peeter de Clerck II († 1642). The early Baroque appears in the *Christ on the Cross*, (1635) by Jan Cauthals III ((ca 1585-1640), for the monumental cross on the *Meir* in Antwerp, now in the Cathedral.

In Antwerp copper work, which had flourished during the 16th century, also held its own. A large quantity of gilt brass decoration was applied to the cabinets intended for export. Many baluster bars made of brass for the screens of choirs and chapels from the second quarter of the 17th century have an Antwerp hallmark; there are examples in Antwerp itself (1625-1628, St James's Church), in Geel (1625-1628, St Dympne's Church), Termonde (ca 1635-1637, Our Lady's Church), Ghent (1630, St Bavo's Cathedral) and Bruges (ca 1626, St Saviour's Cathedral; ca 1626-1634, St Anne's Church). These were supplied by Hendrik de Ridder, from Utrecht, Guilielmus Pluymaeckers and Hans Heyndrickx. Baroque copper work was of a high standard. The large gilt charger from St Michael's Abbey in Antwerp, with a portrait of the Cardinal-Infante Ferdinand on horseback as the *Victor of the Battle of Nördlingen in 1634* (now in Averbode Abbey), was made in 1635, based on a painting by Rubens (Madrid, Prado). The gilt relief with the *Adoration of the Magi* for the epitaph of Abraham Melijn († 1646) in St Paul's Church in Antwerp, was made by his brother, the silverchaser Matheus Melijn.

On a more modest scale, bronze and copper work was also done in other towns in Flanders. In Brussels, Gaspard Turckelsteyn cast a late Renaissance *Recumbent lion* (1610) from a wax model by Jan van Montfort. This was for the new marble mausoleum for Duke John II of Brabant and Margaret of York in St Michael's Cathedral. The well-known bronze cherub *Manneken Pis*, based on a model made by Hieronymus Duquesnoy I in 1619, was cast again in 1630 by Jacob van den Broeck (Broodhuis Museum).

Jaques du Blon from Bruges signed the brass screen bars in St Saviour's Cathedral, dating from 1628/29. Cornelis Rulandt († 1641), who had come from Aix-la-Chapelle, worked in Ghent from at least 1629. In addition to bars for some screens, he cast in about 1630 the late Renaissance choir lectern for the acolytes in St Bavo's Cathedral. Although there were copper chasers and engravers in most of the towns of the Southern Netherlands after 1650, it was the copper workers from Antwerp who set the trend in the high and late Baroque style until the first half of the 18th century.

Guilliam de Vos I († 1674), who was already exporting copperwork in the United Provinces in 1642, made in 1672 the ornamental Baroque candlesticks for the new rood-screen in the choir of St James's Church. In 1684 Jacobus Persoons made four large embossed tripodal candlesticks, together with a (now missing) crucifix for an altar in St Nicholas' Church in Ghent. Guilliam II and Hendrik de Vos cast the large open-work door for the magistrate's chapel in the Town Hall of Antwerp in 1681. This was based on a design by Artus Quellinus II, and is now at the city library. In about 1700 they cast a pair of choir candlesticks with dolphins on a three-sided foot for the Potterie Monastery in Bruges. In 1708 Guilliam made three choir doors behind the high altar; and in 1711 the doorleaves for the Chapel of St Sebastian in St Bavo's Cathedral at Ghent.

Ornamental basin with the Cardinal-Infant Ferdinand on horseback, as the victor in the Battle at Nordlingen in 1634, from St Michael's Abbey at Antwerp, chased brass, 95 cm, engraving by Paulus Pontius after P.P. Rubens, Antwerp, 1635. Scherpenheuvel/Zichem, Averbode Abbey.

The copper chaser Jacobus Steenot signed the choir lecterns of St Nicholas' in Edingen (1717) and of St Julian's in Ath (1723); as well as a pair of brass candlesticks with copper fittings (1721) in St George's in Antwerp.

Sculptors from Antwerp produced the models for copper work. The vase-shaped brass sacristy fountain with two copper dolphin spouts in St Augustine's Church in Antwerp was made around 1690, based on a design of Hendrik Frans Verbrugghen. Michiel van der Voort I made the model for the choir lectern with a large figure of the archangel Michael standing on a devil (1725) for St Michael's Church in Ghent.

Gold and silversmiths were often involved in copperwork, too. In 1705 Wierik Somers III signed the contract for the large door at the back of the choir of St Saviour's Cathedral in Bruges. In 1711 Joannes Bernaerts chased a choir lectern for Our Lady's Church in Courtray,

Wierick Somers III, *Rood-loft door with two wings*, engraved cast and chased copper, Antwerp, 1705-1708, finished in 1726. Bruges, St Saviour's Cathedral.

Joannes Pilsen, *Altar-set of St Sebastian's Altar:* antependium with the coat of arms d'Hane-Steenbrugse, 107 × 217 cm,, gilt chased brass, Ghent, 1729, St Michael's Church.

based on a design by Jan Anthony Le Pies. The gold and silversmith J. J. Picavet not only chased in 1712 the gilt brass side panels of the tabernacle chest for the Corpus Christi Chapel in Antwerp Cathedral, but he also made the tabernacle doors for the new high altar of St Bavo's Cathedral in Ghent from 1717-1720. The prolific silversmith Jan Baptist Verberckt (1735-1819) chased in 1774/75 the door of the tabernacle on the altar in the wedding choir of St James's in Antwerp.

Some of the pieces made by coppersmiths in other centres should also be mentioned. In Bruges, Gillis Moerman cast in 1683 the brass bars for the choir doors in St James's Church; and in 1722/23 Jacobus Ramé cast the candle brackets, placed under the statues of the Apostles in the nave of St Saviour's Cathedral, based on a design by the sculptor Hendrik Pulincx. The most monumental of them, with the coat of arms of Bishop H. van Susteren, is now in the Gruuthuse Museum. The two large choir lecterns with Ramé's signature (1727) were donated by the same bishop. In 1695 the bell founder Ignatius de Cock from Heestert cast the choir lectern with a large figure of an angel for Our Lady's Church in Courtray.

In the Chapel of St Sebastian in St Michael's Church in Ghent, there is a complete altar set in the late Baroque style, with an antependium, predella, crucifix and six candlesticks, chased in gilt brass in 1729 by Joannes Pilsen (born 1695) from Ghent. As a deacon, he donated in 1736 the crucifix (now disappeared) and the four surviving candlesticks, to the Smiths' Chapel in the Augustine Monastery.

CARILLON ART

During the 16th century the bell founders of Malines specialized in making carillons, but during the 17th their monopoly in the Netherlands gradually disappeared. Some of the van den Gheyn family moved away, one to Tirlemont via St-Trond and one to Louvain. Only in Louvain were bells and carillons still cast until the 20th century.

The most famous carillon founders in the 17th century were the brothers François and Peeter Hemony (ca 1609-1667; 1619-1680) who came from Lorraine.

Clock, 105 × 103 cm, Willem Witlockx, 1730. Antwerp, Vleeshuis Museum. This clock comes out of Our Lady's Tower and served there as '11 o'clock' or watch-clock. Each bell is a work of art as far as the decoration is concerned. This big clock is a fine example of these decorations, it has several friezes above each other. On a medallion in front the city-arms are represented, with below the text: 'I am disquiet in this way/I have each night every citizen from the streets and urge the watchers to watch/I close the inns by my sound/I make each one rest and sooth all uneasiness.' At the back there is an oval medallion with a male portrait and the inscription: 'Guilielmus Witlockx, clock and carillon caster'.

Ignatius de Cock, *Choir-lectern with angel figure,* bronze and brass, height 200 cm, Heestert/Courtray, 1695. Courtray, Our Lady's Church.

In 1653 they moved from Zutphen to Antwerp, and in 1655 they cast thirty-two new bells for the collegiate carillon (most of which are now in St Catherine's Tower in Hoogstraten) as well as thirty-three bells for the town carillon, all bells were installed at the time in Our Lady's Tower. However, the Hemonys were attracted by the more prosperous city of Amsterdam and François moved there in 1657. Peeter first established a bell foundry in Ghent, where the new belfry carillon was made in 1659-1662. After 1664 he also went to Amsterdam to work with his brother again. The Hemony workshop in Amsterdam also produced carillons for the Southern Netherlands, such as the one in St Sulpitius' Church in Diest (1671) and the carillon of St Rombout's Tower in Malines (1674). Meanwhile, the carillon founder Melchior de Haze (1632-1697) continued to work in Antwerp. In 1674 he cast the carillon for the Escorial, and in 1695 he sold a carillon with thirty-five bells for the *Neuburg* in Salzburg. Guilielmus Witlockx (ca 1670-1733) from 's-Hertogenbosch followed in his footsteps as a bell and carillon founder. Amongst other works, he cast the carillon for the *Grote Kerk* in Breda in 1715/16.

The carillon foundry in Antwerp continued for a short time under Joris du Mery (1699-1784) from Hoves near Edingen, who acquired citizenship in 1736. But in 1743 he went to Bruges to work at the belfry carillon. There his bell foundry remained in operation until his death.

Ceramics

During the reign of Empress Maria Theresa (1740-1780), the Southern Netherlands once more acquired a significant position in the faience and porcelain industry. Opening one's own workshop was encouraged, which fitted in very well with the economic policy of the second half of the 18th century. The products were not simply utilitarian, but formed part of the decorative elements of the interiors of burghers' houses. As an enormous quantity was imported from abroad, the faience and porcelain factories had to supply accurate copies, which were of a sufficiently high technical standard to compete with the imported ceramic ware. Apart from a small number of workshops, the majority only existed for a short time and were quickly closed down; so that their economic importance – compared with other industries during this period – was not so great. Other workshops, such as those in Brussels and Tournai, remained in existence for many years and produced faience, faience-fine and porcelain. The manufacturers not only produced articles for the local population, but also for wholesalers; and as such, they did not have to become members of an organization of potters, or sellers of stoneware, porcelain and glassware.

COURTRAY In Courtray (West Flanders) faience was manufactured from 1783 to 1792 in a short-lived business, established by Robert Ignatius van Beveren (1734-1792) in the former barracks of *De Thienen*. From 1785 two kilns were used; only six signed examples of the work produced there are known to have survived. These are plates, soup tureens and flower stands in faience or faience-fine, decorated in blue, manganese purple, green and yellow. Both the shape and the decoration are quite different from those of articles made in Bruges; though similarities can be detected with the products from Tournai, Luxembourg and northern France. The *fabryke van Galeyers* was situated between Ghent Gate and St John's Gate, and within the towpath which ran along the canals.

LOUVAIN Little is known about faience in Louvain, and there is only a limited number of signed articles. A certain Joannes-Franciscus Verplancke, who ran a faience business in Brussels, submitted an application in 1767 to start a *manufacture van porseleyn* in Louvain. Three years earlier he had already requested a grant from the central government authorities to produce English stoneware or faience-fine in Brussels, together with his partner, Jan van Gierdegom. However, the business had not done very well, and he now thought to try his luck in Louvain. Verplancke obtained permission from the magistrate in Louvain "to manufacture porcelain, usually known as faience, consisting of common, fine and finely japanned ware, as well as Holland tiles and brown faience for the fire *etc*". He was exempt from civil guard and excise duty for the duration of his business, and started his enterprise in 1768 near Tirlemont Gate. He worked together with Joannes-Baptista van Cutsem, but he ran the business. The faience factory was situated in the *Nieuw Huys* in Tirlemont Street, which had been acquired in 1768 by van Cutsem's brother, an elderly bachelor from Brussels. The Verplancke faience factories were very short-lived, both in the capital and in Louvain; and in 1770 Joannes-Baptista van Cutsem took over the business. They produced ordinary household pottery, but also more delicate products, such as a polychrome hanging flower basket dated 1771, a blue cache-pot, and a soup tureen in maganese purple. As in the other centres, very few objects were signed and therefore our knowledge of the finished articles is incomplete. Although the faience factory in Louvain had a team of artisans, including a miller, figurist or modeller, potters working at wheels, painters and apprentices, it closed down in about 1771. The potential marked was too small and the competition of imported products from Brussels, Tournai, Luxembourg and abroad too great, so that the business was no longer viable.

Bird-whistle in so-called Torhout pottery, height 18 cm, first half of the 19th century. Bruges, Gruuthuse Museum.

Wine-cooler (?), height 18.4 cm, Bruges, atelier Hendrik Pulinx, second half of the 18th century. Bruges, Gruuthuse Museum.

477

Fountain, height 49 cm, Bruges, atelier Hendrik Pulinx, second half of the 18th century. Bruges, Gruuthuse Museum.

Console in Louis XV style, height 26.3 cm, Bruges, atelier Hendrik Pulinx, second half of the 18th century. Bruges, Gruuthuse Museum.

Clock-stand in Rococo style, height 26.5 cm, Bruges, atelier Hendrik Pulinx, second half of the 18th century. Bruges, Gruuthuse Museum.

Ornamental basin for Franciscus Banckaert, diameter 22.7 cm, Bruges, atelier Hendrik Pulinx, 1778. Bruges, Gruuthuse Museum.

BRUGES   One important artist who bridges the opulent Baroque and the charming Rococo period was the versatile Hendrik Pulinx the Elder (1698-1781). In his time he was a highly esteemed architect, sculptor, graphic artist and potter in Bruges. He was largely self-taught, and his work contrasts markedly with the often rather soulless and impersonal artefacts of his contemporaries. His great artistic productivity was quite remarkable. Under the influence of the new artistic fashion from Paris, Pulinx established a faience factory in 1750 in the old tile works on the *Minnewater*, for which he had to sell his wine and linen business. Initially a one man concern, it was ravaged no less than four times by fire; so in 1754 he felt obliged to form a company, together with his son Hendrik, and Jan Chauvet from Ghent. He himself made the designs and took care of the illustrations and the faience, which was remarkable for its colouring. Initially, Pulinx employed thirty-eight workers; later on even sixty, which was a considerable workforce at that time. His work was not only sold in the immediate vicinity, but also exported abroad through Dunkirk in northern France.

The demand for ceramic ware from Bruges became so great that the orders could no longer be met, and in 1760 Pulinx had to expand. In the reorganization the families of Heyl and Alexander Emmery took the place of Chauvet as the third business partner. Although Pulinx had acquired all sorts of privileges, even an imperial patent for thirty years, a heated dispute arose between the father and the son. As a result the business found itself in deep financial trouble after three years, and it was sold. On 31st January 1763 the younger Pulinx signed an underhand agreement with a rich businessman from Bruges, Pieter de Brauwere. The factory rapidly recovered in the hands of the capable de Brauwere (1743-1817), and by 1764 there were once again thirty-four employees. In 1771 he even started to manufacture fine English ceramic ware, for which he had previously attracted skilled craftsmen. In 1780 this daring and market-oriented business was no longer healthy, and in 1781 it went bankrupt.

The bankruptcy announcement in 1764 shows that both ordinary and decorative or painted faience was manufactured by the *Societeyt Hendrick Pulinx en Cie* and his successors. The earliest articles were made in the style of St Cloud and Rouen, and included statues, garden ornaments and table accessories such as bundles of asparagus, artichokes, small animals *etc*. The fact that decorated wall tiles and possibly also tableaux made up of painted tiles were also made in Bruges, is borne out by the fairly recent discoveries of waste material from potteries. However, the shards discovered in the *Arsenaalstraat* in 1978 were only fired once, so that there was no decoration at all on these tiles. The faience from Bruges comprised a whole range of glazed work, including the well-known fireplace tiles, vases, statues and figurines, dinner and coffee services, and Eastern, Dutch and French faience. The articles that were signed or attributed to Pulinx' workshop are mainly to be found in the Gruuthuse Museum in Bruges; but some objects are in museums in Ghent, Brussels and St Omer. These are monochrome blue, purple or polychrome pieces of faience, regularly with a marbled effect.

Some Pulinx fireplaces in the Louis XV style in Bruges, Damme and St Omer are examples of this, as well as consoles, wall brackets for candles, fountains, mantlepiece decoration and clock cases. As in other Flemish cities, very little polychrome faience pieces have survived. Those who have include a dated soup tureen (1754), a beautiful vegetable or fruit bowl, a butter dish and a flower pot. Our knowledge of this important faience factory in West Flanders is certainly incomplete, but archaeological research can remedy this.

TOURNAI Past and recent excavations have shown that earthenware articles were made in Tournai from the Middle Ages onwards. The oldest known faience workshop was established in about 1670 by one Scorion, but it closed down completely in 1674. A new business was established in Tournai in 1687 by the Dutchman Calué who formed a company in 1696 together with Verschure and Beghin. The factory went bankrupt in 1698 but the business, which remained in Beghin's hands, continued to exist until 1704. Even so, the faience industry did not really get properly established in Tournai until Pierre Fauquet established a factory in the same year. He took over Beghin's workforce and materials. This factory too had to close down in 1725, but Pierre Fauquet had already opened another one in St Amand-les-Eaux in 1718. A workshop was then established in 1750 by François, which passed into the hands of François-Joseph Peterinck a year later. The latter recruited his workforce from famous French ceramic centres such as Rouen, Lille, St Amand, Lunéville and Valenciennes. He did not only make

Soup-tureen or vegetable dish, 13.3 × 22.2 cm, Bruges, Atelier Hendrik Pulinx, second half of the 18th century. Bruges, Gruuthuse Museum.

Basin with typically verdigris scenery, 31 × 25 cm, Brussels, Atelier Artoisenet, middle of the 18th century. Brussels, Broodhuis Museum.

Tankard, height 27.8 cm, Brussels, atelier outside the Gate of Laken, period of van Bellinghen (1802-1820) or Stevens (1820-1866). Bruges, Gruuthuse Museum.

faience, brown Rouen earthenware and English grès, but was the first potter in the Netherlands to manufacture porcelain. Objects were made in his *manufacture impériale et royale* that display a high degree of craftsmanship and perfection. This fame was to some extent due to the painters Michel Duvivier and the brothers Robert and Gilles Dubois, who had previously worked in St Cloud with Chiconeau. 18th-century Tournai porcelain had an international character and was remarkably similar to that of Meissen, Sèvres, Chelsea-Derby and Worcester, Japan and China. However, at the end of the 18th century the industry went through a bad period. On 26th December 1793 there was a serious fire in the factory. In 1798, a year before Peterinck's death, the factory passed into the hands of his daughter, who was married to Jean-Maximilien de Bettignies. He was a director until 1802, and at the beginning of the 19th century the factory passed into different hands.

A variety of beautiful household articles were made in Tournai; and a distinction can be made between faience, faience-fine and porcelain. Some well-known objects are the multi-coloured flower vases and pot-pouris, plates, dishes, jugs, coffee pots and sauce boats, even litre jugs. The porcelain included extremely fine groups of figurines and statuettes, including busts, shepherds, enamoured couples, gardeners, couples of pugs, Leda and the Swan *etc.* Nicolas Levreux, Antoine Gillis and Jozef Willems were some of the artists who made them. Characteristic Tournai features were the scalloped and the Ronda decoration, which consisted of a floral edge with *Fleurs des Indes*. But there were also nosegays, sometimes with sharply defines outlines, and fruit decorations which often incorporated insect life.

BRUSSELS   In the middle of the 17th century there were already a number of faience workshops in Brussels, as the archives reveal. In 1641 Guillaume de Decker was given a patent by the council of Brabant to produce earthenware in Brussels. Twelve years later the same privilege was granted to Jacques van den Haute and Jean Symonet. The latter moved to Hanau, Heusenstamm and Frankfurt. However, it is not known which finished products were made by which identified potters, and the style is very similar to Dutch faience of the same period. Some apothecaries' pots have been attributed to this city on the basis of the painted representation of St Michael and the date 1680.

In 1705 and 1754 two factories were founded: by Cornelis Mombaers and the Dutchman Dierick Witsenburg, and Jacques Artoisenet respectively. Despite the fact that conditions were in his favour, Mombaers' business foundered as a result of numerous external factors. His cunning and businesslike son Philippe, *Meester Porselijnbakker*, raised again the standards of the business and the quality of the work with his dynamic approach. He had previously visited the most important workshops in France and in the Netherlands; and started his faience factory in the *Lakenstraat* after his father's death in 1724. The range of objects produced was quite diverse, including not only a variety of services, but also ornamental tableware and even candlesticks.

Jacques Artoisenet, who was married to Philippe Mombaers' only daughter, started a business in competition with that of his parents-in-law when his wife died at an early age in 1751; his business, called *De Moriaen*, was situated on the *Bergstraat*. After he had acquired his own patent, he broke Philippe Mombaers' monopoly, and his children worked in the family concern in the

Duck, height 37 cm, length 44 cm, Brussels, atelier Artoisenet, middle of the 18th century. Brussels, Broodhuis Museum.

Lakenstraat until about 1822. After this, Artoisenet's factory passed into the hands of Ghobert de Saint Martin (1784-1806) and the brothers Bartholeyns (1806-1824), and continued to produce until 1824. In 1791 Jean-Baptist Artoisenet, the oldest son of Joseph-Philippe, and great-grandson of Philippe Mombaers, started a pottery which passed into the heads of the van Bellinghen brothers in 1802. They in turn sold the factory to Mathieu Stevens in 1820; and in 1866 the latter's son, Héliodore Stevens, went bankrupt.

It is rather difficult and risky to attribute ceramic articles to any one of these complex Brussels workshops, as signatures are very rare. Some exceptions are the unpainted bust of a weeping man (1743) in the Museums of Art and History in Brussels; and an octagonal tureen, dated 1746, in the Brussels Town Museum. Only in the 19th century the faience produced in this city was stamped with the rectangular mark STEVENS/BRUSSEL. As regards the colouration used, late 18th and early 19th-century work was predominantly cobalt blue or manganese purple, with a great variety of shading. The beautiful copper green, used in natural scenes, was unique to the capital. These include not only the well-known cauliflowers, but also teapots and cruet sets, serrated plates, jugs with lids and baskets.

Other ornaments which were typical of this coveted ceramic work include Rouen ware, a flowering hedge (a basket of flowers in imitation of Japanese *Kakiemon*) and a motif depicting a scene framed in between two trees, which is also found in French ceramic ware. Unusual articles were produced with the Sinceny style of decoration, which takes its name from the town of Sinceny in northern France, situated on the Oise between St Quentin and Laon. This fashionable style

with charming little Chinese figures, used particularly by Joseph-Philippe Artoisenet, can also be found in the French workshops of Rennes, Aprey, Goult, Marseilles *etc*. The typical beer tankards 'Jacques' and 'Jacqueline' were also decorated in this way; as were sauce boats, large soup tureens, cache-pots, cooling pots, pots with handles, large vases and even double candlesticks. Ornamental articles were also produced in Brussels, including large figures, Bhuddas, semi-recumbent men, *putti*, Bacchus figures, Brussels firemen, and even clowns and lawyers. Animals were also popular, including turkeys, ducks, doves, dogs, cats and lions. Less well-known objects include water bowls, egg dishes, tea caddies, flower holders or tulip vases, tobacco pots, brasiers or portable stoves and plaquettes. A large number of the well-known litre jugs and half litre jugs was made in blue and purple.

The history of Brussels porcelain, the first to be made in Belgium, is also rather complicated. Charles of Lorraine, the governor of the Netherlands, was responsible for the porcelain factory in the immediate vicinity of his own castle at Tervuren. The painter, Georges-Christophe Lindemann, who had previously worked in Nymphenburg and Höchst, took over the workshop from 1758-1766. It was not a commercial venture but more of a laboratory to amuse the Prince, and after his death it closed down in 1780. From 1876-1791 there was a workshop in Monplaisir Castle. Another one opened from 1787-1803 in Terloozen Castle. A third factory was opened by Louis-Pierre Cretté in 1800-1813 in the *Rue de l'Etoile*, now the *Ernest Allardstraat*. Together with Windisch, the painter Frédéric Faber established the first company in 1824 on the *Chaussée d'Etterbeek*, now the *Waversesteenweg* in Elsene, and this closed down in 1870. Finally, Charles-Christophe Windisch separated from Faber in 1830 and started his own factory, the last owner of which stopped producing in 1953, though he is still one of the most important porcelain dealers in the country.

The porcelain factories of Brussels produced very fine articles which vied with the artefacts from Paris and Sèvres, where the most beautiful porcelain in Europe was being produced at this time for the wealthy. Initially French and German painters were commissioned to work in these factories, but later local people were employed. A typical feature of this porcelain is the gilt and the painted tableaux, as seen on the monumental crater-shaped vases which are sometimes over-decorated. On a smaller scale there are dinner and coffee services in the Empire style (1818-1830) or the Louis-Philippe style (1830-1844), decorated with nosegays, foliage, love scenes, landscapes, the woodland imitations copied from Strasbourg work, and the well-known figurines of Our Lady, which reflect the spirit of the time very accurately. Thus, during the middle of the 19th century the two factories of Windisch and Faber, together with the factories of Baudour, Andenne and Tournai, formed the five major porcelain centres in the country.

Musical instruments

During the 17th and 18th centuries musical instruments were adapted to the new requirements of the music being written. Gradually a greater diversity of instruments emerged, both in string and in wind instruments. There was an increasing tendency to build the instruments. There was an increasing tendency to build the instruments in different sizes, so that each instrument had a specific tonal colour. During the 18th century the variety still augmented: recorders and flutes were now being made in several parts; and the clarinet, the oboe and the bassoon attained their final form. Only a very few 17th-century musical instruments have survived; but there are more examples of original instruments from the 18th century. At the international level, Flemish harpsichords were very much in demand for export.

THE HARPSICHORD

FROM *ca 1600 – ca 1660*   During the 16th and 17th centuries clavichords and virginals were made in Antwerp. A workshop was established at the end of the 16th century when Hans Ruckers came to the city, probably from Germany, like the organ builder Hans Suys before him. For generations this workshop produced instruments for musicians throughout Europe. When Joannes Ruckers (Antwerp 1578 – 1642) took over this workshop in about 1600 the first wing-shaped instrument was produced, and it was called a 'harpsichord'. In this instrument the strings were plucked with the same sort of jacks as in the 16th-century virginal. The harpsichord had become indispensible in ensemble music and had more possibilities than the virginal, and consequently there was a great demand for it. In general, the Antwerp

instrument was preferred to the contemporary Italian one, the export of which was restricted to the Iberian peninsula.

In addition to the Ruckers family other craftsmen made these instruments during the 17th century: Daniel Bader, the Britsen family (Joris I, Joris II, Joris III), Gomaar van Everbroeck, the Hagaerts family (Cornelius and Simon), Reynier Leunis, Christiaan Pelle, François van Uffel, Peter Verheyden, Dirk de Vries and Thomas Watson. Only five instruments made by Gomaar van Everbroeck, the Britsen and the Hagaerts families have survived, and there are none from the others. On the other hand, about a hundred instruments can be attributed to the Ruckers-Couchet family. This is obviously indicative of a more important production, giving the impression that this family monopolized the building of harpsichords. Probably other builders, in particular the Britsen and Hagaerts families, worked for them. Presumably the Ruckers owe their position of monopoly to their musical experience, their control of acoustics, and above all, their organizational skill. With the deaths of Andreas I (1579-1651/53), his son Andreas II (1607-1654/55), and his nephew Joannes Couchet (1615 – 1655), all within a few years of each other, the monopoly was broken. The business was kept going until about 1660 by Couchet's widow, Angela van den Brant.

Antwerp harpsichords made during the Ruckers' period can be described as follows: the sound box, usually made of lime or poplar, was painted on the outside with *trompe l'œil* motifs and an imitation marble

Harpsichord, Andreas Ruckers, 1646. Paris, Musée instrumental du Conservatoire national supérieur de musique.
This is one of the finest examples of how a 17th-century harpsichord was adapted to 18th-century fashion concerning decoration. This instrument was indeed 'revalorized' in 1780 by Pascal Taskin. The *Encyclopédie méthodique* refers to this builder as being an excellent master in the enlarging of Antwerp harpsichords.

The Senses, painting (detail), J. Breughel, about 1615. Madrid, Prado.
This detail shows a wide variety of the instruments that were used at that moment. From the left to the right one can notice a typically Antwerp harpsichord with at the outside an imitation of marble. This kind of marble was at those times also used in the architecture (see the Town Halls). Further on there is a decoration with printed paper above the keys. The two keyboards are not parallel, but transponant, which was typical for the beginning of the 17th century. Below the harpsichord is a trum and a trumpet. There are different sizes of gambas with bow around an open case in leather meant for flutes and in the front a lute. Moreover one can notice at the right side a *lira da braccio* with bourdonchord, two cornets (black), a pommer and recorders.

effect. In this respect they followed the general fashion of contemporary furniture. Only few examples of these have survived, and they give some idea of the real appearance of the cases. As laid down in the rules of St Luke's Guild, they were signed with the mark of the workshop: a rose, usually in lead, which filled the sound-hole, and which contained a kneeling, winged angel and the initials of the person who had built the instrument: H[ans] R[uckers], I[oannes] R[uckers], A[ndreas] R[uckers] or I[oannes] C[ouchet]. In addition, the sound-board was often painted with flowers and insects, reminiscent of the numerous paintings of flowers by 17th-century masters from Antwerp. The third predominant decorative element consisted of bands of printed paper which were glued onto the edges around the sound-board and above the keyboard. Some of the motifs used recall Cornelis Bos or the Floris' style, but there is also evidence of another source of inspiration: Francisque Pellegrin's *La Fleur de la Science de pourtraicture* (1530). Recently it has been shown that this type of decoration was also used on wall paper, glued on and between the ceiling joists in house decoration.

There was usually a piece of paper glued to the inside of the lid, with a Latin proverb – generally in praise of the friendship and harmony that is created by music, but sometimes referring to the transitory nature of life. Other lids were painted with scenes on the inside. The names of the artists who painted these scenes can be found in the archives: they include P.P. Rubens, Frans Francken the Younger, Frans Borsse, Otto Venius,

Harpsichord, Joannes Petrus Bull, 1779. Antwerp, Vleeshuis Museum. Joannes Petrus Bull was the last builder who was active at Antwerp. Typical for his instruments is the green colour; this paint was applied directly on the wood, without priming coat, a technique which is also used for some pieces of 18th-century furniture.

Spinet or polygonal virginals, Hans Ruckers, Antwerp, 1591, with gilt leaden rosette with the initials HR. Forty-five numbered low keys, top keys are new. This instrument was drastically restored. The front of the resonance box is original as is the sound-leaf on which the painting has been wiped out. Bruges, Gruuthuse Museum.

Daniel de Vos, Marten de Vos and a member of the Snellinckx family. In some cases these painted lids lasted longer than the instruments themselves, and are now exhibited as paintings on their own; though they can be recognized by their specific shape and size.

Technically the following details are characteristic of 17th-century Flemish harpsichords. The range of the instrument comprises four octaves with a short octave in the bass, which means that there are 45 keys; 27 white lower keys in bone, and 18 black upper keys made of black stained wood, sometimes beechwood. There were two strings of different lengths for every key so that – analogous to the organ – one might say there were two registers.

Antwerp harpsichords were exported throughout Europe. Thus we know the correspondence on an instrument offered for sale to Charles I, painted by Rubens. A virginal (New York, Metropolitan Museum of Art), commissioned by Philip II, was offered to the Margrave of Oropesa and was finally rediscovered in Peru. Constantijn Huygens praised the superior quality of his harpsichord built by Joannes Couchet, and had it moved to his house in The Hague. The fact that many instruments were exported to the United Provinces is evident from a number of paintings by Vermeer, Metsu and Terborgh depicting Dutch interiors, and showing a

Virginals, 175 × 50 × 24 cm Joannes Couchet, 1650. Antwerp, Vleeshuis Museum.
This type of virginal was already designed during the last quarter of the 16th century. In the case of a muselaer, as is printed here, the key-board is placed more to the right. This is a nice example with typical decorations: arabasques on paper in black and white; scattered flowers on the sound board and a view on the roads of Antwerp on the inside of the cover.

Flemish instrument. These were also exported to France, as is shown by numerous inventories of 18th-century instrument builders' workshops.

It is therefore clear that even in their own time Ruckers' instruments were in great demand and were highly thought of. However, it were 18th-century documents that confirmed their lasting fame. In 1788, the *Encyclopédie Méthodique* stated: "The best harpsichords which have been made up to now, with the most harmonious sound, are those made by the three Ruckers (Hans, Jean and André), as well as those made by Jean Couchet. They were all established in Antwerp during the last century in large numbers, and many of them are now in Paris, recognized by connoisseurs as originals".

In his work *The Present State of Music in Germany, the Netherlands and the United Provinces* (1773), which also discusses Antwerp, Charles Burney praised the work of these instrument makers, too. "The famous harpsichord-makers, of the name of Ruckers, whose instruments have been so much, and so long admired all over Europe, lived in this city; there were three, the first, and the father of the two, was John Ruckers, who flourished at the beginning of the last century. His instruments were the most esteemed, and are remarkable for the sweetness and fullness of their tone". These days Antwerp harpsichords can be found in the most important museums of musical instruments. If a museum possesses one, it always has a place of honour.

FROM *ca* 1660 TO THE END OF THE 18th CENTURY   The closure of the Scheldt resulted in an economic recession, and this also led to the end of harpsichord building in Antwerp. Probably other reasons were still more decisive in this respect. In the first place, the manufacture of these instruments had actually been a monopoly of a single family, *viz* the Ruckers-Couchet family. It was therefore fatal for the business when the three leading figures died within a few years, between 1653 and 1655, leaving only children under age. The heirs of Joannes Couchet were trained in the trade by Simon Hagaerts, who was still working at this time, as was Joris Britsen. As mentioned above, few instruments made by these masters have survived. They were evidently unable to cope with the innovations which had to be incorporated into instruments during the 17th century, and which eventually led to the typical 18th-century instrument. Thus a document dating from 1657 already refers to three instead of two registers, and a complete rather than a short octave in the bass.

The typical 18th-century harpsichord comprised five octaves and three registers; in other words, three strings per key. The first step was taken by completing the bass octave. A larger number of strings resulted in more tension on the sound-board, and therefore the design which had been used by the Ruckers had to be fundamentally altered. The 17th-century case was not large enough for 18th-century music. A whole octave, consisting of twelve keys, had to be added. The extension of the instrument with keys and strings was described in detail in the *Encyclopédie*. Actually the Ruckers' instruments were so highly esteemed that as many features as possible were retained. A method for achieving this was known as *ravalement*: "Harpsichords *à grand ravalement* are those that have sixty-one keys". The *Encyclopédie* also said: "The majority of Ruckers' harpsichords and of the old-fashioned ones had only two strings for each key." This extension of the instrument meant the end of the proportions used in Ruckers' design, and as a result the sound also altered. The new design of the case also required a new form of decoration, which was obviously adapted to the fashion of the times. 18th-century furniture is very different from the sober 17th-century style. And so the simple Antwerp harpsichords were adapted to the French taste as regards their shapes and decoration incorporating for example gold paint and *vernis Martin*. The disappearance of the Ruckers

family between 1655 and 1660, and the lack of successors at this crucial moment, encouraged the development of a large number of workshops abroad, particularly in France and England. The trends described in the *Encyclopédie* are confirmed by the instruments of the time, in that the style designed by Ruckers was always followed. A large number of fakes now also came onto the market; and instruments with the rose of Ruckers' workshop were often quoted at four times the price of a French harpsichord.

Meanwhile production in Antwerp slowed down. Towards the end of the 17th century, Jacobus van den Elsche (*ca* 1689 – Antwerp 1772) was working in Antwerp. He was described in contemporary documents as "an unusually gifted master, both in the manufacture of harpsichords and in rebuilding old instruments with *unison*, or adapting a short keybord into a longer one", which meant that in Antwerp Ruckers' instruments were being extended and adapted in the same way as described by the term *ravalement* in the *Encyclopédie*. Apart from van den Elsche, Alexander Britsen also continued to work until the 18th century. None of his instruments has survived and only one of van den Elsche's has (Antwerp, Vleeshuis). Another in Berlin Museum was destroyed during the Second World War.

In France and England the development of harpsichords took place in different ways, on the basis of the Flemish model. A number of German harpsichord builders settled in Antwerp. This happened after a resolution was passed in 1738, aimed at stimulating the arts and crafts of the Netherlands. Joannes Daniel Dulcken (? – Antwerp 1757) was one of the most prominent masters, and the first of a long line of instrument builders who made harpsichords, and later on pianofortes as well. The building of harpsichords in Antwerp flourished again because of his family; about ten instruments have survived. As one of his instruments is now in the Smithsonian Institution in Washington, today's builders are again inspired by the historic way of building. No instrument builder in the world would not wish to know more about the 'secrets' of a Ruckers or a Dulcken, depending on whether he wants to reconstruct instruments of the 17th or of the 18th century. Finally, Joannes Petrus Bull (Erckrath 1723 – 1804) was also working in Antwerp, four of his instruments have survived.

The end of the 18th century also brought the end of the harpsichord. History repeated itself... New ideas about composition required yet another type of sound, and this time there was no longer any place for the harpsichord.

Harpischord, Joannes Daniel Dulcken, 1745. Washington, Smithsonian Institution.
Joannes Daniel Dulcken came from Germany to live in Antwerp shortly after 1738, and he became the founder of a family of harpsichord-builders. Shortly after the 2nd World War, this instrument roused particular interest. It served as model for numerous builders, who followed again the historical example. Having five octaves, this instrument is contemporary to the grandmasters of harpsichord-music: J.S. Bach, F. and L. Couperin, A. Scarlatti and J.Ph. Rameau.

THE ORGAN

During the 17th century organ cases became more elaborate: the new instruments were built on a broader design and the older organs were adapted to the musical requirements of the time. Increasingly the organ was placed in a specific position, either above the portal or in the centre of the church by the choir screen. The registers became more numerous, and the adaptation of older organs often resulted in the disappearance of a number of the original components. An original *block-werk* was very often replaced by a large console with many registers. The Counter Reformation had a very favourable effect on new commissions. The need to repair damaged or destroyed organs, or to adapt or replace them, attracted a number of masters from other countries. The tradition of organ building in Flanders and Brabant was continued, and during the 16th century it was dominated mainly by three families from the Southern Netherlands: the Moors and Brebos families from Lier, and the Langhedul family from Ypres. Various members of these families worked in Germany, Spain, Scandinavia and France. During the 17th century a number of masters also came from the United Provinces: the emphasis was no longer exclusively on the Southern Netherlands.

Matthys Langhedul (Ypres ? – Brussels 1635/36) was the official organ tuner at the court in Madrid from 1592-1599 until he settled in Paris, where he realized the organ in St Gervais' Church (1602). In 1605 he returned to Ypres; then he moved to Ghent, to Brussels to the court of the Archdukes, to Antwerp and to Tongres. After the death of this founder of the 17th-century Baroque organ in the Southern Netherlands, two distinct groups evolved, in Flanders and in Brabant.

In Flanders the most influential area was still centred around Bruges and Ghent. Nicolaas Helewoudt (a contemporary of Matthys Langhedul) worked in Bruges, where he was also the organist at St Donate's Church. His organs include that of 1624 in the Augustine Church; and those in the Churches of St James and St Anne, both dating from 1629. Boudewijn Ledou from Bruges worked from 1643 to 1656. The instrument that he made in Watervliet (East Flanders) has all the typical 17th-century characteristics; the organ cases of Damme (*ca* 1640) and Lissewege (1652) have also survived. In addition, Jan van Belle from St-Winoksbergen (French Flanders) should be mentioned. He made the organs in Poperinge and Dixmude. Jacobus van Eynde, the last organ builder in the great Langhedul tradition, produced the single manual organ in St Anne's Church in Bruges (1707); as

Organ, Nicolas II Le Royer, 1648. Leerbeek/Brabant, St Peter's Church. One-manual organ with three groups of pipes within levels, which are separated by typical Baroque columns.

Organ, Hans Goltfuss, 1630. Steenokkerzeel/Brabant, St Rumoldus' Church.

Organ, Nicolaes van Haeghen, 1658. Antwerp, St Paul's Church. The design for the organ-case is made by Erasmus Quellin (1607-78) and it was performed by Pieter Verbruggen the Elder (1615-86).

well as the majestic instrument situated above the choir screen of St Saviour's Cathedral, built from 1717-1719. An unusual feature of the latter instrument is the fact that the organist's back would be towards the choir, while the main body of the instrument faces the nave. Organs dated between 1696 and 1728 occur in Assebroek, Oostkamp, Poperinge and Ypres.

In Ghent the van der Haegen family were the most prominent, especially with Luypold, who repaired the organ in St Nicholas' Church in 1629; Pieter, active between 1622 and 1669; Nicolaas, Jan and Gregorius, who worked between 1672 and 1693. Finally, a mention should be made of Niclays and Jacobus Bauwens.

In Brabant the main centres were Brussels (where Matthys Langhedul spent the last twenty-five years of his life) and Alost. Composers such as Pieter Cornet, Peter Philips and John Bull worked in Brussels and Antwerp and stimulated organ building. Eventually a number of organ builders from Germany replaced the local masters. After Matthys Langhedul the le Royer family, who came from Namur and settled in Brussels, were the main organ builders during the 17th century. The tradition of organ building was passed on from

Large organ, Jean Baptiste Forceville, 1720-22, Antwerp, St Carolus Borromeus' Church.
Two-manual organ, built to a very special composition in which the lower central party comes between two higher towers. Music-making angels reign supremely on the different columns. Remarkable are the trophies of the musical instruments below.

father to son by Nicolas I, Nicolas II and Jean consecutively. Some of Nicolas II's work from 1654-1662 has survived in Brussels, Lede, Ghent and Hamme; Jean worked in Turnhout, Tournai, Ghent, Brussels, Malines and Courtray from 1662-1675. However, this family never worked in Antwerp, where organ building was developing on a significant scale. A large number of masters was attracted to the city, though without settling there. First, there were Anthoon and Peter de Lanoy, who eventually settled in Brussels after working for Our Lady's Cathedral and St James's Church in Antwerp. In addition, there were the German immigrants, Daniel Baders and Hans Goltfuss. The latter, born in Cologne at the end of the 16th century, went to Haacht after being involved in building organs in 's-Hertogenbosch in 1632 and in Antwerp between 1636 and 1642. He worked in Steenokkerzeel, Tervuren, Tongerlo, Zwijndrecht and Herentals between 1650 and 1658, the year of his death. His colleague, Jan Bremser, settled in Malines and built organs there, as well as in Aarschot, St Gillis-Waas, Westerlo, Zele, Belsele and Nieuwkerke between 1650 and 1676. Joan Gottfried Baders, another German immigrant, worked in Halle and Brussels. Christiaan Penceler and Jean Baptiste Forceville eventually brought about a major change. The latter altered the organ in St Paul's Church in Antwerp so fundamentally in 1736 that nothing was left of the original instrument, which had been a large work by Nicolaes van Haegen, dating from 1654-1658. The style was clearly influenced by the Dutch tradition – grand and majestic. The work was designed by Erasmus Quellin and executed by Pieter Verbruggen the Elder. Nicolaes van Haegen made the organ in the *Grote Kerk* of Dordrecht, based on this example.

J.B. Forceville, the main representative of a number of masters from French Flanders, gave a new impetus to organ building in the Southern Netherlands at the end of the 17th century. This took place after the German influence, which could only be detected in Brabant. Born in Lille or Abbeville *ca* 1660, Forceville's name appears in the Southern Netherlands in 1680. He went to Antwerp in 1686, and made organs for Antwerp, Loenhout, Hemiksem, Haasdonk, Ekeren, Kruibeke, Bevel, Alost and Ghent between 1685 and 1705. He then settled in Brussels and completed important works in Malines, Liege, Antwerp, Ninove, Zaffelare and Brussels between 1713 and 1738, the year of his death. His organs are very individual: they have a broad structure with a low middle section flanked by two towers.

The late Baroque and Rococo periods were dominated by the families of de la Haye and van Petegem. A large number of instruments made by various members of these organ building families have survived, so that we now have a thorough understanding of their work.

Louis de la Haye was the founder of a lineage of organ builders. His name first appears towards the end of the 17th century; he settled in Ghent and in Antwerp. There his son, Louis II, succeeded him; working in Alost, Ghent, Eeklo, Gouda, Bergen-op-Zoom and Nieuwenbos from 1738-1773. Dieudonné Joseph (1725-1811) worked in Antwerp and was succeeded by

Jacobus Josephus († 1845). The extension of the organ in Our Lady's Cathedral is a good example of his work.

A high point was reached in organ building with the van Peteghems, who came from East Flanders and settled in Ghent. They also built organs in France and the Northern Netherlands. The founder, Pieter (1708-1787), was an apprentice to the Antwerp master Gilliam Davidts, and worked under J.B. Forceville after 1725. His most representative work can now be found in the seminary in Bonne Espérance, though it was originally made in 1768 for Affligem Abbey. Between 1758 and 1784 he carried out important works in Alost, Denderhoutem, Courtrai, Valenciennes, Malines, Tirlemont, Vicogne, Amsterdam and Louvain. His son, Lambert-Benoît (1742-1807), worked together with him from 1776. The instrument built by them in Gyzegem in 1776 illustrates the break from the traditional way of organ building, and the development of the front of the organ in Rococo style. This was also related to the extension of the registration in the 18th century. Another son, Egide-François (1737-1803), worked predominantly in the provinces of Antwerp and Brabant; one of his works is the organ of St Rombout's Cathedral in Malines. The van Petegem tradition was carried on into the 19th century by a number of Pieter van Peteghem's grandsons.

A survey of the many organ builders show that this tradition is firmly rooted in Flemish culture. These works of art carry us along small villages, and in larger cities they can be admired in nearly every church. However, the monumental sculpture of these skilful ensembles can only be appreciated when translated into beautiful music. The organ casing allows the different registers to function so that they can come into their own. Like anyone who builds an instrument, the organ builder is an artist, who transforms the available acoustic space into an aesthetic experience.

THE CARILLION

The carillion assumed its final form and was provided with a keyboard during the 16th century. In the 17th century this reached a high point; the largest carillions comprised three and a half to four octaves, which means that there were 44 to 49 bells.

During the 16th century the main bell founders' families had been the Waghevens and the van den Gheyn's. Members of the latter were still working during the 17th and 18th centuries. One of them, Matthias van den Gheyn (1727-1785), was a well-known composer. In the 17th century, Melchior de Haze (1632-1697), who cast a carillion for the Escorial (Madrid) in 1674, should be mentioned. In 1675 he completed his carillion for the Halle Tower in Bruges, already destroyed by lightning in 1741. He also manufactured carillions for Breda, The Hague, Madrid (Prado), Aranjuez, and finally Salzburg. During the 17th century the Hemony brothers also made carillions, though they focused on the Northern Netherlands. François (1609-1667) and Pierre (1619-1680) came from Lorraine and settled in Zutphen in 1640. They also made carillions in the Southern Netherlands in Antwerp, Ghent, Malines and other places. In the 18th century W. Witlockx is worthy of note. However, the flourishing art of bell founding, and therefore of carillions, came to an end during the 18th century.

Clock, 49 × 44 cm, Jacob Waghevens, 1550. Antwerp, Vleeshuis Museum. Often the clocks were given a name, as it appears clearly from the inscription on this clock: 'In the year MDL of Martin, I have been cast by Jacob Waghevens'. Below the portrait of St Martin is pictured in a round medallion.

Clock, 30 × 23 cm, Andreas Jozef van den Ghein, 1766. Antwerp, Vleeshuis Museum.
Remarkable in the case of this clock is the crown with two eagle heads.

Robert Hoozee
Custodian of the Museum of Fine Arts at Gent

THE 19th AND 20th CENTURIES

ROBERT HOOZEE and WIM BLOCKMANS
Introduction

JEAN VAN CLEVEN
Architecture

MONIQUE TAHON-VAN ROOSE
Sculpture

ROBERT HOOZEE
Painting

LIEVEN DAENENS
Decorative arts

Introduction

During the 19th century there was no specific Flemish art that was clearly distinct from the art of the rest of Belgium. Flemish art was significant to the extent that it participated in an international European context with authentic individual creations, even if these originated from a provincial background; for example, the poetry of Guido Gezelle or the first sculptures of George Minne.

In the course of the 19th century, the Belgian art would too finally freed itself from the inherited guild structures. Artists were trained in centralized establishments such as the academies; and the public was involved by means of public events such as group salons and individual exhibitions. The following chapters reveal how virtually all artists were oriented towards other countries during their formative years; many of them also studied abroad. The progressive circles of artists, which became active particularly during the second half of the century, sought to make contact with the artistic circles of the neighbouring countries, and also invited foreign artists to come to Belgium. The fact that quite a few of them spent time in Belgium was very important: one only has to remember the impact of artists such as David or Rodin. Although there were active artistic circles in cities such as Ghent and Antwerp, the capital city of Brussels played a central role for the whole country.

In a modern evaluation of the art produced in Belgium in the last century, it soon becomes apparent that work of international importance was produced only towards the end of the century. George Minne and Constantin Meunier were the first Belgian sculptors to have a decisive influence on the course of European art – their predecessors had merely been able to *follow* this course. The same applies in the field of painting for figures such as James Ensor, Fernand Khnopff and Theo van Rysselberghe. In architecture there was Victor Horta, in the applied arts Henry van de Velde. All this suggests that in these different branches of art a synchronized development was taking place, and that the young state of Belgium actually needed half a century to overcome the gap between the 18th and the 19th century. It would probably be an exaggeration to

George Minne, *The kneeled one from the Fountain*, 1898, plaster, 79 cm. Private collection.

describe this as a cultural decline. Nevertheless, the image of the *Pauvre Belgique* conjured up by Baudelaire in the 1860's, as well as the many exhortations by Flemish writers for a cultural revival, refer to a very real situation.

Moreover, at the beginning of the century a great deal of energy was needed to reorganize art education and to expand a structured artistic scene with salons and prizes, which made it possible to follow a normal artistic career. The occupation by Austria and France played a complex role, for they were responsible for establishing academies, museums, salons *etc*. On the other hand, the occupying nations robbed Belgium of many of its art treasures, which eventually found their way to museums in other countries. Nevertheless, even this had a positive effect – by virtue of the fact that their removal automatically made these works of art become objects of publicity; and led to the foundation of the first museums in Belgium.

In attempting to establish a general outline of the state of art in Belgium in the 19th century, one has to refer to the constant influence and attraction exerted by Paris. This influence had a political basis, both during the period of French domination and after the establishment of the French-oriented state of Belgium; but the supremacy of Paris during the 19th century was also an art historical fact. Up to the end of the century there was a close relationship between Belgian and French art, fostered by artists and critics. The links with Germany and England were far more tangential.

The relations between the different artistic disciplines during the 19th century have never really been studied with reference to Belgian art. Nevertheless, different scientific approaches generally lead to the same classification of periods: 1830-1860, 1860-1880, 1880-1900, the period to the First World War, and the years between the two World Wars. Equivalents can be found in literature and music for the Romantic period in painting during the 1840's, and for the Realism of the 1860's.

The focal points of interest in the 19th century, such as social awareness, the love of nature, the study of the past – especially the Middle Ages, the view of man as an individual *etc*, can be discerned at some point in every discipline. These ideas and circumstances determined the atmosphere of the period not only in Flanders, but throughout Europe. On the other hand, the Flemish Movement was one unique factor in Belgium, though it hardly influenced the development of the visual arts, unlike its effect on literature and music. It is probably more appropriate to indicate some of the turning points in the history of Belgian art during the 19th century, which were accompanied by a definite integration of the various disciplines.

The 1860's constitute a first important period, in which the breakthrough of a new positivist aesthetic theory took place in all the branches of the arts. For the first time the different disciplines combined in Belgium, to form the sort of artistic concentrations which would henceforth develop the art of this country. Also for the first time the role played by Brussels emerged very

493

strongly – it had already been a temporary home for a number of influential foreigners, including Victor Hugo, Charles Baudelaire and Pierre-Joseph Proudhon. Furthermore, there was a continual movement of artists between Brussels and Paris, which fed the first avant-garde movement in Belgian art with ideas. These were opposed to the academic idealist tradition and the related artistic establishment. They made two fundamental requirements: art should reflect contemporary life, and it should be the free expression of the individual artist.

The avant-garde movement materialized around groups of artists and journals, and visual artists soon gained the support of literary circles. An example was Charles de Coster, a critic and the author of *Légendes flamandes*, which was illustrated by a number of different painters of the Realist school. The magazine *Uylenspiegel: Journal des ébats artistiques et littéraires*, which published the first modern views on art in Belgium, first appeared in 1857. In 1868 the Brussels avant-garde formed the *Société Libre des Beaux-Arts*, and in 1871 and 1872 its members published the journal *L'Art libre*. This contained virtually all the contemporary Realist artists, as well as work by literary figures such as Léon Dommartin and Camille Lemonnier.

This concentration of progressive ideas was repeated twenty years later in Brussels. At that moment an important generation of writers and poets was working for the magazine *La jeune Belgique*, first published in 1881. This group included Emile Verhaeren, Georges Rodenbach, Charles van Lerberghe, and Maurice Maeterlinck. These Flemish literati wrote in French and were drawn towards the visual arts; their literary work itself stimulated many artists to produce illustrations. In 1883 an artistic circle was founded in Brussels, led by the lawyer Octave Maus. It was called *Les Vingt* ('The XX'). The approach adopted by this group immediately showed that art in Belgium had come of age. The aim of *Les Vingt* was to secure the acceptance of modern art in all its diversity, and for this purpose its members appealed to anyone in Europe who was producing new ideas. In this way the whole complex world of European art, with individuals such as van Gogh and Gauguin, and movements as Neo-Impressionism and Symbolism, eventually appeared in Brussels. *Les Vingt* was a group of visual artists, but it also organized lectures and concerts, and its exhibitions also covered the applied arts. The journal that was closely connected with *Les Vingt* was *L'Art moderne*; this brought together poets and critics in a mutual appreciation of modern art and society.

Les Vingt were not an isolated phenomenon. The group had developed from earlier groups, *La Chrysalide* and *L'Essor*. When *Les Vingt* was dissolved in 1893, its work was continued by *La libre esthétique*. In Antwerp, Henry van de Velde was one of the founders of *L'art indépendant* in 1887, while the painter Emile Claus was one of the founders of *De XIII* in 1891. There was no such circle of artists in Ghent; though many important *fin-de-siècle* poets and painters maintained close contacts with each other and organized lectures and meetings there. In fact, this was the background of both

Maurice Maeterlinck and Karel van de Woestijne. Finally, the literary magazine *Van Nu en Straks* ('Of now and later') was founded in Antwerp in 1893, which was representative for the whole of Flanders. Artists from different disciplines worked for it, including many of the members of *Les Vingts*, and it also aimed at providing an appreciation of the whole of modern cultural life.

A chronicle of this period of Belgian art has yet to be written. In any event, the last decades of the 19th century were a highpoint of Flemish – and in general Belgian – art. It is not surprising that this period is now the subject of international study. It incorporated all the trends of European art, and it was determined by some first class artists in Belgium. Brussels was one of the centres of Art Nouveau and Symbolism. In the other cities the avant-garde was active and adopted a clear left wing, anarchist or socialist viewpoint, at a time when labour movements were forming everywhere. Social awareness was actually a fundamental theme, found in all the different artistic disciplines of the period. It was a starting point for the socially aware Realists, such as Constantin Meunier, Eugene Laermans and Léon Frédéric; and for ditto writers such as Camille Lemonnier, Georges Eekhoud and Emile Verhaeren. It formed a philosophical basis for critical figures such as James Ensor, and for desperate *fin-de-siècle* artists like Maurice Maeterlinck and George Minne. For their part, most of the Art Nouveau artists were idealist dreamers of a new society in which art would have universal meaning. Figures such as Victor Horta and Henry van de Velde, Octave Maus and Edmond Picard, the esoteric Fernand Khnopff and the many artists who led to a true revival of the applied arts in Belgium at the turn of the century, will be considered in this context.

During the 20th century progressive art had a much more individual look; and only after the First World War an organized avant-garde arose in Brussels, centred increasingly around galleries such as *Selection* and *Le Centaur*. In these circles much attention was devoted to the design of the environment; and experiments in the various artistic disciplines, both Belgian and foreign, were confronted with each other. Expressionism and abstract art were the two main currents of the 1920's; and at the end of the 1920's and during the 1930's Surrealism may be considered as the most progressive force in Belgian art.

Eugène Laermans, *Strike-evening*, oil-colours on canvas, 106 × 115 cm, 1893. Brussels, Museums of Fine Arts.

INDUSTRIALIZATION AND PAUPERIZATION

During the last two centuries profound changes have taken place in virtually all sectors of Flemish society. This process is often described as the process of modernization. However, these fundamental changes manifested themselves in Flanders generally later than in the neighbouring areas such as Wallonia, northern France, the east of England and the Rhineland. The relatively late and gradual urbanization and industrialization gave the power structures in Flanders the opportunity to adapt to the new situation, and relatively speaking, they managed to survive without too many problems.

Three big oppositions split the political world: between capital and labour, between Catholics and atheists, and between the Dutch and the French-speaking population. It was characteristic of the development of Flanders that during some periods one or other of these confrontations took the prominent position (or was thrust to the fore), but that no important conflicts were ever restricted to just one of these three problem areas. Class conflicts were always combined with the polarities in the religious or social fields. In this way strong polarization was avoided and adaptation gradually took place.

Throughout the entire 19th century agriculture continued to be the most important source of income for Flanders. While industrial production started to super-

cede agricultural one for the state of Belgium in about 1870, this state of affairs was only achieved in Flanders in the middle of the 20th century. The marked increase in population – for every thousand people there were thirty-five births a year – did not lead to a growth in the cities, up to a degree that was reached in neighbouring countries. A significant proportion of the rural population depended on commuting or seasonal work in France or the coalmines of Wallonia. The poorest of them emigrated in tens of thousands to America, where they settled above all in Detroit.

In Flanders itself there was actually only one real industrial centre, *viz* Ghent. At the beginning of the 19th century a number of family enterprises in that city introduced the most modern mechanized linen and cotton mills on the continent. Elsewhere the production relied on craftsmen, and the development lagged behind that in other countries. Only the port of Antwerp, with its related shipbuilding and repair docks, expanded to any significant extent. However, for the most part, production took place in small workshops.

Apart from the textile industry of Ghent – which built on traditions handed down through the centuries – Flanders lacked the elements which had stimulated the first wave of industrialization in England, France and Wallonia; *i e* raw materials such as coal and iron ore, and capital investment. The most important fortunes in Flanders continued to be in land ownership. Admittedly the French era had resulted in the public sale of many of the church lands, and these 'black goods' had mainly fallen into the hands of bourgeois investors. However, the Dutch and early Belgian periods had succeeded in restoring the material position of the aristocratic landowners. In 1847, 57% of the wealthiest landowners were still nobles. Only towards the end of the century the bourgeois ownership of land equalled that of the aristocracy. As wealth determined eligibility for election for political careers, and the electoral system was to the advantage of rural areas vis-à-vis the urban districts, the landowners kept a close control over the political system. This policy systematically protected their sources of income, as well as their rights. The baron remained the indisputable lord of the village as its mayor.

From the Middle Ages the family holdings in what is now West and East Flanders were quite scattered and small. The general trend towards growth in population increased the pressure on profitability. The census of 1846 showed that 84% of agricultural land in West Flanders was taken up by farming holdings with an area of less than twenty acres, while in East Flanders this proportion was even higher. By the end of the century 90% of the land was worked by tenants. The rise in population was very much to the advantage of the landowners; the price of products rose, as did the rents from the tenants. They were able to serve notice on their tenants without offering them any reimbursement.

The poor sandy soil of the area did usually not produce enough, because the farms were so small, to provide a decent standard of living for the farmers' families. Therefore the householder often had an additional income from the craft carried out at home, such as the traditional weaving during the winter months, as long as the mechanized mills of the cities still allowed this. Increasingly farmers also had to find work by commuting to the city or to the industrial areas of Wallonia or northern France. This phenomenon of 'migrant workers' from the poverty stricken area of Flanders was facilitated by the construction of an intricate railway network. In this way Flemish farmers formed a docile reserve labour force for the crafts and industries in the cities and neighbouring areas. At the same time village life of Flanders was not totally disrupted, because the men and sons always returned to the family home beneath the church tower.

The vulnerability of the Flemish agricultural economy became evident when the grain harvest failed in 1846, and in 1847 the potato harvest was reduced to one tenth by blight. Because there was no alternative source of income – the crafts carried out at home collapsed in the same decade as a result of competition from factories – more than thirty thousand people died in the two provinces of Flanders. In addition, hunger increased the susceptibility to infectious diseases, which spread rapidly. During these years, fourteen thousand destitute people left the land. Like Ireland, Flanders was all too familiar with the tragic and disastrous consequences of a potato famine, resulting from overpopulation in a traditionally agriculturrally structured society.

The so-called 'second wave' of industrialization, which offered new opportunities to areas without coal, led to changes in Flanders in about 1870, as in the Netherlands, Switzerland and northern Italy. The massive importation of American grain through the port of Antwerp solved the food problem. At the same time this led to the demise of unprofitable farms and an improvement in the conditions of those who remained. Many were able to change over to cattle farming, or specialized in market gardening. The proportion of farmers in the active population was drastically reduced. In 1937 it was 17%; now it is less than 3%.

However, the process of industrialization in Flanders significantly differed from that in Wallonia. The port of Antwerp attracted chemical and metal industries; the 'iron Rhine', the railway link between Antwerp and the Ruhr, stimulated the establishment of glass and nonferrous metal industries in the Campine. The area between Antwerp and Brussels became a virtually uninterrupted industrial area. The discovery of rich seams of coal in Limburg shortly after 1900 gave a new lease of life to this province, the most traditional of all. However, the great majority of Flemish industries were still run on a small scale, supported by individual financing. The Brussels bank houses had invested in large projects, and the management of these was completely in the hands of the French-speaking bourgeoisie. Gevaert and Bekaert were exceptions; they were large modern industries with a true Flemish orientation. The late industrialization of Flanders meant that the advantages of its position on the coast, the large rivers and canals and intricate railway network could be used to the full. In addition, capital was attracted by the presence of an abundant docile and poorly paid workforce. The gradual establishment of industry, learning from earlier developments in Wallonia, explain why the original power structures were better able to maintain themselves in Flanders.

In the middle of the 19th century the prosperous bourgeoisie of the major Flemish cities, who determined the political scene, were predominantly liberal and French-speaking. However, in rural areas, which still had more influence at a national level, the Church was still sovereign and had a good relationship with the landed aristocracy. This bastion of conservatism was totally opposed to any change or modernization. The belief that the lord of the manor preferred to keep the people poor while the priest kept them uneducated, was quite accurate for that time. The French régime had admittedly abolished feudal rights, but the status of the aristocracy survived, the burden of rents was onerous, and the law served the ruling class. The humility of the Flemish peasants as expressed so poignantly by the novelist Cyriel Buysse was rooted in profound social inequality and extreme dependence. However, the agricultural crisis and the changes which took place in about 1880 had a deep and disruptive effect on the social order. The isolation of the village was penetrated by the increased mobility, resulting from the railway network and improvements in communication, with the arrival of newspapers and later on film and radio. The dangerous ideas which had originated in the cities percolated into the villages, threatening the traditional harmony based on the sanctity of the church and the home. In the large cities and old industrial centres the Church was unable to retain control, and the rapid expansion of housing for the workers was followed inadequately in pastoral care. In Wallonia this had led to a mass abandonment of the Church.

When socialism also reared its head for the growing working class in Flanders, the Church reacted by expanding in a powerful and organized way, aimed at caring for its flock from the cradle to the grave, so that the sheep would not stray from the straight and narrow path of Catholicism. 1890 was an important year in this respect. In that year the Farmers' Union was founded, an 'anti-socialist union' of workers' associations, together with the 'anti-socialist' newspaper, *Het Volk*. The Catholic movement harked back to the medieval model of corporatism in the spirit of *Rerum Novarum*, attempting to encourage the harmonious relationship of employers and employees in accordance with the Gospels. The Church expanded its party, a pillar of strength comprising women's organizations, youth movements, banks and investment groups, aimed at the propagation of the Catholic ethic.

As a result of this strategy the Labour movement was deeply divided on the subject of religion. In Ghent the socialists had established their first assistance fund in 1857, as well as a series of workers' cooperatives and a newspaper in the 1870's. The universal franchise for men during the 1920's led to an increase from 25% to 29% for the socialists, but this was the historical maximum. The old clerical elite succeeded in preventing the loss of support which had taken place in Wallonia by expanding its organization with branches in every parish throughout the state to the Vatican. The strength of the Catholic 'pillar' even today remains unaffected by the wave of secularization and by those who have abandoned the Church.

If the class conflicts between tenants and landowners, and those between workers and industrialists were permeated with religious ties, the language conflict was a contributory factor in ensuring that the confrontation between Catholics and liberals did not become an absolute schism. Nevertheless, this did seem to happen on a number of occasions, *e g* during the struggle over educational policy in 1880-1884, which was followed by thirty years of government monopoly by the Catholics. However, the Flemish movement appealed to the intellectuals and middle class elements of the three great political families, and for certain purposes such as the 'Dutchification' of the University of Ghent, politicians from the three 'national' parties acted together. On the other hand, the superior strength of the Walloons in the Belgian Workers' Party always prevented socialists from considering the Flemish movement merely as a struggle for emancipation.

Permeated with language barriers and divisions of religious belief, the acute class conflicts in Flanders have always been concealed by illusory conflicts about 'the soul of the child' or by regional interests. Gradual adaptation has ensured a remarkable degree of political stability at a time of far-reaching modernization.

497

Architecture

In Flanders too, 19th and 20th-century architecture has recently become the object of increasing interest. Even so, no thorough scientific studies provide a complete or profound insight into the architecture of the period; let alone make it possible to view it in the entire historical and cultural context. Two determining factors were the political conditions – with the state of Belgium as a 19th-century creation – and the powerful economic development which took place in the country during this period.

Traditional and purely descriptive art history looks down upon the 19th century as an era of utter confusion, in which totally diverging historical styles were employed side by side, and in combination with each other. However, these Neo-styles are increasingly found to represent a progressive liberation from the confines of the prevailing architectural system; and as they were often employed for specific architectural commissions, they also allowed for the expression of new religious, philosophical, political or social views. In fact, the apparent diversity of the architectural production in Flanders should be understood in the light of two great international movements, *viz* French rationalism and the mainly English inspired picturesque trend.

The creation of new building types, particularly in the commercial sector, was also characteristic of the 19th century. These formed the perfect experimental opportunity for the new materials and construction techniques available, such as iron and glass architecture, or the later concrete buildings. Again, these aspects cannot be viewed separately, at the risk of producing a deterministic or superficial historical description which merely looks on the 19th century for the precursors of particular 20th-century ideas.

19th-century Belgium has already been described as a sort of microcosm of Europe at the time, where the great intellectual and architectural developments were reflected, though initially with some delay. At first the French example still dominated through Neo-classicism; but when the full diversity of Neo-styles emerged in 1830, an expansion of international influences can be discerned, too. A further development followed after 1860 with *inter alia* the Second Empire mode, the continued evolution of the Neo-Gothic and the success of the Neo-Flemish Renaissance, which added an original aspect. Meanwhile an exceptional building such as Poelaert's Palace of Justice testified to an original creative force; which, together with the openness to international developments, anticipated the leading role which Belgium was to play in the Art Nouveau movement at the end of the century. However, the early 20th century was soon characterized by the return to a more traditionally oriented architecture. Against this background, Modernism only managed to gain a foothold with difficulty and under foreign influence.

1800-1830

The internationally popular, severe Neoclassicism or Romantic classicism was also in Flanders at its height in the period up to about 1830. French architects who continued to work in Belgium, determined the development of architecture: for example, Louis Damesme (1757-1822), who had previously worked with Claude Nicolas Ledoux, and who built the Munt Theatre and a prison in Brussels; and the versatile architect François Verly (1760-1822), who originated from Lille and lived first in Antwerp (1801-1814) and then in Brussels (1814-1818). He made plans for both urban projects and for public buildings, castles, houses, gardens and factories.

A determining factor in the training of architects was the institution of the Rome prize. The most gifted architects also often went to Paris to complete their training, for example in the ateliers of Percier and Fontaine. During the French period the city architects of Ghent, Jean Baptiste Pisson (1763-1818) and Pierre-Jean de Broe (1761-1852), as well as Joseph-François van Gierdegom from Bruges (1760-1844), were amongst the most important figures. Only a few of the

Brussels, *Palace of Justice*, the monumental staircase in the colonnade at the front, Jozef Poelaert, 1866-1883.
The statues of Domitius Ulpianus and Marcus Tullius Cicero were sculptured by Felix Bouré in 1882-1883.

Ghent, *mansions of the Recollettenlei*; from left to right mansion by J.B. van de Capelle, 1821; the Hôtel Grenier-Wambersie by J.B. Pisson, 1797-1798 and a mansion by architect C. de Schilder, 1828.
This is one of the most intact ensembles of Neoclassicistic or so-called Empire-architecture.

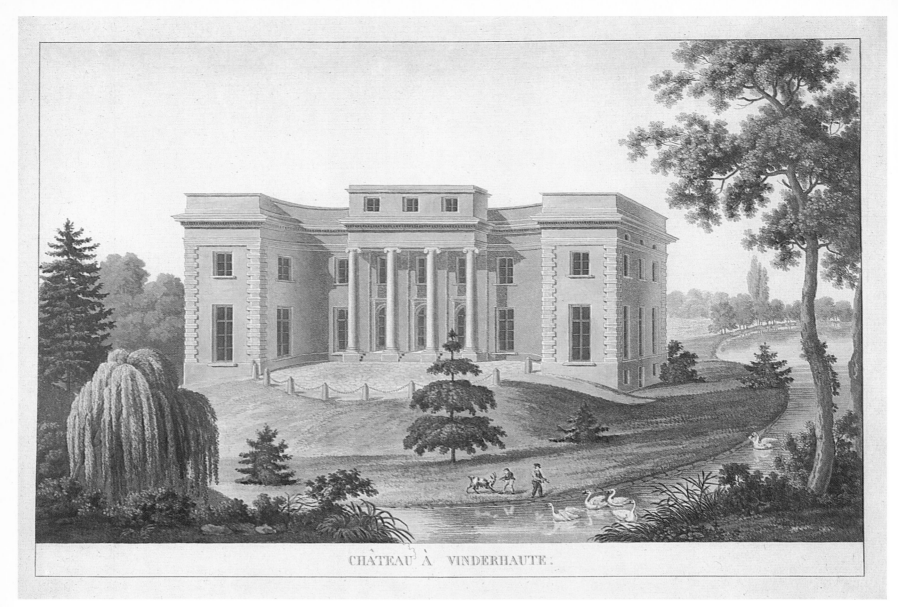

CHÂTEAU À VINDERHAUTE.

Drongen/Ghent, *Château van de Woestijne-Clemmen ('Blue House')*, near the boundary with Vinderhoute, architect Dutry Senior, 1807, expanded by J.B. van de Capelle Senior, 1817. Engraving from: P.J. Goetghebuer, *Choix des monuments, édifícés et maisons les plus remarquables du royaume des Pays-Bas*, Ghent 1827, Pl LXXII.

Brussels, *Palace of the Prince of Orange, now the Palace of Academies*, Charles van der Straeten, 1820-1826, finished by Tilman-François Suys. The strict geometry, the explicit horizontalism and the preference to place equal elements next to each other, are very characteristic for this period. Goetghebuer published the designs for the interior, which was finished by Suys; it has an impressive grand staircase and a banquet-hall with a gallery of Graecian-Doric columns.

ambitious government projects were actually executed. In Ghent Pisson and de Broe built a few city gates which bore a distant resemblance to the work of Ledoux in Paris. De Broe built the fire station in the *Hoogpoort* in Ghent (1808) and the facade of St Saviour's Church (1811) in a similar strict and monumental style.

The Empire style was more successful in private architecture, and it continued to be a leading style during the Dutch period. There are still many elegant houses in Ghent dating from this time, including some by Pisson, Jean Baptiste van de Cappelle (1772-1833) and Louis Minard (1801-1875). In Courtray, these houses also determine the townscape to a large extent. Many mansions were commissioned by the enriched bougeoisie who were profiting from the boom in trade; like the hotel of the banker Spitaels in Geraardsbergen (1812, L. Roelandt).

The same owners often had luxurious estates outside the city, which were furnished or rebuilt in the same style. One of the finest was designed by van Gierdegom for Baron de Peelaert in St Andries-Bruges. However,

500

Brussels, *Green-house of the botanical garden*, now cultural centre 'Le Botanique', Tilman François Suys and Gineste, 1826-1829.

it was probably only partially built in 1813-1817, and has only survived in a mutilated condition. According to the original plans, the main building – with a characteristic rotunda with a dome – had to be flanked by extensive colonnades with entrances in the shape of triumphal arches. Many other country houses bring variations of these elements on a smaller scale; *e g* at Beernem (Château *Driekoningen*, 1802), Oostakker (J.B. Pisson), Bellem (*ca* 1815, B. Renard), Drongen (1807, Dutry; enlarged 1817, van de Capelle), Destelbergen (1821-1823, van de Capelle) or Waasmunster (Château Ortegat, 1814, attributed to J. Dubois).

After 1815, the United Kingdom of the Netherlands led first of all to a revival of public architecture by erecting buildings such as palaces, courts of justice, town halls, theatres, hospitals, barracks, prisons *etc*; by which it wished to emphasize its authority and prestige. Again Neoclassicism was totally dominant, although sometimes employed in a richer version.

The most prominent figures were now, above all, the court architects Charles van der Straeten (1771-1834) and Tilman-François Suys (1783-1861). Van der Straeten, the elder of the two, was undoubtedly the more

traditionally oriented. He designed the hunting pavilion of the Prince of Orange in Tervuren (1819) as a strict Palladian villa integrated into the landscape by means of pillared entrance porches, terraces and staircases. Both this pavilion and van der Straeten's interior of the Parliament building were destroyed by fire in the 19th century, so that the palace of the Prince of Orange, now the Palace of the Academies in Brussels (1820-1826), is the best surviving example to judge his work. In 1827 van der Straeten was succeeded as court architect in Brussels by Tilman-François Suys, who completed the Royal Palace. The Herb Garden Conservatory (1826-1829) in Brussels was an important work in every respect. The plans were probably executed in a simplified version by Gineste. In the building the Neoclassicistic style was already being very successfully combined with the new techniques of iron and glass construction.

A number of public buildings were designed entirely in the spirit of Neoclassicism, with Roman-inspired temple porticos, on the model of the Pantheon or Magdalen's Church in Paris. One example of this is the Munt Theatre in Brussels (1817-1819) designed by

501

Brussels, *Portico of the Royal Munt Theatre*, Louis Damesme, 1817-1819.
Of the works of Damesme only this typical portico has been preserved in intact condition. The interior was redecorated by Poelaert after the fire of 1855; he also introduced important changes in the facades. The side facades were heightened by an attic in 1875 by G. Bordiau.

Antwerp, *Royal Theatre*, now the so-called Bourla Theatre, Pierre Bourla, 1829-34.
The interior was re-furnished after a fire in 1863.

Damesme. In the (disappeared) Palace of Justice in Brussels (1818-1823) by François Verly, the portico was placed in front of the existing buildings simply as a screen; on the other hand, L. Roelandt created a real sense of space with his Aula for Ghent University.

In religious architecture the pillared portico was also a favourite theme, often combined with the type of hall church on the model of the St Philippe-du-Roule's in Paris. Pierre Bourla built St Laurence's Church in Antwerp (1824-1825) on this type. Smaller (monastery) chapels sometimes had galleries, and one of the best surviving examples is in Bruges (*Naaldenstraat*), erected in 1830-1833 by the architect Cools.

A number of buildings with a predominantly functional character were also typical of Neoclassicism, and often revealed the influence of the French architect

and theorist J.N.L. Durand (1760-1834). Examples are those designed by Henri Louis François Partoes (1790-1873), an architect who had been trained in Napoleon's corps of engineers. His *Fermerijgodshuis* (1824-1826, now the *Hospice Pachéco*) in Brussels is characteristic, both for the strict arrangement around two rectangular inner courtyards opening onto different wings with galleries, and for the repetitive character of the facades.

The most interesting projects concerning factories or workers' housing were undoubtedly carried out in Wallonia, *viz* the complex of Grand Hornu (1820-1832) and the workers' district in Bois-du-Luc. Examples of the interest in larger urban structures are the *Barricadenplein* (1824, by the architect Vifquain) and the surrounding of the *Fermerijgodshuis*, both in Brussels. The Munt Theatre was also surrounded by Neoclassicistic buildings, originally even planned with galleries, as in the Rue de Rivoli in Paris.

Towards the end of the Dutch period the renewal in Neoclassicism was particularly evident in the work of architects such as Louis Roelandt (1786-1864) and Pierre Bourla (1783-1866); like Suys, they had both worked with Percier and Fontaine, where they had come into contact with a more eclectic approach. One particularly important work is the *Théâtre Royal Français* or *Grand Théâtre* (1829-1834, now the Royal Theatre) by Bourla in Antwerp, a personal version of the existing Neoclassicistic theatre with a curving entrance lobby.

However, next to the dominating Neoclassicism, the picturesque counter-movement had emerged in Flanders long before 1830 in the shape of a number of buildings built mainly in the Neo-Gothic style. The first of these even date from the French period and were, characteristically, often the work of prominent Neoclassicistic architects. Thus Joseph François van Gierdegom

Original design for St Georges' pavilion at Courtray, Benjamin Dewarlez, 6th August 1810. Courtray, St Georges' Guild.
The building was later expanded at three sides: but the back facade shown here is still the same as on the design of Dewarlez, except for some details like the decoration of the walls.

rebuilt the Lanchals Chapel in Our Lady's Church at Bruges in 1812-1816 in the characteristic 'troubadour' mode. As the result of a donation by Napoleon himself, he provided a romantic decor for the mausoleums of Charles the Bold and Mary of Burgundy. A few years later he renovated the medieval buildings of the *Poortersloge* in Bruges, in which he combined a classical feeling for symmetry with meticulously copied Gothic forms. However, these curious manifestations of the early Neo-Gothic style disappeared later in the purist restorations of these monuments.

The close connection between the earliest Neo-Gothic and exoticism with the predominantly English-influenced garden architecture, can be clearly seen in the pavilion of the archery guild of St George in Courtray (1810, by the architect B. Dewarlez) and in the garden pavilion of vander Straeten's house in Ghent (1821, by van de Capelle), which has not survived.

However, an entire country house was actually transformed in the Neo-Gothic style with the rebuilding project of the Château Wissekerke in Bazel near Antwerp (1825, by François Verly). This work is very reminiscent of the 'Rococo-Gothic' of Strawberry Hill or similar French examples in which a playful and airy character predominates. In the gardens Verly built a suspension bridge, which is supposedly the first to be build on the continent.

The revolution of 1830 in no way brought an end to building activities; on the contrary the universal doctrinaire Neoclassicistic style was now definitely being replaced by a freer choice of form and style. Roelandt and Suys continued to be the main figures; though they increasingly had to compete with their own pupils or with other young and progressive architects, such as Louis Minard (1801-1875), Ferdinand Berckmans (1803-1854), Jozef Jonas Dumont (1811-1859), Louis van Overstraeten (1818-1849) and Alphonse Balat (1818-1895).

Within the Neoclassicistic movement the greatest attention was paid – as in other countries – to the Italian Renaissance, which tended to push classical antiquity as a source of inspiration into the background. Louis Roelandt clearly indicated this trend in three works executed in Ghent during the 1830's: the Casino (1835, now disappeared); the monumental, entirely detached Court of Justice (1836-1840), and the *Grand Théâtre*, now the Opera (1837). While Roelandt often chose resolutely in favour of medieval styles in his later works, Suys remained faithful to Neoclassicism for longer, although he increasingly applied it in a freer and more eclectic manner. An example of this is St Joseph's Church (1842-1849) in the Leopold district of Brussels, which was also designed by Suys, and which was one of the most important urban projects of this period.

Following the Italianist mode, Balat built the Hôtel d'Assche in Brussels (1856-1858), which bore a strong resemblance to the work of Charles Barry in England in his subtle approach to the *palazzo* theme. Other ex-

Bazel, *Château Wissekerke* (Vilain XIIII), rebuilt by François Verly, first quarter of the 19th century. Verly did certainly not aim at an exact reconstruction of the historical castle, but tried – as his contemporary J.P. Goetghebuer expressed it – to undo medieval architecture from its strict and gloomy character. The constructions which rest on pillars in the water, date for the most part from later alternations in the 19th and the beginning of the 20th century.

Ghent, *Court of Justice*, Louis Roelandt, 1836-1840.
The typical dome-shaped roof, which covered the central *Salle des pas perdus*, was not repaired after the fire of 1926.

amples of this involved Neoclassicism as applied to a variety of building projects, including the Jesuit churches in Ghent (1840-1844) and Brussels by Herman Meganck, the Brussels Entrepôt (1843-1847) by Louis Spaak, and the former museum of Antwerp (1839-1843) by Bourla. In about 1850 J.J. Dumont drew the attention by some richly decorated facades in the *Kunststraat* in Brussels, which heralded a new and even more eclectic phase.

At the same time, Dumont, together with architects such as Matthias Jozef Wolters (1793-1859) and Ferdinand Berckmans, was one of the pioneers of the increasing interest in medieval art. Ample opportunity for this resulted from the numerous restoration and rebuilding projects of historical monuments. In addition, the foundation of the Royal Commission for Monuments in 1835 was significant, as was the appearance of publications on antiquity, such as the *Mémoire sur l'architecture ogivale* (1841) by A.G.B. Schayes. The competition for the Neo-Gothic choir stalls of Antwerp Cathedral, which was won in 1837 by Durlet, can clearly be considered a milestone in this context.

The 1840's saw the real breakthrough of the Gothic revival in church architecture with the building of Our Lady-ter-Sneeuw's in Borgerhout (1841-1848) by Berckmans (clearly inspired by the *Mariahilfkirche* in Munich by D. Ohlmüller), St Bonifatius' in Elsene by Dumont (1847) and St George's in Antwerp (1847-

1853) by Léon Pierre Suys. The village churches followed, as a result of the work of Wolters (*e g* the church in Heusden, 1844) and provincial architects such as Pierre Buyck (1805-1877) and Pierre Nicolas Croquison (1806-1887). Most of these creations had few or no archaeological pretensions and are probably best summed up by the contemporary term 'pointed style', which meant that basically a number of separate stylistic elements and decorative motifs were borrowed from Gothic. They were often simply transposed, using contemporary materials such as stucco or cast iron; without departing from the essence of classical aesthetics, with its rules of proportion and sense of symmetry.

The Neo-Gothic style emerged in civil architecture in about 1840 with the building of the Town Hall in Duffel (F. Berckmans), which has not survived. However, the Episcopal residence in Ghent by Wolters, dating from 1841-1845, was still characterized by plastered facades in a fanciful 'pointed' mode. The continued evolution was revealed in the House for the Blind in Ghent (1852-1855, Ch. van Huffel), which was a more or less faithful copy in profiled brick of the well-known medieval facade of the nearby Bijloke Hospital, though again the strict rules of symmetry were observed.

The progress of a more archaeologically oriented Neo-Gothic style took place mainly during the 1850's, partly as a result of a remarkable, directly English influence. In 1850 the English architect Thomas Harper

Antwerp, *interior of St Georges' Church*, Léon-Pierre Suys, 1847-1853. The wall-paintings with religious themes are done by Godfries Guffens and Jan Swerts between 1858 and 1871.

Vive-Kapelle/Damme, *interior of Our Lady's Church*, Jean Baptiste Bethune and assistants, 1861-1867. Flemish Neo-Gothic has got in many aspects its final expression in liturgical furniture and wall-paintings. The whole was realized in a period of about forty years by a group of artists round Bethune,

504

King, who was living in Bruges, published a translation and adaptation of the writings of the well-known English Neo-Gothic artist A.W.N. Pugin, entitled *Les Vrais Principes de l'Architecture ogivale ou chrétienne*, clearly outlining the new views on functional and rational design. However, Magdalen's Church in Bruges (1850-1853), which should have been the first 'model church' for the movement, largely lost its impact because King had to restrict himself to making a few alterations to the existing outdated plans of Pierre Buyck.

Eventually Baron Jean Baptiste Bethune (1821-1894) became the major representative of this strongly religiously inspired movement. Like Pugin, whom he knew personally, he preferred his works to be executed by a limited team of artists whom he instructed himself in medieval techniques. He was also the director of a glazier's atelier. His work is best judged in unified masterpieces such as the Château van Caloen in Loppem (1859-1862, in collaboration with Edward Pugin), or the complex in Vijve-Kapelle. The last example reveals clearly how he combined a total concept and a type of church, which obviously owe a lot to Pugin, with the brick Gothic architecture of Bruges. As one of the founders of the St Luke's schools, to became very influential in the further development of the Gothic revival.

Apart from Neo-Gothic, the German-inspired *Rundbogenstil* was also remarkably successful between 1840-1860. This comprised elements from both Romanesque and early Christian art, as well as Italian Gothic and Renaissance; and can – in a certain sense – be considered as a compromise with Neoclassicism.

Louis Roelandt's son-in-law Louis van Overstraeten (1818-1849), who died young, was a pioneer in this movement with his Our Lady's Church in Schaarbeek (1845-1853). This domed church on a centrally positioned ground plan takes excellent advantage of the irregular site, and is also integrated perfectly in the town planning context of the *Koningstraat*. Our Lady's in St Niklaas (1844) is by Louis Roelandt himself, as is the entrepôt (1844), the military manège (1853) and St Anne's Church in Ghent. A number of these buildings comprise interesting spatial and technical experiments; *e g* both the manège and the impressive single nave of St Anne's have an iron roof structure. The functional and decorative possibilities of the *Rundbogenstil* were actually thoroughly explored in such diverse buildings as the school, hospital and asylum in Ghent by Adolf Pauli, the casino of St Niklaas (1853, J. de Somme-Servais), the Château of Olsene and the relatively late church of Wetteren (1865), both by Louis Minard.

During the 1860's the *Rundbogenstil*, like the 'pointed' style, had to make way – albeit more slowly – for an archaeological form of Neo-Romanesque; as illustrated in St Joseph's Church (1862-1867) in Ant-

Loppem, *Castle of Caloen de Gourcy*, chimneypiece in the Blue Drawning Room or St-Carolus-Borromeus-Drawning Room, sculptured by Leopold and Leonard Blanchart after designs by baron Jean-Baptiste Béthune, 1863-1865. The sculpture shows *inter alia* scenes from the life of the saint after whom the drawing room was named. For the same room, the German painter August Martin made wall paintings representing historical scenes to which Guido Gezelle wrote sub-titles consisting of Old Dutch poems.

Brussels, *St Hubert's gallery*, Jean-Pierre Cluysenaar, 1846-1848. By its dimensions and grand concept, Cluysenaar's gallery is in its kind one of the most important realisations of this period, and anticipates Mengoni's Galleria Vittorio Emmanuele (1865-1877) at Milan.

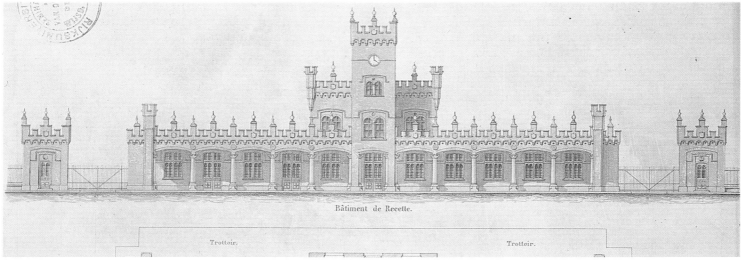

Alost, *Station*, Jean-Pierre Cluysenaar, 1853-1854. Look on the front.
From: P.J. Cluysenaar: *Chemin de fer de Dendre et Waes* (...), Brussels 1854.
Except for the crowning ornaments, the facade composition realized by Cluysenaar in Neo-medieval castle-style, has been preserved fairly well.

Laken, *interior of Our Lady's Church*, Jozef Poelaert and others, 1852-1907.
The hall-church is built on a ground-plan in the form of a cross. It has a wide three-aisled nave, which is even enlarged by galleries at the outside. These galleries give admission to the churchyard. The explicit verticalism is remarkable for this interior; the details were probably adapted by the successors of Poelaert and they were finished in a more 'correct' Gothic style.

werp, by Eugène Gife. Two architects who simultaneously represent their own time very well and made an important contribution to the future, were Jean-Pierre Cluysenaar (1811-1880) and Jozef Poelaert (1817-1879).

Cluysenaar, born in Holland, was trained at the Brussels academy under Suys. His St Hubertus' Galleries in Brussels (1847) formed a significant stepforward in the evolution of covered shopping arcades; his Magdalen's Market (1847), also in Brussels, is another striking example of commercial architecture. Here the front facade was designed in a *quattrocento* version of the *Rundbogenstil*, with arcades in the style of the Florentine *Loggia dei Lanzi*, but divided into two stories. He used variations of this style in the Château at Dilbeek, and in the buildings in the Bas-Fonds of the *Koningstraat* in Brussels (1847-1857), which were intended to form an urbanistic connection between the upper and the lower city at the Congress Column. In the

Dilbeek, *Château Viron, now Town Hall*, Jean-Pierre Cluysenaar, middle of the 19th century.
The colourful Rundbogenstil of Cluysenaar already refers to the later Neo-Flemish Renaissance style.

stations of the Dender and Waas lines (1852-1856), he was consciously aiming at a picturesque contrast of various styles and types of architecture in order to express the function of the buildings and their relationship with the environment, as he put it himself.

The visionary Poelaert contrasts curiously with the clever technician Cluysenaar. They both studied at the academy in Brussels, but Poelaert completed his training in Paris. One of his first important works was the Congress Column in Brussels (1850-1859), conceived in the Neoclassicistic style but with the emphasis particularly on the rich sculptural decoration. As part of the same ensemble, he also designed the large houses around the square in the characteristic Italian *palazzo* mode. Poelaert's own personality was more clearly expressed in two school buildings in Brussels on the *Zuidlaan* (1849-1851) and the *Schaarbeeksestraat* (1853-1865). In these he opted for an original, strict and powerful classical architecture which has been compared to that of Alexander Thomson in Glasgow. A striking feature was the massive character, which is reminiscent of Ancient Egyptian art; while the use of rows of rectangular pillars is probably borrowed from the work of the German architect Schinkel. Poelaert's most important church commission during this period was the Neo-Gothic Our Lady's in Laken (1854-1908). Erected as a burial church for the royal house, and to commemorate Queen Louise-Marie, it reminds of the most elaborate Gothic fantasies by Schinkel; the very nature of the commission made the project for the memorial church of Queen Louise of Prussia an obvious example. The monumental aspects of Our Lady's in Laken can also be considered to anticipate Poelaert's Palace of Justice.

One of the first buildings to reveal the changes emerging in about 1860 was the National Bank in Brussels, built by Hendrik Beyaert in 1859-1864 in collaboration with Wynand Janssens. Within a facade in which the composition has a predominantly Neo-Louis XVI character, the new feeling for plasticity and sculptural effects – also characteristic of the French Second Empire style – is expressed here very convincingly in powerful bossages, free-standing Ionic columns, caryatids, decorative vases, and richly sculpted pediments and statues.

The building of pavilions and the high attic roofs, other characteristics of the Second Empire mode, had already been used in the old North Station (1840-1862, by the architects J.F. Coppens and F. Laureys); though these were possibly due to changes in the original plans and can be sufficiently explained by the specific example of the Town Hall in Paris.

Beyaert's bank represented the beginning of the new evolution, which soon found its most creative expression in the Palace of Justice of Brussels (1866-1883) by Poelaert. The significance of this building extends far beyond a Belgian context, both for its exceptional dimensions and for the originality of its design. Poelaert revealed himself here primarily to be a worthy inheritor of the whole tradition of classical architecture, though extended with vague references to Ancient Egypt and Mesopotamia, as in his early school buildings. He also showed to be a visionary artist in the tradition of *e g* Piranesi or the English painter John Martin. Situated at the highest point in Brussels, this building on its gigantic substructure dominates the entire city; the over-

Brussels, *Side facade of the Palace of Justice*, Jozef Poelaert, 1866-1883.

Brussels, *Palace of Justice* (detail of the front), Jozef Poelaert, 1866-1883. Now that the facades have been cleaned, the typical play of colours in the use of materials is again shown to its full advantage.

whelming monumentality originates from piling up different volumes, which were first to culminate into a cube shape, as can be seen on a model known from photographs. The effective play of light and shadow is particularly evident in the deep entrance porticos and colonnades, which conceal staircases on the facade. Inside, the *Salle des pas perdus* ascending right up to the dome, and the staircases are amongst the most impressive features.

Closer to the French Second Empire was the architecture which arose along the present central lanes of Brussels; built entirely in accordance with Haussmann's principles, after the Zenne was filled in. The designs of the facades – the best of which were rewarded in the competition of 1872-1876 – were produced by Beyaert, Janlet, de Keyser, Laureys, Almainde Hase, Maquet, Samyn, Bordiau and Hendrickx. They are comparable to the richest French work from this period, and the additional fact that the Baroque architecture of the *Grote Markt* was so close by, was probably an added stimulus. However, the eye-catcher in this new district of the city was the Stock Exchange (1868-1873) by L.P. Suys, which seems to compete with the Paris Opera, both for the way it is integrated into the urban development and for the richness of its ornamentation.

In Brussels the Cité Fontainas (1867, by the architect Trappeniers) and the barracks of Etterbeek (1875, Pauwels), can also be mentioned as variations on this style, and in Ghent the Institute of Sciences (1883-1890) by Adolf Pauli. Even the small city of Bruges did not entirely escape 'Haussmannization' in the theatre district, when Gustave Saintenoy – who was also the architect of the palace of the Duke of Brabant in Brussels – built the new Theatre there (1866-1869); precisely because of its small scale, it has one of the most attractive interiors of this period.

Towards the 1880's there was an increasing calm and

St Joost-ten-Node (Brussels), *St Juliana's Chapel*, Joris Helleputte, 1882. One of the most complete and perfect interiors of this period.

academic trend in the foreground, which had already emerged in the work of architects such as Auguste Payen, who had designed the South Station in Brussels (1864-1869). The major representative here was undoubtedly Alphonse Balat (1818-1895). His Palace of Fine Arts, (1875-1881) now the Museum of Ancient Art in Brussels, has a well-proportioned and soberly decorated facade, arranged round the central motif of pillars crowned with statues in the Roman style. On the other hand, the rich use of materials such as the shining granite pillars with contrasting bronze capitals and statues, is entirely characteristic of the second half of the 19th century. The classical Beaux Arts mode was particularly popular in the building of museums during the years that followed, as is revealed in the *Jubelpark* complex of Brussels (1880, G. Bordiau; triumphal arch, 1905, Ch. Girault), the Museum of Antwerp (1879-90, J.J. Winders and F. van Dijk), and finally, in a modernized version, in the Museum of Ghent (1896-1902, Ch. van Rysselberghe).

On the whole, Neo-Gothic and Neo-Romanesque continued to develop during this period parallel to other European countries. In general there was a better understanding of medieval design and techniques of construction, while the most talented artists only withheld concepts such as rational construction or the 'honest' use of materials, as a basis for more original creations. Some important buildings erected by foreign architects contributed to the introduction of the new movement; for example, Edward Pugin was commissioned to build the monumental pilgrimage church in Dadizele (1859-1892) by the Bishop of Bruges, Jean Baptiste Malou. This cathedral-like construction had five aisles with an imposing west wing and a crossing

Brussels, *Stock Exchange*, Léon Pierre Suys, 1868-1873.
The design seems to be inspired by the Opéra of Paris as well as by a design which T. Suys drew for the Palace of Fine Arts at Ghent. For the decorations, he was assisted by Rodin (between others).

Dadizele, *Pelgrimage Church of Our Lady*, Edward Welby Pugin, finished by J.B. Bethune and A. Verhaegen, 1859-1892.
This church, which was designed by Edward Pugin, son of A.W.N. Pugin, knew a long and complicated history of building. It was only finished in 1892 by J.B. Bethune and A. Verhaegen. The furnishing was for the greater part done by them. Engineer Vierendeel drew the metal construction of the spire.

Ghent, *interior of St Joseph's Church* (detail), August van Assche 1880-1883.
This is a remarkable synthesis between the High-Victorian polychromy and forms which are borrowed from early Scheldt-Gothic.

Bruges, *interior of the Jesuit Church of the Sacred Heart*, Louis Pavot, 1879-1885.
This typical Jesuit church combines early Gothic style elements with light effects, which remind of the Baroque. The furnishing consists, among others, of works by the sculptors H. Pickery and Mathias Zens, by the painters Th. Lybaert and E. Wante and by the glass painter S. Coucke.

tower, but the progressive characteristics were rather reduced by imperfect execution and changes to the plans. The well-known Dutch architect P.J.H. Cuypers showed a consistently individual approach to Neo-Gothic with his Franciscan Church in Brussels (1870).

Obviously an important proportion of the Neo-Gothic production was contributed by the St Luke's schools; which achieved a first success when one of the pupils, Pieter van Kerkhove, won the competition to build the new Town Hall of St Niklaas in 1875. Apart from Bethune, some of the leading figures included the architects August van Assche (1826-1907), Arthur Verhaegen (1847-1917) and Joris Helleputte (1852-1925) – the latter two were also influential Catholic politicians – and later, Louis Cloquet (1849-1920). Outside the circle of the St Luke's schools, Neo-Gothic was also employed by architects such as Louis de Curte (1817-1891), Modeste de Noyette (1847-1923) and Louis De la Censerie (1838-1909). The only difference with the latter was possibly the fact that Bethune and his followers put a stronger emphasis on the study of local architecture.

In fact, all of the architects were affected by the influence of the same international movements. Thus, on the one hand, one could detect a shift of interest towards the early Gothic; mainly under the influence of Viollet-le-Duc, whose work and writings were well-known in Belgium. A good illustration of this was François Baeckelmans' St Amands' Church in Antwerp (1867-75), which appears to have been inspired by Viollet-le-Duc's church in Aillant-sur-Tholon. The St Luke's architect Pieter Langerock also designed his Basilica of Koekelberg in 1907 as a sort of 'ideal cathedral', as depicted in the *Dictionnaire raisonné...*, but it was never actually built. However, on the other hand, there was a marked preference for the constructional polychromy of the English high Victorian style. One of the most characteristic projects was van Assche's Church of St Joseph in Ghent (1880-1883), in which the interior is entirely constructed of multi-coloured bricks. The parish hall of St Anne in Ghent (1866, F. de Noyette) and Pauwels' tobacco factory in Antwerp (1875, J.J. Winders), are also striking examples.

The majority of the work combined the various characteristics in differing proportions, particularly emphasizing the archaeological character of the buildings. Jean Baptiste Bethune produced an impressive and sober interpretation of local early Gothic in Maredsous Abbey (1872-1890). In civil architecture the Town Hall of St Niklaas (1875) marked the breakthrough of a nationalistically inspired movement, aiming at a local style of building; which later continued to be adopted *e g* in the public buildings by De la Censerie in Bruges.

Iron structures as an individual form of expression sought its place within the context of Neo-Gothic

Laken, *Interior of the Royal Orangeries*, Alphonse Balat, 1875-1893.
Engineer Vierendeel mentioned already in 1902 this masterly creation of
Leopold II, which was unsurpassed, even abroad.

rationalism; as in the work of Joseph Schadde (1818-1894), who constructed the metal roof for the Antwerp Stock Exchange (1868-1872) and the now no longer existing railway station in Bruges (1877). These can be considered as the local response to the writings of Viollet-le-Duc, or to buildings such as the University Museum in Oxford.

The numerous restorations – which were really more like fastidious recreations – were another characteristic of this period. Charle Albert rebuilt Gaasbeek Castle (1887-1898), and De la Censerie 'restored' the great Gothic hall of the Town Hall (1886-1905) and the Gruuthuse House in Bruges (1883-1911) in the spirit of Cardiff Castle or Pierrefonds.

Apart from Neo-Gothic and classical, the Neo-Flemish Renaissance became a full-fledged alternative during the 1870's, so that it was used in the Belgian pavilion by Emile Janlet at the World Fair in Paris in 1878. However, this pavilion cannot really be considered as the beginning of the movement, but rather as the official recognition of a trend which had emerged in the first half of the century. We have referred before to the interest in the Renaissance during the second quarter of the century in figures such as Dumont. Some of the important, rather French-inspired buildings made after 1860 included the Law Courts of Antwerp (1871-1874) by Lodewijk and Frans Baeckelmans, and the Conserva-

tory of Music in Brussels (1871-1876) by Cluysenaar. In addition, pioneering projects were carried out by the architect and decorator Charle Albert, who had already built his own house in Watermaal-Bosvoorde in 1869-1870 as a *Castel Fleuri* or *Maison Flamande* in the 16th and 17th century-style. Hendrik Beyaert (1823-1894) can also be considered as one of the initiators of this movement; although his original and many-sided talents mean that he cannot be classified under a particular genre. Apart from the National Bank, he designed the Concert Noble building in a Neoclassicistic or Second Empire mode, which is characterized by a cleverly elaborated succession of spaces with different axes and proportions. The castle and the church in Faulx-les-Tombes were again built in a Neo-Gothic and Neo-Romanesque, comparable to the work of Viollet-le-Duc.

On the other hand, the house known as *De Kater en de Kat* in Brussels (1874) and the National Bank complex in Antwerp (1875-1880) may be considered as contributions to the Neo-Renaissance movement, although not yet with a clearly Flemish character. Beyaert particularly revealed his skilled treatment of volume in building the National Bank on a triangular site. The real peak of Neo-Flemish Renaissance came later with figures such as Emile Janlet (1839-1919), Jean Baes (1848-1914), Jean Jacques Winders (1849-1936), and the brothers Leonard (1840-1918) and Henri

Watermaal-Bosvoorde, *Castle Charle-Albert*, Charle-Albert, 1869/70. The interior and the garden were also conceived in Old-Flemish style and exercized much influence.

Brussels, *'Volkshuis'*, Victor Horta, 1895-1899, pulled down 1965-1966. The house was erected almost completely by co-operative societies. It housed between others an inn, offices of the co-operators, a gymnasium and a large meeting-room for about 1500 persons.

(1845-1923) Blomme; as well as Juliaan Jacob van Ysendyck (1836-1901), the author of the *Documents classés...*, which may be considered as the main source book of this movement.

The Neo-Renaissance resulted in some remarkably monumental town and municipal halls; e g at Kuregem-Anderlecht (1875-1879) and Schaarbeek (1885-1887) by van Yzendyck, and at Borgerhout (1890) by the Blomme brothers. However, the style was also adopted in buildings such as the school on the *Anneesensplein* in Brussels (1878-1880) by Emile Janlet, the Entrepôt Steenackers by J.J. Winders in Antwerp, or the stations in Malines and Schaarbeek. Jean Baes made interesting use of iron, both in the Royal Flemish Theatre (1885-1889) and in his own house (1889); but one of the most attractive houses is certainly J.J. Winders' one, known as *In the Compasses* (1883) in Antwerp.

The Neo-Renaissance style continued to be used for a long time, particularly in mansion building, until it was eventually replaced by 20th-century regionalism. One of the merits of the Neo-Renaissance was that it permitted the reconciliation of certain elements from the Neo-Gothic and Neoclassicistic styles – though to a lesser extent than, for example, in the English Queen Anne mode. It was therefore able to contribute to a certain relaxation of the Neo-styles, the benefit of which would eventually be reaped by Art Nouveau.

1890-1914

The period beginning in about 1890 is not only important because it formed a transitional period which anticipated 20th-century art, but also because Brussels became an international centre of the Art Nouveau movement. Art Nouveau grafted upon the constructive logic, conscious asymmetry and polychrome use of materials of the Neo-Gothic; apart from this, it definitively abandoned all references to historical styles and evolved a new kind of ornamentation which was – at least initially – based on the study of nature.

While Art Nouveau in England was particularly prepared by the development of the decorative arts, the continent contributed to this movement with iron and glass architecture, as described theoretically by Viollet-le-Duc, and put into practice by Eiffel. Important works were also designed in Belgium, e g by the engineer Marcellis and the above-mentioned Joseph Schadde. Horta's master, Balat, built the remarkable Royal Conservatory in Laken (1875-1893); Ernest Hendrickx (1844-1892) designed the now no longer existing building of the Free University of Brussels (1884-1885), in accordance with the concepts put forward by Viollet-le-Duc. Later on, the Louvain professor Jules Arthur Vierendeel (1852-1940) emerged as an internationally recognized authority in the field of metal construction.

A pupil of Beyaert, the Walloon Paul Hankar (1861-1901), probably provides the best illustration of the transition towards this new movement. The link with the Neo-styles can still be clearly detected in his own house on the *Defacqzstraat* in Brussels, built in 1893; but a later work such as the *Villa ter Vaart* in Ghent (1897), reveals the influence of English domestic architecture.

Victor Horta (1861-1947) began his career with the restrained classicism of his master Balat; as is revealed in his early houses in Ghent (1885-1886), and the already freer interpreted Lambeaux Temple in Brussels (1889). However, the Tassel House in Brussels, which is considered to be his first mature work, marked the real breakthrough of the Art Nouveau movement in 1892/93. The hall is particularly striking. The omnipresent whiplash ornamentation does not overwhelm the spatial character, but rather reinforces it. On the other hand, the new spirit was expressed more modestly in the curved lines of the bay window, reminiscent of Rococo, and in the characteristic iron work of the elegantly proportioned windows on the still strictly symmetrical facade of the house. Similar features were developed by Horta in the years that followed in a series of mansions designed for the progressive bourgeoisie in Brussels. The Hotel van Eetvelde (1896) deserves particular mention for the spatial creation of the drawing room, covered by a glass dome. The aim to create a unity between the building and the furnishings designed by the architect can be seen today in the perfectly preserved Hotel Armand Solvay (1894-1898), which was commissioned by the famous chemist of that name. Horta reached the peak of his creativity in the last few years of the 19th century, when he built two houses (one for himself) in the *Amerikastraat* in Brussels. Once more his talent appears here from his masterly treatment of ironwork. Also around 1900 he pushed his experiments on freer plan concepts to their utmost consequence, in the (disappeared) Aubecq House.

Horta's most important large constructions in Brus-

Brussels, *dining-room in the house of V. Horta, Amerikaanse straat*, Victor Horta, 1898-1901.

Ukkel, *'Bloemenwerf'*, house of Henri van de Velde, 1895-1896.
Van de Velde had this house built for himself and his young wife Maria
Sèthe, shortly after his marriage. It was meant to be a manifesto of his artistic
views. The request to build was introduced on 11th April 1895.

sels, *viz* the *Volkshuis* (1895-1899), and the department store *à l'Innovation* (1901-1903), have both unfortunately not survived. The former particularly had an international significance, which can only be compared to the importance of Sullivan's work in the United States. The plan was ingeniously adapted to the irregular site, the facade was almost entirely made of metal and glass, and both the constructive and decorative properties of the metal were availed of in the auditorium on the top floor.

Apart from Horta, Henry van de Velde (1863-1957) is usually mentioned as one of the creators of Art Nouveau in Belgium, although his more controversial contribution should be evaluated on a completely different basis. Unlike Horta, he came to architecture through painting and only made his debut as an architect in 1895-1896 with his own house, *Bloemenwerf*, in Ukkel. This differs from the sophisticated character of Horta's creations, both as regards construction and the use of space and decoration; van de Velde's simple painted house is, by contrast, almost naive and rustic. Arranged

around a hall two stories high, which is also used as a living space, it links up best with the work of Voysey in England. The influence of Ruskin and Morris also determined the social emphasis in the work of van de Velde. After 1895 he increasingly pursued his career abroad, *inter alia* in Paris and Weimar, and exercised a particularly strong influence in Germany as an architect, teacher and designer of useful household articles. His main achievements from this period include the interior decoration of the *Folkwangmuseum* in Hagen (1902), the buildings of the *Kunstgewerbeschule* in Weimar (1904-1911), and above all, the (now destroyed) theatre of the *Werkbund* exhibition in Cologne (1913-1914), which can be considered as his masterpiece. Here van de Velde moved further and further away from Art Nouveau in the direction of 20th-century functionalism. In fact the *Kunstgewerbeschule*, of which he was the director, became the cradle of the later Bauhaus.

Some of the best known buildings which illustrate the popularity of the so-called 'floral' Art Nouveau in Brussels include the shop *Old England* (1899) by Paul

Saintenoy (1862-1952), the house of Ernest Blérot (1870-1956) in Elsene (1901-1908), and the house of de Saint-Cyr (*ca* 1900) by Gustave Strauven. However, it soon became clear how this trend deteriorated into mere decoration in the hand of lesser masters. In other cities Art Nouveau only came into its own after it had passed its peak in Brussels. In Antwerp the Liberal folk house *Help U Zelve* (1898-1900) by Emile van Averbeke (1876-1946) and J. van Asperen, was one of the most interesting projects. But even an eclectic architect such as Jos Bascourt (1863-1927) occasionally worked in the Art Nouveau style; the increasing trend for exuberance is clearly expressed in the ship owner's house *'t Bootje* (1901) by F. Smet-Verhas, in which the balcony was constructed in the shape of a keel. In Ghent numerous Art Nouveau houses were built in the new parts of the city by architects such as Constant van Hoecke-Dessel (1873-1918) and Prosper Buyck (1873-1938). Apart from Oscar van de Voorde (1871-1938) and Albert van huffel (1877-1935), Geo Henderick (1879-1957) belonged to the most important figures. His *Coliseum* or *Salle du Valentino* (1911) remains the most beautiful example in Flanders of an auditorium from this period constructed in iron, now that Horta's *Volkshuis* has been demolished.

From 1900 the return of the straight lines as a transition towards the later functionalist movement can be detected in Belgium. Like van de Velde, Horta also introduced this second stage of Art Nouveau in later works, such as the department store Waucquez (1903), the Hotel Max Hallet (1904) and the Brussels Bruggman Hospital (1906-1923). Joseph Hoffman provided an excellent model when he built the Stoclet Palace in Brussels (1905-1911), drawing on his own Viennese background – this was simultaneously one of the most refined and luxurious houses to be built at this time anywhere. Many other artists came to a similar change in direction through a variety of developments: Emile van Averbeke's powerful brick architecture for the fire station in Antwerp (1910-1911) for example was clearly influenced by Berlage, while the house of the painter Paul Cauchie (1905) is more reminiscent of Mackintosh. In the work of Octave van Rysselberghe this evolution can be discerned in the fixedness of the design in his impressive Hotel Belle Vue in Westende (1905), in which the perfect geometry inadvertently calls to mind the work of Boullée or Ledoux. One of the most powerful and personal works of this period was undoubtedly the clinic of Dr van Neck in Brussels by Antoine Pompe (1873-1980), which was built in 1910. The curved lines are almost entirely banned from the brick facade, which has a simple rhythmic structure through the functional element of the air vents, set at different heights; while three angular bay windows accentuate the top floor.

The disappearance of floral Art Nouveau also created new opportunities for the more traditionally oriented architecture which had continued to exist. It manifested itself in the form of mainly French-inspired *Beaux Art* classicistic buildings, of which the new facade of the Royal Palace in Brussels (*ca* 1900) by Maquet is a good example. However, the exuberant Neo-Baroque trend was more interesting as seen, for example, in the central station of Antwerp (1905) by De la Censerie, or in the buildings on the *Leysstraat* there. Possibly the most original creations in the Neo-Gothic style were designed by Professor Louis Cloquet (1849-1920) from Ghent. He managed to produce similar effects to Art Nouveau by expanding the design in an eclectic fashion, and by experimenting with a variety of new materials and techniques. However, apart from this, a rather dry academic atmosphere prevailed: the St Peter and St Paul's Church in Ostend (1905) by De la Censerie can be considered as an archaeologically correct exercise in style in the genre of the fifty years older *Votivkirche* in Vienna, but in comparison the younger church brought hardly any renovation.

On the other hand, old and new were reconciled in a very plausible fashion in house building. The English cottage architecture for example influenced both Octave van Rysselberghe, who designed a curious group of villas in Westende (1896), and Valentin Vaerwijck (1882-1952), trained at the St Luke's school. Jozef Viérin (1872-1949), also from St Luke's, designed the house *Het Lijsternest* in Ingooigem (1904-1905) for the author Stijn Streuvels; providing the basis for an intimate form of architecture inspired by Flemish farm buildings, which still has an influence today. At the same time a number of projects by the German civil engineer Stübben would spread new urbanistic ideas.

Berchem/Antwerp, *Cogels-Osylei*, end 19th-beginning 20th century.
The pearl on the crown of the eclecticism from the belle-époque period, work by (between others) Jos Bascourt and Ernest Stordiau.

After the First World War, the so-called 'traditionalism' in all its various forms continued to represent a large proportion of architectural creations.

The direct continuation of 19th-century views was revealed in the rebuilding of cities such as Ypres, Dixmude, Nieuwpoort, Louvain and Termonde, which were reconstructed as far as possible in their original form, or were restored in one of the Neo-styles with little inspiration. For a long time the simplified academic classicism was predominant in the building of banks. On the other hand, there were also some essentially progressive architects such as Antoine Pompe or Albert Van huffel, who continued to attach a great deal of importance to ornamentation and craftsmanship in building. A good illustration of this was Pompe's (disappeared) villa in Ukkel (1926), which won the first van de Ven prize in 1928. Other aspects of traditionalism were represented by the villas in the rustic or regional style on the coast and in the Leie region, the meritorious public buildings by Valentin Vaerwijck, such as the Law Courts of Termonde (1927), and Horta's architecture for the Palace of Fine Arts in Brussels (1923).

In church architecture a transition from Neo-Gothic and Neo-Romanesque towards a freer form of expression can be discerned, partly as a result of liturgical innovations. This style combined elements from the entire tradition of religious architecture. Van huffel's much maligned Basilica of Koekelberg (1927-1970) was therefore much more of an important step forwards in the context of its time. Later, during the 1930's, the sober brick architecture of the Dutch architect Kropholler, who worked on Affligem Abbey in Flanders, was upheld as an example by the St Luke's schools.

The dividing line between old and new is also difficult to draw in the so-called Art Déco of the 1920's, which combined modernistic characteristics with decorative motifs, often derived from historical or exotic styles. Extremely progressive features in the field of comfort and equipment could go along with traditional architecture and rich decoration, as in the Résidence Palace in Brussels (1926) by Michel Polak.

The modernist architects assembled principally in the *Société des Urbanistes belges* (1919), changed in 1923 to the *Société belge des Urbanistes et Architectes modernes* (SBUAM). They published their views in journals such as *La Cité* (1919-1935) and *Opbouwen* (1928-1937). The founding in 1927 of the Advanced Institute for Decorative Arts in Ter Kameren, under the direction of Henry van de Velde, who had returned to Belgium, was of great significance for the training of architects. The teachers included some of the most prominent Belgian architects from this period, such as Louis van der Swaelmen, Jean Jacques Eggericx, Raphaël Verwilghen, Albert Van huffel, Victor Bourgeois and Huib Hoste. Through their very diversity, they revealed the heterogeneous character of Belgian modernism.

Huib Hoste (1881-1957), a former pupil of Cloquet, became an important pioneer of the new movement immediately after the First World War. Initially influenced by Berlage and the Amsterdam school, he built one of the most progressive churches of his time in Zonnebeke in 1922. However, his most important work of the 1920's was the house *de Beir* in Knokke (1924), which reveals a personal assimilation of the influence of *De Stijl*. In his later buildings, beginning with a house in Zele in 1931, Hoste evolved towards a consistent interpretation of the International Style.

After the foundation of the National Society for Cheaper Housing in 1919, social building was an important field for experimentation for modernist archi-

Brussels, *Concert-hall of the Palace of Fine Arts*, Victor Horta, 1923. In this much discussed work too, Horta's talent shows undeniably in the interiors.

Tervuren, *the 'Nieuwe Huis' ('New House')*, Henry van de Velde, 1927. The rounded corners and the use of brick are typical for van de Velde in this period.

Koekelberg, *National Basilica of the Holy Heart*, Albert Van huffel, finished off by Paul Rome, 1920-1970. Van huffel's design was much appreciated by V. Horta, H.P. Berlage and H. van de Velde, and it was rewarded with the great architecture prize on the Exposition Internationale des Arts Décoratifs at Paris. The original construction technique using terracotta-elements which also function as lost shuttering for concrete, made it possible to arrive at the nice finish of the interior, which was wanted by Van huffel.

Knokke, *House De Beir*, Huib Hoste, 1924. Hoste gave the plane game of the International Style a personal touch by choosing the materials and colours in accordance with the environment of the building.

Watermaal-Bosvoorde, *block of flats 'Fer à Cheval'* in the garden-suburb Floréal, Jean J. Eggericx, 1921-1929.
For family houses Eggericx used a more traditional design with inclined roof.

St Agatha-Berchem, *'Cité Moderne'*, Victor Bourgeois, 1922-1925.
One of the most daring Cubist realizations of the 1920's.

Ghent, *University Library*, Henry van de Velde, 1932-1940.
The tower building houses the book-stores and is crowned by a belvedere.

tects for a long time. Some of the truly significant projects included the garden suburb *Klein Rusland* in Zelzate (1921) by Hoste, *Le Logis* and *Floréal* in Watermaal-Bosvoorde (1921-1929) by J.J. Eggericx, the *Cité Moderne* (1922-1925) by Victor Bourgeois in St Agatha-Berchem, and *Kapelleveld* in St Lambrechts-Woluwe (1923-1926) by Hoste and Pompe. The town planning for most of these projects was designed by Louis van der Swaelmen (1883-1929), who had made a valuable contribution during the war with his *Préliminaires d'Art civique mis en relation avec le 'cas clinique' de la Belgique* (Leyden, 1916), in which he presented the rebuilding projects as unique opportunities for pushing through new views on town planning.

The influence of the first modernist generation is clearly visible in the work of architects who continued to use traditional materials, such as Geo Henderick and Jules Lippens (1893-1969) in Ghent, or Emile van

Averbeke in Antwerp. Richard Acke also followed Berlage with his cinema *De Gouden Lanteern* in Courtray (1918); while Henderick, in some of his brick constructions, made use of the flowing Expressionist forms of the Amsterdam school.

During the 1930's the Dutch architect Dudok became the prime protagonist of the Romantic modernists, who tried to reconcile the new Cubist forms with the local tradition of brick building. His influence was particularly noticeable in figures such as Jules Lippens, J. de Bruycker (1891-1942), and Marc Neerman (1900-1943). The Town Hall of Heist (1930-1932) by F. Langeraert and G. Bailyu also incorporated the typical Dudok tower solution.

Henry van de Velde, who had returned to Belgium in 1925, also followed this tempered tendency in his late work, recognizing the value of existing elements of culture and landscape, as Frank Lloyd Wright did in

America. He preferred to design buildings in brick, such as the Kröller-Müller Museum in Otterlo (the Netherlands, 1937-1954), and his own *Nieuwe Huis* in Tervuren (1927); while the concrete library of the University of Ghent (1932-1940) was carefully integrated into the existing town architecture.

On the other hand, modernism was expressed in its purest form in the work of Victor Bourgeois (1897-1962) and Louis-Herman de Koninck (1896-1984). Bourgeois made completely concrete buildings as early as 1922-1925 in his *Cité Moderne*, though for technical reasons they were rendered. In 1928 he designed the house with an atelier for the sculptor Oscar Jespers in St Lambrechts-Woluwe, revealing the close links between architecture and the plastic arts during this period. If possible, pure form and technical ingenuity are even more dominant in the work of de Koninck. In 1928 he used the first concrete facade in Belgium, after making an important contribution to the development of the minimum dwelling with two constructions in Ukkel, including his own house (1924). His meticulous attention to proportion and spatial quality is revealed very clearly in buildings such as the house and atelier Lenglet (1926) and the Villa Ley (1934), also in Ukkel.

The real breakthrough of the International Style took place at the end of the 1920's under the influence of the *Congres Internationaux d'Architecture Moderne*

(CIAM), and of le Corbusier, who built the house of the painter René Guiette in Antwerp in 1927. A response to this work was made by Gaston Eysselinck (1907-1953), an architect from Ghent, who designed his own house in Ghent as a 'typical living machine', with separate levels for working, living and resting, and a typical roof terrace. On a more monumental scale he also built the Post Office in Ostend (1939). The fact that modernism had by now also gained a foothold in public buildings is revealed by the Naval Colleges of Antwerp (Jozef van Kriekinge) and Ostend (Pierre Verbruggen), and above all, in the beautiful swimming pool in Alost (1935) by Willy Valcke. Churches were also being built in Cubist style; the church of Dessel-Witgoor (1934) by Stan Leurs was one of the first. The arrival of high rise buildings is anticipated in the rather Art Déco-like *Boerentoren* in Antwerp (1930-1932) by van Hoenacker, van Averbeke and Smolderen. Again there was a development in the direction of the use of pure lines, as is clearly revealed in the two-part complex of the *Résidence Léopold* in Brussels (1935) by Eggericx and Verwilghen. However, by giving the go-ahead for the gradual demolition of the old Leopold quarter, this building also clearly demonstrates the isolation of the modernist architect, and his alienation from those inhabiting the buildings, which was to become – like elsewhere – the central problem in Belgian architecture in the years to come.

Antwerp, *Guiette House*, le Corbusier (Charles-Edouard Jeanneret), 1927. Le Corbusier also drew a urbanization design for the Antwerp left bank, for which plans Huib Hoste served as intermediary.

Ghent, *Eysselinck House*, Gaston Eysellinck, 1931. The modernistic architecture was often technically imperfect. As M. Dubois pointed out, Eysselinck replaced the white plastering of the facades later on by a covering of freestone plates. This ruined the typical dematerialization effect of the International Style.

Sculpture

19th-century Flemish sculpture is fairly recent, but curiously it has not yet been studied much. Therefore it has remained largely unknown, and hence unappreciated. Nevertheless, important sculpture was produced during the last century.

The independence of 1830 and the reign of Leopold II were two periods during which sculptors secured numerous commissions from official sources. The new state of Belgium was proud of its politicians, scientists, figures from its national history and artists, and honoured them with statues which were integrated into the decoration of the city. Just one statue was erected in honour of a celebrated woman, Margaret of Austria; which is characteristic of a period when women only represented allegorical figures. During the reign of Leopold II a number of projects were completed which gave a grandiose character to the capital, such as the sculpture on the triumphant arch of the *Jubelpark*, and the statues on the *Kleine Zavel* and in the Botanical Gardens. These official commissions enabled sculptors to establish workshops; although they could hardly escape from the style which dominated the salons, competitions and academies.

The situation changed towards the end of the century. In addition to the traditionally and academically trained sculptors who were able to rely on official recognition, there were a number of sculptors during the last two decades of the 19th century who developed independently of the academic tradition. Two names were to achieve an international reputation: Constantin Meunier and George Minne. In fact the latter was discovered abroad. Generally speaking, Belgian sculptors were always following a few steps behind the international developments of the 19th century, and innovations were assimilated slowly but systematically.

The close relationship with artistic circles in France did not end after the French domination, but remained constant throughout the 19th century. The *Ecole des Beaux-Arts* in Paris and the French sculpture workshops attracted Flemish students. Their participation in Parisian salons resulted in many friendships between French and Flemish artists. Leading French sculptors stayed in Brussels, including Auguste Rodin in the 1870's. Towards 1900 the French innovations were assimilated much more rapidly, partly through progressive circles of artists such as *Les Vingt* and *Le libre esthétique*, which had a foreign orientation.

George Minne, *Mother mourning her dead child* (detail), 1886, plaster, 45.5 cm. Private collection.

During the first half of the 19th century, Neoclassicism and the influence of Gilles-Lambert Godecharle continued to exist, alongside the late Baroque tradition. In this, the academies played a dominant role: Antwerp and Malines followed the Baroque; while Neoclassicism, based on the French example, was popular in Bruges, Ghent and Brussels. However, the Belgian academies offered only a basic training, and artists usually continued their studies in Paris or Rome. Paris was the important centre of attraction for artists. Until the end of the French domination, Belgians had to be registered at the *Ecole des Beaux-Arts* in Paris if they wished to compete for the highly coveted Rome prize, which gave them the chance to visit Rome. More than anywhere else, Rome was the place where artists could study the art of antiquity, and where famous figures – such as Canova and Thorwaldsen – attracted and influenced artists from all over Europe. Jan Robert Calloigne (1775-1830), who came from Bruges, was one of the few Flemish artists to win the Rome prize at the *Ecole des Beaux-Arts* in Paris. In 1811, Jan Lodewijk van Geel (1787-1852) from Malines won the second prize – after David d'Angers, but before Rude. Later, when Rude stayed in Brussels from 1815 to 1827, these two artists continued to be rivals and competed for several commissions. Van Geel completed a number of busts for the Royal House of Oranje-Nassau, and the Prince of Orange appointed him as the first sculptor. However, his most popular work was the *Lion of Waterloo* (1820-1828), standing on an artificial hill to commemorate the battle of 1815.

Jan Lodewijk Van Geel, *The Lion of Waterloo*, 1823-1826. Charles Van der Straeten, architect to the court of Willem I, designed this monument, a lion on a rectangular pedestal on top of a constructed conical hill. It was erected on the spot where the Prince of Orange was wounded in the Battle of 1815. The monumental lion (height 445 cm, weight 28 tons) was cast by Cockerill in Liege.

Willem and Jozef Geefs, Charles Auguste Fraikin, Eugène Simonis, *Congress Column*, 1850-1859, Brussels.
This monument was erected in remembrance of the National Congress in 1830, after designs and drawings by the architects Joseph Poelaert and Louis Mélot. This column is crowned on top by a bronze statue of Leopold I by Willem Geefs.

A lot of artists worked in well-known sculptors' ateliers in Paris, where they acquired much skill in the Neoclassicistic style, which they in turn spread abroad. Philippe Parmentier (1784-1867) worked in the atelier of François Joseph Bosio, and later became a teacher of sculpture at the Academy of Ghent from 1836-1850. Jan Robert Calloigne, mentioned above, worked in the atelier of Antoine Chaudet; as did Jean Baptiste Joseph de Bay, from Malines (1779-1863), who later settled in France, where he secured numerous official commissions. Jacob de Braekeleer (1823-1906) from Antwerp worked in the studio of Francisque Joseph Duret (1804-1865), where the late Baroque tradition was still followed. De Braekeleer himself was a Baroque and theatrically inclined artist.

The real extent of the renewing influence of François Rude has not been studied, but this French sculptor certainly contributed to a tendency which can be discerned from 1830: sculpture threw off the rigidity of the dominant forms used at the time, to make way for an increasingly natural style.

Rude remained in Brussels, as a voluntary exile, from 1815 to 1827. At this time he was still working in the classicistic style. His Romantically inspired work only originated after his return to France, including *La Marseillaise* for the *Arc de Triomphe* (1833-36). In Brussels, Rude secured many commissions thanks to the architect Charles van der Straeten, the court architect of William I, with whom he had come into contact through Louis David. Rude introduced new atelier habits, which would influence sculpture in Belgium. He worked from a live model, and considered a keen observation of nature more important than the study of classical works.

1830-1860

The period following the independence of Belgium led to enormous activity for sculptors and their ateliers. There was no earlier period in Belgian history in which so many monuments had been erected. Public competitions were issued, and the execution of a monument would be entrusted to the winning designer.

Willem Geefs, *Statue of General Belliard*, 1836, in the Victor Horta street at Brussels.

Auguste Fraikin, *Caught Love*, 1849, marble, 183 cm. Brussels, Museums of Fine Arts.

Three artists produced an impressive amount of work: Willem Geefs (1805-1883), Charles Auguste Fraikin (1817-1893) and Eugène Simonis (1810-1882) from Liege (who deserves a mention, as he trained a number of Flemish artists of the next generation when he became a teacher and director of the academy in Brussels). These names are related to a national monument from this period: the Congress Column in Brussels (1859), from the plans of the architect Joseph Poelaert.

Willem Geefs, born in Borgerhout near Antwerp, had six (minor) brothers who worked as sculptors. His greatest merit was his feeling for simplification, his attempt to create natural poses and expressions, and the realism that he achieved in some of his works. These qualities make his earliest monumental commissions – such as the *Statue of Belliard* (1836) in Brussels, and the *Sepulchral Monument of Frédéric de Mérode* (1837) in St Gudula's Church in Brussels – not simply masterpieces of his own oeuvre, but also important examples of Romantic sculpture in Belgium. During the 1830's his work was valued as high as that of his friend Gustaaf Wappers, the leading figure of pictorial Romanticism. In 1835 a medallion was minted depicting the likenesses of these two artists.

The spontaneous creative force of Geefs' early works is seldom found in his later period, when he had to complete numerous commissions as an officially recognized artist. It was particularly in his portraits that he retained his natural inclination for realism. Willem Geefs led an important atelier which produced not only statues, sepulchral monuments, groups of figures and busts in marble or bronze; but also church ornaments in the popular styles of the time: Neo-Romanesque, Neo-Gothic, Neo-Renaissance or Neo-Graecian.

Charles Auguste Fraikin, born in Herentals, made a large number of statues throughout the country; but above all, mythological and allegorical groups carefully executed in marble, which were very popular both in official circles and with the wealthy bourgeoisie. These works combine the characteristics of Neoclassicism and Romanticism with a remarkable feeling for elegance, to the point of being mannered.

During the Romantic period there was an increasing interest in Flanders in Gothic art, and the Neo-Gothic style can be clearly discerned in sculpture from the 1830's – especially in ecclesiastical art. At its craddle stood the Antwerp sculptor Karel-Hendrik Geerts (1807-1855), who taught at the Academy of Louvain the

Karel Hendrik Geerts, Jan Baptist De Boeck and Jan Baptist Van Wint, *Choir stalls*, 1841-1883 after a design by Frans Durlet. Antwerp, Cathedral.

523

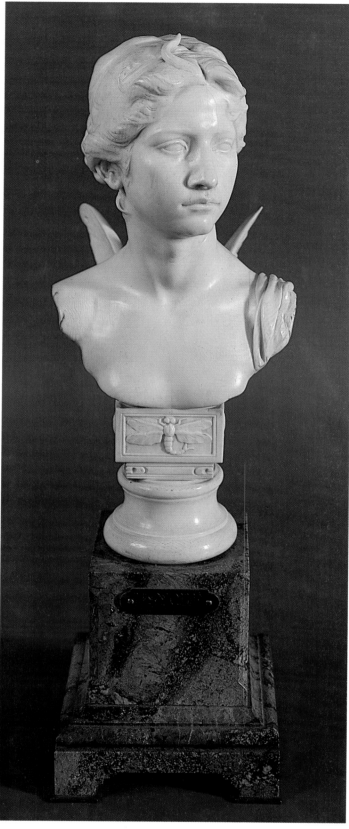

Paul de Vigne, *Psyche* (not-dated), ivory, 30 cm. Ghent, Museum of Fine Arts.

later leading figure of Neo-Gothic sculpture, Jean Béthune (1821-1894).

However, Neo-Gothic sculpture developed particularly in Bruges. Geerts was closely involved in important restoration projects there, *e g* of the fireplace of the *Brugse Vrije* and of the series of statues of the Town Hall in Bruges, destroyed in 1792. He created two altars in Magdalen's Church in Bruges, based on drawings by Thomas Harper King, the translator of A.W.N. Pugin. He also worked on the masterpiece of Neo-Gothic sculpture in Flanders, the choir stalls in Antwerp Cathedral. Geerts also wanted to rehabilitate wood sculpture, at a time when marble had been the favoured medium for many years. Church furnishing from Geerts' atelier can be found throughout Belgium, but it was also exported to England, Holland, Germany, America and Russia.

The first of the St Luke's schools was founded in Ghent in 1861. Gothic art was studied and copied there, and in the training a strong emphasis was placed on craftsmanship. The churches and monasteries, which had been closed down as a result of the anti-clerical activities of the French domination, were now refurnished in the Neo-Gothic style. In many cases even the preserved Baroque interiors had to make way for a Neo-Gothic one. Large ateliers such as that of the brothers Leopold (1832-1913) and Leonard (1834-1905) Blanchaert, or of Aloïs de Beule (1861-1935), both in Ghent, produced statues, retables, pulpits, choir stalls and altars, carved in wood and then polychromed. Aloïs de Beule even continued working right up to the First World War.

1860-1880

During this period sculpture sought its inspiration more and more from life, in terms of both design and content. The classical models and continually repeated allegories made way for more lifelike representations. In France this tendency is first noticeable in the work of François Rude. It developed to the full in Carpeaux' *Neapolitan fisherman* (1858). In Belgium the work of the brothers Bouré and of Victor van Hove introduced Realism in design, while Joseph Ducaju might be considered as the precursor of Constantin Meunier as regards content. Antoine Felix Bouré (1831-1883) was the only sculptor in the *Société Libre des Beaux-Arts*, an association of artists which was founded in Brussels in 1868 to promote Realism. The monumental lion on the Gileppe Dam is his. The work of his elder brother Paul (1823-1848) is known through some promising pieces, completed before his untimely death. His *Child playing with marbles* (1846) was a step towards Realism in sculpture, although it did not quite achieve the loose and uncomplicated pose of Rude's famous *Child with a tortoise* (1833).

Victor van Hove (1826-1891) was born in Ronse and trained under François Rude in Paris. His work reveals and almost brutal force; and his statue *Nègre après la bastonnade*, inspired by Harriet Beecher-Stowe's *Uncle Tom's Cabin* (1853), earned him a gold medal at the World Fair in Paris. Realism was also anticipated in the work of Joseph Ducaju (1823-1891), not so much in his academic style, but rather as regards the content of his work. Born in Antwerp, he became a pupil of Gustaaf Wappers and made a large number of statues there, such as those of the painters Teniers and Leys. The bas-reliefs with scenes depicting workers in the old South Station in Brussels reveal his attempt to depict working people. However, only in 1885 Meunier succeeded in representing this new subject matter satisfactorily.

From about 1870 artists such as Paul de Vigne, Julien Dillens, Charles van der Stappen and Thomas Vinçotte tried to escape academic strictures and the Graeco-Roman world of the gods, to return to nature and mankind. To achieve this they attempted to follow the Renaissance art of Florence, which they considered to be the best approach to reality. They found a stimulating figure at that time in the French sculptor Jean Baptiste Carpeaux, who stayed in Italy from 1856 to 1859. He was not so much interested in the study of classical arts as in enjoying life to the full, and he transformed the excitement of daily life into powerful sculptures. His work was popular in Belgium. In 1863 he showed his *Neapolitan fisherman* (1858) on the *Exposition nationale des Beaux-Arts* in Brussels; and in 1873 he had a one-man exhibition in St Luke's Gallery in Brussels, with thirty-two works in marble, bronze and terracotta.

Paul de Vigne (1843-1901) was the son of Pierre de Vigne-Quoy, who made the Artevelde monument in

Julien Dillens, *Minerva*, 1892, ivory and gilt bronze, 39 cm. Brussels, Gallery L'Ecuyer.

Antoine Felix Bouré, *Child with lizard*, marble, 62 × 112 × 40 cm. Brussels, Museums of Fine Arts.

Ghent. From 1870 to 1875, he stayed in Florence and later in Rome. Before his years in Italy he considered Rude – whom he described in a letter as "the Rubens of sculpture" – to be his most important influence. However, in Florence he discovered the early Renaissance art: Della Robbia, Verocchio, and above all, Donatello – artists who had not been very well-known in Belgium. Back in Belgium, de Vigne sculptured the decoration of the Conservatory of Music in Brussels. He met Rodin, who became a friend, and whose influence can be recognized in de Vigne's early portraits, which were taken directly from life and presented a psychological analysis of the subject. Between 1877 and 1882 de Vigne shared an atelier in Paris with the Walloon animal sculptor Léon Mignon, whom he had met in Rome. These new influences resulted in some of his most important works, including *The Triumph of Art* (1880), which was erected in 1885 on the facade of the Museums of Fine Arts in Brussels. This groups is reminiscent of another one, *La Danse* (1863-1869) by Jean-Baptiste Carpeaux for the Opera in Paris, which caused a great deal of controversy and was widely criticized.

Charles van der Stappen (1843-1910), born in Steenokkerzeel, became a teacher of sculpture (1883) and director of the Academy in Brussels from 1898 until his death. He produced *Education in Art* (1880), a pendant of the above-mentioned group by Paul de Vigne, but above all he was an excellent teacher, able to encourage his pupils to develop their own personalities. In 1882 he founded a free workshop for sculptors – the first of its kind in Brussels. This extremely eclectic artist stood open to all new ideas. His work was very varied, and at an advanced age he became one of the protagonists of Art Nouveau in Belgium.

Julien Dillens (1849-1904) from Ghent was among the founders of *L'Essor*, an association of Realistic artists. Together with Paul de Vigne, he is considered to be the most Italianate sculptor from the second half of the 19th century. He was primarily interested in monumental sculpture, as is revealed not only by the surviving monuments in Brussels and elsewhere, but above all by the many models which were never executed. Dillens would always adapt his sculptures to the architectural context, a skill which he had acquired during his training under Carrier-Belleuse. From 1871 to 1873 he worked under Carrier-Belleuse and alongside Auguste Rodin, on the sculptural decoration of the Stock Exchange in Brussels. Being interested in historical figures, he restored statues on the facades of the *Grote Markt* in Brussels, and made others for the town halls of Brussels and Ghent. However, Julien Dillens' sensitive personality is revealed mainly in his funeral sculpture, although he was clearly influenced by other artists here.

The work of Thomas Vinçotte (1850-1925) from Antwerp was moulded by his experiences during his journey to Italy, and his apprenticeship in the workshop of Jules Cavelier in Paris. The latter was well-known for his reaction against the exaggeration of the Romantic artists. Cavelier's work was permeated with classical art, though a tempered Realism made it more vivid. Vinçotte, who was particularly well-known for his portrait busts, in his turn adopted this classical style, which ensured his success as an official artist.

Jef Lambeaux (1852-1908) was a contemporary of the four artists mentioned, but he can be distinguished from them by his Baroque vitality and exuberance. Giovanni Bologna's *Mercurius* inspired him in his well-known *Brabo* monument on the *Grote Markt* in Antwerp. In 1883 Lambeaux was one of the founder members of *Les Vingt* (the XX), but dropped out after the first exhibition. He failed to win the Rome prize because of his non-academic, nervous and personal art. Lambeaux was a friend of Rodin and was profoundly influenced by the latter's powerful and vital sculptures.

1880-1900

At the end of the 19th century two original artists emerged in Belgian sculpture: Constantin Meunier and George Minne. They represented respectively the breakthrough of Realism and Symbolism in Belgian art. These movements coincided with a period of increasing contact between the national and foreign art circles as a result of, amongst other things, the influence of *Les Vingt* in Brussels. In 1889 Rodin became a member of *Les Vingt*, so that his work was still more a stimulus for modern sculpture. His famous sculpture *L'Age d'Airain* was actually created and first exhibited in Brussels.

Constantin Meunier, *The Coal-heaver*, 1905, bronze, 220 cm. Antwerp, Open-Air museum for Sculpture Middelheim.

Jef Lambeaux, *The Kiss* (1881), in bronze, 161 cm. Antwerp, Museum of Fine Arts.

Constantin Meunier (1831-1905) had already participated as a painter and as a member of the *Societé Libre des Beaux-Arts* in the breakthrough of Realism, before he took up sculpture in 1885. In the exhibition of *Les Vingt* in that year he exhibited a number of busts, and the wax models of *The Puddler* and *The Boatbuilder*. However, the press considered these works only as an attempt by a painter to embody his figures in sculpture. But when he exhibited his life-size *Smith* at the Salon in Paris the following year, he became famous overnight. The French critics Gustave Geffroy and Octave Mirbeau praised his work and the public was struck by its originality, as no one before Meunier had succeeded in depicting the working man in such an honest, simple and yet characteristic fashion. These statues of workers, especially miners, made Meunier internationally famous. These socially inspired works, with a slightly heroic character but quite lacking in anecdotal detail, are masterpieces of 19th-century sculpture. No other artists achieved the same conviction in this genre.

In 1887 Meunier became a teacher at the Academy in Louvain, a profession that had often been refused him. The way in which he justified his appointment was characteristic of the man himself: "My life has been hard at times but I have always persisted in following an artistic path and I still have the strength not to abandon it, left to my own resources. However, this position would give me the opportunity to get my breath back, and from time to time, produce a work with greater care. That is my only ambition". One of his works created in Louvain was his masterpiece *Fire-clamp*: a statue of a mother bending over her dead son, a modern Pietà. In 1896 Meunier had his first large one-man exhibition in the gallery *L'art nouveau* of the art dealer Samuel Bing in Paris; probably at the suggestion of Henry van de Velde, with whom he was in close contact, and who also introduced his work in Germany. There he participated successfully in the most important exhibitions. At the end of his life he was commissioned to make the Zola monument in Paris, which was eventually completed in 1924 by Alexandre Charpentier.

The great importance of George Minne (1866-1941) from Ghent lies particularly in his early work done before 1900. From 1895-1899 he lived in Brussels, where he was a member of the artistic circle *Les Vingt*. While he was a student in Ghent, Minne was already adopted by a circle of poets which included Maurice Maeterlinck, Grégoire Le Roy and Charles van Ler-

Constantin Meunier, *The Fire-damp*, 1888-1889, bronze, 150 × 212 × 110 cm. Brussels, Museums of Fine Arts.

berghe. These artists were directed towards Paris, participating in the Symbolist vision and the sensibility of the *fin de siècle*. Maeterlinck typified the young Minne thus: "He was twenty years old and had seen nothing and read nothing. He didn't speak - he babbled. He smiled continuously and calmly at something which only he could see. We regarded him amicably and not without respect, like a sort of primitive, a marvellous *minus habens*. He didn't know anything, and even in his first drawings and sketches, all his art was there in embryo, all he had become and all he would be tomorrow."

Minne's art, which impressed Maeterlinck and his friends so much, because it embodied also their feelings so powerfully, contained references to Rodin, Michelangelo and Giovanni de Bologna – but at the same time differed fundamentally from them. Minne made small figures, delicately moulded, enclosed and sensitive; they could not merely be considered as Symbolist, but also as precursors of Expressionism because of the simplification and expressive force in them.

Minne was only interested in sculpting people: mother and child in tragic lamentation, father and the prodigal son, and above all, the lonely young man. He portrayed the latter in different poses, from the delicate *Small, wounded boy* (1889) to the powerful *Man with water pouch* (1897), and gradually developed the kneeling figures for his famous *Fountain of the kneeling youths* (1898). Minne executed several commissions for the German industrialist and arts patron Karl Ernst Osthaus, through the mediation of Henry van de Velde, with whom he became acquainted in Brussels. Van de Velde also introduced him to Julius Meier-Graefe, and influential German critic and gallery owner in Paris. Through these contacts Minne became well-known by 1900 in the important centres of Art Nouveau, such as

George Minne, *The Fountain with Kneeled Figures, ca* 1898, plaster, 168 cm, diameter with step, 240 cm. Ghent, Museum of Fine Arts.

George Minne, John the Baptist, 1895, plaster, 72 cm. Ghent, Museum of Fine Arts.

Paris, Berlin and Vienna. His rather small output reveals a number of fundamental links with artists of that time: Puvis de Chavannes, Paul Gauguin, Edvard Munch and Ferdinand Hodler. Some modern artists from the beginning of the century show Minne's influence: for example Oskar Kokoschka, Egon Schiele, Gustav Klimt, Wilhelm Lehmbruck and Käthe Kollwitz.

In ten years, both in Ghent and in Brussels, Minne expressed his sensitive feeling for life in numerous drawings and at most, thirty sculptures. He never worked in stone or in wood, but he was essentially a modeller, so that we gain the best impression of his work from the surviving original plaster models. In 1899 George Minne settled in St Martens-Latem in the vicinity of Ghent. He was a member of a small colony of artists there, which included the painters Gustaaf van de Woestijne and Valerius de Saedeleer. During the First World War he lived in Wales. In this period he concentrated predominantly on drawing, while his apprentices made statues based on the old models dating from before 1900. After the war he began to sculpt again himself, repeating earlier compositions of mother and child sculptures.

Various sculptors mentioned above shared in the strong Art Nouveau current in Belgium. Artists such as Julien Dillens and Charles van der Stappen created works which were entirely in the aesthetic tradition of Art Nouveau in their decorative essence, the lines based on plant shapes, and the eclectic use of materials. Many works were made in ivory during this period, largely due to the intervention of Leopold II. In 1892 he provided ivory for artists to encourage the use of a product from the Belgian Congo. The first exhibition of 'chryselephantine' sculpture in Belgium (*i e* a technique using a combination of ivory with gold or other metals) took place at the World Fair in Antwerp in 1894. Fourteen Belgian sculptors took part in this exhibition with a commercial rather than an artistic character.

A second exhibition, at the World Fair in 1897 in Brussels, was considered to be the most innovatory and revealing artistic event of the *fin-de-siècle*. Eighty sculptures by thirty-eight Belgian sculptors were presented at the salon of honour in the Congo Pavilion in Tervuren. All the current trends in Belgian sculpture of this period were represented.

George Minne, *The Man with the water-skin*, 1897, bronze, 64.5 cm. Brussels, Museums of Fine Arts.

George Minne, *The Little Injured person II*, 1898, marble, 26 cm. Private collection.

Fernand Khnopff, *Mask of a young English woman*, 1891, polychromed plaster, 40.5 cm. Brussels, Museums of Fine Arts.
In the 1890's Khnopff made some characteristic statues. With the same sensibility as in his paintings, the artist manages to depict his refined and mysterious female types in his statues.

THE TWENTIETH CENTURY

Rik Wouters (1882-1916) from Malines, one of the most remarkable Flemish artists from the period just before the First World War, created from 1907 to 1913 some masterpieces striking for their spontaneous character, animation and vitality. In addition to a number of portraits and children's heads, the image of his wife Nel was a constantly recurring theme. She was the inspiration for *Household Cares* or *Contemplation*. *Insane Violence* is undoubtedly his boldest creation and was inspired by the dancer, Isidora Duncan. Rik Wouters' figures were sculpted nervously, with rough strokes; rendering a play of light to the surface, similar to that in some of Rodin's work. Although a sculpture like *Household Cares* is reminiscent of Bourdelle's *Penelope*, the sculptural approach of both artists is essentially different. The unity of Bourdelle's figure lies in its architectural structure, while in Wouters' work it results from an inner tension. To him a statue was a synthesis of a pose, a movement or a condition, the most characteristic feature of a person. He worked primarily from nature and reproached Bourdelle for his borrowing from classical art.

One of the first artists in Belgium to follow this classicistic path was Ernest Wijnants (1878-1964). Like Bourdelle's works, his were inspired by the art of Ancient Greece, Egypt and Assyria. Before the First World War he was among the first sculptors to use the *taille direct* method. He preferred to execute nude figures of women and girls, who had great vitality and

Ernest Wijnants, *The Echo*, 1913 lime-wood, 135 cm. Ghent, Museum of Fine Arts.

Rik Wouters, *Crazy Force*, 1912, bronze, 200 cm. Antwerp, Open-air museum for Sculpture Middelheim.

sometimes a certain sense of sensuality, as in *The Echo* (1913). When the new trends of Abstract art, Cubism and Expressionism emerged after the war he remained faithful to his traditional figurative art.

AFTER 1918   In the 1920's Flemish sculpture underwent Cubist and Expressionist influences. These influences already manifested themselves during the First World War, but only developed later. Without doubt, Oscar Jespers (1887-1970) was the leading and most representative sculptor of this period in Flanders. With Paul Joostens he was part of an avant-garde circle of friends in Antwerp, surrounding Paul van Ostaijen. During the period 1917-1921 Jespers went through an experimental phase. He alternately resorted to abstract designs and abstractions. In this he was inspired by the Cubists, particularly Archipenko, whose work had been exhibited in Brussels in 1911. He destroyed virtually all his works from this period, because he did not consider them to be representative experiments. Up to 1935 his sculpture displays a debt to Cubism, Expressionism, Negro art and Egyptian art. As a result of his sense of plasticity, he was able to assimilate many influences in a personal way. His sculptures were usually in *taille direct*, carved in wood or stone.

Jozef Cantré and Henri Puvrez were closely related to Jespers. They also combined elements from Cubism and Expressionism, and worked in *taille direct*. Jozef Cantré (1890-1957) lived in Holland during the First World War. There he probably came under the influence of the work of Zadkine, which he got to know

in collections. This influence can be discerned throughout Cantré's work. In common with Jespers he had a liking for enclosed forms, though he always approximated the natural appearance of man, and kept a great eye for detail. Henri Puvrez (1893-1971) worked in the abstract style around 1919. His work initially reveals a great deal of the influence of Oscar Jespers, Zadkine and Negro art; but he later developed an individual style, serene and elegant, with a preference for stylized designs.

The most radical creations were undoubtedly those in the field of abstract sculpture. They were also the least understood, despite exhibitions, lectures, and reviews in magazines such as *Het overzicht*, which supported this tendency. Rather than a movement, abstract art consisted of individual experiments, which reached an international level with Georges Vantongerloo (1886-1965). He belonged for a short time to the *De Stijl* movement. As a geometric abstract sculptor, in whose work mathematical formulae and laws of natural science were of fundamental importance, he is accepted as a pioneer of modern sculpture. This is understandable, because his idea expressed in colour and space becomes more important than the making the work of art itself. He settled in France at the beginning of the 1920's, where he lived up to the time of his death.

The Antwerp avant-garde artist Paul Joostens (1889-1960) started experimenting in many ways from 1917, influenced by Expressionism, Cubism and Futurism. However, above all the Dada movement led him to develop his own personal form of expression. During the 1920's he made assemblages in the form of quasi-arbitrary constructions with a harmonious structure, indicating a high degree of ingenuity, also as regards the interplay of the materials used.

From 1930 the artists rejected the experimental art and the deformities of the Expressionists, to return to a more serene image of man. In this they followed the example of French and Italian art, especially of Maillol and Despiau. The influence of Despiau is clearly visible in the work of Charles Leplae (1903-1961), they have met each other in Paris. By the 1930's Jespers, Cantré and Puvrez had also adopted this trend. In 1935 the great Flemish Expressionist painter Constant Permeke (1886-1952) created his first sculptures. These display the same sense of monumental brutal force, which is so characteristic of his paintings.

Oscar Jespers, *Angel*, sepulchral monument for Paul van Ostayen, 1932, freestone, 63 × 60 × 165 cm. Antwerp, Municipal cemetery Schoonselhof.

Painting

NEOCLASSICISM

French Neoclassicism enjoyed a great following in Belgian art circles, both in Flanders and Wallonia. The well-known portrait of the Hemptinne family (Brussels, Museums of Fine Arts) by François Navez (1787-1869) proves that in 1816 the severity of David and the voluptuous refinement of Ingres had been simultaneously assimilated in Belgium. It could indeed pass for the model of the many skilled portraits of the bourgeoisie and heads of state, which were produced in Belgium at the beginning of the 19th century. In the decades before the Belgian revolution French-oriented artists were active in most artistic centres in Flanders. During this period, cities as Ghent and Bruges were important, but they played a far lesser role in artistic life after 1830.

In Flanders each of the three centres had its dominant figure: Joseph Odevaere (1778-1830) in Bruges, Joseph Paelinck (1781-1839) in Ghent, and Matthieu van Bree (1773-1839) in Antwerp. These three painters all secured official commissions from Napoleon, and after 1815 they worked for William I. Most representatives of Neoclassicism had a similar career. They studied in one or more cities in their own country, went to Paris, and finally spent some years in Italy. A few, such as Paelinck and Odevaere, succeeded in studying under David. This long period of study was enabled through grants and prizes, and in some cases through patronage. Promising artists would be sent by local authorities to the great centres of art, because there alone they could learn the skills to be used back at home in the service of the community. The local press regularly reported on the progress of artists, while they themselves sent home works of art to participate in local art salons. Flanders seemed to consider itself to be a *departement* of France – as indeed it was at that time politically – and most provincial artists could only make their career via Paris.

There were also artists whose careers took place virtually entirely abroad. The man who represented the transition between the Baroque tradition of the 18th century and Neoclassicism, Joseph Suvée (1743-1807), came originally from Bruges. He became first the director of the Academy in Paris and then of the *Académie de France* in Rome. From these centres Suvée in fact attracted his compatriots. Josse Sebastiaan van den Abeele (1797-1855) painted more in Italy than in his own country. Martin Verstappen (1773-1860), who

James Ensor, *Self-portrait with masks*, 1899, painting in oils on canvas, 120 × 80 cm. Private collection.

Joseph Paelinck, *The beautiful Anthia and her suite in the temple of Diana at Ephese*, 1820, painting in oils on canvas, 230 × 300 cm. Ghent, Museum of Fine Arts.

Josse Van den Abeele, *Self-portrait*, painting in oils on panel, 81.5 × 57 cm. Ghent, Museum of Fine Arts.

Gustaf Wappers, *Scenery of September-days 1830, on the Great Market at Brussels*, 1835, oil-colours on canvas, 444 × 660 cm.
Brussels, Museums of Fine Arts of Belgium.

specialized in landscapes, and Jean Baptiste Maes-Canini (1794-1856), worked in Italy up to their deaths. François Simonau (1773 or 1783-1859) and Charles Picqué (1799-1869) secured many commissions in England as portrait painters.

The Neoclassicists mainly painted portraits, as well as landscapes and historical or mythological scenes. In Belgian art history their work forms a homogeneous whole which until recently was confined to museum storerooms, with one or two exceptions. Nowadays the Neoclassicists are once more a subject of interest as representatives of an era, and executors of a unified style which permitted little deviation, and as painters with a strong métier. Their severe and sober technique, delicate use of line, fine colouration and suggestion of precious materials – in short all the qualities which artists such as Ingres combined to create great works of art, and which his followers employed to a standard of high craftsmanship – are now justifiably reappreciated.

Before 1830 there were also specialists in the other genres, such as landscapes, animal painting and historical scenes. The most representative landscape painters included Jean Baptiste de Jonghe (1785-1844)

and Henri van Assche (1774-1841); the animal painters Balthazar Ommeganck (1755-1826) and Eugene Verboeckhoven (1789-1881), and the historical painters Ferdinand de Braekeleer (1792-1883) and Joseph Geirnaert (1790-1859). No original talent may be expected from these artists or their contemporaries. They were purely academic painters, who imitated past traditions and did not feel called upon to renew their own specialized fields. This style would be found in salons until the end of the 19th century; Verboeckhoven himself produced his artificial animal scenes until the 1880's.

Amongst the later generations there was always a section of secondary figures to continue this academic tradition. This group of painters developed very slowly, and only followed to a limited extent the artistic changes in tempo which took place during the 19th century. So, after the breakthrough of Realism a whole line of artists painted works of anecdotal Realism, who gradually dared to replace their smooth finish with a rather livelier technique. The same class of artists – worthy craftsmen – continued with great conviction to work with a tempered and outdated Impressionism during the era of abstract painting and Expressionism.

ROMANTICISM

The development of painting in Belgium from 1830 was determined, as in France, by a few individual innovators. They recognized the importance of new developments abroad and assimilated them, to occupy a place in their own country with this new art, and literally to found new schools. The historical painter Gustaaf Wappers (1803-1874), who trained and became a director at the Academy of Antwerp, was the first major figure. His significance is twofold. On the one hand, he was the first artist to share the ideals of French Romanticism consistently; on the other, he worked openly in the Baroque tradition of Antwerp – and as such he became the symbol of the rediscovery of a local heritage in painting. His breakthrough coincided with the appearance of a number of ambitious canvases at the triennial salon in Brussels. In 1830 he exhibited *The Sacrifice of Burgomaster van der Werff* (Utrecht, Central Museum). At this salon, which was overloaded with academic entries, Wappers' work attracted most of the attention. The content appealed to the patriotism of the 1830's, the form linked dignity and intensity, and in many people's view was far superior to the formula-bound compositions of Neoclassicism. Five years later Wappers exhibited *An Episode from the Belgian Revolution* (Brussels, Museums of Fine Arts), with which he set himself up as the leader of the modern movement. Wappers' work refers back to the great French examples: Géricault, Gros and Delacroix. He shared their interest in past and present heroic events and in the exotic, though he never matched their solid pictorial force.

A similar, rather flat synthesis of Romanticism with a classic design characterized the work of Nicaise de Keyser (1813-1887), another artist from Antwerp, who competed with and later succeeded Wappers as the director of the Academy in Antwerp. In 1836 de Keyser became prominent with his *Scene from the Battle of the Golden Spurs* (Courtray, Museum of Fine Arts). Three years later he exhibited the *Battle of Woeringen* (Brussels, Museums of Fine Arts) at the salon. De Keyser was not deeply concerned with new pictorial problems, because he continued to use his tempered Romantic formula as a true academic painter until his death.

Little original talent marked the other Romantic historical painters: Louis Gallait (1810-1887), Godfried Guffens (1823–1901) and Edouard De Biefve (1808-1882). To discover this quality one has to look amongst the less exalted genres such as landscape painting, portraits and thematic paintings. As in other European countries, this originality was coupled in Belgium with an increasing lack of interest in large spectacular works; but with a search for contemporary themes and a return to the sources: nature, and in some cases, medieval art.

Henri Leys (1815-1869) made his debut with historical works, preferably violent scenes in the true Antwerp tradition, until he followed a different path in 1839 with his *Flemish Wedding in the 17th Century* (Antwerp, Museum of Fine Arts). Against the Baroque style of Wappers, he posed a depiction of daily events from the past, based on 17th-century genre painting.

Leys' art would develop entirely in this vein. His works seem historical reconstructions of daily occurrences and conditions, usually set in the 16th century. These scenes were always portrayed without pathos, almost by coincidence, as in the work of Gustave Courbet or later in Edgar Degas. Nothing is suggested or sketchy, each figure is sharply defined, and the architectural backgrounds framing the scenes are depicted with archaeological precision. The isolation of all the figures is remarkable, and in many works results in a climate of resignation, reminiscent of the Pre-Raphaelites and of Khnopff.

Henri Leys was strongly influenced by the Flemish Primitives and by German Renaissance artists such as Dürer and Holbein. The Realism of Courbet and Millet must have fascinated him as well. All these influences form a curious synthesis in characteristically sharply

Henri Leys, *Church-goers*, oil-colours on panel, 60 × 35 cm. Brussels, Museums of Fine Arts.

537

outlined figures, in which both the physical appearance and the clothing is depicted with an analytical attention to detail – a material Realism that is later rediscovered in Leys' most important pupil, Henri de Braekeleer. The technique of shining, saturated colours, painted on panels rather than canvas, is also indicative of Leys' study of medieval art.

A few years after Leys, Charles De Groux (1825-1870) from Comines was one of the first to turn to Realism, after starting as a historical painter. He was a pupil of the classicist Navez, and studied at the Academy of Düsseldorf in 1851. In contrast to Leys, he depicted contemporary daily life, with an emphasis on village life and the poor social conditions. However, his work again shows a curious synthesis of Realism cast in a decorative composition dominated by elegant, almost Gothic lines. De Groux' work was very unequal; he only occasionally succeeded in producing a noble Realistic composition or a powerful sketch. Yet these few works have more lasting value than the historical scenes painted by Leys. De Groux is actually the direct precursor of social Realism, as seen in the work of Meunier, Frédéric and Laermans at the end of the 19th century.

The development towards Realism, early hints of which can be discerned in the work of Leys and De Groux, is very evident in landscape painting. While academic landscapes continued to be painted up to 1900, a few transitional figures were already breaking away from the traditional concepts in the 1850's. Painters began to work from nature in order to observe better light and colour, and to capture them on the canvas more truthfully. There was a growing interest in the specific aspect of the artist's own surroundings, rather than in an academically formulated type of nature. In short, the new developments of the English landscape painters (including above all John Constable) and of the French

Henri Leys, *Lucie Leys, daughter of the painter*, oil-colours on panel, 107 × 36 cm, 1865. Antwerp, Museum of Fine Arts.

Charles De Groux, *The Prayer of Thanks, ca* 1860, painting in oils on canvas, 80 × 154 cm. Brussels, Museums of Fine Arts.

538

Charles Degroux, *The pelgrimage to St Guy at Anderlecht*, oil-colours on canvas, 157 × 216 cm, about 1856. Brussels, Museums of Fine Arts.

Paul Lauters, *A sunken Road*, 1847, painting in oils on canvas, 38 × 30.5 cm. Brussels, Museums of Fine Arts.

school of Barbizon also spread to Belgium. The first artist to break away from the smooth painting technique and the conventional representation of nature of his contemporaries was Theodore Fourmois (1814-1871) from Hainault. With studies he tried to retain his direct impression of nature in the large atelier works, which were still largely conceived in the spirit of the 17th-century Dutch landscapes. Most artists who fell between the academic and Realistic landscape painters remain little known; they include Jean Baptiste Kindermans (born 1821 or 1822), Jozef Lies (1821-1865), François Roffiaen (1820-1898), Paul Lauters (1806-1875), Alfred de Knyff (1819-1886), Edouard Huberti (1818-1880), and the brothers Xavier (1818-1896) and Cesar (1823-1904) de Cock. In their works one gradually discerns the specific aspect of Belgian nature with its own light and atmosphere.

The tendency towards greater realism was also growing amongst painters in related genres: city views, animal paintings and sea scenes. One interesting figure in this context was Paul Jan Clays (1819-1900), who radically broke with the stereotyped Romantic seascapes in the 1850's, to concentrate for the rest of his life on the study of the North Sea and the Scheldt estuary.

A special place was taken up by the Antwerp landscape painter François Lamorinière (1828-1911). Although he had worked in Barbizon for some time, like de Knyff and the de Cock brothers, his work – unlike that of all the transitional figures mentioned above – was not oriented towards France. The precision and meticulous detail, with which he painted the woods and heathland surrounding Antwerp, were more in the tradition of the English Pre-Raphaelites or of the German and Austrian schools with painters such as Waldmüller and Friedrich. Lamorinière was sometimes referred to as the 'Leys of landscape painting' or 'the painter with a Gothic soul'. His extremely delicate use of oils on panels makes one certainly think of the Middle Ages, and was far removed from the fluent and resilient style developed by the French and most of the Belgian landscape painters of the 19th century.

Paul-Jean Clays, *Turbulent Sea*, 1866, painting in oils on canvas, 60 × 100 cm. Liege, Musée du Parc de la Boverie.

François Lamorinière, *Autumnal Landscape*, 1857, painting in oils on panel, 110 × 140 cm. Private collection.

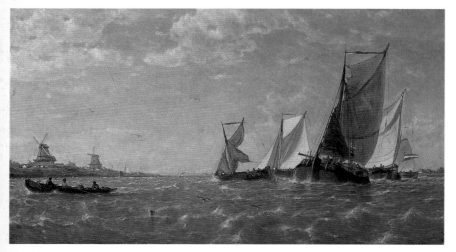

REALISM

From the 1860's progressive Belgian artists seemed better organized than their predecessors. The latter had to find their own way, compromising with the dominating system on the academies, or entirely autonomously. In the wake of the pioneers a number of progressive artists' circles appeared, which began to play a role in artistic life. In Antwerp an anti-academic circle of artists developed around Henri Leys; in Brussels a number of younger artists started a free atelier as an alternative to the Academy. These circles stood open to stimuli from other countries, the most important undoubtedly being the French works of art which were sent to Belgian art salons, e g by Courbet and Millet. When Courbet exhibited his *The Stone-breakers* in Brussels in 1851, he caused a real sensation. In 1862 Courbet visited Antwerp in person to lecture on the principles of Realism at an international conference. In the meantime this style had become a subject of discussion in the press.

In Brussels particularly many artists were sympathetic to this new form of expression. In 1868 this led to the foundation of the *Société Libre des Beaux Arts*, which was directed against the artistic establishment and was clearly inspired by French Realism. The society's activity was aimed at placing modern art as an acceptable force in the art world. To this end it organized its own exhibitions; although the members also tried to penetrate in the official salons. They were supported by the critic Camille Lemonnier, and published a journal called *L'Art Libre* in 1871 and 1872, still the best source to understand the thoughts of the Belgian Realists. These ideas contained two main principles: the desire for an art form which expresses contemporary life in a truthful way, and the consideration of a painting as a personal expression of the artist, not dictated by laws.

All the Belgian Realists were associated more or less directly with the *Société Libre*; some of them were personally establishing contacts with Paris. From the 1840's Jozef Stevens (1819-1892) participated in the official salons with animal paintings, social allegories which made him one of the first Realist painters in Belgium. He spent time in Paris on several occasions and built up a reputation as a painter of animals.

His younger brother Alfred Stevens (1823-1906) was a typical exponent of the *belle peinture*. Even in socially aware Realists (such as Courbet and Millet in France or De Groux in Belgium) artistic freedom sometimes led to the display of mere good painting – *l'art pour l'art* – which was especially evident in portraits, genre tableaux and landscapes. It was above all as an artist with a splendid métier that Alfred Stevens deserves his place amongst the Realists. His best works are portraits of ladies, which depict the visual richness of the subject

Alfred Stevens, *Lady in pink*, oil-colours on canvas, 87 × 57 cm. Brussels, Museums of Fine Arts.

with all her paraphernalia. Stevens became a much sought after portrait painter in Paris. He befriended the best known painters of contemporary life: Courbet, Fantin-Latour, Whistler and Manet. Alfred Stevens was a stimulus for many rather traditionally oriented second-rate figures, who painted enjoyable and well-constructed Realistic portraits, as well as painting in other genres.

Louis Dubois (1830-1880), an interesting artist in many respects, who painted still lifes, figures and landscapes, was a central character in the *Société Libre des Beaux-Arts*. He was deeply influenced by Courbet, although his landscapes sometimes express a rather personal and melancholy feeling. He knew Courbet personally, and was an active proponent of positivist aesthetics. Under the pseudonym *Hout* (meaning 'wood') he was one of the spokesmen for Realism in the journal *L'Art Libre*. The famous sculptor Constantin Meunier (1831-1905) was also one of the founders of the *Société Libre des Beaux Arts*. He had trained as a painter and sculptor in the Academy in Brussels, and from 1860-1870 he worked exclusively as a painter. He painted mainly religious subjects, but increasingly took the life and appearance of ordinary people as the subject of his work; such as during his trip to Spain in 1869, which broadened the scope of his art both technically and thematically. From 1878 he made studies of labourers from the Belgian mining regions in drawings and paintings – from 1885 also in sculpture – and during the 1880's he produced his best work on this theme. Stylistically Meunier already belongs to a later generation than Dubois and De Groux. He is one of the

Alfred Stevens, *Remember*, 1863, painting in oils on panel, 63 × 52 cm. Brussels, Museums of Fine Arts.

Louis Dubois, *Swamps in the Campine*, oil-colours on canvas, 105 × 181.5 cm, 1863. Ghent, Museum of Fine Arts.

542

many exponents of a school of Realism that was still rooted in the 1860's by its themes and dark colouration, but that is inconceivable without Impressionism; from a pictorial point of view. One could call this a transitional style between Realism and Impressionism, though many consider it as an 'autochtonous Impressionism', in which the dark palette, the heavy coating and the serious subject matter form an original Belgian contribution to the painting of the 1880's.

Two artists developed through these two stages of Realism and 'autochtonous Impressionism' in Antwerp: Jan Stobbaerts and Henri de Braekeleer. Jan Stobbaerts (1838-1914) caused a scandal when he exhibited his *Slaughterhouse* (Antwerp, Museum of Fine Arts) in 1873. The slitting of the animal's throat is depicted on a large scale at the front of the composition. This testified to a conscious rejection of idealistic subjects, and emphasized the métier as a sufficient *raison d'être* for a painting. A number of Realistic paintings of livestock farming depicting cattle and horses followed. In his treatment of these themes, it is easy to see Stobbaerts' evolution towards Impressionism. The artist began to pay more attention to the effects of light than to tangible objects. The colouration became lighter and the brush strokes flakier. Gradually Stobbaerts' work took on a hazy, atmospheric character. In his late work Stobbaerts only used this hazy technique for mythological scenes painted in his atelier.

A student colleague of Stobbaerts at the academy and in Leys' atelier was Henri de Braekeleer (1840-1888), the son of the thematic and historical painter Ferdinand. However, he was trained above all by his uncle Henri Leys and made study journeys, not to the classical countries of France and Italy, but to Germany and the Netherlands. Like his father, Henri de Braekeleer was inspired above all by 17th-century Dutch interior and still life painters. He painted his major works between 1870 and 1880, interrupted by a nervous breakdown until 1883. His interiors, with usually only one or a small number of figures, were depicted with photographic precision. The artist was particularly interested in the material appearance of the objects surrounding

Henri De Braekeleer, *The Man in the Chair*, 1875, painting in oils on canvas, 79 × 63 cm. Antwerp, Museum of Fine Arts.

Constantin Meunier, *Coal-mine in the snow*, oil-colours on canvas, 40 × 54 cm. Brussels, Museums of Fine Arts.

the figures, and in the soft interior light shining on the objects and the textures. On the other hand, the effects of perspective with open doors and windows, the emphasis on emptiness and silence, and the multiplicity of meticulously depicted detail, imbue these works with a penetrating atmosphere that reminds one of Friedrich and is later found in the work of Symbolists such as Mellery and Khnopff. In some of de Braekeleer's works the excessive attention to rich textures is rather disturbing; though this very sense of opulence develops to add a new quality in the artist's later paintings.

During the 1880's his work became increasingly sketchy. His form of Impressionism was to express on the canvas the visual richness of an interior, a figure and particularly a still life with increasing frankness in an abstract manner. These late works are an extremely personal pictorial expression, pointing to Expressionism and comparable to the works from Ensor's sombre period. In his etchings too, de Braekeleer made excellent use of an emotionally charged and nervous handling; in this respect he can also be compared to Ensor.

543

Henri de Braekeleer, *Still life*, oil-colours on canvas, 35 × 52.5 cm, about 1885. Antwerp, Museum of Fine Arts.

LANDSCAPE PAINTING:
FROM REALISM TO IMPRESSIONISM

Realism and Impressionism had an especially great impact on landscape painting. Transitional figures such as Fourmois and Lamorinière had been exponents of a tendency to paint landscapes that were more locally inspired, a tendency that had first appeared in England at the beginning of the century, and in France with the school of Barbizon in the 1830's. The Barbizon experience was repeated in Belgium, and in this context there are many interesting though barely studied artists.

Hippolyte Boulenger (1837-1874), French in origin, was born in Tournai and died in Brussels. It is disputable which national school Boulenger might belong to, but he holds such a central position in the development of Belgian art that he should certainly be mentioned in this survey. In 1863, Boulenger began to concentrate on landscape painting, and in this he followed the path of the French Romantic-Realist painters of the school of Barbizon. With the encouragement of the painter Camille van Camp (1834-1891) he settled in Tervuren near Brussels, where he became the central figure in the school of Tervuren, a name that he introduced himself. Boulenger sought the intense contact with nature that had imbued the art of his great models, Rousseau, Daubigny and Troyon, with such verisimilitude and originality. For Boulenger, this contact – in

Hippolyte Boulenger, *Rainy Weather*, 1870, painting in oils on canvas, 65 × 81.5 cm. Liege, Musée d'Art Wallon.

544

Adrien Joseph Heymans, *Sunset on the moors*, 78 × 146 cm, about 1877. Ghent, Museum of Fine Arts.

Tervuren as well as in the Ardennes – was twofold: it was the observation of natural phenomena, but also an emotional response. In his sketches and paintings he achieved a representation of light and atmosphere. He developed a differentiated technique to depict clouds, trees, grass, mud, *etc* together with a natural colouration – qualities which were quite new in Belgian art. He was also much more an emotional painter than Fourmois, attracted as he was by extreme weather conditions and by wild nature, in which he found a medium for his tormented personality. Boulenger died at an early age in 1874, so like van Gogh, his major work was created in the space of ten years. During these years Boulenger worked outside in nature as if possessed, even though his health was rather poor. He painted increasingly turbulent and expressive canvasses with a melancholy interpretation of nature.

None of the other figures who worked with Boulenger in Tervuren ever achieved his expressive force. Painters such as Joseph Theodore Coosemans (1828-1904), Alphonse Asselbergs (1839-1916), Jules Montigny (1840-1899), Edouard Huberti (1818-1880) and Theodore Baron (1840-1899) were highly specialized and dedicated landscape painters, who worked not only in Tervuren but also in other favourite surroundings. Their work usually bears the traces of a painstaking, hesitant realization. Virtually all the other landscape painters from this period worked at the same level. They are found in local schools, such as those of Kalmthout and Termonde, and their work reveals a gradual lightening in the colouration and a freer style of painting under the influence of Impressionism. Adriaan Jozef Heymans (1839-1921), the leader of the Kalmthout school, is

Franz Courtens, *The Fisherman*, painting in oils on canvas, 80 × 60 cm. Private collection.

usually described as the representative of the 'grey school'. This gentle artist, who was sensitive to the depiction of half light, preferred to paint the nature around Kalmthout in the early morning or evening light. The soft grey tonality of his work, and the controlled brushwork that seems to complement it, are reminiscent of Corot. This 'grey' quality is found in the work of many Belgian landscape painters, including that of Huberti and Baron, mentioned above. In fact, the 'grey school' was another Belgian version of Impressionism.

Art criticism has conjured up a number of names to illustrate the specific qualities of the Belgian Impressionists, such as the 'autochtonous Impressionism' in connection with Meunier. Other terms denoting less respect were *peinture grasse*, tachism and *vlekkenschilders* ('blot-painters'). These terms can well be applied to the work of Franz Courtens (1854-1943), who took to the extreme the dramatic representation of nature, following Boulenger's example. Courtens painted above all in the region of Termonde and on the Scheldt, as well as in the Netherlands, where he owned an estate. He had a preference for woods and rivers, where fertile spring and the colour wealth of autumn particularly inspired him to create large virtuoso canvasses with a generous use of paint. Courtens' art was

excessive and seems rather superficial to modern eyes. Nevertheless, he was very successful in his own time, both in Belgium and abroad, and his dexterous technique influenced many landscape painters after him.

The most typical representative of *peinture grasse*, whose work warrants a thorough study and deserves re-evaluating, is Willem Vogels (1836-1896). His paintings again display the familiar ingredients: the atmospheric effects of rain, snow and twilight, the use of a rich, exuberant impasto, a lot of grey with sketchy brushwork and a pallet knife technique. With these effects Vogels achieved a more suggestive representation of nature than the other 'tachist' painters, because he observed nature more closely and profoundly, and created a pictorial equivalent more easily. Vogels actually achieved the same results when he allowed himself certain technical extravagancies or different themes. For example, he was just as proficient at depicting the bright light of the Belgian coast as the greyness of a city on a rainy day.

Among the many painters somewhere between Realism and Impressionism, the seascape painter Louis Artan (1837-1890) is worth mentioning. He was born in the Netherlands; his father was French and his mother Portuguese. Artan was trained in Belgium but also spent time in Paris and in Normandy. He knew

Willem Vogels, *The Snow, evening*, oil-colours on canvas, 105 × 154 cm. Brussels, Museums of Fine Arts.

Guillaume Vogels, *The Beach at Ostend*, painting in oils on canvas, 18.5 × 43 cm. Brussels, Museum of Fine Arts at Elsene.

Corot and Courbet, and like his friend and compatriot Dubois, was influenced by them. In 1868 Artan was among the founders of the *Société Libre des Beaux-Arts* in Brussels. He was also active with the progressive movement in Antwerp, where he worked from 1873-1874 and was in contact with de Braekeleer, Stobbaerts and Heymans. Artan's most important works date from the 1870's, the period when he definitely specialized in painting seascapes. In accordance with the principles of Realism, he abandoned anecdotal and artificial seascapes to concentrate exclusively on representations of the North Sea. In this he was preceded by Paul Jan Clays in the 1850's. However, unlike Clays he was not so much concerned with creating compositions with boats; but confined his subject matter to the clouds, the water and the sand. Artan eventually settled on the North Sea coast and built his studio right on the beach. The far-reaching thematic limitation and constant contact with his subject imbue Artan's work with great authenticity. He was the first artist in Belgium to develop an expressive form to represent the changing views and character of the North Sea coast. Typical Artan's work is dark in tone, and like most of his contemporaries, he was particularly fascinated by overcast and stormy weather conditions. The North Sea never inspired him to sunny seascapes.

The work of Alfred Verwee (1838-1895) was similarly restricted to a single theme. He was also influenced by contacts with French art and was a founder of the *Société Libre des Beaux-Arts* in 1868. He had a studio in Brussels and made friends with many young artists, including the Dutchman Hendrik Willem Mesdag, who owned a number of his works. In his work Verwee searched to combine his two special fields, landscape and animal painting. He painted almost exclusively horses and cattle in the polders of Flanders. He depicted the open clear nature of the coastal area with an Impressionist technique and used predominantly bright, silvery colours. His impressive animals – either singly or in

Louis Artan, *Sea-sight at Blankenberge* 1871, painting in oils on canvas, 83 × 121 cm. Ghent, Museum of Fine Arts.

Alfred Verwee, *Fight between young bulls*, 1883, painting in oils on canvas, 132 × 157 cm. Ghent, Museum of Fine Arts.

groups – were usually placed statically in the foreground, against a sweeping and atmospherically accurate background. The combination of these two elements is not always as successful, probably because he designed his animals in the studio in the academic tradition, while he usually painted his backgrounds in the open air. As an animal painter Verwee worked with a great deal of understanding; his studied representation of the animal was neither flattering nor heroic, but fascinating because of its anatomical precision and artistic objectivity. Verwee was probably the purest and most uncompromising of the Belgian Realists.

IMPRESSIONISM AND NEO-IMPRESSIONISM

For most of the artists discussed above, the compromise between the dark tones of Realism and elements from Impressionism marked a terminus. However, during the 1880's a new generation of 'autochthonous Impressionists' appeared, who either gradually or radically departed from this starting point. Nevertheless, 'tachist' painters continued to work for a long time, even into the 20th century. The new approach of the 1880's went hand-in-hand with a more direct and intense contact with foreign art than had ever taken place before. Journals and groups of artists played an important part; but it was above all the activities of *Les Vingt* ('the XX'), founded in Brussels in 1883, that were both the exponents and the motivation behind this new movement.

Les Vingt initially consisted of twenty artists, painters and sculptors, representatives of the different progressive currents at the end of the 19th century. The activities were directed by the secretary Octave Maus, and consisted of exhibiting the artists' own works, as well as the work of artists invited from Belgium and abroad, and the integration of different disciplines. Although this group was opposed to the official institutions such as the academies and salons, it was able to hold annual exhibitions in official buildings. These were always very popular and controversial events, which put on show all the contemporary movements of European art. A few

James Ensor, *The bourgeois' Drawing Room*, 1881, painting in oils on canvas, 133 × 109 cm. Antwerp, Museum of Fine Arts.

James Ensor, *Satan and the phantastic legions torture the Crucified*, coloured etching, 17.2 × 23.5 cm, 1895. Brussels, Royal Library.

James Ensor, *The Entry of Christ into Jerusalem*, 1885, Glued on canvas. Conté pencil, pencil, brown and black crayon, collage, 206 × 150.3 cm. Ghent, Museum of Fine Arts.

names from the long list of invited artists give a clear indication of the international scope: they included Monet, Renoir, Pissarro, Gervex, Bracquemont, Signac, Seurat, Rodin, Toulouse-Lautrec and Gaugin, as well as Rodin, Cézanne, van Gogh, Filliger, Denis, Whistler and Klinger. The school of The Hague was also represented. In 1893 *Les Vingt* was disbanded, though Octave Maus continued the activity with *La Libre Esthétique* until the First World War. Throughout this period he published the journal *L'Art moderne*, together with the influential art collector Edmond Picard. Though the journal was independent, it was the mouthpiece of the two succeeding avant-garde groups.

Initially 'autochthonous Impressionism' was strongly represented in *Les Vingt*. The atmospheric sketchiness and dark mood of Willem Vogels could be discerned in the work of a number of members, or artists who were invited by the group to exhibit: Anna Boch (1848-1933), James Ensor (1860-1949), Willy Finch (1854-1930), Pericles Pantazis (1849-1884), Theo van Rysselberghe (1862-1926), Jan Toorop (1858-1928) and Henry van de Velde (1863-1957). The early works of these artists would form a remarkably homogeneous ensemble, in which landscapes, city views and interiors predominate. Within *Les Vingt* the young Ensor and the older Vogels with their daring sketchiness were considered as the central figures of modernism, although they soon had to relinquish this status to the Neo-Impressionists. However, the work of James Ensor in his so-called 'sombre' period led 'tachism' to a new expressive form.

James Ensor, *The intrigue*, oil-colours on canvas, 90 × 150 cm, 1890. Antwerp, Museum of Fine Arts.

James Ensor, *Temptation of St Anthony*, 1887, painting in oils on canvas, 117.8 × 167.6 cm. New York, The Museum of Modern Art.

Ensor's early sensitive registration of light and atmosphere can already be discerned in some of the oil studies which he painted as a young man on the beach of his birth town, Ostend. By 1880 these studies were clearly conceived in the 'tachist' palette knife technique, and in some seascapes and city views Ensor's work bears a close stylistic resemblance to Vogels and Finch. However, he did not restrict himself to these themes but began to make studies of figures in bourgeois interiors. Using a dark palette of shining colours and a great pictorial freedom, he arrived at a subjective analysis of the light and atmosphere in these barely illuminated rooms. These contain one, sometimes two figures in a contemplative mood, reminiscent of Khnopff and Whistler. Both in the town views, such as *The Roofs of Ostend* (Antwerp, Museum of Fine Arts), and in the interiors, such as *The Bourgeois Salon* (*ibid*), Ensor arrived already before 1885 at a very expressive and sensitive use of oils, revolutionary in his circle.

During the next ten years he went through a period of great creativity, and developed completely independently as an innovator of European stature. He became isolated from the art world of Brussels because he remained aloof from the latest developments taking place in *Les Vingt*, particularly Neo-Impressionism and Symbolism. Ensor also got isolated in his own bourgeois milieu, of which the hypocrisy and the rules irritated him increasingly. His complex personality is strongly present in his mature work, and he belongs to that unadapted group of *fin-de-siècle* artists – like Munch, Gauguin, van Gogh – who assimilated all artistic innovations in a completely personal interpretation of reality. Ensor's landscapes and seascapes became visions, such as *The domain of Arnheim* (private collection) and *Christ stills the storm* (Ostend, Museum of Fine Arts), with a strength of colour that is reminiscent of Turner, and highly differentiated and sensitive use of paint. In these ten years Ensor evolved from his sombre period to bright canvases, in which a pure use of colour predominates. He expressed his strongly conflicting feelings with the greatest possible freedom in scenes peopled with symbols of his tormented personality:

550

Theo Van Rysselberghe, *Family in an orchard*, 1890, painting in oils on canvas, 115.5 × 163 cm. Otterlo, Rijksmuseum Krïller-Müller.

Theo Van Rysselberghe, *Portrait of Mrs. Charles Maus*, 1890, painting in oils on canvas, 56 × 47 cm. Brussels, Museums of Fine Arts.

saints and demons, masks, skeletons, human faces, Christ and himself, usually in the midst of hostile surroundings. The critical tone of many of his works sometimes merged into pure mockery. However, some of his masterpieces such as *The Old Lady with masks* (Ghent, Museum of Fine Arts) and *The Man of Sorrows* (private collection), testify to an extraordinary tenderness which the painting artist seemed to develop.

Ensor was also important as a graphic artist. His evolution from an Impressionist phase to more individual themes and an increasingly expressive style of drawing can be followed in his numerous sketches — both in studies and finished drawings — as well as in etchings. The latter originated between 1886 and 1904. In 1885-1887 Ensor made a series of autonomous drawings, as large and ambitious as paintings. He entitled the series *Les auréoles du Christ ou les sensibilités de la lumière*. These were studies of an all-penetrating light with a figure of Christ in the centre, which Ensor often used as a central theme, and with whom he identified. He was obsessed with capturing the essence of light. In the *Auréoles* this unrealistic light penetrates the architectural background and the surrounding human crowd. The concept of light revealing all and pervading everywhere, and the use of light as a means of expression reminds of some of the artists from the past whom Ensor admired: Rembrandt, Piranesi and Turner.

In the art circles of his time Ensor stood alone, despite the influence he exerted on other artists. His use of colour and paint can be found in the early work of a number of painters. The way his work inspired Rik Wouters and the later Expressionists, Permeke and van den Berghe, who will be discussed below, was of more fundamental importance. In a wider context Ensor should be considered as one of the precursors of modern art, and particularly of Expressionism. His pure and sensitive use of colour, often set in daring contrasts, as well as his expressive handling of the paint, which is not dependent on the scene depicted but has an autonomous life on the canvas, are fundamental elements which were elaborated by others in the twentieth century.

During the 1880's French Impressionism and Neo-Impressionism exerted a strong attraction. This influence did not always lead to a compromise, as in the work of Vogels or Artan: in some artists it was so radical that they changed their technique and colouration overnight as a result of the French stimulus. Most of the artists employing the 'imported Impressionism' were members of *Les Vingt*. Outside this circle Emile Claus was the most influential Impressionist. A few older artists such as Heymans evolved spontaneously from Realism to French Impressionism and Neo-Impressionism, combining their external stylistic characteristics.

Theo van Rysselberghe (1862-1926) from Ghent was one of the first artists to fall under the influence of the French. He first came across Impressionism in Paris, but the radical change in his work coincided with his discovery of Seurat, and particularly his work *La grande Jatte*, which was exhibited by *Les Vingt* in 1887. A year later van Rysselberghe painted his *Portrait of Alice Sèthe* (St Germain-en-Laye, Musée du Prieuré), which was painted entirely in the pointillist technique. He specialized in landscapes and portraits, which can be considered to be among the finest assimilations of pointillism in European art. For the rest, van Rysselberghe had little to do with Impressionism properly speaking. His early work includes a number of sensitive portraits in the style of Whistler. He also painted landscapes in the 'tachist' style of Willem Vogels. Van Rysselberghe fits better in a Symbolist context, and his attraction to pointillism can be explained through his natural inclination towards hieratic portraits and rigidly structured poetic landscapes. Seurat and Signac considered van Rysselberghe as a kindred spirit and they regularly exhibited work together. In 1898 he settled in Paris and in 1910 he moved to Saint-Clair on the Mediterranean coast. During these years he gradually abandoned the severe stylistic principles of pointillism, and his best known work, *The Lecture*, dating from 1903 (Ghent, Museum of Fine Arts), reveals a return to realistic designs and a more cohesive style of painting. In his

Theo van Rysselberghe, *Marguerite van Mons*, oil-colours on canvas, 90 × 70 cm, 1886. Ghent, Museum of Fine Arts.

orthodox and Neo-Impressionist phase van Rysselberghe certainly made an original contribution to this European movement, being able to use the pointillist technique and non-realistic colours perfectly to evoke a melancholy mood. In his drawings he also achieved remarkable results as, for example, in the many portrait studies of Emile Verhaeren. Here too he had abandoned the rigours of pointillism in favour of a more linear style of drawing already before 1900.

Van Rysselberghe's sudden conversion to Neo-Impressionism was not an isolated event. At this time a similarly radical change of style took place in a number of artists who had started off as 'tachist' painters: Henry van de Velde (1863-1957), Willy Finch (1854-1930), Georges Morren (1868-1941), Georges Lemmen (1865-1916) and the Dutchman Jan Toorop (1858-1928), who was working in Belgium at that time. However, the Neo-Impressionist phase in their work did not last long. After a few years Finch and van de Velde turned to the applied arts. Toorop began to work in a purely Symbolist style; while Morren and Lemmen, like van Rysselberghe, developed towards a less systematic Impressionism in which elements of the Nabis and Fauvism can be discerned.

In comparison with the brief adventure of Neo-Impressionism, the French oriented Impressionism of Emile Claus and his many colleagues and followers was

Emile Claus, *Cows crossing the Leie*, 1889, painting in oils on canvas, 200 × 305 cm. Brussels, Museums of Fine Arts.

Emile Claus, *The Ice Birds*, ca 1890, painting in oils on canvas, 148 × 205 cm. Ghent, Museum of Fine Arts.

a more lasting phenomenon in Flemish art. Claus did not turn to Impressionism until the 1890's. Before that he had painted anecdotal Realistic genre scenes and was assimilating the influence of Bastien-Lepage, which could be detected throughout Europe. This was a brighter form of Realism: Impressionist in its 'open air' quality and bright colouration, Realistic in form and content. However, during the 1890's he came into contact with Le Sidaner and was stimulated by the critic Camille Lemonnier, to turn to Impressionism, and from then on the direct influence of French painters, especially Monet and Pissarro, is found in his work. Emile Claus began to paint his pastoral scenes exclusively in sunny and bright colours. However, he never went so far as to dissolve form in the interplay of colour and light, although some works painted during his period in London during the First World War reveal him as a faithful follower of Claude Monet. Usually Claus' brush strokes remain small in comparison with the total composition. They do not form or animate the whole but remain subordinate. Emile Claus continued to paint in the Impressionist style until his death in 1924, developing only a looser style of brushwork. He had a considerable influence on his contemporaries and on the next generation.

553

Fernand Khnopff, *Memories*, 1889, pastel on paper on cardboard, 127 × 200 cm. Brussels, Museums of Fine Arts.

SYMBOLISM

A number of Impressionist artists have already been mentioned in relation to Symbolism. In fact, Symbolism was the predominant artistic movement at the end of the 19th century. It was a fundamental reaction against the positivism that had overpowered aesthetic theory throughout the second half of the century, though without replacing Romanticism entirely. This Symbolist or *fin-de-siècle* spirit, this Post-Impressionism, was one of the major ingredients in the work of figures such as Ensor, van Rysselberghe, and even Vogels and Claus. However, at the end of the century there were also artists working in the art circles of Brussels and the cities of Flanders, who renounced the entire heritage of Realism and Impressionism and joined the idealist movements of the past, such as the Romanticists and the Pre-Raphaelites. The most radical of these artists joined the French *mouvement symboliste* and shared the dogmatic ideals of the Rosicrucians, an 'order' of artists founded in Paris around the influential Sar Péladan.

The most important of these was Fernand Khnopff (1858-1921). His significance lies, on the one hand, in his consistent dedication to the esoteric and idealist views of the Symbolists; and on the other, in the fact that he transcended his extravagant iconography with his sensitivity and painterly quality. Khnopff's sensitivity is at once apparent in a less well-known aspect of his work, *viz* the landscapes he painted during the 1890's. These were studies of nature (or memories) in which he abandoned any interest in organic or atmospheric conditions in order to evoke a spiritual climate and an emotional content. He interpreted nature as a delicate dreamworld through his use of light and restrained colour. His views of the city of Bruges, which he painted and drew in 1904, are rather similar to these. They were based on photographs and concentrate on enchanting effects which anticipate Surrealism.

The typical allegories and enigmatic figures of women to which Khnopff owes his international fame, are related to the artist's aesthetics and ideals. He shared the Rosicrucians' yearning for an ideal beauty and liberation in the hereafter. This lamentation is indeed of all times, and was expressed by the Symbolists in an endless variety of allegorical themes, taken from the past. Hence for instance the timeless symbol of the angel-sphinx, the androgyne. In drawings, pastels and oil paintings Khnopff constantly repeated a particular langourous type of woman, based on the work of the Pre-Raphaelites. He admired her enormously, and represented her in theatrical poses, usually based on photographic studies. Very often these scenes were loaded with covert eroticism, which adds another element to the already ambiguous content of his work. His art was purest when he depicted a figure in complete simplicity with merely a few attributes, and when he succeeded in transmitting the ideas of the *fin-de-siècle* by purely pictorial means. This can be seen, for example, in his well-known work *Memories* (Brussels, Museums of Fine Arts), or in the *Portrait of Marguerite Khnopff* (private collection).

The other Symbolists in the circle of the Rosicrucians were rarely able to achieve this poetic simplicity. Jean Delville (1867-1953) was a highly motivated follower of idealism, who produced literary and artistic work. He founded the group *L'Art idéaliste*, based on the model of the Rosicrucians in Paris. However, his work was over-emphatic and concentrated too much on esoteric themes, lacking the necessary pictorial quality to be truly fascinating. The Symbolists strove to imbue life and the environment with an aesthetic quality. In this context they were also concerned with the applied arts and tried to revive mural painting. In fact, the monumental tradition was one of the ways in which the idealism of classical and Romantic art had continued to exist in the background. By way of illustration, one could cite the names of Nicaise de Keyser, Henri Leys, Godfried Guffens (1823-1901), Jean Bethune (1821-1894) and Theodore Canneel (1817-1892). They produced wall decorations which were reminiscent of the Nazarines and the Pre-Raphaelites, and their work was connected with Belgian Symbolism.

In this monumental tradition figures like Constant Montald and Xavier Mellery can be placed. Montald (1862-1944) belonged to Delville's group *L'Art idéaliste*, and specialized in murals in the manner of Puvis de Chavannes, assimilating many influences from the Renaissance and Eastern art. In the work of Mellery (1845-1921), one of the oldest representatives of Symbolism and Khnopff's teacher, the aim to create a new monumental art led to dichotomy. He designed murals with allegorical figures of men and women, either nude or draped, and usually depicted in a frieze. However, his true significance is concealed in less ambitious black and white drawings, interiors and still lifes, in which the forms and shadows are animated with a life of their own. He gave these works, which reveal a cyclical relationship because of their restricted theme, the title *L'âme des choses* ('The spirit of the things').

At the end of the 19th century Impressionism and Symbolism were the two dominant movements in Belgian art. However, a discussion of the latter brings us back to a late flowering of Realism – often incorporating social comment – which acquired a Symbolist content in the work of a number of artists. There were certainly occasions to produce Realistic paintings of the environment; as Belgium (with its industry, city proletariat and its contrasting, though equally uncertain rural community) provided a real-life background for artists to ponder the meaning of human existence. This was the tenor of the work of the many Realistic painters of daily life: Léon Frédéric (1856-1940), Charles Mertens (1865-1919), Eugène Laermans (1864-1940), and the

above-mentioned Meunier, de Braekeleer and Mellery. The Symbolist element is particularly strong in the work of Frédéric. Apart from landscapes he also painted scenes from country life with a strong emotional emphasis. The philosophical aspect is particularly evident when the scenes are represented in triptychs with significant titles such as *The life of the farmer*. Frédéric's work eventually evolved into pure Symbolism in the context of *L'Art idéaliste*. The best known example of this is *The river* (Brussels, Museums of Fine Arts).

Eugène Laermans might be one of the most underrated figures in 19th-century Belgian art, which was probably due to the unequal quality of his work. Laermans was deaf and virtually mute, even as a child; which explains the strong sense of isolation and the tragic tone of his work. Like Frédéric, Laermans painted scenes from country life, and his concern about the social unrest of his time often appears in his work. He usually painted social outcasts; though his portraits of children and bathing women, and his landscapes, were also dominated by a tragic overtone. Laermans' work is all emotion, expressed in a completely non-academic form. The compositions usually have a very naive and flat structure, with monumental figures in the foreground. The high degree of simplification and the twisted unrelenting linearity, supporting both the figures and the landscape, sometimes bring his works to the border of exaggeration, even caricature, though in some cases they achieve a poetic strength which anticipates Expressionism.

Eugeen Laermans, *The Intruders*, painting in oils on canvas, 152 × 202 cm. Liege, Musée d'art Moderne.

THE 20th CENTURY

The fundamental changes in European art from the beginning of the 20th century also had an influence in Belgium, where close contact was maintained with the art centres of other countries, as in the previous century. Many different influences acted simultaneously, made the younger artists form groups, and sometimes led to abrupt changes in their styles. This all took place while the great figures of the previous century continued to work in the background: Emile Claus with his luminism; James Ensor, who repeated himself and seldom regained the quality of his earlier work; van Rysselberghe with his serious art, rather lacking in inspiration and reminiscent of the Nabis. Symbolism continued to be influential until the First World War. In about 1900 a group of artists who were still permeated by the *fin-de-siècle* spirit and who were reacting against the superficial luminism in search of a new meaningful art, settled in each other's company in St Martens-Latem. The Latem group included the sculptor and graphic artist George Minne, the poet Karel van de Woestijne, and his brother Gustave, a painter, as well as Valerius de Saedeleer and Albijn van den Abeele.

George Minne (1866-1941) had at that time already passed through the most creative years of his life, but his personalized art continued to stimulate younger artists around him. The poet Karel van de Woestijne (1878-1929) admired Minne and was more or less the spiritual leader of the Latem group. He wished to create the favourable conditions for the development of authentic and profoundly felt art through reading, a knowledge of classical art, and spiritual discipline. With this vision he had a great impact, particularly on his younger brother Gustave, who was the purest representative of the Latem Symbolism. Gustave van de Woestijne (1881-1947) lived a pious life amongst the artists of St Martens-Latem. He was absorbed in the art of the Flemish

Gustaaf Van de Woestijne, *Peasant Woman*, 1913, painting in oils on canvas, 37 × 32 cm. Ghent, Museum of Fine Arts.

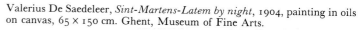

Jacob Smits, *The well*, oil-colours on canvas, 100 × 104 cm, about 1920. Antwerp, Museum of Fine Arts.

Valerius De Saedeleer, *Sint-Martens-Latem by night*, 1904, painting in oils on canvas, 65 × 150 cm. Ghent, Museum of Fine Arts.

primitives, Bruegel and the Pre-Raphaelites. From all these influences he developed a highly personal style to express his mild, though sometimes ironic view of humanity. Besides a number of views of villages and allegorical scenes, he preferred to draw or paint portraits. These are sharp and yet tenderly observed studies, depicted in soft colours with a subtle linear style that is almost medieval. Over the years van de Woestijne's art became increasingly complicated, losing some of its naive qualities and revealing the contemplative side of his nature.

Valerius de Saedeleer (1867-1941) was influenced by Franz Courtens until he went through a personal and artistic crisis in St Martens-Latem. In comparison with the complex personalities of van de Woestijne and Minne, he was a rather discreet and disarming figure. His work consists of serene and stylized landscapes in which he attempts to evoke a spiritual climate. The same results were intuitively achieved by Albijn van den Abeele (1835-1918). He was the village secretary in St Martens-Latem and an amateur painter. His landscapes were scrupulous and diffident studies of copses,

Leon Spilliaert, *Boxes in front of a Mirror, ca* 1904, pastel, 57.9 × 39 cm. Brussels, Museums of Fine Arts.

fields and hedges – all simple and understated. Their poetic strength is comparable to that of the landscapes of Khnopff.

Jacob Smits (1855-1928), who originated in the Netherlands, lived in the Campine near Antwerp, in a situation similar to that of the Latem school. His career started under the influence of the school of The Hague, especially Mauve and Maris. When he got to know the Campine through his friend, the painter Albert Neuhuys, he found an ideal environment for his pre-dilection to depict pastoral scenes in intimate paintings full of atmosphere. Like Gustaaf van de Woestijne, he settled among the farmers so that he would be com-pletely immersed in this new environment. This milieu inspired him to create biblical scenes, interiors of farmhouses, desolate landscapes and village scenes. Both in the watercolours (before 1900) and in his later oil paintings, Smits resorted to stylization and simplifica-tion of colouration, *clair-obscur* and the composition. In his oil paintings he kept working over the surface of the paint to create a thick, grainy texture; which produces a simplifying effect and seems to retain the light on the canvas. Jacob Smits is rightly considered a painter of

light, though it is always a static presence, whether outdoors or indoors, not a natural light.

Another figure in the context of Symbolism at the beginning of the 20th century is Léon Spilliaert (1881-1946), from Ostend. Unlike his contemporaries in the Latem school or Jacob Smits, Spilliaert did not paint scenes from rural life, but chose the same themes as Khnopff or his fellow-citizen James Ensor. The poet Karel van de Woestijne, who was a fine art critic, considered that Spilliaert's art testified to a sometimes frightening and certainly troubled originality, which only cleared very occasionally. It is true that Spilliaert's self-portraits, his mysterious interiors echoing the work of Ensor and Mellery, his still lifes, and his beach scenes reflect an unfathomable source of inspiration in which many foreign influences, including Munch, played a role. Spilliaert's art is usually evocative and poetic, but sometimes becomes mere illustrative painting. Like most Symbolists, Spilliaert rarely worked in oils and preferred pastels, watercolours and gouache.

The late Symbolists were only one movement in artistic life at the beginning of the 20th century, and by no means the most forward looking. Meanwhile, a number of different vital forces were developing in other countries in Europe, which abandoned introspection and emotion, and were more in line with the strongly sensory art of Impressionism. Art was again experienced more as a sensuous than as an intellectual adventure. In Belgium too, the introspective Post-Impressionism made way for a renewed painterly drive, which was to be conditioned by the European movements of Fauvism, Futurism, Cubism and Expressionism. Flemish painters, including artists working in the provinces and inspired by specific local influences, were eager to be in contact with the artistic adventures taking place in the capitals of Europe.

One fascinating figure in this respect was Rik Wouters (1882-1916), a man who had no affinity whatsoever with cerebral Symbolism, but who was inspired by Fauvism and challenged by the great painters of the turn of the century: Bonnard, Ensor and above all, Cézanne. Wouters worked predominantly as a sculptor until he was thirty. His painting phase lasted at most five years, first in Belgium, and during the First World War in the Netherlands. He spent the last years of his life in Amsterdam, where he died after a pro-tracted illness at the young age of thirty-four. Apart from his paintings he produced numerous watercolours and sketches. These are almost all interiors and portraits of his wife, Nel. His works were spontaneously and sometimes even hurriedly, with the informal use of paint, abstract colouration and deliberate sketchiness of the French Fauves. On the other hand, his simplifi-cation of form and heightened contrast of colour in his last works can be related to German Expressionism.

In the field of Belgian art, the work of Rik Wouters neatly followed that of Ensor's sombre period; in that they both would scan the space inside a room as they sketched, with as much interest in light and atmosphere, seeking a relationship between the interior and the space outside. The figure of the woman is present without dominating the scene. In comparison with Ensor's work,

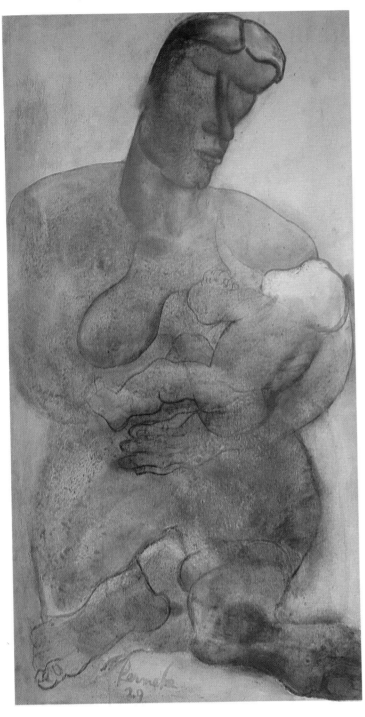

Constant Permeke, *Maternity*, 1929, charcoal and thinned oil-colours on canvas, 180 × 90 cm. Ostend, Museum of Fine Arts.

who included Ferdinand Schirren (1872-1944) and Willem Paerels (1878-1962). Wouters' characteristic sketchiness can also be seen in the work of Hippolyte Daeye (1873-1952), who painted charming portraits of women and children. His paintings were more hesitant, in hazy pastel shades. The later Expressionists, Edgard Tytgat and Jean Brusselmans, also worked initially in a style reminiscent of Wouters.

During the First World War and later, the dominant style – apart from Fauvism – was Flemish Expressionism. The main exponents of this movement were the painters from Ghent, Gustaaf de Smet (1877-1943), Frits van den Berghe (1883-1939), Constant Permeke (1886-1952) and Albert Servaes (1883-1966). The movement, which only really broke through after the First World War, was supported by a few progressive galleries in Brussels, especially *Le Centaure* and *Sélection*, which both published a journal. The main promoters were Paul Gustave van Hecke and André de Ridder. Although Flemish Expressionism was not well received by the general public, it was acclaimed by artistic circles as an authentic expression of Flemish art which fundamentally followed the northern tradition, beyond the Latin influences of Impressionism and Fauvism. Flemish Expressionism arose during the First World War: Frits van den Berghe, Gustaaf de Smet and a few others sought refuge in the Netherlands, where they came into contact with the international avant-garde. They broke away rather suddenly from the Impressionism with Symbolist overtones, which they had adopted earlier. Their process of assimilation during their Dutch period is easy to follow; the Futurists, Cubists and German Expressionists clearly made a great impression. They were also influenced directly by local artists who were themselves in contact with the avant-garde, especially Sluyters and the Frenchman Le Fauconnier, who was living there at the time.

Constant Permeke spent the war in Devon after having been wounded in action. He had already turned

Albert Servaes, *Farmers on the Field*, 1909, painting in oils on canvas, 150 × 191 cm. Brussels, Museums of Fine Arts.

Wouters' style is more volatile, the paint thinner, and the colouration completely cleared up. The colours are lying purely and applied in separate brushstrokes on the white canvas. Ensor actually sought to achieve the same elucidation, when he started to paint brighter versions of his earlier work after 1907. Rik Wouters' pure and sensuous art came to a premature end at the moment that he was recognized by the City Museum in Amsterdam, in the form of a retrospective exhibition and the purchase of three pieces of sculpture. His work was an important innovatory force in Belgium, and his name is often associated with the so-called 'Brabant Fauvists', away from Impressionism before the war, and the influence of van Gogh can be detected in some of his early works. Nevertheless, it was in South England that Permeke painted his first ambitious Expressionist canvases. These were landscapes with vivid colours, reminiscent of Turner, and representations of farmers in which the artist used constructive deformations for the first time. The fourth figure, Albert Servaes, did not go through an Impressionist phase as he had joined the Symbolists van de Woestijne and de Saedeleer. He combined their styles even before 1914 in scenes of farmers, using dark colours and heavy brushwork. After 1918 he applied himself to religious art.

On their return to Flanders after the war, Permeke, de Smet and van den Berghe must have had the conviction that art was heading in the right direction. During the 1920's these artists evolved along parallel lines, and finally elaborated Flemish Expressionism. Constant Permeke, undoubtedly the most powerful figure, was to leave his mark on many artists in the following generations. When he returned from England to Ostend, which had been ravaged by the war, he painted sombre canvases conceived on a grand scale. He spontaneously assimilated the attainments of Expressionism and Cubism – especially Picasso – in his heavy, enclosed compositions, which had a broad and angular structure and were dark in colour. He was particularly interested in farmers and sailors, interiors of Flemish houses, farms and the overcast Flemish landscape. To portray this life and this milieu dominated by the forces of the elements, he used a powerful expressive style, which owes its originality to its great strength and solidity. Permeke produced his most important paintings in the 1920's. During this period he was very successful in the deforming use of line, and his constantly varied and constructive use of paint.

Frits van den Berghe had a more contemplative spirit. He was a well-read man with an inquiring mind, and the expressive force of Permeke's paintings is rarely found in his work. During the 1920's he worked in the company of Gustaaf de Smet, and they arrived at a similar poetic Expressionism. They also employed abstract and Cubist distortions. Both painters sought rich textures through their use of paint, and their colour is sunnier and more decorative than in Permeke's work. They worked in the neighbourhood of St Martens-Latem, and in their works they idealized the unhurried pace of country life. Gustaaf de Smet pursued this rather naive Expressionist style until his death. In contrast, van den Berghe attempted already after a few years to express his much more complex fantasy. By 1924 he was expanding his themes and he introduced strange compositional effects in his work. In this he was probably fascinated by the work of Chagall. Van den Berghe

Frits van den Berghe, *Portrait of Lady Brulez*, 1919, oil-colours on canvas, 84.5 × 65 cm. Private Collection.

Gustaaf De Smet, *Sunday*, painting in oils on canvas, 197.5 × 139 cm. Antwerp, Museum of Fine Arts.

Jean Brusselmans, *Sunny Landscape*, 1933, painting in oils on canvas, 97 × 100 cm. Antwerp, Museum of Fine Arts.

Georges Vantongerloo, *Composition*, painting in oils, 53 × 33 cm. Paris, Musée National d'Art Moderne.

spontaneously evolved in the direction of the new spiritual climate of the 1930's, which gave birth to Surrealism. He participated in this new school himself in working on the Brussels magazine *Variétés*, which was significantly subtitled *Revue de l'esprit contemporain*. From 1928 his work was permeated with the surrealist world of ideas, which was also featured in *Variétés*.

Edgard Tytgat (1879-1957) and Jean Brusselmans (1883-1953) developed their form of Expressionism later than the above-mentioned major figures, and it pays to compare their divergent elaboration. Brusselmans specialized in the problems of form which were implicitly present in van den Berghe and de Smet's work. He chose similar subjects, though they always gave rise to virtually abstract constructivist compositions, in which he arranged the visual elements freely about the picture plane. This rather oppressive 'order' of Brusselmans' work is somewhat less apparent in some of the landscapes he painted during the 1930's. In contrast, Tytgat had few form problems and spontaneously applied himself to the narrative element, satire and fairytale. His freedom was predominantly iconographic. He gave full rein to his ironic, sometimes rather piquant vision of mankind, in particular the relationships between men and women, in playful compositions with an extremely informal structure. In contrast to the cerebral Brusselmans, Tytgat was an epicurean poet.

The Flemish artists also used the specifically Expressionist techniques of wood and lino cuts. During their period in Holland, de Smet, van den Berghe and Jozef Cantré (1890-1957) discovered German woodcuts and they themselves achieved fine results in this medium. These formed the basis of a tradition which would live in Flemish art fairly constantly, and of which the socially committed Frans Masereel (1889-1972) was the most important representative.

The Flemish Expressionists referred in their work to all possible form experiments that were taking place (or had just done so) in contemporary European art. They had an eclectic approach; and in this respect differed fundamentally from the first Belgian abstract artists, who were working at the same time, mainly in Brussels and Antwerp. The vision of these abstract artists was related to the *Bauhaus* and *De Stijl*. They were searching for a purely visual, non-figurative language, which could be a universal language of the community and could give new form to modern society. Their wide range of interests and their being active in the field of the applied arts was also characteristic of this. Although Belgian abstract artists appear to have been a homo-

561

geneous group from a distance, they were, nevertheless, very divergent artists. The more theoretically inclined included Jozef Peeters (1895-1960), who was one of the publishers of the magazine *Het overzicht*, and organized a number of conferences; and Georges Vantongerloo (1886-1965) who subscribed to the *De Stijl* Manifesto in the Netherlands. Other important artists included the more decorative Victor Servranckx (1897-1965), the futurist Jules Schmalzigaug (1882-1917), and the least orthodox figure of that group, Paul Joostens (1889-1960), who made Dadaist collages from 1917.

The first Belgian abstract artists, who are also sometimes referred to collectively as 'pure vision', formed the most progressive factor in Belgian art in the 1920's, together with the Flemish Expressionists. However, neither of these schools was able to survive the critical 1930's. The 'pure vision' movement disappeared from the scene almost entirely, while the Expressionists went their separate ways. During the 1930's the most important current in Belgian art was Surrealism, which was particularly prevalent in Wallonia and Brussels. The art world of Brussels turned spontaneously to this French movement, which once more united poets and painters, as in the era of Symbolism. The effect of this new orientation is found in the above-mentioned periodical *Variétés*, published by Paul Gustave van Hecke. This dealer from Ghent had previously supported Expressionism, but turned to Surrealism in 1927 with a

new gallery, *L'Epoque*, and a new magazine. In other milieus, *e g* at the Gallery *Le Centaure*, the new Surrealists could also be found at the end of the 1920's, alongside the Expressionists. The work of foreign artists such as De Chirico, Ernst, Chagall, and the first Belgian Surrealists, including René Magritte (1898-1967), could also be found there. Exhibitions of Surrealist photography were also held.

Surrealism had a profound effect on a number of Flemish Expressionists. This was the case with Edgard Tytgat, and particularly Frits van den Berghe, in whose work of the 1930's the fantastic element was dominant. Van den Berghe abandoned the 'realism' of his Expressionist works as early as 1924 in a few series of gouaches, in which he began to experiment freely with parts of the composition. After 1928 he broke completely away from Expressionism, and under the influence of Max Ernst he developed a technique of drawing and painting in which he made use of random material effects. This was completely in accordance with the interest in automatism, which was characteristic of the Surrealists. The element of Surrealism was also present in the work of Flemish abstract artists: Paul Joostens made use of Surrealist effects in his Dadaist collages already at an early stage. In 1927 Victor Servranckx departed from his purely geometric abstract work, to paint lyrical works in which he attempted to evoke a cosmic, surreal world.

In Western art a general tendency can be discerned during the 1930's to return to an accurate observation of reality; which is referred to in terms as New Realism or *Neue Sachlichkeit* ('new objectivity'). It was a truly international trend which appeared in America and all the European countries. In painting an attempt was made to portray reality emphasized in such a way, that the Realistic representation acquired its own expressive force without Expressionist exaggeration. Stylistically the arts adopted a classical style with carefully modelled and sharply outlined forms in sober colours and with restrained pictorial effects. This style was related to photography and also lent itself to the manipulation of reality by Surrealism, as in the work of De Chirico and Magritte. In Belgian art, Jos Albert (1886-1981) followed objective Realism from the beginning of the 1920's. After the war, Gustaaf van de Woestijne was influenced by Expressionism; though much of his later work, especially penetrating portraits and still lifes, should be considered in the context of New Realism.

The return to reality did not always lead to such striking results. In Belgian art many artists in a traditionalist reaction in the period before the Second World War turned a blind eye to any form of experiment, in order to produce a muted Realism. This phenomenon was termed 'animism', and the tendency was found not only amongst the younger artists such as Albert van Dijck (1902-1951), but also in the very first Expressionists and their followers. The later work of Gustaaf de Smet is the best example of this. It consists of landscapes, portraits and interiors which became less and less abstract and Expressionist in form; but instead revealed an increasing attention to realistic detail and the play of light.

Albert van Dyck, *Gusta at five years old*, 1934, oil-colours on canvas, 50 × 40 cm. Priory Corsendonk.

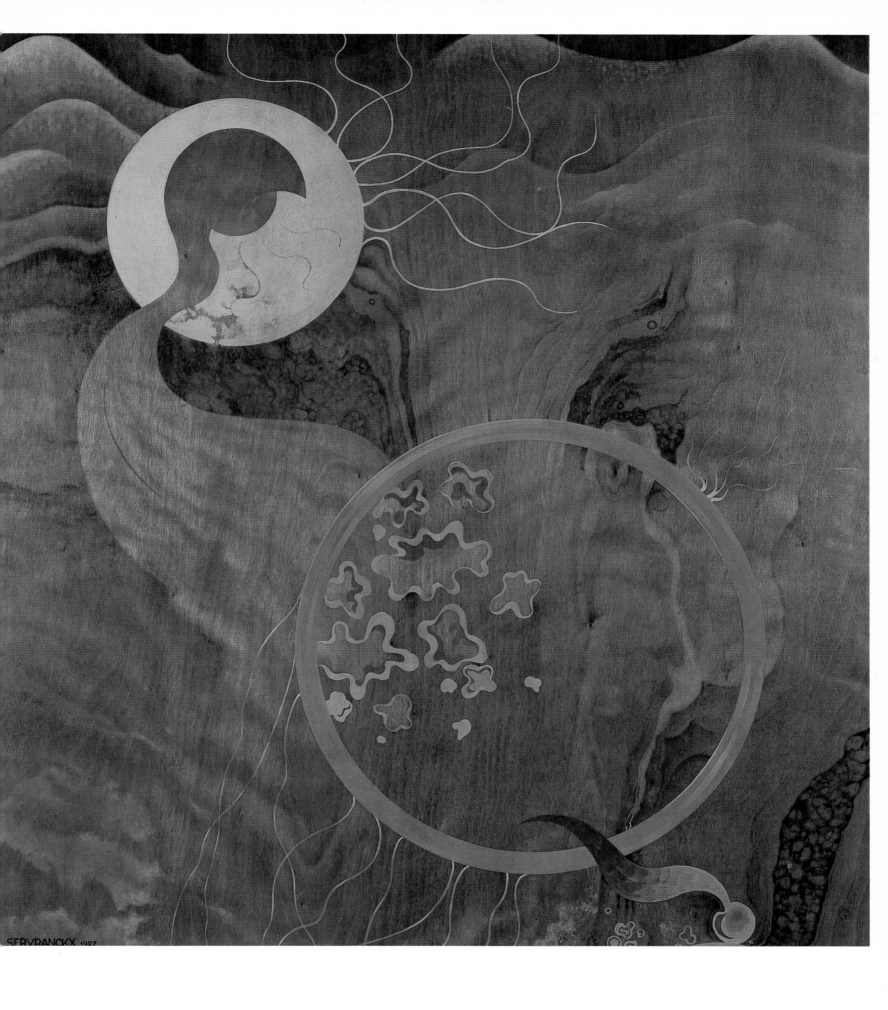

Victor Servranckx, *The domain of the water (Opus 2)*, 1927, triplex,
70 × 45 cm. Antwerp, Museum of Fine Arts.

Decorative art

The applied arts during the first half of the 19th century remained very indebted to the French sources of inspiration. French Neoclassicism and the Empire style had exercised a dominating stylistic influence throughout Europe during the second half of the 18th century, supported by the expansionist policy of the Napoleonic era.

The French Revolution dealt a serious blow to the corporate system, in which the guilds and trades had worked since the Middle Ages. When the guilds and trades were dissolved in 1795 the safe little world of craftsmen collapsed, and everyone had to fall back on his own resources. Moreover, the increasing industrialization, together with the far-reaching mechanization, formed stiff competition for the craftsmen who continued to work in the traditional manner. One can hardly speak of a separate style in Flanders during the first half of the 19th century: at best, adequate work was produced in the French style. As the century wore on, the strict lines of the Empire style also weakened.

In the art of silverwork the best pieces were produced by craftsmen whose designs were based on the training methods of the Ancien Régime: for example, Pierre Joseph Tiberghien and Joseph Schitz in Ghent, Joseph G. Dutalis and Josse Allard in Brussels, Johannes Petrus Verschuylen and P. Dandelooy in Antwerp. The same also applied to pewtersmiths: Louis J. Caluwé and Jan Baptist Duvivier in Ghent, Henri Bartholomé in Brussels and J. vande Casteele in Bruges were unusual exceptions to the artistic petrification which had affected most craftsmen.

The mechanization in the textile industry yielded a few innovations during the first half of the 19th century. First, the invention of machine-made lace made it possible to produce wide strips in a much shorter time than hand-made lace. However, because of its poor quality compared with needlepoint and pillow lace, machine-made lace definitely has less artistic value. Brussels, Malines and Antwerp were the most important centres of production for hand-made lace. The large cotton production in Flanders at the end of the 18th century, also stimulated by the high degree of mechanization, achieved an artistic merit during the 19th century through the medium of printing. Some fine cotton printing-shops were established, particularly in Ghent, such as those of Abraham Voortman and Frans de Vos.

During the first half of the 19th century ceramic work in Flanders was produced mainly in West Flanders and in the Brussels area. Glazed earthenware was made in workshops in Courtray, Torhout and Bruges, while faience was produced by family concerns such as the Bartholeyns and Stevens families. In addition, there were the porcelain factories in Brussels of Faber and Vermeren-Coché. In Halle J.B. Capellemans ran a porcelain factory from 1846-1869. With the exception of Brussels porcelain, which was comparable in quality to work produced in Paris, Flemish ceramic work from

Staircase of Hotel Solvay, Victor Horta, 1894-1898. Louisalaan, Brussels.

Coffee-pot, silver, height 26 cm, Ghent, Joseph Schitz, beginning of the 19th century. Ghent, Bijloke Museum.

Interior, from the house of painter George Buysse, Paul Hankar, 1897. Wondelgemkaai, Ghent.

this period was lacking in inspiration. From an artistic point the work was still made in a local 18th-century tradition, both as regards design and decoration.

The French influence was most evident in furniture making. The publication of books of designs by French designers, such as those of Percier and Fontaine, provided plenty of inspiration for imitators of the Empire style. During the first decades of the 19th century Flemish furniture was characterized by the imitation of the severity of the French Empire style, though without adopting the often brilliant decoration or majestic designs. The abolition of the guilds led to opportunities for foreign craftsmen to settle in Flanders. The best known of these was undoubtedly J.J. Chapuis, who worked in Brussels from 1795-1830. His furniture shows flexible lines and elegant decoration. French furniture was also imported into Flanders; for example from the workshop of François Honoré Jacob-Desmalter, the ebony worker of Napoleon I and Louis XVIII.

During the second half of the 19th century a new 'style' evolved everywhere in Europe, which was unparallelled in any other century as regards diversity.

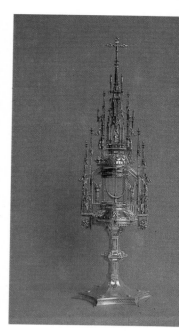

Banner of the Fraternity of the most Holy Sacrament (detail), embroidery by Jeanne Maes after a design by baron Jean-Baptiste Béthune, 1806. Ruiselede, Our-Lady's-Church.

Cylinder monstrance, height 78.5 cm, diameter base 24.2 cm, precious metal-work by Armand Bourdon after a design by baron Jean-Baptiste Béthune, 1860. Bruges, Nunnery of the Ladies of St Andreas.

Interior in Flemish Neo-Renaissance and Neo-Baroque style, 1886. Ghent, Museum of Decorative Arts.

The new bourgeoisie enjoyed expressing its growing power, and to do so, harked back to the former glory of its own national past. Architecture, both in design and ornamentation, was based on a revaluation of designs and motifs from the Gothic, Renaissance, Baroque, Rococo and Empire styles. The Flemish bourgeoisie was influenced by this nostalgia, too.

This hankering for the past was certainly very beneficial for the art of tapestry making. After the closure of the last factory in Audenarde (J.B. Brandt, 1772) and in Brussels (van der Borgtht, 1794) the thread with the past was once more tied in Ingelmunster in West Flanders, where Baron Charles Descantons de Montblanc established a new tapestry workshop for the brothers Alexandre and Henry Bracquenié. However, its production consisted mainly of copies of older work. In 1870 the brothers left Ingelmunster to settle in Malines, where their work in a new factory was based on cartoons by *inter alia* W. Geets and L. Gallait. In 1899 three other factories developed from the Bracquenié workshop in Malines: those of Theophyle de Wit, Laurent Geets and Frans Opdebeeck. In Brussels there had been a *Manufacture de Tapisserie d'Art* of the painter/weaver Arthur Lambrecht since 1878. This was later taken over by George Chaudoir. Embroidery underwent a complete renovation through the work of the Grossé workshop in Bruges, which secured important commissions for religious vestments abroad from 1850.

The neo-styles were also expressed in furniture. A number of workshops were productive in Malines, specializing in Neo-Renaissance and Neo-Baroque fur-

Drawing-room furniture, Jacob Desmalter, beginning of the 19th century. Ghent, Private collection.

Vase, china, from the Brussels Faber-manufacture, beginning of the 19th century. Brussels, Broodhuis Museum.

niture. This work fitted very well into the general urge of the bourgeoisie for nostalgic expression; and furniture from Malines found an eager market abroad.

Neo-Gothic furniture was related to architecture and was based on the same theoretical principles. The work of the English architect and theorist A.W.N. Pugin (1812-1852), had a great influence on the Neo-Gothic style in Flanders. His *Gothic Furniture*, published in 1835, clearly inspired that of J.B. Bethune (1821-1894), the great promoter of Puginian Neo-Gothic in Flanders. Bethune's colleagues included Bourdon, a gold and silversmith from Ghent, who executed many examples of Neo-Gothic church gold and silverwork. Beautiful Neo-Gothic furniture was also produced in the workshops of K. Smitz from Eeklo and Petrus Pauwels from Ghent.

The ceramic industry continued to operate at a low level in Flanders. There were still some workshops producing earthenware in Torhout and Courtray; but the major production came from Wallonia, where important porcelain factories were established in Tournai, La Louvière, Jemappes, Andenne and Nimy.

567

Interior (detail) from the architect's mansion in the *Amerikastraat* at Brussels. Victor Horta, 1898-1900, now Horta Museum.

Interior, House de Craene-van Mons (Brussels), Henry van de Velde, 1898. Ghent, Museum of Decorative Arts.

Cutlery, silver, design: Henry van de Velde, about 1903. Private collection.

The first reaction against the unimaginative imitation of works from the past came from England, where John Ruskin and William Morris campaigned for a new consciousness of the unity of art and life. The 'Arts and Crafts' movement, which developed a new sense of decoration, feeling for colour, purity of style and honesty in the choice of materials, also affected Flanders.

Curiously enough, these new ideas were propagated by architects. As a result, the relationship between architecture and the applied arts, which had been lost, was reinstated. This was already very apparent in the furniture and interiors of Paul Hankar (1859-1901). In his early work Hankar still borrowed from the Neo-Flemish Renaissance style of his teacher, Hendrik Beyaert. For Hankar, architecture was a true synthesis

of expressive forms in the plastic arts: furniture, interior decoration and the building itself should form a whole. Hankar's furniture and interiors are characterized by severe lines, which can be partly explained by the application of the skeleton building principle. This severity made him a protagonist of the new movement, which pushed aside Art Nouveau in Flanders during the first decade of the 20th century.

Henry van de Velde (1863-1957) came to architecture through the plastic arts. He also aimed at an artistic unity between building and the applied arts; and practised this in his first major work, his own house *Bloemenwerf* in Ukkel. He designed not only the house but also all the accessories and furniture – including even the door knockers, dinner service and silverware. This emphasized the diversity of van de Velde's talents, which he employed successfully throughout the rest of his career. His early work was remarkable for its sober and harmonious design, in which the ornament is an integral part of the whole, in the form of a flowing line. Construction and decoration seem to fuse to become a single unit. From about 1897, and certainly after 1899 during his German period in Berlin and Weimar, van de Velde removed all ornamentation from his design; and by about 1905 decoration had almost completely disappeared from his work. The rationalism penetrated his work totally from about 1920 during his Dutch and second Belgian period, resulting in a strict and almost geometric style of design.

As in the work of Hankar and van de Velde, the furniture designed by Victor Horta (1861-1947) is inseparable from his architectural work. Any elements that were not in complete harmony with his architecture were rejected. His early work from before 1900 was characterized by a forceful dynamism resulting particularly from his use of the spiral and the whiplash line. The spatial openness of Horta's architecture can also be found in his furniture. The characteristic Horta spiral was a frequent source of inspiration for his followers in numerous furniture workshops throughout Flanders.

The British artist Frank Brangwyn (1867-1956), born in Bruges, was less well-known for his furniture than for his paintings. After a period in the spirit of the Arts and Crafts movement – for some time he was active in the workshop of William Morris – his work reflected the influence of the Vienna Secession shortly before 1900. Inspired by the rational and constructive character of the Viennese school, Brangwyn's interiors and furniture (*e g* for the British Pavilions for the International Exhibition in Venice in 1905 and the World Exhibition in Ghent in 1913) revealed a clear affinity with it.

In the wake of the innovations brought about by Art Nouveau architecture, interior design and furniture,

Furniture, design: Frank Brangwyn, 1913. Bruges, Arentshuis.

Vase, glazed pottery, height 30 cm, Torhout, atelier Leo Maes, beginning of the 20th century. Ghent, Museum of Decorative Arts.

Vase and Basins, glazed pottery, A.W. Finch, about 1895. Ghent, Museum of Decorative Arts.

Candlestick, silvered bronze, 58.5 × 50 cm, design: Henry van de Velde, about 1898-99. Brussels, Museums of Art and History.

Belt-clasp, silver and diamonds, 7.5 × 9.5 cm, design: Henry van de Velde, about 1900. Trondheim, Nordenfjeldske Kunstindustrimuseum.

tion at all on a larger scale. Fashion in Flanders was concentrated completely on Paris at the turn of the century. Ladies' fashion designs were characterized by a shallow S-line, decorated with a wealth of ribbons and bows and supported by tight corsets. Only Henry van de Velde created new designs for his wife and for a small circle of intimate friends. Usually these were softly flowing dresses in Liberty prints, or plain dresses decorated with embroidery in abstract organic designs. Nor did the tapestries follow the new artistic ideas; and only Hélène Du Menil introduced some new ideas in her symbolic embroidery, usually based on the designs of her husband, Isidore de Rudder. Art Nouveau jewellery was undoubtedly dominated by the work of Philippe Wolfers, who succeeded in combining Art Nouveau iconography with a perfect technical skill in a very impressive manner. The jewellery of Henry van de Velde was less ostentatious and matched his total artistic vision. He

attempts were also made to liberate other applied arts from the eclectic morass in which they had been foundering since the middle of the 19th century.

An important contribution to this renovation was made by the *Groupe des XX (Les Vingt)*, an association of artists founded in Brussels in 1884. From 1888 the applied arts were exhibited at the annual *Salon des XX*, though initially with traditional products. From 1893, partly through Henry van de Velde, new and daring experimental works were exhibited.

In the ceramic arts an important innovation was made by the painter Alfred William Finch (1863-1930). Finch put a definite end to the sickly Romantic decoration which had been common practice in the ceramic industry up to that time; and produced glazed earthenware decorated with simple, warm engobe decoration. The strength and harmony of his design and decoration did not go unnoticed; and in 1897 Finch was invited by Count de Sparre to manage workshops in Borga (Finland) of the ceramic factory IRIS. His influence on the work of the Dutch ceramist W.C. Brouwer and on the ceramic industry in Finland, raised Finch to become one of the great innovators in Art Nouveau ceramics.

The Maes workshop in Ghent, the Laigneil workshop in Courtray (1898-1926) and the Leo Maes workshop in Torhout produced work inspired more by folk motifs. Some important artistic influences on ceramic art came from Omer Coppens, Arthur Craco and Isidore de Rudder, who extended their artistic views from sculpture into ceramic art. The same applied to painters such as Combaz and Lemmen, who produced designs for tiles and panels of tiles; these became a speciality of some ceramic factories, *e g* 'Majolica' in Hasselt, 'Helman Céramique' in Berchem near Brussels, and the ceramic factories of Hemiksem.

The principles of Art Nouveau did hardly penetrate into textiles. Even if Victor Horta and Henry van de Velde designed carpets and runners as part of their architectural *Gesamtkunstwerk*, there was no produc-

Interior (detail), from Hotel Solvay, Victor Horta, 1894-1898. Louisalaan, Brussels.

Furniture from the Geerardijn house in Bruges, Huib Hoste, 1927. Ghent, Museum for Decorative Art.

also produced many designs for table silverware. The aesthetic qualities of glass were not adopted with any enthusiasm by glass workers in Flanders around 1900; only in Val-Saint-Lambert in Liege important Art Nouveau works were produced. Victor Horta made optimum use of the fresh attitude of Val-Saint-Lambert, where he had the unique chandelier made for the Hotel Solvay in Brussels.

In Victor Horta and Henry van de Velde, Flanders was fortunate to have two of the major figures of the Art Nouveau movement. However, Henry van de Velde's departure to Germany in 1900 and Horta's return to an academic formalism after 1903, brought a rapid end to the new movement. The building of Stoclet Palace in Brussels from 1905 by the Viennese architect and designer Josef Hoffmann marks the influence of new movements, which soon replaced the Art Nouveau style. The late flowering of Art Nouveau did not see any more important creations in the applied arts in Flanders, and the work of followers of the movement was given its *coup de grâce* with the outbreak of the First World War.

The more constructive trend in architecture led by C.R. Mackintosh and the Viennese school replaced the floral style of Art Nouveau shortly after 1900. The influence of this movement on the applied arts can also be discerned in Flanders, *e g* in the interiors and furniture of Oscar vande Voorde and Albert van huffel. After 1918 this tendency was taken up once again; but the applied arts from the period between the wars cannot be categorized as a single stylistic movement, and they borrowed from the many new artistic movements in architecture and the plastic arts. In Flanders this diversity was most evident in furniture making. The designs

by Huib Hoste (1881-1957) reveal how this artist evolved from the sober stringency under the influence of H.P. Berlage, through the neoplasticism of *De Stijl*, to the modernistic tubular furniture, under the influence of Le Corbusier's *Esprit Nouveau*. The architect Gaston Eysselinck (1907-1953) was closest to Le Corbusier's theories. He was already designing a series of tubular furniture towards the end of the 1920's, which he later produced in his own factory (FRATSTA).

Tea-set (Gioconda), silver, Philippe Wolfers, 1925. Private collection. This tea-set was shown at Paris in 1925 in the Belgian Section on the Exposition International des Arts Décoratifs et Industriels Modernes.

572

Other designers such as Karel Maes and Jules Boulez were more inclined to design sober and functional furniture with no ornamentation. More luxurious furniture was produced in the workshops of *Kunstwerkstede de Coene* in Courtray and of Charles van Beerleire in Ghent. Appliqué work in precious woods was used there on furniture, in which the geometric designs revealed an obvious French influence. The furniture of Willy Kessels, Richard Acke and Louis de Koninck, who designed the combination kitchen CUBEX for the Antwerp firm Vandeven in 1930, had a more sober and simple design. After his return to Belgium, Henry van de Velde became the artistic advisor for public projects; and as such, he produced designs for the interior decoration of railway carriages and ferries.

Between the wars the production of ceramic and glass ware was concentrated mainly in Wallonia, where the firms of Boch (La Louvière), Nimy (Manufacture Royale et Impériale) and Val-Saint-Lambert had the lion's share of the work.

The traditional 'Flemish pottery' was still made by well-known companies, such as Laigniel (until 1926) and Noseda in Courtray, Maes in Ghent and Torhout. Jewellery was made by the Brussels company *Wolfers Frères*, which had a virtual monopoly on jewellery making through its association with the Antwerp house

Emile Anthony, and the Ghent one of A. Bourdon. In addition, Wolfers produced silverware together with his partners; of which the *Giaconda* service, designed in 1925 for the Parisian *Exposition internationale des arts décoratifs et industriels modernes*, was of an international standard.

The artistic renovation got underway at a fairly late stage in Flemish tapestry making. During the 1920's some handsome tapestries were woven in the workshop of Gaston Woedstad in Ghent, based on designs by Maurice Langaskens and Woedstad himself; but the real revival only came at the end of the 1930's, when large tapestries were made in the workshops of Gaspard de Wit and Braquenié in Malines, and of Chaudoir in Brussels.

New creativity also affected the production of carpets. The workshop of Elisabeth de Saedeleer in Etikhove in particular produced technically perfect work, based on designs by *e g* Albert Van huffel, Victor Servranckx, Gustave van de Woestijne, Edgard Tytgat, Jozef Peeters and Gust de Smet.

An important stimulus for the revival of the applied arts was given in 1927 by the foundation of the Higher Institute for Decorative Arts, in Ter Kameren Abbey in Brussels. Henry van de Velde had been especially commissioned by Camille Huysmans to realize this project; his insights on artistic education were predominantly based on his earlier teaching experience at the Art College in Weimar, the later Bauhaus. The interplay of technical skill and artistic creativity ensured that during the 1930's especially, Ter Kameren was open to a wide range of artists dedicated to the applied arts.

However, the outbreak of the Second World War ruined any possibility of its further development.

Les guirlandes, hanging, 105 × 74 cm, Gaston Woestad, about 1925. Ghent, Museum for Decorative Art.

Nike, brooch with pendant, 6.5 × 5 cm, Philippe Wolfers, 1901. Private Collection.

Index

Photographic acknowledgments

Amsterdam, Rijksmuseum
Amsterdam, Stichting Koninklijk Paleis
Antwerp, A. De Belder
Antwerp, Koninklijk Museum voor Schone Kunsten
Antwerp, Museum Mayer van den Bergh
Antwerp, Museum Plantin-Moretus
Antwerp, Museum Vleeshuis
Antwerp, Openbaar Kunstbezit
Antwerp, Provinciaal Museum Sterckxhof
Antwerp, Rubenshuis
Antwerp, Stedelijk Prentenkabinet
Antwerp, Filip Tas
Baltimore, The Baltimore Museum of Art
Baltimore, The Walters Art Gallery
Barcelona, Archivo Mas
Berlin, Bildarchiv Preussischer Kulturbesitz
Berlin, Kunstgewerbemuseum
Berlin, Staatliche Museen Preussischer Kulturbesitz
Berlin, Staatsbibliothek Preussischer Kulturbesitz
Bern, Historisches Museum
Bourg-en-Bresse, Roger Gay
Bruges, Generale Bankmaatschappij
Bruges, Grootseminarie
Bruges, Groeningemuseum
Bruges, Gruuthusemuseum
Bruges, Hugo Maertens
Bruges, Memlingmuseum
Bruges, Provinciale Dienst voor Cultuur
Bruges, Sint-Godelieveabdij
Bruges, Sint-Janshospitaal
Brussels, Airprint
Brussels, Bibliothèque Royale Albert Ier
Brussels, Ministerie van de Vlaamse Gemeenschap, Bestuur voor Monumenten en Landschapszorg
Brussels, Musée Instrumental
Brussels, Musées Royaux d'Art et d'Histoire
Brussels, Musées Royaux des Beaux-Arts de Belgique
Brussels, François Lahaut
Brussels, Jean-Jacques Rousseau
Brussels, Hotel Solvay
Cambridge (Mass.), Fogg Art Museum
Chicago, The Art Institute
Cologne, Erzbischöfliches Diözesan-Museum
Cologne, Rheinisches Bildarchiv
Cologne, Schnütgen-Museum
Cologne, Wallraf-Richartz-Museum
Copenhagen, Niels Elswing
Courtray, De Kortrijkse Verzekering
Courtray, Peter Labarque
Culemborg, Fotostudio Chris Martin
Den Haag, Mauritshuis
Diest, Stedelijk Museum
Dordrecht, Dordrechts Museum
Dresden, Staatliche Kunstsammlungen
Dublin, The National Gallery of Ireland
Elsene, Museum voor Schone Kunsten
Essen, Museum Folkwang
Florence, Scala
Florence, Uffizi
Frankfurt, Historisches Museum
Frankfurt, Städelsches Kunstinstitut
Ghent, Bijlokemuseum

Ghent, Foto-atelier De Rammelaere
Ghent, Foto-studio Claerhout
Ghent, Museum voor Schone Kunsten
Ghent, Museum voor Sierkunst
Ghent, Saint Bavo's Cathedral
Ghent, Jean Van Cleven
Ghent, Piet Ysabie
Hasselt, Foto-Team
Innsbruck, Tiroler Volkskunst-Museum
Karlsruhe, Staatliche Kunsthalle
Kassel, Staatliche Kunstsammlungen
Kasterlee, De Vroente
Kolen-Kerniel, Klooster Mariënlof
Liège, José Mascart
Liège, Musée de l'Art Wallon
Lier, Leo Deprince
London, The British Library
London, The British Museum
London, Courtauld Institute Galleries
London, A.F. Kersting
London, The National Gallery
London, National Monuments Record
London, Royal Collection
London, The Tate Gallery
London, Victoria and Albert Museum
London, The Wallace Collection
Louvain, Foto L. Oosterlynck
Louvain, O.C.M.W.
Louvain, Paul Stuyven
Louvain, Stedelijke Musea
Louvain-la-Neuve, C.R.C.H.
Madrid, Museo del Prado
Madrid, Patrimonio Nacional
Malibu, The J. Paul Getty Museum
Malines, Aartsbisdom
Malines, Hendrik Acket
Malines, Stedelijk Museum
Mantova, Palazzo Ducale
Melbourne, National Gallery of Victoria
Minneapolis, The Minneapolis Institute of Arts
Munich, Bayerisches Nationalmuseum
New York, The Frick Collection
New York, The Metropolitan Museum of Art
New York, The Museum of Modern Art
New York, The Pierpont Morgan Library
Nürnberg, Germanisches Nationalmuseum
Nürnberg, Stadtgeschichtliche Museen
Ostende, Provinciaal Museum voor Moderne Kunst
Ostende, Stedelijk Museum
Otterlo, Kröller-Müller-Stichting
Oudenaarde, Foto Paul Maeyaert
Oxford, Bodleian Library
Paris, Bibliothèque Nationale
Paris, Documentation Photographique de la Réunion des Musées Nationaux
Paris, Giraudon/Lauros-Giraudon
Paris, Musée de Cluny
Paris, Musée d'Art Moderne
Paris, Musée Instrumental du Conservatoire National Supérieur de Musique
Paris, Photo Bulloz
Paris, Publimages
Planegg, Artothek
Rome, Arte Fotografica
Rome, Galleria Doria Pamphilj

Rome, Galleria Spada
Rome, Soprintendenza per i Beni artistici e storici de Roma
Ronse, Stedelijk Museum
Roskilde, Nationalmuseet
Rotterdam, Museum Boymans-van Beuningen
Saint-Albans, The Earl of Verulam
Saint-Omer, Musée
San Francisco, The Fine Arts Museums
Sint-Niklaas, Stedelijk Museum
Stockholm, Kungl. Husgerådskammaren
Stockholm, Statens Konstmuseer
Tielt, Drukkerij-Uitgeverij Lannoo
Tienen, Stedelijk archief en Museum
Toledo, The Toledo Museum of Art
Torino, Museo Civico
Trondheim, Fotografi Svein Lian
Trondheim, Nordenfjeldske Kunstindustrimuseum
Urbino, Palazzo Ducale
Vienna, Gemäldegalerie der Akademie der Bildenden Künste
Vienna, Kunsthistorisches Museum
Vienna, Lichtbildwerkstatte Alpenland
Vienna, Österreichische Nationalbibliothek
Vienna, Photo Meyer
Washington, National Gallery of Art
Washington, Smithsonian Institution
Windsor Castle, Royal Collection

Contents

THE 17th AND 18th CENTURIES

THE 19th AND 20th CENTURIES